Conrad C. Reining
Oxford, 1954.

TRIBAL STUDIES IN
NORTHERN NIGERIA

PLATE I

A WOMAN OF THE BOLEWA TRIBE

TRIBAL STUDIES IN NORTHERN NIGERIA

By

C. K. MEEK

B.A., F.R.A.I.

Government Anthropologist, Nigeria.

VOLUME ONE

LONDON

KEGAN PAUL, TRENCH, TRUBNER & CO., LTD.

BROADWAY HOUSE : 68–74 CARTER LANE, E.C.

1931

TRIBAL STUDIES IN NORTHERN NIGERIA

By

C. K. MEEK

B.A., F.R.A.I.

Government Anthropologist, Nigeria.

PRINTED IN GREAT BRITAIN BY
STEPHEN AUSTIN AND SONS, LTD., HERTFORD.

PREFACE

THESE volumes are published as a contribution to the ethnography of the Northern Provinces of Nigeria. They embody a collection of tribal reports submitted by me to the Nigerian Government at various times during the last five years. The reports deal with upwards of fifty non-Muslim tribes and are essentially of a survey character, as it was felt that tribal surveys covering large areas would, as a rule, be of more practical assistance to the Administration at the present stage than intensive research confined to small areas.

Although some of the reports are little more than hurried notes taken during the course of a few days' work, it is considered that the whole of the material collected should be placed on permanent record in order that it may be made accessible to administrative officers and others interested, and serve as some kind of basis for future investigations. Most of the data are new, but the paper on the Katab tribe has appeared in the *Journal of the African Society*, while that on the Bachama tribe has been published in *Africa*, the magazine of the International Institute of African Languages and Cultures.

The reports have not been subjected to any close recension, and no attempt has been made to reconcile varying opinions, where these occur. There is some amount of repetition, due to the desire to make each report independent of the others. The linguistic material is only such as could be obtained in conjunction with the cultural survey-work, and, although the schedules of words and phrases are of value for purposes of classification and establishing tribal relationships, they cannot be regarded as accurate guides to the morphology of the languages.

The photographs are, with the one or two exceptions indicated, my own.

C. K. MEEK.

CONTENTS OF VOLUME I

LIST OF ILLUSTRATIONS

VOLUME I

ix

TRIBAL STUDIES
IN NORTHERN NIGERIA

CHAPTER I

THE BACHAMA AND MBULA

The following notes on the Bachama tribe were made during a fortnight's visit to the Numan Division.[1] The tribe, which numbers 8,500 people. occupies the country on both banks of the Benue in the neighbourhood of Numan. They call themselves the Gboare or Men, a term which is doubtless the same as Gbari (the name of the large tribe in the Niger and Zaria Provinces), Bari (in the Eastern Sudan), and Ka-Bwari (Tanganyika). The root *gba*=man is also found in the Upper Ituri regions of Central Africa under the form *mu-gba* or *ba-gba*. The words for man and the male organ are commonly interchangeable in the Sudanic and Bantu languages, and it is therefore interesting to find that in the language of the Kanakuru—neighbours of the Bachama—the word for penis is *gware*.

The Bachama say that the term Bachama means " The place to which tribute was taken ", but this is certainly a fictitious derivation. *Ba* can only be the plural prefix, and the root *cham* as a tribal term is found in Cham-ba, or Tsam-ba. The Chawe of Zaria Province call themselves the A-Tsam. Outside Nigeria there are the Ba-Samba of Upper Congo, the Kuamba of Upper Ituri, and the Kamba of British East Africa. Sama is the name by which the Fulani are known to some Benue tribes ; and it is possible that the present line of Bachama and Bata chiefs was of Fulani origin.

The Bachama speak a language which is classed in the Central Sudanic division on the ground principally that plurals are formed by suffix or by internal change, and that gender occurs in the form of a third personal feminine pronoun. Relative pronouns are also inflected for gender. The language is remarkable for its use of

[1] Adamawa Province.

B

inclusive and exclusive first personal plural pronouns—a characteristic of Fulani, Bura, Pabir, Kilba, and Yungur. Whether the other tribes have adopted this characteristic, which is not peculiar to West Africa, from the Fulani, or whether it is a common inheritance from some ancient civilization of which the Fulani are the modern representatives is a matter of speculation.

The Bachama and Bata speak the same language, and they are clearly sub-divisions of a single tribe. Both claim to have come from Sokoto.[1] Others say that the tribe came from Gobir which they left under their leader Jaro Palami in consequence of a dispute at a well between a daughter of Jaro and a daughter of the king of Gobir, of whom Jaro was a relative. They travelled by way of Zim and Maifoni to the region surrounding Garua. The claim of a tribal connection with Sokoto (or Gobir) is untenable on historical, linguistic, and cultural grounds, and it is probable that the tale was merely an invention made for the purpose of securing immunity from the attacks of the Adamawa Fulani. The Bata say that the Shehu dan Fodio forbade Adama to attack the Bata on the ground that they were his relatives ! It may be that the present line of Bachama and Bata kings is in fact of Fulani origin ; but if this is so it is clear that even if they were pre-Jihad Fulani they were not the originators of the Bata and Bachama kingship. The Bata were the predominant people of the present Adamawa Division in the days prior to the Jihad. They were broken up and scattered in all directions—the main body retreating south and west by various stages (Gurin, Yola, Namtari, Ngorore, and Mamwomo) until they reached the vicinity of Demsa. Here, it is said, the tribe split in two as a result of an intrigue by the younger brother Jaro Dungi[2] against his elder brother who occupied the throne. The brothers were twins. The elder decided to kill the younger during a hunt, but the younger, forewarned by his father's sister, fled towards Numan, having previously stolen the sacred pot—the rain cult of the tribe. The elder brother followed in pursuit, but when he reached Demsa he found that his younger brother was half-way across the Benue. He called on him to return, but the younger brother refused. So seizing a long roll of cloth he hurled it towards his brother, holding on to one end. The younger brother caught the other end.

---

[1] The capital of the Fulani Sultanate established at the beginning of the nineteenth century.

[2] I.e. the Black Twin. A variant gives the names of the twins as Jejumse-Atingno (elder) and Bitiparomo.

The elder then drew a knife and slit the cloth in two, saying " Henceforth you must live on the northern bank, and I shall live on the southern. We must never look on each other's face and we must neither of us see the Benue. Yours shall be the duty of sitting at home, a slave of the cults ; mine will be that of hunting game and of fighting our Fulani foes ". And hence it is that the supervision of the religious rites is the business of the Bachama and not of the Bata chief.

It is remarkable how persistent throughout the Benue regions is the story of the elder brother being outdone by the younger. It is found among the Kona and Jukun, and among the latter also it occurs in connection with twins.[1] It is current in fact throughout the Sudan, being found for example in the Soninke and Sokona story of how Tere-Khine was robbed of his birthright, i.e. the royal insignia, by his younger brother Jabe, and how his blind father compensated Khine by conferring on him the rain-making cult. The details of the story, as quoted by M. Delafosse, make it quite clear that the Soninke legend is the Jacob-Esau legend of the Bible. The story is perhaps a survival of an ancient custom of ultimogeniture or succession by the youngest son—a custom which is still in existence in one group of the Hill Verre pagans.

Government and Law.—The chief or king is known as the Hemen. He is elected by the Jege kindred of the town of Hadio. In former times the election was frequently the occasion for free fighting between the various households of the royal clans. On election the chief is taken to the shrine of Fara Borungti and there sits down for a few minutes on the sacred stone which is the emblem of the cult. His feet are ceremonially washed by an official known as Dawodi Gungrung. He is then escorted to the shrine known as Ramo Mbakauwen which contains the sacred Bachama stool. Here a curious rite is performed. A monitor lizard is brought with its forelegs tied behind its back, in the same way that a human prisoner is bound. The people then jokingly address the lizard, saying " Yes, you were not all that you should have been in bygone days—you even ran after the chief's wife ! " The lizard is then taken to the royal graveyard and released. The idea underlying this ceremony is that the new chief must not use his new power to wipe off old scores—all private resentments must be laid aside. The chief-elect then enters the hut of the

---

[1] See *A Sudanese Kingdom*, p. 36.

shrine and there lives a life of seclusion for fifteen days—undergoing a kind of dynamization which converts him into a semi-divine being and " a son of the cult ". He is attended by four officials, the Zǫpwato, Dandowǫdi, Doitiga, and Zeekei, who counsel him in his new duties, reminding him that he must show neither favour nor ill-feeling to man, woman or child, for he is the father of his people. On the conclusion of this period of segregation he takes formal possession of the palace by stepping over a cow slain at the threshold. Two explanations were given of this rite: (i) that in crossing over the body of the cow he left behind him all conduct of a kind which would be inconsistent with his new position ; and (ii) that the sacrifice of the cow at the threshold secured the palace against invasion by the late chief's ghost. The king is then given a crown which is worn on occasions of public dances and festivals. It is known as Pawalato and consists of strips of brass worn round a red fez, the forehead being covered with a band of white cloth. A few ostrich plumes protrude at the sides. The crown is handed to the chief without any formality. Its appearance is as follows :—

The election rites closely resemble those of the Mbum, Bata, Kam, and Kona which are described elsewhere. Like the chiefs of these peoples the Bachama chief was accustomed to eat in private his food which was cooked by a favourite wife provided she was not in a menstruous condition. This taboo against menstruous women is not however general among the Bachama as it is among the Jukun and Arago. A Bachama nevertheless will remove his

charms and poisons from his house while his wife is in this condition. The reasons assigned by the Bachama for the secret
eating ritual of the chief are (*i*) the chief is a divine being and is
not therefore supposed to eat at all, and (*ii*) the ritual secures
protection from witchcraft and poisoning. (In point of fact it is
clear from the Jukun data that the ritual repast of the chief is a
Holy Communion with the gods, the chief himself being a son of
the gods.)

In former times, when the chief died, his body, it is said, was
placed on a bed over a hole in the ground which afterwards
served as a grave. It was allowed to decompose, and after an
interval of eight to fourteen days the head was removed by
members of the Jege clan and was buried in mud until all the flesh
had disappeared. It was then dug up and washed, wrapped in a
cloth and given to the new chief, together with the heads of
former chiefs, to serve as a royal talisman. A dead chief, it may be
noted, was known as Njefin—a title which recalls the Ajifin of the
Jukun.[1]

The government was to a considerable extent decentralized,
many senior officials and members of the royal family being
placed in charge of outlying towns. The chief's right-hand man
was the Kpana who at the present time resides at Rigangen.
The Vulpi village-area was in charge of the " Gboare Vulpi " ; the
" Daudi Zekin " was responsible for the riverain villages, while
the Indowodi Waduku, head of the original royal house and rival
of the chief, had his headquarters at Waduku. The ruler of the
town of Njimoso was and is a woman—the Gboarata Njimoso.
The original chieftainess was said to have been a sister of Hamabulki, one of the early Bachama leaders, and the reason assigned
for the chieftainship being held by a woman is that the female
deity of Njimoso had so willed it. The chieftainess is thus also a
priestess, for she is responsible for the maintenance of the local
cult. In addition to the local village-area head there was also an
official called the Kasalla (i.e. Kachella) who was the leader of the
village-area in time of war. To him the central chief sent a spear
shaft when he wished to call on the war-services of the village-area.
The town of Njimoso, being governed by a woman, was exempt
from military service.

Closely associated with the chief at the capital was the
Kpanatai, one of whose principal duties was to see that all large

[1] See *A Sudanese Kingdom*, pp. 154–156.

animals killed in the bush were duly delivered to the chief. The chief's spokesman and the leader in war was the Induǫmato. Other officials were the Ingurgima and the Gbafǫye, the former of whom looked after visitors to the town. The Dowǫde and Zǫpwato were the chief's personal guards ; the Kpadue and Zǫpukai were messengers to the Mbula tribe ; Dowǫde Zutika, Njege and Gura were the respective messengers to the Boso, Fare, and Bulki cults. Gura was also the guardian of the royal burial place. The women of the palace were under the supervision of the Kpanato who was either a senior wife or female relative of the chief. She had charge of the shrine of Gboara Bitikin—a deity who is said to have been originally a sister of the first chief of Lamurde—and was also keeper of the royal insignia, which includes a horse's tail and a spear.

Tribute was formerly paid to the chief by (a) Fulani herdsmen in the form of cattle and (b) by all villages in the form of gowns, goats, guinea-corn or fish. The chief had full rights over all fishing grounds, subletting them to individuals in return for gifts and a claim to 50% of all fish caught (the gifts of dried fish being paid periodically). The chief had the power of life and death, murderers being decapitated and the head given into the charge of the Piri kindred who were the official keepers of skulls. The cults of Nafaran and Boso however provided a sanctuary to criminals who succeeded in making their escape. The criminal resided ten days at the shrine and became the slave of the cult. He could then leave the shrine, and no one dared lay hands on him, for he was believed to have come under the protection of the deity. He was obliged however to make continuous gifts to the officials of the cult, and if he failed in this it was said that the deity would cause his death.

Social Organization.—The social system of the Bachama is of a mixed and indeterminate character due to the fact that the Bachama are a fusion of heterogeneous elements. The social unit is the kindred or grouping of several families related to each other patrilineally. This unit, which is always exogamous, may be self-sufficient, claiming no relationship with any other kindred. On the other hand a number of kindreds may share a common name and claim a common forefather and sometimes also share a common cult. It is difficult to find a suitable term for this second larger grouping. It resembles the Scottish clan ; but as the term clan has been arbitrarily appropriated to describe a purely matrilineal exogamous grouping it may be safer to use the term " kindred-group ". The kindred is usually localized in a village, but the kindred-group may extend over a number of villages and in some cases elements of a single kindred-group may be found living among the neighbouring Bata and Mbula tribes and regarding themselves as members of those tribes. In such cases the sense of relationship is maintained by the meeting of the various kindreds at funeral feasts or the annual religious rites. The kindred-group is sometimes, like the kindred, an exogamous unit, but sometimes intermarriage is permitted between kindreds of the same kindred-group.

The following is a list of some of the kindreds and kindred-groups : (1) Waduku, (2) Nikedimin, Numupo, Magbilaro, Kauwo, (3) Piri, (4) Jeno, (5) Vwiti or Vo, (6) Mwomi, (7) Kwati, (8) Muja, (9) Killa, (10) Fwa, (11) Filo, (12) Ndaka, (13) Mọmo, (14) Mbo, (15) Mbako, (16) Pukur, (17) Mbamo, (18) Mo, (19) Nje, (20) Indiuno. The Waduku, who are located in the village-area of the same name, was the original royal family. It is taboo for any member of this family to eat the flesh of leopards or of lions, a prohibition common to most royal families in Nigeria. The conception appears to be that lions and leopards hold, in the animal world, a position analogous to that of royalty in the human world. Indeed among some tribes, e.g. the Mbum, it is believed that a chief on his death becomes a lion or leopard. Hunters, therefore, who kill lions or leopards are usually required to make formal apology to the chief on the ground that, in killing the lion, they had killed the chief's brother : and skins of leopards or lions become the property of the chief. At the present time the chief belongs to the Nikedimin kindred who are closely related to the Numupo and less closely to the Magbilaro and Kauwo.

The Piri, Jeno, Vwiti or Vo and Mwomi kindreds are not really Bachamas at all, though they are now so regarded. The Piri, as their name implies, are a kindred who belonged originally to the Piri tribe. They hold a special position at Numan as the keepers of skulls (human and animal) and to this reference will be made later. Their totem or emblem animal is the chameleon. The Jeno are the remaining representatives of the Jen tribe who were the original inhabitants of Numan and were driven out by

the Bachama. The Vwiti are of Chamba origin, and the Mwomi
are said to have belonged originally to the Mumuye tribe. The
Kwati are of Tula origin. The next two social groups, the Muja
and Killa, are primarily occupational groupings; they are medicine
men and blacksmiths respectively. They form hereditary castes
apart within the tribe, and their membership extends into the
neighbouring tribes of the Bata and Mbula. We have thus an
instance of a social grouping which is wider than the tribal
grouping. Neither of these groups have any " totem." The
Killa appear to respect all snakes but no particular species of
snakes. The Fwa clan who are found at the villages of Tsogbon,
Yimburu, and Numan are said to have come originally from
Gwompa, a non-Bachama town close to the country of the Yungur
tribe. But there are Fwa among the Mbula tribe. The Ndaka
clan, whose emblem is the water tortoise, are found both at
Yimburu and Numan. But there are Ndaka also in the neighbouring tribe of Bata (who do not respect the tortoise). The
Mbamo clan are found at the Bachama town of Namzo, and their
taboo animal is the bush-cat. There are Mbamo also at Demsa,
the Bata capital, and these also respect the bush-cat.

It has been said that where the various kindreds of a kindred-
group do not live in close association the sense of relationship is
maintained by the meeting of the kindreds at funeral feasts or
religious rites. In some cases the kindred-group has its own cult.
Thus the Mbamo group, who have a special association with the
bush-cat, assemble every harvest at the bush-cat shrine of the
village of Bolen. The priest takes in his hands the emblem of the
cult—the stuffed skin of a bush-cat—and addressing the members
of the kindreds says " We have received this cult from ancient
times and it has given us untold help. If we cling to it it will not
fail us." Offerings of beer and food are placed before it, and all
the members of the Mbamo kindreds then join in a sacred meal.
Some of the consecrated food is carried home to those sick
relatives who were unable to attend. In other cases the kindred-
group may have no special cult, but the various kindreds meet
and group themselves together at general feasts such as the spring
festival at Fare.

Each kindred included in a kindred-group is an independent
social unit, i.e. there is no central social authority other than the
priest of the cult (where a kindred-group has a cult of its own).

PLATE 2

WOMEN DANCERS

(Photograph kindly lent by Mr. K. V. Elphinstone)

[face p. 8

BACHAMA YOUTHS AT A FESTIVAL

(Photograph kindly lent by Mr. K. V. Elphinstone)

Each kindred has its own recognized headman to whom quarrels within the kindred are referred and who is held responsible by the chief if he fails to control unruly members of the kindred. If the kindred follows a special profession he sees to it that all the male children are brought up to that profession. He may assist them in meeting their marriage expenses and, in cases of sickness or ill-fortune, takes gifts to one or other of the cults on behalf of the afflicted. He is entitled to the skin, liver and heart of animals killed by members of the kindred.

Usually the local group in a village-area is composed of a number of unrelated kindreds, so that the ward or hamlet and not the kindred or kindred-group is the administrative unit. Thus the town of Numan consists of three wards : (*i*) Nikaun (*ii*) Mba Kauto and (*iii*) Mba-Uro. In the first we find members of five kindred-groups, viz. Piri, Muja, Fwa, Filo, and Ndaka ; in the second there are Ndaka, Momo, Mbo, and Mwomi ; in the third Mbako, Fwa, and Filo. Each ward has a headman to whom all owe allegiance. In bygone days fights between the wards were frequent, and members of the same kindred-group might be ranged against each other. When this occurred they would avoid engaging each other as far as possible. It is evident, therefore, that from many points of view the local grouping into wards was of greater social importance than the kinship grouping.

Some of the kindreds or kindred-groups stand to each in a special relation of comradeship. Thus the Muja or leech-craft group are the special friends of the Killa or blacksmiths. If a Muja man dies members of the Killa group are summoned to prepare the body for burial and vice versa. On such an occasion the members of the friendly group summoned are entitled to help themselves to any small articles of property they can lay their hands on : it is usual therefore to conceal all property before announcing a death.

From the above summary it is apparent that the Bachama, who appear at first sight to be a homogeneous people with a common language and culture, are in fact composed of hetero-geneous elements, which, by reason of war or other political circumstances, have been thrown together and coalesced under a vigorous invading chief. It is easy to understand how in the absence of a central authority various groups of a tribe like the

Vere, though speaking the same language and sharing a common culture, may be found to differ fundamentally from each other in the character of their social organization, clear evidence that the tribe is composed of groups of diverse origin.

Totemism.—A feature of the social and religious life of the Bachama (as also of the Mbula, Kanakuru and Longuda tribes) is the presence of totemic beliefs. These occur in two forms, viz. (*a*) a sense of relationship between an extended family or kindred and a species of animal, and (*b*) a sense of relationship between an individual and an animal. As regards the former the totem is transmitted in the male line, the family group being formed on patriarchal principles : but in the latter case the totem is transmitted by females, so that there is (or may be) a totem-kin as distinct from the family group. But not all kindreds, nor yet all individuals have totems. Indeed the possession of a totem appears to be exceptional, and there are reasons for believing that such totemism as exists was introduced from the Mbula tribe, a people who speak a language which is definitely Bantoid.

The Mbamo kindred respect the bush-cat, and, as already noted, carry out harvest rites at the bush-cat shrine, just as though the bush-cat were some deity. If a Mbamo loses his way in the bush he will call on the bush-cat to show him his way home, in the same way as members of other tribes will call on the Sun or the Supreme Being. The Mbamo regard themselves as " children" of the bush-cat, and believe that all that they have in life—their food, their health and children—are the gifts of the bush-cat. If they fall sick, or if anything goes wrong, they resort to the bush-cat shrine at Bolen ; and one whose son has been sick for a considerable period will hand him over permanently to the priest of the Bolen cult. So much do they respect the bush-cat that it is taboo to eat the flesh of any animal bearing similar stripes. No Mbamo, therefore, will touch the flesh of a leopard or hyena. If any non-Mbamo had killed a bush-cat and subsequently touched the person of a Mbamo the body of the latter would immediately be covered with sores, and he would have speedily to find a " medicine ". There is, however, no personal association with individual bush-cats, though an enemy of the Mbamo may charge one of their number with having, as a bush-cat, stolen one of his chickens during the night. On the other hand the bush-cat takes a personal interest in the welfare of all members of the Mbamo clan. If anyone thieves from a Mbamo the bush-cat will cry outside the thief's house, and the members of the household will know that one of their number had committed an offence against one of the Mbamo group. The thief, stricken with fear, will, it is said, betake himself forthwith to the person from whom he stole, confess his offence and solicit his protection. The Mbamo concerned will take him to the shrine at Bolen and say to the priest of the cult : " This man stole from me : I bring him to the bush-cat, for the bush-cat went to him." The priest will question the thief who will straightway confess his guilt and offer to the priest a white cloth in recompense. This the priest binds on to the roof of the shrine. He then takes some cotton and passes it round the offender's head, and there the matter ends. Or if a Mbamo loses a cow by theft he immediately sets out for the bush-cat shrine at Bolen, taking with him the cow's halter. Before reaching the shrine he strips himself of all his clothes, and girds his waist with leaves—the ancient custom. He states his case to the priest, who deposits the halter in the shrine ; and thereafter the thief will be pursued by bush-cats, who will micturate on his flour, poison his food and bring sickness on the whole of his kindred. If he dies, the vengeance of the bush-cats will pursue his heritors. The afflicted kindred will then resort to a diviner to ascertain the cause of their misfortune ; and being told that one of them who is no longer alive had stolen from a Mbamo, they will go to the bush-cat shrine at Bolen, confess the offence of their dead fore-father, and by numerous gifts secure the forgiveness of the cult. It is of interest to note that stolen goods subsequently restored become the property of the priest and are not returned to the complainant. The bark of the Bauhinia Reticulata tree is sacred to the bush-cat, and strips are deposited beside the symbol of the cult. These strips are issued as charms by the priest to members of the clan ; bracelets for men and necklaces for women. The priest is attended by a boy who, every evening, is required to light a fire in the hut of the priest. Some of the embers are carried to the shrine, as the bush-cat is believed to be fond of warmth.

There are one or two other kindreds which have totem animals. Thus the Ndaka of Yimburu associate themselves with water-tortoises. But the water-tortoise does not appear to be a totem for the whole of the Ndaka clan, as there is a group of Ndaka in the

Bata district which has no totem. It may be said generally that the majority of the Bachama kindreds or clans are non-totemic,

Turning now to the individual relationship of a man or woman to some animal, derived from his or her mother, this appears to be fairly common. The general conception is that the man and his animal counterpart are each the double or *alter ego* of the other. The fortunes of the two are so closely bound together that nothing can happen to the one without a corresponding reaction on the other. The sickness or death of the one connotes the sickness or death of the other. The man can influence and direct the movements of his animal counterpart, and the latter can visit at night his human counterpart and warn him of possible dangers. If a man who is associated with a hippopotamus knows that his fellow-townsmen are going to hunt hippopotami he can warn his hippopotamus *alter ego*, together with other hippopotami who are his relatives, to leave the herd that day. If a hippopotamus upsets a canoe his human counterpart is fully aware of the fact, however far away he may be. If the man is himself in a canoe, and his hippopotamus *alter ego*, or even hippopotami who are the counterparts of members of his totem-kin, come to attack his canoe he merely orders them to be gone, and off they go. Totemic conceptions of this character occur among the Bura, Kilba, Kanakuru and Yungur tribes. Among the last, for example, there is a kindred at Waltandi which has a special association with roan antelopes. None of the kindred, therefore, may shoot a roan antelope. Any member of another kindred who wishes to shoot a roan antelope will first present himself before one of the roan kindred with a gift of a pot of beer and two hoes, soliciting the assistance of the kindred. The person approached will then indicate to the petitioner where the roans are accustomed to graze, but he will warn the hunter that he must avoid shooting the leader of the herd, as the leader of the herd is his own second self. From this it appears that although all of the roan kindred have animal counterparts not all roans have human counterparts.

A parallel to this West African conception has been given by Matthews with reference to the Wotjobaluk (of North America) who says : " Each individual claims some animal, plant or inanimate object as his special and personal totem, which he inherits from his mother." In commenting on this Professor Durkheim says it is evident that if all the children in the same family had the personal totem of their mother neither they nor she would have personal totems at all. Matthews, he says, probably means to say that each individual chooses his individual totem from the list of things attributed to the clan of his mother. But Professor Durkheim's difficulty would be removed, in so far as the Bachama are concerned, by the fact that not all of a woman's children are conscious of or assume the animal relationship : indeed it was stated that some of her children might fail to attain it, just as the gift of possession or second-sight is transmitted to some children, but not necessarily to all. Moreover, as daughters on marriage leave their mother's home and are scattered in various villages, they are regarded in those villages as having a private, individual totem. Sons are unable to transmit the totem even if they receive it.

The question of the origin of such beliefs is always of interest, and the recent letters to the *Times* (April 1927) purporting to give well-attested instances of human children suckled and brought up by wolf-mothers in India and subsequently rescued in a condition physically and mentally resembling that of animals rather than of human beings, may have some bearing on the problem.[1] Among the Malabu tribe (who are really a sub-tribe of the Bata and therefore of common origin with the main body of the Bachama) there is a kindred whose totem is the leopard and who gave as their reason for the respect paid to the leopard that the ancestress of the kindred, a human being apparently, bore first a leopard and then a human son. They played together, for they had drawn milk from the same breast ; and when each founded its own family the children of the one became identified with the children of the other. Each human being had its leopard counterpart, and vice versa. An interesting point is that the members of the existing Malabu leopard kindred state that they no longer have leopard counterparts, as the " medicines " by which they maintained the connection were burnt. Thus at the present time they merely respect the leopard, without claiming

---

[1] It is hardly credible that a human child could survive the environment of a wolf's den ; and it would seem to be wholly impossible that a human being could in the course of a year or two abandon physical and mental qualities which are the result of hundreds of thousands of years of evolution. The belief may have arisen as an explanation of human monstrosities, or of children suffering from diseases such as myxoedema, cretinism, etc., which produce an inhuman appearance.

the intimate association and identification with leopards, such as other kindreds claim with other animals.

Exogamy. Among the Bachama the essential principle is that intermarriage between persons who are genealogically related on the father's side is totally taboo. The kindred, therefore, which is a patrilineal grouping, is always an exogamous unit. Where there are a number of kindreds bearing the same name (and united usually by a common cult and common animal emblem or totem) the exogamous rule is in some cases applied to the whole clan ; in others it is confined to the local group of the clan, i.e. to a single kindred or two kindreds which are very closely related. A few examples will illustrate the system. The Piri at Numan are a single kindred and a Piri may not marry a Piri. There are two kindreds of the Mbo clan located in different wards in Numan. They may not intermarry. It was stated that there are also kindreds of the Mbo clan among the Mbula tribe and that the Mbo of Numan may not marry the Mbo of Mbula. A Muja may not marry a Muja anywhere. On the other hand the Ndaka of Yimburu may marry the Ndaka of the Bata tribe (and instances of such marriages were obtained). Intermarriage with close relatives on the mother's side is also taboo ; but it appeared that the taboo in this case did not extend so far as in that of patrilineal relatives. It was stated that a man might marry a second cousin on his mother's side, but no instances were obtained to show that this was so.

It might be concluded that as the exogamy of the Bachama is primarily governed at the present time by consanguinity there is no connection between their exogamy and their totemism. But totemism does play a part in the regulation of marriage. Among those kindreds which have patrilineal totems intermarriage between members of the same kindred is forbidden ; but it was difficult to ascertain whether the prohibition was dependent on the common possession of the totem or on consanguinity. The general opinion appeared to be that consanguinity was the governing factor, and that totemism only acted as a bar to marriage if two persons with different totems who were each capable of transmitting the totem proposed to marry. Thus a Ndaka man who is a water-tortoise (and can transmit his totem, the Ndaka being a patrilineal kindred) may not marry a woman whose mother belongs to an elephant totem-kin (in which the

totem is transmitted matrilineally). The reason given was that if
two persons with different totems married and transmitted their
totems the totems would fight one another and the children
would die. The same reason was given among the Mbula tribe ;
but the Mbula stated that no persons who had inherited different
totems could marry, whether they could transmit the totem or not,
as the partners to the marriage would themselves, together with
their totems, fight and kill each other. A man or woman who is
the owner of a totem must, therefore, marry a woman or man who
has no totem.

It might be supposed that these regulations would prevent
marriage between the majority of the members of the tribe, and
would lead eventually to complete tribal exogamy. But actually
the majority of the people are totem-free, partly because the
totemism appears to have been introduced by a small group, and
partly because it is not always hereditary.

Mother-Right. Though the Bachama are organized on a
patrilineal basis there are many social practices of a so-called
mother-right character. Thus in the matter of inheritance
though the eldest son (in the absence of a brother) inherits his
father's spear, shield, bow and arrow and also the compound (if
old enough) all other property such as horses, goats, clothes, cash,
and cattle are heritable by the sister's son. The latter is even
entitled to all standing crops and corn in the granary ; but in
actual practice he would allow his uncle's son a share in these as it
would be considered disreputable to leave the son without
sufficient corn for his immediate necessities. The deceased's
widows may be married by his brother, son, brother's son or
sister's son—according to the wishes of the widow ; there is no
fixed rule and the widow may decide to re-marry outside the
family altogether. In this case the bride-price is divisible by the
deceased's brother and sister's son, the deceased's son having no
share. If the sister's son is too young to be given control of his
uncle's property the uncle's brother may act as trustee, using it to
provide a wife for the lad and in meeting other expenses on the
lad's behalf. He may even use some of it on his own account,
knowing that the lad will one day inherit from him also. The
privileged position occupied by the sister's son is reflected in the
relationship terminology, for you address your father's sister's
child not as " brother " but as " father ", on the ground that

your father's sister's child is the heritor of your father's property and that on your father's death you treat him with the same respect that you formerly accorded to your own father, giving him a share of all game animals killed in the bush, even though he may be your junior in years. This might suggest that the Bachama have changed from a purely mother-right to the present father-right organization, but there is no evidence, traditional or other, of any such change. On the other hand there is at the present time clear evidence of a tendency in favour of abandoning the custom of matrilineal inheritance. I was told by responsible persons at Numan that many Bachama are of the opinion that, under present conditions, it would suit everyone better if a man's property were made wholly heritable by sons. This opinion has recently crystallized to such an extent that it is now permissible for a man to declare publicly that on his death his property should go to his eldest or some favourite son, and that the sister's son should be disqualified, on the pretext that he had not shown his uncle sufficient respect. In some groups succession has become purely patrilineal.

The sense of kinship with the mother's family was undoubtedly in former times greater than that with the father's family : for if a man was murdered or killed in a fight it was incumbent on the sister's son, not the son, to exact vengeance. If he was unable to kill, in return, the actual murderer of his uncle, he would kill the murderer's brother or sister's son. Vice versa the maternal uncle was obliged to exact the penalty for any wrong done to his sister's son ; uncles therefore constantly warned their nephews against any hot-headed action which would involve themselves. The hypothetical case was raised as to whether a man would kill his own father's brother (by the same father) who had killed his sister's son, and the answer given was that in such a case vengeance would be taken by a maternal uncle who was not related to the murderer. The question was also put as to whether a maternal uncle would take action against a man who had killed his sister's son while the latter was engaged in some criminal act. It was stated that in such a case no action would be taken, the uncle being ashamed of the disgrace brought on his family. It is noteworthy also that in cases of witchcraft it was the uterine relatives alone who were implicated. If a person was convicted of witchcraft he and his brothers and sisters (by the same mother),

PLATE 3

YOUTHS DANCING

(Photograph kindly lent by Mr. K. V. Elphinstone)

and his sister's children were sold into slavery and all their property confiscated. Sons were not involved.

The Household. The family being organized on a patrilineal basis the household, if large, may consist of a man and his younger brother or brothers, and their wives, his sons and brothers' sons and their wives and children. Widowed mothers may also be found living with their sons. In many households one may find a sister's son who of his own accord, or because his father's family has died out, has taken up his abode with his maternal uncle. There may also be descendants of uterine relatives. Occasionally one may find in a household a person of slave origin who has been adopted into the kindred ; or a member of another kindred who has attached himself to the household. The following is an example of a household at Numan, the list of members being given by sex and seniority.

Males, Name.	*Clan or kindred.*
Legam (head of the household)	Muja.
Atamasa (son of Legam's eldest brother)	,,
Jibaro (son of Legam's eldest brother)	,,
Ibrahim (son of Legam)	,,
Bawo (son of Legam's eldest brother)	,,
Tamino (son of Legam)	,,
Bubuko (son of Legam's second eldest brother)	,,
Betohula (a distant uterine relative)	Nzonzo.
Ndawula (brother of Betohula)	,,
Pwovima (brother of Betohula)	,,
Piri (no relative of any of the above)	Piri.
Mbake (a very distant uterine relative)	?
Tadimiba (of slave origin).	
Nzakolle (son of Legam)	Muja.
Tawomi (son of Legam)	,,
Peprage (son of Jibaro)	,,
Habila (son of Ibrahim)	,,
Amadu (grandson of Legam's eldest brother)	,,
Tugbe (son of Jibaro)	,,
Ndonde (son of Jibaro)	,,
Gissang (son of Jibaro)	,,
Mahadeng (son of Jibaro)	,,
Andoha (son of Jibaro)	,,

Females, Name.	*Clan or kindred.*
Filo (mother of Jibaro)	Filo.
Momdaki (grandmother of Amadu)	Fwa.
Kalaya (daughter of elder sister of Ibrahim's paternal grandmother)	Zumo.

Females, Name.					Clan or kindred.
Ashettu (mother of Ibrahim)	.	.	.	.	Indiuno.
Damo (widow of Legam's elder brother)				.	Chamba tribe.
Dembinim (wife of Jibaro)	.	.	.	.	Ndaka.
Audi (wife of Jibaro)	.	.	.	.	Zumo.
Moriama (wife of Ibrahim)	.	.	.	.	Tsoato (Bata tribe).
Tamodi (wife of Jibaro)	.	.	.	.	Piri.
Womtipilim (wife of Ibrahim)	.	.	.	.	Tera tribe.
Kasamu (wife of Jibaro)	.	.	.	.	Mbo.
Meale (wife of Bawo)	.	.	.	.	Nzonzo.
Dabo (wife of Bawo)	.	.	.	.	Bata tribe.
Sumbur (wife of Tamino)	.	.	.	.	Kwati.
Shidenu (wife of Nzakolle)	.	.	.	.	Killa.
Somti (wife of Betohula)	.	.	.	.	Chamba tribe.
Gilamto (wife of Betohula)	.	.	.	.	Jeno.
Suko (wife of Ndawula)	.	.	.	.	Filo.
Suwogen (wife of Betohula)	.	.	.	.	Ndaka.
Dabo (wife of Ndawula)	.	.	.	.	Bata tribe.
Pedo (wife of Pwovima)	.	.	.	.	?
Tima (wife of Pwovima)	.	.	.	.	Mbo.

Also various female unmarried children.

This household which constituted a kindred of the Muja clan embraced about fifty-five people. In the event of the death of the head of the house (Legam) the headship would pass to Atamasa the son of Legam's elder brother. It was stated that Legam's spear would be inherited by Atamasa and not by his eldest son Ibrahim (see page 15) as the spear is the symbol of authority.

The following is a list of the relationship terms :—

> Father = Ba.
> Mother = Nuwo.
> Child = Nze (male), Nzito (female).
> Elder brother = Shibiya (male or female speaking).
> Younger brother = Mufwe (male or female speaking).
> Elder sister = Sebeto (male or female speaking).
> Younger sister = Mafwuto (male or female speaking).
> Father's elder brother = Jiji.
> Father's younger brother = Ba.
> Younger brother's child = Nzojo (male speaking).
> Elder brother's child = Nze (male speaking).
> Father's elder brother's wife = Kuko.
> Father's younger brother's wife = Nuwo.
> Husband's younger brother's child = Nzojo.
> Husband's elder brother's child = Nze.
> Father's brother's child = Shibiya (male), Sebeto (female) if older ; Mufwe (male), Mafwuto (female) if younger.
> Father's elder sister = Kuko.
> Father's younger sister = Nuwo.

Younger brother's child = Nzojo (female speaking).
Elder brother's child = Nze (female speaking).
Father's elder sister's husband = Jiji.
Father's younger sister's husband = Ba.
Wife's younger brother's child = Nzojo.
Wife's elder brother's child = Nze.
Father's elder sister's child = Jiji (male), Kuko (female).
Father's younger sister's child = Ba (male), Nuwo (female).
Mother's elder brother = Jiji.
Mother's younger brother is addressed by his personal name or as the "father" of so and so.
Younger sister's child = Nzojo (male speaking).
Elder sister's child is addressed by his personal name.
Mother's elder brother's wife = Kuko.
Mother's younger brother's wife is addressed by a male by her personal name and she does likewise. By a female she is addressed either by her personal name or by the term *Mashi*, a term which is used reciprocally.
Husband's younger sister's child = Nzojo.
Mother's elder brother's child = Nze.
Mother's younger brother's child = Nzojo.
Mother's elder sister = Kuko.
Mother's younger sister = Nuwo.
Younger sister's child = Nzojo (female speaking).
Elder sister's child = Nze (female speaking).
Mother's elder sister's husband = Jiji.
Mother's younger sister's husband = Tsogi.
Wife's younger sister's child = Nzojo.
Wife's elder sister's child = Tsogi.
Mother's elder or younger sister's child = Shibiya (male), Sebeto (female) if older ; Mufwe (male), Mafwuto (female) if younger.
Sister's son's wife = Metinza (male speaking).
Sister's son's child = Nzojo (male speaking).
Sister's daughter's husband = Muro disin (male speaking).
Sister's daughter's child = Nzojo (male speaking).
Father's or mother's father = Jiji (male or female speaking).
Son's or daughter's child = Nzojo (male), Nzojeti (female), male or female speaking.
Father's or mother's mother = Kuko (male or female speaking).
Husband = Mure.
Wife = Meto.
Wife's father = Sherua.
Wife's mother = Sherosin.
Husband's father = Sherua.
Husband's mother = Sherosin.
Daughter's husband = Muro disin (male or female speaking).
Son's wife = Metinza (male or female speaking).
Wife's elder brother = Sherua.
Wife's younger brother = Tsogi.
Wife's elder sister = Sherosin.
Wife's younger sister = Mashi.

Younger sister's husband = Muro disin (male speaking).
Elder sister's husband = Tsogi (male speaking).
Younger sister's husband = Muro disin (female speaking).
Elder sister's husband = Mashi (female speaking).
Husband's elder brother = Sherua.
Husband's younger brother is addressed simply by his personal name, and he so addresses his elder brother's wife. They may also call each other " husband " and " wife " (*mure* and *meto*).
Younger brother's wife = Metinza (male speaking).
Husband's elder sister = Sherosin.
Husband's younger sister = Mashi.
Younger brother's wife = Metinza (female speaking).
Elder brother's wife = Mashi (female speaking).
Wife's elder or younger sister's husband = Tufo.
Husband's elder brother's wife = Sherosin.
Husband's younger brother's wife is addressed by her personal name or as *zhuna*.

A noteworthy feature about this system is that in a tribe which has inheritance by the sister's son there is no special term for maternal uncle. On the other hand there is a special mode of addressing the children of the father's sister by terms implying seniority. You address the son of your father's eldest sister as *Jiji*, a term which is applied to all male blood relatives who are senior to your parents, and you address your father's younger sister's son by the term *Ba* or " father ". It would seem to be clear that the use of these terms is directly due to the circumstance that the property of your father or of your father's senior brother is heritable by your father's sister's son who in consequence becomes a second father to you. You treat him with a respect similar to that which you accorded to your own father during his lifetime, and if you kill an animal in the bush you would send to him the same portion of the quarry which you would have given your own father, even though he (your cousin) may be junior to you in years. The Chamba have precisely the same practice of addressing the father's sister's child as " father ", and the explanation of the extraordinary respect paid in numerous Benue tribes to the father's sister is due, without doubt, to the custom of matrilineal succession.

As already indicated relatives senior to parents are addressed by a term (*Jiji* (male) or *Kuko* (female)) which includes grandparents. This is unusual among tribes in other parts of Nigeria, among whom the difference of two generations creates a social equality, grandsons and grandparents being able to joke with and abuse each other. It is noteworthy therefore that among the Bachama (and most tribes of the Adamawa Province) there is a complete absence of joking familiarity between grandparents and grandchildren.

The classification of elder brothers with members of a senior generation is noteworthy though in no way remarkable. A husband's or wife's elder brother or sister always occupies the same social status as a parent-in-law ; while a husband's or wife's younger brothers or sisters are people towards whom all deference is abandoned. The derivation of the term *Tsogi* (used between a man and his wife's younger brother), and *Mashi* (used between a man and his wife's younger sister) could not be ascertained, but they have the connotation of " playmate ". The term *Zhuna*, which a woman applies to her husband's younger brother's wife, means " rival " and is of course dependent on the practice of the junior levirate marriage. The term *Muro disin* means " the husband of my daughter ", and the term *Metinza* " the wife of my son ". The term *Tufo* used between a man and his wife's sister's husband means " the same road ", and implies that those who use the term are on the same footing as regards matters of social etiquette. The rules of etiquette are observed with a degree of accuracy which implies a close knowledge of the life history of everyone in the community. As an example, among the Bachama, a man who normally addresses his father-in-law as *Sherua*, may also address him as " father ", provided that his own father is of approximately the same age as his wife's father.

In speaking of matters of etiquette two points came to my notice which are perhaps worth recording. A Bachama would no more think of applying the second personal singular pronoun *hye* to one who was older than himself or his social superior than a Frenchman would use *tu* to a person he had never seen before. The singular form is however used towards an equal or inferior. Similarly though *pokauna* is a general word for " good morning ", *hukeda* is the word used in addressing a junior or social inferior. Another point (which has no connection with the above) is that among the Bachama (as among the Jukun) it is the height of bad manners on entering a house to pour forth immediately a volume of salutations. You must stand patiently until your host finishes what he is doing. He then assigns you a place to sit, and when you have both comfortably settled yourselves you begin to greet each other. The normal mode of saluting a superior is by clapping the hands, a custom which extends throughout the Adamawa Province. When people enter the presence of the chief they seat themselves before him, and when the last comer has taken his place they all begin to clap their hands solemnly and keep the clapping up for as much as thirty seconds. It may even last considerably longer, for in answer to each enquiry by the chief as to their welfare, the welfare of their town, of their wives and children and cattle, the volume of clapping increases (it is considered indecorous to give any reply by word of mouth).

In this section we have seen that the Bachama word for " mother " is *nuwo*, and this reminds one of Dr. Barth's assertion that the word *Benue*, or *Binue* as it is generally pronounced, means in the Bata language " mother of waters ". In *Northern Nigeria*, vol i. (p. 10, footnote) the opinion of Dr. Bronnum [1] (who has an intimate knowledge of the Bachama language) is recorded that the word means " great death " from *gbin* =great and *wei* =death. This is the derivation given by the more intelligent Bachama, and like most native derivations, is, I think, fictitious. The word *mbe* is used by some Bata-speaking peoples for water, and it may be that Benue or Gbinuwe is a combination of *mbe* " water " and *nuwo* " mother." In favour of this view there is the fact that among the Bantu-speaking peoples of South Africa it is quite usual to apply the term " mother of waters " to any large river. On the other hand in the Bachama (and Bata) language the dependent genitive follows the noun, so that " mother of waters " would be *nuwo* (*da*) *mbe* and not *mbe* (*da*) *nuwo*. Among the Jukun the Benue is known as Anu or Nu and *nu* is a common Sudanic root for water. It occurs also in the forms *ni* or *ne*.[2] I am inclined therefore to think that the word Binue either means " the great water " (*bin* = great and *nu* = water), or that it is one of those reduplicated words such as are commonly found in Sudanic, and is composed of two roots (*mbe* and *nu*) each meaning " water ". The word *mbene* (river) is found among distant peoples such as the Okande and the Ngkomi of Central Africa. It is worth noting, incidentally, that the

---

[1] Dr. Bronnum has an intimate knowledge of the Bachama, and I am indebted to him for a number of suggestions. He has written, in Danish, a monograph on the Bachama.

[2] See Westermann's *Die Westlichen Sudansprachen*, p. 266.

names Donga and Gongola—both important tributaries of the Benue—occur as words for "river" among the Mbunda and Lujazi of the Zambesi region, and the Lumbila or ancient Busongo of the Kasai region of Central Africa.

Before passing on to the subject of religion a few remarks may be made concerning the material culture of the Bachama. The huts are of the ordinary circular type, with conical thatched roofs, the thatching being carried out on the system of having the head of the straw pointing upwards and not downwards as among the Munshi, Mambila, and Yoruba. This system, which is that of the Hausa and the majority of tribes in the Northern Provinces, gives a neater appearance to the thatching; but it is stated by tribes who follow the reverse system of having the head of the straw pointing downwards that their method is superior, in that the roof is rendered waterproof by a minimum use of straw. I observed that in a number of houses the outer thatching was supported not by rafters (of bamboo or other trees) but by a bell-shaped "dome" of plaited grass-matting reinforced by concentric circlets of grass. This system is common among the Fulani, and in the middle reaches of the Benue is believed to be characteristic of the "Wurbo" or riverain Jukun. It has been adopted by the inland Jukun from the Wurbo. The Bachama and Bata claim that it is their ancient method of roofing. Another feature of Bachama houses is the absence of mud or wooden bedsteads, the normal couch being merely a mat of plaited grass. Head rests of cane are used; as the Bachama, male and female, have elaborate coiffures. The kitchen mills for grinding corn are of a type that I had not observed elsewhere, in that a pot is sunk at the lower end of the grinding stone to receive the flour. Among the Bura and Jukun the flour descends into a well or hollow at the lower end of the mill. A further feature observed in huts was the use of over-head shelves made of reeds woven in checker-work fashion. Checker-worked baskets are commonly employed for depositing or carrying any kind of materials.

The Bachama and Bata, like the Bura of Bornu, make brass pipes and ornaments by the *cire-perdue* method, the industry being in the hands of the Killa clan. Bows are of the usual Benue pattern (devoid of the side niche or shoulder characteristic of most of the Hausa bows). I was particularly struck by the close resemblance of the Bachama and Bata shields to those of the

Borom of Kanam, a photograph of which is given in *Northern Nigeria*, vol. i, p. 30. As regards farming implements the only noteworthy feature is the miniature hoe—an implement so small that it would rank with the Hausa *fatanya*. Of musical instruments there was nothing noteworthy except the use of the xylophone, a description of which appears on page 38. It is clear that this instrument is of foreign importation (from the Sara tribe of French Equatorial Africa) ; it is found among the Kanuri and Bura, but its use has not, to my knowledge, spread any farther west.

In the matter of pottery it is particularly noticeable that the three-legged pot which is in common use among the Bachama and Bata does not appear to extend further westwards than the Jukun-speaking Kona, among whom it is a characteristic feature, and the Chamba of Donga and Takum who came from the east within recent times. It is not found among the Jukun of Wukari ; this affords a further proof that though the Jukun of Kona and the Jukun of Wukari were in close association, religiously and governmentally, there was a definite cultural breach in other respects (at least in later times), the former looking east and the latter being influenced from the west and south.

Characteristic types of pottery among the Bachama are the following :—

But I observed also a pot of peculiarly graceful and classical design of which the following sketch is a rough imitation :—

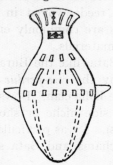

This type of pot is stated to be of non-Bachama origin and was in fact imported from the Piri tribe. With it we may compare the photograph of a Jera pot given in *Northern Nigeria*, vol. i, p. 164.

Religion. The Bachama and Bata appear to differ considerably from other Benue tribes in the general character of their religious ideas. They believe in a remote Sky God, Pua or Hemen Pua, the Lord of the Heavens, but they do not, like many of the Adamawa tribes, associate him with the Sun nor do they perform any rites to the Sun. They have no earth god or goddess like the Jukun and other tribes of Benue Province; nor are they, like the Jukun and Igala, dominated by witchcraft and the cruder forms of "fetishism". They venerate their ancestors by pouring libations of beer and food on the graves of chiefs and forefathers, but the skull cult of neighbouring tribes is not practised except (formerly) in the case of chiefs. Their religion is rather a religion of gods or demi-gods; and their steadfast belief in the power of these deities to protect and regulate their lives tends to throw the more banal religious conceptions into the background.

The gods appear for the most part to have been originally human beings, noted for their bravery or adroitness, who subsequently became deified and endowed with supernatural qualities. Some, however, may have been animal gods in origin, for, though they are credited with a human birth, they are associated with certain animals. Thus though Ngbirrim, the god of Biempti, is said to have been a son of Venin, mother of all the Bachama gods, he is associated with the hyena, which to the Bachama and Bata is the symbol of astuteness. Similarly Gbeso the deity of Boso is known as the Bush Vulture (*Zokarko*).

The cult of *Ma Tiya vene* (i.e. the builder of the house) at Lamurde has however to do with the deified first chief of Lamurde; and that of *Ndzo-Mewa* at Bulki is also a royal cult in honour of Hamabulki, who is said to have been the second son of Venin. The dæmon of Gemen (*Ado minna gwe* = he bit you and entered the ground) was also a royal personage.

The most honoured cult of the Bachama, Bata and Mbula is that of Nzeanzo who is enshrined at Fare, a Bata village some 7 miles east of Numan. Nzeanzo is also known as Zanzo or Njanjo, and the word is said to mean " the boy who is not a boy ". He is believed to have been the youngest of the five sons of a woman Venin, who herself receives divine honours, her death being mourned annually at the feast of Fare held in April. She is said to have come from the skies, and her brother was Wun the God of Death. The names of her father and mother are not known. Nzeanzo's brothers were Hamabulki, Hamagenin, Ngbirrim, and Gbeso (others say Marka) — the founders of the rival Bachama cults. Though Nzeanzo was the youngest son he outshone all his brothers in ability and astuteness, and he corresponds to some extent to the Auta of Hausa tradition. There are numerous tales of his exploits.

While still in his mother's womb he asked her to permit him to be born before his time, but his mother said she had never heard of such a thing, but if he could devise a means of being born, then let him do so. Nzeanzo thereupon came out of his mother's thigh.[1] While he was still a small child his mother left him behind while she went with her other children to visit her brother Wun in order to purchase cattle. Wun pretended to receive his sister joyfully, but resolved to devour her children. So he set her sons to sleep with his four daughters. Nzeanzo, fearing that some evil might befall his brothers, had decided to follow them to the house of Wun, and arrived in the middle of the night. Divining the wicked intention of Wun, he transferred the clothes of Wun's daughters to his brothers, and the loin coverings of his brothers to the girls. Wun rose up in the darkness, and feeling along the line of sleeping children, he seized each child that was wearing a boy's loin cloth and cast it into a pot of boiling water. He then lay down again to sleep. Nzeanzo thereupon roused his brothers, showed them the children of Wun boiling in the pot and the fate they had escaped. He set his mother and his brothers on the road back to Earth and himself followed riding on a hunting-dog. When Wun woke up and found how he had been tricked he hurled a river in front of Nzeanzo, but Nzeanzo caused the river to become a stream and leapt across. Wun then cast a marsh in his way, but Nzeanzo caused it to become merely a pool and, leaping over it, reached home in safety. Thereafter his brothers knew that they were no match for Nzeanzo. It may be that this tale is an attempt to account for the pre-eminence of the later Nzeanzo cult over the pre-existing cults of the Bachama.

---

[1] Compare the Egyptian " Patch comes, appearing from the thigh of Horus " (see Budge, *Osiris*, vol. i, p. 118). Compare also the Jukun story in *A Sudanese Kingdom* (Meek), p. 193.

Many of the tales of Nzeanzo are ætiological. It is said that one day while he was tending his cattle he placed his grandmother in a palm-tree and left her there with a supply of milk. A hippopotamus came along and demanded the milk. But the old lady had drunk all the milk, and so the hippopotamus killed her. Nzeanzo on his return, discovering what had happened, went to the river bank, found the hippopotamus and killed him. As the animal died he said : " Henceforth no one shall cross the Benue except with the aid of wood ; for if a man attempts to swim across he shall be devoured by one of us." And this is the origin of canoes.

Another story of Nzeanzo is that once upon a time Nzeanzo collected all the flies in the world and put them in a calabash. He warned his brothers not to open the calabash. But during his absence they opened it, and hence the plagues of flies which men are now forced to endure.

The Muja and Killa clans believe that they obtained their leechcraft and smithing arts from Nzeanzo.

Among the Mbula there is a tradition, which is not known at Fare, that Nzeanzo was the leader of a tribal movement which embraced the Bachama, Bata, Mbula, and some Tikar, bringing them down-river in a huge iron canoe.[1] He left his brother at Boso while he himself went to Kwolle, but the croaking of the frogs at Kwolle disturbed him, and so he moved to Fare. He then ordered the Mbula of Zuren to make a roof for his house and bring it to Fare. They brought it and were themselves transformed into the wooden posts which supported the roof. This story is paralleled among the Kanakuru in the tale that one of their chiefs, Kadang, directed his young men to weave a huge mat and hold it over their heads. Immediately the young men were turned into posts and Kadang had a house to sit in.

The same informant stated that one of Nzeanzo's brothers went to Kona, and that when Nzeanzo visited his brother he was attracted by the women of Kona, and took one to wife. It is for this reason that the priestess of the cult at Fare is a woman of Kona origin.

The end of the god's life on earth is not clear. Some say that he died for the people, others that he withdrew from the earth

---

[1] Compare the Kede story of Edegi who is said to have come up the Niger in an iron canoe.

because the potency of his person was causing the death of many. With this we may compare the story of Mukasa the boy-god of the Baganda who is said by some to have died, and by others to have disappeared as suddenly as he had come (Roscoe's *Baganda*, p. 292).

The anthropomorphic tales told of Nzeanzo do not lessen the belief in his real divinity, for he is regarded as the giver of rain, the corn-god and even as the creator of man. He is not a remote god, but is immanent on earth, ever present with his people and engaged in a ceaseless contest with Wun the god of death.

The epithets applied to Nzeanzo imply an omniscience and loving care which is quite remarkable in West African theology. He is called the " all-seer " (*dukutun*), " the power that over-shadows all " (*dembu*), " the hollow in the tree " (i.e. the place of refuge). Everything that happens is carried to his ear by the wind ; he is likened to the house lizard (*nzo teko vene*), for he beholds all that takes place ; and to the small black ant (*fafelo*) ; for just as this ant scents out food, so Nzeanzo discerns your innermost thoughts. He is called " Hillocky ground ", for just as the mounted hunter cannot gallop over hillocky ground, so a man cannot over-ride Nzeanzo. He is " The little horn "—you may think you may play with an animal whose horn is small, but you find your mistake. He is *digenno kwalti*, i.e. not an orphan whose ears you may box with impunity. He is like " a milch cow which feeds its calves ", and a " mother-hen which gathers its chickens under its wings ". These similitudes are not the result of Christian teaching at Numan—they have been applied to Nzeanzo from time immemorial. He is even likened to " a rubbish heap "—the place on which people deposit their troubles and offences. Perhaps one of the most remarkable expressions applied to Nzeanzo is *hino hino*, i.e. I am I—I have complete power over all and there is none but me. It has precisely the same meaning as the name of the God of the Hebrews, viz. Yahweh (JEHOVAH).

The cult of Nzeanzo is in the hands of a kindred at Fare whose head bears the title of Kisami. He is assisted by a relative known as Nzo Bellato who acts as spokesman on all public occasions. The third principal official, Nzo Duato, belongs to another kindred, and his duties are to brew the beer and prepare the food offered in the rites—he is in fact the cook of Nzeanzo.

PLATE 4

THE PRIEST OF FARE (with crook)

[*face p.* 28

The medium of the god is a woman known as the Mbamto. She is chosen as a virgin from the town or district of Kona ; which suggests, as has actually been stated, that the cult is of Jukun (Kona) origin, though there is no cult of this name at Kona. Nevertheless the Fare cult does not differ in its general character (though it differs materially in the conception of the deity) from the Jukun cult of Yaku ; for the priestess is in each case regarded as the medium of the god and capable therefore of conveying to the god the wishes of the people and to the people the wishes of the god. Moreover the Fare priestess is commonly addressed as Kuko or grandmother, and this is the meaning also of the Jukun term Yaku.

The Mbamto lives a life of perpetual virginity, being regarded as married to the god who is believed to come to her house in the town every night from his shrine in the bush.[1] During her menses she withdraws from the sacred enclosure to a special hut (compare Roscoe's *Baganda*, p. 276," The female mediums could not perform the temple duties, nor act for the gods during their menses "). She wears her hair long, and is clothed in a skirt of strips of blue ribbon. When she goes abroad she wears, in addition, sandals and anklets of palm leaves smeared with red earth. She is not subject to any food or other taboos, except that her hair must be greased with no other kind of oil save that derived from the manatee fish. It is said that the smell of other oils is offensive to the god, and also that manatee oil has special properties for promoting the growth of the hair.

She is not apparently chosen for any special psychic qualities. On first arrival from Kona, attended by a slave girl, she gives way to many tears at being torn from her home and set among a strange people ; but being well treated she soon resigns herself to her lot. If she displays early signs of qualities inconsistent with her position as wife of the god she is sent away, the god repudiating her. Should it appear that her hair was incapable of growing to at least a moderate length that also would be a sign that Nzeanzo desired her not. Apparently she is not subject to possession

---

[1] The conception of the priestess as the wife of the god is common. In ancient Egypt for example the high priestess was identified with Hathor, the wife of the Heliopolitan Sun-god (see *ERE.*, vol. xii, p. 777). And in Babylon women were set apart as the human wives of Bel. In the Hausa *bori* worship the priestess Arifa was not allowed to have a human husband (see Tremearne, *Ban of the Bori*, p. 275). See also Ellis, *The Tshi-speaking Peoples of the Gold Coast*, p. 121 ; and Talbot, *Peoples of S. Nigeria*, vol. ii, p. 132.

by the god, like some mediums—indeed it was stated that the hysterical symptoms usually regarded as evidence of possession would, in her case, be considered a sign of the god's repudiation.

The shrine of Nzeanzo is in the bush some three quarters of a mile from the village. It was formerly in Fare itself, but was removed to the bush as the god could not endure the noise of the village. The priestess occupies a compound inside the village, the innermost hut being sacred to the god—no one being allowed to enter it save the Mbamto. A fire is kept burning there all night long ; and with this we may compare the sacred fire of the temples of the gods of the Baganda, whose religion appears to bear a striking resemblance to that of the Bachama and Bata (see Roscoe's *Baganda*, p. 275). Here she holds nightly converse with Nzeanzo with whom she is believed to have sexual inter-course.

He reveals to her his divine desires, and expression is given to these desires in the Bata tongue, and not in a gibberish as is frequently the case in cults of a similar character. He is believed by many to have a white skin, to be clothed in white, and to ride a white horse.

It may be noted in passing that Fare is not the only town distinguished by a priestess. The Bachama town of Nzumoso is governed by a woman ; and it would appear that the *raison d'être* for this is religious rather than political. For in this town there is a female spirit known as Gyengoro, and though a male looks after her shrine he takes his orders from the priestess-chief. She is said to have been given her position by her brother Hamabulki, the founder of the town and cult of Bulki. In this connection I note in a report of Major Glasson that, among the Chamba Tsugu of South Cameroons, one Ganlugeni is said to have made his sister head of the town of Debbo, and high priestess of the important cult there. Elsewhere in Nigeria I have only met with chieftainesses among the Gwari of Niger Province ; and as far as I can recollect they belonged, not to the Gwari tribe, but to the pre-Fulani ruling families of Zaria. The famous Queen Amina, who conquered all the Hausa States, was also traditionally connected with Zaria. It may be recalled that Thebes was at one time governed by sacerdotal princesses.

To the shrine of Nzeanzo all Bachama, Bata, and Mbula (the last in particular) constantly resort, either to solicit help in times

PLATE 5

SYMBOLS OF THE CULT OF NZEANZO

of trouble or to offer thanks in times of prosperity. Those who are sick go to the shrine or send a representative. They take with them a gift of beer and a piece of cloth, or a chicken, and these are handed to Kisami, who places the beer and cloth on a three-forked stick outside the hut of Mbamto. There they remain overnight, and the god is believed to accept the " substance " of the gifts (which are actually appropriated and used by the officials of the cult).

In the morning the suppliants, accompanied by the Kisami, sit outside the hut of Mbamto and clap their hands in salutation. They state their request, which the Kisami repeats. The Mbamto may reply that the cause of the sickness is due to an offence against Nzeanzo or some other deity, and direct that a further offering be brought ; or she may remain silent, being regarded merely as the medium by which the prayer is brought to the notice of the god. Heads of families present themselves before the god at the beginning of the agricultural year with some such prayer as : " I come to you, Nzeanzo, as we purpose soon to begin planting : do you look after me and all my family : let no evil thing befall us in our work. If you turn your back on us then we shall be sore beset ; but if your face is turned towards us no harm can overtake us." The Kisami repeats this prayer saying : " Your slave says so and so : do you hold him by your right hand." Thanksgiving offerings are also brought to Fare by farmers on the conclusion of the harvest. On the death of a relative a man may betake himself to Fare and make some such prayer as : " Your slave whom you cared for in the world, you have taken. I come therefore to beseech you to help all of us who are left." The suppliant on the conclusion of his prayer takes a little dust from the ground near the sacred symbol and casts it over his left and right shoulder.

The cult is of some judicial importance ; for one who suffers a loss by theft will go to the shrine and call on the god to take vengeance on the thief. The thief, hearing of this, may be stricken with fear and present himself at the shrine, confessing his crime and asking the forgiveness of the god : for it is believed that the god takes vengeance on an unrepentant thief, not merely by killing the thief himself, but by extirpating his entire family. In political matters also the cult was in former times at least not unimportant, for if a chief oppressed his people, the Kisami, directed by Mbamto as the mouthpiece of the god, could warn the chief that if he did not mend his ways he would be slain by Nzeanzo.

The principal festival of the cult is held at the end of April, and is attended by hundreds of people from the surrounding districts. It marks the opening of the agricultural season, being a necessary preliminary to planting, and is directed towards securing the good offices of the god in all farming operations. But it is also a mourning festival commemorating the death of Venin the mother of Nzeanzo ; for it is believed that by thus showing respect to his mother the favour of the god himself is enlisted. The festival lasts three days. It is not attended by the chiefs of the Bachama and Bata, as these chiefs are regarded as being in a sense the " sons of the god ". The chief of the Mbula, however, is present ; for the Mbula tribe are considered to be in a special way " the slaves of Nzeanzo ".

A word may be said in passing about the position of the chief in regard to cults in general. The chief does not himself perform religious rites, and it is perhaps misleading to apply to him the term priest-king. He is, however, the overseer or president of all the cults and is held responsible for the due performance of the rites. This entails the provision of gifts at stated periods, or on special occasions such as the occurrence of a drought.[1] If he fails in this, any misfortunes that befall the tribe are ascribed to his failure : if he is punctual in his duties no blame can be laid at his door.

On the other hand, the gifts sent by the chief are not to be regarded merely as dues paid. Before despatching them the chief addresses them, as though they were endowed with life and under-standing, saying : " I send you to my forefather (a general description of all the cults)—do you salute him. And do you, my forefather, assist me in all matters affecting my welfare and that of my people—grant that we may increase in numbers, that sick-ness may be driven away and that rain and food may be abun-dant." These spoken words are believed to have a compelling effect on the deity. From this point of view the king may be regarded as a priest. But he is more than a priest, for the gods are thought to be close to, or even immanent in, his person. It is for

---

[1] On the occasion of a drought the Bachama chief, like the Jukun, presents a black cloth to the cult.

this reason, therefore, that the person of the chief is believed to be
charged with a dynamism which makes it dangerous for anyone
to sit close to him and still more to be touched by him. It is taboo
for the chief to point his finger in anger at a man, or to strike the
ground with his hand ; for by so doing he projects against the
people the destroying force of the divinities attendant upon him.
Even articles which are in constant association with the chief are
dangerous to touch—his bed, mat, gown are all charged with
dynamic force. It is for this reason that a chief's mat or stool is
commonly used as the medium on which oaths are sworn. (A
chief may however give away one of his gowns without endanger-
ing the recipient. The fact of bestowing the gift with his own
hands is believed to insulate it.) It will thus be seen (and this
conception extends the whole length of the Benue) that the chief
is much more than a priest—he is so closely in touch with divinity
that he is almost a divinity himself—a relative of the gods (as
one chief stated).

Some twenty days before the Fare rites are begun Kisami goes
to Lamurde and announces that the time of the festival is at hand.
The chief of the Bachama presents him with eight *taji* (bars
of iron formerly used as currency), pieces of cloth, fish, sauce, some
Bomanda salt, a hippopotamus skin, and eight spear shafts. Some
days later the Mbamto presents herself before the chief and
receives similar gifts, together with a skin bag (which she carries
on her shoulder during the festival) and a cloth skirt. In express-
ing her thanks she says : " As the gifts have been given in good
time we shall have health and a bountiful harvest. Had you
delayed beyond the appointed time misfortune would have
overtaken us." Finally, two days before the festival begins, the
chief is visited by yet another official of the cult, the Zikeno
Kpake (compare the Jukun title Zikê) who informs the chief and
the general community of the time-table for the entire
ceremony.

I was present during the greater part of the festival. On the
morning of the first day all proceeded to the shrine of Nzeanzo in
the bush. The senior members present took up a position close
to the shrine, the younger men sitting behind. Each elder held in
his hands a hoe, and on his right shoulder had a crozier-sceptre
made of the hide of a hippopotamus and covered with some
crocodile skin. These sceptres are similar in shape and size to the

D

sceptres of the Pharaohs of Ancient Egypt, which were originally part of the insignia of Osiris.[1]

All sat on their heels—the supreme attitude of respect. The official Nzo Bellato then rose and, taking a hoe, made three furrows in the ground. The leader of the younger men thereupon stepped forward, and, placing his hands over those of Nzo Bellato, pressed the hoe against the ground. Then taking the hoe into his own hands he began hoeing vigorously along the path that led to the town, followed by the other young men who had taken the hoes from their elders.

Meanwhile the drums had struck up a chant, and the old men danced a slow one-step behind the young men as they hoed their way forward. When they reached a point some 300 yards from the shrine of the god they raised a small mound of earth, in which the leader of the young men stuck two fragments of his hoe handle which he had formally broken in two. The explanation given for the breaking of the hoe handle was that when you hoe the farm of the king—and the king was in this instance the god— you must put all your vigour into the work ; and a broken hoe handle is a common result of vigorous hoeing. All then danced slowly back to the shrine of Nzeanzo, and were there met by the Kisami who danced a solo step round the staves of Nzeanzo-sticks, surmounted by brass ornaments, planted in front of the shrine. Mbamto then appeared, attended by four old women and three young men, and began dancing slowly towards the shrine of the god. When they reached the entrance of the hut Mbamto danced forward by herself, entered the shrine and soon reappeared still dancing the one-step with bent body.

It is noteworthy that in these hoeing rites there is no formal planting of seed. Towards the end of the wet season, however, seed provided by the chief of the Bachama, who like the Jukun king is believed to be the earthly repository of the life of the corn, is formally planted close to the shrine of the god. The intention attached to this planting of seed at the end of the agricultural year was stated to be that the seed given by the god should be formally returned to him for safe-keeping during the dry season. It is analogous to the Verre custom of " burying the life of the corn ", a custom which may be related genetically to the ancient Egyptian practice of burying effigies of Osiris made of earth and

---

[1] See *Encyclopædia of Religion and Ethics*, vol. vi., p. 648.

PLATE 6

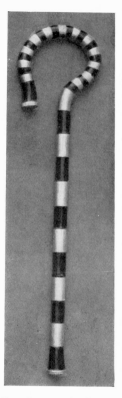

THE BACHAMA PRIEST'S CROOK

THE PHARAOH'S CROOK

corn. Nzeanzo is, as Osiris came to be,[1] the corn god, and it is said of him that he first gave hoes and seed to men.

On the conclusion of the Mbamto's dance the male members of the various villages grouped themselves by villages in a circle. There was no general intermingling ; and the reason given was that the god wished to view the numbers of each village in order that he might know what havoc Death had played with them during the preceding year. If he observed that they had become reduced he would, it was said, send back to them some of their brethren who had died (for the Bachama like most Nigerian tribes believe in the re-incarnation of at least some of the dead).

The younger men then engaged in wrestling bouts, two grown-up men, known as Balagwe, acting as judges and masters of the ceremonies. They carried in their hands long ropes which they swung round the ring to keep it clear. They invited candidates to come forward by calling out : " Where is the young man who would seek a fall with his brother ? " A candidate would enter the ring and sit on his heels until one of his own age and size appeared. The contest began by each young man assuming a crouching position and picking some dust from the ground in order to give him a better hold. Contact was obtained by the opponents clasping each other round the neck with the left hand, the right being used to obtain an opening. It was a catch-as-catch-can contest and the legs were freely used to trip up the opponent and land him on his back. If, during the encounter, one of the contestants touched the ground with both hands or turned his back on his opponent, the bout was given against him. Every now and then the contestants broke away for a few moments, and resumed after rubbing their hands again in sand. The contests were carried out in solemn fashion ; and though the victor was greeted by his townsmen, who surrounded him and danced with him round the ring, he betrayed no sign of emotion.[2]

While the wrestling was going on all the grown-up women,

---

[1] It would appear that Osiris was originally conceived as the Nile-god and hostile to humanity, but as the Egyptians learned to use the annual inundation he became transformed into a beneficent power and identified not only with the soil but with the grain.   In the " Coffin Texts " he expresses himself as " I am Osiris . . . I live as grain, I grow as grain . . . I am barley " (see *ERE.*, vol. ix, p. 219*b*). Breasted (p. 23) speaking of the god says, " The ever-waning and reviving life of the earth, sometimes associated with the life-giving waters, sometimes with the fertile soil, or again discerned in vegetation itself—that was Osiris."

[2] Among the Ibo wrestling is an important feature of the new yam festival (see Talbot's *Some Nigerian Fertility Cults*, p. 114).

those subject to possession, had formed themselves into a company numbering about a hundred, and began marching slowly up and down a cleared space some distance from the wrestling ring. Each had a cloth skirt of blue, white, and yellow (red being taboo to the god). In her right hand she carried a staff to which streamers of cloth were attached (I have seen similar staves used by the Gwari women of Niger Province).

Oblivious of all others present they marched with the slow step used by troops attending a funeral, for they are the horses of the god, and, just as a king rides slowly, so they must proceed discreetly. As they marched they sang a monotonous chant, some sentences of which were as follows :—" Nzeanzo says, let horses in plenty be assembled on the morrow, that he may mount them and drive away Death. For Death shall be put to flight and no longer shall he deplete the land." " Nzeanzo is like a father of a son—a father permits no one to chastise his offspring and Nzeanzo will not permit Death to chastise mankind." " Afore-time Death was amongst us, but a thing will happen and men shall no longer die." " Nzeanzo went to the house of Death, but found him not for he had flown." " March gently, march gently, that Nzeanzo may not be angry with us. We are the steeds of Nzeanzo and he has put the bit in our teeth." " Nzeanzo, the youngest of all, excels the gods of Bulki and of Boso and of the White Men, for he seeks out Death to pierce him with his spear." " Kisami is ruler of the Fare festival ; he alone may summon the people and we give him thanks." The funereal character of the women's march and song was in keeping with the main idea of the festival, a commemoration of the death of the mother of the god. The march was maintained for four hours with occasional intervals of a few minutes. Every now and then a woman would be seized by the spirit and become dazed or semi-conscious. When this happened two of her friends supported her and walked her back-wards and forwards in the opposite direction to the others, until she recovered her equanimity.

Throughout the morning the older men, sitting apart, regaled themselves with beer (but I did not observe a single case of drunkenness during the three days of the festival). Occasionally they too would rise and dance round the wrestling ring in the slow one-step which was alone employed. They first stripped themselves of all clothes above the waist and danced with cloths

PLATE 7

MARCH OF THE MOURNING WOMEN

[face p. 36

girt about their waist in Jukun fashion. The younger men wore
triangular loin coverings of blue, white, and yellow cloth, and
leglets and armlets of plaited grass. All weapons were taboo, and
as one came along the road from Fare to the shrine one
saw the branches of trees littered with knives, spears, swords,
bags, and articles of unrequired clothing. No one had any fear of
losing his clothing or property ; theft during the festival is un-
thinkable, and anyone finding property, obviously lost, takes it to
the Kisami who restores it to the owner on application.

About 2 p.m. the proceedings at the shrine terminated, and all
returned to the village where, in the evening about 5 p.m., the
women—the horses of Nzeanzo—resumed their solemn march.
At sunset the Kisami and his followers appeared dancing, carrying
short swords in their right hands. All the men joined in behind
them, the seniors holding the " Staves of Nzeanzo," the hereditary
possession of each family-head. They danced towards the house
of Mbamto, and the procession was followed up by the Mbamto
herself, who also danced, holding in her right hand a forked stick.
She was preceded by two women carrying each a basket filled with
pots used in the rites, and behind her were two old women, the
wives of Kisami and her personal attendants. This concluded the
ceremonial for the first day.

On the second day, the day that draws the greatest crowds, the
entire proceedings took place in the village of Fare itself. The
mournful atmosphere of the previous day gave place to one of
unrestrained joy. Everyone, man, woman and child, turned out in
his most gaudy attire, and one saw no more of the company of
mourning women. The proceedings were opened about one
o'clock with wrestling bouts, the judges vigorously cracking their
whips like showmen at a circus. While the wrestling was going on
the young men from neighbouring villages began arranging their
toilet for the dance, and a gorgeous toilet it was. In their braided
hair they set two parallel rows of stork feathers, after the fashion of
North American Indians. In this they assisted each other, and
looking-glasses were used to see that all was correct. Some of the
men did not use feathers but decked their hair with oval pieces of
copper arranged after the fashion of a Roman helmet. On
their waists they wore corselets of decorated plaited grass, and on
their arms bracelets made from the beards of goats. Around
their loins were triangular cloths pulled between the legs from

back to front, and decorated in various colours, a number having streamers attached. Some wore fringed kilts of leather and a few had baggy blue trousers. Leglets of plaited grass, corresponding in colour to the corselets, were also worn, and on the right ankle each had an iron rattle with which he stamped time to the dance. In their right hands they held short swords or knives. The costume of the women was even more striking. Their braided hair was studded with oval pieces of copper arranged in helmet fashion. On the back they wore corsets of blue and white beads, the strings of which were fastened tightly across the breasts and the abdomen. Over their waists were short, fringed skirts of many colours. A notable feature was that each woman carried a spear in her right hand. Even the small girls carried spears, the points being tipped with wood as a safeguard against accidents.

The members of each town held a preliminary dance on their own account ; but about four o'clock the dancers had formed a huge circle and kept moving slowly round and round. The musical instruments used were the oblong, single, and double membrane drums beaten by hand, and also small single membrane drums of pottery, the lower end of which was open.

There were two xylophone players (the xylophones were of the type known as " Sara "—graded cow-horns mounted on a wooden framework, the joints sealed with wax, being used as resonators : the tip of each horn was cut off and blocked with beeswax, a small aperture being left which was covered with some spider's web. A wooden block was suspended over the mouth of each horn. The player used two forked sticks as strikers—one in each hand).

On the conclusion of this, the main dance of the day, all the onlookers proceeded to take up a position on the raised ground surrounding the wrestling ring, round which the dancers (who must have numbered two or three hundred) slowly performed their one-step in a crouching position, the men shaking their swords to the beat of the tune and the women their spears. The women danced with eyes closed, and a waggle of the head which gave them appearance of being half-witted. About 5 p.m. the dance was stopped on the appearance of the Kisami and the senior men of Fare, who all sat down in the centre of the ring. Nzo Bellato then rose, his crozier-sceptre hanging on his shoulder,

PLATE 8

MALE DANCERS AT THE FARE FESTIVAL (second day)

[face p. 38

and holding in his right hand a short knife surmounted by a rattle and covered over with hibiscus fibre. Shaking the knife-rattle up and down as he spoke, he delivered himself of an oration —of which the following is a rough summary : " The ' spear ' I hold in my hand was given us of old by Nzeanzo, not for purposes of war, but that it might be planted in his house, and that we might become his servitors. Nzeanzo also gave us horses that we might go to the bush and hunt, and that we might bring the quarry killed and lay it before this spear as a gift to him. For all bush animals are his, and the lions of the bush are merely the dogs of Nzeanzo. Even women know this, for we are told of old that in the earliest days a woman bore a child ; and for a moment she left her child to go and fetch some water. But when she reached the well she saw some vultures hovering in the bush, and she straightway left her pitcher saying ' A lion has killed some bush animal ' ; and she bethought herself nought about the child, but went and found the flesh and laid it before the ' spear '[1] of Nzeanzo. Moreover Nzeanzo demands that fish be brought to him ; for did he not appoint Bemin to have control of the river that fish might be brought and laid before the ' spear ' ? Nzeanzo took fish in his right hand and gave them to the men of Fare, and he took corn in his left hand and gave it to the men of Fare. But now he has turned his back on us, and people are making mock of us. Aforetime Nzeanzo apppointed the men of Mbula to be the slaves of the men of Fare—he gave them corn so that if the men of Fare lacked corn they would find it with the Mbula. But now both we and the Mbula lack corn, for Nzeanzo has turned his back on us. Nzeanzo is without a peer. Once upon a time a youth of Waduku (a rival Bachama cult), his name was Belim—a man of surpassing strength—bethought himself that he would go to Fare and overthrow the strongest of the men of Fare in a bout of wrestling. But when he reached Numan his strength began to fail, and he was hurled down by a Fare stripling before the ' spear ' of Nzeanzo. A youth of Yimburu thought likewise and met with a similar fate. A youth of Duom set out in the morning with all his strength, but in the afternoon he was tumbled upside down before the ' spear ' of Nzeanzo. A young man of Kedimin, the strongest they had, was sent to overthrow the youths of Fare ; but

---

[1] The emblem of the cult, though styled a spear, is in reality an iron rod with lugs at the top.

his strength flowed away at the first stream on the road. The day of rejoicing is here, and all the people are assembled before the spear of Nzeanzo. Aforetime there was good fellowship; but husbands are now jealous of their wives—if a husband sees a man making friendly conversation with his wife at Fare he goes and sharpens his sword! But if a man pursues a woman by reason of what she did at Fare, Nzeanzo will pursue him and strike him dead, and ants will enter his nostrils, and his whole kindred will perish. If one man has followed another for a debt, and meets him at Fare, let him but point a finger at him and Nzeanzo will slay him. Nevertheless, you women, think not that, because there is freedom at Fare,[1] you can offer yourselves to men as a bitch in heat offers itself to a dog. For if you do, it will recoil on your own heads. Let all the people avoid adultery and theft and evil-feeling. May Nzeanzo grant us rain and crops in plenty, and if a man goes hunting in the bush and nurses no evil in his heart may he return home in safety."

The main points of interest in this speech are :—(i) The jealousy displayed towards other cults; (ii) The warning to the women that the special licence permitted at Fare is not to be taken as the normal standard of behaviour; (iii) The dissatisfaction expressed at the general condition of things at the present time. With regard to the last point the primary concern of the officials of the cult is, of course, their own personal advantage; for they are not slow to ascribe a bad harvest, such as that of last year, to a neglect of the god and incidentally of themselves. Nevertheless throughout the pagan tribes of the Benue there is a firm belief that sickness and death have reached a pitch which was never known before, and which is ascribed, not to the opening up of communications facilitating the spread of epidemic diseases, but to the abandonment of ancient customs as a result of European intrusion. The worth of our Government is gauged by the signs of the times; and when a series of epidemics is followed by a bad harvest, the European administration is blamed; if it could be personified it would be put to death (in accordance with the custom of slaying the king in times of adversity).

At the conclusion of the Nzo Bellato's speech, which was listened to in silence, the people of Fare, led by the Kisami and Mbamto, performed a dance of their own in honour of Nzeanzo.

[1] The sexual freedom permitted at Fare is no doubt symbolical of fertility.

PLATE 9

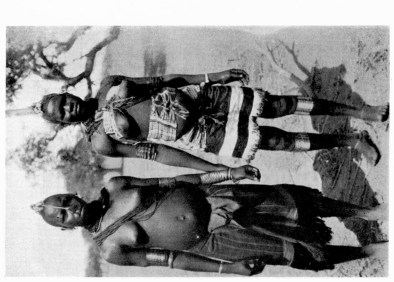

FEMALE DANCERS AT THE FARE FESTIVAL (second day)

[face p. 40

This concluded the ceremonial of the second day. Many of the visitors set out for their homes, but large numbers remained until the following morning, most of them being obliged to sleep out in the open. On the following morning the men of Mbula mounted their horses and went off hunting. They returned in the evening and handed over the quarry—one or two small antelopes—to Kisami, who gave them gifts of beer in return. Informal dancing was carried on in the village throughout the morning, and the wrestling bouts were also continued. In the evening dancing was renewed ; but by this time most of the visitors had returned to their villages.

In connection with the cult of Nzeanzo there is a sacred pot which is kept at Fare. When a Bachama chief dies or when the pot gets worn out or broken there are special rites for the making of a new one. Application is made to Ndako of Yimburu who is the priest-guardian of a deep pool of water, at the bottom of which innumerable spirits are believed to have their home. It is Ndako's business to procure some of the mud from the bottom of the pool, for the mud in which the spirits reside is believed to be charged with magical power. A large canoe is brought into the pool, and three or four bamboos are lashed together and are thrust down into the bottom of the pool. By this Ndako descends, and it is said that when he reaches the bottom he inquires for the spirits, but finds only the children of the spirits, the father-spirits having gone off to the bush that day. The children ask Ndako what has brought him to their abode. He says that if they will bring him some mud from their houses he will give them some salt. The young spirits go off and bring the mud, and Ndako allows them to lick his fingers which have been smeared with Bomanda salt. He promises the spirits that if they will go to their houses and return in a few minutes he will give them some more salt. So off they go. Immediately Ndako sticks pieces of the mud in each of his finger and toe-nails, and by shaking the bamboo pole he makes it known to the canoe-men above that he wishes to return to the surface. The canoe-men pull up the pole and Ndako falls unconscious into the canoe. The crew paddle off as fast as they can, and make for the village of Duom and then of Numan, at both of which they are given gifts. They then return to Yimburu where they are given further gifts from the chief of the Bachama. The sacred mud is mixed with mud from the village of Kiken, and parings of the nails of the deceased chief are included. With this mixture the pot is made (by any skilled old woman). The pot is sent by the Bachama chief to the Mbamto at Fare in charge of a virgin girl, who remains at Fare as an attendant on the Mbamto. The pot is used for making first-fruit offerings of beer to the god. It is also a royal talisman. It is said that if the chief displays apathy towards the cult the pot is set out in the midday sun and the chief is immediately assailed with sickness. This is similar to the Kona practice. If the chief of the Kona offended the priest who was keeper of the royal skulls, the latter retaliated by exposing the skulls to the rays of the sun. The chief, it was said, immediately fell sick, and if he did not promptly tender his apologies (accompanied by gifts) he would be " gathered to his forefathers ".

In leaving the subject of the Fare festival a few speculative remarks may be permitted. There are features about the character and personality of Nzeanzo which at first sight suggest that this Bachama and Bata god is a distant reflection of Jesus received perhaps from the Christianized peoples of North Africa or of Abyssinia. The miraculous birth of the god, the respect paid to his mother, the Jesus-like similitudes applied to him (such as that he is like a mother-hen which gathers her chickens under her wing, and that he is a rubbish-heap on which men may deposit their offences), and the conception of the fatherhood of God, are all suggestive of Christian influence.

On the other hand it is becoming increasingly evident that much of the doctrine which was formerly believed to have originated with Jesus was current in Ancient Egypt and in other countries surrounding the Mediterranean many centuries before the Christian era. Venin and Nzeanzo would appear to belong to the same group of gods and goddesses as Osiris, Horus, and Isis ; Adonis and Aphrodite ; Baal and Astarte ; Demeter and Dionysus ; and Cybele and Attis. The cult of Isis and Horus pervaded the ancient world from the time of the VIth. Egyptian dynasty to the latter days of the Roman Empire. In Egypt, Horus appears under three aspects : (a) as the greater Horus, brother of Osiris ; (b) as son of Osiris and avenger of his father ; and (c) as Horus the child—Harpekhroti (Harpocrates)—son of Isis. It was the last aspect that was the most popular, and the combination of Isis with Horus led to a world-wide devotion to her

PLATE 10.

THE FARE FESTIVAL

CHALLENGERS TO A BOUT AT WRESTLING

[face p. 42

as the mother-goddess.[1] In Christian times, when the antagonism between the religion of Jesus and the cult of Isis had subsided, Horus became identified with Christ and Isis with the Virgin Mary. The rites practised in Roman times on the first day of the Isis festival were carried out with manifestations of the deepest grief, figuring the search for the body of Osiris ; whereas on the ensuing day there was unrestrained joy in honour of the resurrection of the god. Among the Bachama the first day is a day of grief, Venin mourning for her son, who has disappeared and is engaged in a mortal combat with Death. Just as Horus the son of Isis waged constant war against his uncle Set, so Nzeanzo fought and overcame his uncle Wun, the god of Death. The fight apparently recurs annually and figures the death and resurrection of the crops. It may be recalled that in classical times the cult of Dionysus the infant god and son of Demeter was a reflection of the Osiris myth. One form of the legend of Dionysus was that he descended into Hades to bring up his mother from the dead, just as Nzeanzo is said to have rescued his mother and brothers from Wun, the god of the lower world. In this connection we may quote Sir James Frazer who, speaking of Dionysus, says : " His return from the lower world, in other words his resurrection, was annually celebrated on the spot by the Argives. Whether this was a spring festival does not appear, but the Lydians certainly celebrated the advent of Dionysus in Spring ; the god was supposed to bring the season with him. Deities of vegetation who are believed to pass a certain portion of each year underground naturally come to be regarded as gods of the lower world or of the dead. Both Dionysus and Osiris were so conceived " (*Golden Bough*, abr. ed., p. 389). In the Verre and Kugama custom of burying the corn-spirit we would seem to have a definite instance in Nigeria of this Osiris-like conception ; and when Sir James Frazer continues (p. 378) to remark that " possibly in prehistoric times the kings themselves played the part of the god ", we are immediately reminded that in the Benue regions, especially among the Jukun, the king is identified with the corn ; and that just as the body of Osiris was dismembered, so parts of the body of Jukun, Kona, Bachama, and Bata chiefs were preserved with the object of securing the continuance of the life of the crops.

---

[1] See Flinders Petrie in *E.R.E.*, v, p. 247.

Still another parallel cult in classical times was that of Cybele and Attis, the Great Mother and her stripling son. Under the Roman Empire the rites were held during the latter part of March. On 15th March, the College of Cannophori, or reed-bearers, carried reeds in procession, a custom said to be a commemoration of the finding of Attis by Cybele on the reedy banks of a river. With this we may compare the carrying by the Bachama women of staves with cloth streamers. On 24th March, *dies sanguinis*, fasting and mourning symbolized the grief of the mother at the death of Attis. 25th March was the day of rejoicing at the god's resurrection, and it was a day of universal licence. Attis was regarded as the symbol of the plant kingdom. His death and burial symbolized the death of plant life through the winter : his resurrection the return of spring. He and the Great Mother were also thought of later as parallel to Christ and the Virgin.

A few further remarks may be made on the subject of Bachama religion. As already indicated the cult of gods overshadows that of ancestors. Nevertheless a Bachama is not neglectful of his ancestors and frequently offers prayers at the graves of his forefathers. If a Bachama was killed in war it was considered necessary that his wandering soul should be brought home to the family burial-hut. A diviner or seer was accordingly dispatched to the bush to discover the ghost and lead it back. Armed with a calabash of water he started off ; and, as he hunted the bush, he kept striking the calabash with a grass-stalk to attract the ghost's attention. Suddenly he would descry the ghost, speak to him, and invite him to enter the calabash that he might be taken home to join the company of his departed relatives. The ghost did as he was bid, and the seer, hastening home, emptied the calabash of water at the threshold of the family burial-hut. This rite is exactly paralleled among the Ngizim of Bornu for the recovery of souls stolen by witchcraft. The Ngizim seer retrieves the stolen soul in a calabash of water and hurrying home empties the water over the patient, who, conscious of the restoration of his soul, heaves a sigh of relief and is, it is said, speedily restored to health.

The Bachama like most Nigerian tribes believe in re-incarnation, or it might be more correct to say in the possibility of re-incarnation. For re-incarnation ideas in Nigeria are hazily held and never amount to an absolute faith. This is the explanation of the apparently illogical custom of continuing to offer sacrifices to

PLATE II

WRESTLING AT THE FARE FESTIVAL

[face p. 44

a dead ancestor who at the same time is believed to have returned to the world as a grandchild or child of a friend (i.e. who is re-born from the womb of his son's wife or the wife of a friend). Re-incarnations are the exception rather than the rule. If a child shows a marked physical resemblance to a deceased ancestor he is regarded as that ancestor re-born and is treated with silent respect. If a child cries a lot and the divining-apparatus declares him to be a returned forefather, he will be given a small loin-covering and miniature bow and arrow as though he were some grown-up person. His mother will even take him out to the fields and, pointing to the cows and sheep and goats, say to him; " See, there are all your cows, just as you left them ; so cry no more, for they are yours and we have not robbed you of a single one ! "

Ideas as to the condition of life in the next world are as hazy as our own. The abode of the dead is known as Jia Palami or the Red Country, but I was unable to obtain any explanation of this term.[1] Life there is a replica of that on earth, with the exception that people rest from their labours. Retributive ideas are present to some extent, for it is said that the ghosts of evil men are tied up and subjected to beatings at the hands of their fellows, by direction of the presiding spirits.

There are special hunting and head-hunting rites. In every village may be seen a collection of standing stones surrounded with the heads of the larger game. When a Bachama kills a lion, leopard, rhinoceros, buffalo, elephant, hippopotamus, or wart-hog, the fame of his exploit is soon made known, and on returning he is saluted on the outskirts of the town by everyone who owns a horse. He is escorted to the hunting shrine before which he sits down. The chief or some senior man takes the tail of the dead animal and, speaking words of congratulation, touches the arm of the hunter with the tail. He then smears some flour over the head and body of the hunter, with the intention, it was stated, of pro-tecting him from pursuit by the ghost of the dead animal. In the dry season the hunter's friend, who had previously carried home

---

[1] The Red Country is a term used by the Hausa for the abode of the " *bori* " spirits. It is said to be situated between Ghat and Asben, but no living person has ever seen it. Anyone entering it would never appear again (see Tremearne, *Ban of the Bori*, p. 255). It is perhaps worth noting that in the Osiris cycle Set, " the Red Fiend," seems to stand for the red desert soil as opposed to the black soil of the alluvial plain (see *ERE.*, vol. ix, p. 220).

the head of the animal, seeks out a monolith in the bush and brings it to the town. The hunter and his brethren, mounted on horses, attack this stone with sticks as though they were beating the life out of the animal itself. The stone is then deposited with the other stones in the shrine, and offerings are made to it periodically, presumably to pacify the ghost of the dead animal. On the same principle one who had killed an enemy in war deposited in his compound a stone symbolizing his dead enemy, and to this made periodical offerings. The enemy's head was, as in the case of dangerous animals, brought home by the slayer's friend and not by himself. It was deposited with a kindred of Piri (and not Bachama) descent, because the Piri rites were considered superior for allaying the dead man's ghost. The slayer carefully avoided sleeping in his own house until some days after the conclusion of the rites.

The use of stones as the symbol or abode of dead ancestors is common among the Jukun and many tribes of the Southern Cameroons.

A few words may be said about the agricultural rites of the Bachama. We have seen that the Fare festival is primarily connected with the opening of the agricultural year, and it would appear that among the Bachama the rites preceding the sowing of the crops are of more importance in the minds of the people than the harvest rites of thanksgiving. It is said that in former times one of the king's own children was sacrificed annually during the fertility rites of " Pilla " carried out at Lamurde, and that in comparatively recent times the human victim was replaced by a black cow. This reminds us of the ancient custom of the sacrifice of the king's son and we may here once more quote Sir James Frazer who, in speaking of the custom, says : " We may fairly infer that in Thessaly and probably in Bœotia there reigned of old a dynasty of which the kings were liable to be sacrificed for the good of the country . . . but that they contrived to shift the fatal responsibility to their offspring . . . As time went on, the cruel custom was so far mitigated that a ram was accepted as a vicarious sacrifice " (*Golden Bough*, abr. ed., p. 292).

At Nafaran no one may sow his crops until the priest of the Nafaran cult performs certain rites and distributes the seed, which has been under his keeping and is therefore believed to be charged with magical power. Among the Jukun, Kona, and Mbum the seed-corn is distributed by the chief—the product of the royal farm. This was apparently also the ancient custom of the Bachama kings, for to this day the product of the royal farm is considered the property of the community. It is not used for the daily requirements of the king and his household, but is set aside for the benefit of the hungry and of those farmers who still believe that the product of the royal farm has special reproductive properties, and that by mixing a little of the royal seed-corn with their own the chances of a successful harvest will be considerably increased. The harvesting of the king's crop is carried out by the king's slaves and any commoners who wish to assist. In the case of the latter they are at liberty to help themselves to a bundle or two of the corn without asking the permission of anyone. It is refreshing to find among peoples whom we are over-ready to regard as " primitive ", the humane idea that the poor and hungry man may apply to the king for assistance ; and that among the Bachama, though the king may be a despot, he is also the father of his people.

The necessities of the royal household are met by gifts of corn from every farmer according to his ability. It might be considered that under present conditions, as a chief receives a regular salary, the presentation of corn to the chief should be discouraged. This would, in my opinion, be taking a very short view. The gifts of corn are in no sense an exaction ; they are the free gifts of the people to the chief as an expression of the loyalty they feel, and as a form of payment for services rendered—services which are not always obvious to the European.

In point of fact a large proportion of the corn presented to chiefs throughout the Benue regions is expended in the provision of beer and food to those (generally senior men) who consider it their duty to pay their daily respects to the chief. The curtailment of such customs can only have the effect of creating doubt in the minds of the people as to the validity of present-day chieftainship. The custom is, among the Jukun, carried on secretly, for it is felt by the people and the chief that the Government would, if it were aware of it, forthwith prohibit it. Any secrecy of this kind is detrimental to the kind of relations which ought to exist between the Government and the people ; and it would be better if the matter were brought into the open and received the formal approval of Government provided that anything in the nature of exactions was sternly forbidden.

In concluding this report (which is, I hope, not to be regarded as the work of someone claiming to have any close acquaintance with the Bachama but merely as a help to Political Officers in charge of the Bachama and Bata tribes) it may be of use to point out that numerous instances have been given of points of cultural contact with the Bura (and Pabir) who, incidentally, like the Bachama and Bata, do not practise circumcision and who also use the inclusive and exclusive first personal plural pronoun. Looking westward the connection between the Bachama (and Bata) with the Kona is noteworthy. The priestess of Fare must be a Kona woman or a woman of Kona origin, and on the death of a Bachama chief it was customary to send to the chief of Kona gifts of two slaves, a horse, and the late chief's spear. This relationship with Kona may have been merely a deferential tribute to the earlier authority of Kona and need not imply any inferiority of culture (in point of fact the Bachama are in many ways culturally superior to the Kona and Jukun). It is usual for all invading peoples to adopt an attitude of religious subservience towards the peoples conquered or displaced, for animistic reasons. The land conquered from the living can never be regarded as land conquered from the dead, and to ignore the dead is to invite an hostility which will manifest itself in a succession of misfortunes— sickness, infertility, and drought. It is for this reason that even Fulani Muslim Emirs and District Heads frequently insist that the former pagan rites of a conquered territory are scrupulously carried out. Points of cultural contact between the Bachama and Chamba have already been noticed (such as the great respect paid to the father's sister and the common application of the term " father " to the father's sister's sons). A special point observed was that in the commemoration ceremony for the dead during the dry season the Bachama and Chamba ritual is the same. Both go to a cross-roads and smash up the pots and calabashes of the deceased. They advance to the cross-roads with the same dancing step—a syncopated one-step—and on the return journey adopt a different step which might be described as a gyrating one-step. There are, however, differences in matters of detail, for among the Chamba (of Donga) at these funeral processions there is a definite order of procession. First come the male paternal relatives, followed by the female paternal relatives who carry the pots which are to be broken. (The daughters of the deceased are exempt on the ground that it would break their hearts to take any part in the funeral proceedings.) The paternal aunt of the deceased follows on and is succeeded by the maternal relatives. General friends bring up the rear. Among the Bachama there appeared to be no fixed order, friends and relatives being intermixed.

Attached is a full schedule of words and phrases of the Bachama language, and to this are appended a few additional notes made by Dr. Bronnum and kindly lent to me by the Director of the Sudan United Mission at Numan :—

SCHEDULE OF WORDS AND PHRASES

1. Head	Ne	ne
2. Hair	Shewǫne	ʃewɔne
3. Eye	Dito	dito
Two eyes	Diekpe	di ɛkβe
4. Ear	Kwake	kwake
Two ears	Kwakekpe	kwakɛkβe
5. Nose	Shine	ʃine
6. One tooth	Linto hido	lɪnto hidˇo
Five teeth	Linye tuf	lɪnje tuf
7. Tongue	Jime	dʒime
8. Neck	Wura	wura
9. Breast (woman's)	Bop'e or bupto	boβe or bupto
10. Heart	Huboto	hubɔto
11. Belly	Yede or yedie	jede or jedie
12. Back	Beto	beto
13. Arm	Tufa or tafe	tufa or təfe
14. Hand	Vaktutufe or wura tafe	vaktutufe or wura təfe
Two hands	Tufekp'e or wure tefekpe	tufekβe or wure tefekβe
15. Finger	Gelto	gɛlto
Five fingers	Geletuf or gelietuf	gɛletuf or gɛlietuf
16. Finger-nail	Pup'e or gele	puβe or gɛle
17. Leg	Mbwara	mbwara
18. Knee	Duge or ḍige	dˇuge or dˇige
19. Foot	Vombwara	vombwara
Two feet	Mbǫekpe	mbɔekβe
20. Man (person)	Gboara	gboara
Ten people	Gboare bau	gboare bəu
21. Man (not woman)	Mure	mure
Two men	Muyekpe	mujekβe

E

22. Woman	Meto	meto
Two women	Mandekp'e or mandi ekpe	mandekβe or mandi ekβe
23. Child	Nze	nze
24. Father	Bato	bato
25. Mother	Nuoto	nuoto
26. Slave	Kasa	kəsa
27. Chief	Hamin	həmɪn
28. Friend	Indewai or indewe, plural Indewogi	indewai or indewɛ, plural indewogi
29. Smith	Kalla	kəlla
30. Doctor	Inzo bwato	inzo bwato
31. One finger	Gelto hido	gɛlto hiɗo
32. Two fingers	Geliekpe	gɛliekβe
33. Three fingers	Gelie mwakin	gɛlie mwakɪn
34. Four fingers	Gelie fwọt	gɛlie fwɔt
35. Five fingers	Gelie tuf	gɛlie tuf
36. Six fingers	Gelie tukoltaka	gɛlie tukɔltaka
37. Seven fingers	Gelie tukolukp'e	gɛlie tukɔlukβe
38. Eight fingers	Gelie fwofwot	gɛlie fwɔfwɔt
39. Nine fingers	Gelie dombi hido	gɛlie dombi hiɗo
40. Ten fingers	Gelie bau	gɛlie bəu
41. Eleven fingers	Gelie bau ambidi hido	gɛlie bəu ambɪdi hiɗo
42. Twelve fingers	Gelie bau ambidi kp'e	gɛlie bəu ambɪdi kpe
Thirteen fingers	Gelie bau ambidi mwakin	gɛlie bəu ambɪdi mwakɪn
43. Twenty fingers	Gelie bau tukp'e gin	gɛlie bəu tukβe gɪn
44. A hundred fingers	Bau ta bau	bəu ta bəu
45. Sun	Fere	fɛre
46. God	Pwa	pwa
47. Moon	Likito	lɪkɪto
Full moon	Likito ne dingira	lɪkɪto ne dɪŋgɪra
New moon	Likito hwelto	lɪkɪto hwɛlto
48. Day	Fere	fɛre
Night	Tukoto	tukɔto
Morning	Kaha kidato	kaha kɪɗato
49. Rain	Bole	ɓole
50. Water	Habe	haβe
51. Blood	Zambe	zambe
52. Fat	Mare	mare
53. Salt	Fito kwana	fito kwana
54. Stone	Fara, plural Fare	fara, plural fare
Iron	Ta	ta
55. Hill	Hagbalato	hagɓalato
56. River	Binue, plural Benewe	ɓɪnue, plumal, bɛnewe
57. Road	Tufe	tufe
58. Stream	Tadaha	tadaha
59. House	Vine	vɪne
Two houses	Vani ekpe	vəni ekβe
Many houses	Vanie furfuri	vənie furfuri
All the houses	Venie kat	vənie kat

60. Roof	Pi vine	pi vɪne
61. Door	Kwa vine	kwa vɪne
62. Mat	Kidzeto, plural Kaje	kɪdzeto, plural kadʒe
63. Basket	Inzakada, plural Zukade	ɪnzəkada, plural zukade
64. Drum	Ganga	gaŋga
65. Pot	Duato, plural Due	duato, plural due
66. Knife	Sungato, plural Sunge	suŋgato, plural suŋge
67. Spear	K'ufe, plural K'ofe	ƙufe, plural ƙofe
68. Bow	Rage	rage
69. Arrow	Galnbato, plural Galnbe	galnbato, plural galnbe
Five arrows	Galnbe tuf	galnbe tuf
70. Gun	Mbudigito	mbudɪgito
71. War	Kawato	kawato
72. Meat (animal)	Hara	hara
73. Elephant	Wonge, plural Wonji	wɔŋɛ, plural wɔndʒi
74. Buffalo	Indoaka, plural Indoake	indoaka, plural indoake
75. Leopard	Jara, plural Jare	dʒara, plural dʒare
76. Monkey	Burame	buraːme
77. Pig	Tumbirime	tumbɪrɪme
78. Goat	Hwoto, plural Hwoye	hwoto, plural hwoje
79. Dog	Sakke, plural Saike	sakke, plural saike
80. Bird	Bakare, plural bakaje	bakare, plural bakaye
Feather	Dire	ɗire
81. Crocodile	Gilinge	giliŋe
Sheep	Bagato	bagato
Horse	Duwe	duwe
Lion	Tukume	tukume
82. Fowl.	Deke	ɗeke
83. Eggs	Dule, plural Dole	ɗule, plural ɗole
84. One egg	Dule hido	ɗule hiɗo
85. Snake	Rukune	rukune
86. Frog	Gweenda	gwɛɛnda
87. Spider	Kurakurato	kurakurato
88. Fly	Jide	dʒide
89. Bee	Jumato	dʒumato
Honey	Marin jumato	marin dʒumato
90. Tree	Kada	kada
Ten trees	Kade bau	kade bəu
91. Leaf	Jide Kade	dʒibe kade
92. Guinea-corn	Zumwe	zumwe
93. Maize	Dawa	dawa
94. Ground-nut	Biara	biara
95. Oil	Mare	mare
96. Fulani	Biriye	birije
97. Hausa	Fufe	fufe
98. Jukun	Kwana	kwana
99. Beriberi	Mi Bornu	mi bɔrnu

100. The tall woman	Meti dukoto	meti dukoto
The tall women	Mandi dukoto	mandi dukoto
101. Large dog	Sako kpane	sako kpane
102. Small dog	Sako belange	sako belaŋe
103. The dog is biting	Sake adi aa	sake adi aa
104. The dog is biting me	Sake adi ari	sake adi ari
105. The dog which bit me yesterday	Saka ari tukun	saka ari tukun
106. I am flogging the dog	Na di liep sakoi	na di lɛp sakai
107. The dog which I have flogged	Saka na liebo	saka na lɛbo
108. I see him	Na nin	na nɪn
I see her	Na naro	na naro
He sees you	Nda nau	nda nəu
He sees us	Nda nainu	nda nəinu
We see you (pl.)	Hin naunu	hin nəinu
	Hum naunu	hum nəinu
We see them	Hin naran (excluding person addressed)	hin narən
	Hum naran (including person addressed)	hum narən
109. Beautiful bird	Bakaro feme	bakaro feme
110. Slave	Kesa	kəsa
My slave	Kesade	kəsade
Thy slave	Kesado	kəsado
Our slaves	Kesadeno	kəsadeno
111. The chief's slave	Kesa da hemin	kəsa da kəmɪn
His slave	Kesadan	kəsa dan
112. We see the slave	Hin na kesa (including person addressed, Hum na kesa)	hin na kəsa
113. We call the slave	Hin wa kesa	hin wa kəsa
114. The slave is coming	Kesa ne dishi	kəsa nɛ diʃi
115. He came yesterday	Nda shi tukô	nda ʃi tukô
He is coming to-day	Sane (or nda) ba shi supo	səne (or ndə) ba ʃi supo
He will come to-morrow	Nda ba shi kada	ndə ba ʃi kəda
116. The slaves go away	Kese mudo	kəse mudo
117. Who is your chief ?	Wono hemedo ?	wono həmedo
118. The two villages are making war on each other	Hwodie kpei ta dipa kawato ka so	hwodie kpei ta dɪpa kawato ka so
119. The sun rises	Fere ne difila	fɛre ne dɪfɪla
The sun sets	Fere imbiro	fɛre ɪmbɪro

120. The man is eating	Gboara sa ne dizimche	gboara sə ne di zɪmʃte
121. The man is drinking	Gboara sa ne di so-abwa habi	gboara sə ne di so-abwa habi
122. The man is asleep	Gboara sa ne di chini	gboara sə ne di tʃini
123. I break the stick	Na bia kada	nə ɓia kada
The stick is broken	Kada bio	kada ɓio
This stick cannot be broken	Kadano ko bito	kadano ko ɓito
Break this stick for me	Bia kadano	ɓia kadano
124. I have built a house	Na no vane	na no vəne
125. My people have built their houses yonder	Jinogi tano vane garo	dʒinogi tano vəne garo.
126. What do you do everyday ?	Da wula so ye di da nagi ndo fero ?	da wula so je di da nagi ndo fero.
127. I work on my farm	Na dida le into a gashede	nə dida lɛɪnto a gaʃede
I am going away	han ba mudo	hən ba mudo
I am hoeing	Na di hawo	nə di hawo
I am going away to hoe	Na wudo hauto	nə wudo hauto
I am going to my farm	Na wudo gashede	nə wudo gaʃede
128. The woman is coming	Meto nie dishi	meto nie diʃi
She is coming	Nga dishi	nga diʃi
The woman is laughing	Meto adi keḍoko	meto adi keɗoko
The woman is weeping	Meto adi tuo	meto adi tuo
129. I ask the woman	Ma dio meto	nə dio meto
130. Why do you laugh ?	Gamino yedi kedoko ?	gʌmɪno jedi kedoko
131. Why do you cry ?	Gamino yedi tuo ?	gʌmɪno jedi tuo
132. My child is dead	Nzede am biro	nzede am bɪro
133. It is not dead	Ndam biro	ndaːm bɪro
134. Are you ill ?	A amo ?	a amo
135. My children are ill	Jede amore or amo jede	dzede amorɛ or amo dʒede
136. Her child is better	Nzedaro dum piato	nzedaro ɗum piato
137. Yes	E	e
No	O'o	ɔ'ɔ'
138. A fine knife	Songati pepeto	soŋgati pepeto
Give me the knife	Vi songato	vi soŋgato
I give you the knife	Na vu songato	nə vu soŋgato

139.	I am a European	han baturo	hən baturo
	You are a black man	Hye gboara dungo	hje gboara duŋo
	You are a Bachama	Hye gboara Bachama	hje gboara batʃʌma
140.	Name	Kwakai	kwakəi
	My name	Kwaka	kwaka
	Your name	Kwakinga	kwakɪŋa
	What is your name ?	Kwakinga shia ?	kwakɪŋa ʃia
141.	There is water in the gourd	Habie nie do a vǫr hu boto	habie nie do a vɔr hu boto
	There is a knife lying on the stone	Songato nie a no fara	soŋgato nie a no fara
	There is fire under the pot	Die nie a puko doato	die nie a puko doato
	There is a roof over the hut	Dulise nie a no vine	dulise nie a no vine
142.	You are good	He hula	he hula
	This man is bad	Mano a hula	mano a hula
143.	The paper is white	Malimto puat puat	malimto puat puat
	This thing is black	Sano a dembino	sano a dembɪno
	This thing is red	Sano bimbim (or sano akpalamo)	sano bɪmbɪm (or sano akpalamo)
144.	This stone is heavy	Faratino dagsuk	faratɪno dəgsuk
	This stone is not heavy	Faratino a dagsuko	faratɪno a dəgsuko
145.	I am writing	Han edi dore	hən ɛdi dore
	I give you the letter	Han vu malimto	hən vu malimto
	Carry the letter to the town	Wudo ka malimto gara hodi	wudo ka malɪmto gara hoɗi
146.	Go away	Mudi	mudi
	Come here	Hwa	hwa
147.	Where is your house ?	Hwodo baundoha ?	hwoɗo bəundoha
148.	My house is here	Hwode no ga	hwoɗe no ga
	My house is there	Hwode do garo	hwoɗe do garo
149.	What have you to sell ?	Mino yedi doden	mɪno jɛdi dodɛn
150.	I want to buy fish	Namo ati nadir vakye	namo ati naɗɪr vakje
151.	The fish which you bought is bad	Vakye he daro a hula	vakje he dəro a hula
152.	Where is the man who killed the elephant ?	Wono ma bil wonge ?	wono ma bɪl wɔŋɛ

He has killed many elephants	Nda bil wonge han-anang	nda bɪl wɔŋɛ han-anʌŋ
How many elephants were killed yester-day ?	Wonge ea mea bilo tukô ?	wɔŋɛ ea mea bɪlo tukô
153. Un-tie it	Paran	paran
Tie this rope	Bue somwano	bue sɔmwano
Make the boy un-tie the goat	Tsa nze manda para hwoye	tsa nze manda para hwoje
154. My brothers and I, we are going but no one else	Hino ka zinogi baw-udo di sa reno	hino ka zɪnogi baw-udo di sə reno
Brothers, let us go and tell the chief	Zinogi da kamen ma wuda buemo hemin	zɪnogi da kamɛn ma wuda buɛmo hə mɪn
155. This tree is bigger than that	Kadano pirga aro kalato	kadano pirgə aro kalato

156. Last night I was in my house with a white man ; we heard a movement outside ; he said, " You hear that ; they are thieves ; let us go and see." We went, and I said, " Who are you ? " and they answered, " Nothing " ; but I said, " You are thieves " ; so we called the police and put them in prison.

Tukô ka tukoto hini a hwode ka a baturo ; hina kila humurto a ha bwange ; nda tsa " Yekil sana ; mahari ; dakan ma wudo adinaren " Hina duma. Han na cha " Huno ro wono ? " Tana luwa " ati talido ". Han na cha " Hu ma hari ". Galangen hina wa dan sanda hina dikden a vano gberauye.

Tukó ka tukoto hini a hwode ka a baturo ; hina kɪla humurto a ha bwaŋe ; nda tsa " jɛkɪl sana ; mahəri ; dakan ma wudo adinarɛn " Hina duma. hən na tʃa " Huno ro wono " Tana luwa " ati talido ". Hən na tʃa " Hu ma həri " gələŋɛn hina wa dan sanda hina dɪkdɛn a vəno gbɛrəuje.

Notes by Dr. Bronnum

Prepositions.—*Gaka* = with, *Gɛkɛlo* = on account of, *Pukko* = in, *A* = in, *Avor* = in, *Ahumwa* = before, *Abetso* = behind, *Pwa* = above, *Ana* = on.

Adverbs.—*Ga, ge, gano* = here, *Duma* = where, *Garo, haro, aro* = there, *Aha, ha* = where, whence, *Gwodi, naya* = when.

Adjectives follow the noun except those adjectives which are compounded with the particles *ma-* or *ndso-*, e.g. *Duwe gban* = big horse, but *ma-gban duwe* = big horse.

Nouns.—Terminations usually are -*a*, -*e*, -*i*, -*o*, -*ei*, -*tso*. Those ending in " *a* " take plural form " *ei* ". Those ending otherwise take plural form "*ye.*" Nouns ending in " *tso* " seem to be regarded as feminine. Some words undergo internal change for plural and some have irregular plurals, e.g. *tuffe* (road) plural = *tuffegye*, *ditso* (eye) plural *diye*, *rukune* (snake) plural *rokoniye*, *kwotso* (quiver) plural *kwosariye*. Nouns may be formed from verbs by adding the termination -*tso* or -*ha* to the stem of verb. (This is the same form as past participle.) *Hεmo, ndse* or *ma* may be prefixed to nouns to indicate ownership (cf. Hausa *mai*). They may also be prefixed to verbs.

The final consonant of verbs may be altered to create concord with the object.

Intransitive verbs seem to be changed frequently into transitive by the addition of " *do* ", e.g. *mado* = to rise, *madodo* = to raise. By altering final vowel of verbs different shades of meaning are given (cf. Hausa *fitta, fitto*), but no rules are yet available.

Pronouns.—*Mano* = this and *maro* = that, are used in referring to persons. *Sano, saro, seno* and *sero* are used in referring to things. Pronouns are inflected for gender, e.g. *ma* = which, feminine = *mache.*

I go	= Hon mudo or na mudo	We go	= Hi mudo
Thou goest	= Hye mudo		= Hum mudo
He goes	= Nda mudo	You go	= Hu mudo
She goes	= Nga mudo	They go	= Pan mudo
He gave me	Bovi		
He gave you	Bovu		
He gave him	Boven		
He gave her	Bovirro		
He gave us	Boveno or bovum		
He gave you (plural)	Bo vauno		
He gave them	Bo veren		
Give me (imperative)	Vini (plural Vimi)		

Future is formed by inserting *ba* between pronoun and verb, e.g. *hon ba minna* = I will return.

Future is used to express purpose, e.g. *nda sa ba belti* = he came to kill me.

Possessive.—*Ingi* = my, *Ungu* = yours, *Ungen* = his, *Ungero* = hers, *Ungeino* = ours (or *ungum*), *Ungauno* = yours, *Ungeren* = theirs. Sometimes the form of first and second pronominal suffix varies, e.g. my house = *hwadei*, your house = *hwadau*.

PLATE 12

A CLOWN AT FARE

[face p. 57

Passive.—

Miye bo di	= They hid me (bo = hide)
Miye bo da	= They hid you
Miye bo den	= They hid him
Miye bo do	= They hid her
Miye bo deino or dum	= They hid us
Miye bo dauno	= They hid you (plural)
Miye bo den	= They hid them

Imperative.—

Ma di	= begone (singular)
Ma dum	= begone (plural)

THE MBULA .

The Mbula are close neighbours of the Bachama and Bata of Demsa, with both of whom they have coalesced to such a degree that they are likely, in view of the paucity of their numbers, to lose their tribal identity within the next two generations. They belong, however, to an ethnic group which is totally distinct from that of the Bachama and Bata. For whereas the latter speak a suffix language of the Central Sudanic type, the Mbula speak a language which is so Bantoid that it might almost be described as Bantu. It is the same language as is spoken by the Tambo of the Adamawa Emirate, and is practically the same as that of the Bare (in the Numan division) and of the Kulû (in the Wurkun district). It is also closely related to Jarawa, and the so-called Semi-Bantu languages of the Bauchi Plateau and surrounding country.

The word Mbula means " The Men " or " People," being a variant of Bura. (In the Mbula language itself the word for men is *bua bura*.) They claim to have come into their present habitat from the East. According to one tradition they, in company with the Bata and Tikar tribes, were brought down the Benue in an iron canoe by Nzeanzo, the god of the Bata, Bachama, and Mbula. Some say that their former home was Rai Buba in the French Cameroons, others that it was Mundang (also in the Cameroons) and that they proceeded to their present locality via Malabu and Tambo. Among others, again, Mboi near Song is indicated as a former home of the tribe.

The social organization of the Mbula closely resembles that of the Bachama ; that is to say that the community is composed of a number of kindred-groups or clans in which descent is reckoned patrilineally, but movable property is inherited matrilineally. These groups are : (a) The Muja, (b) The Fwa, (c) The Mana, (d) The Zumo, (e) The Muzong, (f) The Killa, (g) The Mbo, and (h) The Jee. Of these the first two are the original Mbula. The Mana are of Bachama origin, and the Zumo belong to the Jirai-Bata groups.[1] The Killa, as their name implies, belong to the blacksmith group which is scattered among the Bata, Bachama, and neighbouring tribes. It may be observed that groups of Muja and Fwa and Mbo are also found among the Bachama.

Each kindred of the kindred-group is an exogamous unit, but the kindred-group or clan as a whole is not usually exogamous, though it is sometimes. Membership of the kindred is reckoned on patrilineal lines, and fixed property such as houses and farms are normally transmitted in the male line. But all movable property is transmitted matrilineally, i.e. it passes to brothers by the same mother or to sister's sons, but never to brothers by different mothers or to sons. The family group is patripotestal, but the mother's relatives have considerable authority. They can assume the custody of children who are not being properly treated by the father or the father's family. (But normally, even in such cases, the children would be allowed to assist their father in his agricultural work.) They can also appropriate the first-born child, if the father of the child had not completed his marriage-payments ; and for this reason it is not uncommon to procure the abortion of a child conceived before the final payments had been made.[2]

A maternal uncle is also primarily responsible for the debts of his nephew, just as nephews, who inherit from their maternal uncles, are responsible for debts left by the latter. Witchcraft is regarded as being transmitted matrilineally, and in former times all the uterine relatives of a person convicted of witchcraft were sold into slavery. The witch herself was bound hand and foot, laid on the ground, and covered with the roof of a hut which was then set on fire.

As among the Bachama so among the Mbula there is a totemic complex. The totems are usually transmitted matrilineally, but

---

[1] See the paper on the Bata-speaking peoples (ch. II).
[2] Abortion may be procured by massage, or by inserting into the neck of the womb a pellet of " dedeki " leaves or of pounded " garahunu " seeds soaked in water. (Garahunu = *Momordica balsamina*.)

some are transmitted patrilineally. Thus the lion, hippopotamus, leopard, and elephant totems are handed down from a mother to her children, but the crocodile and monkey totems from a father to his children. Not all Mbula, however, have totems; for the Mbula marry outside the tribe to a considerable extent, and it also appeared that many children do not in fact inherit the totem from parents who own totems, or if they do they lose it in childhood. It was stated that a man may be born a hippopotamus or elephant because his mother was such, but that if he annoys his mother as a small child she may cancel the relationship by depriving him of that second-sight which enables him to be one with his totem. The totemic relationship is, for this reason, considered to be an individual relationship.[1]

No man who has a totem may marry a woman who has a totem; for this would lead to fighting between the repective totem-animals, who would kill each other and so cause the death of the human counterparts, i.e. of the husband and wife. A man who has a totem must, therefore, seek as his wife one who is totem-free, and vice versa.[2]

The general conception regarding the totem is the same as that described in my paper on the Bachama. A member of the Misara totem-kin,[3] which has the hippopotamus as a totem, stated that on the day he was conceived his hippopotamus counterpart was also conceived, and that on the day he dies his counterpart will also die. In a herd of hippopotami he can distinguish the particular hippopotamus which is his own second-self, and he can also distinguish those hippopotami who are relatives of his mother. If anyone does him an injury he will, in his hippopotamus form, upset that person's canoe. On the other hand he will tell a friend who wishes to hunt hippopotami where he can find his own herd. But during the night he and his relatives will leave the herd secretly so as not to be killed by his friend. Secrecy is necessary, because the other hippopotami would, on their betrayal, attack

---

[1] It is also an individual relationship from the point of view that the relationship is with one particular animal and not with the whole species.

[2] Marriage is contracted by agricultural service and gifts. The lad has also to repair the house of his fiancée's mother during the dry season. When the girl reaches the age of puberty her fiancé sleeps with her in her own home. During the ensuing wet season the lad presents the girl with numerous bundles of corn which are converted into beer. The beer-feast, which is held on the lad's farm, constitutes the wedding ceremony, and the girl is then escorted to the bridegroom's home.

[3] This totem-kin is now almost extinct.

those hippopotami who belonged to the Misara totem-kin. His
own group of hippopotami fights with other hippopotami, just as
among men one kindred fights with another. If his counterpart
upsets a canoe he himself becomes automatically aware of the
occurrence, however distant he may be ; and if his counterpart
threatens his own canoe he has merely to tell him to be gone, and
off he goes. He can control also all hippopotami who are the
counterparts of his own (maternal) relatives. Although his
relationship is with a particular hippopotamus he refrains from
injuring, killing, or eating the flesh of any hippopotamus, out of
respect for his own hippopotamus ; and if in any house he saw a
person eating hippopotamus flesh he would immediately rise and
walk out. If he came accidentally on the corpse of a hippopotamus
he would run away in fear. He would never wear an ornament
made of hippopotamus ivory. The members of his totem-kin call
themselves Barama, i.e. Hippopotami, but they object to others
calling them by this name, as they consider that this would, at the
present time, be tantamount to a charge of sorcery. At the head
of the totem-kin there is a leader, who knows all the secret rites
by which the animal-relationship is sustained. When a female of
the totem-kin bears a child she takes the child to this leader, who
is regarded as the " keeper " of the hippopotami. He informs the
mother that on the day of the child's birth a fellow hippopotamus
had been born. If the child subsequently falls sick the mother
reports the sickness to the leader of her totem-kin, who will
prescribe a remedy, stating that the sickness of the child was due
to the circumstance that his hippopotamus counterpart had
eaten something which disagreed with him. Vice versa, it is
believed that if a hippopotamus of the totem-kin is wounded by a
man it will go secretly at night to the leader of the kin who will
remove the spear which had caused the injury.

A Mbula whose totem is an elephant stated that the relationship between his totem-kin and elephants arose in the following
way. One of his ancestors was a mighty hunter, and in the course
of his life time he slew animals innumerable. So all the ghosts of
the slain animals held a meeting and decided that the children of
the hunter should be born as elephants.

The Mbula do not identify the Supreme Being with the Sun.
They call the sun Pọri and the Supreme Being Bakuli, a word
which seems to mean, " He of the skies." They share with the

Bata and Bachama the cult of Nzeanzo or Janzo whom they sometimes describe as the creator of men. For details of this cult the reader is referred to the chapter on the Bachama, and it need only be added here that every Mbula who is in trouble, or wishes to seek some favour from the gods, has recourse to the priest of Nzeanzo. It is even said that if a Mbula has an evil dream he will set out for Fare the next day. The chief of the Mbula is expected to visit the shrine at Fare once every three months.

Some attention is, however, devoted to the ancestors; and it is customary to seek the assistance of ancestors by pouring a libation over the graves and uttering a petition. The paternal ancestors in this respect appear to be of more importance than the maternal, and in carrying out the rites it is usual for a man to secure the services of his paternal grandmother or aunt if she is still living. They go together to the grave of the man's father or father's father, and there the grandmother or aunt makes a declaration that she is not responsible for her grandson's (or nephew's) ill-fortune : but if her dead brother or father is responsible then let him desist.

Graves are of the shaft and tunnel pattern. Sticks are laid across the floor of the chamber, and over these some mats and (if the deceased had been rich) some gowns. The body is laid lying on its side, and the face is covered with a calabash held in position by a strip of cloth. When the body has been deposited a senior male relative addresses the dead man, saying : " You have left us to go to another place. If you find that place pleasant abide there in peace : but if it pleases you not then return again to us." If the deceased had borne a bad character he is told to go to the other place and remain there for ever. The mouth of the grave is blocked with sticks and mats over which a plaster of mud is laid. The grave may be under the deceased's hut, and in this case the hut is redecorated immediately after burial by friends (not relatives) of the deceased. Or it may be made in the open and covered with a hut specially built. Offerings of porridge are set outside the hut every morning and evening for a considerable period. They are removed after twelve hours and given to junior members of the household to eat. Every six months libations of beer and further offerings of food are made, and at the end of two years the hut covering the grave is broken down, the thatched

roof being burnt in the bush.   The site of the grave is marked by
a stone.

A grave may be used again after a number of years, the bones
and skull [1] of the former occupant being sewn up in a cloth and
deposited at the side of the chamber.   But in times of epidemics
several bodies may be buried together.   The bodies of married
women are always buried in their homes, a rule which is found
also among the Yendang and neighbouring tribes.   Grave-
diggers, like blacksmiths and medicine-men, are a kindred or clan
by themselves, the occupation of grave-digging being hereditary.
They are rewarded for their labours by gifts of beer, and the heads
of animals killed in the chase at the time of the burial ceremonies.

As regards material culture the huts are of the same pattern as
those of the Bachama and Bata.   The roof has usually no rafters,
being supported by a bell-shaped lining of woven straw.   Sometimes two or three huts may be joined together with a partition
of matting, a piece of the matting being cut out to serve as an
entrance.   Beds are usually woven grass-mats laid on the ground,
but occasionally bedsteads of indurated mud may be seen.   The
mills for grinding corn consist of a stone set at an angle on a
platform of dried mud, with a well at the lower end of the stone.

The clothing of the Mbula is generally the same as that of the
Bachama.   Women wear a flap of cloth over the pubes and
buttocks.   Youths affect many modes of hair-dressing.   Some
leave a frizzled elongated patch of hair on the centre of the head ;
others have this patch braided, with the side-locks plaited.

It may be noticed in conclusion that the Mbula do not practise
circumcision.

Mbula Vocabulary

1.	Head	Ba muru	ba muru
2.	Hair	Nyûu	njûu
3.	Eye	Misu	mɪsu
	Two eyes	Misi bari	mɪsi bari
4.	Ear	Kirʉ	kɪrʉ
	Two ears	Kiri bari	kɪri bari
5.	Nose	Lulu	lulu
6.	One tooth	Mini mǫshet	mini mɔʃɛt
	Five teeth	Mini tǫngno	mini tɔŋno
7.	Tongue	Lasu	lasu

[1] But among the Tambo Mbula the skull of a chief was ceremonially removed
and given to his successor.

8.	Neck	Meli	mɛli	
9.	Breast (woman's)	Kyure	kjure	
10.	Heart	Kikili	kɪkɪli	
11.	Belly	Lungo nu gule	luŋo nu gule	
12.	Back	Inzim	ɪnzɪm	
13.	Arm	Bu	bu	
14.	Hand	Babu	babu	
	Two hands	Babu bari	babu bari	
15.	Finger	Munebu	munɛbu	
	Five fingers	Munebu tọngno	munɛbu tɔŋno	
16.	Finger nail	Kolebu	kolɛbu	
17.	Leg	Kusu	kusu	
18.	Knee	Kunu	kunu	
19.	Foot	Bakusu	bakusu	
	Two feet	Bakusu bari	bakusu bari	
20.	Man (person)	Buá ma pinde	buá ma pɪnde	
	Ten people	Abuana lum	abuana lum	
21.	Man (not woman)	Bua bura	bua bura	
	Two men	Bua bura bari	bua bura bari	
22.	Woman	Bua ma	bua ma	
	Two women	Amamna bari	amamna bari	
23.	Child	Muna	muna	
24.	Father	Dada	dada	
25.	Mother	Nana	nana	
26.	Slave	Guro	guro	
27.	Chief	Murum	murum	
28.	Friend	Beam	beam	
29.	Smith	Mintul	mɪntul	
30.	Doctor	Munggala	muŋgala	
31.	One finger	Munebu mọshet	munɛbu mɔʃɛt	
32.	Two fingers	Amunebu bari	amunɛbu bari	
33.	Three fingers	Amunebu taru	amunɛbu taru	
34.	Four fingers	Amunebu ine	amunɛbu ine	
35.	Five fingers	Amunebu tọngno	amunɛbu tɔŋno	
36.	Six fingers	Amunebu tọngno nọng mọshet	amunɛbu bari nɔŋ mɔʃɛt	
37.	Seven fingers	Amunebu tọngno bwọmdi bari	amunɛbu tọngno bwɔmdə bari	
38.	Eight	Amunebu ine ine	amunɛbu ine ine	
39.	Nine fingers	Amunebu tongno ine	amunɛbu tɔŋno ine	
40.	Ten fingers	Amunebu lum	amunɛbu lum	
41.	Eleven fingers	Amunebu lum nọng mọshet	amunɛbu lum nɔŋ mɔʃɛt	
42.	Twelve fingers	Amunebu lum nọng bari	amunɛbu lum nɔŋ bari	
	Thirteen fingers	Amunebu lum nọng taru	amunɛbu lum nɔŋ taru	
43.	Twenty fingers	Amunebu lume bari	amunɛbu lume bari	
44.	Fifty fingers	Amunebu lume tọng-no	amunɛbu lume tɔŋno	
45.	A hundred fingers	Amunebu lume lum	amunɛbu lume lum	

46. God	Bakuli	bakuli
47. Sun	Pọri	pɔri
48. Moon	Zomo	zomo
Full moon	Zomo gbaliki	zomo gbaliki
New moon	Bissa zomo	bɪssa zomo
49. Day	Ni pọri	nə pɔri
Night	Ni du	nə du
Morning	Ni dimbari	nə dɪmbari
50. Rain	Mur	mur
51. Water	mur (nuna)	mur (nuna)
52. Blood	Nkila	nkɪla
53. Fat	Muru	muru
54. Salt	Tu	tu
55. Stone	Tali	tali
Iron	Bolo	bolo
56. Hill	Nbangban	nbaŋban
57. River	Ngesala (Benue = gbinuwen)	ngɛsʌla (gbɪnuwɛn)
Stream	Tuli mur	tuli mur
58. Road	Njergula	ndʒɛrgula
59. House	Kurum (Compound = bala)	kurum (Compound = bala)
Two houses	Akurum bari	akurum bari
Many houses	Akurum pas	akurum pas
All the houses	Akurum pirakpirá	akurum pɪrakpirá
60. Roof	Bangsa	baŋsa
61. Door	Kumþala	kumbala
62. Mat	Kalmarim	kalmarɪm
63. Basket	Ndakade	ndakade
64. Drum	Gangga	gaŋga
65. Pot	Kwering	kwɛrɪŋ
66. Knife	Biau	biau
67. Spear	Kọngo	kɔŋo
68. Bow	Nta	nta
69. Arrow	Mundi	mundi
Five arrows	Mundi tọngno	mundi tɔŋno
70. Gun	Bindigi	bɪndɪgi
71. War	Lua	lua
72. Meat (animal)	Nyama	njama
73. Elephant	Nzu	nzu
74. Buffalo	Ndoakọng	ndoakɔŋ
75. Leopard	Mumbri	mumbri
76. Monkey	Nyaû	njaû
77. Pig	Timbirim	tɪmbɪrɪm
78. Goat	Bulpinda	bulpɪnda
79. Dog	Imvwa	ɪmvwa
80. Bird	Nyal	njal
Feather	Imbur inyal	ɪmbur ɪnjal
81. Crocodile	Gandu	gandu
82. Fowl	Ingukulek	ɪŋgukulɛk
83. Eggs	Inkinggu	ɪnkiŋgu

84. One egg	Inkinggu mọshet	ɪnkɪŋgu mɔʃɛt
85. Snake	Iyau	ijau
86. Frog	Dọlung	dɔluŋ
87. Horse	Pir	pɪɾ
Cow	Inda	ɪnda
88. Fly	Ngi	ngi
89. Bee	Nyi	nji
Honey	Murunyi	murunji
90. Tree	Ngun	ngun
Ten trees	Angun lum	angun lum
91. Leaf	Bumbu	bumbu
92. Guinea-corn	Misa	mɪsa
93. Maize	Misa Kono	mɪsa kono
94. Ground-nut	Biara	biara
95. Oil	Muru	muru
96. The tall woman	Bua ma mi dare	bua ma mə dare
The tall women	Amamna ami darike	amamna amə darike
97. Large dog	Mvwa mi gule	mvwa mə gule
98. Small dog	mvwa mi kewe	mvwa mə kɛwe
99. The dog bites	Mvwa mi nimban	mvwa mə nɪmban
100. The dog bites me	Mvwa nda nini mam	mvwa nda nɪnɪ mam
101. The dog which bit me yesterday	Mvwa man nimam yilung nga	mvwa man nɪmam jiluŋ nga
102. I flog the dog	N wọl mvwa	n wɔl mvwa
103. The dog which I have flogged	Mvwa man n woli	mvwa man n wɔli
104. I see him or her	N si ni	n sə ni
He sees you	A sinino	a sɪnɪno
He sees us	A sinasim	a sɪnasɪm
We see you (pl.)	Si sinawun	sə sɪnawun
We see them	Si sinniya	sə sɪnnija
105. Beautiful bird	Nyel bọrjiam	njɛl bɔrdʒiam
106. Slave	Guro	guro
My slave	Guromem	guromem
Thy slave	Guromô	guromô
Our slaves	Guromasim	guromasɪm
107. The chief's slave	Guro ma murun	guro ma murum
His slave	Guromale	guromale
108. We see the slave	Sin sina guro	sɪn sɪna guro
109. We call the slave	Si tunu guro	sə tunu guro
110. The slave comes	Guro ndia kiyu ka	guro ndia kəju ka
111. He came yesterday	Yu yilung	ju jiluŋ
He is coming to-day	Ni yu yelung	nə ju jɛluŋ
He will come to-morrow	Ni yu li	nə ju li
112. The slaves go away	Aguro a wuma	aguro a wuma
113. Who is your chief ?	Murum mo nda yen le ?	murum mo nda jɛn le ?

114. The two villages are making war on each other — La bari anda aki muno a raria — la bari anda akə muno a raria

115. The sun rises — Pǫri nda ki yau ka — pɔri nda kə jau ka
    The sun sets — Pǫri kpana — pɔri kpana

116. The man is eating — Bua india ki lili ka — bua india kə lili ka

117. The man is drinking — Bua india ki nu mur ka — bua india kə nu mur ka

118. The man is asleep — Bua india ki nang tulo ka — bua india kə nʌŋ tulo ka

119. I break the stick — N bun gara — n bun gara
    The stick is broken — Gara buno — gara buno
    This stick cannot be broken — Gara manga bine buno — gara maŋa bine buno
    Break this stick for me — Bum bam gara mini-angga — bum bam gara mını-aŋga

120. I have built a house — M banga kurm — m baŋa kurum

121. My people have built their houses yonder — Abǫna mem a banga kurum a kano — abɔna mɛm a baŋa kurum a kanó

122. What do you do every day ? — Mwo kala turo mani a pakile ni pǫro le ? — mwo kala turo mani a pakile nə pɔri le
    I work on my farm — Men ingge pak turo a baban amem — mɛn ıŋge pak turo a baban amem

123. I am going away — Min u wo — mın u wo
    I am hoeing — Min ingge riria — mın ıŋge riria
    I am going away to hoe — Mining karia — mınıŋ karia
    I am going to my farm — Mining ka baban mem — mınıŋ ka baban mem

124. The woman comes — Mbwama nda ki yuka — mbwama nda ki juka
    She comes — Nda ki yuka — nda kə juka
    The woman laughs — Mbwama nda ki wǫlka — mbwama nda kə wɔlka
    The woman weeps — Mbwama nda ki boaka — mbwama nda kə boaka

125. I ask the woman — M diche mbama — m ditʃe mbama

126. Why do you laugh ? — Acheman sa awolo ? — atʃeman sa awolo ?

127. Why do you cry ? — Acheman sa awo boa le ? — atʃeman sa awo boa le ?

128. My child is dead — Mune miim wu na — munɛ miim wu na

129. It is not dead — Wu ro — wu ro

130. Are you ill ? — Maro su ro chenduro ? — maro su ro tʃɛnduro ?

131. My children are ill — Amunemi ingga ria chenduro — amunɛmi ıŋga ria tʃɛnduro

132. Her child is better — Mumemale ri chendina — mumɛmale ri tʃɛndına

133. Yes — ie — ie
    No — ao — ao

134. A fine knife	Biau bǫjem	biau bɔdʒɛm
Give me the knife	Pam biau	pam biau
I give you the knife	M pano biau	m pano biau
135. I am a European	Minda bature	mɪnda bature
You are a black man	Nyira awunda bwa mpinde	njira awunda bwa mpɪnde
You are a Mbula	Nyira awunda bwa Mbula	njira awunda bwa mbula
136. Name	Lulo	lulo
My name	Lulam	lulam
Your name	Lulomô	lulomô
What is your name ?	Luloamen ?	luloamɛn ?
137. There is water in the gourd	Mur dagam a ba du	mur dagʌm a ba du
The knife is on the stone	Biau da mutali	biau da mutali
The fire is under the pot	Bissa nda tang kwor-ing	bɪssa nda taŋ kwɔriŋ
The roof is over the hut	Mini bangsa kurum	mɪnɛ baŋsa kurum
138. You are good	We a bǫjam fwat	we a bɔdʒam fwat
This man is bad	Bua man biki jam fwat	bua man biki dʒam fwat
139. The paper is white	Malim che mangga ma pǫshe na	malɪm tʃe maŋga ma pɔʃe na
This thing is black	Gimangga ma pinde na	gɪmaŋga ma pɪnde na
This thing is red	Gimangga ma bangye na	gɪmaŋga ma baɲje na
140. This stone is heavy	Tali mangga dim bire fwat	tali maŋga dɪm bɪre fwat
This stone is not heavy	Tali mangga dim biriro	tali maŋga dɪm bɪriro
141. I write	Mining ga bala	mɪnɪŋ ga bala
I give you the letter	M pano malimche	m pano malɪmtʃe
Carry the letter to the town	Keni malimche a la	kɛnə malɪmtʃe a la
142. Go away	Kene	kɛnə
Come here	Yuu	juu
143. Where is your house ?	Bala mo na ke ?	bala mo na ke ?
144. My house is here	Bala mem na kane	bala mem na kane
My house is there	Bala mem nda kano	bala mem nda kano
145. What have you to sell ?	Mani a kulki le ?	mani a kulki le ?
146. I want to buy fish	N yere ni ma mini kuru nji	n jɛre nə ma mɪnə kuru ndʒi

147. The fish which you bought is bad — Nji mana kuro ka bo ro — ndʒi mana kuro ka bo ro

148. Where is the man who killed the elephant ? — Bua ma wọn zuka nda ke le ? — bua ma wɔn zuka nda ke le ?

He has killed many elephants — Wọn zu pas — wɔn zu pas

How many elephants were killed yesterday ? — Anzu shen a wọl yilung le ? — anzu ʃen a wɔl jiluŋ le ?

149. Untie it — Panzi ki — panzə ki

Tie this rope — Kur ungur miniangga — kur ungur miniaŋga

Make the boy untie the goat — Ne muna bi panzi mbul pinda — ne muna bə panzə mbul pɪnda

150. My brothers and I, we are going but no one else — Sinda sinimi yambam sinu wo nimbubari sim — sənda sənəmi jambam sənu wo nɪmbubarə sɪm

Brothers, let us go and tell the chief — Mi yambam lo sinika bam murum sinibang giwi — mi jambam lo sənəka bam murum sənəbaŋ giwi

151. This tree is bigger than that — Ngun mangga ku timo nugulo — ngun maŋga ku timo nugulo

Last night I was in my house with a white man ; we heard a movement outside ; he said, " You hear that ; they are thieves ; let us go and see." We went and I said, " Who are you ? " and they answered, " Nothing " ; but I said, " You are thieves " ; so we called the police and put them in prison.

Yilungga minda balamen sini bature ; su wo gir ki digrikia aban fwana, nu a ma " Awọng a le ; a me ina ; cheme sini puro sini sinea ". Si purag bal. Nia ni ma " Wundaka yani le ? " A ere " Ka gir ki gir pa kam ro " ; Mem ga banga ni ma " Wunda ka mi yi " ; acheman ana le si tuna a dan sanda si bwọlia si wọshia so lo.

jiluŋga mɪnda balamem sənə bature ; su wo gɪr kə dɪgrəkia aban fwana ; nu a ma " awɔŋ a le ; a me ina ; tʃɛme sənə puro sənə sɪnea ". sə purag bal. nia nə ma " wundaka jani le ? " a ere " ka gɪr kə gɪr pa kam ro " ; mem ga baŋa nə ma " wunda ka mə ji " ; atʃɛman ana le sə tuna a dan sanda sə bwɔlɪa sə wɔʃia so lo.

CHAPTER II

THE BATA-SPEAKING PEOPLES OF THE ADAMAWA EMIRATE

This paper deals with a variety of tribal groups in the Adamawa Emirate which speak the Bata language or a dialect of Bata. They do not describe themselves as Bata, each group being known by its own local title. But in many instances it is apparent that the group contains a Bata element, in the ruling kindred or clan. This is not surprising when it is remembered that the Bata formerly held in these regions the position which is now held by the Fulani. They were displaced by the Fulani at the beginning of the nineteenth century. Just as the Fulani have in recent times broken down many of the former tribal divisions, so it must be supposed that Bata invaders had previously disrupted tribes whose names are no longer preserved, imposing on them their own language and culture. Local tradition suggests that this is so, and inquiry into the form of social organization would seem to prove it beyond any doubt.

The groups under consideration are the following :—

        (*a*) Zumu (or Jimo) and Bulai.
        (*b*) Malabu.
        (*c*) Kofa.
        (*d*) Muleng.
        (*e*) Bolki.
        (*f*) Holma.
        (*g*) Gudu.
        (*h*) Njai or Nzangi.

All are situated on the North bank of the Benue from Yola, and are administered by the Fulani Emir of Adamawa. The first five units contain a common ethnic stratum known as Jirai, and these five groups may, therefore, be classed under the single designation of " Jirai ".[1] The term Jirai also includes the pagan groups found at or near the villages of Wapango, Midauro, Mivezo, Wadi, Firda and Maio Jirai. It is probable that the

---

[1] The term Jirai apparently contains the root *ji* or *ju* = man, which occurs as a tribal title further down the Benue in the forms Jibu and Jukun. The Gudu group of Bata-speaking peoples call themselves the Ji Gudu or " men of Gudu ". Jirai may possibly mean " The men of Rai ", i.e., of Rai Baba in in the French Cameroons.

Holma, Gudu, and Njai groups contain a Jirai stratum, so that the term Jirai might be conveniently applied to all these Bata-speaking peoples, unless they are to be described as Bata or as Jirai-Bata. But those groups which have become Muslim, viz. Zumu, Holma, and Gudu, resent any other description than the local term by which they call themselves.

As there are considerable variations between the customs of the eight units enumerated above it will be advisable to give some account of each unit separately. But a few general remarks may first be made.

First of all there is a tradition common to all the groups (except Njai) that the group was founded by Bata-speaking immigrants from Mandara, or was invaded by a body of Mandara immigrants who became the masters of the aboriginal inhabitants. These aboriginal inhabitants were known collectively as Jirai, a term which is a variant of Jibu and Jukun ; and it is not improbable that the Jirai formed part of the Jukun kingdom of Kororofa prior to the advent of the Bata.[1] The Bata conquest of this region does not appear to have occurred at any very remote date, for the royal kindreds in many of the Jirai groups still speak a different dialect from the aboriginal kindreds, and in some cases observe different customs. The tradition of the Bata conquest is still so fresh in the minds of the people that the exact route taken by the immigrants from Mandara is definitely indicated. They first established themselves a few miles to the North of Wuba in a town the remains of which can still be seen. Thence they proceeded to Baza, and from Baza they scattered themselves in all directions. The groups now represented by the inhabitants of Holma, Zumu, Gudu, and Demsa Mosu (near Numan), are stated to have formed a single migratory group from Baza, while the Bata of Demsa Poa and Malabu are said to be another group of the same stock.

At Baza itself the tradition is different, for the old Margi ruling families of Baza claim to belong to the same stock as the Pabir chiefs of Biu. But the Pabir also claim a Mandara connection. It is possible, therefore, that Baza became a distributing centre for Mandara immigrants who established themselves as chiefs over the Bura and Kilba tribes, the Southern Margi, and various

[1] There are a number of cultural traits among the Jirai suggestive of close contact with the Jukun. At Zumu the family of royal grave-diggers is known as the Aba-Kuru, a pure Jukun term.

groups of Bata-speaking peoples to the South. On the other hand, the Pabir migration from Mandara seems to have been long antecedent to that of the Bata-speaking groups from Baza, and if we accept the tradition of the latter the main body of the immigrants worked South or South-West.

It is to be noted that although the Bura-Kilba-Margi linguistic group is clearly connected in vocabulary with that of the Bata group, a connection which only becomes apparent when we insert the intervening Higi-Fali group, there is a marked difference in phonology. In grammar the two groups have many points in common, such as the absence of feminine pronouns,[1] the use of suffixes and of the inclusive and exclusive first personal plural pronoun. But there are notable differences. The pronouns are different in form, and the Bata do not suffix the pronoun to the verb (as e.g. the Margi who, in this respect, may have been influenced by the Kanuri). It would require an intensive study of both groups of languages before ethnological arguments could be adduced on the basis of linguistic differences between the two groups. And even if this were done the conclusions would be doubtful, in view of the fact that grammatical differences may exist between dialects of the same group. Bura and Margi, for example, though almost identical in vocabulary, vary from one another in some points of grammatical construction.

The Zumu.—The Zumu or Zomo or Jimo are a group of between 1,600 and 1,700 people who live in and around the town of Zumu. This town is now mainly a Fulani settlement, and the Zumu are fast becoming Muslims. They have been subservient to the Fulani for the greater part of a century. They have in recent times adopted the practice of circumcision, and they clothe themselves and build their houses in the Fulani fashion. They formerly practised kindred exogamy, but marriages with second cousins are now permissible. In a few years the entire group will have become Muhammadan.

The Zumu claim to have come into their present habitat from Mandara. They state that from Mandara they proceeded to Baza, north of Wuba, and that Baza was the centre from which most of the Bata-speaking groups were distributed. Their tradition is, therefore, the same as that of the Holma and Malabu, and of

---

[1] But the Zumu and Gudu groups of Bata-speaking peoples employ feminine pronouns.

Muleng and Bulki in the Song area. They may be described as Jirai-Bata.

They speak a dialect of Bata. It is the same dialect as is spoken by their neighbours of Bulai, Malabu, and Kofa, and is practically the same as Holma and Nzangi. It is closely connected with Gudu. But a remarkable feature which differentiates it from most Bata dialects is the use of second and third personal singular feminine pronouns. The pronouns, like those of the Kanakuru, are strongly suggestive of Hausa, and the grammatical structure is also like that of Hausa. A noteworthy feature of the North-Eastern languages of Adamawa Province and the mandated area as a whole is the large number of characteristic Hausa words.

The chief of the Zumu has lost much of his former prestige and has abandoned many of the customs of his forefathers. He no longer wears a hair-lock, and there are no taboos attached to his person. But he eats his food alone and signifies to his boy attendant the conclusion of the repast by giving a cough. It is still customary to bury the body of the chief sitting in charcoal. The chief also continues to observe many of the ancient pagan rites, and among these there is one of remarkable interest. It is carried out every month in connection with a cult known as Dagire, whose symbol is a pot containing some medicine or material object, the nature of which was not disclosed. The pot is set on a forked branch inside a shrine, the custodian being an old woman who has passed the age of menstruation and for whom sexual relations are taboo.

On the evening of each month when the new moon is sighted the priestess prepares a supply of sweet beer which she deposits in a pot before the symbol of Dagire. On the following morning the chief and all the members of his kindred repair to the shrine, each taking with him a small supply of cotton as a gift to the god, a gift which is subsequently appropriated by the priestess. The chief also binds a strip of cloth round the sacred symbol. The priestess then pours some of the consecrated beer into a gourd which she hands to the chief, who speaks as follows : " We are now about to perform the monthly custom which has been handed down to us by our forefathers. By the grace of God and of Dagire may no evil thing befall me or any member of my kindred. Whoever attempts any wickedness against me or mine shall be confronted by Dagire and killed. May we live in harmony, one with the other." The chief then drinks some of the beer and is followed by the priestess, who hands the gourd to each member of the royal family, including females and children old enough to drink beer.

No member of the royal kindred may absent himself from these rites unless he is prevented from attending by illness. Otherwise he will, it is believed, fall sick and die. If illness had prevented him from attending he must, as soon as he has recovered, betake himself to the shrine with the customary gift to the priestess, who puts some water in the pot which had contained the beer at the new moon rites. He is given this water to drink.

At the end of every four months the priestess removes from the sacred pot the strips of cloth which had been offered by the chief, and when the number of strips is sufficient she makes them into a skirt.

The rites are said to have the sole intention of protecting the royal kindred from illness, especially illness produced by witchcraft or sorcery. They are not associated in any way with the Moon as a god. But it is not unlikely that they were at one time so associated. In my Jukun monograph[1] it is noted that the Jukun chief is likened to the moon, and that the Hona and Gabin title for chief, viz. Kutira or Kudira, probably means "The lord of the Moon", *ku* being a common Nigritic root for king or lord, and *tɪrra*, *ndirra*, and *tera* being the word for moon among these and neighbouring tribes.[2] It is possible, therefore, that the Zumu royal rites are a relic of times when the chief was associated with the moon as the lord of fertility. [3]

The Zumu state that the cult was originally received from the Bata of Bulki in order to put a stop to the constant conflicts which occurred over the election of a chief. The symbols of the cult are the same as those of the well-known Bata cult of Nzeanzo which is also served by a priestess. A description of this cult is given in the paper on the Bachama tribe (Chapter I).

The cult of Dagire is also used for general purposes. Thus if a person is charged with theft or any other offence he may appeal to

---

[1] *A Sudanese Kingdom*, p. 123.
[2] But there is another possible interpretation of Kutira, viz. "The lord of the rain." (See the paper on the Gabin, Vol. II, Chap. XIII.)
[3] Among the Baganda at each new moon a ceremony is performed which seems to be intended to ensure the king's life and health throughout the ensuing month. (Roscoe, *J.R.A.I.* xxxii, 1902, pp. 63 and 75, quoted by Frazer in *Adonis*, p. 375.)

the chief for leave to swear his innocence at the shrine of Dagire. If he falls seriously ill within a few months of having sworn his oath he is adjudged guilty and has not merely to pay compensation and a fine, but has also to seek absolution from the god, in order that he may be freed from his illness. The fee for taking an oath of this character is one dish of cotton paid to the priestess. But the priestess shares all fees with the chief who is the real owner of the cult. In bygone days if a person were convicted by the cult of a serious offence, such as witchcraft, all his property became forfeit to the chief.

Similarly, if a man is assailed with illness, and it is ascertained by divination that Dagire is the cause of his illness, he will go to the shrine and confess any offences of which he may have been guilty and ask the god to remove the illness. The method of divination is one frequently practised in Nigeria. The diviner lays a number of wisps of grass before him, each representing some question (e.g. is Dagire the cause of this man's illness ?). He then places his left hand on his head and asks the questions one by one, at the same time watching to see if certain muscles of his upper arm move. If the answer is in the negative there is no movement, but if in the affirmative the muscle flickers violently.

The cult of Dagire is not used for fertility purposes ; but the chief is himself regarded as so intimately connected with the crops that the crop sown and harvested ritually each year on a section of his farm is believed to contain the life-giving principle or spirit in a special degree, and is, therefore, set aside to serve as consecrated seed.

When the time arrives for planting, the senior members of the community are summoned by the chief and directed to dig up certain tubers which are grown in his garden specially for the purpose. The tubers are ground in a mortar, and the juice is mixed with the soil produced by the red worms which come out of the ground during the wet season. Some of this mixture is laid on one side for use by the chief on the ensuing day. The rest is rolled in seed from the royal farm, and from the resultant ball a small quantity is taken and given to each of the senior men for mixing with his own seed and planting. Early next day the chief proceeds alone to his farm and scatters to each point of the compass a few fragments of the mixture, calling on the Supreme Being to give him and his people food. The senior men than plant on the chief's farm the remainder of the ball of worm-earth, tuber-juice, and seed. The patch planted is carefully marked, and at harvest the bundles of corn obtained are set aside for the rites of the following spring.

Among the Jukun the royal seed is regarded as sacred and magical, and the tuber used by the Zumu in these rites is also used by the Jukun in numerous magico-religious rites. The red-earth worm also plays a prominent part in Jukun beliefs, being regarded as the sole food of the dead.

On the occurrence of a drought two rites are carried out. The drought may be due to the wrath of some royal ancestor. The chief, therefore, calls on the senior members of the kindred known as the Aba-Kuru,[1] who are the grave-diggers and custodians of the royal tombs, to inspect the grave of each former chief. If he finds (as he no doubt does) that some of the grass shelters covering the graves are in a state of disrepair the head of the Aba-Kuru takes immediate steps to put matters right, blaming his subordinates for not attending to the work (for which he was himself respon-sible). When the repairs are completed he lays an offering of a number of pumpkins in the hut of the latest deceased chief, apologizes for his neglect, and calls on the chief to send them rain. Among numerous tribes drought is ascribed to royal ancestors, and even among the Muslim Bolewa one of the first actions of the reigning chief during a drought is to have the royal cemetery put into a state of repair.

The second rite is carried out at the instance of the Kiladima, the senior non-royal official. He dispatches two members of his family to the top of a hill where a spirit known as Tingno is thought to abide. The young men are provided with a chicken and some flour. When they reach the hill-top they kill the chicken, cook it, and eat it with porridge. One of the lads then strips himself naked, while the other yells loudly (with the idea of driving away the evil spirit causing the drought). The youth who had discarded his garments then re-clothes himself, and both make for home as speedily as possible. It is said that before they reach home they are drenched with rain.

Another cult found among the Zumu is that known as Pukol which is symbolized by a gourd containing some decoction. The

---

[1] This is a Jukun expression. One of the towns of the Jibu Jukun is known as Abakuru.

gourd is covered with a dish into which ground benniseed is placed when the services of the godling are required. The cult is used principally as a court of appeal in cases of charges of witch-craft or theft, the accused being required to eat some of the benniseed after having proclaimed his innocence. This cult is not, apparently, an ancient cult of the Zumu. It was introduced by an immigrant from Kofa.

The Zumu still observe a form of male initiation which is now associated with circumcision (though it is stated that in former times circumcision was not practised by the Zumu or, at any rate, by all the Zumu). The rites extend over a month, and the boys sleep in shelters specially erected in the confines of the village. But they spend the day in the bush. They are circumcised in the bush, and when the wound has healed they spend their time learning to spin. For among all the tribes of North-Eastern Adamawa spinning is carried out by men and not by women (as is usual elsewhere). The boys are not subjected to the usual form of physical hardship, but they must avoid all social intercourse with women. They may only be visited by senior male relatives. At the end of the month's seclusion their heads are shaven, but there is no feast to celebrate their return to normal life. There is no change of name and there are none of the formalities usually connected with initiation rites, except that the boys refuse con-versation with female relatives until they have been given a gift.

As regards the form of social organization it was stated definitely that prior to contact with the Fulani the patrilineal kindred was an exogamous unit, but that nowadays there was no objection to a man marrying his second cousin (on either side of the family). When it was put to them that the Fulani commonly marry the first cousin they stated that feeling was against marriage between relatives so closely related, and that even marriages with second cousins were infrequent. Nevertheless, two instances were obtained of marriage between a man and his maternal uncle's daughter. But in both cases it appeared that the man's mother and the maternal uncle were not full brother and sister. They had different mothers. Had they had the same mother the marriage would not have been permitted, on the ground that " milks may not be intermingled ".

Inheritance follows the patrilineal principle, and in former times was by primogeniture. But nowadays younger sons are given a minor share, on the ground that everyone is now free to pursue his own way independently of his brothers. Brothers only inherit in the absence of sons, or on behalf of sons who have not reached the age of discretion. Until recently sons could inherit and marry their father's widows (their own mothers, of course, excepted) ; but at the present time, owing to the influence of Muslim ideas, this practice is regarded with disfavour. A widow may be married by the deceased husband's younger brother. If she elects to marry outside her late husband's family her husband's heritor is entitled to claim a bride-price, if the woman had not borne a child by her first husband. (For among the Zumu the birth of one child cancels the bride-price.)

In view of the strong patrilineality of the Zumu it is surprising to find the rule that on the death of a man his sister's son is entitled to retain any property which he can purloin from his late uncle's estate. Normally among patrilineal peoples in Nigeria a sister's son is entitled to make inroads on his uncle's property during the latter's lifetime, but he has no claim on the latter's estate after death. Among the Zumu the legal heritors, i.e. eldest son or younger brother, will usually take immediate steps to secure custody of the deceased's effects ; but if a sister's son is able, by any device, to obtain possession of any article, he is entitled to retain it. If the article had any special sentimental value it would be redeemed from the sister's son by barter. The reason given for this licence is interesting : it is contended by the sister's son that if his mother had been a male she would have been entitled to inherit from her deceased brother !

Authority within the kindred is patriarchal, but this does not mean that wives are chattels or that maternal relatives are of small account. On the contrary, the position of a wife is high ; for once she has borne a child to her husband she is free to change her husband for another " without prejudice ". She may change her husband at any time ; but if she has borne a child by the first husband the latter cannot claim any refund of his bride-price. The rule that children belong to the legal husband prevents wives who are devoted to their children from contracting new alliances indiscriminately. Nevertheless, a large percentage of women leave their husbands and children in order to live with other men.

When a wife bears her first female child the husband is required to pay to her maternal uncle a gift of five gowns and eleven pieces of cloth. Among the Jirai of Bulai this gift is paid when the child is born, whether that child is a female or not. This would seem to suggest that the wife's family had at one time an automatic claim on the first child. But the Zumu explanation is that, as a man receives no bride-price for his sister, it is right that he should derive some advantage from one of her children in order to help him to provide a wife for one of his sons. He or his heir, therefore, claims the five gowns and eleven pieces of cloth as soon as his sister's daughter bears her first female child. Another explained the matter by saying that the gift compensated the maternal uncle for his expenditure in obtaining a wife and enabled him to provide a bride-price for his son. A third statement was that as a man is entitled to a share of his sister's property so he is entitled to derive some advantage from her children. He is expected to contribute something towards the marriage expenses of his sister's sons.[1]

It will be seen that the natives look at this matter not from the point of view of " patriarchy " and " matriarchy " but from that of give-and-take. It is erroneous, therefore, to suppose that payments made for a first-born child are necessarily an indication of a former mother-right complex.

It may be noted also that a maternal uncle has a right to veto the marriage of his niece to any particular individual. This again need not be regarded as indicating former mother-right principles, for if a maternal uncle is entitled to a substantial gift from the husband of his niece, when the latter bears a female child, it is natural that he should have some say in the choice of her husband.

It may be added in conclusion that the pre-marriage payments amount to the equivalent of fifty pieces of cloth, of which the father of the girl appropriates about three-fourths, the remaining fourth being given to the mother.

As regards the dissolution of marriage the main principle is, as already stated, that the birth of one child cancels the bride-price. If, therefore, a woman, who has borne a child, becomes the wife of another man, that man is under no obligation to make any payment to her former husband. But custom requires that he shall give one gown to the woman's father. Per contra, if a wife

---

[1] For other views on the subject of the claim to the first-born child the reader is referred to the paper on "The Mumuye and their neighbours". (Vol. I, Chap. VIII.)

PLATE 13

A CAIRN AT ZUMU

abandons her first husband without having borne him a child he becomes entitled to a refund of all his marriage expenses. And if a man dies before his wife bears him a child his heir can reclaim the full bride-price from anyone who marries the widow.

As the Zumu have abandoned the principle of exogamy they have abandoned also the wife-sharing system which is characteristic of the tribal group to which they belong. This system is fully described in the chapter on the Malabu (p. 91 et seq.).

The relationship terms are as follows :—

Ba-gi is applied to a father and his brothers and male cousins.
Mo-gi is applied to a mother.
Nzêai is applied to sons and daughters and most relatives of a junior generation.
Na-gi is applied to a father's and mother's sisters.
Wu-ʒo is applied to a mother's brother and sister's child.
Jiji is applied to male grandparents.
Kaka is applied to female grandparents.
Jejen is applied to all grandchildren.
Sheru-wo (f. sheruti) is applied to parents-in-law and senior brothers-in-law and senior sisters-in-law.
Mashi is applied to junior brothers or sisters-in-law.
Mausenu is a general term for brother or sister in the classificatory sense.
An elder brother or sister is called *zibo*.
A junior brother or sister is called *mafe*.

These terms are the same as those used by the surrounding tribal groups, the only difference being that in most of these groups the father's elder brothers are classed with grandfathers.

In the plains between Zumu and Gola there are a large number of cairns of which the local inhabitants can give no explanation. They are built of loose stones, thrown together without arrangement (unlike the cairns of the Gongola valley). They are circular or elliptical in shape, and some are 20 to 30 feet high, with a base diameter of 30 to 60 feet. One of the cairns observed was unlike the rest, in that it had a flat top cemented with hard clay. The cairns had not the appearance of great age, as the surface stones showed no signs of excessive weathering. Pieces of pottery were found in all of the cairns between the boulders. Captain Skelly opened one of the cairns and found at the base a hoe, some beads, and fragments of pottery. I continued the digging of a central trench to a depth of 3 feet but discovered nothing further. A complete examination (which would require a week's work) might have disclosed that the cairns marked the sites of the graves of chiefs. In the vicinity of one set of cairns a large number of small circular collections of stones clearly indicated that the place had been used as a cemetery.

There are numerous cairns in Kenya Colony, some of which are said to be the burial places of the chiefs of the Maanthinle (or " tall people "). Among the Masai the bodies of medicine-men are laid in a trench and covered with stones. Afterwards when anyone passes the spot he throws a stone on the heap and this is done for all time.[1] Elsewhere in Northern Nigeria there are a number of cairns in the valley of the Gongola River. For an account of these the reader is referred to the paper on the Longuda tribe. (Vol. II, Chap. XIII.)

A full schedule of words and phrases is attached :—

ZUMU (JIMO)

1. Head	ngino	ŋino
2. Hair	showo	ʃɔwo
3. Eye	din	din
Two eyes	di bak	di bək
4. Ear	limo	lɪmo
Two ears	limogi bak	lɪmogi bək
5. Nose	chino	tʃino
6. One tooth	nintsu hiḍo	nintsu hiɗo
Five teeth	neni tuf	nɛni tuf
7. Tongue	genna	gɛnna
8. Neck	wura	wura
9. Breast (woman's)	watsu	watsu
10. Heart	diva	dɪvə
11. Belly	sikka	sɪkkə
12. Back	batsu	batsu
13. Arm	waḍi	waɗi
14. Hand	dabadaba or sikko waḍi	dʌbadʌba (palm) or sɪkko wadi
Two hands	dabadaba bak	dʌbadʌba bək
15. Finger	geli	gɛli
Five fingers	gelituf	gɛlituf
16. Finger-nail	papi	pəpi
17. Leg	Shiḍo	ʃiɗo
18. Knee	magirsho	magɪrʃo
19. Foot	suka shiḍo	suka ʃiɗo
Two feet	suka sheḍi bak	suka ʃeɗi bək

[1] See G. W. B. Huntingford in *Man*, December, 1927.

20.	Man (person)	ndo	ndo
	Ten people	nyi pu	nʤi pu
21.	Man (not woman)	muro	muro
	Two men	mori bak	mɔri bək
22.	Woman	mitu	mitu
	Two women	mangti bak	maŋti bək
23.	Child	nzo	nzo
24.	Father	ba	ba
25.	Mother	mo	mo
26.	Slave	mava	mava
27.	Chief	hamo	hamo
28.	Friend	sobagi	sobagi
29.	Smith	killa	kɪlla
30.	Doctor	dadgowo	dədgowo
31.	One finger	geltsu hiɗo	gɛltsu hiɗo
32.	Two fingers	geli bak	gɛli bək
33.	Three fingers	geli mwakin	gɛli mwakɪn
34.	Four fingers	geli fat	gɛli fʌt
35.	Five fingers	geli tuf	gɛli tuf
36.	Six fingers	geli kwakh	gɛli kwax
37.	Seven fingers	geli miskata	gɛli mɪskata
38.	Eight fingers	geli fofat	gɛli fɔfʌt
39.	Nine fingers	geli tambiɗo	gɛli tambiɗo
40.	Ten fingers	geli pu	gɛli pu
41.	Eleven fingers	geli pu ka ido	gɛli pu ka ido
42.	Twelve fingers	geli pum bi bak	gɛli pum bi bək
	Thirteen fingers	geli pum bi mwakin	gɛli pum bi mwakɪn
43.	Twenty fingers	geli gba mashetso	gɛli gba maʃɛtso
44.	A hundred fingers	geli haru	gɛli haru
45.	Two hundred fingers	geli haru bak	gɛli haru bək
46.	Four hundred fingers	geli haru ofat	gɛli haru ofʌt
47.	Sun	foto	fɔto
	God	fito	fɪto
48.	Moon	ligiɗo	ligɪɗo
	Full moon	ligiɗo pupul	ligɪɗo pupul
	New moon	ligiɗo muja	ligɪɗo mudʒa
49.	Day	fotel mur kano	fɔtɛl mur kano
	Night	viɗo	vɪɗo
	Morning	dupati	dupəti
50.	Rain	famo	famo
51.	Water	koti	koti
52.	Blood	bizo	bizo
53.	Fat	maro	maro
54.	Salt	powo	powo
55.	Stone	firra	fɪrra
	Iron	riengo	riɛŋo
56.	Hill	mbo	mbo
57.	River	gara	gərə
58.	Road	tavo	təvo

59. House	vino (Compound = hwoɖo)	vino (Compound = hwɔɖo)
Two houses	veni gi bak	vɛni gi bək
Many houses	veni gidigau	vɛni gɪdɪgəu
All the houses	veni gidbiga	vɛni gɪdɪgba
60. Hoof	kwashi	kwaʃi
61. Door	magarango	magaraŋo
62. Mat	kazetu	kəzɛtu
63. Basket	paktako	pəktako
64. Drum	ganga	gaŋga
65. Pot	wuda	wuda
66. Knife	ngilla	ŋgɪlla
67. Spear	kuvo	kuvɔ
68. Bow	rago	rago
69. Arrow	afthu	afθu
Five arrows	avo tuf	avo tuf
70. Gun	binduko	bɪnduko
71. War	vuretu	vurɛtu
72. Meat (animal)	lio	lio
73. Elephant	chiwa	tʃiwa
74. Buffalo	ndoka	ndɔka
75. Leopard	aruwo	aruwo
76. Monkey	robo	robo
77. Pig	dagilla	dagɪlla
78. Goat	hutu	hutu
79. Dog	kida	kɪda
80. Bird	kotoko	kotoko
Feather	deti	deti
81. Crocodile	gilengo	gilɛŋo
Sheep	baga (pl. bagi)	baga (pl. bagi)
Lion	ivo	ivo
Horse	kara (pl. karagi)	kara (pl. karagi)
Cow	piritsu (pl. porio)	pɪrɪtsu (pl. pɪriɔ)
82. Fowl	dieko	diɛkɔ
83. Eggs	kwali	kwali
84. One egg	kwali hiɖo	kwali hiɖo
85. Snake	iso	iso
86. Frog	ngwanda	ŋwanda
87. Fly	jeddo	dʒɛddo
88. Bee	bozongsu	bɔzɔŋsu
89. Honey	bozongo	bɔzɔŋo
90. Tree	kadi	kadi
Ten trees	kadi pu	kadi pu
91. Leaf	guɖa	guɖa
92. Guinea-corn	gweo	gweo
93. Maize	mapinawo	mapinawo
94. Ground-nut	walatu	walatu
95. Oil	maro	maro
96. The tall woman	mikun chuchu	mikun tʃutʃu
The tall women	mangtin chuchu	maŋtɪn tʃutʃu
97. Large dog	kidan digau	kɪdan dɪgau

98.	Small dog	kidan filek	kɪdan fɪlɛk
99.	The dog bites	kidan ma ado	kɪdan ma ado
100.	The dog bites me	kidan ma iditai	kɪdan ma ɪdɪtai
101.	The dog which bit me yesterday	kidan mo iditai hwodi	kɪdan mo ɪdɪtai hwɔdi
	I	no	no
	You	iyo	ijɔ
	You (f.)	ki	ki
	He	zano	zano
	She	kano	kano
	We	hinno	hinno
	You	hun	hun
	They	tinno	tɪnno
	Fulani	Pirasali	pɪrasali
	Hausa	Hausi	hausi
	Beri-Beri	Koli	koli
	We (inclusive) go	ma du	ma du
	We (inclusive)	hina du	hina du
102.	I flog the dog	na killa kidano	nə killə kɪdano
103.	The dog which I have flogged	kidano na killin	kɪdano nə kɪllɪn
104.	I see him	na nan	nə nan
	I see her	na nato	nə nato
	He sees you	min nau	mɪn nau
	He sees us	min namno	mɪn namno
	We see you (pl.)	hin nauno	hɪn nauno
	We see them	hin natin	hɪn natɪn
105.	Beautiful bird	kotokon ma ulia	kotokon ma ulia
106.	Slave	mava	mava
	My slave	mavan gi	mavaŋ gi
	Thy slave	mavan gu	mavaŋ gu or mavau
	Our slaves	mavan gin	mavaŋ gɪn
107.	The chief's slave	mava hamo	mava hamo
	His slave	mavan gano	mavaŋ gəno
108.	We see the slave	hin na mavan	hɪn nə mavan
109.	We call the slave	hin ya mavan	hɪn ja mavan
110.	The slave comes	mava na mashi	mava nə maʃi
111.	He came yester-day	mishi wodi	mɪʃi wɔdi
	He is coming to-day	za shi supo	za ʃi supo
	She is coming to-day	ka shi supo	ka ʃi supo
	He will come to-morrow	za shi wodi	za ʃi wodi
112.	The slaves go away	mavin na ma pitto	mavɪn nə ma pɪtto
113.	Who is your chief ?	wona ham anga ?	wona ham aŋa ?
114.	The two villages are making war on each other	berigin bak ma bero ta suwo getin	bɛrigɪn bək ma bɛro ta suwo gɛtɪn

115.	The sun rises	fatin ma dima	fətɪn ma dima
	The sun sets	fatin ma ndi	fətɪn ma ndi
116.	The man is eating	ndɛn mangoso shin	ndɛn mangoso ʃin
117.	The man is drinking	ndɛn ma sa kotin	ndɛn ma sa kotin
118.	The man is asleep	ndɛn ma chini	ndɛn ma tʃini
119.	I break the stick	na bian zualan	nə bian zualan
	The stick is broken	zualan ma bii	zualan ma bii
	This stick cannot be broken	zualan ma karo bii kin	zualan ma karo bii kɪn
	Break this stick for me	biashi zualan to	biaʃi zualan to
120.	I have built a house	na hidda vinin	nə hɪdda vinin
121.	My people have built their houses yonder	njeringi mu hidda venigin getin a gato	ndʒerɪŋgi mu hidda vɛnigin gɛtɪn a gato
122.	What do you do every day ?	nin tsimi ninwu ma han ma kidda fa ?	nɪn tsɪmi nɪnwu ma han ma kɪdda fa ?
	I work on my farm	na man nino ninkin auyegi	nə ma nnɪno nɪnkɪn auʃegi
123.	I am going away	na dinge	nə dɪŋe
	I am hoeing	na ma wwza	nə ma wwza
	I am going away to hoe	na ma du wuza kin	nə ma du wuza kɪn
	I am going away to my farm	na du yegi	nə du ʃegi
124.	The woman comes	mikin ma si	mikɪn ma si
	She comes	kina ma si	kɪn ma si
	He comes	zina ma si	zɪn ma si
	The woman laughs	mikin ma moso	mikɪn ma mɔso
	The woman weeps	mikin ma tiwa	mikɪn ma tiwa
125.	I ask the woman	na do mikino	nə do mikɪno
126.	Why do you laugh ?	kami ya ma moso ?	kami ʃa ma mɔso ?
127.	Why do you cry ?	kami ya ma tiwa ?	kami ʃa ma tiwa ?
128.	My child is dead	zange mam bitto	zaŋɛ mam bɪtto
129.	It is not dead	am bitto	am bɪtto
130.	Are you ill ?	pigo kwangkwang ?	pigo kwaŋkwaŋ ?
131.	My children are ill	wojinge a go kwangkwang	wodʒɪŋe a go kwaŋkwaŋ
132.	His child is better	zangin ma ḍumo dama	zaŋɪn ma ɗumo dama
	Her child is better	zangato ma ḍumo dama	zaŋato ma ɗumo dama
133.	Yes	ho	ho
	No	angnge	əŋŋe

134. A fine knife	ngilla kin ma wulya	ŋɪlla kɪn ma wulʝa
Give me the knife	vi ngilla kin	vi ŋɪlla kɪn
I give you the knife	na vu ngilla kin	nə vu ŋɪlla kɪn
135. I am a European	no na Nasara	no nə nasara
You are a black man	iyo indu dungwo	iʝɔ ɪndu duŋwo
You are a Zumu	iyo indu Zomo tsu	iʝɔ ɪndu Zomo tsu
136. Name	limo	limo
My name	limangai	lɪməŋai
Your name	limanga	lɪmaŋa
What is your name ?	atimi limanga ?	atimi lɪmaŋaga ?
137. There is water in the gourd	kotin na asako hubo kin	kotin nə asəko hubo kɪn
The knife is on the stone	ngilla kin angna firran	ŋɪlla kɪn aŋnə fɪrran
The fire is under the pot	ɗuwin a firro wudan	ɗuwɪn a fɪrro wudan
The roof is over the hut	nyin zuma vinin	nʝɪn zuma binɪn
138. You are good	iyo i ma wulya	iʝɔ i ma wulʝa
This man is bad	ndin no a wulya	ndɪn no a wulʝa
139. The paper is white	derewol nono pudo	dɛrɛwɔl nɔno pudo
This thing is black	sono so dungo	sono so duŋo
This thing is red	sono eem	sono ɛɛm
140. This stone is heavy	firrano purut	fɪrrano purut
This stone is not heavy	firrano aga purut	fɪrrano aga purut
141. I write	na ma vinda	nə ma vɪnda
I give you the letter	na vu derewollin	nə vu dɛrɛwɔllɪn
Carry the letter to the town	du ta derewollin ta biri	du ta dɛrɛwɔllɪn ta biri
142. Go away	dinga	dɪŋa
Come here	suwa gano	suwa gano
143. Where is your house ?	ma hagu ?	ma hagu ?
144. My house is here	hagi a gano	hagi a gano
My house is there	hagi a gato	hagi a gato
145. What have you to sell ?	mi derungwu ?	mi dɛruŋwu ?
146. I want to buy fish	na ɗirro horfin	nə ɗirro horfin
147. The fish which you bought is bad	horfin ya derra au wulede	horfin ʝa dɛrra au wulɛdɛ
148. Where is the man who killed the elephant ?	andua den a billo chuwan ?	andua dɛn a bɪllo tʃuwan ?

He has killed many elephants	mu billo chuwan diggau	mu bıllo tʃuwan dıggau
How many elephants were killed yester-day ?	chuwan bawa ya billo hodi ?	tʃuwan bawa ja billo hodi ?
149. Untie it	parran	parran
Tie this rope	tang pallu hirkin	tʌŋ pallu hirkin
Make the boy un-tie the goat	mano zento za pirra honto	məno zɛnto za pırra honto
150. My brothers and I, we are going but no one else	no tamafinge hina dingyin hidegin	no tamafıŋe hina dıŋjın hidegın
Brothers, let us go and tell the chief	mafinge zanungwun huma du mano hamin	mafıŋe zanuŋwun huma du məno hamın
151. This tree is bigger than that	kadan to ma pudugo noto de gaunin	kadan to ma pugugo noto dɛ gaunın

The Bulai.—The Jirai of Bulai have retained their ancient customs to a greater extent than those Jirai who now call them-selves Zumu. Thus they still possess the characteristic Jirai organization by which two or more kindreds, not necessarily related, form a single exogamous group within which wives may pass from one husband to another. Under this system, as practised by the Malabu and other typical Jirai communities such as Kofa, Muleng, and Mivezo, there is no refund of bride-price when a wife passes from one husband to another of the associated kindreds, as wives are held to be common to the group. But this rule has at Bulai become modified in recent times so that the bride-price is now reclaimable from a secondary husband, if the wife had not borne a child to the primary husband. This modification is due partly to the influence of Muslim ideas and partly to the fact that the associated kindreds are no longer wholly localized, the pax Britannica having made it possible for anyone to establish a home wherever he pleases.

Society is organized on a dual basis, there being two groups of associated kindreds. The first consists of the Kambi, Jikombai, and Jejinjongwe kindreds. The second consists of the Kovangi, Wadi, and Jumayo kindreds. Each group is exogamous : that is to say that no Kambi man may marry a Kambi woman, nor yet may he marry a Jikombai or Jejinjongwe woman. But he may marry a Kovangi or Wadi or Jumayo woman. This rule of exogamy is not ostensibly based, according to native ideas, on blood relationship, and it is clear that originally there was no blood relationship between the associated kindreds. For (to take an example) the Kovangi are immigrants from Kofa and the Wadi are immigrants from Wadi. The rule of exogamy, they say, arises from local association, i.e. it is loyal exogamy and not kinship exogamy. But actually there is no real distinction between local exogamy and kinship exogamy, for, owing to the practice by which wives may pass from members of one kindred to members of another associated kindred, kindreds which were originally in no way related become related in a very short period of time. And the blood relationship becomes still more pronounced where, as among most Jirai groups, any male member of the associated kindreds may have extra-marital relations with the wife of any other member of the associated kindreds who is of the same age as, or senior to, himself.

At the present time it has become the fashion at Bulai to view with disfavour promiscuous sexual intercourse between men and the wives of fellow members of their own kindred or of an associated kindred ; and where such intercourse occurs it is carried out *sub rosa*, and not openly as among most other groups of Jirai. If detected the paramours are mildly rebuked by the husband and there the matter ends. There are no penalties, such as would be inflicted if a husband discovered that his wife was having extra-marital relations with a member of some foreign group.

The present position, therefore, among the Jirai of Bulai may be summarized as follows. A Kambi man may not marry a woman who belongs to the Kambi, Jikombai, or Jejinjongwe kindreds. But he may marry a woman of the Kovangi, Wadi, or Jumayo kindreds. On the other hand, he may marry any woman who is already married to a man of the Kambi, Jikombai, or Jejinjongwe kindreds, but he may not marry a woman who is the wife of any member of the Kovangi, Wadi, or Jumayo kindreds, even if that woman is not debarred to him by the rule of exogamy, i.e. even if she belongs to some foreign community. The rule that a man may marry a woman who is the wife of any member of his own (or of an associated) kindred has one exception, viz. that he may not appropriate the wife of a brother or first cousin. Where the

Jirai of Bulai differ from most other groups is in the new-fangled custom by which a refund of bride-price may be demanded by a man from one of his own exogamous group who deprives him of his wife (if the wife had not borne him a child). They also differ (as already indicated) in refusing any longer to countenance the open paramour relationship practised by the Malabu, Kofa, Muleng, and several other Jirai communities.

As regards the arrangement of marriage with a virgin girl the procedure is as follows. The suitor (or his father acting on his behalf) makes an early application (soon after the girl's birth) by offering gifts of oil and a cow's horn. If the suit is accepted gifts of meat are sent to the girl's father at each new moon, and the suitor (or his representative) is required to render agricultural service on the occasions when such help is necessary. The main payments consist of 2 gowns, 70 pieces of cloth, salt, corn, and beef, all of which are paid during the year prior to that in which the suitor lays formal claim to his bride. In making these payments the suitor is assisted by his father, paternal uncles, and numerous friends. The entire kindred in fact contributes towards the marriage expenses of any member of the kindred, and on this account it is held in most Jirai communities that the wife obtained is justifiably regarded as the wife of all, i.e. that no member of the kindred can bear resentment if his wife chooses to abandon him for some other member of his kindred. A maternal uncle may also contribute something towards the marriage expenses of his nephew. There is no seclusion of the young bride, as among the Malabu, and it is normal among the Bulai for a girl to take up residence with her husband before she has attained the age of puberty, provided that the bride-price has been fully paid. There are no sexual relations until the girl is considered old enough to bear a child. When she bears her first child the husband is required to present two gowns and twenty pieces of cloth to his wife's father, who hands them to the girl's maternal uncle. The reason for this payment has already been discussed in the preceding notes on the Zumu. But it may be added that among the Kofa and some other groups of Jirai the gifts received at this stage are not handed to the girl's maternal uncle, but are given by the girl's father to his younger brother who uses them to secure a bride for his son. If the payment is not made the girl's first female child can (among the Kofa) be claimed by her father in order to become the wife of his younger brother's son. And for this reason we find among the Kofa an unusual form of marriage, viz. that between a woman and her mother's younger paternal uncle's son. Among the Bulai it is permissible for a man to marry his maternal uncle's daughter, provided his mother and maternal uncle had different mothers.

If a wife who has not borne a child passes as a secondary wife to some other man within the associated exogamous group the bride-price has (as already stated) to be refunded. But it is obvious that no man can pay down in a lump sum the gifts which the first husband had gradually accumulated with the assistance of numerous relatives and friends. The new husband is, therefore, permitted to extend his payments over a number of years, and they generally take the form of the products of a specially-planted cotton farm, the crop of which is, for a period of five years, handed over to the former husband.

Inheritance follows the patrilineal principle, the chief inheritor being the eldest son. But if the son has not reached the age of discretion the deceased's younger brother or cousin takes charge of the estate on the son's behalf. Widows are regarded as heritable property and may become the wives of the heritor if they so desire. A woman, therefore, may become the wife of her late husband's son (provided, of course, she is not his mother). If the deceased's brother or cousin acts as the administrator of the estate and marries the deceased's widows he must compensate the sons later by providing them with wives to the same number as he had himself inherited. If the deceased had no male relatives and left a young son the boy's mother would act as trustee ; and if any of the other widows remarried, the bride-price due would be handed to the son as soon as he was old enough to receive it. If she herself remarried her son would not claim a bride-price, as that would be regarded as selling his own mother. But the person who married his mother would assist the boy later in obtaining a wife.

The relationship terms are the same as those used by the Zumu, with the exception that a father's and mother's elder brother are both classed with grandfathers, the title used being *zizo* or *zuo*.

The Jirai of Bulai do not devote much attention to religion, and little information was obtained on the subject. The principal cult appears to be Gedi, a word which means " East " in a number of languages spoken further North. Among the Yungur the word for the Supreme Being means " The East " or " He of the East ". Possibly the cult of Gedi was at one time associated with the Sun. At the present time Gedi is regarded as a spirit which tenants a particular spring, and prior to the harvest the chief and priest of the cult, accompanied by the senior men, go to the spring with gifts of cotton-wool. The chief offers a prayer that the harvest may be abundant and that he and all his people may have health. He also calls on Gedi to bring evil on those who would rob them of their crops or of any other property. The priest slays a chicken, and the blood is allowed to flow out close to the edge of the spring. All present then deposit their gifts of cotton beside the spring, and each man drinks a little of the sacred water.

Many householders also possess a home-cult of Gedi, the symbol being a pot containing some earth and water taken from the sacred spring. This pot is set on a forked stick and is used as a general means of securing health and preventing theft.

The chief is believed to be closely associated with Gedi ; and it is important, therefore, that the chief's peace of mind should not be disturbed, for otherwise a drought might ensue. In this event the people would go to the chief and confess some offence against him. If the drought persisted it would be considered that the chief had offended Gedi and he might be called on to resign. Or it might be ascertained by divination that the drought was due to the neglect of some royal ancestor. The royal graves would then be repaired, and the chief would offer a petition to the forefather to relent. The royal graves are normally repaired every year before sowing, a libation of beer being poured in the centre of the graveyard.

Chiefs are buried sitting on a stool, clothed in gown and fez. The legs are drawn up slightly, and the hands are placed between the knees. The head is kept in position by an upright stick fixed under the chin, and resting on a calabash placed on the ground between the legs. The body is then covered with calabashes, and the grave is filled up with charcoal. The mouth of the grave, which is flagon-shaped, is blocked with a stone, and a grass hut is built over it. The charcoal method of burial for chiefs appears to be typical of the whole of the North-Eastern region of Nigeria.

All the Bulai and neighbouring Jirai now practise circumcision, and there are special circumcision rites similar to those practised by the Zumu.

The Bulai dialect is identical with that of the Zumu.

The Malabu.—The Malabu are a small group of some 2,050 people who occupy, in scattered hamlets, the area known to the Fulani as Vango Malabu, which is situated about 45 miles north-east of Yola. Their territory formerly extended to the vicinity of the present Fulani town of Malabu, but they were forced to withdraw from that area as a result of political troubles at the beginning of the present century. They have a chief of their own who is directly responsible to the Fulani district head of Malabu. Until recently they were almost entirely a pagan people, but within the last few years Islam has made advances, and those villages which are situated nearest to the Fulani settlements have ceased to maintain the pagan cults of their forefathers. There are indications also in these villages that the social regulations governing marriage, which have hitherto served as a barrier to intermarriage with the Fulani, are being relaxed ; and it is not improbable that they will have been completely abandoned within the next fifteen or twenty years.

The Malabu are almost entirely an agricultural people ; but spinning, weaving and dyeing are carried on as subsidiary occupations by the men. It would appear that these crafts were introduced into the tribe from the direction of Mandara. They have no wealth in livestock, but state that in former times they had numerous herds of the small unhumped cattle characteristic of the pagan tribes. They lost these cattle when they fell under the yoke of the Fulani.

They have no tribal marks, but state that their women used to affect the bodily marks now worn by the women of the Margi tribe.

The Malabu have a dual organization of royalty and commoners. The royal kindred or clan is known as the Baza and claims to have come from Mandara. The chief of the Malabu asserts that he belongs to the same stock which provided the chiefs of the Bata capitals of Demsa Poa and Demsa Mosu, as well as of Song and Kofa. As evidence of his relationship with the chief of Kofa he states that he may not meet this chief face to face, just as the chief of the Bata at Demsa Mosu may not meet the chief of the Bachama, both being descendants of the same ancestor.

Not merely does the family of the tribal chief belong to the Baza kindred, but so also do the families of all the village headmen. The Baza are in fact the aristocratic caste, and they enjoy numerous privileges, especially as regards marriage. They speak pure Bata, in contrast to the commoners who speak a dialect of Bata, and they describe themselves as " Gboate ", the Bata tribal title which means " The Men " or " People ".

The commoners may be described, generically, as Jirai. They speak the same dialect of Bata as is spoken by the Jirai of Zumu, Bulai, Kofa, and Muleng. It closely resembles Strumpell's Wadi (Wapango), Kovoci, Njei (my Njai or Nzangi), Holma, Maiha, and Gudu. Where it diverges from Bata it shows a general connection with the North-East as far as Mubi.[1] All the groups speaking this Jirai dialect have, or had until recently, the same characteristic form of social organization (to which reference has already been made and which will be described in fuller detail in the following paragraphs), and the same religious cult known as Gedi. All, moreover (with the possible exception of the Zumu group), have practised circumcision from ancient times. The pure Bata are a non-circumcising people.

It is apparent, therefore, that although the Malabu have now a tribal title of their own, they are not really a distinct tribe. They are Jirai with a Bata infusion, precisely like the other groups of Jirai. All might be described as Jirai-Bata.

It is not clear whether the Mandara conquerors of the Malabu and the surrounding Jirai groups imposed their language on the aboriginal inhabitants. It might be supposed that they did, as all speak dialects of Bata. On the other hand, the variations between the dialect spoken by the royal families and that of the commoners suggest that the aboriginals (i.e. the Jirai) already spoke a dialect of Bata before they were conquered, and that they have adhered to this dialect. It is possible, therefore, that there was a double conquest by Bata-speaking peoples, one in the seventeenth or eighteenth century, and the second not long prior to the Fulani " jihad " of the nineteenth century.

---

[1] To take a few examples, the Malabu word for ear is " *limo* ", and the Mubi " *limin* ". The Bata word is " *kwake* ". Men = *nji* in the Malabu language, *anji* in the Mubi, and *gboate* in the Bata. Belly = *sikko* in Malabu, *sika* in Mubi, and *edi* in Bata. Leg = *shido* in Malabu, *sida* in Mubi, and *mbare* in Bata.

We may now turn our attention to the social system of the Malabu, which is one of quite exceptional interest. As a preliminary it may be remarked that the Malabu do not appear to contain a " Laka " element as stated in Mrs. Temple's book (*Tribes, Emirates, etc.*, p. 160). There may be one or two small groups of " Laka " settlers in the Malabu district, but if so they are not Malabu, in the present-day acceptation of the term.

The Malabu consist of the following kindreds, who live intermixed in the various hamlets :—

> Baza.
> Tafafwando (or Diginchi).
> Gogen.
> Ngwoi.

> Magdari.
> Tara.
> Jekin.

> Mwaio.
> Belemo.
> Habiro.

> Minmo.
> Ngwalo.

The kindred known as Dadirmi or Badawo is omitted from the list, as there are only one or two representatives left. A group of Jirai who have become associated with the Mwaio are also excluded, owing to inadequate information as to their history and social status. The bracketed kindreds form distinct social groups. Each group of bracketed kindreds is an exogamous group. That is to say that a Baza man may not marry a Baza woman nor may he marry a Tafafwando or Gogen or Ngwoi woman. A Magdari man may not marry a Magdari or Tara or Jekin woman, and so on. From the point of view of exogamy, therefore, the bracketed groups, being no longer localized (as they were apparently at one time) might be described as a " clan ". This term generally implies that the constituent kindreds of the " clan " believe themselves to be related through a common ancestor, the exogamy being ascribed to this sense of relationship. But the Malabu do not regard the social grouping quite from this angle. The bracketed kindreds, in their view, form a distinct social group not because of a common ancestry necessitating exogamy, but because the various kindreds of the group have (to use their own words) their " wives in common ". This expression does not imply that there is any general state of sexual promiscuity, but rather that a wife of a member of one kindred may pass to a member of another kindred of the same group without recrimination, and without the repayment of the original bride-price or any other consideration. Nevertheless, it will be seen later that there is a measure of sexual promiscuity in the paramour relationship which may exist between a man and the wife of a member of one of the kindreds which are associated with his own.

It is obvious that in an association of this kind actual blood relationship is speedily established between kindreds which were not in any way related when the association was formed, and that a rule of exogamy would have to be made, unless the members of the associated kindreds were prepared to run the risk of marrying close blood relatives including, possibly, half-sisters. All the male members of the associated kindreds regard themselves as " brothers ", and it is clear that many of them are in fact half-brothers.

It is not suggested that the fear of consanguineous marriages is the only or even the primary reason for the rule of clan or of kindred exogamy of the character found among the Malabu. A variety of considerations may all have tended in the same direction. Thus there is in all tribes a sense of shame in meeting daily a person with whose relative one is having regular sexual relations, whether marital or extra-marital. This shame is, perhaps, inherent in human beings. It is possibly the explanation of the avoidance of parents-in-law, and also of the custom of local exogamy. Among the Malabu there is a definite rule that if two men of different but associated kindreds live cheek by jowl and share their meals together (as is the custom where compounds adjoin) they shall not exercise the sexual privileges which would otherwise be allowed.

Another reason commonly given for the rule of kindred exogamy is the necessity for the maintenance of the kinship bond. For if two families of the same kindred intermarry the inevitable quarrels between husband and wife are liable to cause a breach between the two sections of the kindred. This also may be a reason for the practice of local exogamy, i.e. the local exogamy may be the result of a desire to prevent local friction.

A more potent reason still for the practice of exogamy may be the sense of the necessity for reciprocity between groups, the sense of fair-dealing. If both groups marry internally and externally trouble will ensue, as one side or the other will, by accident or design, absorb more women than is due in proportion to its numbers. To effect a fair and square deal there must be a rule that no woman may marry a man of her own group. If one group exceeds the other in numbers the matter is adjusted by relations with a third or fourth group, or by a bisection of the larger group. But the principle of exogamy must be maintained.

Finally, it is only by a rule of clan or local exogamy that a workable system of secondary marriages and extra-marital relations can be arranged. These secondary marriages provide an easy escape from uncongenial partners and from sterile marriages ; and the freedom of sexual relations within the group provides a natural outlet for the sexual impulses of young men who have not yet been able to obtain a wife of their own.

This is, perhaps, rather an academic discussion, hardly suited to a government report. But it is important to direct attention to questions of this kind, with a view to gaining a greater under-standing of the people. From the purely academic point of view the points raised are of interest as suggesting that many factors may govern the rule of exogamy ; there may in fact be an exogamy " complex ". Some of the suggestions made may help towards a new or at least a more comprehensive view of the subject.

From the practical point of view the " clan " organization, or the " wife-sharing " organization, whichever term we choose to apply, is of political as well as social importance. The associated kindreds act as one in cases of dispute. Though they might originally have been blood relatives they took and take common action against any other group on the ground, not of kinship, but of " community in wives ". They have their leader appointed by the chief, and this leader is permitted by the chief to appoint sub-leaders from each of the associated kindreds.

Turning now to the history of the various kindreds composing the wife-sharing group, the first group consists of four kindreds, viz. Baza, Tafafwando (or Diginchi), Gogen, and Ngwoi. As already stated the Baza are the royal kindred. The story goes that the founders of the kindred came from Mandara via Wuba as hunters into the region of the present Fulani settlement of Malabu. They became friendly with the Ngwalo kindred which was at that time regarded as the ruling kindred. The Baza had no women with them ; so the chief of the Ngwalo gave one of his daughters as wife to the leader of the Baza. In due course the leader of the Baza resolved to become chief of the whole group. He disclosed his intention to his wife, who thereupon devised for him the following plan. He was to go out hunting and collect as many skins as possible. Then he was to suggest to the Ngwalo and others that he could provide for them fine leather coverings for their weapons. This scheme was adopted, and the Ngwalo and others brought their weapons to the Baza leader who sewed them up in leather and then fell upon his dupes, reducing them to the position of subjects. Stories of a similar ruse are current among numerous tribes of Bornu, and also among the Bolewa.[1]

A variant account is that the Baza originally fell in with the Tafafwando, the leader of whom gave, not a daughter, but one of his wives to the leader of the Baza ; or in other words the Baza were adopted into the exogamous and wife-sharing group composed of the Tafafwando, Gogen, and Ngwoi.

The second exogamous and wife-sharing unit consists of the Magdari, Tara, and Jekin kindreds. All three believe themselves to be related to each other and claim to be aboriginal, it being said that the forefather Magdari came out of a hole in the ground, and that Tara and Jekin were offshoots from the original kindred. It is not possible to prove a genealogical relationship between these three kindreds, and it may be that originally Magdari, Tara, and Jekin were local family-groups who, for purposes of wife-sharing, adopted a system of local exogamy.

The next group consists of Mwaio, Belemo, and Habiro. It is certain that these three kindreds were not originally related. The Mwaio were Jirai immigrants from Zumu, the Belemo were blacksmiths from Rai, while the Habiro were the aboriginal (Jirai ?) kindred.

The final group is composed of the Minmo and Ngwalo kindreds. The former were Jirai who migrated from Kofa. The Ngwalo, as already noted, were aboriginals. It is stated that the association between the Ngwalo and Minmo arose because a Ngwalo man used to have sexual relations with the wife of a Minmo man during the latter's absence while hunting. When this was discovered it was decided that there should be a community of wives between the two kindreds, and in consequence of this arrangement it became impossible for the two kindreds to marry

[1] See the paper on the Bolewa tribe. (Vol. II, Chap. XIII.)

each other's daughters.   This may be putting the cart before the horse, but that is how the matter was stated.

Totemic ideas do not play any significant part in the life of the Malabu.   It was stated that the royal clan respect the crocodile, on the ground that once upon a time a Baza maiden was, on the day of her marriage, seized by a crocodile.   The Gogen also respect the crocodile.   The Magdari, Tara, and Jekin have a special association with leopards, and this would suggest that all these three kindreds belonged, as their tradition indicates, to a common stock.   The association is ascribed to the circumstance that an ancestress of the group bore twins, one of which was a leopard and the other a boy.   The two lived in close association, the leopard visiting the boy at night and bringing him a share of his quarry, and the boy feeding the leopard when the leopard had failed to kill game.   And just as the original leopard and man were brothers so their offspring also became brothers, each assisting the other, and being identified, so that any (human) of the three kindreds could turn himself into a leopard if he so desired. In later times the association became lost because the " medicine " necessary for its maintenance was destroyed in a fire.

It is possible that totemic ideas of this character are connected with the widespread belief that some wild animals can suckle human children who grow up like animals, walking on all fours and tearing their food like their foster-mother.   This belief is not confined to Negroes or Oriental peoples, for a recent series of letters to *The Times* (April, 1927) shows that many Englishmen who have lived in India share the belief, some even stating that they have themselves seen such children under the care of missionaries. (There is usually an important missing link in the chain of the evidence adduced, and beliefs of the kind appear to run counter to all existing scientific knowledge.)   The Jekin, Tara, and Magdari kindreds do not describe themselves as " Leopards " ; but members of other kindreds may, on an occasion of some dispute, charge them with being leopards and, in the guise of leopards, stealing their neighbours' stock by night.

The Habiro kindred has a special relationship with the monitor lizard.   The Habiro are the rainmakers ; and during a drought the head of the kindred is called on by the chief to perform the rites.   Accompanied by the senior members not merely of his own kindred but also of other kindreds, he proceeds to a certain spot,

H

marked by a forked stick, close to the river's edge. There he sits
down and claps his hands, the normal mode of salutation among
all tribes which are or have been asssociated with the Bata.
Immediately, it is said, a monitor lizard comes out of the water
and makes for the hills where in former times the Habiro kindred
had its home. A goat is then sacrified, the strip of white cloth by
which it had been tethered being tied round the forked stick. The
head and skin of the goat are handed to a young man who hurries
up the hill and deposits them on a rock at the site of the old village.
It is said that rain usually descends before the young man has had
time to return home. It was admitted that in some cases the
monitor lizard failed to appear ; and when this happened it was
presumed that the rainmaker was offended with the chief or the
people. The chief would then go to the rainmaker and apologize,
offering a further gift of another goat.

The monitor lizard is not taboo to the other kindreds of the
exogamous group to which the Habiro belong. The Tafafwando
are said to avoid all reptiles. None of the remaining kindreds has
any animal or plant emblems.

Reverting now to the regulations governing marriage the
following table shows the form of marriage permissible for each
kindred, and for the exogamous or wife-sharing group :—

A.—*Baza* men may marry girls of (*a*) Tara ; (*b*) Mwaio, Belemo, and
    Habiro ; and (*c*) of Minmo and Ngwalo. They may take as
    wives women married to men of (*a*) Baza ; (*b*) Tafafwando,
    Gogen, Ngwoi ; and (*c*) of Magdari. It would seem to be
    against the normal rule that Baza men should be permitted to
    marry the daughters of Tara, and also to marry women who
    had been wives of Magdari men, as Tara and Magdari are
    members of the same social group. But Baza, being the royal
    kindred, has special privileges ; and the rule of exogamy is
    not broken, as Magdari men have no reciprocal right of appro-
    priating the wives of Baza men. It will be observed that Baza
    neither marry the daughters nor steal the wives of Jekin. The
    reason given was that there had been a quarrel at one time
    between the two kindreds. It will be observed also that Baza
    men may appropriate wives of other Baza men. This is against
    the normal rule of Vango Malabu, where it is held that it is
    indecent for a man to appropriate the wife of a member of his
    own kindred. It is a privilege only accorded to the royal
    kindred. A Baza man will not, however, appropriate the
    wife of a close blood relative.

  Tafafwando men may marry the daughters of any kindred save
    Baza, Gogen, and Ngwoi. They may appropriate wives from

Gogen and Ngwoi ; but not from Baza, on the ground that Baza is the royal kindred and must be treated with special deference.

Gogen men may marry the daughters of any kindred save Baza, Tafafwando, and Ngwoi, from all three of which Gogen may appropriate wives. It will be observed that Baza men permit Gogen men to appropriate their wives, a privilege not accorded to Tafafwando or Ngwoi who are members of the same wife-sharing group.

Ngwoi men may marry the daughters of any kindred save Baza, Tafafwando, and Gogen. Ngwoi men may steal wives from the Tafafwando and Gogen, but are not permitted to steal wives from the royal kindred.

B.—*Magdari* men may marry daughters of any kindred save Tara and Jekin, whose wives they appropriate. They may not marry the daughters of Baza, as Baza men appropriate the wives of Magdari men.

Tara men may marry the daughters of any kindred save Magdari and Jekin.

Jekin men may marry the daughters of any kindred save Magdari and Tara. In practice they do not marry the daughters of Baza.

C.—*Mwaio* men may marry the daughters of any kindred save Belemo and Habiro, whose wives they may appropriate.

Belemo men may marry the daughters of any kindred save Mwaio and Habiro, whose wives they may appropriate.

Habiro men may marry the daughters of any kindred save Mwaio and Belemo, whose wives they may appropriate.

D.—*Minmo* men may marry the daughters of any kindred save Ngwalo, whose wives they may appropriate.

Ngwalo men may marry the daughters of any kindred save Minmo, whose wives they may appropriate.

This is the theoretical scheme. But in practice it appeared that certain kindreds seem to avoid marrying the daughters of certain other kindreds with whom intermarriage is theoretically permissible. Thus Mwaio does not intermarry with Tafafwando, Gogen, Ngwoi, and Minmo. Jekin intermarries entirely with Mwaio, Ngwoi, and Minmo ; Magdari with Mwaio, Ngwalo, and Minmo ; Tara with Mwaio, Ngwalo, and Baza. There is no doubt a reason for this which I was unable to ascertain. It was stated that the reason why Magdari and Tara do not, like Jekin their associated kindred, marry the daughters of Ngwoi was that the Ngwoi were not of sufficient numerical strength to permit of this.

In the above table it has been said that kindreds of the same " wife-sharing " group may " appropriate " each other's wives. Both terms, viz. " wife-sharing " and " appropriate ", require some explanation. There is among the Malabu no group-marriage in the sense that several men may live with several women in the same household in a state of sexual promiscuity. But a wife who has been married as a virgin for a bride-price may abandon her husband at will and become the wife of a member of a kindred which is associated with her husband's kindred. Thus the wife of a Magdari man may abandon her husband and take up residence with a Tara man. There are no formalities, and the Magdari husband makes no claim for the return of the heavy expenditure he had incurred in obtaining his wife as a virgin girl. Moreover, it is stated by all Malabu that the husband who has lost his wife neither displays nor feels ill-will towards his supplanter. The latter is to him a younger " brother ". A woman may in this way become the wife of several men in succession ; but excessive changing of husbands is not looked on with favour. She may eventually return to her first husband.

If, however, a wife attempted to leave the group into which she had married, and to remarry a stranger or a member of a neighbouring tribe, she would be restrained both by her own social group and by that of her first husband ; and if she persisted the husband's group would take common action for the immediate repayment by the new husband of every tittle of the bride-price, a sum which no ordinary man could afford to pay under several years. There can be no doubt that the abnormally high bride-price among the Malabu was designed to keep women within the community, and that the freedom allowed to a woman after marriage had the same object, by keeping her contented.

There are three restrictions placed on the practice of wife-sharing. The first is, as already stated, that a man may not appropriate the wife of a member of his own kindred. The Baza are exempted from this rule. Those Ngwalo also who live at the village of Korache do not observe this rule at the present time, as instances were obtained of a Ngwalo man marrying the wife of a Ngwalo woman. By some it was stated that this was a breach of custom due to contact with Fulani, most of the Malabu at Korache having become Muslim, and having abandoned the high bride-price system of the other Malabu. By others it was stated that even in the olden days a Ngwalo man could take the wife of another Ngwalo who was not closely related, provided he refunded the bride-price to the original husband. It may be observed that at Korache there are only two social groups, viz. Baza and Ngwalo, and that they marry each other's daughters. As Baza men marry each other's wives it would be a hardship on the Ngwalo if they could not do likewise.

The second restriction is that in a wife-sharing group it is against custom for a senior man to appropriate the wife of a junior. That would be *infra dignitatem*, just as much as it would be for any senior man to accept financial assistance from his junior.

The third restriction is that it is improper to take the wife of a man who is a very close neighbour. Thus in a small hamlet where all grown-up men eat their evening meal together it would be improper for a Magdari man to appropriate the wife of a Tara man.

It may be contended that these secondary marriages are not marriages at all, but merely cicisbeism ; but the natives regard them as marriages, and this view is borne out by the rule that children born to a woman while she is living with her secondary husband belong to the secondary husband. Marriage with a virgin is known as " *nebatso* ", and marriage with a married woman is known as " *nebanguru* ".

We come now to the third feature of Malabu social life, and that is the paramour relationship known as " *sarati* ". By this custom it is permissible for any man in a wife-sharing group to have sexual relations with any wife in that group (who desires such relations), without incurring any social censure and without causing any apparent sexual jealousy on the part of the husband. The only restrictions imposed are (*a*) that a man shall not have sexual relations with the wife of one who is junior to himself ; (*b*) that a man shall not have sexual relations with the wife of a member of his own kindred, if that kindred is a small kindred. If a husband discovers that a younger brother or cousin has been having sexual relations with his wife he will rebuke him by asking him why he is " forestalling his inheritance ", the junior levirate being practised by the Malabu. (*c*) Normally (though not invariably) a married woman who has borne a child does not seek extra-marital sexual relations, it being said that a mother has passed the stage of desiring intercourse with a number of men. To use their own words " her daughter will carry on where she left off ".

Several reasons are offered as sanctions for these extra-marital relations. A wife is given every opportunity of bearing children. If she continues infertile it is due to her own barrenness. A sterile husband, on the other hand, can become the legal father of children. It appears to be immaterial to a husband whether the children borne by his wife were begotten by himself or by one of his kindred group. It is stated on all hands that a man does not treat a legal son, *qua* legal son, differently from a natural son, *qua* natural son. It is hard for a European who believes in the " instinctive " love of parent for child to allow this point of view. To the Malabu the question does not normally arise at all. Among tribes who follow matriarchal principles, such as the Gure of Zaria Province, a child's " father " in our sense of that term is his maternal uncle, and the maternal uncle regards the child as his own offspring. Among the Jukun, where the social system is of a bilateral character, the parental feeling of the maternal uncle is equal to that of the father, and the feeling of the child towards either is a matter of circumstance. Even under purely patriarchal conditions, where adoption by paternal uncles is a regular feature of social life the distinction between a biological and a social father is not drawn. A paternal uncle who has brought up a child regards himself as the " father " of that child, and the child regards his paternal uncle as his " father " *par excellence*. It is easily understandable, therefore, that a Malabu husband entertains no feelings of dislike for a child begotten to his wife by one who belongs to his own social group and whom he regards as a brother and in fact as part of himself.

The Malabu custom provides an outlet for the sexual feelings of young men who, owing to the high bride-price, have to postpone marriage to a comparatively late age. It also enables an elderly man, who is losing his powers, to retain a wife, the loss of whom would be an economic disaster, as he might have no one to cook his meals (unless he had married sons). It is not uncommon, therefore, among the Malabu for a husband to request his wife's paramour to accompany her when she sets out to visit her relatives. For the husband may have fears that, during her visit, she may become attracted to some stranger. Accompanied by her paramour this is less likely to occur.

The " *sarati* " relationship has, however, in the case of un-married men, certain obligations. The husband can require the young man who has had access to his wife to perform various economic duties. He can call on him to assist him in farm operations, such as harvesting, which demand special assistance ; and the paramour will on such occasions not merely offer his own services but will also requisition the services of his friends. The paramour may also be sent on messages to distant towns. These services are regarded as a contribution towards the original bride-price paid by the husband. The Malabu system resembles a form of fraternal polyandry such as is met with in Kashmir and other parts of India, with the exception that the brothers are " clan " brothers and not blood brothers.

The social organization of the Malabu is paralleled by that of the Katab tribe in Zaria Province, a description of which is given in my paper on that tribe. A similar organization will, no doubt, be discovered elsewhere in Nigeria,[1] but it is fortunate that it has been possible to obtain some account of the Malabu system before it has disappeared, as it certainly will disappear with the next generation.

A main point of difference between the Katab and Malabu systems is that the paramour relationship is not, as far as I know, recognized among the Katab as a social institution. Among the neighbours and relatives of the Malabu the form of social organization is practically of the same character as that of the Malabu. There is, however, this difference that in some of the groups, if a wife passes to a secondary husband within the wife-sharing group, the bride-price has to be refunded, unless she has borne a child to her first husband.

It may be noted finally that there is among the Malabu no custom of lending wives to friends of other communities such as is followed by the Verre, the Berom, and a number of other tribes.

It will be of interest now to describe the procedure for obtaining a virgin girl as a primary wife. The suitor for the girl's hand, who must not be a member of her own kindred or of any kindred associated with her own, makes his advance to the girl's father or paternal uncle while the girl is still a baby. He or his father may, a few days after the girl's birth, send a preliminary gift of mahogany oil for the girl's anointing. Later he sends periodical gifts of meat and fish sauce and, if these are received, he becomes the accepted suitor. As such he may be called upon to assist his prospective parent-in-law in various ways, e.g. by

[1] It appears from a recent report that in some groups of the Cross River area (e.g. among the Atam) the members of an age-grade have free sexual access to each other's wives, towards whose bride-price all contribute.

helping him at harvest, by running messages, or by roofing a hut. It is not the Malabu custom, as it is among some tribes, to accept more than one suitor.   In due course he makes the substantial payments which entitle him to take the girl to his home.   These payments consist of two or three blue gowns, two or three pieces of cloth, and thirty rolls of the narrow cloth woven by the Malabu. Among the Baza it was customary in former times to offer a cow in lieu of this narrow cloth.   These gifts are amassed by the efforts of the suitor and his father.   The paternal relatives of his kindred and his brethren of the associated kindreds may assist ; but it does not appear that at the present time this assistance is ever very substantial.   The maternal uncle also may offer some help ; but this depends purely on his inclination, the Malabu being essentially a patrilineal people.   The gifts are appropriated in the main by the girl's father.

Before the girl takes up formal residence with her husband she lives a life of seclusion, discarding all ornaments, doing no manual work, and being attended by an old woman.   It was suggested by the natives that the reason for this seclusion is that the girl may be instructed in all her marital duties by the old woman, and that she may go to her husband in good physical condition.   There was also the suggestion that by the month's seclusion her virginity could be guaranteed.   There may have been originally some religious intention of marking the transition from one state of life to another, and the custom would thus belong to what M. van Gennep calls " rites de séparation ".   The practice of divesting oneself of ornaments would seem to be paralleled in England, for in Shropshire a peasant-bride strips herself entirely of every article of clothing and begins " absolutely *de novo* to attire herself in new and unwashed garments, rejecting even pins that have ever been used before ".[1]

On the conclusion of this period the bride is carried on the shoulders of the bridegroom's sister's son to the bridegroom's home.   The relatives of the bride are at this time made the recipients of numerous gifts by the bridegroom, and in this he is liberally assisted by the members not only of his own kindred, but also by those of the associated kindreds.   For some ten days or so the bride is attended by her girl friends, and the husband

---

[1] Miss Burne, *Shropshire Folk*, p. 289.   See also the papers on the Margi and Higi tribes.   (Chap. IV.)

makes no attempt to establish sexual relations. It is said that the object of this rule is to allow the girl to become gradually accustomed to her new surroundings. The bride may not hand any article to the bridegroom, and she may not speak to him until he has " ransomed her mouth " with the gift of a cloth. This would suggest that there is an underlying fear of evil influences.

The marriage payments are not concluded by the formal taking-up of residence in the husband's home ; for after the birth of the first child the husband has to make further gifts to the girl's father of two or three gowns and twenty to thirty rolls of cloth. If these payments are not made a debt is incurred, which is eventually cancelled by the appropriation on the part of the woman's father of a proportion of the marriage payments made on behalf of his daughter's first female child.

The bride-price among the Malabu of Vango Malabu is thus comparatively speaking very high, and this may have had a direct connection with the custom of wife-sharing. Kindreds which were poor might experience difficulty in providing their members with wives, and hence may have arisen the system by which a number of kindreds became federated so that a wife could pass readily from one to another, or even be partially shared. It is possible that there was at one time a regular system among the Malabu of fraternal polyandry ; for even at the present day it is scarcely an offence for a younger brother to have sexual relations with an elder brother's wife, and it is no offence at all for men of one kindred to have sexual relations with the wives of senior men of another kindred. We have seen that the men of one kindred regard those of the associated kindreds as brothers, and it must often happen that men in one kindred are actually half-brothers or first cousins of the men in another associated kindred.

The necessity for a high bride-price may have been due to a number of causes, such as a scarcity of women or a desire to prevent women leaving the Malabu community for other communities. At the present time the females outnumber the males by 1,119 to 922.

The tendency nowadays is towards a gradual reduction of the bride-price, and a reduction in the number of cases of secondary marriages.

The Malabu are patrilineal, and all intermarriage with close paternal relatives is forbidden, even if not prohibited by the rule of exogamy. Thus marriage with the father's sister's daughter is taboo ; and in this respect the Malabu may be contrasted with the Bata-speaking peoples of Bolki, whose customs are in most respects the same as those of the Malabu, but who permit marriage with the father's sister's child. Marriage with maternal cousins is permissible, provided the rule of exogamy is not infringed. I was unable, however, to obtain a single instance of marriage with a daughter of a mother's sister or mother's brother. It was said that marriage with the mother's brother's daughter was exceptional, as in the absence of other relatives a man might have to act as guardian, i.e. as the social father, of his maternal uncle's children. Moreover in the ordinary way a man possesses a certain amount of social responsibility towards his maternal uncle's daughters. A suitor for a girl's hand generally approaches her father through his sister's son, who keeps an eye on the suitor's conduct and reports to his uncle any behaviour which would be likely to show that the suitor was an undesirable person.

As regards inheritance, property passes either direct to sons, if old enough, or through the mediumship of the deceased's younger brothers. The sister's son has normally no share. Wives are heritable by younger brothers or " clan " brothers or by sons, according to circumstances and the wishes of the widow. A woman who had borne children would normally unite herself to her late husband's younger brother. But one who had not borne children could, if she wished, marry any " clan " brother, without any monetary consideration. A young widow might elect to become the bride of her late husband's son. As already noted, instances were obtained of men inheriting their paternal grandfather's young widows, but such instances are necessarily rare. It may be added that if a man marries a " clan " brother's widow who has young sons he is bound to provide for the marriage of the sons.

As regards authority in the family there is among the Malabu little of the bilateral authority such as we find among the Jukun and the Bachama. The maternal uncle has no claim to the custody of the first of his sister's children, and it seldom happens that any child goes to reside with his maternal uncle. As among most tribes, however, the maternal uncle can make occasional calls on his nephew's economic services, and he may even send him off on a journey occupying several days. Per contra, if a lad finds himself in difficulties, he will usually seek the assistance of his maternal uncle.

The relationship terminology used by the Baza is that commonly employed by the Bata. But the peasants have a number of independent terms. The most noteworthy feature is the classification of the father's or mother's elder brother with the grandfather, all three being called *jijo*. The corresponding term is *ja* or *jeni*. All grandmothers are known as *kaka* (kəkə), and there is the usual jocular relationship between grandparents and grandchildren, i.e. a grandfather may address a grandson as " robber of my wife ", a grandmother may address her grandson as " husband ", and he may call her " wife ". Grandmothers and granddaughters call each other " rival wife ". Junior uncles (whether paternal or maternal) are addressed as *zo-gi*, the corresponding term being *zongi* (zʌŋi). But junior uncles may also address their nephews as *nza*, i.e. " son." Paternal and maternal aunts are addressed as *na-gi*. If a person's mother is dead he will address his mother's sister as *mo-gi*, i.e. mother, but he would not use this term in addressing his father's sister. An elder brother or sister is addressed as *zebangi* and a junior as *mafani*. These terms are also used between all cousins, and between persons belonging to the same " clan " or group of associated kindreds, if they are of the same generation. A person calls his or her parents-in-law " *sarausi* ", a term which is also applied (*a*) to a husband's elder brother or elder " clan "-brother, (*b*) to a younger brother's wife or a younger " clan "-brother's wife. A woman applies the term " husband " to any member of her husband's group who is of the same generation as her husband ; and a man applies the term " wife " to any woman who is married to a senior member of his group. Thus if the wife of a Magdari man visits the home of a Jekin man who is junior to her husband she addresses him as " husband ", and he addresses her as " wife ". She addresses his wife as *ma regi*, i.e. " rival wife ". But if the wife of the Jekin man visits the house of the Magdari man, who is senior to her husband, she avoids addressing her husband's elder brother's wife as " rival wife ", if her husband's elder brother is present. A man applies the term *sarausi*, i.e. " in-law ", to his wife's elder sister, but he addresses his wife's younger sister as " my wife ". A Malabu may not, however, marry his wife's sister, either during the life-time of his sister or after her death.

Each group has its own religious cult. Thus the Jekin, Tara, and
Magdari have the cult which is known as Gedi (gədi) ; the Baza,
Habiro, Gobel, Ngwoi, and Tafafwando have a common cult called
Diginchi ; the Mwaio and Belemo cult is Fokel ; that of the Minmo
kindred is Bongon ; that of Badawo is Fare ; and that of Dadirmi
is Bagin. Gedi is a well-known cult in all Jirai groups, though the
symbols and ritual vary in different localities. In some groups
Gedi is a water-spirit, with whom the chief is supposed to be in
close touch. Among the Malabu the cult is in the hands of a
Magdari official known as Kiladima, and the symbol of the cult is
a pot set on a three-pronged stick. Rites are performed when the
corn is about 1 foot high. The male members of the Jekin, Tara,
and Magdari kindreds assemble ; and the Kiladima, after a
prayer for health, deposits some porridge in the pot. Similar rites
are performed when the guinea-corn begins to sprout. It is noteworthy that the rites are always carried out at the new moon ; and
with this we may compare the Zumu custom by which oblations
are offered to Dagire by the chief at the rising of each new moon.

The Fare cult of the Badawo kindred is of interest. It is the
same cult as that described in my paper on the Bachama tribe, and
was in fact derived from the village of Fare near Demsa. The
deity is Zanzo and the priestess, who is known as Kizarhemi or
Bamchi Fare, is an old woman selected by the chief. She is
subject to possession by the god and declares oracles at night,
wandering round the town and warning the people of threatening
dangers which can be averted by gifts to Zanzo. The cult is
supervised (as at Fare) by an official known as Kizami who is sent
by the chief every two years to the Kizami of the original cult in
order to obtain seed-corn, which is distributed by the chief among
the heads of the various kindreds. The seed is obtained from Fare
at a cost of a gift of one horse or cow, an expensive proceeding.

The ritual in connection with the death and installation of the
chief is interesting for purposes of comparison with that of the
Bachama, Bata, and Jukun tribes. The duty of burying the chief,
removing his skull, and installing the new chief is in the hands of
the Kiladima, head of the Magdari kindred. The death of the
chief is kept secret, in order, it is said, to avoid an interregnum.
This was not, perhaps, the original reason ; for among many of the
Benue tribes the king, being a divine being and the personification
of the crops, cannot die ; he leaves the world for a space and

returns in the person of the new king and in the form of the next
year's crops. The Malabu bury their chief secretly at night, and it
is noteworthy that one reason given for this was that it would
detract from the dignity of chieftainship if the chief's widows and
the general populace were allowed to look on his dead body. The
body is not buried immediately. It is preserved for four days, a
fire being kept burning in the hut in order to allay the odour of the
corpse. The body, clothed in gown and cap, is then taken to the
royal cemetery and deposited in a sitting position in a cone-shaped
grave. It is covered up to the neck in charcoal, over which a
coating of mud is smeared. The mouth of the grave is sealed with
a stone. In the following spring the skull and bones of the late
chief are formally removed from the tomb to the royal skull-hut.
All the senior males of the tribe assemble at the graveside. A cow
is killed and the skin is set on one side. The Kiladima then enters
the tomb and brings up the skull and the bones of the chief, the
latter being sewn up in the cow's skin. A feast is held and all
spend the night close to the grave. Next morning the skull and
bones are deposited in the skull-hut by the Ndohoḍo (the head of
the Habiro kindred), the skull being placed on the top of a forked
branch, and the bones (wrapped in the cow's skin) on a wooden
stool. The Ndohoḍo then addresses the skull, saying : " To-day
we have brought you home, so that you may not be left abandoned
in the bush. Hinder us not, therefore, from obtaining sufficient
rain this year, and send not sickness amongst us ; but grant that
we may have health and prosperity." He then pours a libation of
beer over the skull and all hasten home ; for it is believed that on
the conclusion of these rites, which coincide with the beginning of
the rainy season, rain will immediately fall. If this does not
happen for some days resort is had to a professional diviner in
order to ascertain the cause. It will usually be declared that the
people had offended the chief on some occasion during his life-time.
All the seniors, therefore, accompanied by the new chief, go to the
royal skull-hut and make formal apology. It is clear that the cult of
deceased chiefs is primarily directed towards securing a successful
harvest ; and it is appropriate, therefore, that at the guinea-
corn harvest libations of beer are offered to all the skulls of dead
chiefs. It is a noteworthy rule that at harvest the reigning chief,
if the son of a former chief, must himself personally pour the
libation on his father's skull. The Ndohoḍo may not usurp this

right. A reigning chief may not pour a libation on the skull of a deceased chief who was a brother and not a father. I was unable to ascertain the reason for this rule.

The new chief is selected by the Kiladima in consultation with two other officials known as the Birma and Ndokpokei. He is warned on election that he must give his undivided attention to the ancestral cults, i.e. that he must be scrupulous in providing the gifts required for sacrifice, and must avoid giving offence to the priests of the cult. He is further advised, nowadays, that he must avoid making mischief with the Fulani administration and thereby bringing trouble on the community ; and that if he does not observe these injunctions he will be removed from his office. The Malabu did not, apparently, practise king-killing ; but they did not hesitate to depose a chief after a succession of bad harvests, or if the people had begun to leave the district. The new chief is formally installed four days after the burial of the former chief, being robed in a gown presented by the Kiladima and a cap presented by the Birma. He is set on a seat outside the palace, and after the royal drum has been beaten—the formal announcement at once of the death of the old chief and the election of his successor—he is saluted by the entire populace, all the seniors coming forward and holding up to him their right hand and saying : " To-day you enter upon the chieftainship held by your forefathers. God grant that you may hold it well." At the present time the election is ratified by the Fulani district head, who presents to the new chief a turban and a cap on his own account.

These notes on the Malabu may be concluded with the remark that in the Malabu market pre-war German 5 pfennig pieces are being used as currency, together with French francs. Ten 5 pfennig pieces are standardized as being the equivalent of 2d. in English money.

A short vocabulary of the Malabu language is attached, the more purely Bata variations of the Baza kindred being indicated in brackets. It will be seen that Malabu is the same language as Zumu (i.e. Jirai), of which a full schedule of words and phrases has already been given :—

MALABU VOCABULARY

1.	Head	ngino (nei)	ŋıno (nei)
2.	Hair	shewe (shewe)	ʃewe (ʃewe)
3.	Eye	diti (die)	diti (die)
	Two eyes	diti bak (diekpe)	diti bək (diekpe)

4. Ear	limo (kwaka)	lɪmo (kwakə)
Two ears	limigi bak (kwaka ekpe)	lɪmigi bək (kwakə ekpe)
5. Nose	chine (chine)	tʃine (tʃine)
6. One tooth	linti hiɗo (linchi hiɗo)	lɪnti hiɗo (lɪntʃi hiɗo)
Five teeth	leni tuf (leni tuf)	lɛni tuf (lɛni tuf)
7. Tongue	shimo (zhimai)	ʃimo (ʒiməi)
8. Neck	wurai (wurai)	wurəi (wurəi)
9. Breast (woman's)	wati (wache)	wati (watʃe)
10. Heart	zomti (zomchi)	zɔmti (zɔmtʃi)
11. Belly	sikko (edi)	sɪkko (ɛdi)
12. Back	bati (bechi)	bati (betʃi)
13. Arm	hwigi (tuvai)	hwigi (tuvəi)
14. Hand	sikko hwi (edituvo)	sɪkko hwi (ɛdituvo)
Two hands	sikko hwi bak (teviekpe)	sɪkko hwi bək (teviekpe)
15. Finger	gelo (gelo)	gɛlo (gɛlo)
Five fingers	geli tuf (geli tuf)	gɛli tuf (gɛli tuf)
16. Finger nail	papi geli (papi geli)	pəpi gɛli (pəpi gɛli)
17. Leg	shiɗo (mbare)	ʃiɗo mbarɛ
18. Knee	na diggo (na diggo)	nə dɪggo (nə dɪggo)
19. Foot	sikka shiɗo (edim-bwara)	sɪkka ʃiɗo (ɛdim-bwara)
Two feet	sikka shiɗo bak (edim-bwarekpe)	sɪkka ʃiɗo bək (ɛdim-bwarekpe)
20. Man (person)	ndeo (gboate)	ndeo (gboate)
Ten people	njin bu (gboate bu)	ndʒɪn bu (gboate bu)
21. Man (not woman)	muro (mure)	muro (mure)
Two men	muri bak (murekpe)	muri bək (murekpe)
22. Woman	meti (meiche)	meɗi (meitʃe)
Two women	manti bak (manti ekpe)	manti bək (manti ekpe)
23. Child	inzo	ɪnzo
24. Father	bagi (baba)	bagi (bəba)
25. Mother	mogi (nwo)	mogi (nwo)
26. Slave	kizza (kizze)	kɪzza (kɪzze)
27. Chief	haman	həmən
28. Friend	bajigi	badʒigi
29. Smith	killa (killai)	kɪlla (kɪlləi)
30. Doctor	duguzi (duguzhi)	duguzi (duguʒi)
31. One finger	gelti gi hiɗo	gɛlti gi hiɗo
32. Two fingers	geli bak (geli kpe)	gɛli bək (gɛli kpe)
33. Three fingers	geli mwakin	gɛli mwakɪn
34. Four fingers	geli fwat	gɛli fwat
35. Five fingers	geli tuf	gɛli tuf
36. Six fingers	geli tukoldaka	gɛli tukɔldaka
37. Seven fingers	geli tukolakpe	gɛli tukɔlʌkpe
38. Eight fingers	geli fwafwat	gɛli fwafwat
39. Nine fingers	geli tanggido	gɛli taŋgido
40 Ten fingers	geli bu	gɛli bu
41. Eleven fingers	geli bu bidi hiɗo	gɛli bu bidi hiɗo

42. Twelve fingers	geli bu bidi bak (kpe)	gɛli bu bidi bək (kpe)
Thirteen fingers	geli bu bidi mwakin	gɛli bu bidi nwakın
43. Twenty fingers	geli bu bak (bo kpe)	gɛli bu bək (bɔ kpe)
44. A hundred fingers	geli haro	gɛli haro
45. Two hundred fingers	geli haro bak (kpe)	gɛli haro bək (kpe)
46. Four hundred fingers	geli haro fwat	gɛli haro fwat
47. Sun	fatir (fete)	fatır (fete)
God	pua	pua
48. Moon	ligitsa	ligıtsə
Full moon	ligitso laba	ligıtso laba
New moon	ligitso kangsupo	ligıtso kaŋsupo
49. Day	kafate	kafate
Night	vido	vid̵o
Morning	kakitte	kakıtte
50. Rain	fame	fame
51. Water	mbaiye	mbəije
52. Blood	ulo	ulo
53. Fat	mari	mari
54. Salt	fite	fite
55. Stone	fara	fara
56. Iron	ta	ta
57. Hill	mwai	mwəi
58. River	gari = small river ; gbinuwe = big river nogambe = mother of waters	gəri = small river ; gbinuwe = big river nogʌmbe = mother of waters
59. Road	tuve	tuve
60. House	vine. Compound = hodo	vıne. Compound = hod̵o
Two houses	vane gi bak (kpe)	vəne gi bək (kpe)
Many houses	vane ge firafiro	vəne ge fırafıro
All the houses	vane ge gbaka	vəne ge gbaka
61. Roof	pir vine	pır vıne
62. Door	mada vine	madə vıne
63. Mat	kidzasa	kıdzəsə
64. Basket	kenevo	kɛnɛvo
65. Drum	ganggai	gaŋgəi
66. Pot	duai	duəi
67. Knife	suga	suga
68. Spear	pira	pita
69. Bow	ragai	ragəi
70. Arrow	galbatsa	galbatsə
Five arrows	gabe tuf	gabe tuf
71. Gun	bundukaru	bundukaru
72. War	burutsa	burutsə
73. Meat (animal)	hatai	hatəi
74. Elephant	chuwai	tʃuwəi
75. Buffalo	indoaka	ındoaka
76. Leopard	bangai	bʌŋəi

77.	Monkey	burame	burame
78.	Pig	tumbirime	tumbɪrɪme
79.	Goat	hwo	hwo
80.	Dog	kadai	kədəi
81.	Bird	ngulai	ŋuləi
	Feather	deti	deti
82.	Crocodile	gilinge	gɪlɪŋe
	Sheep	bagai	bagəi
	Horse	duwe	duwe
	Lion	taskui	tʌskui
83.	Fowl	deikai	deɪkəi
84.	Eggs	ḍongli	ḍɔŋli
85.	One egg	ḍongli hiḍo	ḍɔŋli hiḍo
86.	Snake	gwanda	gwanda
87.	Fly	jeddo	dʒɛddo
88.	Bee	nzumachi	nzumatʃi
	Honey	mari nzumai	mari nzuməi
89.	Tree	kadi	kadi
	Ten trees	kadi bu	kadi bu
90.	Leaf	jibi	dʒɪbi
91.	Guinea-corn	zumwe	zumwe
92.	Maize	dawai	dawəi
93.	Ground-nut	unatsa	unatsə
94.	Oil	mare	mare
95.	Fulani	Prisali	prɪsali
	Hausa	Hausi	hausi
	Beri-Beri	Ufi	ufi

Kofa.—The people of Kofa speak the same language as the Jirai of Zumu, and like the Malabu and most other Jirai groups claim that their chiefs came from Baza. The royal kindred is, as among the Malabu, known as the Baza kindred, and the names of three of the other six kindreds, viz. Mwaio, Tara, and Ngwalo, are also found among the Malabu. The Kofa and Malabu may, therefore, be regarded as one and the same people. The form of social organization is identical with that of the Malabu, and may be summarized as follows :—

There are seven kindreds :

1. ⎰Baza.
2. ⎱Demsa.
3. ⎰Mwaio.
4. ⎱Jetin.
5. ⎰Ngwalo.
6. ⎱Tara.
7.   Mahaya.

Each kindred is exogamous, and each bracketed pair of kindreds is also exogamous, e.g. a Baza man may not marry a Baza woman nor yet a Demsa woman. But a member of any kindred may marry a girl belonging to any other kindred (i.e. other than of his own or a bracketed kindred). To this rule there appeared to be two exceptions, viz. that a Demsa may not marry a Mwaio, nor may a Ngwalo marry a Mahaya. It was stated that the Demsa and Mwaio regarded themselves as kin in virtue of some former association, and that Ngwalo and Mahaya did not intermarry owing to a former feud.

The next point is that a man may appropriate (with her consent) any wife of a member of his own kindred or of a kindred bracketed with his, e.g. that the wife of a Baza man may leave her husband and become the wife of another Baza man or of a Demsa man. No ill-feeling results in consequence, and no claim for the return of a bride-price is preferred. For it is held that wives are common to the group. The only exceptions to this rule are that (a) a man may not take the wife of one who is regarded as junior to himself, and (b) he may not take the wife of his own brother or first cousin.

It is clear from the history of the kindreds that the rule of exogamy is based on the fact of local association and not of blood relationship. For, to take an example, the Baza were immigrants from Baza North of Mubi, while the Demsa are Bata from Demsa Poa. And yet a Baza may not marry a Demsa. At the present time it is asserted that Baza and Demsa were originally related, but this statement is clearly fictitious and is based on the fact of the existing relationship resulting from interchange of wives and from the paramour relationship, both of which practices are consequent on the local association. Similarly the Ngwalo and Tara kindreds were not originally related, as the Ngwalo came from the North and the Tara from the East.

It may be noted that as Demsa and Mwaio do not marry each other's daughters it is permissible for the wife of a Demsa man to become the wife of a Mwaio man and vice versa, provided of course that the rule of exogamy is not broken. But a bride-price would be demanded, as these two kindreds do not constitute a wife-sharing association.

Like the Malabu the Kofa recognize the paramour relationship, i.e. any man may become the lover of a wife of any member of his own or of an associated kindred, provided the husband is not junior to himself. This relationship is so open and well recognized that a wife, after having provided her husband with his evening meal, may bid him good-night and go off openly to the house of her lover, taking some of the cooked meal to him. If the two men are of the same age-seniority they may exchange wives for the night. If one is senior to his wife's paramour he may exact certain services from the paramour. He may call on the paramour to assist him in farm work, or to carry messages. If his wife wishes to attend a market at some distant town he will direct the paramour to accompany her. If he has to absent himself from home he will request the paramour to sleep with his wife during his absence. If his wife proposes to absent herself in order to visit her relatives he will send the paramour with her to secure her chastity!

The relationship terms among the Kofa are the same as those among the Malabu, with the exception that the Kofa (like the Jirai of Muleng) use the Fulani term *kawo* for maternal uncle. A distinction is drawn between a father's elder and younger brother, the former being classed with grandfathers, and the latter being addressed by a term which, in some other Jirai communities, is applied to the maternal uncle. The term *mise* = " my wife " is applied (as we should expect) to any wife of the kindred or associated kindred.

There is a noteworthy rule at Kofa that a woman's first-born female child may be claimed in marriage (without bride-price) by her father's younger brother's son, if her husband had failed to give the customary gift of twenty pieces of cloth to his wife's father when she had borne her first child (whether male or female). For this gift is normally used as a principal part of the bride-price for the younger brother's son.

Muleng.[1]—The inhabitants of Muleng in the Song district claim to have come into their present habitat from Baza via Zumu. They have the typical Jirai form of social organization.

The kindreds are as follows, those which are associated for purposes of wife-sharing, and which constitute a single exogamous unit, being bracketed together :—

{ Gewo (the royal kindred).
{ Murfane.
{ Garagi.
{ Baburaî.

[1] The term Muleng means " The Men."   See p. 122 (No. 21.)

{ Kofa.
{ Minmo.
{ Jekin.
{ Hwalmi.
{ Ngwale.
{ Parakeo.
Mulpoli.

The usual rules apply. The men of the Gewo kindred, for
example, may not marry girls belonging to the Gewo or Murfane
kindreds, but may marry girls belonging to any other kindred.[1]
Per contra, a man of Gewo may appropriate, without repayment
of the bride-price, the wife of any other man of Gewo [2] or of
Murfane ; but he may not appropriate the wife of a member of any
other kindred.

The paramour relationship between men and wives of members
of their own kindred or of the associated kindred is practised,
with the proviso that no man may become the paramour of a
woman who is married to a man who is junior to himself. Nor
may he become the paramour of the wife of his brother or first-
cousin. Married men of the same age-group may sleep with each
others' wives (if the wives so desire) : and a married or unmarried
man may become the lover of the wife of any senior. One who
becomes a recognized paramour may be called on by the husband
to assist him in farm-work and to perform other economic services.
When the wife absents herself temporarily from her husband's
village, the paramour is sent with her by the husband to protect
her and prevent her from committing adultery with a stranger.
But a recognized paramour must not abuse his privileges by
attempting to appropriate the woman. The woman can only
become his wife after he has ceased to be a paramour, his place
as paramour having been taken by someone else. This is
the general Jirai rule.

Wives are inherited by brothers, sons, or any member of the
kindred, the matter being determined by the widows, who, if
they have young children, will consider which home is likely to
be the best for the children. (For young children accompany
the mother until weaned.) If her children are grown up she may
elect to marry her late husband's brother or son in order to be

[1] But Kofa men do not marry Mulpoli women, owing to some dispute in
the past.
[2] Except the wife of a junior or of a brother or first-cousin.

with her children (for grown-up children remain in the father's home).

The relationship terms are as follows :—

bagi is applied to a father, and generally to any male of a senior generation.

mogi is applied to a mother, and generally to any female of a senior generation.

zogi is applied to a father's younger brother.

zizo is applied to a father's elder brother, and to all male grandparents.

kagi is applied to all female grandparents. Also to the father's or mother's elder brother's wife, and to the father's or mother's elder sister.

kawo-gi is applied to maternal uncles.

na-gi is applied to junior maternal or paternal aunts.

anzangi is applied to sons and daughters, and generally to all of a junior generation.

jengai is applied to all grandchildren, and also by a man or woman to his or her younger brother's child, and by a woman to her husband's younger brother's child.

zibangi = elder brother.

zibase = elder sister.

mafangi = younger brother, and is the general term for " brother ".

mose = younger sister.

moronge = husband.

meso = wife, and is applicable to the wife of any member of the kindred, or of an associated knidred.

sheruwo is applied to parents-in-law, and senior brothers and sisters-in-law.

mashi is applied to junior brothers and sisters-in-law. But a husband's younger brother's wife is called by a special term, viz. *gazai* = the person who comes after.

maa-regi = rival wife.

Paternal cousins are called " brothers " or " sisters ", but maternal cousins have a special title, viz. *zomogi*.

The Muleng, like many other Jirai communities, have adopted some Fulani terms such as *kawo* = maternal uncle. The Fulani term *esam* is often used instead of *sheruwo*.

The Muleng speak the same language as the Zumu.

Bolki.—The people of Bolki in the Song district claim to be Bata and to have come into their present habitat from Baza, North of Mubi. Actually, however, it would seem that only the royal kindred, who are known as the Gboate, are Bata in the strict sense of the term. The remaining six kindreds are Jirai.

The composition of the Bolki group is, therefore, precisely the same as that of the Malabu ; for among the Malabu the royal kindred is Bata-speaking and claims to have come from Baza, while the other kindreds are Jirai, speaking a Bata dialect (which differs slightly from the pure Bata spoken by the royal group).

The Bolki kindreds are :—

{ Gboate.
{ Gbwamin.

{ Badawo.
| Geteme.
{ Pokin.
| Gbwame.
{ Hwarme.

The bracketed kindreds form a single exogamous and wife-sharing group, according to the typical Jirai system. The only variation from the normal rule is that if a wife passes from one husband to another a bride-price can be claimed, if the woman had not borne a child to her first husband. This variation was found also among the Jirai of Bulai. It is not permissible for a man to appropriate a wife from a member of a non-associated kindred.

The paramour relationship is also recognized, the paramour being usually a young unmarried man. No one may become the paramour of the wife of his own brother or first-cousin, and no man may appropriate as his wife the woman to whom he stands in the relation of recognized paramour. Further a man can only become the paramour of a woman married to a member of his own kindred or of the kindred or kindreds associated with his.

At Bolki there is a cult known as Pilai which is typically Bata, being served by a priest and priestess. The former is known as the Do Pilatso and the latter as the Bamso, the same title as is borne by the Bata priestess of the Fare cult of Nzeanzo. The symbol of the god is a pot set in the fork of a branch stuck into the ground. The Bamso, who must be a woman who has passed the age of menstruation, lives beside the shrine and sweeps the ground round the symbol every morning and evening. She also prepares the beer and cooks the food used in the rites. As at Fare the main rites are held immediately before sowing. The Do Pilatso ties a strip of cloth round the sacred pot, and having poured a libation of beer over the pot speaks as follows : " This cult is not a thing of our own invention. It was received by us from our forefathers who, when they sought rain, came to you, Pilai, and were not denied. You

are our corn and our health. Bless us, therefore, and accept
these gifts." A ram provided by the chief is then sacrificed,
and some of the cooked flesh, together with porridge, is set
beside the sacred symbol.

Near to Bolki there is a village known as Murke. This is
composed of three elements: (a) a Bata-speaking group from
Baza, (b) a Jirai group, and (c) a Yungur group.

The Holma.—The Holma are a small group of people situated
between the Njai (Nzangi) and the Jirai of the Zumu area. They
are administered by the Emir of Adamawa, through the Fulani
district chief of Holma. They claim to have come into their
present habitat as part of an extensive migration of Bata-speaking
peoples from Mandara, who established themselves North of
Wuba, then at Baza, and finally scattered, leaving groups at
Holma, Zumu, Gudu, and Demsa Mosu. They speak a Bata
dialect which shows a greater affinity with Njai than with Zumu.
This is striking in view of the fact that the Njai do not claim a
Bata or Baza origin, like all the other groups under consideration.
It may be supposed that the pre-Fulani chiefs of the Holma were
of Bata origin, while the aboriginal inhabitants were cognate with
the Njai.

The Holma have become Muslims to a man, and have adopted
the culture and language of their Fulani conquerors. A few old
men only are able to speak the language of their forefathers, and
the schedule of words and phrases attached may prove to be the
last obtainable.

The old men interviewed were able to give definite information
on two matters of considerable interest. Firstly, they could
remember some of the details of the former mode of burying their
chiefs. The body of the dead chief was deposited in a cave, or
rather in the mouth of a cave, being set on a ledge of rock (lower
than the ground surface) which led to a subterranean passage.
It was clothed in numerous gowns and covered with charcoal
(after the Pabir fashion). A layer of logs was laid over the body,
and in the centre of the logs a pot was placed, the symbol of the
god known as Terau. No information could be obtained with
regard to this deity; but one is tempted to think that the word
Terau is not unconnected with the common word for moon,
viz. *Tirre*, among many neighbouring tribes. The inference might
be that chiefs were at one time associated with the Moon. Over

the grave a hut was built ; and close to this hut a man, accompanied by his wife, lived as a constant custodian of the chief's body and of the cult of Terau. Every evening he had to light a fire inside the pot which was the symbol of the cult. He acted as the servant of the priest, who at sowing or on occasions of drought attended personally to carry out the necessary rites. This lighting of an evening fire in the house of the gods was, until recently, followed by the Kilba, and a parallel may be drawn between the Kilba practice and that of the sacred fire of the Baganda.[1]

For the three months following the death of a chief his widows sent morning and evening gifts of food. These gifts were deposited beside the body of the dead chief, and after an interval of twelve hours were removed and given to members of the priest's family to eat.

When a Holma chief died the announcement of his death was proclaimed by fire to the inhabitants of Zumu and Demsa Poa. The body of the former chief was thrown down the subterranean passage in order to make way for that of the newly deceased chief. For the prosperity of the land was believed to be bound up with the personality of the last chief.

The second point of interest, which is of peculiar value, inasmuch as the informants are now professing Muslims, is concerned with the former system of marriage. It was stated that, until the Holma fell under the domination of the Fulani, wives were regarded not as the property of individuals, but as the property of the kindred group. Not that there was a general system of polyandry ; but that a man's wife might leave him, and become the wife of any member of his kindred or of any associated kindred without recrimination or ill-feeling or any repayment of the bride-price. Moreover, any wifeless young man might have sexual access to the wife of another man of his own kindred without prejudice.

These rules were stated by the old men of Holma to be due to the fact that the bride-price for a virgin girl (obtained from a neighbouring community) was high, and that the means of obtaining the bride-price were limited, as the people were cooped up in their hills and unable to add to their wealth by expeditions abroad. When, therefore, a man married he was assisted by all

---

[1] See the paper on the Kilba tribe. (Chap. IV.)

the members of his kindred ; and if a wife chose to change her husband within that kindred there could be no recrimination, as all the members of the kindred had contributed towards her purchase.

Moreover, young men within the kindred who had not been able to obtain a wife were allowed to satisfy their sexual feelings by having access to any wife of the kindred. Sexual jealousy on the husband's part, if it existed, was discounted by the view that if the young man were not allowed such local privileges he would seek them outside the local group. In this way he would not merely expose himself to danger (and the kindred might be robbed of one of its number), but he would also render the entire kindred liable to attack by members of the other group among whom his intrigue had been discovered. It was said at Holma that the paramour relationship was so well recognized that if a husband who intended sleeping that night with his wife found a spear standing at the door of her hut he would withdraw to his own hut, and would not even take the trouble on the following morning to ascertain the name of his supplanter.

HOLMA VOCABULARY.   PER BUBA OF HOLMA

1.	Head	kilin	kɪlɪn
2.	Hair	shewon	ʃɛwɔn
3.	Eye	din	din
	Two eyes	din bak	din bək
4.	Ear	lekoɗen	kɛkoɗɛn
	Two ears	lekoɗen bak	lɛkoɗɛn bək
5.	Nose	chinin	tʃinɪn
6.	One tooth	lin kin	lin kɪn
	Five teeth	len in tuf	lɛn ɪn tuf
7.	Tongue	gennan	gɛnnan
8.	Neck	wulan	wulan
9.	Breast (woman's)	unetsa	unɛtsə
10.	Heart	duven	duvɛn
11.	Belly	jemen	dʒɛmɛn
12.	Back	bikin	bikɪn
13.	Arm	tivin	tivin
14.	Hand	dabadaban	dabadaban
	Two hands	dabadaban bak	dabadaban bək
15.	Finger	gele	gɛlɛ
	Five fingers	gele tuf	gɛlɛ tuf
16.	Finger-nail	papin	papin
17.	Leg	shiden	ʃidɛn
18.	Knee	magilshen	magɪlʃɛn
19.	Foot	hajema shiden	hĭdʒɛma ʃiden
	Two feet	hajema shiden bak	hĭdʒɛma ʃiden bak

20.	Man (person)	minde	mɪndɛ
	Ten people	bali pu	bali pu
21.	Man (not woman)	mulen	mulɛn
	Two men	mwalin bak	mwalin bək
22.	Woman	madukin	madukɪn
	Two women	madin bak	madin bək
23.	Child	nzenzen	nʒɛnʒɛn
24.	Father	dedekin	dɛdɛkɪn
25.	Mother	nuokin	nuokɪn
26.	Slave	mavan	mavan
27.	Chief	mon	mɔn
28.	Friend	sobaji	sobadʒi
29.	Smith	killa	kɪlla
30.	Doctor	ndahalin	ndahalɪn
31.	One finger	gelen hiɖe	gɛlɛn hiɖɛ
32.	Two fingers	gelegin bak	gɛlɛgɪn bək
33.	Three fingers	gelegin mwakin	gɛlɛgɪn mwakɪn
34.	Four fingers	gelegin fwat	gɛgɛgɪn fwat
35.	Five fingers	gelegin tuf	gɛlɛgɪn tuf
36.	Six fingers	gelegin kwa	gɛlɛgɪn kwa
37.	Seven fingers	gelegin miskata	gɛlɛgɪn mɪskata
38.	Eight fingers	gelegin fwafwat	gɛlɛgɪn fwafwat
39.	Nine fingers	gelegin tamide	gɛlɛgɪn tamide
40.	Ten fingers	gelegin pu	gɛlɛgɪn pu
41.	Eleven fingers	gelegin pu kaba hiɖe	gɛlɛgɪn pu kaba hiɖɛ
42.	Twelve fingers	gelegin pu bidi bak	gɛlɛgɪn pu bidi bək
	Thirteen fingers	gelegin pu bidi mwakin	gɛlɛgɪn pu bidi mwakɪn
43.	Twenty fingers	gelegin gḅwam ma satsa	gɛlɛgɪn gḅwam ma satsə
44.	A hundred fingers	gelegin haru	gɛlɛgɪn haru
45.	Two hundred fingers	gelegin haru ag bak	gɛlɛgɪn haru əg bək
46.	Four hundred fingers	gelegin haru ofwat	gɛlɛgɪn haru ɔfwat
47.	Sun	feetn	fɛtɛn
	God	fitte	fɪtte
48.	Moon	ligide	lɪgide
	Full moon	ligide mubile	ligide muɓile
	New moon	ligide ja	ligide dʒa
49.	Day	sa feten	sa fɛtɛn
	Night	na birin	na bɪrɪn
	Morning	habire	habɪre
50.	Rain	famen	famɛn
51.	Water	batin	bɛtɪn
52.	Blood	bizen	bizɛn
53.	Fat	matsubga	matsubga
54.	Salt	powon	powɔn
55.	Stone	kwakin	kwakɪn
	Iron	lengin	lɛŋɪn
56.	Hill	matufoken	matufɔkɛn

57.	River	mabolekin	mabolɛkɪn
58.	Road	tuven	tuvɛn
59.	House	jellen (Compound = hoḍen)	dʒɛllɛn (Compound= hɔdɛn)
	Two houses	jellin bak	dʒɛllin bǝk
	Many houses	jellin pas	dʒɛllin pas
	All the houses	jellin dugḅa	dʒɛllin dugɓa
60.	Roof	kille jellen	kɪllɛ dʒɛllɛn
61.	Door	bagarangin	bagaraŋïn
62.	Mat	hedzekin	hɛdzɛkɪn
63.	Basket	pekteke	pɛktɛkɛ
64.	Drum	dangin	daŋɪn
65.	Pot	wudan	wudan
66.	Knife	hamalkin	hamalakɪn
67.	Spear	udima	udimǝ
68.	Bow	lagin	lagɪn
69.	Arrows	afkin	afkɪn
	Five arrows	avin tuf	avin tuf
70.	Gun	bindugaru	bɪndugaru
71.	War	konokin	konokɪn
72.	Meat (animal)	borka	bɔrke
73.	Elephant	chuware	tʃuwarɛ
74.	Buffalo	uvuden	uvudɛn
75.	Leopard	tsauyekin	tsauʝɛkɪn
76.	Monkey	birvangin	birvaŋɪn
77.	Pig	bellen	bɛllɛn
78.	Goat	hotsi	hɔtsi
79.	Dog	yangba	ʝaŋba
80.	Bird	kodekekin	kodɛkɛkɪn
	Feather	shewo kodekekin	ʃɛwo kodɛkɛkɪn
81.	Crocodile	giradangin	gɪradaŋɪn
	Horse	kalan	kalan
	Cow	pilikin	pilɪkɪn
82.	Fowl	dekin	dɛkɪn
83.	Eggs	kulengyi	kulɛŋji
84.	One egg	kelengga hiḍe	kɛlɛŋg hidɛ
85.	Snake	ise	isɛ
86.	Frog	gwandasa	gwandasǝ
87.	Fly	yedin	ʝɛdɪn
88.	Bee	mwozan kin	mwozan kɪn
	Honey	mwozangin	mwozaŋɪn
89.	Tree	kadin	kadin
	Ten trees	kadin pu	kadin pu
90.	Leaf	gudan	gudan
91.	Guinea-corn	maudzen	maudzɛn
92.	Maize	mapinawin	mapɪnawɪn
93.	Ground-nut	onekin	onɛkɪn
94.	Oil	malin	malɪn
95.	Hausa	Nji Hausa	ndʒi hausa
	Bata	Batin	batin
	Fulani	Pirasali	pɪrasali

The Gudu.—The people of Gudu, who live some 10 miles north-west of Song, call themselves the Ji Gudu, i.e. The People of Gudu. They are described in Mrs. Temple's compilation as Mandara,[1] presumably because they claim to have come from Mandara. There is no justification for singling out the Gudu for this description. With the Gudu are associated the villagers of Kante, Sigere, and Or ; and in the Shellen district of the Numan division sections of the villages of Kula and Deben are offshoots of Gudu. The villagers of Kumbi (or Gombi, as it is pronounced by the Fulani) and of Duwa, in the Gola district, claim to be " Gudu " and this claim is borne out by their language. But the former have adopted the customs of the Kilba tribe, and the latter of the Hona. At Sentere near Gudu, on the other hand, there is a mixed community of Kanakuru and Jirai who have adopted the Gudu dialect.

All these people, with the exception of Sentere, claim a Mandara origin, and it is clear that from the linguistic point of view they may be grouped with the Jirai-Bata communities who have also a traditional connection with Mandara. It is not contended, however, that all the groups classed as Jirai-Bata belong to a single ethnic stock, for it is apparent that the Mandara invaders became fused with aboriginal peoples. In the case of the village-area of Gudu itself, the fusion was with a Yungur-speaking group.

There is no uniformity of culture among the various Gudu groups. The people of the villages of Gudu and Or are Muslims, but those of Kula, Gombi, and Dawa are pagans. It is asserted at Gudu that their Muhammadanism is not of recent introduction as a result of close association with the Fulani, for prior to the Fulani " Jihad " they had no less than fifteen chiefs all of whom were professors of Islam. This claim cannot be accepted in view of the fact that several of the Gudu groups are still pagan, and of the tradition found in all the other Jirai-Bata groups that the invaders from Mandara were a non-circumcising people. None of the first fifteen chiefs of Gudu bore Islamic names, unless we are to suppose that Shak, the name of the first chief, is a form of Isiaku. Shak, it is said, left Mandara because one of his brothers had been appointed king of Mandara, and it was the Mandara custom for a newly-appointed king to cut off the ears (or one ear)

---

[1] *Tribes, Emirates, etc.*, p. 270.

of all possible rivals, who were usually brothers or cousins.   For
no one with a physical disfigurement could succeed to the kingship.   To avoid this fate Shak left his own country and journeyed
westward, accompanied by his younger brother, who became the
chief of Or, and by his father's sister's son, who became the chief
of Holma.   The Gudu and the Holma are, therefore, " playmates "
at the present time.[1]   There is no doubt that the Gudu and Holma
are intimately connected.   For the Gudu dialect bears a closer
resemblance to Holma (and Njai) than to any of the other dialects
which we have classed as Jirai-Bata.   In this connection it will be
remembered that the Holma have only become Muslims during
the last century, and we shall see later that the Njai, who are
virtually the same people as the Holma, are still pagan.

When Shak arrived at Gudu he found groups of Yungur-
speaking people there.   This is probable, as a Yungur dialect is
spoken in the town of Mboi, which is only a few miles distant
from Gudu.

The sixteenth chief of Gudu, Dewi by name, obtained a flag
from Modibo, the first Fulani governor of Adamawa ; and in
return for this honour attempted to introduce Islam by force
among the surrounding pagan villages, and a more purified form
of Islam among his own people.   He met with so much opposition
that he was forced to fly.   It is said that he concealed himself in a
bundle of hay in his own stable, having told his slave to announce
that he was dead.   His infidel brother from Sigere was appointed
chief in his stead, but one day Dewi sprang out of the hay and
killed him.   He then resumed the chieftainship.   Many of his
people fled, and it is to this time that the foundation of the Kulu
settlement of Gudu is ascribed.   Thereafter the people of Gudu
became the satellites of the Emirs of Adamawa, who used them as
an outpost for slave-getting among the Gabin and Rǫba tribes.

The villagers of Gudu have adopted the Fulani system of
social organization, i.e. the community consists of a number of
patrilineal family groups which are not exogamous, marriage
being permitted between all classes of cousins.   The principal
terms of relationship are :—

ba = father and paternal uncle.
ma = mother.
na = mother's sister, father's sister.

[1] The Gudu and Bata are also " playmates ".

huzo = mother's brother, sister's child.　But the Fulani term
　　kawo is also used.
jiji = male grandparent.
kai or *kaka* = female grandparent.
jejen = any grandchild.
surkwan (or at Ḍuwa *sirifi*) = parent-in-law (male or female),
　　senior brother-in-law, senior sister-in-law.　Junior brothers-
　　in-law or sisters-in-law are called *reau minsin* or *mashi*.　But
　　a man may address his wife's younger sister as *madi*, i.e. my
　　wife, and a woman may address her husband's younger brother
　　as *mori*, i.e. my husband (*miri* at Ḍuwa).[1]
ziban = elder brother or male cousin.
mafan = younger brother or male cousin.
dai = elder sister or female cousin.
mabsin = younger sister or female cousin.
za = son, daughter.

It was said that, in spite of their Muhammadanism, the people
of Gudu still practised some pagan rites.　But no evidence of
this was obtained.　At Ḍuwa, however, all the inhabitants are
pagan.　One of their cults is known as Gabawur, which is
symbolized by a pot containing a piece of iron and is used for
swearing oaths.　Another of their cults is known as " Malam
Babir " and was adopted from the Kilba.　A third is " Wuli ma
hondatsu " which is the " Sambariya " cult of the Hona.[2]　It may
be noted further that while the villagers of Gudu practise circumcision, those of Duwa and Kumbi do not. Generally speaking, it
may be said that the people of Ḍuwa have become identified with
the Kilba, while those of Kumbi have become identified with the
Hona.　Thus at Kumbi the houses are built according to the Hona
pattern, with the typical grass porch.　The women wear a fringe
in front and a strip of cloth or a bundle of leaves behind.　They
pierce the upper and lower lip, and they carry their children in a
satchel on the back.

A full schedule of words and phrases is attached.　This should
be compared with (*a*) Holma and Njai, (*b*) Zumu, and (*c*) Bata.
It may also be compared with Strumpell's Mubi and Wadi.　In
phonology it displays a closer connection with the Bura-Margi
group than do all the other Jirai-Bata languages (e.g. in the use
of the so-called Welsh *l*).　But the most striking feature is
the employment of a third personal singular feminine pronoun.
To this reference has already been made, and taken in conjunction

---

[1] The junior levirate only is practised at Gudu.
[2] See the paper on the Hona tribe.

with the fact that many typical Hausa words are found in this part of Nigeria it suggests that the Hausa influence at one time extended to these regions ; or it might be safer to say that in North-Eastern Nigeria there is linguistic evidence which suggests that this part of Nigeria and Hausaland were at one time subject to a common influence, which was at least pre-Kanuri. By typical Hausa words I do not refer to the common stock of Nigritic roots which Hausa shares with the Bantu and Sudanic languages, but to those which seem to be specially associated with Hausa culture. It is significant that the Gudu word for "maize" is *zakzak*, the name by which the ancient Hausa state of Zaria is still known.

A short vocabulary of the Kumbi dialect of Gudu is also appended. In this the word for maize is, apparently, "the guinea-corn of the Buzu." Were, then, the Hausa "Buzu",[1] i.e. Berbers from the North, as Mr. H. R. Palmer has suggested as a result of his own investigations ?

N.B.—The notes on the Njai or Nzangi will be found in the paper dealing with the tribes of the British Cameroons.

GUDU VOCABULARY.

1.	Head	iyin	iɲin
2.	Hair	jeva	dʒevə
3.	Eye	di	di
	Two eyes	di bak	di bək
4.	Ear	hlim	łim
	Two ears	hlim bak	łim bək
5.	Nose	chin	tʃin
6.	One tooth	leen tsajang	leɛn tsədʒʌŋ
	Five teeth	leen tuf	leɛn tuf
7.	Tongue	geana	geana
8.	Neck	wura	wura
9.	Breast (woman's)	wachi	watʃi
10.	Heart	guraksa	guraksə
11.	Belly	kap	kaːp
12.	Back	bia	bia
13.	Arm	waksa	waːksə
14.	Hand	didaruwa (palm of hand)	dɪdaruwa
	Two hands	didarawa bak	dɪdarawa bək
15.	Finger	deltsa	dɛltsə
	Five fingers	del tuf	dɛl tuf
16.	Finger nail	machi pietsing	matʃi pietsiŋ

[1] The term "Buzzi" may be regarded as synonymous with Tuareg, though to the enlightened it means "low-class Tuareg" or even "Tuareg-slaves".

17.	Leg	shetsa	ʃɛtsə
18.	Knee	udidi	udidi
19.	Foot	kabshet	kabʃet
	Two feet	kabshet bak	kabʃɛt bək
20.	Man (person)	minda	mɪndə
	Ten people	niji pu	midʒi pu
21.	Man (not woman)	mir	mɪr~
	Two men	mgir bak	mgɪr~bək
22.	Woman	maditsa	madɪtsə
	Two women	miet bak	miɛt bək
23.	Child	inza	ɪnzə
24.	Father	ba	baː
25.	Mother	ma	maː
26.	Slave	kiza	kɪza
27.	Chief	mmom	mmom
28.	Friend	bazhi	baʒi
29.	Smith	mala	mala
30.	Doctor	ndangum	ndəŋgum
31.	One finger	deltsa zhang	dɛltsə ʒaŋ
32.	Two fingers	del bak	dɛl bək
33.	Three fingers	del makan	dɛl makan
34.	Four fingers	del fwat	dɛl fwat
35.	Five fingers	del tuf	dɛl tuf
36.	Six fingers	del kwa	dɛl kwa
37.	Seven fingers	del miskata	dɛl miskata
38.	Eight fingers	del fwarfwat	dɛl fwarfwat
39.	Nine fingers	del zhetapan	dɛl ʒɛtapan
40.	Ten fingers	del pu	dɛl pu
41.	Eleven fingers	del pumbit zhang	dɛl pumbit ʒaŋ
42.	Twelve fingers	del pu mbit bak	dɛl pu mbit bək
	Thirteen fingers	del pu mbit makan	dɛl pu mbit makan
43.	Twenty fingers	del po bak	dɛl po bək
44.	A hundred fingers	del aru	dɛl aːru
45.	Two hundred fingers	del aru bak	dɛl aru bək
46.	Four hundred fingers	del aru fwat	dɛl aru fwaːt
47.	Sun	fota	fotə
	God	fitea	fitea
48.	Moon	leeda	leɛɗə
	Full moon	leeda bir	leɛɗə bɪr~
	New moon	leeda kessung (Have adopted Fulani expression)	leɛɗə kɛssuŋ
49.	Day	fuetagaa	fuɛtəgaə
	Night	vit	vɪt
	Morning	war	wʌr
50.	Rain	nyanzim	njanzɪm
51.	Water	nya	nja
52.	Blood	mamshi	mamʃi

53.	Fat	mar	mar~
54.	Salt	ngirada	ŋɪrədə
55.	Stone	mmomo	mmomo
	Iron	tubos	tubos
56.	Hill	mmomo	mmomo
57.	River	mobora	moborə
58.	Road	tava	təvə
59.	House	vin (Compound = hoḍo)	vin (Compound = hoɗo)
	Two houses	vin bak	vin bək
	Many houses	vin pas	vin pas
	All the houses	vin kima	vin kɪma
60.	Roof	panglata	pʌŋlata
61.	Door	mahunda	mahunda
62.	Mat	hija	hɪdʒə
63.	Basket	tsilla	tsɪlla
64.	Drum	danga	daŋgə
65.	Pot	wuḍa	wuɗã
66.	Knife	luta	luta
67.	Spear	baura	baura
68.	Bow	ragha	ragə
69.	Arrow	ava	avə
	Five arrows	ava tuf	avə tuf
70.	Gun	bindiga	bɪndɪgə
71.	War	ghatsa	gatsə
72.	Meat (animal)	hat	haːt
73.	Elephant	ong	ɔŋ
74.	Buffalo	sapanda	sapanda
75.	Leopard	dava	dəva
76.	Monkey	ruaba	ruaba
77.	Pig	ngirdim (cf. Kanuri)	ŋɪr~dɪm
78.	Goat	hwa viratsa	hwa vɪr~atsə
79.	Dog	khidda	xɪdda
80.	Bird	cho	tʃo
	Feather	bibet	bibet
81.	Crocodile	gira	gira
	Horse	duhu	duhu
	Cow	la	la
	Sheep	nbaha	nbəhə
	Hausa	Nji Hausa	ndʒi hausa
	Fulani	Pileshir	pileʃɪr
	Beri-Beri	Ivetsa	ivetsə
	Bata	Ɓete	ɓete
	Burra	Huve	huve
	Gaanda, Gabun, and Hona	Huene	huene
	Yungur	Gbinna	gbɪnna
82.	Fowl	ḍiegha	ɗiɛgə
83.	Eggs	ḍiela	ɗielə
84.	One egg	ḍiela diksa	ɗielə dɪksə
85.	Snake	ruhun	ruhun

86. Frog	ngibaha	ŋibaha
87. Fly	jeɖa	dʒeːɖə
88. Bee	mmua	mmuə
Honey	nya mmua	nja mmuə
89. Tree	kada	kada
Ten trees	kada pu	kada pu
90. Leaf	yuaɖa	ɟuaɗə
91. Guinea-corn	gawa	gawa
92. Maize	zakzak	zəkzək
93. Ground-nut	kere	kere
94. Oil	mar	mar
95. The tall woman	maditsa nderi yirkir	madɪtsə nderi ɟirkir
The tall women	meet nje yir rira	meɛt ndʒe ɟir rira
96. Large dog	khidda da burooma	xɪdda da burooma
97. Small dog	khidda da toɓa	xɪdda da toɓa
98. The dog bites	khidda da adua	xɪdda də adua
99. The dog bites me	khidda a dishi	xɪdda ə diʃi
100. The dog which bit me yester-day	khidda a a dishi mbide	xɪdda a ə diʃi mbide
101. I flog the dog	n magbil khidda	n məgbɪl xɪdda
102. The dog which I have flogged	khidda ya na bil ta yii	xɪdda ɟa nə bɪl ta ɟii
I	an	ən
You (m. and f.)	i	i
He	atsa	ətsə
She	ir	ɪr~
We	in	in
You (m. and f.)	wun	wun
They	ara	ara
We (incl. person addressed) are going to the town	amam taza hara	amam tazə hara
We (excl. person addressed) are going to the town	in taza hara	in tazə hara
103. I see him	n ma daba	n mə ɗəba
I see her	n ma dabar	n mə ɗəbar
He sees you (f.)	atsa ma dabu	ətsə mə ɗəbu
He sees us	atsa ma ḍaba mam	ətsə mə ɗəbə mʌm
We see you (pl.)	in ma ḍabun	in mə ɗəbun
We see them	in ma ḍabera	in mə ɗəbɛra
He is coming	ta shige	ta ʃige
She is coming	a shige	a ʃige
He has come	atsa ma shi	ətsə mə ʃi
She has come	ir ma shi	ɪr mə ʃi
04. Beautiful bird	choksa nderzhi dankir	tʃoksə ndɛrʒi dankɪr
105. Slave	kiza	kɪza
My slave	kizai	kɪzai

Thy slave	kizau	kɪzau
Our slaves	kizayin	kɪzajin
Their slaves	kizaara	kɪzaəra
106. The chief's slave	kiza mmomtsa	kɪz mmomtsə
His slave	kizaa	kɪzəa
107. We see the slave	in ma ɖiba kiza	in mə ɖiba kɪza
108. We call the slave	in ma yea kiza	in mə jɛə kɪza
109. The slave comes	kiza shiggai	kɪza ʃiggai
110. He came yesterday	atsa ma shi bide	ətsə mə ʃi bide
She came yesterday	ir ma shi bide	ɪr mə ʃi bide
He is coming today	ta shi gai su bo	ta ʃi gai su bo
He will come tomorrow	ta shi gai dirra	ta ʃi gai dɪrra
111. The slaves go away	kizhe a put	kiʒe a put
112. Who is your chief?	au chimmom uwo ?	au tʃi mmom uwo ?
113. The two villages are making war on each other	viratsa baka a ra ha tamijira	vɪratsə bəkə a ra ha tamidʒira
114. The sun rises	fota dima	fotə dima
The sun has risen	foten ma dima	fotən mə dima
The sun sets	fota a fuan	fotə a fuan
115. The man is eating	minda ta zim ishi	mɪndə ta zɪm ɪʃi
116. The man is drinking	minda ta sha nya	mɪndə ta ʃa nja
117. The man is asleep	minda cho na	mɪndə tʃo nə
Horse	dufu	dufu
My horse	dufwi	dufwi
118. I break the stick	in ma bata diapa	ɪn ma bata diapa
The stick is broken	diapa ma batsa	diapa ma batsə
This stick cannot be broken	diapa na mangar batsasa	diapa na mangər batsəsə
Break this stick for me	kum batsei diapana	kum batsei diapana
119. I have built a house	in ma an vin	ɪn mə ən vin
120. My people have built their houses yonder	minzhi ma an vinira gara	mɪnʒi mə ən vinira gara
121. What do you do every day ?	tene michi ya hlen kil fotkin ?	tɛne mitʃi ja ɬɛn kɪl fotkɪn ?
I work on my farm	na hwuza yu wi	nə hwuza ju wi
122. I am going away	in tiruwe	ɪn tɪruwe
I am hoeing	na hwuza	nə hwuza
I am going away to hoe	in ta we hwuzatsa	ɪn ta we hwuzətsə

	I am going away to my farm	in ta we yui be	ɪn ta we ɟui be
123.	The woman comes	madɪtsa a shige	madɪtsə a ʃige
	She comes	a shige	a ʃige
	The woman laughs	madɪtsa a hi met	madɪtsə a hi met
	The woman weeps	madɪtsa a tu	madɪtsə a tu
124.	I ask the woman	in ma daha madɪtsa	ɪn mə daha madɪtsə
125.	Why do you laugh ?	michi ya himedi yau ?	mitʃi ɟa himedi ɟau ?
126.	Why do you cry ?	michi ya tui yau ?	mitʃi ɟa tui ɟau ?
127.	My child is dead	nji ma ru	ndʒi mə ru
128.	It is not dead	da ru	də ru
129.	Are you ill ?	da i jam ?	də i dʒam ?
130.	My children are ill	uji da jam	udʒi da dʒam
131.	Her child is better	inzair merie da ma	ɪnzəɪr mɛrie da ma
132.	Yes	woo	woo
	No	awo	awo
133.	A fine knife	luta dangaa	luta daŋaa
	Give me the knife	vi luta	vi luta
	I give you the knife	in mu vu luta	ɪn mu vu luta
134.	I am a European	in chi bature	ɪn tʃi bature
	You are a black man	ichi minde chikchik	itʃi mɪnde tʃɪktʃɪk
	You are a Gudu	ichi du gudu tsagho	itʃi du gudu tsəgo
135.	Name	hlim	ɬɪm
	My name	hlimi	ɬimi
	Your name	hlimu	ɬɪmu
	What is your name	amgitsa hlimu wo ?	amgɪtsə ɬimu wo ?
136.	There is water in the gourd	nya ge kap gura ki	nɟa ge kap gura ki
	The knife is on the stone	lutai yin ma moktsa	lutai ɟin mə moktsə
	The fire is under the pot	ɖu gai kitta wuḍa	ɗu gai kɪtta wuɗa
	The roof is over the hut	vina ma za fite	vina mə za fite
137.	You are good	in nga	in ŋa
	This man is bad	utsa a da ka danga	utsə a də ka daŋa
138.	The paper is white	ɖeryuel puput	ɗerɟuɛl puput
	This thing is black	ndea ishi chik chik	ndea iʃi tʃɪk tʃɪk
	This thing is red	ndea ishi bi bî	ndea iʃi bi bî
139.	This stone is heavy	mumukya ḍap ḍap	mumukɟa ɗəp ɗəp
	This stone is not heavy	mumukya da ḍap	mumukɟa da ɗəp
140.	I write	na dor	nə dɔr
	I give you the letter	in ma vu deryuel	ɪn mə vu dɛrɟuɛl

Carry the letter to the town — we ta deryuel kya hwoḍo — we ta dɛrjuɛl kja hwoɗo

141. Go away — wei — wei
Come here — shu wa — ʃu wa

142. Where is your house — ma hwoḍo ? — ma hwoɗo ?

143. My house is here — vini gana — vini gana
My house is there — vini gara — vini gara ?

144. What have you to sell ? — michi ya dereiyo ? — mitʃi ja dɛrɛijo ?

145. I want to buy fish — in ma wum ma nidir hirfu — ɪn mə wum mə nɪdɪr hirfu

146. The fish which you bought is bad — hirfya yi diri danga — hirfja ji diri daŋa

147. Where is the man who killed the elephant ? — manda bilen ongya on ? — mandə bɪlɛn oŋja on ?
He has killed many elephants — ma bilen on pas — mə bɪlɛn on pas
How many elephants were killed yesterday ? — uen am ara bilen bide wo ? — uɛn am ara bɪlɛn bide wo ?

148. Untie it — siḍa — siɗaː
Tie this rope — kwonga zo kya — kwɔŋga zo kja
Make the boy untie the goat — woḍa nja ma ta siḍa ho kya — wɔɗa ndʒa ma ta sɪɗa ho kja

149. My brothers and I, we are going, but no one else — in ta mizhi in tar wi reshin ngal — ɪn ta miʒi ɪn ta we reʃin ŋal
Brothers, let us go and tell the chief — un mizhiya be wun naza bwan dara mmom — un miʒija be wun neze bwan darae mmom

150. This tree is bigger than that — ndiya kada ma hirdira duburum — ndija kada ma hɪrdɪra duburum

THE KUMBI DIALECT OF GUDU

1. Head — yiin — jɪm
2. Hair — shibte — ʃɪbte
3. Eye — ji — dʒi
Two eyes — ji bak or kulia — dʒi bək or kulia
4. Ear — hlim — ɬim
Two ears — hlim kulia — ɬim kulia
5. Nose — chin — tʃin
6. One tooth — hlin jang — ɬin dʒaŋ
Five teeth — hlin tuf — ɬin tuf

7. Tongue	geana	geana
8. Neck	wura	wura
9. Breast (woman's)	than	θan
10. Heart	kubitsa	kubɪtsə
11. Belly	yau	ʝau
12. Back	bia	bia
13. Arm	hwa	hwa
14. Hand	yawohwa	ʝawɔhwa
Two hands	yawohwa kulia	ʝawɔhwa kulia
15. Finger	zamohwa	zamohwa
Five fingers	zamohwa tuf	zamohwa tuf
16. Finger-nail	matifa	matifə
17. Leg	shiḍa	ʃiɖə
18. Knee	ina kukun	ina kukun
19. Foot	yawa shiḍa	ʝawa ʃiɖə
Two feet	yawa shiḍa kulia	ʝawa ʃiɖə kulia
20. Man (person)	minda	mɪndə
Ten people	minji pu	mɪndʒi pu
21. Man (not woman)	mir	mɪr~
Two men	mir kulia	mɪr~ kulia
22. Woman	maditsa	madɪtsə
Two women	mitia kulia	mitia kulia
23. Child	za feda	za fɛdə
24. Father	da	da
25. Mother	ma	ma
26. Slave	mava	mava
27. Chief	mum	mum
28. Friend	bazhi	baʒi
29. Smith	maala	maala
30. Doctor	ndungum	nduŋgum
31. One finger	zamohwa dzang	zamohwa dzʌŋ
32. Two fingers	zamohwa kulia	zamohwa kulia
33. Three fingers	zamohwa makin	zamohwa makɪn
34. Four fingers	zamohwa fwat	zamohwa fwat
35. Five fingers	zamohwa tuf	zamohwa tuf
36. Six fingers	zamohwa kwakh	zamohwa kwax
37. Seven fingers	zamohwa miskara	zamohwa mɪskara
38. Eight fingers	zamohwa fwarfwat	zamohwa fwarfwat
39. Nine fingers	zamohwa zhatapan	zamohwa ʒatapan
40. Ten fingers	zamohwa pu	zamohwa pu
41. Eleven fingers	zamohwa pu kama dzang	zamohwa pu kama dzʌŋ
42. Twelve fingers	zamohwa pum bir kulia	zamohwa pum bir kulia
Thirteen fingers	zamohwa pum bir makin	zamohwa pum bir makɪn
43. Twenty fingers	zamohwa pu putu kulia	zamohwa pu putu kulia
44. A hundred fingers	zamohwa aru	zamohwa aru
45. Two hundred fingers	zamohwa aru kulia	zamohwa aru kulia

46. Four hundred fingers	zamohwa aru fwat	zamohwa aru fwat
47. Sun	mabir	mabır~
God	vunia	vunia
48. Moon	lida	lidə
Full moon	lida bir	lida bır~
New moon	lida ma wea	lida mə wɛa
49. Day	tabiri	tabıri
Night	vada	vədə
Morning	tawuri	tawuri
50. Rain	nyazim	njazım
51. Water	nya satsa	nja satsə
52. Blood	ajin	ədʒın
53. Fat	mar	mʌr~
54. Salt	ngirda	ngırdə
55. Stone	woum	woum
Iron	sablissa	sablıssə
56. Hill	shauwom	ʃauwom
57. River	mabur	mabur
58. Road	tava	təvə
59. House	hunda (Compound = hwaḍa)	hunda (Compound = hwaɗa)
Two houses	hunda kulia	hunda kulia
Many houses	hunda hanini	hunda hanini
All the houses	hunda pupwa	hunda pupwa
60. Roof	gabaza	gaɓəzə
61. Door	mahwada	mahwada
62. Mat	buchi	butʃi
63. Basket	tsilla	tsɪlla
64. Drum	birni	bır~ni
65. Pot	wuda	wuda
66. Knife	sangatsa	saŋatsə
67. Spear	pir	pir~
68. Bow	ragha	ragə
69. Arrow	ava	avə
Five arrows	ava tuf	avə tuf
70. Gun	bindiga	bındıgə
71. War	hatsa	hatsə
72. Meat (animal)	hada	hadə
73. Elephant	wong	wɔŋ
74. Buffalo	hivin	hɪvın
75. Leopard	aru	aru
76. Monkey	rubu	rubu
77. Pig	ngirdim	ngir~dım
78. Goat	shintsa	ʃıntsə
79. Dog	khidda	xıdda
80. Bird	kwadang	kwadaŋ
Feather	bibiḍa	bibiɗə
81. Crocodile	kirim	kırı̄m
Horse	kara	kara
Cow	la	la

	Sheep	puɗa	puɗə
	Hausa	Hausa	hausa
	Fulani	Filasar	filasar
	Beri-Beri	Shuwatsa	ʃuwatsə
	Bata	Bitia	bitia
	Burra	babaɗa	babəɗə
	Hona	Khenia	xenia
	Yungur	Yungur	juŋur
	Kanda	Bawa	bawa
82.	Fowl	kwadang	kwadaŋ
83.	Eggs	ngya	ngja
	One egg	ngya dzang	ngja dzʌŋ
85.	Snake	ruhun	ruhun
86.	Frog	gubada	gubada
87.	Fly	jiɗa	dʒiɗə
88.	Bee	mwuatsa	mwuatsə
	Honey	mwuatsa	mwuatsə
89.	Tree	kada	kada
	Ten trees	kada pu	kada pu
90.	Leaf	yiada	jiadə
91.	Guinea-corn	gawa	gawa
92.	Maize	gau buza	gau buzə
93.	Ground-nut	wanatsa	wanatsə
94.	Oil	ɗan	ɗan

PLATE 14

AN ALBINO

CHAPTER III

THE BURA AND PABIR (BABUR) TRIBES

Bura should be spelt with a single " r ", the " r " being trilled. The spelling " Babur " represents the pronunciation used by the Kanuri, Hausa, and some neighbouring tribes. The tribe calls itself Pabir or Babir, and some neighbouring tribes apply the term Babira. The " r " in Pabir is trilled.

Both tribal titles mean " The men " or " People ", being variants of the common Nigritic root *bur* or *bir* = man or male or male organ.[1] The names Bura or Pabir are thus cognate with Mbula, Igbiri, Igbira, and Burum, all of which are titles of Northern Nigerian tribes. There is a Babira tribe situated in the north-east corner of the Congo Basin and mentioned by Stanley (*Darkest Africa*). Johnston refers to a pygmy tribe of Bagbira or Babira as speaking an unclassified Sudanic language (*Comparative Study*, vol. ii., p. 121). Johnston's Ki-bira are apparently the same people as Stanley's Babira. There is a Bura tribe in the Northern Territories of the Gold Coast (see Armitage's *Tribal Markings*, p. 11).

Language. The Pabir and Bura speak a common language, which with Margi, Chibuk (Kibaku), and Kilba forms a group of what may provisionally be termed the Benue-Chad subdivision of Struck's Central Sudanic Division.

In phonology and vocabulary there are striking resemblances with the Bantu languages of South Africa. Thus the laterals *tl*, *dl*, *hl*, the labialized θ, and palatalized *s*, are common to Bura and the Zulu and Kafir languages. A list of Bura roots is given below showing the resemblance with the various Bantu groups as given in Johnston's *Comparative Study*. A remarkable circumstance is the identity of the Pabir and Bura word for Chief (viz. Kusi) with

[1] In the Mbula language " man " = *bua bura,* and in the Kulû language *ba bira.* In the Hausa language the male organ is " *bura* ".

137

that of the South African, e.g. Se-Cuana, Amazulu (Zulu) group.

We shall see later that there are numerous cultural parallels between the Pabir, Bura, and the South African tribes. The crocodile " cult ", for example, is common to both, and just as the Pabir Chief is associated with a crocodile, so the Chief of the Bakuenas [1] was known as " The Great Man of the Crocodile " (Casalis, *The Basuto*, p. 211). Incidentally the Basuto use the word Melimo for spirits—the Pabir and Bura word being Melim. It is worth noting also that the word Kusi for Chief is used by the Avatime of Togoland, and that in the Volta regions— where the crocodile cult is notable—there is a Bura tribe of Grunshi origin. It is remarkable that the quite distinctive mouth marks of the Nigerian Bura are exactly paralleled among the Fra-fra Grunshi.

English.	Bura.	Bantu (and Semi-Bantu).	Ref. No. in Johnston's *Comp. Study.*
Back	Hili	Ili	137.
Bee	Chiri	Uchi, chue, dzuchi	13, 67, 68, 125, 6a.
Bird	Dika	Daka, deke	124–33, 167, 75.
Blood	Manshi	Masi	39.
Buffalo	Fur	Fulu, furu	133, 238.
Chief	Kusi	Kusi, kosi, etc.	259, 80, 75, 76, etc.
Come	Asi	Asa, nzie, nzi	1, 5a, 200.
Egg	Hlihli	Huli, holi, kili	2e, 147, 132, 133.
Eye	Ncha	Cho, ncho, etc.	128, 191, etc.
Father	Tida	Tada, teta	253, 114, 205, 230.
Finger	Kuliañ	Nekele	155.
Frog	Whonda	Swamba, onda, whawha	100, 195, 74.
Go	Mwaru	Wuara, bwaro	234, 267.
Goat	Kwi	Buli, buzi, bui, ke	1, 5, 32, 232, 228, 208.
House	Mba	Mba, umba	2, 17, 56b, 65, 69.
Iron	Liya	Ira, era, ela, bia lini	81, 13, 1, 5a, 237.
Knife	Inla	Ela, ele, landa	75, 9c, 40–4, 83, 90, 39, 193.
Leopard	Tunvwa	Umvwa, tumbala	2a, 265.
Man	Sal (pl. Shil) Mda	Silisa Ndu	75a. 70, 75, etc.
Meat	Kum	Koma	114.

---

[1] The word Kuena or Cuana (Bechuanaland) would appear to be the same word as the Nigerian Kwana (Kona) and Hwana (Hona) and the Huana of Johnston's Kwango-Kasai group. Compare also the Kunna of El Masudi, iii, 51.

English.	Bura.	Bantu (and Semi-Bantu).	Ref. No. in Johnston's *Comp. Study.*
Moon	Siya	Etsi, esi, seetsa	38, etc., 101–28, 73.
Night	Viri	Ria, irima, iro	145, 2f, 5.
Salt	Una	Onu, nma	2f, 250.
Snake	Pwapu	Hlwatu, hwaa, pwi	75a, 254, 61a.
Spirit	Melim	Melimo (spirits Basuto)	—
Stone or Hill	Pyela	Pili, bila, lola, yala	44, 77, 84, 166, 110, 51, 57, 62, 21.
Sun	Chi	Sui, jui	228, 229, 232, 227.
Ten	Kuma	Kumi	Universal Bantu root.
War	Lira	Bira, bila, liye	208, 226, 5.
Water	Yimi	Mi, nyi, dyii	241c, 111, 239, 220.
Woman	Mwala	Mwali	167.
		Muwoli	Wahenga (Hamitic).

Bura does not, however, display any of the typical morphological characteristics of the Bantu and Semi-Bantu languages (e.g. classification of nouns by means of pronominal affixes and showing concord between noun and verb or adjective by the use of the same pronominal affix).

The Pabir occupy the country betweeen 12 and 12·50 longitude and 10·50 and 10·30 latitude : the Bura the country between 12 and 13 longitude and 10·40 and 10·15 latitude (roughly). The Pabir are centred entirely in the Province of Bornu but a number of Bura extend into Adamawa Province. The Pabir number 13,400 and the Bura 83,000.

The Pabir and Bura though speaking a common language differ considerably in culture and appearance (these differences will be noted later), the Pabir having been subjected for four (?) centuries to cultural influences from the North, introduced by the royal " clan " of the Woviri. This influence (Tida-Kanuri or Mandara) resulted in the establishment among the Pabir of a central authority which the Bura never had. The Pabir did not, however, adopt the Muslim religion, though Islam is now making some impression among the tribe. (The royal clan has for a number of generations professed a spasmodic adherence to Islam, while practising all the pagan rites.)

The Bura and Pabir have to some extent intermingled, as is shown by the possession of common clan titles, but intermarriage between Bura and Pabir is uncommon. The Bura also have foreign elements, chiefly of Tera origin (e.g. at Birni, Nyawi, Balbiya, and Kokwal).

There is no evidence to show whether the Pabir and Bura were indigenous or strangers. Such traditions as exist centre round Yemta-ra-Wala, the founder of the Pabir royal family. Nothing is known of his parentage but the story runs that he was at one time a candidate for the throne of Birnin Ngasr-Gamo The Mais of the Kanuri capital claimed a connection with the Tida of Kawar, and it is curious that Dirku and Zeila are mentioned in Yemta's " kirari " or chant.[1] Yemta may therefore have been of Tida origin. On the other hand tradition also connects Yemta with Mandara, and it may be that he was of that " Kwana " stock to which reference has already been made. Mr. H. R. Palmer has somewhere stated that the " Fika written chronicle as also the tradition of the Dera and Tera of the Shani region are unanimous in declaring that the Kwana came into this country from Mandara, debouching from the hills in the region of Mubi and the Hawal river—the rock of Walama being one of the earliest centres of the Jukun cult ". Certainly the chiefs of Biu were in close touch with the Pindiga Jukun, the chief of whom used to send an annual gift of salt (from Wase) and two gowns stuffed into two ox-horns,[2] the return present being natron and an ox. The three-leafed "Rum spear" was the emblem of royalty of the chiefs of Biu, Pindiga, and Ngasrgamo.

Yemta, it is said, came from Birnin Ngasrgamo to Mandara and thence on to Pabir via Diwa and Zlimbir. He was not apparently a Muslim, as the story goes that he was rejected at Ngasrgamo because he did not know the Muslim ritual for killing animals. There is a story that before his death his son Mari invited him to "prepare porridge" for him, as he (Mari) was going to bring fresh milk in order that both might be mixed for a meal This is a typical Sudanic declaration of war, and it may point to the common African practice of sons fighting their fathers for the succession. The message enraged Yemta who forthwith sank into the ground, his pigtail being cut off by his daughter before he disappeared. Every Pabir Chief wears a pigtail which he assumes

[1] Yemta's *kirari* is " Su-sataha Dirgiri ka Zeila ka siaha Mandara karwa ", i.e. " the thing arose from Dirku and Zeila and came to Mandara."

[2] Two horns seem to have been an emblem of kingship in Yemen. El Sa'ab was known as Dhu el Karnayu—the two-horned—and it is noteworthy that his brother Abraha (born 134 B.C.) made an incursion into the Sudan as far as the Moghrab.

six months after his royal baptism (cf. page 184). On his death it is cut off and put in a satchel containing the pigtails of all former Chiefs. This satchel which is known as Mizpar is carefully kept by the reigning Chief as a talisman. The names of twenty-three Pabir Chiefs have been preserved (see Major Edgar's *Gazetteer*).

Political Organization.—Both tribes are now administered by the Pabir Chief of Biu, whose chiefdom is divided into a number of districts under district headmen. Formerly the authority of the Chief of Biu was confined to the Pabir tribe and the hill Bura in the vicinity of Biu. The chiefdom was divided into two sections with centres at Gur and Gunda, each section being under a Hiedima with whom were associated officials responsible for village areas. The Hiedima and subordinate officials of Gur belonged to the Hiamtiga clan, those of Gunda to the Minta clan. The Pabir organization was thus of a dual character. An independent section of the royal Woviri family was established at Mandaragarau, but I had no opportunity of investigating the relations of this section to the Woviri of Biu.

The Bura in the vicinity of Biu were controlled by a Hiedima of the Dangwal clan, with headquarters at Kidda.

In Biu itself apart from the members of the royal family all the office-holders were of slave origin. The royal title-holders were the Wakshama, Yerima, Chamalwa, but their official duties were nil—each lived in an outlying village in which he exercised a purely local control, having rights over captured runaway slaves and a portion of bush animals killed within the village boundary. The office of Medala was held by the Chief's eldest son who was heir to the throne. The vizier was known as the Birma and was always a slave. He, with the chief office-holders, dealt with all minor cases, but the major cases came before the Chief.

The Bura were, with the exception of the Kidda area, devoid of any central government, each village area constituting an independent political unit under the headship of the senior member of the oldest established clan. Inter-clan and inter-village feuds were of common occurrence. The Bura east and south of the Hawal river acknowledged the suzerainty of the Yola Fulani represented by the Chief of Gola.

Clothing and Ornaments, etc.—There is a marked difference

between the two tribes in appearance, clothing, and ornaments. The tribal markings are totally distinct, as the following sketches show :—

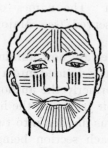

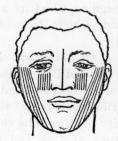

Bura.   Pabir.

Pabir women are known at once by their distinctive manner of dressing the hair over a raised pad (like the Bolewa of Fika) with a plaited lock hanging down on either side. Bura women, on the other hand, wear their hair, which they plaster with red earth, in bowl-shaped fashion, and bound with pieces of brass.

The Bura men used to wear their hair long, plaiting it with rags and metal ornaments and plastering it with red earth and fish-oil, but they are now becoming ashamed of these practices and have taken to shaving the head completely (like the Pabir), or partially so as to leave a circular tuft on the back of the head thus :—

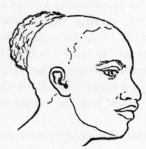

This is the fashion affected by all who exercise priestly functions (as these are forbidden by custom to shave the head). Pabir men circumcise, Bura do not.   There is no female circumcision.

Bura men wear loin-coverings of cloth or hide which they pull through the legs from front to rear—in the Hausa fashion.   The

PLATE 15

A PABIR MOTHER

A PABIR PLAYING A XYLOPHONE

[face p. 143

Pabir, on the other hand, like the Kanuri, wear their loin-cloths behind and pull the end through from rear to front. The Pabir has always worn the short trousers and short sleeveless jumper known to the Hausa as the "yerchiki". On occasion also he wears the large "gumaji" gown which resembles the Hausa "kwakwata." Bura men did not usually wear gowns but would throw a cloth over the shoulder.

Pabir women wear large cloths, Bura small ones. The breasts are left uncovered as a rule. Bura girls are often seen wearing a cloth flap which hangs down in front or is pulled through the legs to the back. Or they may be seen with fringes of string or of string bound round with metal. They often wear circlets of beads on their heads and plugs (brass rings or strings of beads or reed or guinea-corn stalks) in the upper and lower lips (a practice not followed by Pabir women, who, however, wear ear-plugs and metal earrings and perforate the right nostril, inserting lead plugs, threepenny bits, etc.).

Children are carried (by both tribes) in a leather satchel which is also sometimes covered with a cloth binding. The heads of children are protected with a calabash (of Bede, Kare-Kare, etc.). Women carry loads on calabashes poised on the shoulder.

Several albinoes were noticed among the Bura. They are regarded with disfavour, refused the tribal marks, and no girl will marry one.

Weapons.—The bow-and-arrow is the usual weapon. Short swords of the type found among the Plateau tribes are carried by the Bura (and Kilba). Bossed oval shields of bush cow hide, precisely the same pattern as is used by the Borom of Kanem, were seen among the Bura. Spears are carried by the Pabir, and the Chief of this tribe provided some of his followers with suits of chain-mail, and quilted cotton for their horses.

Musical Instruments.—The Bura have a xylophone called the Tsindza—seven blocks of wood which rest against a series of cows' horns as resonators, the whole being supported on a circular framework of wood. The player sits on the ground with the instrument between his legs and uses a pronged stick as a striker.

Salutations.—No one but a Malam [1] may enter the Chief's compound wearing any form of headgear, and all, including members of the royal family (but not the senior members of the household), would remove their headgear on meeting the Chief

---

[1] A "Malam" is a Muslim teacher.

outside his compound (compare Bolewa and Kanuri custom). A Pabir woman salutes the Chief by going down on her knees and throwing dust with the right hand over the left and right shoulder three times and then clapping her hands three times. A Pabir man salutes a superior by going down on his knees, touching the ground with his forefinger which he then draws up from the tip of his nose to his forehead three times, and clapping his hands three times.

Time Reckoning.—The Bura and Pabir have had from time immemorial a seven-day week of named days as follows : Hlumawa (Friday), Sibduwa, Laduwa, Litininwa, Talakwa, Larabawa, and Liamsuwa—all of Arabic origin.

A year consists of twelve lunar months and an intercalary period called Bilam by which the first month of the year is made to coincide with the beginning of the wet season when the home guinea-corn is planted, i.e. the calculation of the year is dependent on the farming season.

The months and farming periods are :—

1. Slientang—the first month of the wet season when the home guinea-corn is planted.
2. Sliensuda—first hoeing.
3. Slienmagir—middle of wet season.
4. Slienfwar—maize and ground-nut harvest.
5. Slientufu—early guinea-corn harvest.
6. Slienkwa—conclusion of wet season when the early millets are eaten.
7. Slienmurfa—general guinea-corn harvest.
8. Slienchisso—corn taken to bins.
9. Slienimla—bush fired and work of house repairing begun.
10. Slienkuma—house repairing continued.
11. Mafarmiyaviya—farm clearing.
12. Simnaw or Simarari—seed selection.
13. Bilam, i.e. " look out " (for the new year) the intercalary period.

It is obvious that on this method of reckoning there may be a lack of uniformity, and that one district may be in Silentang while others are still in Bilam.

Currency.—Among both tribes the medium of exchange was (*a*) thread (Bura only), (*b*) narrow strip of cloth (*kuntu*), (*c*) *bul* (gown), and (*d*) metal bracelets.

10 rolls of small (wadari) thread = 1 strip (kuntu).
10 strips = 1 bul.
5 brass bracelets = 1 bul.

There was apparently no cowry currency.

Firemaking.—Both Pabir and Bura use the drill method—one piece of guinea-corn stalk (that which carries the grain) being twirled in a groove made in another (part of the main stalk). The latter is placed over a hole in the ground in which a piece of cotton or cloth has been deposited to catch the flame. To increase the friction a little sand may be placed in the groove. Sometimes a piece of the shell of the fruit of the monkey-bread tree is used as a base (instead of the guinea-corn stalk).

Houses.—Pabir and Bura huts are of the circular mud or plaited straw type with conical thatched roof. When the walls are of plaited straw they are cemented on the inside with a smearing of mud, as a protection against weather and fire. This, I was informed, was the only type of hut in former times (with the exception of the Chief's which was of mud ; the Chief also had a flat-roofed building at the doorway of his house).

The Bura build their compounds in scattered groups of three or four. The Pabir are more gregarious and their villages more compact. The husband has a hut of his own (unlike many other tribes where the husband uses the porch by day and one of his wives' huts by night). Each wife has her own hut in front of which is a stack of wood. The ground beside the stack may be tessellated to serve as a place for cooking when the weather is fine. Scattered in the compound are several bins of mud and straw and having a top-covering of thatch. These bins, which stand 4 feet high, are made by the women and are used for storing cereals. A smaller type of bin divided into three compartments is used for storing various kinds of seasoning leaves, peppers, etc. Inside the Bura woman's hut there is a milling arrangement of peculiar type, consisting of a quern inset in a hollow mud platform at the end of which is a well for receiving the ground grain.

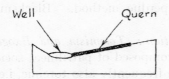

In the woman's hut another peculiar feature is the mud

frame-work built out from the wall so as to form a pen for goats and provide receptacles for flour, peppers, etc.

It is shaped something like the following :—

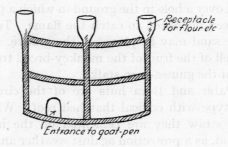

Here and there inside the hut are numerous small bins resembling vases of classical pattern. They are used for storing beans, ground-nuts, and seasoning vegetables.

The bedstead is of mud and has a hollow underneath. But a fire is not, as among many Plateau tribes, lighted on the ground close by.

Every Bura woman has a " habtu " in her hut—a sacred pot set within another pot. This receives the blood of the sacrifice.

Pottery.—The mud used has a powder, made from crushed pieces of old pots, intermixed. This is said to prevent cracking during the process of baking. The base of the new pot is shaped on the base of an old pot and is then built up by the addition of coiled strips, the surface being smoothed by a piece of calabash dipped in water. The fire consists of dry cow-dung and grass, the pot being carefully covered with the cow-dung. A wood fire would burn too quickly and crack the pots.

Smithing.—The Pabir and Bura use the cire-perdue method (fata) for manufacturing brass bracelets, necklaces, and girdles. The design of the girdle beads resembles that of the tin discs dug up on the Bauchi Plateau and suggests that these discs were also made by the cire-perdue method. Blacksmiths are honoured among the Bura.

Social Organization : Totemism and Exogamy.—Both tribes were found to be composed of patrilineal social units which are exogamous and are frequently also totemic, i.e. associated with a species of animal or tree which serves as a badge or symbol of the group. These clans or gentes are in reality enlarged families, and

PLATE 16

A BURA POT

A BURA MAN

[face p. 146

consist of people who are descended from a common (human) ancestor. The clan, which may include anything from fifteen to five hundred biological families, may have its own name or may share a common name with two or more other clans, the combination of clans forming a " phratry " (though these phratries are not exogamous).

The members of one clan will usually deny any kinship with the members of another clan of the same name, but as they will sometimes share the same religious cult and are also sometimes recognized as related by themselves and other clans for purposes of the blood feud, it would appear that the original clan has become subdivided, i.e. that kin exogamy had become localized.

It would also appear that the phratry occasionally cuts across the tribe, e.g. that one or two clans of a phratry may call themselves Pabir, while a third may call itself Bura. Thus the Bwola (Bola), Kusuku, and Bwola Dam are Pabir clans, while the Bwola Bura is a Bura clan. Each Bwola clan is an exogamous unit, but the clans may intermarry (I had no opportunity of finding out if such marriages did actually occur). If any member of one of these clans killed a member of another Bwola clan no blood feud resulted, as they regarded each other as related, and conversely if any member of a Bwola clan killed a member of a non-Bwola clan vengeance was taken on any of the three Bwola clans.[1]

On the other hand the Dangwal is a Bura phratry consisting of clans at Kidda, Pama, Milala, Dagwa, Wakshapindar, Bangam, Kumba, etc.—each clan being of course an exogamous unit. The clans may intermarry. But for purposes of the blood feud the clans at Kidda and Pama formed one unit, while those at Milala, Dagwa, etc., formed another. That is to say that if a Dangwal of Kidda killed a non-Dangwal man the murdered man's clan would, in lieu, murder any Dangwal of Kidda or of Pama, but would not murder any Dangwal of Milala. Moreover, while the Dangwal of Kidda and Pama share the same religious rites, the Milala, Dagwa, etc., clans have their own separate religious rites. The Dangwal thus appeared to be divided into moieties, but it is possible that there are other groups of Dangwal of which I did not

[1] The position would appear to be the same as that described by Professor Sidney Hartland in speaking of the Herero: " The blood feud still attaches to the *eanda* and has not been transferred to the *oruzo*."

hear. The Pabir Bola also apparently have a dual organization consisting of the Sheduma Halshini and Gambila clans.

We may digress for a moment in order to refer to this law of blood revenge. In a case of homicide done by a member of another clan, the clan (*yangur* or *dur*) of the murdered man proceeded to take immediate vengeance in the form of the *lex talionis*. The murderer's clan fled. The members of the murdered man's clan then proceeded to track down a specially selected individual of the opposing clan (no fool or weakling would be chosen). He might be shot as he went to close up his compound at night : or his sleeping-place would be discovered by one of the murdered man's clan, who would make a hole in the wall of the hut and then shoot his adversary with an arrow (first micturating on the arrow to make the poison active). He would then, if satisfied that he had accomplished his purpose, run off home and announce his success with a loud shout. All would rush out to greet him and a dance of vengeance would be held on the murdered man's grave. But among the Pabir, where there was a central authority, the Chief made himself responsible for the apprehension of a murderer, who was handed over to the murdered man's clan and then (in Jewish fashion) stoned to death (by women and boys—no grown-up man would condescend to lend a hand).

Individuals were sometimes exempted from the operation of blood revenge. Thus if a member of clan A killed a member of clan B, all the members of clan B might notify X, a member of clan A, that his life would be respected in the subsequent feud, provided he came and put his hands on the clan B "fetish".

The clan does not coincide with the local group, for in most village-areas you find groups of several clans living together, and where this is the case the authority, civil and religious, is usually vested in the senior member of the senior clan. The clan as a whole is, however, localized (in contradistinction to the phratry which is scattered). Descent is patrilineal, but the sense of kinship is not confined to the clan (in which the descent from a common ancestor may be fictitious or at any rate cannot be demonstrated), but extends to relatives on the mother's side whose relationship can easily be traced. Among the Bura all cousin marriage is forbidden, but among the Pabir cross-cousin marriage is practised in the Woviri or royal family group.

The sense of association with a totem is vague. In some instances the clan disclaimed any such association, but it is possible that in such cases a closer inquiry than I was able to give would have revealed the totem. Thus the Gamsama clan of the Mbeiya phratry, while stating that one of the African mahoganies (*Afzelia africana*) might not be burnt by any Gamsama (if it were their children would be injured by fire), could give no account of this taboo. Usually all the three main characteristics of totemism could be traced, viz. the association of an animal or tree species with the exogamous group (clan), the belief in the sense of relationship between the members of the clan and the animal or tree, and the respect shown by the members of the clan to the animal or tree.

In at least two instances the name of the totem was identical with that of the social group. The Bwola phratry respects the *Ficus platyphylla* and the name for this tree in the Bura language is Bwola. The Minta clan of the Pabir respects the *Afzelia africana* tree and the Pabir name for this tree is Minta. The members of a clan refer to the totem animal species as their brethren, but they do not usually claim descent from the totem (as is the case with some of the Zaria tribes). The relationship is rather one of alliance. The following are instances of how the relationship is said to have arisen. The Lasama totem is the *Mamba*. Once upon a time a Lasama was captured in war and was put in the stocks to await sacrifice. In the early morning a *Mamba* crawled up to him and so frightened him that he gave a lurch, which freed his legs and he escaped. All *Mambas* were therefore proclaimed to be friends of the Lasama and no Lasama may kill or injure a *Mamba*. *Mambas* will not, it is said, injure a Lasama, and any Lasama coming across the dead body of a *Mamba* must bury it.

The Mbeiya of Sakwa state that their totem is the *tsala kokwa* snake. The founder of the clan was troubled because he was getting old and had no children. In his sleep he dreamed that someone bade him go and dig in the ground, and when he found the tail of a living thing he was to cut it off, sew it up in leather, and give it to his wife ; so he dug and came across a tail and gave it to his wife and she bore a child and eventually had a large family. The man wondered at the marvel, and went again to the hole and dug deeper and found the body of the snake. And

so he forbade any of his children to kill any of that species of
snake, and if they came across its dead body they were to bury it.

The totem of the Gauja clan is the *Varanus niloticus*,
Any member of the clan eating it would be covered with sores,
and his body would waste away. The dead body of the *Varanus*
must be buried respectfully," its secret must not be discovered."
An injured *Varanus* in the possession of any member of another
clan must be ransomed.

The members of the Gwayar clan (the name Gwayar is said to
have been the name of the town they formerly inhabited) pay
respect to the crocodile, and every year at the beginning of the
rains the two most senior men of the clan resort to the sacred
pool where the crocodiles, which embody the souls of Gwayar
forefathers, reside. Maize porridge and a chicken are placed on
the sacrificial stone near the water's edge and the crocodiles are
addressed : " You are our head (i.e. source), here is our offering,
permit us to take what we seek (viz. fish). If any people (clan)
other than our own join in the fishing let them fish unharmed."
The blood of the chicken is mingled with the porridge, and next
day people of various clans go there and catch fish (by hand) in
the pool—the crocodiles being pushed aside if they get in the way.
This practice is confined to one day in the year. The head of the
Gwayar clan sits and watches the operations and may order
certain of the largest fish caught to be replaced (he himself takes
a share of the catch and sends a share also to the Chief of Biu).
No member of the Gwayar clan will eat crocodile's flesh, and
everyone is bound to bury in a cloth the body of any dead
crocodile he comes across.

The Ngima clan (Bura) became associated with their leopard
totem in the following way : During a famine the founder of the
clan kept himself alive by eating the fruit of a certain monkey-
bread tree. But one day he found a leopard at the base of the
tree and so he ran away. But, coming to the conclusion that it
was better to be killed than to die of hunger, he returned. The
leopard offered no opposition and in fact became friendly, and
used to spend the nights in the old man's compound. And to this
day leopards come and sleep in Ngima compounds and always
appear when an old man is about to die. Here we seem to have
the idea of the bush soul rather than of a " totem ", for when a
Ngima dies his leopard double dies (first stealing chickens and

goats and behaving in an unfriendly way). The dead body of a leopard is buried ceremonially.

The Dangwal stock are known as the Mshel Isa and are said to have come from Hwong in Kilba country. Formerly it is said they never intermarried, but as the Bura among whom they settled would not give them their daughters in marriage their leader Alam Beji bade them abandon their old rules of exogamy. Hence the Bura call the Dangwal " Hamtakima " = " turn your head away ", i.e. disregard the old rules of exogamy. This is quite a reasonable account of how an originally exogamous clan became subdivided into several small exogamous groups which may intermarry.

The Yiringau group are stated to respect the *Vitex cienkowskii* because the child of the founder of the stock was marvellousy protected from death, during a tornado, by this tree. The order therefore went forth that no member of the stock must ever cut or burn the *Vitex cienkowskii*.

A wife respects her husband's totem while she is living with him, but husbands could not usually state, without making inquiries, what were the totems of their wives' families.

We have said that each clan was an exogamous unit, but there was one exception. Any member of the royal group of the Woviri could marry another member of that group. (The Children of the Sun marry into their own stock—see Perry's *Children of the Sun*, p. 377.) Cross-cousin marriage is practised among the Woviri.

The following is a list of some of the Pabir and Bura clans :—

Pabir.	Sacred Animal or Plant.	Bura	Sacred Animal or Plant.
Woviri (royal family, not a clan)		Amaza [1] Tilla Amaza Vina, etc.	Mamba
Bandau	Crocodile.	Dangwal Kidda, etc.	African Ebony (?) Reedbuck.
Gawa	*Ficus platyphylla.*	Idawi	—

[1] Compare Amazingh (Berbers), and their language T'amazhek (*Nachtigal*, p. 245).

Pabir.	Sacred Animal or Plant.	Bura	Sacred Animal or Plant.
Kwafwa	—	Kingal Sheldiaha	—
Pubara	—	Kingal Zhimani	—
Gwayar	—	Kulnjin	—
Minta	*Afzelia africana.*	Lasama	*Mamba.*
Bola, Sheduma, Halshini, Garubila	*Afzelia africana.*	Malgwi	
		Mbeiya Sakwa	Snake (*tsala kokwa*)
		Mbeiya Moram	
Muskodawa	—	Mbeiya Gamsama	*Afzelia africana*
Tidiba	—	Mbeiya Milala	
Ganga i	—	Mbeiya Ingiling	
Ganga ii or more	—	Mbeiya Ingiling, etc.	
Nganjua i	—	Ndahi	
Ngangua ii or more	—	Ngima	Leopard.
Diramza	—	Bwola (Bola) Gwa	
Daba	—	Bwola Sakwa	
Zizi or Hiamtiga	Crocodile.	Bwola Bilatim	
		Bwola Biladuniya	
Gauja	*Varanus niloticus.*	Bwola Tanga	
Gaga Tilo	—	Sasowa	
Ganga Laraba	—	Silla	
Mbeiya Mimbilim	—	Tura	
Mbeiya Pankpa	—	Wawkirwa	
Mbeiya Agala	—	Wharja	Snake (?)
Mbeiya Shala	—	Worgum	
		Zuwaga	
		Gumdowi	
		Kwodami	
		Basi	
		Chara	
		Yiringa (Hinna)	*Vitex cienkowskii*
		Berde	—
		Bizya	—
		Kwari	—
		Tauri	—
		Mizowi	—
		Gwari	—
		Zlakwa	—
		Tarfa	Crocodiles, snakes, monkeys, pigs.
Mizoi	Mamba, monitor lizard, tortoise, rat.	Nda Tanga	—

Pabir.	Sacred Animal or Plant.	Bura	Sacred Animal or Plant.
Billa	Pig, monkey.	Gasi	—
Zooka	Fish, chickens	Vereti	—
Mbaiya of Galkidda	Locusts.	Balami	—
		Viya	—
		Kinim	—
		Dara	—

No close examination was made of the political powers of the clan leaders. The constitution is the usual gerontocracy found in Africa. The clan head is responsible for the religious rites, and for this reason some clan heads are said to be averse to accepting the position of village-area heads under the existing Administration on the ground that they might be called away at a time when they should be carrying out their clan duties at home. It was said that Medugumari had refused the headship of the Garubila Bola on the ground that his present official position might prevent him from carrying out the clan religious rites. As an example of the character of these clan rites we may instance those performed annually before harvest by the head of the Gawa clan (Pabir). He salutes the clan tree (*Ficus platyphylla*) in Pabir fashion three times (dust rubbed thrice up the bridge of the nose and the hands clapped thrice). He then takes some benniseed and, addressing the tree, says: " I come to thee ; grant that we—all the men and women and children of my clan, great and small— may be blessed by thy presence. May we bear many children and obtain much corn, and may good fortune abound, everything that we do turning to good." He then throws the benniseed on the base of the tree three times, and also deposits some cotton. Beer is poured on the grooved stone beside the tree. A chicken is left at the base of the tree ; it is not sacrificed, but is allowed to go its own way—a scapegoat no doubt.[1] During the performance of these rites he is accompanied only by one or two lads who carry the paraphernalia. On returning to the town he informs the clansmen that the rites have been duly performed.

It is noteworthy that among the Pabir the political offices were, apart from the royal family, held almost entirely by the

[1] The Dangwal of Kidda also release a chicken at the base of their sacred African ebony tree.

Zizi (Hiamtiga) and Minta groups. The sense of clan kinship has been considerably weakened by the abolition of the blood feud. All members of the clan stood by one another in trouble, and ransomed any of their members who had been captured and enslaved.

Pabir young men are loosely organized for work and play under a Madi or leader of the young men, who holds the office until he becomes old. In the large towns such as Biu there are two Madis each in charge of one-half of the young men of the town. The Madi may also have an under-officer in each quarter. The Bura have no regular Madi, but appoint a temporary Madi for the wet season's festival. A Bura youth, therefore, who wants young men to help him on his prospective parent-in-law's farm has to go round and canvass his friends for himself, unlike the Pabir youth who would apply to the Madi. Pabir girls have an organization similar to that of the young men, but the Bura have not.

Among the Pabir a wife works three days per week on the husband's farm : the other four days she devotes to her own farm, the produce of which she stores for her own use. At the beginning of the dry season the husband hands over to his wife corn sufficient (with the addition of the wife's) to last the household until the beginning of the wet weather. During the wet season he hands out a supply for each month. The wife can dispose of all excess supplies. Among the Bura, wives only assist husbands in farming one day in the year. The husband hands over to his wife at the beginning of the dry season, and at the beginning of the wet, corn sufficient, with the addition of the wife's, to meet all requirements. Any surplus is regarded as the wife's perquisite.

Marriage.—Marriage is by "purchase" in both tribes ; there is no regularized form of marriage by exchange, capture, or elopement. Both the junior and senior levirate are permitted. Sororate marriage is not countenanced. The inheritance and marriage of the wives of one's father is permitted and practised (as among the Yabga, Aworraw, Munshi, Arago, Idoma, Ganagana, Ayu, Makangara, Kamuku, and Zumper). The inheritance and marriage of the wives of one's grandfather is also permitted and practised, and this type of marriage, which is of great social interest and importance—I hope to deal with the matter in a separate paper—has a widespread distribution (Gade, Arago, Gwari, Igbira, Nupe, Katab, etc.), and where it is no longer found the evidence of its former existence is seen in the relationship terminology of every tribe in the Northern Provinces. The widows of both grandfathers may be married, but in practice a man is by the laws of inheritance more likely to marry the widows of his father's father than of his mother's father. Cousin marriage is not permitted (except among members of the royal family), but as a man's " *abokin wasa* " [1] is his father's sister's or mother's brother's child it may be that cross-cousin marriage was at one time practised (when the social organization was perhaps of a dual character).

The marriage ceremonies have been fully described by Major Edgar in his *Gazetteer*. The following are a few additional notes : When a Bura female child is born a suitor immediately presents himself, staking his claim by throwing into the mother's hut a branch of the *Ficus thonningii* (it is on a bed of the leaves of this tree that the child is received at birth). When the girl is weaned (the weaning period is three years, and during this time the father lives apart from the mother) the accepted suitor presents the child with a bracelet, and later on a necklace. When she is between seven and nine gifts are given at various times as follows : 1 cloth, 3 strips (Kuntu) of cloth, 4 strips, 6 strips, and 4 bracelets. 14 strips are then given to the girl's father and mother. As the time for marriage draws near 2 strips, 4 " buls " (Bura shirts), and 5 buls are successively given. Finally, on a single day a girdle, girdle-ring, 14 brass armlets, 12 brass bracelets, 10 " *kworrias* " [2] of cloth are brought, the father of the girl receiving these and retaining them, or sharing them with his wife and relatives as he thinks fit. A gift of salt is made to the girl's mother together with two strips of cloth—compensation it is said for the loss of the girl's services in grinding corn—an interesting sidelight on the purchase system. The girl is captured by the bridegroom's friends and taken to his compound. Her brothers and sisters arrive and lodge a formal protest, which is withdrawn on receipt of gifts from the bridegroom (a brother gets an arrow and a sister a strip of cloth). Games are held, and for twelve days the girl remains in the hut with one male and two female friends of the bridegroom. She is then taken to a specially prepared hut ; the bridegroom enters, the door is blocked, and coitus takes place.

---

[1] *Abokin wasa* = playmate.   [2] *Kworria* = a calabash of standard size.

No Bura girl goes to her husband's house as a virgin—she has invariably had prior sexual relations with her fiancé or other men, and to this no stigma attaches. Indeed Bura girls sometimes go to their husband's house enceinte by another man. Occasionally fiancées were carried off by men of other clans. This led to a clan feud unless the girl's betrothed agreed to accept compensation. Wife-stealing between members of different clans was practised, but not on the organized scale found among the Semi-Bantu tribes of Bauchi and Zaria.

A woman bears her first child either in her husband's compound or at her own home, whichever she prefers. A child is named by the father who may, after consulting his wife, bestow his own father's or mother's name or that of his wife's father or mother. Every Bura (but not Pabir) has two names, a private and a public, the first being used only by his parents and close relatives.

It is not unusual for a child to be handed over after it is weaned to relatives on the father's or mother's side or to friends. This gives the mother an opportunity to rest and prevents the undue prolongation of the lactation period. (A mother will plaster her breasts with pepper when she thinks it is time the child had given up breast-feeding.)

Twins were not viewed with favour, being regarded as reincarnations ever ready to take offence and die, with a view to being reborn somewhere else. (Among the Hausa there is the same idea and twins are therefore treated with great leniency.) When twins are born pots (Bwol) are made as an amulet, a custom found also among the Gwari.

The Pabir and Bura follow the usual custom of cutting off the tip of the uvula of every child. It is pounded up so that no one may use it to injure the child.

Among the Pabir pre-nuptial chastity was expected. Immediately after coitus the bride goes off for three days to the house of a friend. Next day the husband takes two chickens, plucks them, removes the entrails, and sews them up again. They are frizzled and inspected by the bride's friends. If the chickens are not sewn up it is a sign that the bridegroom had not found the bride to be a virgin, and she might be asked to name her paramour who could be fined by the Chief. After three days' absence the girl returns to her husband.

PLATE 17

A PABIR WOMAN AND CHILD

[face p. 156

Among other social regulations we may note that no Pabir or Bura man will eat food cooked by his wife during her menses nor will he drink water from her water-pot (if he did it would cause blood to collect on the calf of his leg and prevent him from hunting or fighting).

Relationship System.—A table of relationship terms was prepared. This will be included in a later paper dealing with the relationship systems of a dozen or more Nigerian tribes.

Rules of Inheritance.—Primogeniture is the guiding principle, but the eldest son must make provision for the marriage of his younger unmarried brothers. Brothers of deceased only inherit if deceased had no sons or if his sons are under age, in which case the property would eventually be passed on to the deceased's children. But the deceased's brother commonly inherits the mother of the eldest son. Full brothers take precedence of half-brothers, irrespective of age. A grandson if of suitable age may inherit his grandfather's young widow. A man may inherit his father's brother's widow and other property if his father's brother had left no sons. The eldest son also inherits his mother's property with the exception of purely feminine property. If a woman has no son her property goes to her male relatives who also act as trustees for the property of children under age. A husband has no share in his widow's estate. Among the Pabir the Chief of Biu appropriated the property of any who died and left no relatives. A new Chief of Biu inherits the widows of the former Chief, retaining such as he wants and giving the others in marriage (without exacting a bride-price).

Religion.

(a) *Islam.*—Yemta-ra-Wala, the founder of the Woviri dynasty of Biu, is said to have been a Muslim. But the account of his rejection by the Kanuri of Ngasrgamo (see the story of the origin of the Pabir in Palmer's *Bura Grammar*) would indicate that, if he were a Muslim at all, he had an indifferent knowledge of Muslim practices.

Major Edgar states in his Biu *Gazetteer* that Ari Paskur, the twentieth chief, was the first Muhammadan Chief of Biu; but it was stated by the Shafir that Marwa Tirwa (Ari Paskur's father) was undoubtedly a Muslim. The Shafir, however, also stated that Ari Paskur and Marwa Tirwa had sixty wives at the time of their death, and that Garga had one hundred!

Mr. Elder reported that the present Chief of Biu became a Muslim in 1910 ; but my information is that he, like his father Garga, always professed Islam, though prior to 1910 he failed to observe the public Friday rites and was addicted to beer-drinking. Whatever his profession, the Chief carries out punctiliously all the customary pagan rites, and is said to have many more than the prescribed number of wives. A number of the Woviri clan and all the district headmen and their followers are also professing Muhammadans, but the rest of the population is pagan. In fact the only Muslims worthy of the name are strangers. (The Liman and Ladans of Biu are Kanuri or Hausa.)

(b)   *Animism.*—The religious conceptions and practices of the Pabir and Bura (the few professing Muslims included) are of the animistic type, a combination of ancestor-worship, spiritism, and naturism. But a Supreme Deity is recognized under the title of Hyel. This word has the appearance of being a form of the Semitic " El ", and if this is so it might have been introduced as a result of Jewish or Jewish-Christian influence from North Africa. There is evidence of such influence elsewhere in Nigeria. Among the Bura it is noteworthy that the word Shaitan is applied to spirits, and it is possible that the use of this word is pre-Muslim. It is noteworthy that most of the religious rites of the Bura are performed on a Saturday. On the other hand, circumcision is not practised, and I am inclined to think that the word Hyel is connected with the word for moon, viz. Hya. Among the Chibbak, who are neighbours of the Margi, Hyel is pronounced Hyal. It is possible, therefore, that Hyel was originally a moon-deity.

The Chief of Biu belongs to the order of divine kings. When he dies it is said that " God has fallen." He does not die, but like the kings of the Jukun (and Bavenda and Buganda of Central Africa) he " goes away for a time". With his person is bound up the well-being of the Pabir and much of the Bura country. He is responsible, therefore, for the due performance of numerous religious rites, and is subject to numerous taboos.

Like some Igara Chiefs who may not put foot to the ground, the Benue and Busa Chiefs who may not look on the Benue or Niger rivers, the Mashonaland chiefs who may not cross a river, and the chiefs of the Ewe and of Dahomey who may not look on the sea, so the Chief of Biu may not look on the waters of Tilla where his double resides in a certain crocodile. (The present chief has broken this taboo several times.) No evidence was found of the ceremonial killing of the Pabir chief, but tradition says that Yemta-ra-Wala did not die, but merely sank into the ground after a fracas with his son. It is considered a solecism, therefore, to speak of his " grave " which is always referred to as the " house " of Yemta. Many of the religious rites are associated with Yemta, and here we have an example of the illustrious ancestor who has become a god.

With the Chief is bound up the productiveness of the crops— no one may clear his farm until the Chief has first cleared his, and none may plant until the royal farm has been sown.[1] In time of drought the Chief takes action, sending gifts to the priests of Dewa, Gurgur, Wasira, and Shambar and ordering them to perform the rain-producing rites.

When a Chief dies his successor undergoes a period of probation —a process of rebirth no doubt, such as Mr. Hocart records of the coronation ceremonies of Fijian chiefs. He is given by the Birma the royal spear known as Rum and is taken to the Maigira's village of Kwagu where he resides for seven days. He does not enter the royal palace for a year, nor does he assume the title of Kusi (being called the Kadala). He does not shave for two years. At the end of a year he is taken to a rock in the middle of the river Surakumi (near Kidda) and is there ceremonially washed by the Mairem of King-gal,[2] who says : " I am about to pour water over you : in your time may there be good fortune without end : may the people and their possessions increase, may all evil things and epidemics be kept from us in your reign, and may all fear you as a lion." He is then given his royal robes by the Galadima of Gur and formally enters the palace. At the conclusion of a further year he goes to the " house " of Yemta-ra-Wala at Limbir and is there shaven.

These rites, we have observed, resemble a process of rebirth— a process no doubt by which the Chief is converted into a god.

---

[1] Moret, iii, 210–19, describing the divine Egyptian kings of the Fifth Dynasty, says, " As king of the harvest he turns over the earth and presides over the sowing. Sickle in hand he cuts the grain." Compare the ceremonial first hoeing carried out annually by the chief of the Fika Bolewa. " The people of Western Vanua Levu (Fiji) believe that they have less food now than formerly because the government head of the province is not their proper chief ; when the last one who was their proper chief died the food was buried with him," Hocart, iii, 637, 640. Compare the Jukun chief, the giver of food and water.

[2] Another informant said that this was done by the blacksmiths of King-gal, who also fashion the iron supports which are put into the grave to prop up the dead body of the chief.

Ceremonial lustration of the Pharaoh before and at coronation was apparently customary in Egypt (see Breasted, *Ancient Records*, ii, 222 and 99). The priest representing the god addressed the king saying: " I purify thee with the water of all life and good fortune, all stability, all health and happiness."

Ancestor Worship.—The central religious festival of the Pabir year is that known as the Mambila. The word means " ghost", and it is a feast of all souls, more particularly of the souls of the Chief's forefathers. The Pabir conception is that on a man's death his soul goes to join his grandfather's but returns to the town each year at the Mambila feast. The festival is held at harvest and the Chief takes a prominent, in fact the principal, part. A Bura woman of the Kachi clan at Mahashi brings fresh clay from Mahashi to Biu, and with this fashions two pots wherein the souls of the Chief's father and mother are supposed to take up their abode. A white bull and ram are sacrificed—the bull for the Chief's father, the ram for his mother—and offerings (heart and kidney) are made by the Chief before the pots with some such prayer as: " I leave for thee, my father, food for thy service. Grant by thy graciousness that I and my family and my people may have plenty and prosperity, increase of children and crops, and freedom from sickness." Next day (Sunday) the offerings are removed, the spirits having eaten the soul of the food. (Not merely the spirits of the Chief's father and mother but of all his ancestors are supposed to attend.) All the senior members of the royal (Woviri) family make similar offerings on behalf of their own immediate forefathers. In the evening a feast is held in the Chief's compound, Zara Gana, Janfada, Kyafir, and Chapola attending, together with the royal daughters (no other males are present, as no males, not even the Chief's sons, are allowed to enter his compound at night).

The Chief remains in seclusion from the Saturday night until the Monday morning. During this interval he discards his trousers and dons the " bul " shirt of the Bura—a symbol of humility (compare the custom of the Sarkin Musulmi and the people of Sokoto in wearing humble attire at the Salla). Feasting and dancing are carried out from the Monday to the Thursday, the Chief giving a gift of eight cows (to the Chiefs of Gur and Gunda and the more important office-bearers).

At the beginning of the rains rites are carried out at Viyu Kusa where the royal graves are situated. The Chief of Biu attends himself with his followers, all discarding their sandals and head-gear. The graves are cleared of grass and the Chief, planting his Rum (a three-leafed) spear in the ground and casting pieces of cotton [1] on the graves, says : " I come to seek your blessing for my-self and all my country : may good fortune of every kind attend me : may my people increase and their crops and their cattle : may sickness be stayed : may we hear of evil things at a distance and not close at hand." Offerings of milk are laid on a stone (an old quern) at each grave and a white ox is sacrificed, the flesh being eaten by the custodians of the royal graveyard. During this festival all householders at Biu, whether professing Muslims or not, make similar offerings and petitions to their forefathers.

These rites closely resemble those of the South African Baronga as described by M. Junod, who notes that it is to the ancestors of the reigning Chief that prayers and sacrifices are presented when the interest of the tribe as a whole is concerned and that, as the ancestors of the Chief are worshipped on national occasions, so the ancestors of the family are worshipped on occasions of family interest. Incidentally also, among the Baronga the Chief's nails and beard are cut off and become a sort of national palladium just as the pigtail of the Pabir Chief is carefully preserved by his successors.

The Bura have no public Mambila feast, but each year at the maize harvest every Bura who has lost a father or mother selects three heads of corn, dresses them carefully, burning off the sheath, and places them on a tray which he sets by his head at night. The spirits of the dead father and mother come and eat the soul of the corn (the three heads are actually eaten by the boys of the household next day). No Bura will eat fresh corn until he has first performed these rites with the first-fruits. The Bura also make offerings and prayers at harvest at the family graves, pouring beer on the stones which mark the grave. The formula for the prayer is : " Grant that our town may have health and that evil may be heard of only at a distance, by your gracious-ness who are in the tombs and by the graciousness of Hyel and of the Chief."

Further when a Bura kills a goat he invariably lays aside the

---

[1] Cotton and benniseed play an important part in all Pabir and Bura religious rites.

M

entrails and liver as food for his forefathers. When he offers sacrifice to the indwelling spirit of a rock or tree he introduces the names of his father and mother and grandparents in making his petition : he associates Hyel and his ancestors with the spirit (Shaitan) whose abode is in the rock or tree.

The " house " (grave) of Yemta-ra-Wala is situated at Sokfwi near Limbir 14 miles north of Biu. It has a thatch covering, and is surrounded with a circle of " African myrrh " trees. Zara Gana is its custodian, and when the thatch is renewed the operation is carried out at night, for no one may look on the spot into which Yemta-ra-Wala sank. It is said that if the enclosure were removed the world would go to pieces (compare the " Muni " of the Kanuri, and the royal burial ground of the Baronga Chiefs, which is also a holy grove). Any Pabir or Bura may resort to the house of Yemta in time of need and offer a petition through the priest of Limbir, who, throwing pieces of cotton on the sacred enclosure, addresses the spirit of Yemta with a fixed formula (the Dirku and Zeila " kirari "). [1] This formula is repeated by the petitioner who also throws cotton on the grave and then makes his request. The priest then pours a little beer on a stone receptacle and sacrifices a goat which is cooked and eaten *in situ*, the priest reserving for himself the skin, head, and one shoulder.

Spiritism and Naturism.—Side by side with the cult of ancestors numerous objects or phenomena of the natural world are regarded as mysteriously divine or as the abode of an immanent spirit vaguely conceived but invested with some personality. They are collectively known as Melim [2] or Melimnga, a word which appears to be etymologically connected with the Bantu Mulungu, Milungu, Mulenga (not = a personal God as some travellers would have us believe, but rather the aggregate of spirits).

The material object worshipped may be a hill, pool, tree, or rock. As in Kordofan monoliths play a prominent part (e.g. at Shangam, Pashi, Kabura, Tabira and in the " kurti-kurti " cult of the Vina section of the Amaza clan). The cult though commonly open to all is controlled by a particular clan (and it is noteworthy that in the absence of the priest the object loses its dynamism).

The Chief of Biu makes himself responsible for the regular

---

[1] See p. 140.   [2] The Basuto use the word *melimo* for spirits.

performance of rites before certain Melim of special potency. Thus every harvest he sends a goat to Kobata for sacrifice and in spring another to Leya where the "Bulamina" rites centre round a tamarind tree. In spring also he goes to Shaha Wiyaku and there hands to the priest of Kula Ngir a he-goat, which the priest sacrifices, saying: "The Chief has brought you blood: grant us health, etc."

Every March the Chief is present at the rites of Kamji Karwa— a female dæmon apparently. Again there are the Moda Kasama rites performed each harvest near Viyu Kusa. The object of worship is a tree associated with Yemta-ra-Wala, and as the Chief pours the blood of the sacrifice on to the stone at the base of the tree he says: "You were the protector of my grandfathers and my father. Be mine also and may my people have health, peace, and prosperity." Here we see the connection between Naturism and ancestor worship—the Nature spirit being a magnified ancestor.

East of Biu there is another rock—Fela Umji—also associated with Yemta-ra-Wala, and there the Chief-elect sacrifices an ox as he goes to his coronation "baptism". Passers-by always stop here to sharpen their weapons.

In addition to the personification of natural objects we find also the personification of abstract ideas. Thus among the Bura the spirit of sickness is driven out each year. Bundles of corn are lighted and each man purges himself and his neighbour with the smoke. The ceremony is called "Al lukwa Hinara", i.e., Let it go to Hinna country!

Special powers may become associated with a particular clan (and we can see here the origin of an organized and centralized priesthood). Thus in any village-area the head of the oldest clan may perform rites every harvest on behalf not merely of his own clan but of all other clans resident in that area. But each clan may have its own cult, the clan head going down on his knees, saluting the tree or stone three times by rubbing dust up the bridge of his nose three times, and offering a chicken, beer, cotton, and benniseed. The Medalla, head of the Vina section of the Amaza, swings the chicken thrice round his head, cuts its throat, and pours the blood on the sacred tree. Among the Bandau the head of the clan provides the sacrifices but is not himself the priest. The sacred object is a pool and into this benniseed and the entrails of the sacrifice are thrown, the priest saying : " As you have cared for us in the past, so do in the future." It appeared that in some cases the head of the clan carried out the rites *solus* or attended by a boy, and that in other cases all the members of the clan (including clan daughters, but not wives) were present.

The Melim are natural objects worshipped publicly in the bush, but families and individuals protect themselves with minor objects known as "habtu" which are amulets or "fetishes", according as their efficacy is transmitted from outside or is due to the presence of an indwelling spirit.

The commonest habtu is a pot with a covering, and at the beginning and end of the dry season, or in times of stress, the family head offers a chicken to this pot for the health of his household. Benniseed is thrown back over the left and right shoulder in turn with the words, " May evil things go behind us." He then throws benniseed in front and on to the pot saying, " But may good things come in front." For this purpose a family would consist of a man and his brothers, sons, daughters, brother's children (but not sister's children or wives).

The cult passes from father to son, but an uncle would not accept the rites from his brother's son—he would in such a case obtain a habtu for himself, and his method of doing so would be as follows : He goes to some public object of worship (Melim) accompanied by the priest, and there with his offerings makes some such prayer as : " I have come to thee—thou art my father and my mother—assist me in all that I desire in life—by your graciousness may I obtain it." He then scatters the benniseed and cotton. The priest then gives him [1] a small piece of the Melim pot with which to make a pot for himself, at the same time disclosing the necessary formula. And so the man goes home and has a pot made for himself which he duly consecrates before the Melim with the sacrifice of a chicken. The dynamism of the Melim has been transferred to the pot. Incidentally we may note that any Pabir or Bura may consecrate a tree by sprinkling it with benniseed and pouring over it a libation of beer. If he has good luck the tree becomes sacred and people will approach it via the man who originally consecrated it.

There is another type of pot sacred to the Bura and known as

---

[1] Sometimes the suppliant waits for a year to test the potency of the Melim before making his habtu from that particular Melim.

Hyel Kir or " God at the head ". It has two necks, and on the body has a design which is said to represent the female pudenda. Young Bura men put this pot beside their heads at night to bring them luck, and every year at harvest and sowing make offerings (cotton is stuck on it and a chicken sacrificed). The owner, with his most trusted friend, drinks beer ceremonially from the pot, and when he dies the pot is buried with him. A specimen of this remarkable pot was obtained.

Habtu Pwapu is a striking representation in iron of a snake (*pwapu* means " snake ") which is commonly seen in houses. Or it may be attached to the leg as an amulet. In the houses they may be seen set in pairs (male and female) in the shell of a baobab nut. They are said to ward off evil influences and appear to have a fertility significance. Their custodians are women, but every householder must at harvest offer benniseed and cotton and the blood of a chicken to his Habtu Pwapu, otherwise one of his household will be bitten by a snake. It may be noted here that the figure of the serpent appears as a personal or house-protecting amulet all through Egyptian history. A specimen of a Habtu Pwapu was obtained.

Conception of the Soul.—A few details only were obtained of beliefs relating to the personality. The conception of the multiple soul is widespread among both tribes, and we have seen that the ghost of a dead man may reappear on earth (at the Mambila festival). His " soul " may be reincarnated. A woman who keeps bearing children who die will come to the conclusion that it is the same soul that is being reborn and will cut off the ear of the last child who has died, in order to deter the soul from again seeking reincarnation. It was stated by a priest that a man's soul is about 2 feet high and resembles the man in every way. A man who dies normally takes his soul to Lahira, but the soul of a man who is killed by lightning has to be destroyed by certain rites.

Both the Pabir and Bura share the belief (common in West Africa, Melanesia, and elsewhere) in the bond which may exist between a man and an animal, the welfare of the one being dependent on the welfare of the other, so that if the animal counterpart dies the man dies also. The animal kinsfolk may not therefore be shot at or molested.

Thus the royal clan of the Woviri and the Lasama and Amaza Bura clans believe themselves, and are believed by others, to be associated with the crocodiles of Tilla, a lake occupying a volcanic crater, 7 miles south of Biu. The belief takes the form common elsewhere in West Africa of the " bush soul", i.e. each member of the above clans believes that his external soul is deposited in a particular crocodile.[1] It did not appear that the crocodiles were regarded as soul animals, i.e. as embodying or being actually the souls of the dead, nor that the Chief went through any ceremony by which his soul was deposited in a particular crocodile for safe-keeping (see *Golden Bough*, iii, 407, and *J.R.A.I.* xx, 13). There is not apparently any ceremony for procuring the crocodile as a tutelary genius (another common African custom),[2] nor yet do the members of the above clans appear to change into crocodiles (as is recorded of some Calabar tribes). The Pabir and Bura belief is exactly that recorded (*Golden Bough*, abr. ed., p. 686) of the people of Eket in North Calabar where there is a sacred lake, the fish of which are carefully preserved because the people believe that their own souls are lodged in the fish and that, with every fish killed, a human life would be simultaneously extinguished. " In the Calabar river not many years ago there used to be a huge old crocodile popularly supposed to contain the external soul of a Chief who resided in the flesh at Duke Town." And so at Tilla the external soul of the Chief of Biu is deposited in a crocodile, and when the Chief is seized by fatal illness his crocodile is believed to leave the water and betake himself to the shrine at

[1] The Zidi—a Bura clan—also believe that their souls reside in crocodiles. One of the Shalumbi stated that his Shangur (soul or shadow) resided in a hyena, and that when, a few days previously, his neighbour's dog had been killed by a hyena he knew that it was he who had killed the dog, for he woke up in the morning with a sense of fullness in his stomach !

[2] The belief in the bush soul is no doubt connected with, if it is not the direct consequence of, the practice of procuring animals as tutelary genii, an interesting example of which was given me by the head of the Shalumbi (Bura) clan. He had eight brothers all of whom died, and so his father, fearing he would have no one to bury him, took his sole surviving son to a family in Kilba who could ally men to protecting animals by certain magic rites. He was made to sit down on an axe and a brass image was set against his back. His feet were enclosed in a leather bag, and beside him a pot, with some concoction in it, was placed. The liquid was stirred and from the froth was taken a small animal that typified the larger animal who was to become the lad's tutelary genius. Thus if the tutelary genius desired was a crocodile, the typical animal taken from the froth would be a lizard. A small harmless snake represented the python, a rat with skin of the same colour as a lion represented a lion, and so on. As soon as the animal appeared from the froth its good or evil disposition was tested. If it ate the goat-dung laid near the pot it was killed, as it would bring evil on the person associated with it. If its disposition was good it would climb on to the back of the man with whom it was to be associated. He took the animal home with him and it was supposed to turn into the larger animal which it typified. The priest made the man promise that he would not use his alliance with the animal for any evil purpose. A man can be associated with several animals at one time.

Gar Limbwar where the Kadala, who is priest of the Tilla rites, goes to him and sprinkling him with benniseed, says : " By your leaving the water we know that there is illness, but by the grace of God let not the ' pigtail ', i.e. royal office, fall to the ground and be taken by someone else." Word is sent to the Birma at Biu that the Chief's crocodile has come out of the water, and the Birma, knowing that the Chief is at the point of death, sends a gift of salt to the Kadala and a winding-sheet in which the crocodile is buried on the top of Gar Limbwar hill, care being taken that no earth touches the corpse. It is only the Chief's crocodile which will in this way betake itself to the sacred grove.

But it has already been said that every member, male and female, of the royal clan, as well as of the clans of the Lasama and Amaza, has his or her crocodile *alter ego* in Tilla Lake. The story of the origin of this association is given as follows. When Yemta-ra-Wala came from Birnin Ngasr-Gamo and was sitting down at Limbir he ordered the Chief of Taula to build a village beside " a big open space " which he had seen. And so the Lasama clan came and settled there together with the Bwola. Suddenly one night the waters rose in the open space and the place became a lake. The Chief of Taula called the men of Bwola and said, "Come and see this extraordinary thing—what can you see inside—are there frogs or fish ? " The men of Bwola could see nothing, so the priestly clan of Lasama was summoned. They planted their divining-rods by the water's edge and went off for the night. When they returned next morning they found a number of crocodiles on the banks and these were proclaimed by the Chief of Taula to be the children and relatives of Yemta-ra-Wala. Thereafter the Chiefs of Biu might not look on the lake, for if they set eyes on their crocodile double they would fall sick. The taboo extended also to all male members of the Woviri who, if they had to pass the lake, kept wiping their bodies with pieces of cotton which they cast behind their backs—a sympathetic rite designed to wipe away the disease that would otherwise assail them. (Among the Ba-Kuena of South Africa the crocodile is sacred and the sight of a crocodile is supposed to cause inflammation of the eyes.)

The crocodile " cult " is common among the Volta peoples of the Gold Coast, and in Nigeria is found at Wukari, and numerous other places. There are " sacred " crocodiles at Musawa (Katsina Division) before whom natives and strangers make petitions and offerings of meat, money, etc. The father of the family is at present

Dan Datijo and to him women offer prayers for fertility. These crocodiles, like those at Wukari, live in small caves surrounding a shallow pond in which people bathe without fear. They come out at night scavenging through the town, but do not interfere with domestic animals. The crocodiles of Musawa are well fed (perhaps because a hungry crocodile would be an unpleasant neighbour !).

In ancient Egypt it was the practice to feed the crocodiles associated with the god Souchos (Sebek), who was himself believed to take crocodile shape.

The sacred lake of Tilla occupies the crater of a volcano with a diameter of ½ to ¾ mile. It offers a remarkable parallel to the two lakes of Deriba (Darfur) described by Mr. MacMichael in his *History of the Arabs in the Sudan*, vol. i, p. 111. These two lakes, he says, lie at an altitude of 4,704 feet above sea-level. One of the lakes is salt, and the other contains fresh water ; one is known as the male and the other as the female (Tilla is known as the female and her husband is Tanga Hill). One of the lakes forms the centre of a large crater, and is 1,550 yards long by 900 broad. There is no outlet of any kind unless it be a subterranean one. This lake, he says, is regarded with much superstition and fear by the inhabitants of Jebel Marra to whom its mystic properties are well known. The Fur of the Jebel say it is haunted, regard it as an oracle, and ask it questions.

Tilla is similarly regarded with awe, not merely by the Woviri, Lasama, and Amaza clans, but by all Pabir, Bura, and neighbouring tribes. Every six years rites are performed at Tilla by the Kadala of the Lasama for the general welfare of the people, the Chief of Biu providing the sheep, ram, grain, benniseed, and cotton required by the ritual. The Kadala goes to the banks of the lake with the members of the Lasama all carrying the staves [1] characteristic of

---

[1] The Kadala's staff is made of iron and is shaped thus :—

The staves of the other members of the clan are made of the African ebony and may have two, three, or four prongs, on which pieces of cotton are stuck during the performance of religious rites.

this priestly clan. They pile their staves at the banks of the lake and the priest taking the benniseed and sprinkling it towards the lake and on the sacrificial stone, says: " We come to thee, Tillayimi, Tillayawa (' water of Tilla, Tilla the giver of birth '—Tilla being considered the great mother, bearer of all the children of Pabir and Bura) grant us increase, may our fields bear fruitfully and all the world be filled with prosperity." The priest (Kadala) then kills the sheep, and twice again scatters benniseed and cotton round the sacrificial stone beside which is laid a calabash of pounded grain. They then retire, taking with them the sheep, (certain parts of which only (liver, etc.) are eaten by the seniors, the rest being cut up and given to juniors and strangers. The following year the same rites are performed, the only difference being that a cow is used instead of a sheep.

Those afflicted with sunstroke, hysteria, epilepsy, and insanity are taken to the priest of the Lasama at Tilla for treatment. The rites are performed on a Saturday and all the senior Lasama are present. They climb to the sacred grove on Gar Limbwar hill and there deposit the goat brought by the sick man's relatives. Then all descend to the water's edge, and there the priest, with offerings of benniseed and bitter tomatoes, addresses the lake saying : " I have brought this man—an evil spirit follows him to destroy him. But you spirits who are in the lake kill this evil spirit or drive him out." A young man takes the patient's right hand and another his left and they plunge him into the water, swimming by his side and continually ducking him. The priest directs the proceedings from the shore. They then return to Gar Limbwar, put the goat on the shoulders of the patient, and go to a distance and watch the pair. The priest then orders one of his men to catch the goat and kill it. The evil spirit is believed to enter the goat and be destroyed when the goat is killed. One shoulder, one thigh, the head and skin are given to the priest (with nine rolls of cloth) and the rest of the goat is eaten *in situ*. It may be noted that the custom of transferring sickness to a goat is practised among the Kaffir tribes of South Africa[1] and that the Jewish rite of sending a goat into the wilderness laden with the sins of the people is practised in West Africa.[2]

When anyone is killed by lightning the rites of burial and purification have to be performed by the Lasama of Tilla district, who dance round the body twisting their sacred staves and

[1] See Frazer, *Golden Bough*, abr. ed., p. 540.   [2] See Burdo, *Niger*, p. 182.

beating drums. The priest (the Kadala) goes with four of the dead man's relatives to the corpse, and says : "Dead body, what did you do that Hyel has killed you ? " The reply comes back : " Here is the evil that I did—I took (or intended to take) the soul out of the crops or fertility from such and such a woman." A place where a hole had been made in the ground by lightning is selected as the burial ground, and all the burial rites are performed by the Lasama. The relatives of the dead man are purified by lying down and being covered with leaves and ashes.

Seven days later the ceremony of destroying the dead man's evil spirit is carried out. The Lasama assemble at the dead man's haunts and there dance and toss up in the air a goat which, as it falls, is caught on the sacred staves. Suddenly one of the Lasama espies the wicked soul and catching it wraps it in grass and deposits it in the dead man's grave. The fee paid to the Lasama for these services is one goat, fourteen strips of cloth, and a beer feast.

Death and Burial.—When the Pabir Chief falls ill he is attended by the Kwatam, his official sister, who alone is present at his death. When this occurs the members of the royal household are collected by the Birma and a guard is placed over the palace. The Pukuma and Kwatam alone may touch the dead body of the Chief. The fencing round the compound is smashed (compare the Bede custom). The Chief-elect is brought by the Birma and is led round the corpse three times. A cow is killed and the body of the Chief is wrapped in the skin (also a Bantu custom, e.g. among the Warundi). Next day another cow is killed and a fresh skin is put on the body, the old one being removed, and so on for seven days, the idea being to delay putrefaction. The body is not apparently buried in a cow's skin (as stated by Major Edgar) but in a gown and wearing a red hat. The grave is shaped thus :—

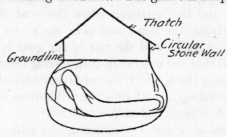

The body is buried in a sitting position, a slab of iron being put under the buttocks and Y-shaped props being placed under the arms, knees, and back of neck. The grave is circular and has a recess to receive the feet. Charcoal is sprinkled freely in the grave and over the body as a protection against termites. The body is covered with numerous gowns and an iron pot is put over the head. On the surface the grave is marked by a circular wall of stones and mud, and the whole is covered over with a protection of thatch.

The following is a description of the burial rites of a Bura girl. As the dead body lay in the hut the mother performed a dance of grief and chanted a funeral dirge. Other relatives sat round in front of the compound watching the mother. Meanwhile men from the village were digging the bottle-shaped grave, the opening being just large enough to admit the body (feet first). It took ten men four hours to dig the grave which was $3\frac{1}{2}$ feet deep and about 2 feet in diameter. The men then dispersed and the body, wrapped in native cloth, was carried by a villager in his arms to the grave. The brothers of the girl followed close behind, no women coming to the grave. The body was lowered by two men into the grave feet first, some little difficulty being experienced as the protruding arms of the deceased barred progress. The body was laid flat, and a small gourd of oil was placed in the grave. The girl's ornaments had not been removed. The grave was sealed with a stone, the brothers of the girl plastering the edges of the stone with lumps of mud mixed with grass. This was to prevent any loose earth falling on the corpse. The loose earth was then filled in on the top and a stick was set up to mark the centre of the grave, which seven days later would be smeared with mud and surrounded by a stone circle, the interstices being blocked up with mud, and an opening being left for rain-water to escape. One brother threw round the stick four handfuls of loose earth taken from North, South, East, and West—a rite similar to that observed among the Ngizim. The axe-head used in digging was removed and put in a flame to purge the pollution of death. The handle was left lying across the grave.

The grave was shaped thus in section :—

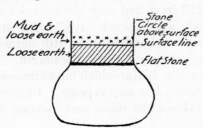

Lustration rites (*pirtua*) are performed on the second or third day after burial, according as deceased was a male or female. The rites of finally plastering over the top of the grave and surrounding it with a stone circle seven days after burial are known as Hir Kula. At the end of a month or two the Kuri Towa rites are performed to mark the conclusion of the mourning. Beer is made and goats are killed. Some of the beer and meat is laid aside for the deceased. Then, when he is supposed to have repleted himself, all take their calabashes and divide the food and drink. Dancing is kept up until next morning. The dead man's friend then takes an amulet —a *habtu pwapu* (snake) or a *mufil* (blacksmith's hammer), and placing it on the head of each wife and child of the deceased, says : " Say not that you are husbandless or fatherless and thereby live in fear of witchcraft, for this amulet will destroy all witchcraft and evil." (Death is ascribed to witchcraft, and a Bura suspected of causing death by witchcraft had to undergo the cactus ordeal described elsewhere.) The dead man's friend then invites all who have claims against the deceased's estate to state them, otherwise he will close them down by striking the amulet.

The dead are buried in a burial ground common to the whole village, each kindred having its own section. But children are buried inside the compound. Graves are not, as among the Hona and other neighbouring tribes, used more than once. The Bura do not subsequently remove the skulls of old people, a custom which is almost universal among the pagan tribes to the South.

Oaths and Ordeal.—Self-imprecatory oaths may be sworn on any of the sacred objects known as Melim (see page 162). The swearer accompanied by the priest stands (or squats if the sacred object is small) in front of the Melim. The priest, throwing benniseed and cotton on the object, says : " This man has come before thee ; if with truth may he have health ; if with falsehood may the evidence of his falsehood be seen on his body within seven days." The swearer then lays his hands on the sacred object saying, " If I have lied may the evidence of any falsehood be seen on my body within seven days." If he has falsely sworn and is overtaken by sickness he may still obtain absolution by going again to the priest and confessing his sin. The priest takes him once more to the Melim which he addresses, saying : " This man told lies hitherto, but now repents. Pursue him no more." The priest then takes some flour, and, putting it in his mouth, spits it over the object before which the repentant person sits with his hands extended to his toes.

The milk of the *Euphorbia Barteri* was the commonest medium for ordeal purposes both among the Pabir and Bura. The Pabir ordeal was conducted generally at Kubala. Among the Bura there were numerous centres. There was an attendant priest—the particular euphorbia used being consecrated by regular offerings. The priest (in a witchcraft case) addresses the euphorbia, saying : " Here is one who has come to drink of you : if he has eaten the flesh of man, let him not pass your roots but die in front of you. But if he has no witchcraft may he vomit and go home in his strength, and his people rejoice in him." The priest then cuts the euphorbia branch with a knife (the knife and a fee of one strip of cloth are brought by the person undergoing the ordeal). The milky juice is smeared on a piece of straw. The man licks it and says : "If I know the flesh of man, and have of will eaten it, may I die here and now." He swallows the juice. The priest has also made a mixture of the juice with water (into which no doubt he introduces an emetic when he thinks fit) [1] and he gives three draughts of this to the swearer who is then made to cross fire, this being supposed to add to the potency of the euphorbia juice. If he is guiltless he vomits and goes home where he is given chicken soup as a sedative and is acclaimed by his friends. Having himself undergone the ordeal he can call on anyone else to prove similarly that he had not caused the dead man's death.

Another form of cactus ordeal which is commonly employed in cases of theft or adultery or for ascertaining the paternity of a child is as follows : The suspected person who offers to undergo the ordeal has his eye-brow smeared, first with some moist earth and then with cactus juice. A piece of straw is stuck on over the juice and the swearer sits thus the whole day. At sunset the presiding official brings a calabash of water and says: "If you have lied may it remain on your brow, but if you have spoken the truth may it become three thorns." The swearer then puts his head into the calabash of water and waggles it about, the official beating the back of his neck with a switch of grass. If the straw patches come off he is guiltless and three thorns (for a woman four) will be found in the calabash ; if not he is guilty and will be punished.

[1] The emetic effects may, however, be dependent on the strength of the mixture.

Schedule of Words and Phrases

Bura

1.	Head	kir	kir̃
2.	Hair	shishir kir	ʃi ʃir̃ kir̃
3.	Eye	ncha	ntʃa
	Two eyes	nchi sūdă	ntʃi suɗa
4.	Ear	Hlim	ɬim
	Two ears	hlim suda	ɬim suɗa
5.	Nose	kuchir	kutʃir
6.	One tooth	hyer or hiir duku	hjɛr or hjiir duku
	Five teeth	hyer ntafu	hjɛr ntʌfu
7.	Tongue	kengyɛr	kɛŋjɛr
8.	Neck	wulya	wuʎa
9.	Breast (woman's)	uwa	uʔwa
10.	Heart	dafu	dəfu
11.	Belly	busu (or kuta)	busu (or kuta)
12.	Back	hili	hili
13.	Arm	tsi	tsi
14.	Hand	tsi	tsi
	Two hands	tsi suda	tsi suɗa
15.	Finger	kulyang	kuʎaŋ
	Five fingers	kulyang tufu	kuʎaŋ tʌfu
16.	Finger nail	mpil	kuʎaŋ mpil
17.	Leg	sil	sil
18.	Knee	bunji	bundʒi
19.	Foot	sil	sil
	Two feet	sil suda	sil suɗa
20.	Man (person)	mda	mda
	Ten people	imji kuma	imdʒi kuma
21.	Man (not woman)	sal	sal
	Two men	shil suda	ʃil suɗa
22.	Woman	mwala	mwala
	Two women	mwanki suda	mwanki suɗa
23.	Child	bzir	bzir
24.	Father	tida	təda
25.	Mother	mama	məma
26.	Slave	mafa	mafa
27.	Chief	kuhli	kuɬi
28.	Friend	pazhi	paʒi
29.	Smith	ya dla or yaha	ja dla or jaha
30.	Doctor	yaha or imdir kuzugu	jaha imdir kuzugu
31.	One finger	kulyang duku	kuʎaŋ duku
32.	Two fingers	kulyang suda	kuʎaŋ suɗa
33.	Three fingers	kulyang makir	kuʎaŋ makir
34.	Four fingers	kulyang fwar	kuʎaŋ fwar
35.	Five fingers	kulyang tufu	kuʎaŋ tʌfu
36.	Six fingers	kulyang kwa	kuʎaŋ kwa

37.	Seven fingers	kulyang murfa	kuʌaŋ murfa
38.	Eight fingers	kulyang chisu	kuʌaŋ tʃɪsu
39.	Nine fingers	kulyang imla	kuʌaŋ ɪmla
40.	Ten fingers	kulyang kuma	kuʌaŋ kuma
41.	Eleven fingers	kulyang kum nyang tang	kuʌaŋ kum njaŋ taŋ
42.	Twelve fingers	kulyang kum nyang suda	kuʌaŋ kum njaŋ suɗa
	Thirteen fingers	kulyang kum nyang makɪr¯	kuʌaŋ kum njaŋ makɪr
43.	Twenty fingers	kulyang sir kumari	kuʌaŋ sɪr¯ kumari
44.	A hundred fingers	kulyang aru	kuʌaŋ aru
45.	Two hundred fingers	kulyang aru suda	kuʌaŋ aru suda
46.	Four hundred fingers	kulyang aru nfwar	kuʌaŋ aru nfwar
47.	Sun	chi	tʃi
48.	Moon	hliya	ɬija
	Full moon	mbulir hliya	mbulɪr ɬija
	New moon	hadda sata	hadda sata
49.	Day	chi or bukchi	tʃi or buktʃi
	Night	viri	viri
	Morning	didipa	dɪdɪpa
50.	Rain	yimi or yimir hyel	jimi or jimɪr hjɛl
51.	Water	yimi	jimi
52.	Blood	mamshi	mamʃi
53.	Fat	malkum	malkum
54.	Salt	una	una
55.	Stone	pyela	pjela
	Iron	lea	lea
56.	Mill	gar	gar
57.	River	hyaha or manda	hjaha or manda
58.	Road	lagu	lagu
59.	House	mba	mba
	Two houses	mba suda	mba suɗa
	Many houses	mbayiri	mbajiri
	All the houses	shanga mbayiri	ʃaŋa mbajiri
60.	Roof	kirambwa	kɪrambwa
61.	Door	nyarmbwa	njarmbwa
62.	Mat	sirpi	sɪrpi
63.	Basket	hlambila or siskhiu	ɬambɪla or sɪsɪxu
64.	Drum	ganga	gaŋga
65.	Pot	tuwum	tuwum
66.	Knife	inla	ɪnla
67.	Spear	mwasu	mwasu
68.	Bow	lali	lali
69.	Arrow	afa	afa
	Five arrows	afantufu	afan tʌfu
70.	Gun	binduku	binduku
71.	War	lira or mpa	lɪra or mpa

72.	Meat (animal)	kum	kum
73.	Elephant	chiwar	tʃiwar
74.	Buffalo	fur	fur
75.	Leopard	tunvwa	tunvwa
76.	Monkey	chandum	tʃandum
77.	Pig	gadu	gadu
78.	Goat	kwi	kwi
79.	Dog	kila	kɪla
80.	Bird	dika	dika
	Feather	shishir dika	ʃiʃir dika
81.	Parrot	aku	aku
82.	Fowl	tika	tɪka
83.	Eggs	hlihli ayiri	ɬiɬi ajiri
84.	One egg	hlihli duku	ɬiɬi duku
85.	Snake	pwapu	pwapu
86.	Frog	hwomba	hwɔmba
87.	Spider	titau	tətəu
88.	Fly	chiri	tʃiri
89.	Bee	chir muma	tʃir muma
	Honey	muma	muma
90.	Tree	fwa	fwa
	Ten trees	fwa kuma or fwayiri kuma	fwa kuma or fwajiri kuma
91.	Leaf	hlali	ɬali
92.	Banana	ayaba	ajaba
93.	Maize	pinau	pɪneu
94.	Ground nut	hwada	hwada
95.	Oil	mal	mal
96.	The tall woman	mwala sabil	mwala sabɪl
	The tall women	mwanki or mwan-keyiri sabil	mwanki or mwan-kwɛjiri sabil
97.	Large dog	kazim kila or kila walaka	kazɪm kɪla or kɪla walaka
98.	Small dog	kuturu kila or kila kuturu or kila fɪlɪnga	kuturu kɪla or kɪla kuturu or kɪla fɪlɪŋa
99.	The dog bites	kila tsa na kalha	kɪla tsa na kalha
100.	The dog bites me	kila tsa ta kalha (or kila tsa ta kigalla)	kɪla tsa tə kalha (or kɪla tsa tə kigalla)
101.	The dog which bit me yesterday	kila na kalle nakhani	kila na kalla naxani
102.	I flog the dog	i ka tsa kila	i kə tsa kɪla
103.	The dog which I have flogged	kila na ti itsa	kila na ti ɪtsa
104.	I see him⎱ I see her⎰	i (or ik) wutu ni	i (or ɪk) wutu ni
	He sees you	tsa wutu nga, or tsak ka wutu nga	tsa wutu ŋga, or tsak kə wutu ŋga
	He sees us	tsa wutu mburu	tsa wutu mburu
	We see you (pl.)	yar ka wutu giri	jar kə wutu giri

We see them	yar [1] wutu da or mbur [2] ka wutu da	jar wutu da or mbur kə wutu da
105. Beautiful bird	dika daku	dika daku
106. Slave	mafa	mafa
My slave	mafarna	mafarna
Thy slave	mafarnga	mafarnga
Our slaves	mafarmburu	mafarmburu
107. The Chief's slave	mafar kuhli	mafar kuɫi
His slave	mafarni	mafarni
108. We see the slave	yar wutu mafa ne, or mbur ka wutu mafa	jar wutu mafa ne, or mbur kə wutu mafa
109. We call the slave	yar kiga mafa ne, or mbur ka ga mafa	jar kiga mafa ne, or mbur kə ga mafa
110. The slave comes	mafa ata si	mafa atə si
111. He came yesterday	tsa ki si naha	tsa ki si naha
He is coming today	tsa ta si ashina	tsa tə si aʃɪna
He will come tomorrow	tsa ta si dipa	tsa tə si dipa
112. The slaves go away	mafayiri ka tira	mafajiri kə tɪra
113. Who is your Chief?	wan kuhlirngiri	wan kuɫiŋɪri
114. The two villages are making war on each other	diyaiyın suda atampa kâ vwa da	dijəijın suɗa atampa kâ vwa da
115. The sun rises	chi ata sibla	tʃi atə sɪbla
The sun sets	chi ka tri	tʃi kə tri
116. The man is eating	mda ta sima	mda tə sɪma
117. The man is drinking	mda ta sa	mda tə sa
118. The man is asleep	mda ta heni	mda tə heni
119. I break the stick	i ka mboli zol ne	ɪ kə mbɔli zol ne
This stick is broken	zol ka mboli	zol kə mbɔli
This stick cannot be broken	zol ni ka gal [3] tambila	zol ni kə gʌl tambɪla
Break this stick for me	mbila a li zol ngini	mbila a li zol ŋɪni
120. I have built a house	i ka nla mbwa	ɪ kə nla mbwa
121. My people have built their houses yonder	imhirna kinla te mbwarda anda	ımdʒɪrna kənla tə mbwarda anda
122. What do you do everyday?	mi ta gana hara tadaga vır ri?	mə tə gana hara tədəgə vır ri?
I work on my farm	yata kihlir a kwa fakırna	jata kɪɫɪr a kwa fakırna

[1] Yara = "we," exclusive of the person you are addressing.
[2] mburu = "we," inclusive of the person you are addressing.
[3] gal = "refuses."

123. I am going away	iya ta tıra	iya tə tıra
I am hoeing	iya ta su<u>kh</u>wa	iya tə suxwa
I am going away to hoe	iya ta ra suxwa	iya tə ra suxwa
I am going to my farm	iya ta lukwa fakırna	iya tə lukwa fakırna
124. The woman comes	mwala ta si	mwala tə si
She is coming	tsa ta si	tsa tə si
She has come	tsak si	tsak si
The woman laughs	mwalane ata kumshi (or mwalana ta kumshi)	mwalane ata kumʃi (or mwalana tə kumʃi)
The woman weeps	mwalane ata tuwa	mwalane atə tuwa
125. I ask the woman	ik yu mwala	ık ju mwala
126. Why do you laugh ?	ga kumshi ka miri	gə kumʃi ka mıri
127. Why do you cry ?	ga tuwa ka miri (or gada tuwa ka myar miri)	gə tuwa ka miri (or gada tuwa ka mjar miri)
128. My child is dead	zirna kamti	zırna kʌmti
129. It is not dead	tsa dim tu wa	tsa dim tu wa
130. Are you ill ?	ga nga waya ?	gə ŋga waja
131. My children are ill	mdarna danga wa	mdarna daŋga wa
132. Her child is better	zirni ka hara la gomi	zırni kə hara la gomi
133. Yes	i	i
No	aʔa	aʔa
134. A fine knife	inlya daku	ınʎa daku
Give me the knife	ni ınlyaja	ni ınʎadʒa
I give you the	i ka naga inlya	i kə naga inʎa
135. I am a European	i baturi	i baturi
You are a black man	ga mdu mangil	gə mdu mʌngıl
You are a Bura	ga Bura	gə Bura
136. Name	hlım	łım
My name	hlimi	łimi
Your name	hlimaga	łimaga
What is your name ?	wa hlimagiri ?	wa łimagiri
137. There is water in the gourd	yım a kwa pıla or yimi adi a kwa kukwa	jim a kwa pıla or jimi adi a kwa kukwa
The knife is on the stone	inlyaja ata kira pyɛla	ınʎadʒa atə kıra pjɛla
The fire is under the pot	uʔu adi a kıra tuhum	uʔu adi a kıra tuhum
The roof is over the hut	mbwa tsa ka kir	mbwa tsa ka kır
138. You are good	ga daku, or gip dago	gə daku, or gıp dago
This man is bad	imdungini dimai	ımduŋıni dıməi
139. The paper is white	kakadune mwopu	kakadune mwopu

		su ngini mungil	su ŋini muŋgɪl
This thing is black			
This thing is red		su ngini mamza	su ŋini mamza
140.	This stone is heavy	pyɛla nangini kugubu	pjɛla naŋɪni kugubu
	This stone is not heavy	pyɛla nangini kugubu wa	pjɛla naŋɪni kugubu wa
141.	I write	i ga rubuti	i gə rubuti
	I give you the letter	i ka naga kakadu	i kə naga kakadu
	Carry the letter to the town	nwantu kakadu ne a kwa kuta dai	nwantu kakadu ne a kwa kuta dəi
142.	Go away	mworu	mworu
	Come here	asir azi	asɪr azi
143.	Where is your house ?	kir nga ma ri ?	kɪr ŋa ma ri
144.	My house is here	kirna azi	kirna azi
	My house is there	kirna anda	kirna anda
145.	What have you to sell ?	ga ta dil miri	gə ta dɪl mɪri
146.	I want to buy fish	i hir ka mas kilfa	i hɪr kə mas kɪlfa
147.	The fish which you bought is bad	kilfa ta ga masa na dagu wa	kɪlfa tə gə masa nə dagu wa
148.	Where is the man who killed the elephant ?	amam dina si chiwar ne ?	amam dina si tʃiwar ne
	He has killed many elephants	tsa ki tsi chiwar hang	tsa kə tsi tʃiwar haŋ
	How many elephants were killed yesterday ?	chiwar yidau antim mda chi naha ri ?	tʃiwar jɪdəu antɪm mda tʃi naha ri
149.	Untie it	mpili ni	mpɪli ni
	Tie this rope	imbwi suni, or imbwi suwa ngini	imbwi suni, or ɪmbwi suwa ŋini
	Make the boy untie the goat	vu bzirne kasa mpiri kwini, or ka bzirne mpili kwi	vu bzɪrne kasa mpɪri kwini, or ka bzɪrne mpili kwi
150.	My brothers and I, we are going but no one else	i ka bzirmarna yɛr ata tira shi yɛro	i ka bzirmarna jɛr ata tira ʃi jɛro
	Brothers let us go and tell the Chief	bzirmarna (or madamarna) ka mbur mwari aha kuhli kambur pila a la ri	bzɪrmarna (or madamarna) ka mbur mwari aha kuɫi kambur pɪla a la ri
151.	This tree is bigger than that	fwa ngini waltan daga	fwa ŋini waltan daga

Last night I was in my house with a white man ; we heard a movement outside ; he said " You hear that ; they are thieves ; let
us go and see." We went and I said, " Who are you ? " and they

answered " Nothing " ; but I said " You are thieves " ; so we called the police, and put them in prison.

naha aviri ya vi yankiya ka nasara laga ; yar ngatsu kwiya su abɪla anta tsa pila " Giring gate nginiya ; hilayiri, mwa libla kam mwa wuta." Yar libla, anti pila " Gir wa ri ? " Anti da pila " suwa " ; amma i pɪla " Gir hila " ; kam nyɛr apani (i.e. " and so ") yar kiga dogari, anti yar vuda a kwa sowa.

naha aviri ja vi jankija ka nasara laga ; jar ngatsu kwija su abɪla antə tsa pila " gɪrɪŋ gatə ŋgɪnija ; hɪlajiri, mwa lɪbla kam mwa wuta." jar lɪbla anti pila " gɪr wa ri ? " anti da pila " suwa " ; amma i pila " gɪr hɪla " ; kam njɛr apani (i.e. " and so ") jar kɪga dogari, antɪ jar vuda a kwa sowa.

PLATE 18

A MARGI MAIDEN

CHAPTER IV

The Kilba and Margi of Adamawa

The Kilba

The following notes on the Kilba were obtained as a result of a week's visit to this tribe.

The Kilba occupy the hill country to the West of Mubi, their neighbours being the Bura and Margi to the North and East, and the Hona to the West. They number about 21,000 people and are administered by the Emir of Adamawa through their own chief who acts as headman of the Kilba district. They were never conquered by the Fulani, though the latter had established an outpost at Bila Kilba, from which they used to raid at intervals the Kilba who farmed on the plains. The Kilba would sometimes at sowing give gifts to the Fulani to secure protection for their crops. But during the dry season they would in turn make raids on the Fulani cattle camps. The Kilba, however, suffered severely from the prolonged presence in their midst of the Bornu adventurer Fadr Allah in 1900. There is a considerable admixture of Fulani blood among the Kilba resulting from intermarriage with Fulani groups who from ancient times were the herdsmen of cattle owned by the Kilba.

The name Kilba was conferred by the Fulani, possibly as a corruption of the term Khibba (Xibba) by which the Kilba call themselves. There is an alternative tribal title, viz. Ndirmā, a word which means " The People of the Hills".

The Kilba speak the same language as the Margi, Chibbak, and Bura, and all four tribes may, therefore, be regarded as units of a single tribe. The Kilba, however, have difficulty in understanding the Bura and Chibbak and the more distant groups of Margi. The language, which is of a suffix type, is characterized by its extensive use of palatalization and of the voiceless "*l*". It employs two first personal plural pronouns, the one inclusive of the person addressed, and the other exclusive. There is no grammatical gender. A full schedule of words and phrases is attached.

181

Though the Kilba have a reputation for lawlessness equalled by few tribes in Nigeria, robbery, murder, and inter-village battles having been constant occurrences in the past and not uncommon during recent years, the tribe, nevertheless, has, from ancient times, recognised a central authority in the person of the chief of Hong.[1] Not merely was this chief the ultimate court of appeal, but members of his kindred acted as heads of the various local groups. The chiefs of Hong are drawn from the descendants of a group of invaders who are stated to have been of Pabir origin, and there is little reason to doubt this tradition as the installation and burial customs of the Kilba chiefs closely resemble those of the Pabir of Biu. The invaders brought with them official titles such as Hedima, Birma, and Kotam[2], which are found among the Pabir[3] (and Tera). They also introduced the doctrine of the divinity of kings which has served throughout the Sudan as a solder by which disorganized units recognising no authority save that of the kindred organization have become welded into a unified whole. The Kilba never became wholly welded together, largely because of the existence of two royal groups which constantly fought each other for the chieftainship. Nevertheless, it must be considered a remarkable phenomenon that a small group of invaders was able to establish a measure, at least, of suzerainty over a warlike people protected by hilly country, a suzerainty which the Fulani were unable to obtain throughout the period of their domination during the nineteenth century. It is noteworthy that the idea of divine chieftainship is not found among the Western neighbours of the Kilba such as the Gabin and Yungur. The chiefs of those peoples were merely rain-makers, who never claimed any administrative authority in virtue of their magico-religious powers. But among the Kilba the chief was not himself a priest—he was a divinely appointed ruler, the priests being servitors of the cults for the maintenance of which the chief held himself responsible. The system of government was, in its crude way, similar to that of the pre-Muslim Sudanic kingdoms and ultimately to that of ancient Egypt.

[1] The authority of the chief of Hong extended also to some of the Margi groups.
[2] The Kotam = the chief's official sister and is known among the Pabir as Kwatam.
[3] According to one tradition at Biu the Pabir of Biu came to Biu from Mandara via Gaya in Kilba.

The chief is known as the "til", or "ptil", a word which seems to embody the final syllable of the Pabir and Bura word *ku-tli*, and of the Tera words *kutir* or *kudil*. It is noteworthy that the name of the traditional founder of the Kilba chiefdom was Fura Kudil. The chief is chosen from one of two royal families represented by the houses of Dawi and Kashere, the first of which became identified with the Mitil area, and the latter with that of Gaya.

The choice of the chief is made by the members of a particular kindred at Hong, which is said to be of Mbula origin. The head of this kindred is known as the Hedima, a title corresponding to Kaigama among the Fulani. The Hedima is the prime minister, and is responsible also for the maintenance of the important cults of Vidigal (or Sirmilim) and Garga. The other senior officials, who are also drawn from the same kindred as the Hedima, are the Biraol (or Mijindadi), the Biratada (or Sarkin Fada), the Kadagimi (or Sarkin Zana), and the Kadafur (or Jekada). At Hong also resides the priestly family of the Killa, the senior members of which are known as the Dubukuma and Tiliihi respectively, and are the servitors of the cults of Garga and Vidigal. This family is responsible for the royal obsequies. For purposes of external government the chiefdom was formerly divided into two sections, the Mitil area being under the control of the senior member of the Mitil branch of the royal family, who resided at Uding, the Gaya area being under the senior member of the Gaya branch with headquarters at Mijili. Each of these officials bore the title of Yerima. In addition each village had a headman or "shel" who was a member of one of the two royal kindreds.

It was an understood rule that each of the royal kindreds (viz. the Mitil or Tilbang branch as it is also called, and the Gaya branch) should take it in turn to provide a chief, and any attempt to break this rule resulted in a battle between the two groups. Many battles were fought on this account as either kindred would, if strong enough, attempt to usurp the chieftainship in perpetuity, having first by bribery obtained the consent of the Hedima.

When a chief dies the Hedima immediately summons to Hong the person whom he had finally decided to nominate as successor. It may be noted that members of the royal families are not allowed to live at Hong ; they must all take up their abode in outlying villages, where the more senior amongst them act as village heads. But all keep in touch with the Hedima, sending him gifts at frequent intervals with a view to obtaining the Hedima's favour at the next election. There was in former times no interregnum at the death of the chief, the Hedima's nominee being appointed without a day's delay. When he had stepped across the dead chief's body his succession was proclaimed by beating the royal drum. The reason for this haste was to forestall, if possible, armed conflict, and also to prevent the escape of any of the late chief's wives. A wife who escaped before the beating of the drum could not be recovered. After the beating of the royal drum the Hedima tied a leather loin-covering round the new chief's waist and clothed him in a white coat and white cap. The goat-skin loin-covering was not the ordinary garment worn by men ; for it still retained the natural hair, a relic of the days when the process of removing the hair by means of acacia juice was unknown. The new chief then went into seclusion for a period of seven days, being attended by an official known as the Batari. He was not allowed to leave his hut for any purpose, and was given the scantiest of meals, consisting of unsavoured soup. Here he sat holding on his right shoulder the royal crook [1] which had been presented to him by the Hedima. On the first day he was also given seven blows with a whip by the Batari, who warned him to treat the people fairly.

It would appear that this period of seclusion symbolized a process of rebirth, for when the chief emerged at the end of seven days he acted as one who was new to the world, failing to recognize his former friends. On emerging he was ceremonially washed and shaven by the Dubukuma, a lock of hair being left on the top of his head. Into this lock was plaited the hairlock of the last member of his family who had held the chieftainship. It may be noted that the wearing of a hair-lock was practised by the kings of ancient Egypt, and that in Northern Nigeria the custom is followed among the Pabir and Jukun at the present time. The chief's leather loin-covering was removed, and he was clothed in blue trousers and gown. A blue cap shaped like a coronet was

---

[1] A crook and flail were the royal symbols in ancient Egypt. The Kilba chief was not formally presented with a flail, but one of his officials, the Kadafur, carries a three-tailed flail, the symbol of the chief's power. The crook is known as Tamba.

placed on his head, and he was told that he must never be parted from this symbol of royalty (which incidentally is always lined with charms). The chief then took up his stand in front of the shrine of Garga, and holding an iron staff in his hand spoke as follows : " I am a river of sand—if anyone takes sand from me it will do me no injury. I am a rock—if a man strikes me I shall not break. I am mist, and cloud the vision of all." On the conclusion of this speech all broke into loud shouts of joy and hailed their new chief.

The chief was regarded as a divine person, and was subject, in consequence, to numerous taboos. He might not visit the village where he had formerly resided, for if this rule were broken disaster would fall on the inhabitants. He might not engage in any agricultural work, nor was he permitted to visit any farm. He might not pick up anything from the ground lest the dynamism of his person should blast the crops. If he struck the ground in anger the people would be confounded with fear. If he shook his fist in a man's face that man would go mad. He might not receive any article from the hand of any save the official known as the Biratada. If he fell off his horse all persons riding in his company had to fall off also. The mat on which he sat was regarded as charged with divine dynamism, and no one could touch it except for the purpose of swearing an oath. The chief was not supposed to require the ordinary nourishment of mortals, and he therefore ate his food in private, attended only by the Biratada. While the chief was eating or drinking the attendant official sat with head averted, and the chief signified the conclusion of the meal by uttering a cough. The official then smoothed the ground in front of the chief in order, it is said, to cover up any of the sacred food which might have dropped on the ground. The chief's meals were cooked by an old woman past the age of menstruation. The morning meal consisted of beer taken at sunrise. The evening meal of porridge and stew was eaten at sunset, and it is said that if the cook had failed to prepare the meal before sunset the meal could not be eaten. In my monograph on the Jukun-speaking peoples of Nigeria it is suggested that the ritual meals of the Jukun king may have had some connection at one time with the cult of the Sun.[1]

[1] See *A Sudanese Kingdom*, p. 122.

The Kilba chief was not permitted to eat from a decorated calabash ; and the remnants of the food were either eaten up by the attendant official (in his capacity of priest in attendance on the god) or else were given to the chief's dogs. If any other were to eat the remnants of the chief's meal he would go mad and die. If the chief had to be absent from Hong he was surrounded by grass matting when he wished to eat or drink. No one might go near the chief's lavatory, and if a new lavatory were required it had to be prepared by a particular family to whom this special duty was delegated. Such were the ancient rules of Kilba chieftainship, but few of them are observed at the present time. They are the rules still observed by the kings of the Jukun.

It does not appear that apart from the ritual eating of meals the Kilba chief of Hong ever performed daily religious rites. But it is stated that in former times the chief and the Hedima were responsible for the lighting of a fire every day at sunset in the shrines of Garga and Vidigal, this duty being delegated to the priestly officials known as Dubukuma and Tiliihi. With this we may compare the Baganda custom of maintaining a sacred fire within the precincts of the royal palace. The daily custom is no longer observed, but a fire is still lit in the shrine of Vidigal at the annual rites which precede the sowing of crops, and also on the evening following the death of a chief, the chief's body being deposited that night in the shrine of Vidigal. Garga has no longer a separate hut, the symbols of the cult being deposited under a large pot which is not protected from the weather. Vidigal and Garga, who are regarded as male and female deities, are together believed to be the custodians of the health and prosperity of the people, and the protectors and ripeners of the crops. The symbols of Vidigal are a number of iron implements, such as are used by blacksmiths, a number of hoes and of iron models of horsemen. Those of Garga are two iron smithing instruments, and seven of the crescent-shaped iron adornments which all women wear over the pubes, and which may, therefore, be regarded as symbols of fertility. Rites are performed at sowing to both deities, a he-goat being sacrificed and the blood sprinkled over the symbols. The skin, liver, and viscera of the goat are deposited before the symbols, but the flesh is eaten ceremonially by members of the Killa kindred who are the officiants of both cults. Rites are also performed on occasions of prolonged stoppage of rain at any time during the agricultural season when rain is necessary for the crops. Goats are provided by the chief and the Hedima for sacrifice, and the priest and six members of the Killa kindred also chew some corn and spit the corn out over the symbols, the priest offering a prayer for rain. The flesh of the goat is cooked and eaten ceremonially by all the senior members of the priestly kindred. Similar rites are carried out in cases of epidemics, such as smallpox.

The spirits of Vidigal and Garga are believed to pervade the whole country of the Kilba, and to be centred particularly in the persons of the priests and of the chief. It is, therefore, in the interests of all that the peace of mind of these human personages shall not be disturbed, and if a drought occurs the priests of the cult may ascribe the drought to the inconsiderate behaviour of certain individuals. In such cases the chief acts as arbiter, and apologizes to the priests for the conduct of the persons concerned. The divine spirits are also believed to rest on the head of the chief; and for this reason no one in former times might shave the head of the chief, save the Dubukuma. This is the reason assigned, but it is well known that the fear of black magic is also a reason for the precautions taken in safeguarding the shaven hair of any royal personage.

The burial rites accorded to the chief differ wholly from those observed for commoners. A chief, unlike an important commoner, is buried without delay on the morning of the day following his death. The body is washed, clothed in three or four gowns, and laid overnight in the shrine of Vidigal.[1] Next day it is laid in a flagon-shaped grave sitting on a stool set on a rug. The feet rest on another stool and the head rests against a cushion placed between the head and the wall of the grave. The left arm, holding the royal knife, is supported in an upright position by a piece of iron, the right arm being left extended at the side. The late chief's shield is cut in half, and one half is placed under each buttock. The legs are protected by two leather flaps. The body is then completely covered with charcoal prepared by the late chief's sons-in-law. A brass plate is placed over the head of the

---

[1] The intention in depositing the chief's body in the shrine is to bear witness to the god that the chief is dead.

corpse and is kept in position by a layer of loose earth. The shaft or narrow entrance to the grave is blocked by a large pot, turned upside down, a hole being made in the base of the pot, presumably with the idea of permitting the egress of the chief's soul. This custom also permits the ingress of rain; and it is noteworthy that the Kilba do not follow the Pabir custom of erecting a shelter over the grave. The chief's favourite dog is killed and buried beside him, and after the interment of the chief a cow is killed, and the meat is used to provide a meal for all the male and female relatives of the chief. A seven days funeral feast is held, accompanied by dancing and a liberal supply of beer during the last three days (the beer having taken four days to prepare). It will have been noted that the number seven recurs in all ceremonies connected with the Kilba chiefs, and seven is also a sacred number among the Pabir, who also bury the chief in a sitting position covered with charcoal. It is not a Kilba custom to place corn in the hand of the dead chief (as among the Hona, Gabin, Yungur, and Kilba commoners), nor is it the custom to make a post-burial effigy of the chief and throw over it seeds of the various crops. The chief's skull is not subsequently removed (as among the Gabin and Yungur), and it is said that if the Kilba chief's grave were reopened drought would assail the land. No regular rites are subsequently performed at the graves of Kilba chiefs but one year after interment a he-goat, taken from the late chief's estate, is sacrificed over the grave, the meat being cooked and eaten by all members of his family. This rite appears to have the purpose of dispatching to the chief the property that was his, and when this has been done it becomes legitimate to divide without prejudice his estate amongst his heritors. It was stated that if the rite were not performed the chief's ghost would haunt all those who had shared in his estate.

All Kilba chiefs are buried on the top of a hill at Hong, and all male members of the royal family must also be buried on the same hill a little lower down. This rite is applied to the senior daughters of chiefs, but not apparently to junior daughters.

Turning now to the system of government it does not appear that the doctrine of divine chieftainship entailed extensive centralization of government. The Kilba local units were much too warlike and independent to allow any excessive interference in their own affairs. Each unit selected a member of one of the royal kindreds as a local authority, but if this personage failed to meet their requirements they turned him out and appointed some other member of the royal family. These local royalties were known as " shel ", and to them were referred by the inhabitants all disputes which could not be settled by the local kindred organization. Any matter which proved to be beyond the competence of the shel was referred to the Yerima or ultimately to the central chief of Hong. The shel was thus the local arbiter, the chief of Hong being the final court of apppeal. But the shel was by no means a king within his own domain, for he was only permitted to adjudicate on such matters as the local inhabitants chose to refer to him. Thus in cases of homicide there was no reference to the shel. The people followed the ancient custom by which the kindred which had lost a member through the culpable action of a member of another kindred sought reparation by slaying a member of the other kindred. There was no question (as among many other tribes) of paying compensation. A life taken deliberately could only be atoned for by the deliberate taking of a life. It was the business of the brother or son of the murdered man to kill a member of the murderer's family, and when he had carried out this duty he returned home and made a pretence of weeping. But the women ululated with joy. In cases of accidental homicide, such as might occur during hunting, the matter was regarded as being on a different plane. The homicide brought home the body of the man whom he had accidently killed and he provided the gown for burial. He was required to do this by the local shel who also called together the two families and pointed out that the homicide was not to blame. Nevertheless the shel required that compensation should be paid, and this was done by a gift of a girl to the brother of the man who had been killed. When the girl had borne a male child this child was regarded as the equivalent of the dead man, and the girl was then at liberty to return to her own family if she so desired. The central chief was not concerned in the matter at all, though he might be referred to on any point of detail in which the shel's decision had failed to give satisfaction.

Similarly in quarrels over the division of an estate the members of the kindred concerned would refer the matter to the shel, or ultimately to the chief of Hong. The shel would normally conclude the matter himself, and require the contestants to swear

friendship on the " shafa " (or family cult) that they would
abandon hostility. He would also make them shake hands in
western fashion. In cases of affray the shel might be called
upon to adjudicate, and might order the aggressor to be
publicly beaten.

There was no regular form of taxation. When the local shel
was appointed he was given numerous gifts, and at harvest those
who felt inclined might present him with a basket of corn.

Similarly, the central chief of Hong was unable to exact any
annual levy, but he was given numerous gifts by the local
inhabitants, and also by the shels of outlying villages, as well as by
members of those villages who wished to prefer any suit. The
central chief could also call on the warriors of outlying villages to
enforce his will on some area which had defied his authority. But
normally his own bodyguard of slaves was sufficient for the
purpose of effecting arrests. Cases of witchcraft were settled by
appeal to the sasswood ordeal, but persons believed to be poisoners
or to be guilty of murder by projecting needles into the bodies of
their enemies were sent to the chief of Hong, who had them
publicly executed in the market-place by his slaves, the method
of execution being by clubbing.

It is to be noted that among the Kilba a conviction of witchcraft entailed no consequences on members of the convicted
person's family (as, e.g. among the Jukun).

In addition to the sasswood ordeal the Kilba were accustomed
to refer matters which called for a divine decision (e.g. suspected
cases of theft) to the test of crossing a pool at Wuba in the territory
of the Margi tribe. This pool is believed to be tenanted by a
spirit known as Guti who prevents the passage of a guilty man.
Such a person becomes paralysed when half-way across, and is
unable to move until his opponent in the case calls out to Guti to
release him, saying : " He is my slave, let him go." The man had
then to admit the charge and pay the necessary compensation.

Minor matters of dispute might be settled by self-imprecatory
oaths, the medium being usually a bundle of leaves enclosing an
arrow and surrounded by grass, and known as " shafa ". Every
householder owns a " shafa", which is regarded as a tutelary deity
and the special protector of property. Another medium for
swearing oaths is the spirit called Kurta, whose cult, symbolised
by two pieces of iron placed in a pot, is maintained by a family at

the village of Jedini. The oath is not sworn on the symbols themselves but on a chip of the sacred pot.

Religion.—The Kilba, like the Bura and Margi, call the Supreme Being " Hel " or " Hyel ". This word suggests the Semitic " El ", and it is possible that there was at one time some Semitic influence in this region of Nigeria, especially as the Bura perform all religious rites on Saturdays and claim to have used the term Shaitan [1] to describe a god of evil long before they came into contact with professors of Islam. We have already noted the constant recurrence of the number seven. On the other hand the Kilba, Bura, and Margi do not practise circumcision, though it was stated that circumcision was practised at one time by a small group of Bura. The Kilba, moreover, have no seven-day week. Hyel is regarded as the sky-god and creator, and to him prayers are directly addressed. He is not identified with the sun, and in this respect the Bura, Kilba, and Margi differ from most of the surrounding tribes.[2] I am inclined to think that Hyel was originally associated with the moon, for the word for moon is " *hya* ". Among the Chibbak Hyel is pronounced Hyal. The word may therefore mean " He of the moon " or " The lord of the moon ". No rites are performed in honour of Hyel.

The principal cults are those of Vidigal and Garga (to which reference has already been made), Ngau, and Jugumi. The two latter cults are served by a priest who lives at Pella. The symbol of Ngau is a pot containing three pebbles, and the mouth of the pot is blocked with certain sacred leaves. This pot is kept in a cave, sitting on a mound of sand. Rites are performed in times of drought, the priest sacrificing a red cock and pouring the blood over the symbols, the meat being subsequently cooked and eaten by the priest and members of his family. For the performance of the rites he must discard his gown and he may not have sexual relations the evening before. He is not permitted to eat the first-fruits of any crop until the guinea-corn crop has been finally gathered in, e.g. he may not eat of hibiscus which had been gathered in the middle of the wet season. The services of the godling are also sought by persons anxious to obtain titles, or

[1] The Kilba have no belief in Satan.
[2] The Kilba word for sun is Pichi, which contains the root " chi ", used by numerous tribes in Africa in the sense of Earth, Moon, Sun, or Supreme Being. I have suggested elsewhere that Chi or Usi (as it is frequently pronounced) is the first half of the word Osiris (i.e. of Usi-ri).

success in hunting, or a cure for leprosy. The cult of Jugumi, which is symbolized by three pots, is used similarly to that of Ngau.

At Hong there are also two other cults, one known as Lim and the other as Micheri. The former is a rain-cult symbolized by four pieces of crescent-shaped iron such as are commonly worn by women over the pubes. These are contained in a pot which is kept in a cave on a high hill, and on the occasion of a drought a ram is sacrificed, the flesh being eaten by members of the family of the Hedima who has charge of the cult. The Micheri cult is also used for obtaining rain, but the Hedima admitted that it was used for more secular purposes. Those seeking official advancement apply to the Hedima in order to obtain supernatural assistance. The Hedima suggested that some self-seekers sought to derive advantage from the cult without paying the necessary fees, i.e. they secretly visited the shrine, chipped off a piece of the sacred pot, ground it up and mixed the powder into a new pot which they fashioned for themselves !

The Kilba do not follow the custom widespread among the Gabin, Yungur, and Longuda by which every grown-up person has a sacred pottery vessel to which he transfers certain classes of diseases, the vessel taking the place of the human body as the abode of the disease-producing spirit. But the Kilba have adopted from the Bura a cult known as Katu Bura to which similar conceptions are attached. When a person is sick he employs a medicine-man to make two pots, one representing a male and the other a female spirit. The patient and medicine-man then go to the bush and sacrifice a chicken, the blood being poured over the pots. The medicine-man next takes some benniseed and circles it round the patient's head, saying : " If this disease is Katu Bura, then come forth and let this man recover." He deposits the benniseed inside the pot, before which he lays offerings of the chicken's flesh and porridge. The two men eat the remainder of the food. After these rites the pots are handed to the patient who secretes them either in his own home or under a rock in the bush. If he ever feels ill again he goes to the pots, smears them with some porridge, and transfers some of the porridge to his own body. When the owner dies the pots are smashed.

Similarly, if a child is afflicted with any nervous trouble, the mother will perform rites known as Huhwa by which the child's disease is exorcised and transferred to a pot. She makes a pot and takes it and the child to a professional exorcist, who sets before him a dish of water into which he drops a pebble. He then takes a wooden instrument to which a number of small pieces of iron are attached, and circles it round the child's head. He inserts this instrument into the dish, shaking it against the sides of the dish. The jingling noise produced is believed to be the cry made by the disease-spirit as it leaves the child.   The exorcist suddenly seizes the pebble and transfers it to the pot, blocking the mouth of the pot with the leaves which are used in the " shafa " cult. He covers the mouth of the pot with a sherd and hands the pot to the mother, who takes it home and deposits it in a cool place, with the intention of keeping the spirit contented.

The Kilba are not much given to the propitiation of ancestors. They describe the ancestral ghost as " mambil ", but they do not, like the Bura, observe an annual feast of All Souls (which the Bura call " Mambila ").   There is, however, a family cult of fore-fathers known as " Katirndo ".   This is maintained by heads of households who use as the symbol of their deceased father or paternal uncle a potsherd taken from the latter's grave. This is placed under a pot which is covered with a lid. When he sets it up the householder kills a cock, sprinkles the blood over the symbol, and shares the cooked flesh with all the members of the household.   Rites are performed before sowing or hunting or on the occasion of illness among any members of the household. In many compounds also there is a household amulet known as " katu " which consists of one or two pieces of iron placed between two potsherds. When this amulet is first set up the owner smears a red cross on the upper sherd and says : " We have received you from our forefathers that you may abide in our house, as a son abides in the house of his father. Be our protector, and if any man comes to steal during my absence do you catch that man." Oaths are sworn on these " katu ", which are also placed on farms to deter people from stealing the crops.

The Kilba have a reputation among their neighbours of being able to enter into a secret mystic relationship with certain animals by means of magical rites, the man and the animal becoming so identified that each is the *alter ego* of the other, and that what happens to the one happens simultaneously also to the other.

Similar beliefs are found among the Pabir of Biu where each member of the royal family is believed to have a crocodile counterpart in Tilla lake ; and when the man is about to die his animal counterpart may be seen coming out of the water to do likewise. Among the Kanakuru and Mbula also the belief in a twin animal soul is so strong that there is a regular totemic kindred organization, the head of the kindred being regarded as the custodian of the totem souls. In both these tribes the totem is transmitted matrilineally. Among the Kilba, however, there is no belief that when a man is born a double of himself in animal form is also born. But it is thought that a man can, by payments made to a certain class of magicians, contract an alliance with some animal which becomes his tutelary genius. The main intention of the alliance appears generally to be directed towards prolongation of life, the man being made and nourished by the food which his counterpart eats. Thus one who enters into an alliance with a lion becomes strong as a lion and is nourished by the quarry which the lion is able to obtain. When he is about to die his lion counterpart roars outside his house. One who allies himself to a crocodile lives to a great old age because crocodiles are long-lived. One who is associated with a hyena maintains his strength to the day of his death. In other cases the object appears to be to obtain the moral qualities of the animal with which he allies himself. Thus a man will identify himself with a leopard in order to obtain the leopard's bravery, and he will also have (in the leopard) a guardian of his home during his absence. He may associate himself with a baboon in order to obtain riches, because a baboon is a wily animal. He may asssociate himself with a python because a python is abstemious. Just as a python maintains his thickness, even though he may go without food for a long period, so a man associated with a python will always present a nourished appearance, even if there is a famine in the land. The inference might be drawn that totemic ideas are sometimes based on the principle of sympathetic magic, but an objection to this view would be that many " totems " do not appear to be endowed with qualities which would make a special appeal to human beings. Even among the Kilba, who allow a free choice of totems, I was unable to ascertain the reason why a man should wish to ally himself to a wart-hog, or a monitor lizard. Among the Bura the totem is frequently some species of tree. It may be, therefore, that the Kilba view is based ultimately on a system of totemic clans, the totem having been adopted for reasons which had no connection with sympathetic magic. Among the Bura a historical explanation is usually given for the kinship emblem.

It was disapppointing to find that among the Kilba, despite the prevalence of the conception that alliances with animals could be and were contracted by numerous individuals, no one could specify any individual who had contracted such an alliance or indicate any Kilba magician who was able to conclude the contract. It was stated that if a Kilba wished to obtain an animal genius he had to go outside his own country. Kofa was indicated as the source from which the Kilba were accustomed in the past to obtain the mystic relationship. A longer acquaintance with the Kilba would probably have revealed that there were a number of Kilba families which claimed the ability of providing a man with an animal guardian. This is suggested by the fact that there is a group of Kilba who claim a Mbula origin, and it is well known that all Mbula inherit a totem through the mother. The Kilba may, therefore, have obtained their conceptions from Mbula immigrants who discerned an easy way of making money by selling the family "totem". The Kilba account of the process by which the animal counterpart is obtained from Kofa corresponds exactly with that formerly given me by a Bura who said he obtained it from the Kilba. And it is worth repeating. The Bura informant stated that he had eight brothers, all of whom died. His aged father, fearing that he might have no descendant left to accord to him the customary rites of burial, took his surviving son to a Kilba magician, in order that the son might be allied to an animal by whose protection the son's life would be made secure. The lad was made to sit down on an axe, and a brass image of a man was placed against his back. His feet were enclosed in a leather bag, and beside him the magician placed a pot of some decocted liquid. This was stirred by the magician, and from the froth was taken a small animal typical of the species of animal desired. Thus if the desired animal were a crocodile a lizard would be taken from the froth ; if a lion a small rat, striped like a lion, would appear. If a python were desired a harmless snake would be produced. The disposition of the animal was tested by applying its mouth to some goat's dung laid beside the decocted liquid ; if it ate the dung it was killed, as it would bring disaster on the person with whom it was to be associated. But if it was friendly to the alliance it would refuse the dung and climb on to the back of the person who sought the alliance. This is exactly the account given by the Kilba of the Kofa procedure, but it was added that if the animal wished the alliance it micturated into the decocted liquid, which was given to the man to drink, this draught effecting the union of the man's soul with that of the animal. The typical animal was then handed over to the man [1] who was supposed to guard it secretly and feed it until it grew up into a full-blown representative of the typified species, when it was let loose to take up its abode in the bush. But despite the new-found freedom the animal visited its master's home each night and brought him food or received food. He became the friend and protector of the man. This is the normal Bura and Kilba belief, though some of the more enlightened people regard the whole thing as chicanery and nonsense. As far as I could ascertain women seldom seek alliances with animals, and, if they do, the animal chosen is always the python which is believed to confer childbirth. In fact it is thought that the woman whose counterpart is a python has sexual relations with the python. Men must always choose a male of the species sought, for it is said that if one man chooses a male and another a female the two animals will go off together and propagate and neglect their human friends. Moreover, their offspring would be liable to be killed by some human being, whereas the parent animals are protected by their human counterparts.

We may conclude this account of the religious beliefs by giving a description of the burial rites, which are of universal interest as they exhibit certain features suggestive of the mummification practices of ancient Egypt.

When any old man or woman dies the body is laid on a trestle-bed in the dead person's hut and is thoroughly washed with soap and hot water. The head is shaven. Friends come to salute the dead man and deposit on the ground round his body gifts of guinea-corn and other crops. Some of this corn is converted into beer, but some is left as food for rats which might otherwise attack the corpse. A cloth bandage is tied tightly round the dead person's abdomen with a view to preventing the extrusion of the

---

[1] But according to other accounts the typical animal grows up in the custody of the magician.

viscera. The body is guarded day and night ; and if the death had occurred during the wet season a fire is lit in order to keep off flies which would deposit worms on the corpse. This precaution is less necessary in the dry season and a fire is not then used ; but two old women fan the corpse with leaves or a whisk made from a cow's tail.

On the evening of the day following the death the body is laid face downwards in a rectangular hole in the ground, leaves being put under the mouth, elbows, and knees. It is then covered over with sand and is left until the following morning. The object of this temporary burial in sand is not to desiccate the body, but rather to hasten decomposition and render easier the subsequent removal of the epidermis.

On the following morning the body is placed on a four-legged table or bier cut out of solid wood, and is thoroughly washed in a sitting position. One of the Killa kindred then proceeds to remove the epidermis with his fingers. The nails on the hands and feet are not removed. The peeled skin is thrown into a pot which is buried in a rubbish-heap, no further notice being taken of it. The viscera are not removed, and the orifices are not blocked.

After the removal of the epidermis the body is smeared with the red juice of acacia berries.[1] This is the juice used in tanning leather, and the object in applying it to a corpse is to harden and preserve. The juice may be mixed with the bark of the *Boswellia dalzielii* tree. A mixture of garlic may also be sprinkled over the body to allay the stench. A loin-covering of sheepskin is then tied round the dead man's waist, and a dance is held until about four in the afternoon. The body is then clothed in a gown and trousers, and the head is completely swathed in a cloth covering. Immediately before burial a head of corn (taken from the deceased's stock) and the symbol of his " shafa " cult are placed in the dead man's hand. The heritor of the dead man's property takes the corn and symbol, saying : " From your hands I now receive the corn which you possess, together with your shafa. May I derive the benefits thereof, even as you did in your life-time. Say not that I stole them from your house, but prosper me in all things." The heritor then runs off towards his house

---

[1] Among the Margi the bark of a mahogany-tree and the red berries of the *Sarcocephalus russegeri* tree are added to the acacia mixture.

with the corn and cult symbol and deposits them in his granary, closing the entrance to the granary as quickly as possible. He is followed by men armed with bows and spears who make a pretence of warding off some invisible assault. The intention appears to be to prevent the corn and " shafa " spirits from returning to the dead man. The rite may also be a substitute for a former custom of burying a dead man's property with him.

The body is buried in a shaft and tunnel grave ; but in most of the Kilba groups there is an unusual custom of filling up the grave with earth, no attempt being made to protect the body from loose earth. In some groups, however, earth is not thrown into the grave, the mouth of the grave being blocked with a stone. But even in these groups earth is thrown directly on the bodies of those who had died young.[1] Beer is poured on the top of the grave, and the loose earth thus moistened is plastered down.

The funeral feast is held during the dry season and only lasts one day. On its conclusion all the relatives go to the grave, and the senior men dig out some of the earth. The female relatives of the deceased pour several calabashfuls of beer into the grave saying, amidst their tears : " We have given you your share (of the feast). To-day we sever our connection with you for ever."

The most interesting features of these rites are the use of a bier and the practice of denuding the corpse of the cuticle. For both customs would seem to have been borrowed from peoples who practised the art of mummification. In ancient Egypt the body was laid on a bier for the mummification rites, and was subjected to a saline bath which resulted in the complete denudation of the epidermis, the bath being given for the purpose of getting rid of fatty ingredients and preserving the tissues.[2]

The Kilba are unable to give any reason for their custom, and there can be little doubt that it was transmitted across the Sudan from ancient Egypt. It is noticeable that the custom of using a bier and removing the epidermis is only carried out in the case of old, i.e. important people, just as in Egypt embalming was the privilege of the rich. The custom of removing the epidermis was followed in such distant localities as the Torres Straits, Canary Islands, and South America, and it is probable that in all these cases it was received from a common centre of civilization.

[1] Children are often buried with the rites of the mother's family rather than of the father's.
[2] See Warren R. Dawson in *J.R.A.I.*, vol. lviii, 1928.

As regards the preliminary temporary burial it is worth noting that Wiedemann considers that primitive Egyptians buried the body first in the ground or under the house, until it had partially decayed, and then transferred it to its final resting-place in the desert necropolis.[1]

We may note in conclusion that among the Kilba a grave may be used more than once, the bones of the former occupant being relegated to one side. (This custom is not followed by the Margi.) Also that if a Kilba dies at a distance from home his forearm is cut off and taken back to his village for burial. Wives may not be buried in their husbands' home—the bodies must be sent back to their own homes for interment. It is also the custom for widows to light a fire in their late husbands' hut each evening, and to deposit there dishes of food which are removed in the morning and given to dogs or small children. This practice is kept up for six months, at the end of which the widows are free to remarry. It is not a Kilba custom to remove the skulls of old men and women. But before the British conquest they removed and brought home the heads of enemies killed in war.

Social Organization.—The Kilba are organized socially on a patrilineal basis, the hamlet being composed usually of ten or twenty households the heads of which are related to one another by descent from a common forefather. But many households contain uterine relatives ; for although a wife's parents have no automatic claim on any of her children it is not uncommon for a male child who is dissatisfied with his father's home to take up residence, temporary or permanent, in the home of his maternal uncle. Or a father, whose wife has borne a number of children, may of his own free will hand over one or more of his children to his wife's brother, should the latter have been less fortunate than himself. A sister's son has the usual privilege among most patrilineal peoples in Nigeria of making inroads on his maternal uncle's property during the latter's life-time, and if he has taken up permanent residence with his uncle he may also be a principal heritor on his uncle's death. But normally inheritance follows the patrilineal principle, and the estate is divided amongst sons rather than among brothers, the eldest son receiving a larger share than younger sons, If a man dies and leaves children who are too young to take charge of his estate his younger brother assumes

[1] See *Enc. Rel. Eth.*, vol. iv, page 459.

control of the property. But he is merely an administrator on behalf of the deceased's children. He must disclose all the deceased's assets to the latter's widow in the presence of witnesses, and he must hand them over intact to his dead brother's son as soon as the son has received his puberty marks. A woman's property, similarly, is heritable by sons and daughters, or failing these by brothers and sisters. A husband has no claim. The social position of women is, as usual among most Nigerian pagan tribes, high ; for a woman can change her husband on the slightest provocation. But the rule that male children who have been weaned must join the father's group acts as a deterrent to change. Wives help their husbands on farm work ; but as women have their own home-farms husbands also help wives. Sons work on the farms of fathers, but daughters work on the farms of mothers. Wives have their own granaries, but they are expected to place stocks at the disposal of the household throughout the period of the dry season. A wife will do this freely in the interests of her husband and children ; but if she decides to sell a portion of her crops for any personal purpose the husband will offer no complaint. At the end of the dry season the husband becomes responsible for the maintenance of the family ; and if the wife has any surplus supplies she is quite at liberty to sell them. But a discreet wife would hold them in reserve, especially if she had an indiscreet husband, one inclined to make excessive inroads on his corn in order to keep himself and his friends liberally supplied with beer. The Kilba are a drunken people.

Wives are heritable by junior brothers or cousins ; and it is also permissible for a man to inherit the young widow of his father or even of his maternal uncle (in the absence of other claimants). But the widows are only inherited by their own consent, which is given if they have no suitor who is capable of refunding the bride-price. A widow who has children will normally seek the protection of her deceased husband's brother. If she has no children and is young she may easily find a mate outside her late husband's family, but financial complications are avoided if she accepts as her new husband a brother, son, cousin, or nephew of her former husband. There is usually a considerable range of choice. It may be noted that among the Kilba a man may marry his deceased wife's sister provided the sisters had not the same mother. This is unusual among most Nigerian tribes ; and the Kilba rule would seem to suggest that matriarchal rules were at one time more potent than they are to-day. At the present time the patrilineal kindred is wholly exogamous and it is not permitted to marry relatives on the mother's side. But whereas a man may marry a maternal relative who is three generations apart, it is not permitted to marry any paternal relative, however distant the known relationship.

There are, as may have been gathered from previous remarks, no kindred totems, i.e. there is no connection between exogamy and such totemic ideas as the Kilba possess.

The following relationship terms are used :—

Ada is applied to a father, and a father's brothers and male cousins. It may also be used in addressing a maternal uncle. The corresponding term is *zirda*, i.e. my child (son or daughter).

Ama is applied to a mother, a father's or mother's sister, a paternal or maternal uncle's wife.

Zamda = brother and all male cousins.

Kwomda = sister and all female cousins.

Sikida is a special reciprocal term used between a man and his sister's children.

Jiji (possessive = *ajida*) is a reciprocal term used between all grandparents and all grandchildren.

Silkida is a reciprocal term used between parents-in-law and children-in-law. It is also applied by a woman to her husband's elder brother.

Khimda is a reciprocal term used between a man and his wife's brothers and sisters.

Malbida is a reciprocal term used between a woman and her husband's sister.

Salda is the term applied by a woman to her husband, and is also extended to the husband's younger brother, who may inherit her.

Malada is the term applied by a man to his wife and is also extended to the elder brother's wife who may be inherited.

The most noteworthy feature is that, while the term *khimda* is applied to a wife's brothers and sisters, the term *malbida* is only applied to a husband's sisters and not to a husband's brothers.

The Marriage Ceremonial.—Among the Kilba there are three methods of contracting marriage, viz. (*a*) that arranged by a father on behalf of his infant son ; (*b*) that arranged by a young man himself with some unmarried girl ; and (*c*) that arranged between a man (who may or may not be already married) and a married woman.

For the first type the procedure is as follows : The father of a small boy approaches the parents of an infant girl in order that she may become betrothed to his son. If his gifts are accepted the father is required to assist both parents of the girl at those periods of the agricultural season when farmers require special assistance. He gives his services each year until his son reaches the age of eleven or twelve. Among the Kilba there are no bush initiation rites such as are found among the neighbouring tribes, but it is customary for a young betrothed couple to go into seclusion together when the boy has reached the age of eleven or twelve. Each occupies a separate hut in the compound of the boy's father. Every morning and evening the boy is smeared with a mixture of mahogany oil and red earth. The girl is also smeared with a similar mixture by her mother on the first day of her seclusion, and by a girl friend on each succeeding day. Both must be content with scanty meals of hot gruel, and must avoid speaking to, or being seen by, any grown-up men or women. They may be visited by young boys and girls who have not reached the age of puberty, and by old men and women who no longer engage in sexual intercourse. No form of physical chastisement is administered. For the first four days of the seclusion large supplies of food are cooked and distributed among the members of the household and also among all friends and relatives in the village. On the fifth or sixth day a brew of beer is set, and when it matures (on the tenth day) a feast and dance are held to celebrate the emergence of the young couple from their seclusion. The boy is then told by his father that he has now become a man and must behave as such ; and from that time forward the boy takes the father's place on the farm of the girl's parents.

When these rites are carried out simultaneously by a boy and girl who are betrothed they are regarded as being little more than a ceremony of betrothal. But it is clear that they are in reality puberty rites, for they have to be observed by all boys and girls whether they are betrothed or not. As far as boys are concerned, they take the place of the month's segregation and hardship in the bush which are usual in other tribes, among whom there is also some form of smearing with oil ; and as far as the girls are concerned the rites correspond to the final cicatrization among other tribes, without which no girl is permitted to marry. It is note-worthy that among the Kilba no significance is attached to cicatrization, the marks being incised without ceremony, and being regarded merely as an ornament. A girl may even refuse to be marked ; but in such a case she would be liable to mockery on the ground of cowardice. It is probable that cicatrization was at one time regarded as an essential preliminary to marriage, for it is said that a Kilba man can claim a reduction of the final marriage payments if his bride had not undergone cicatrization.

The remainder of the marriage ceremonial will be described in connection with the second type of marriage, which is as follows : A young man may make personal advances to an unmarried girl, and if accepted he gives her gifts of bracelets, rings, and girdles. Later he gives her a number of pieces of cloth and gifts of meat. The girl gives the former to her father and the latter to her mother. She informs her lover that he must come and work on her mother's farm during the ensuing wet season. The girl's father also tells his daughter that if she has really decided to marry the young man she must instruct him to come and clear his farm of grass. The youth brings all his friends to help him on these occasions of agricultural work, and it is a point of honour that the duty prescribed by the father and mother on each occasion shall be carried out in a single day. A suitor and his friends studiously refuse to accept any return in the form of beer or food for this work, for if the suitor is subsequently repudiated he is entitled to a refund for the work done, and it is thought that the acceptance of beer and food would prejudice his claim to this refund. After a year or two the youth makes his main marriage payments in the form of pieces of cloth which the father and mother divide equally. He has also to give them liberal gifts of meat, and in the final year has to undertake the entire work of harvesting the crops on the farm of both parents of the girl.[1] After the harvest he is entitled to claim his bride. He comes for her at night, but on the first occasion she refuses to go. She promises, however, to accompany him three nights later. The bridegroom does not take his bride directly to his own home. He deposits her in the house of a friend. For before the bride may enter his home it is necessary for the bridegroom to kill a goat and eat the cooked flesh in the company of his relatives. This ritual constitutes the marriage ceremony ; for it is said that if a bride went to the bridegroom's home without the ceremony of killing and eating

---

[1] If the father of the girl is no longer living with the girl's mother he sends most of the bride-price to his late wife's mother, who hands a proportion to her daughter.

the goat the marriage would be no marriage at all and the wife would be merely a harlot. After this rite the bride takes up formal residence in the bridegroom's house, and to mark the occasion the bridegroom provides a feast for all those who had assisted him in obtaining his wife. The wife has to cook this meal. While they eat it the bridegroom's friends twit her for having given them all so much trouble, and she replies that they have given her great trouble in having to cook so much food.

Among the Kilba it is not customary for a wife to return to her mother's home in order to bear her first child. But six days after bearing the child she returns with the child to her mother's home and there remains until the child is weaned, the weaning period being reckoned as three years for a male child and four years for a female. Throughout this period she must abstain from sexual relations, on the ground that a renewal of pregnancy during the weaning period would interfere with lactation. At the end of the period she returns to her husband, but leaves the child in the custody of her mother. If the wife bears a second child she again goes with her babe to her mother's home, the first child being sent back to the husband. But if she does not again bear, the first child if a male remains in the home of the wife's mother until he is six or seven years old; if a female until her marriage. The husband is required to show his gratitude for this care by building a new hut for his mother-in-law. The mother-in-law also enjoys the advantage of the numerous services which young children are able to perform.

It is a gross offence among the Kilba for a girl to bear a child before she has gone to her husband's home. If she becomes pregnant by her fiancé the latter is required to complete his payments without delay, and the wedding ceremonies are carried out forthwith. But if motherhood is due to some rival suitor, some youth who hoped eventually to abduct the girl from her husband, an attempt is made by her parents to procure abortion, either by massage or by medicine. If these remedies fail the child at birth is deprived of its life by immersion in hot water or by the administration of a draught of charcoal water. A child so born is regarded with the same contempt as is shown towards a bastard by European peoples. Among the Kilba its continued existence would, it is believed, entail certain disaster to the entire household of the mother.

It would appear that in cases of this kind the parents of the girl are primarily to blame. For it is to their advantage to delay as long as possible the final ceremonies which permit a youth to take his fiancée to his home as a wedded wife. They continue to enjoy his agricultural services, and the more unscrupulous accept gifts from rival suitors who make advances to the girl with a view to immediate sexual relations or to ultimate abduction. On the other hand the fiancé may be himself to blame by failure to complete his contract payments. There is no punishment or even censure of a man who causes a woman to become the mother of a child which, according to tribal custom, must be put to death.

This is a matter which calls for active intervention on the part of the Administration, as it is not sufficient or just, from the native point of view, to deal with a single aspect of the complex, by prosecuting for murder those individuals whose observance of the tribal rule happens to come to the notice of the Administrative authorities.

The third form of marriage is by elopement with a married woman. The suitor endeavours to secure the good offices of the woman's mother who will summon her daughter to meet the suitor in her (the mother's) home. If the husband suspects his wife he will accompany her, and prevent the meeting. The suitor will then apply to the woman's father who will summon his daughter, and if the husband again follows her, his father-in-law will send him about his business, telling him his daughter is not a slave. If the woman accepts the suit she instructs the suitor to bring gifts of meat to her parents, and to collect the bride-price, which is handed to her father. She then leaves her first husband and goes to the second. If she had borne no children by her first husband the father hands the bride-price to the first husband ; but if she had borne a child the bride-price is handed to the woman's mother. In the reckoning of the bride-price the first husband's agricultural service is only included if the woman had abandoned him soon after marriage ; but if she had cohabited with him for a year or longer the agricultural service is discounted by the culinary and agricultural services which the wife had rendered to the husband.

The Kilba have a curious custom by which a woman who is anxious to conceive a child is made to creep through a tunnel in the ground. She does this four times, her husband standing at one end of the tunnel, and a friend of the husband's at the other.[1] Similarly, if a woman is ill she scoops out the centre of an ant-heap with a potsherd in which she has put some beer and ashes. She then lies down over this hole and is pulled backwards and forward by her husband and his friend. The intention is apparently to transfer the disease-causing spirit to the ant-hill, which is regarded as a place where spirits assemble.

If a woman is having a difficult labour it is customary to dig up and leave exposed the afterbirth of a former delivery. This sympathetic rite is thought to facilitate delivery and to ensure that the afterbirth will come away.

It is also customary to bury the afterbirth of a horse at cross-roads.

Material Culture.—Kilba men wear loin-coverings of leather ; but cloth gowns or jumpers are also worn. Young boys wear triangular cloth aprons. Women wear loin-coverings of various kinds, some a bundle of leaves before and behind, some a thin strip of cloth which hangs loose, and some a string girdle to which are attached in front half a dozen or more crescent-shaped pieces of iron. Others wear aprons of loose string about six inches long. The girdle with iron attachments is the favourite fashion among the younger women and girls who also disport numerous bracelets and brass-ring necklaces or necklaces of horses' hair, gifts from their fiancés. Iron nails, porcupine quills, or wisps of grass may be worn in the lower lip. Whitened discs of guinea-corn stalk are worn in the ear lobes. The most characteristic feature of feminine dress is the iron girdle mentioned, which is also worn in a more developed form by the Margi. The Bura do not follow this fashion.

There are no distinctive tribal marks, but many men have the single mark down the centre of the forehead which is characteristic of Bornu and Mandara. This mark may be accompanied by four sets of three short marks at each side, but there is a great variety of marks. Many men have no marks at all. Women wear lines of parallel marks on the abdomen and back, and many have a series of keloids on each shoulder.

The principal weapons are bows (of the same pattern as is used

---

[1] This custom is paralleled in certain districts of Europe in which it is common practice to pass sick children and cattle through perforated earth, the rite symbolizing the new birth of the patient who leaves his former afflictions behind him.

PLATE 19

A MARGI MARKET-SCENE

by the Hona, Gabin, and Yungur), short knives (worn at the waist), and short swords with leather grips. In former times shields of buffalo hide were carried. They had a leather grip and were pear-shaped. Small hoes are used for all farming purposes and are fitted by the socketed method. They lack the wooden spur characteristic of the hoes used by the Gabin, Yungur, Kanakuru, and Longuda. Axes are also fitted by the socket method.

The character of the dwellings is also totally different from that of the Hona, Gabin, and Yungur, but is the same as that of the Margi and is generally similar to that of the Bura. All the huts are built of mud and have conical thatched roofs. Rafters are not commonly employed, the thatch being supported by an oval inner shell of woven grass. But some houses have rafters of bamboo or guinea-corn stalks. The most notable feature is the presence inside all the huts of a number of granaries, so that there is scarcely room to turn round. The bedsteads consist of platforms of baked mud, and are protected by a mud screen built out from the wall or from one of the granaries. Each wife is generally assigned three separate huts which are connected together by a flat-roofed enclosure of grass matting. A conical thatch may be placed over this flat roof to render the enclosure, which is used as a sitting-room, partially rain-proof. One of the three huts serves as a sleeping apartment for the husband and wife, one is used as a kitchen, and the third for milling corn. The quern is fixed into a platform of mud. But sometimes in dry weather corn is milled on flat rocks outside the compound ; and in the bush one can always detect the site of a former village by the presence of grooves made in rocks as a result of milling. Milling may be done by girls as young as three or four years. The only house furniture observed consisted of two types of stools, one of wood and shaped like an Egyptian head rest, and the other a circular disc of sun-dried mud, hollow underneath. This mud stool, which is also found among the Margi, has a hole in the centre to permit of it being lifted easily. The Kilba and Margi baskets are characterized by having a head-pad of basketry woven on to the base.

A schedule of words and phrases is appended, and as already stated Kilba, Margi, and Bura may be regarded as constituting a single linguistic group. There are, however, certain grammatical differences between Kilba and Margi on the one hand, and Bura on the other. It may be added, also, that some of the so-called Fali groups of the mandated area speak languages which are so closely related to Kilba and Margi that they may be considered dialects. These " Fali " groups are also, in spite of numerous differences, clearly cultural relatives of the Kilba, Margi, and Bura.

1.	Head	Kir	kɪr
2.	Hair	Shishi	ʃiʃi
3.	Eye	Li	li
	Two eyes	li mahlu	li məłu
4.	Ear	Khimi	ximi
	Two ears	Khimi mahlu	ximi məłu
5.	Nose	Nchir	ntʃɪr
6.	One tooth	Hyir zhang	hjɪr ʒaŋ
	Five teeth	Hyir tufu	hjɪr tufu
7.	Tongue	Kyer	kjɛr
8.	Neck	Wulya	wuʎa
9.	Breast (woman's)	Woʔa	woʔa
10.	Heart	Wuḍufu	wuɗufu
11.	Belly	Ta	ta
12.	Back	Iyi or degreyi	iji or degreji
13.	Arm	Shakho (upper), upurchi (lower)	ʃʌxo (upper), upurtʃi (lower)
14.	Hand	Chi	tʃi
	Two hands	Chi mahlu	tʃi məłu
15.	Finger	Kwarchi	kwartʃi
	Five fingers	Kwiirchi tufu	kwiɪrtʃi tufu
16.	Finger nail	Pilu	pɪlu
17.	Leg	Khi	xi
18.	Knee	Wundi	wundi
19.	Foot	Irikhi	irixi
	Two feet	Irikhi mahlu	irixi məłu
20.	Man (person)	Mdu	mdu
	Ten people	Nji kuma	ndʒi kuma
21.	Man (not woman)	Shili	ʃili
	Two men	Shili mahlu	ʃili məłu
22.	Woman	Malaku	malaku
	Two women	Mahii mahlu	mahi i məłu
23.	Child	Zir	zɪr
24.	Father	Ada	ada
25.	Mother	Ama	ama
26.	Slave	Mava	mava
27.	Chief	ptil	ptɪl
28.	Friend	Bazhi	baʒi
29.	Smith	Iyaku	ijaku
30.	Doctor	Mdir mir ku zaku	mdɪr mɪr ku zəku
31.	One finger	Kwarchi zhang	kwartʃi ʒaŋ
32.	Two fingers	Kwiirchi mahlu	kwiɪrtʃi məłu
33.	Three fingers	Kwiirchi makiru	kwiɪrtʃi makiru
34.	Four fingers	Kwiirchi foḍu	kwiɪrtʃi foɗu

35. Five fingers	Kwiirchi tufu	kwiɪrtʃi tufu
36. Six fingers	Kwiirchi kwa	kwiɪrtʃi kwa
37. Seven fingers	Kwiirchi maḍafa	kwiɪrtʃi mədʃəfa
38. Eight fingers	Kwiirchi chiso	kwiɪrtʃi tʃɪso
39. Nine fingers	Kwiirchi hla	kwiɪrtʃi ɬa
40. Ten fingers	Kwiirchi kuma	kwiɪrtʃi kuma
41. Eleven fingers	Kwiirchi kwa ba zhang	kwiɪrtʃi kwa bə ʒaŋ
42. Twelve fingers	Kwiirchi kwa ba mahlu	kwiɪrtʃi bə kwa məɬu
Thirteen fingers	Kwiirchi kwa ba makiru	kwiɪrtʃi kwa bə makiru
43. Twenty fingers	Kwiirchi mahlo kwu minyi	kwiɪrtʃi məɬo kwu minji
44. A hundred fingers	Kwiirchi haru	kwiɪrtʃi haru
45. Two hundred fingers	Kwirrchi haru mahlu	kwiɪrtʃi haru məɬu
46. Four hundred fingers	Kwiirchi haru foḍu	kwiɪrtʃi haru foɗu
47. Sun	Pachi	pətʃi
God	Hyel	hjɛl
48. Moon	Hya	hja
Full moon	Hya mbilbila	Hya mbilbila
New moon	Hya taka pieda	Hya təka piɛda
49. Day	pachi	pətʃi
Night	vai	vəi
Morning	Umbulḍa	umbulɗa
50. Rain	Paru	paru
51. Water	Bitirsa	bitɪrsa
52. Blood	Mashi	maʃi
53. Fat	Mal	mal
54. Salt	Wuna	wuna
55. Stone	Hanggu	haŋgu
Iron	Liang	liaŋ
56. Hill	Mma	mma
57. River	Ḍil	ɗil
58. Road	Laku	laku
59. House	Vi (compound = ki)	vi
Two houses	Vi mahlu	vi məɬu
Many houses	Vi dangu	vi daŋu
All the houses	Vi dahu	vi dəhu
60. Roof	Zada	zada
61. Door	Nyevi	njɛvi
62. Mat	Buchi	butʃi
63. Basket	Tsilla	tsɪlla
64. Drum	Dang	daŋ
65. Pot	Tim	tɪm
66. Knife	Nggahya	ŋgəhja
67. Spear	Masu	masu
68. Bow	Laga	laga
69. Arrow	Hafa	hafa
Five arrows	Hafa mahlu	hafa məɬu
70. Gun	Bindiku	bindiku

71. War	Pa	pa
72. Meat (animal)	Kum	kum
73. Elephant	Chuwar	tʃuwʌr
74. Buffalo	Fur	fur
75. Leopard	Mapilawu	mapɪlawu
76. Monkey	Bilam	bɪlam
77. Pig	Dagla	dagla
78. Goat	Kwa or kushishi	kwa or kuʃiʃi
79. Dog	Khaya	xəja
80. Bird	Yaku	jaku
Feather	Shishi yaku	ʃiʃi jaku
81. Crocodile	Sirbiti	sɪrbiti
Sheep	Kating	kətɪŋ
Cow	Hla	ła
82. Fowl	Tigga	tɪgga
83. Eggs	Khikhi	xixi
84. One egg	Khikhi zhang	xixi ʒaŋ
85. Snake	Pobu	pobu
86. Frog	Gwǫmba	gwǫmba
87. Spider	zirkahel (i.e. son of God)	zirkəhɛl
88. Fly	Chidi	tʃidi
89. Bee	Chidi	tʃidi
Honey	Momwa chidi	momwa tʃidi
90. Tree	Uwa	uwa
Ten trees	Wuwa kuma	wuwa kuma
91. Leaf	Heli	heli
92. Guinea-corn	Uhi	uhi
93. Maize	Hi biku	hi biku
94. Ground nut	Wada	wada
95. Oil	Mal	mal
Horse	Taku, pl. taku ingga	taku, pl. taku iŋga
96. The tall woman	Mala za gamu	mala zə gamu
The tall woman	Mahii za gamu	mahii zə gamu
97. Large dog	Kheya da galu	xɛja də galu
98. Small dog	Zir kheya	zɪr xɛja
99. The dog bites	Kheya kwǫng ngala	xɛja kwǫŋ ŋala
100. The dog bites me	Kheya kwa ngalḏa	xɛja kwa ŋalḏa
101. The dog which bit me yesterday	Kheya nda ngalda anna	xɛja nda ŋalḏa ənna
102. I flog the dog	Iya kwa digga kheya	ija kwa dɪgga xɛja
103. The dog which I have flogged	Kheya nda ya digga	xɛja nda ja dɪgga
104. I see him or her	Iya la nyi	ija la nji
He sees you	Cha la ngga (or a la ngga ta cha)	tʃa la ŋga (or a la ŋga tə tʃa)
He sees us	Cha la ya (or a la min ta cha)	tʃa la ja (or a la mɪn tə tʃa)
We see you (pl.)	Ya la hi (or a la hi ti ya)	ja la hi (or a la hi ti ja)
We see them	Ya la nda	ja la nda

105. Beautiful bird	Yaku gumaguma	jaku gumaguma
106. Slave	Mava	mava
My slave	Mavada	mavada
Thy slave	Mavanga	mavaŋa
Our slaves	Mava ka min	mava kə mɪn
107. The chief's slave	Mava ptil	mava ptɪl
His slave	Mava nyi	mava nji
108. We see the slave	Ya la mava (or a la ti ya mava)	ja la mava (or a la ti ja mava)
109. We call the slave	Ya nga mava	ja nga mava
110. The slave comes	Mava kwa shili	mava kwa ʃili
111. He came yesterday	Cha shili anna	tʃa ʃili ənna
He is coming today	Cha kwa shili nya	tʃa kwa ʃili nja
He will come tomorrow	Cha kwa shili azaku	tʃa kwa ʃili əzəku
112. The slaves go away	Mavii kwa tira	mavii kwa tɪra
113. Who is your chief?	Wa ptil anga ?	wa ptɪl aŋa ?
114. The two villages are making war on each other	Milim mahlu kwa pa ana kir na nda	mɪlɪm məłu kwa pa ana kɪr nə nda
115. The sun rises	Pachi kwa sadi	pətʃi kwa sədi
The sun sets	Pachi kwa tada	petʃi kwa təda
116. The man is eating	Ndu kwa kwa sa suru suma	ndu kwa kwa sa suru suma
117. The man is drinking	Ndu kwa sa bi ti	ndu kwa sa bi ti
118. The man is asleep	Ndu kwa nji hanyi	ndu kwa ndʒi hanji
119. I break the stick	Iya billuwu zua	ija billuwu zua
The stick is broken	Zuana bil te	zuana bɪl te
This stick cannot be broken	Zuana ada i biluwa	zuana ada i bɪluwa
Break this stick for me	Biluda zuang nga	bɪluda zuaŋ nga
120. I have built a house	Iya khirra vi	ija xɪrra vi
121. My people have built their houses yonder	Nji kiya ta khirri vi hi nanda	ndʒi kija tə xɪrri vi hi nanda
122. What do you do everyday?	Hlirra mia ka kwa mirra ka pachi ?	łɪrra mia ka kwa mirra ka pətʃi ?
I work on my farm	Iya kwa mir ku fada	ija kwa mɪr ku fada
123. I am going away	Iya kwa mai tada	ija kwa mai tada
I am hoeing	Iya kwa zua	ija kwa zua
I am going away to hoe	Iya kwa mai ki zua	ija kwa mai ki zua
I am going away to my farm	Iya kwa mai gu fada	ija kwa mai gu fada

124. The woman comes	Malaku kwa shili	malaku kwa ʃili
She comes	Cha kwa shili (or a shili ta cha)	tʃa kwa ʃili (or a ʃili tə tʃa)
The woman laughs	Malaku kwa gedi	Malaku kwa gɛdi
The woman weeps	Malaku kwa tiwi	Malaku kwa tiwi
125. I ask the woman	Iya jauwari malaku	ija dʒauwari malaku
126. Why do you laugh?	Mi ka kwa geda ?	mi ka kwa gɛda ?
127. Why do you cry ?	Mi ka kwa tiwa ?	mi ka kwa tiwa ?
128. My child is dead	Zirda ta ta	zɪrda tə ta
129. It is not dead	A da tu wa	a da tu wa
130. Are you ill ?	Ga za ka da mina ka ?	Ga za ka da mɪna ka ?
131. My children are ill	Nguli da ada zanda mina kua	Nguli da ada zanda mɪna kua
132. Her child is better	Zirnyi ada ti dama	zirnji ada ti dama
133. Yes	A	
No	Aˤaˤ	
134. A fine knife	Ngahya minaku	ngəhja mɪnaku
Give me the knife	Naa ngahya	naa ngəhja
I give you the knife	A ningita ngahya	a nɪŋtia ngəhja
135. You are a European	Naya nasara	naja nasara
I am a black man	Naka ndu khakya ru	naka ndu kjakja ru
I am a Kilba	Naka Dirma (or Khibba)	naka dirma (or xɪbba)
136. Name	hlim	ɬɪm
My name	hlimda	ɬɪmda
Your name	hlimnga	ɬɪmŋa
What is your name ?	Wa hlim nga ?	wa ɬɪm ŋa ?
137. There is water in the gourd	Biti ada aku taku	biti ada aku təku
The knife is on the stone	Inyeha ato ma	injɛha ato ma
The fire is under the pot	Huu ada ki da tim	huu ada ki da tɪm
The roof is over the hut	Karagida ati kara vi	kəragɪda atî kəra vi
138. You are good	Naka mina ku	naka mɪna ku
This man is bad	Indingga ḍimi	ɪndɪŋga ḍimi
139. The paper is white	Likalikata pirtu	lɪkalɪkata pirtu
This thing is black	Sina kekeru	sɪna kekɛru
This thing is red	Sina dazu	sɪna dəzu
140. This stone is heavy	Mina ta dabu	mɪna tə dəbu
This stone is not heavy	Mina ada ta dabu wa	mɪna ada dəbu wa
141. I write	Iya kwa safa su	ija kwa səfa su
I give you the letter	Nungtia likatkata	nuŋtia lɪkatkata
Carry the letter to the town	Ka maini likatkata iya ku milim	ka maini lɪkatkata ija ku mɪlɪm

142. Go away   Mâi   mâi
Come here   Anda   anda
143. Where is your house ?   Ima kinga ?   ıma kıŋa ?
144. My house is here   Kida tana   kəda tana
My house is there   Kida hina nda   kəda hına nda
145. What have you to sell ?   Mika kwa ḍil nda ?   mika kwa ɗil nda ?
146. I want to buy fish   Kwa iya dilla kalfi   kwa ija dılla kalfi
147. The fish which you brought is bad   Kalfi nda ka dilla aḍimi   kalfi nda ka dılla aɗimi
148. Where is the man who killed the elephant ?   Imana dinda ta tsia chiwar ra ?   ımana dında tə tsia tʃiwʌr ra ?
He has killed many elephants   Cha tsia chuwar da ngu   tʃa tsia tʃuwʌr da ŋu
How many elephants were killed yesterday ?   Chiwar yida wa nja tsia ana ?   tʃiwʌr jida wa ndza tsia əna ?
149. Untie it   Pili nyi   pili nji
Tie this rope   Imbati sii ngga   ımbati sii ŋga
Make the boy untie the goat   Na ringi ana zir cha pilia kwa   narıŋi anə zır tʃa pılia kwa
150. My brothers and I, we are going but no one else   Naya ka zamda ya kwa mai   naja ka zamda ja kwa mai
Brothers, let us go and tell the chief   Kazamda ta yama mina yada ptil mina paringnyi   kazamda ta jama mına jada ptılu mına parıŋnji
151. This tree is bigger than that   Wuna ndieti nanda nda ana digal kur   wuna ndieti nanda nda ana dıgal kur
Horses   Taku ingga   taku ıŋga
Houses   Vi ingga   vi ıŋga
Pot   Tim ingga   tım ıŋga
Cows   Hla ingga   ɬa ıŋga
Hausa   Hausa   hausa
Hona   Hwana   hwana
Bura   Njir Bura   njır Bura
Kanuri   Vwa   vwa
Fulani   Pilahari   pılahari
Bata   Bata   bata

THE MARGI OF ADAMAWA

The Margi tribe, including the Chibbak,[1] number between fifty and sixty thousand people, of whom the majority are located

[1] Chibbak is a better spelling than Chibbuk but the local pronunciation is Kabak (Kəbʌk).

in South-Eastern Bornu. The remainder are found in Adamawa Province. The present notes are concerned only with those groups which are administered by the Emir of Adamawa, i.e. with the Margi of Adamawa Province (including the villages of Palam, Madagali, Duhu, Gulak, Baza, Wuba Mao Bani, and Kofa, which are situated in the mandated area).

These southern Margi are of heterogeneous origin. Thus at Womdiu three of the four kindreds are immigrants, two having come from Mabini in Bornu, and one (of Fali origin) from Fidi in the Mubi area. The royal families of Baza, Wuba, and Dille claim a Pabir origin, like the royal families of the Kilba. At Huyim, Chul, Lasa, and Madagali the ruling groups are immigrants from Gazama (to the west of Mulgwoi in Bornu) and claim ultimately to be Kanuri from the old Bornu capital of Ngasr-Gamo. There are also Gazama groups at Kofa and Moda. At Duhu and Gulak the Margi-speaking groups have become fused with immigrants from Gudur in the French Cameroons; and at Baza, which was in pre-Fulani times an important Margi centre, there are but few Margi left, their place having been taken by Higi from the Mandara Hills. Higi and Margi are also found side by side at Kofa.

We may say, then, that the Margi of Adamawa consist roughly of three strata : (a) indigenous peoples (using this term of course in a purely relative sense), (b) Pabir, and (c) Kanuri.

The indigenous inhabitants belong to the same group as the indigenous Bura and Kilba, a group which has fused to some extent with the Higi, Gudur, and Fali to the East, the Higi in particular showing definite linguistic and cultural connection with the Margi. This stratum provided the common language (with variations to be noted later) spoken by the Bura, Kilba, Margi, and Chibbak, and is characterized by the practice of initiation rites, exogamy, the removal of the epidermis from the bodies of old people (Bura tribe excepted), and the absence of circumcision and of secular chieftainship. Granaries are built inside the huts, and women wear over the pubes brass and iron ornaments. Long iron (or aluminium) nails are worn in the lower lip. The more Eastern groups follow the Higi custom of surrounding their compounds with large stone walls.

The Pabir stratum is distinguished by (a) secular chieftain-ship, (b) the wearing of a hair-lock by chiefs, (c) the custom of

PLATE 20

MARGI WOMEN

[face p. 214

burying chiefs in a sitting position and covering the body with charcoal, and (d) the use of official Pabir titles. In other respects the Pabir immigrants have coalesced with the indigenous inhabitants.

The third stratum, viz. the Kanurified Margi from Gazama, though speaking the same language as the aboriginals, have not coalesced to the same extent, being later immigrants possessed of a superior culture. They wear gowns or cloth garments instead of the leather loin-coverings which are characteristic of the aboriginals. They do not observe the rule of kindred exogamy, marriage with all classes of cousin being permissible, and cross-cousin marriage being particularly favoured. They practise circumcision. They wear the typical bodily marks of the Kanuri, and many are Muslims. They bury their dead in the Muslim fashion, and during the last century they have been closely associated with the Muslim Fulani who were driven out of Bornu. Some of them even resent the description of Margi, though Margi is their mother tongue. Most of them are trilingual, speaking Margi, Kanuri, and Fulani with equal facility. Originally they belonged to the same stock as the " aboriginals ", but owing to contact with the Kanuri and Fulani of Bornu they have lost all the characteristic Margi traits.

We may say, then, that at some period considerably prior to the beginning of the nineteenth century Pabir immigrants from Biu had established a suzerainty over the Kilba and also over the Margi of Baza, Dille, Wuba, and Womdiu, introducing into these areas a new conception of chieftainship. Society had previously been governed through the kindred organisation, the arbiters between two kindreds being the local magico-religious powers personified in the priests. The establishment of Pabir chiefs at Hwong (Kilba) and Baza (Margi) did not lead to an abandonment of the former system, but it introduced a modifying influence, so that the Pabir chiefs became courts of appeal, parallel with, but not antagonistic to, those represented by the gods. It is, perhaps, in this way that leaders of conquering peoples come to be regarded as divinities ; for those who are able to establish authority over several groups, each of which had formerly recognized no external authority save that of the gods, come to be regarded as gods themselves.

It is said that in pre-Fulani times the chief centre of Pabir influence among the southern Margi was Baza, and that the chiefs of Huyim, Dille, Musa, and Multafu all owned the suzerainty of the chief of Baza. Baza was, in fact, a centre of distribution for numerous groups who became chiefs wherever they went ; and it will be found that among most of the Bata-speaking tribes north of the Benue the members of the royal kindreds claim a Baza origin and are indeed known as " Baza ". But among these Bata-speaking peoples it is stated that " the Baza " came from Mandara and not from the Pabir country of Biu. It is possible to correlate the two traditions by recalling that the Pabir chiefs themselves claim to have come originally from Mandara.

The Margi of Womdiu and Wuba appear to have looked to the Kilba chief of Hwong as their leader ; and although they did not permit him to interfere in their domestic affairs they sought his assistance in war, and were accustomed to send him annual gifts of iron currency and other articles. Womdiu and Wuba are in fact more like Kilba than Margi towns. Wuba, it may be noted, was the centre of the cult known as Guti, which was used as a means of obtaining a divine decision not merely by the local Margi groups, but by the whole of the Kilba tribe. Prior to the nineteenth century the kings of Bornu must have exercised some form of political control over sections at least of these southern Margi, but of this there is no recollection at the present time, though Kanuri is spoken in most groups.

During the first half of the nineteenth century most of the Margi communities became subservient to groups of Fulani who had been driven out of Bornu, and, after founding settlements at Sawa, Madagali, Kofa, and Michika, established themselves at Dawari, where they acted as coadjutors of the Emirs of Adamawa. Tribute was paid annually in the form of gowns, corn, chickens, and honey, in order to secure immunity for their persons and crops. It is said that the Fulani seldom respected their engagements, and that the Margi had constantly to redeem members of the group who had been treacherously captured while working on their farms. At the present time the Margi are administered by the Emir of Adamawa through the district heads of Huyim, Madagali, Michika, and Wuba, all of whom are Fulani.

Government.—Every Margi town has a chief or headman known as the *ptil* or *til*, a word which is also found among the Kilba, and is possibly a contraction of the latter half of " *ku-tira* ", which is the term used for chief by the Tera, Hona, Gabin, Hinna, and Jerra. The chief's administrative and executive powers were not very extensive, at any rate during the period of Fulani domination. Thus in cases of murder the whole of the murderer's kindred had to take to flight. The chief had no power to arrest the murderer and adjudicate. But after the lapse of several days or possibly of weeks the people of the town would ask for the chief's intervention, pointing out that it was unreasonable that the death of one man should entail the loss of an entire kindred to the community. The chief would then summon the senior men of the murdered man's kindred and represent this point of view. The latter would agree, and one or two of their number would go as ambassadors to the fugitive family, who, on their return would be required to give a gown, cap, and trousers to the head of the deceased's family. They would also be required to give a virgin girl to the deceased's brother ; and when the latter had obtained a child by her the girl would be permitted to return to her own kindred if she so desired. The chief also called on the two kindreds to lay aside feelings of animosity, by carrying out a rite which was seemingly of a " scapegoat " character. Representatives of the two kindreds met at cross-roads ; and a ram, provided by the murderer's family, was placed on a stone, the fore-legs being held by the murderer and the hind-legs by the brother of the murdered man. A blacksmith then beat the animal to death with his smithing implement, and he appropriated the body. If this were not done sickness, caused presumably by the dead man's ghost, would invade the murderer's family. During the Fulani régime the murderer's family had also to pay a fine of three gowns or three goats.

These regulations only applied between members of the same local group. If a man of one local group killed a man of another local group warfare between the two groups followed automatically. The Fulani were ignored.

The chief had powers of intervention in cases of proved theft. The thief had to refund to the owner the equivalent of the stolen articles, plus 25 per cent compensation for the trouble given. He had also to give gifts to the chief, a portion of which were handed by the chief to the senior members of the community. If the thief was unable to pay, the whole of his kindred was held responsible. Where there was suspicion of theft, but no conclusive proof, the

person charged submitted to the ordeal of " Guti " at Wuba.
Charges of witchcraft were also referred to " Guti ". Thus if a
person fell sick or died, and the diviner indicated that his sickness
or death was due to the witchcraft of some individual, the person
charged was compelled to undergo the ordeal. If convicted he
was sold as a slave to the Fulani chief of Dawari, who presented
the local Margi chief with one or possibly two gowns. It was
stated that in pre-Fulani times the witch was clubbed to death by
members of the injured kindred. The bodies of witches are
believed to swell up after death, blood oozing from the mouth and
nose. If these symptoms were not observed it was concluded
that a false charge has been made, and the kindred responsible for
the charge was required to give a virgin girl to the wronged
kindred in order that she might bear a child by way of compensation. The logical conclusion would be that the " Guti " ordeal
was not always infallible, but I did not pursue this matter. It is
not difficult to understand why the swelling of a corpse, coupled
with the oozing of blood, is regarded as a sign that the dead man
had been a witch. He is swollen with his victims, and the blood
that oozes is the blood of those whom he had eaten in his life-time.

The community protected itself against indiscriminate charges
of witchcraft by imposing a heavy fine on the person who failed to
prove his charge. Such a one had to pay two gowns as compensation to the person charged, and seven gowns to the local chief,
who was required to give a number of these to his Fulani overlord.
Among those villages which recognized the seniority of Baza the
seven gowns were handed to the chief of Baza who gave one to the
local chief, retained one for himself, and handed the remainder to
the Fulani. It is obvious, therefore, that the senior men of a
kindred would discourage any fellow member from bringing a
charge which was not felt to be genuine.

It will have been seen that in cases such as murder, theft, and
witchcraft, the chief acted as administrator of native custom.
In cases of adultery the law was automatic. The husband was
entitled by custom to kill the paramour of his wife. No money
compensation was accepted. But in cases of adultery with a slave-
wife compensation was accepted. The reason for this distinction
was that, if compensation were accepted for a wife who was a free
woman the compensation would be regarded as a refund of the
bride-price, and the adulterer would therefore become the woman's

legal husband. But in the case of a slave-wife, as no bride-price had been paid, the acceptance of compensation would not imply a legal transference of the wife.

It will have been observed that in " legal " matters the chief was a court of appeal, rather than of summary jurisdiction. But he was also the religious leader. For though he did not, like e.g. the neighbouring chief of Sukur, perform daily religious rites by which he was regarded as the embodiment of the " health " of the whole people, he was responsible for seeing that all the customary religious rites were performed, and had himself to provide the sacrificial animals or gifts. He decided, in consultation with the heads of kindreds, all matters relating to aggressive or defensive warfare ; and in social matters he was the arbiter between the various kindred groups, which were ever ready to take arms one against the other. He was the conferrer and depriver of the local official titles, most of which appear to be of Pabir origin. At Womdiu the principal titles are Hedima (= Kaigama), Batari (= Baraya), Kadala (= Galadima), Birma, and Shal. All these titles except the last are found among the Kilba. At Dille, Duhu, and Madagali the title Hedima is not used, the Galadima being known as the Hliffu. The title Birma is not found at Dille or Madagali. At the later place the Kaigama is known as the Makarama, and at Duhu as the Medala.

The chief was not allowed to engage in any manual labour or to enter amongst the crops. Those chiefs who claim a Pabir origin (e.g. Baza, Wombiu, Wuba, and Dille) wear a hair-lock characteristic of their office. Into this is plaited the hair-lock of the preceding chief. On the death of the chief his hair-lock and that of his predecessor are removed and preserved in a leather box. Where there are two royal families (as at Dille) the head of each family is the custodian of the hair-locks of his royal forefathers. The Kilba chiefs, who are also of Pabir origin, have the same custom. Those Margi chiefs who claim to have come from Gazama do not wear a hair-lock.

The burial customs for chiefs also vary according as the chiefs claim a Pabir or Kanuri origin. Among the latter the grave is of the type normally used by Muslims, but among the former the dead chief is buried in a flagon-shaped grave. He is placed fully clothed in a sitting position on a stool or a sheet of iron, the head being kept erect by means of an iron girdle passed round the neck, and fixed into the wall of the grave. A wooden plank is placed between the dead chief's back and the wall of the grave. His left hand is laid on the top of his head, and to it is attached a string which is carried out to the surface. His dog is killed and buried beside him. The body is then completely covered with charcoal, and the mouth of the grave is blocked either by a stone or by an up-turned pot, a small hole being made in the bottom of the pot with the purpose of permitting an egress and ingress for the dead chief's spirit. No form of mummification is practised, and the body is buried within twenty-four hours after death, the dead chief's hair-lock being cut off and handed to his eldest son. The Margi do not follow the Kilba custom by which the successor, who is appointed without delay, is required to step over the dead chief's corpse. But he is required to step over a stick which had been cut to the same size as the corpse by the Hedima. This stick is laid at the threshold of the late chief's compound, and, by crossing over it, the successor receives formal appointment, his head being shaved by the Hedima so as to leave a patch of hair into which his late father's hair-lock is subsequently plaited.

The Kilba custom of removing the epidermis from the bodies of those who had died of a ripe old age is only practised by those Margi communities who are close neighbours of the Kilba. A full account of the ritual, which is clearly connected with mummification ideas, is given in my notes on the Kilba and Higi tribes and need not be repeated here. But the following variations were noted among the Margi of Womdiu. On the morning of the second day after death the body is placed in a hole in the ground which has been well sprinkled with water. It is then covered over with grass matting and is left in this humid atmosphere until the afternoon, the intention being to loosen the epidermis. The body is then removed, placed on a plank, and washed. The cuticle is peeled off completely and deposited in the hole in the ground. The denuded body is then smeared with a mixture of the juice of acacia seeds, mahogany-tree bark, and the red berries of the tree known to the Hausa as " tafashia".[1] It is next carried into the deceased's hut, where it is placed on a wooden table in a sitting position, being held erect by a rope tied round the neck and made fast to the roof of the hut. A dance is held outside the hut throughout the night, and is continued next day well into the

---

[1] *Sarcocephalus russegeri.*

PLATE 21

A Margi Market

[face p. 221

afternoon. The body is then buried in a shaft and tunnel grave as described in my notes on the Kilba, males being laid so that they face the north and females so that they face the east.

Religion.—The composite character of the Margi groups is further exemplified by the variety of names by which the Supreme Being is known. Thus at Womdiu, Wuba, and Baza, the Bura and Kilba title of Hyel[1] is applied. But among the other groups the common term is Iju. Among the Margi of Bornu the Supreme Being is known as Tambi.

The conception in all groups is the same. He is the firmament, the sun, the moon, the stars, the sender of rain. He is male by sex, because he fertilises the Earth (Ii). The Earth is female, because she brings forth. There is thus a form of dualism ; but the Earth is not definitely personified (as among the Jukun and Southern Nigerian tribes), nor are prayers addressed to Ii as they are to Iju.

It is said that, in the beginning, Iju was so close to the Earth that men could touch the place of his abode (i.e. the sky). In those days men did not require to farm, for they had merely to place clean calabashes on platforms outside their houses and Iju sent his children to fill the calabashes with food. Men were like the gods, for they lived for ever.[2] But this state of bliss was ended through the sin of a woman, who, by setting-out a dirty calabash caused a swelling to rise on the forefinger of one of the children of heaven. In his anger at this Iju withdrew to a distance from men, who, left without food, began to make inroads on the farms of Death [3] (Mptu). When Death complained to Iju of the ways of men Iju made a compact with him that if he would allow men to take seed-corn from his farm Iju would permit him to take the lives of a few men each year, one man here and one man there. (Iju did this because he knew that he could restore men to life.) And thus it was that men obtained corn, and death entered into their midst.

[1] Hyel is also the title used by the Higi. The Chibbak pronunciation is Hyal. As hya is the word for moon it is possible that Hyel was originally associated with the moon, and that the word means " The lord of the moon ".

[2] Compare the classical myth of the reign of Cronus (who succeeded Uranus as the sky god) when men lived like gods, free from toil and grief, and the weakness of old age, and the earth brought forth abundantly without the necessity of cultivation.

[3] According to another account it was Iju who led men to the fields of Death that they might break off heads of corn and eat them. But if they approached too closely to the abode of Death Iju pulled them back by the chain necklaces which the first men wore.

When Death took his first victim the brother of the victim espied Death and followed him. But when he overtook him he found him bathing in a field of fire, and fled in terror. But another younger brother resolved that he would face Death and slay him. And when he found Death bathing in fire he attacked him with a sword and cut off one leg. And thus it is that Death is lame. It is also said of him that he has two long teeth reddened with the blood of his victims.

When Iju saw that men were taking the law into their own hands he became angry and put dark colouring into their eyes so that they could no longer see Death. And that is why the eyes of men are dark. For men knew not what they were doing, but Iju knew what He was doing.

When men began to die they sent a messenger to Iju to ascertain the cause. The messenger was a chameleon, and Iju told the chameleon to say to men that if they threw baked porridge on the corpse the corpse would come to life. But as the chameleon, being a slow traveller, had been absent a long time, men resolved to send another messenger, for death was rampant in their midst. So they sent a lizard which arrived in the presence of Iju soon after the chameleon had departed. Angered at this second message Iju told the lizard to dig a hole in the ground and bury the corpse.[1] The lizard arrived home before the chameleon and delivered his message, and the corpse was buried. But when the chameleon arrived with his message men opened the grave in order to throw baked porridge on the corpse, but the corpse was not there. And thus it is that men can no longer be restored to life. According to another account Iju gave the same message to the lizard as he had given to the chameleon, but the lizard falsified the message. The noteworthy features about this story, which is found (with similar variations) in many parts of Africa, are (a) that the downfall of man was due to the sin of a woman, (b) that God did not intend that men should die a permanent death. Man does not in fact die a permanent death. Owing to the mistake or carelessness of the lizard the ghosts of the dead are forced to hover round the grave until they are, by the final funeral rites, released to the realm from which they may be reborn. The interval between the burial rites and the funeral festival (held in the dry

---

[1] According to another account men sent the lizard to ascertain how to treat a man who was sick, and Iju in his anger said," Throw hot gruel over him." This was done, and the man immediately died.

season) is thus explained in terms of the interval between the arrival of the lizard and that of the chameleon.

But a more important feature is the correlation between (*a*) the crops, and (*b*) Death and resurrection, a correlation suggesting that the whole conception of death and rebirth which pervades African society, and indeed the entire world, in various forms, is based on the observation that if you plant a seed, a seemingly dead thing, it will rise into life. The inference would seem to be that much of the religious belief which dominates the world at the present time was introduced by that group of peoples who first introduced agriculture. In the Christian world the doctrine is summarized in the thesis of St. Paul that unless a man dies (to his former self) he shall not rise again (to a higher life), a doctrine which is taught among many Nigerian tribes, noticeably in the form of initiation rites. It may be noted that in this Margi myth we have an adequate explanation of the custom of the Gabin and other pagan tribes of Adamawa Province by which the dead bodies of important people are showered with corn. The native explanation is that the dead man must be supplied with seed for planting in the spiritual world, but there can be little doubt that the original intention was one of resurrection. The custom is parallel with the ancient Egyptian practice of burying a germinating figure of Osiris with the illustrious dead. (This figure consisted of a wooden framework which was shaped into the form of the god and filled with silt from the bed of the Nile. Seed-corn was planted in the silt, and the figure was thus a symbol both of the resurrection of Osiris and of the deceased.)

The Margi believe in the reincarnation of the good. But evil persons cannot be reborn ; for as among the Jukun (and ancient Egyptians) the evil are subjected to a second death. Among the Jukun the dead man's soul suffers annihilation in a region beyond Hades, the mode of annihilation being unspecified ; but among the Margi it is believed that the wicked soul (*shangguda*)[1] is destroyed by fire. The Margi have a belief, like the Platonic doctrine of ideas, that every earthly thing has its " heavenly " counterpart. Human beings have heavenly fathers and mothers, brothers and sisters ; trees and animals also have their counterparts. Among the Jukun it is believed that human beings have counterparts in the spiritual world, this belief being carried so far

---

[1] The *shangguda* of the Margi is the equivalent of the *mambil* of the Bura.

that every grown man is thought to have a female spiritual paramour ; but it was not held that non-human things had heavenly " images". A further parallel between Margi and Jukun beliefs is that the woman whom a man had first married as a virgin will be his one and only wife in the life to come. There will be no wife-stealing or secondary marriages, as on the earth ; and however unsatisfactory his first wife, married as a virgin, had been on earth, he will have to put up with her for the whole of his after-life. It is noteworthy that, among the Margi, one of the main reasons given for the practice of polygyny is the practical advantage derived from the farm work of wives. For Margi women are noted for their farming ability, and a wife who fails to come up to the required standard is, as a rule, speedily dismissed. There are, of course, numerous other reasons for the practice of polygyny, and I merely mention the one given above because it seemed to occupy a prominent place in the minds of husbands.

In addition to the belief in heavenly counterparts there is also the belief that a man may have an earthly counterpart in the form of some animal. Details of this kind of belief have been given in several of my reports (e.g. Kilba, Kanakuru, Bura, etc.). But it may be observed that, among the Margi, it is not considered essential that an animal counterpart should die at the same time as the man with whom he is mystically or soulfully associated. For when the man receives the magical medicine which creates the alliance he may insert a clause in the contract to the effect that when he dies his animal counterpart may live on to bite and injure his enemies ! Another feature of Margi beliefs in this connection is that a person who obtains an animal counterpart hands the miniature animal (see page 195) into the care of his maternal uncle, who feeds it until it grows up and then releases it to lead a free life in the bush. No Margi will admit that he personally has entered into an alliance with an animal ; but he will affirm that numerous other Margi do contract this kind of alliance, and he will say that the reason for giving the animal into the charge of a maternal uncle is because the maternal uncle is a man's most dependent friend. In a fight paternal relatives will run away and leave one to the mercy of the enemy. But maternal relatives will stand by one unto death. A man is an object of jealousy to paternal relatives, with whom he is entitled to share an estate ; but he is regarded with unmixed affection by maternal relatives, for he cannot be a heritor.

This is the explanation offered at the present time for the custom of giving to the maternal uncle the custody of one's miniature animal counterpart ; but it is possible and probable that the custom is merely a reflection of a former matrilineal rule by which a man received his totem from his mother's family (as among the Kanakuru and Mbula at the present time).

Reference has been made to the cult of Guti, which was and is still used as a means of settling disputes. Guti is believed to be a water-spirit inhabiting a certain stream near Wuba, which becomes a deep pool during the dry season. The disputants go to the edge of the pool, and each calls on Guti to catch him if he has lied, and to catch his opponent if his opponent has lied. Both then dive in and swim or attempt to swim across the pool. It is believed that Guti clutches at the guilty party in mid-stream, and causes him to flounder about in a paralysed condition until his successful opponent calls on the spirit to release him. The psychological effect of a guilty conscience no doubt plays a considerable part in this form of ordeal. But frequently it is merely a swimming match, the man who crosses first being declared the winner. It is permissible for one who cannot swim to employ a substitute.

Apparently there is no special priest of Guti, the care of the pool being in the hands of the members of a whole hamlet which is situated near the pool. It is customary for the winner of a dispute to give a gift of a chicken to the members of this hamlet, and it was stated that the chicken must be eaten outside the hamlet, other-wise all the houses would go on fire and an epidemic would break out. In times of drought all householders in the vicinity come to the edge of the pool and deposit gifts of food, with a prayer to Guti that rain may be sent. The godling's assistance is also sought by people afflicted with ophthalmia and by enceinte women who are afraid of aborting.

As among the Kilba, oaths are normally sworn on the sacred symbol known as " shafa ". Most men of importance possess a shafa, which consists of a bundle of leaves (of the *Combretum verticillatum* tree) in which are tied up a piece of lion's tail or some hog's hair, a bug, a louse, an arrow-shaft, a porcupine quill, a stalk of grass, and a piece of stick used in digging a grave. These articles are chosen in order to produce on guilty people the various evil things they symbolize. The person charging the other provides the shafa, and the person charged swears by it, saying : " If I have done wrong to you may Shafa catch me ; but if I have done you no wrong may Shafa catch you." He then steps across the symbol. If he is assailed by misfortune or illness he is believed (and may believe himself) to be guilty, and is compelled to confess his guilt. The Shafa is again produced, and his former opponent addresses the spirit, saying : " You, Shafa, have shown this person to be at fault. He has confessed his fault. Release him now, I pray you, that he may pay me." The guilty person then steps across the symbol, and subsequently pays compensation to his opponent. If, on the other hand, the person who made the charge falls ill, or is assailed by some misfortune, he has to confess before Shafa that he has made a false charge, and he is required to pay damages of one goat to the person whom he had charged.

At Dille there is a cult of a spirit or godling known as Iyal Diri, who is symbolized by a pot. Rites are performed at sowing and before the harvest, a dish of corn being deposited in the shrine. After the harvest all members of the community, including women and children, make offerings to this spirit for their health's sake. It is said that in former times, if a man of Dille was captured in war and uttered the name of Iyal Diri, his captor would derive no advantage from him. Vice versa, if a man of Dille captured an enemy, he shaved his captor's head and took him to the shrine of Iyal Diri, calling on the godling to prevent his escape. It was believed that if the captive escaped he would die of thirst in the bush. There is a similar cult at Musa known as Hyel Musa, and one at Huyim known as Mirhla. At Womdiu there is a deity known as Mizra, symbolized by a number of pots with narrow necks. The priest of this cult offers a sacrifice of a chicken every year immediately before sowing, pouring the blood and libations of beer over the symbols, and asking for a successful agricultural season. At other times any person seeking the favour of the god makes offerings of a chicken and of a calabash containing samples of every kind of crop. At Womdiu, also, there is a private cult of female ancestors, or rather of dead mothers, known as Katir Mama. This cult always appears to be in the charge of younger sons, who carry out rites at sowing and on occasions of sickness. The Margi do not devote much attention to ancestors and I am inclined to think that the cult of Mama was not originally a cult of human mothers at all, but the cult of the Great Mother, the Earth deity known as Ma or Mam among the Jukun and numerous other tribes of the Benue.[1]

There are two festivals known as Yawal and Hladir which are worthy of mention. The former is held in the spring prior to sowing, after the completion of the work of preparing the farms. All householders assemble before dawn and throw lighted brands of guinea-corn stalk into the bush, shouting loudly as they do so. The conception appears to be that at harvest the corn spirits have followed the harvested crop home to the granaries, and that they must, at spring-time, be sent out once more into the bush in order to resume their work. A seven-days feast follows the rites, and it is then permissible to carry out the first sowing. In some communities initiation rites are associated with the Yawal festival. These will be described later. The Hladir festival is held at the end of October or beginning of November and is usually followed by a fishing battue. It is at this time that affianced girls are given in marriage.

Divination is practised to some extent, the usual medium being a land-crab. Three pieces of nut shell are placed near the crab's hole, together with a number of stalks of grass, each stalk representing some question or individual. Thus if a man had died his friends might ask a diviner to ascertain how he had died, and the diviner would assign certain causes of death (e.g. witch-craft, poison, natural causes) to each stalk of grass. If it had already been determined that witchcraft had been the cause of death the diviner would be asked to name the witch. Names of suspected individuals would be assigned to the stalks of grass. The answer is obtained by watching to see if the crab deposits a piece of shell on one of the stalks of grass. In order to obtain a clear decision the crab is expected to deposit the shell on the same stalk of grass three times running.

Divination by means of land crabs is practised in some Jukun-speaking groups, and also among the Chamba.

Social Organization.—As already noted there is considerable variation in the form of social organization. Thus at Womdiu, Wuba, Baza, Duhu, and a number of other villages, marriage within the kindred is regarded with disfavour, and under no

[1] See *A Sudanese Kingdom*, chap. iv.

circumstances would relatives so closely related as second cousins be allowed to marry each other. Among the Gazama or Kanurified Margi, on the other hand, there is no bar to first-cousin marriage and the marriage of cross-cousins is particularly favoured. There is no totemism, but certain groups avoid eating certain animals or groups of animals. Thus those claiming a Pabir origin usually avoid eating the flesh of crocodiles, all snakes, monitor lizards, bush-cats, and monkeys. It was said that anyone breaking these taboos would be assailed with a skin disease. It was added, however, that the evil effect of the taboos could be overcome by fumigating oneself in the smoke of meat roasted in a blacksmith's fire. The Higi of Lasa area also avoid the flesh of monitor lizards and bush-cats, the reason assigned in this case being that all these animals are sacred to the cults. Those claiming a Kanuri origin avoid eating the flesh of bush-pigs, no doubt because these peoples were at one time associated with Muslims. But the reason assigned was that in ancient days, while they were journeying from Ngasr-Gamo to Gazama, they lost their way in the bush and were dying of thirst. Suddenly they saw a wart-hog, and, following him, found water.

Blacksmiths are endogamous, i.e. a member of a blacksmith's kindred will only marry one of his own kindred or of another smithing kindred. And it was stated that no non-blacksmith would marry a blacksmith's daughter. This prejudice is widespread in Northern Nigeria. Members of royal families do not observe the taboo against intermarriage with daughters of smiths on the ground, it was said, that royal persons are above the ordinary rules.[1]

The rules regulating inheritance, custody of children, and authority in the family follow the patrilineal principle. Property is inherited by the eldest son on behalf of himself and his brothers. A younger brother only inherits on behalf of an eldest son who has not reached the age of discretion. But widows are heritable by the deceased's brothers (elder or younger). The Margi do not favour the custom of neighbouring tribes by which sons may inherit the young widows of their fathers or paternal uncles. If the widows elect to re-marry outside the family the eldest son is entitled to a bride-price, provided the widow had not borne a

---

[1] There are good reasons for believing that chieftainship was among many tribes introduced by immigrant blacksmiths.

PLATE 22

A YOUNG MARGI MOTHER

[face p. 228

child by his father. The authority of the maternal uncle is comparatively slight, and no Margi child can (as among numerous tribes) take up his abode in his maternal uncle's home without the consent of his father.

The relationship terminology is as follows :—

Tada or *Ada* = father, father's brothers and male cousins. The term may also be used in addressing maternal uncles and any man of a senior generation. The corresponding term is *bzirda* or *zirda* (i.e. my son or daughter).

Mama = mother, father's or mother's sister (or female cousin), a paternal or maternal uncle's wife, and any woman of a senior generation.

Zamda = brother, and any male cousin.

Kwomda = sister, and any female cousin.

Sikida = maternal uncle, sister's child.

Chiji (possessive = *ijida*) = all grandparents and all grand-children.

Zamia salda = husband's brothers.

Malbida = husband's sisters, or brother's wife (female speaking).

Khimda = wife's brothers and sisters, sister's husband (male or female speaking).

Salda = husband.

Malda = wife.

These terms are the the same as those used by the Kilba, with the exception that the Margi do not, like the Kilba, address the husband's elder brother as *silkuda*; they use a descriptive term *zamia salda*. It will be observed that though the term *khimda* is applied to a wife's brothers and sisters the corresponding term *malbida* is only applied to a husband's sisters (and not brothers). This difference is due, apparently, to the fact that, whereas a man may not marry his deceased wife's sister, a woman may marry her deceased husband's brother. A number of the Margi and Kilba terms (e.g. those for maternal uncle, father, mother, husband, wife) are also found among the Higi.

There are two principal forms of marriage among the Margi (*a*) that contracted with a girl who had not previously been married, and (*b*) that contracted by elopement with a married woman. The first is usually an endogamous union, in the sense that both partners belong to the same local group, parents refusing to give their virgin daughters to strangers [1]; whereas the second is exogamous, in the sense that no man may elope with a married woman of his own local group. This system is, therefore,

[1] This is at least the system followed at Womdiu and Wuba.

the reverse of that folowed by the Jirai, Malabu, and many of the
Zaria and Bauchi tribes, among whom it is a general rule that a
man may not marry a virgin girl of his own local group, but may
marry the wife of a member of his local group. Under the first
form of marriage the bride-price is small, under the second it is
large.

A feature of the first type of marriage is that a young boy and
girl who are betrothed are required to undergo together a form of
puberty rite when the boy has reached the age of ten or eleven.
They go into seclusion for a period of one or two months, each
being assigned a hut in the compound of the boy's father. They
may not speak to anyone, and are smeared, morning and evening,
with ochre by a boy and girl friend respectively. They are fed
liberally. On the final evening of the period of seclusion the father
and mother come to the boy's hut. The father says to his son :
" To-day you have became a man : you must lay aside the folly
of youth. Take to yourself a wife and make a home." He then
hands to the boy two pieces of guinea-corn stalk, one symbolizing
a spear and the other an arrow. The boy hurls one to the right
and the other to the left. He then goes to a cross-roads or ant-hill
and cuts in two a branch of wild paw-paw tree which his father
had planted there. The intention was stated to be that the
spirits which are believed to haunt ant-hills and cross-roads
release the hands of the boy which had grown heavy in consequence of his two months' idleness. On the conclusion of this
rite the boy's mother ululates loudly and then runs off home at
full speed, followed by her son. Whoever reaches the compound
first slays a chicken, which is afterwards cooked and given to the
children of the household to eat. It was stated that the object
of slaying the chicken was to secure protection for the boy at the
beginning of his new life, and to insulate him from the glances of
evil men who had not looked on him for two months.

The boy now presents himself before the chief to whom he
offers a gift of tobacco. The chief informs him that he has become
an adult and that he need not rely on his father any longer, for he
has himself joined the ranks of fathers.[1] That night the boy
returns to his own hut ; but on the following morning he
appears decked in numerous ornaments, and salutes all his

---

[1] A boy becomes entitled to inherit property as soon as he has completed the
puberty ritual.

PLATE 23

MARGI GIRLS (of Womdiu)

relatives and friends who load him with gifts. Meanwhile the girl has returned, without ceremony, to her own home. These rites are carried out at sowing-time.

During the next two or three years the boy is required to make annual gifts of a basket of corn, bundles of cotton grass, and of string to the mother of his betrothed. When the girl has reached the age of twelve small gifts of iron currency are substituted for the string When she is old enough for marriage the boy builds a new hut for his fiancée's mother, and he becomes entitled to claim his bride at the following harvest, the final ceremony being a feast. A cow is killed by the boy's father, and the meat is sent to the girl's parents. During the feast the girl is dispatched to her husband's home.

It will be observed that the pre-marriage payments are inconsiderable [1] and are appropriated by the girl's mother. But we shall see later that, if the girl contracts a secondary marriage, there is a definite bride-price, most of which is appropriated by the father.

Among those Margi groups which claim to be immigrants from Gazama the pre-marriage ritual is somewhat different from that described above. The puberty rites last for seven days only, and though the girl is secluded the boy is allowed to walk about. There is no smearing with ochre. The boy's father is required to give a gift of a goat to the father of the girl. At the end of the seven days the boy presents the girl with a gift (5s. nowadays), and he is then entitled to have sexual intercourse with her for a period of seven days. After this the girl returns to her own home for some months, at the end of which she takes up formal residence with her husband, the occasion being marked by a feast. In this group boys are circumcised at the age of twelve ; but the circumcision is carried out informally and has no connection with the seven days puberty rite.

In some groups (e.g. at Womdiu, Wuba, Ihi, Husara, and Bietso) abortion is practised if a girl conceives before she has gone to her husband's home. The abortifacients used are the juice of of the boiled bark of the *Balanites ægyptiaca* tree, and a strong laxative made from the sticky substance produced by a certain species of fly. If the abortifacients prove ineffective and a child is

---

[1] A suitor is, of course, required to assist his prospective father-in-law in farm work on the occasions when special assistance is required.

born it is generally put to death. Reference has been made to this subject in the notes on the Kilba tribe (page 204).

Turning now to the second type of marriage, viz. that contracted by elopement with a married woman, the normal procedure is as follows : The suitor (who belongs to another village) approaches the woman's father, who refers him to her mother. The mother summons her daughter and asks her if she wishes to change her husband in favour of the suitor. If the daughter consents the suitor is required to give her father four gowns, one cloth, two lumps of salt, one girdle of beads, ten bars of iron currency, and ten bracelets. The father appropriates all of the articles, with the exception of the cloth, girdle, and bracelets. When the payments have been made the mother sends for her daughter, and the father informs the suitor that he will find his new bride at the house of one of his friends. The first husband receives no compensation, as he had not paid any substantial bride-price for his wife. If the woman leaves the second husband and goes to a third, the second husband becomes entitled to a complete refund of his bride-price, unless his wife had borne him a child. The birth of one child cancels the bride-price.[1]

It is obvious from these regulations that many parents must encourage their daughters to contract secondary and tertiary marriages, in order to derive the advantages of the bride-price.

Material Culture.—As regards material culture that of the people of Womdiu, Wuba, and Baza is virtually the same as that of the Kilba, with the difference that the women wear a greater profusion of iron ornaments. The houses are built on the same pattern. But among the other groups there are marked variations. The huts of a compound are still connected by the woven grass enclosures, but they never contain more than a single small granary (unlike those at Womdiu and Wuba which are crowded with granaries). Many of the external granaries are made entirely of woven straw, without the outer smearing of mud. At Duhu the granaries are built on a pattern commonly seen among the Higi. First there is a foundation of stones, then a layer of sun-baked mud, then another layer of stones over which a flooring of planks is laid. On this flooring the grass granary rests, the outer walls being plastered with mud. At Duhu and Gulak, also, all the

---

[1] But at Duhu the birth of one child does not cancel the bride-price if the child had died within three months of its birth. In some other groups the mere fact of conception cancels the bride-price.

PLATE 24

MARGI GIRL WITH LIP ORNAMENT

compounds are surrounded with circular stone walls from 3 to 5 feet high. This practice is followed by most of the tribes of the Mandara Hills.

Bedsteads are usually logs of wood laid across wooden trestles or mud pillars. Grass mats are used as mattresses.

Men wear leather loin-coverings drawn between the legs, the flap being left to dangle down behind. But the use of cloth garments is spreading, and most of the Margi who claim a Kanuri connection wear gowns when they are not at work in the fields. Many of these Kanuri groups of Margi practise dyeing, and claim to have done so from ancient times. Necklaces of blue and white beads are worn, as well as iron and brass bracelets.

The younger women of Womdiu and Wuba are distinguished by their iron hook girdles, but these are not seen at Lasa and Dille or Kofa, their place being taken by an unadorned leather fringe. In some villages, e.g. at Duhu, small iron hooks are worn above the fringe. Many women wear girdles from which bunches of leaves are suspended at the back and in front. Women frequently wear iron or aluminium nails in the lower lip, some of these nails being as much as 3 inches long. Three or four beads strung tightly together may be worn in the ear. Mothers keep their bodies smeared with ochre while suckling their children.

The facial marks are generally a variation of the following pattern :—

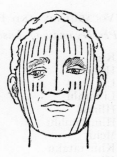

Sometimes the pronounced triple or quadruple marks under the eyes are not seen, and without these the marks resemble those of the Kanuri and Pabir. Among those who claim a Kanuri admixture the typical Kanuri bodily markings are found, viz. long triple lines on the arms, legs, back, and sides.

Bows are, at Womdiu and Wuba, of the single eyelet type described in the notes on the Kilba, Hona, and Yungur ; but at Lasa, Dille, and Madagali some of the bows have no eyelet. Margi commonly carry throwing knives which are more ornamental than useful.

Language.—The Margi language is almost identical with that of the Kilba. There is little difference also between Margi and Bura. But in Margi the subject pronoun is commonly suffixed to the verb, especially in the past tenses. This is a feature of Kanuri, and must, I think, be ascribed to a closer contact with the Kanuri than was experienced by the Bura. Schedules of words and phrases are attached, which show clearly that Bura, Kilba, Chibbak, and Margi are one and the same language ; and if a comparison is made with Higi and Fali it will be seen that there has been some fusion between the Bura-Kilba-Margi group and that of the Higi-Fali.

The characteristic features of the Bura-Kilba-Margi group are (*a*) the absence of feminine pronouns such as are found among the Kanakuru, (*b*) the use of an inclusive and exclusive first personal plural pronoun which is characteristic of most of the Benue-Chad languages (Kanuri excluded), (*c*) the presence of a dual (*mwa* = we two), and (*d*) the use of the so-called " Welsh *l* ", which is only found among tribes of the extreme Eastern regions of Nigeria (including the Tera-Hinna-Hona-Gabin groups).

MARGI VOCABULARY AND PHRASES
Per Nyamdu of Lasa

1. Head	Kir	kɪr
2. Hair	Hlihli	ɬiɬi[1]
3. Eye	Li	li
Two eyes	Li mihlu	mɪɬu
4. Ear	Hlimi	ɬimi
Two ears	Hlimi mihlu	ɬimi mɪɬu
5. Nose	Mchir	mtʃɪr
6. One tooth	Khir tataku	xɪr tətəku
Five teeth	Khir tafu	xɪr təfu
7. Tongue	Kyer	kjɛr
8. Neck	Wuya	wuja
9. Breast (woman's)	Uwa	uˤwa
10. Heart	Wudafu	wudəfu
11. Belly	Wuɗu	wuɗu
12. Back	Dagiriyi	dagɪriji

[1] This lateral has an *s*-like quality.

13.	Arm	Tsi	tsi
14.	Hand	Wuɗu tsi	wuɗu tsi
	Two hands	Wuɗu tsi mihlu	wuɗu tsi mɨɫu
15.	Finger	Gulanda	gulanda
	Five fingers	Gulanda tafu	gulanda təfu
16.	Finger nail	Pil	pɪl
17.	Leg	Khi	xi
18.	Knee	Wundi	wundi
19.	Foot	Wudi khi	wudi xi
	Two feet	Wudi khi mihlu	wudi xi mɨɫu
20.	Man (person)	Mdu	mdu
	Ten people	Mji kumu	mdʒi kumu
21.	Man (not woman)	Asal	əsal
	Two men	Sal mihlu	sal mɨɫu
22.	Woman	Mala	mala
	Two women	Mahidi mihlu	mahidi mɨɫu
23.	Child	Ubzir	ubzɪr
24.	Father	Tada	tada
25.	Mother	Mama	mama
26.	Slave	Mafa	mafa
27.	Chief	Ptil	ptɪl
28.	Friend	Mwǫlda	mwɔlɗa
29.	Smith	Ngkyagu	ŋkjagu
30.	Doctor	Pitipitima	pitipitima
31.	One finger	Gulanda tataku	gulanda tətəku
32.	Two fingers	Gulanda mihlu	gulanda mɨɫu
33.	Three fingers	Gulanda makir	gulanda makɪr
34.	Four fingers	Gulandu fwǫɗu	gulanda fwɔɗu
35.	Five fingers	Gulanda tafu	gulanda təfu
36.	Six fingers	Gulanda nkwa	gulanda nkwa
37.	Seven fingers	Gulanda madafu	gulanda mədəfu
38.	Eight fingers	Gulanda nsisu	gulanda nsisu
39.	Nine fingers	Gulanda nhlu	gulanda nɫu
40.	Ten fingers	Gulanda kumu	gulanda kumu
41.	Eleven fingers	Gulanda kum ga sir-tang	gulanda kum ga sɪrtaŋ
42.	Twelve fingers	Gulanda kum ga pwa mihlu	gulanda kum ga pwa mɨɫu
	Thirteen fingers	Gulanda kum ga pwa makir	gulanda kum ga pwa makɪr
43.	Twenty fingers	Gulanda mihlu kumnyi	gulanda mɨɫu kumnji
44.	A hundred fingers	Gulanda gharu	gulanda ɣaru
45.	Two hundred fingers	Gulanda gharu mihlu	gulanda ɣaru mɨɫu
46.	Four hundred fingers	Gulanda gharu fwǫɗu	gulanda ɣaru fwɔɗu
47.	Sun	Bachi	bətʃi.
	God	Iju	Idʒu
48.	Moon	Khia	xia
	Full moon	Khiambil para	xiambɪl para
	New moon	Mambidu khia	mambidu xia

49.	Day	Bachi	bətʃi
	Night	Avai	əvəi
	Morning	Kulakula	kulakula
50.	Rain	Yimi	jimi
51.	Water	Yimi	jimi
52.	Blood	Mamchi	mamtʃi
53.	Fat	Mal	mal
54.	Salt	Wunu	wunu
55.	Stone	Insika	ɪnsɪka
	Iron	Iyang	ijaŋ
56.	Hill	Ngwudigal	ŋwudɪgal
57.	River	Idil	ɪdɪl
58.	Road	Lagu	lagu
59.	House	Umbwa	umbwa
	Two houses	Umbwa mihlu	umbwa mɪɬu
	Many houses	Umbwa wadi	umbwa wadi
	All the houses	Umbwa papatu	umbwa papaːtu
60.	Roof	Kirambwa	kɪrambwa
61.	Door	Nyumbwa	njumbwa
62.	Mat	Ntafu	ntəfu
63.	Basket	Wururu	wururu
64.	Drum	Akangga	əkaŋga
65.	Pot	Intim	ɪntɪm
66.	Knife	Nyihya	njihja
67.	Spear	Masu	masu
68.	Bow	Laga	laga
69.	Arrow	Ghafu	ɣafu
	Five arrows	Ghafu tafu	ɣafu təfu
70.	Gun	Birnding	bɪrndɪŋ
71.	War	Mpa	mpa
72.	Meat (animal)	Kum	kum
73.	Elephant	Chuwar	tʃuwʌr
74.	Buffalo	Fur	fur
75.	Leopard	Wula	ula (u with lip rounding)
76.	Monkey	Billam	bɪllam
77.	Pig	Fashu	fəʃu
78.	Goat	Ku	ku
79.	Dog	Khia	xia
80.	Bird	Iki	iki
	Feather	hlihli iki	ɬiɬi iki
81.	Crocodile	Khim	xɪm
	Horse	Tagu	tagu
	Sheep	Ntumahu	ntumahu
82.	Fowl	Imtika	ɪmtɪka
83.	Eggs	Ihimtika	ihɪmtɪka
84.	One egg	Ihimtika tataku	ihɪmtɪka tətəku
85.	Snake	Pabou	pabou
86.	Frog	Uhwambou	uhwambou
87.	Hausa	Hausa	hausa
	Beriberi	Uvwa	uvwa

	Hiji	Hiji	hɪdʒi
	Kilba	Khibba	xɪbba
	Bura	Bura	bura
	Pabir	Pabir	pabɪr
	Shuwa	Shuwa	ʃuwa
88.	Fly	Chidi	tʃidi
89.	Bee	Chidi	tʃidi
	Honey	Mamou	məmou
90.	Tree	Shiru	ʃɪru
	Ten trees	Shiru kum	ʃɪru kum
91.	Leaf	Iskwar	ɪskwar
92.	Guinea-corn	Ukhi	uxi
93.	Maize	Masar	masar
94.	Ground nut	Kwalchi	kwaltʃi
95.	Oil	Mal	mal
96.	The tall woman	Mala za gam	mala zə gam
	The tall women	Mahidi za gam	mahidi zəgam
97.	Large dog	Khya dagal	xja dəgal
98.	Small dog	Khya kushu	xja kuʃu
99.	The dog bites	Khya ngal	xja ŋal
100.	The dog bites me	Khya ngal da	xja ŋal da
101.	The dog which bit me yesterday	Khya ngal arda umna	xja ŋal arda umna
102.	I flog the dog	Ni an dabu khya (or Khya ni an dibu)	ni an dəbu xja (or xja ni an dəbu)
103.	The dog which I have flogged	Khya di an dibu	xja di an dəbu
104.	I see him or her	Nia wulari nyi	nia wulari nji
	He sees you	Naja wularingu	nadʒa wularɪŋu
	He sees us	Naja wulari mir (incl. person addressed)	nadʒa wularɪ mɪr
		Naja wulari ya (excl. person addressed)	nadʒa wularɪˤja
	We see you (pl.)	Naya wulari nyi	naˤja wularɪ nji
	We see them	Namir wularnda (incl.)	namɪr wularnda
		Naya wularnda (excl.)	naja wularnda
105.	Beautiful bird	Iki managu	iki mənagu
106.	Slave	Mafa	mafa
	My slave	Mafa giya	mafa gɪˤja
	Thy slave	Mafa ginnyi	mafa gɪnnji
	Our slaves	Mafar mir	mafar mɪr
107.	The chief's slave	Mafa ga ptil	mafa gə ptɪl
	His slave	Mafa ginda	mafa gɪnda
108.	We see the slave	Wular mir mafa	wular mɪr mafa
109.	We call the slave	Angar mir mafa	aŋar mɪr mafa
110.	The slave comes	Mafa vir shili	mafa uvɪr ʃili
111.	He came yesterday	Ashilir ja umna	aʃilir dʒa umna
	He is coming today	Naja ashili ashina	nadʒa aʃili aʃina

	He will come to-morrow	Naje shili a za gu	nadʒe ʃili a zə gu
112.	The slaves go away	Mafayer a tirra	mafajɛr a tɪrra
113.	Who is your chief ?	Wǫngo ptil nginyi ra ?	wɔŋo ptɪl ngɪnji ra
114.	The two villages are making war on each other	Millimu mihlu ampa aga kuvanyi	mɪllɪmu mɪɫu ampa aga kuvanji
115.	The sun rises	Bachi a ya sadu (or bachi uvra asaba)	bətʃi a ja sədu (or bətʃi uvra asəba)
	The sun sets	Bachi a tadu	bətʃi a tədu
116.	The man is eating	Mdu uvir sim	mdu uvɪr sɪm
117.	The man is drinking	Mdu uvir sa imi	mdu uvɪr sa imi
118.	The man is asleep	Mdu agwa uvwa nyi	mdu agwa uvwa nji
119.	I break the stick	Nia bil na zua	nia bɪl na zua
	The stick is broken	Azua a biliri (or azua a bilna kir)	əzua a bɪlɪri (or əzua a bɪlna kɪr)
	This stick cannot be broken	Azua ku a bilmai	əzua ku a bɪlməi
	Break this stick for me	Bilnada azua ku	bɪlnaɗa əzua ku
120.	I have built a house	A pa riyu mbwa	a pa riju mbwa
121.	My people have built their houses yonder	Inji gia a pa rimbwa alufuta	ɪndʒi gia a pa rɪmbwa alufuta
122.	What do you do every day ?	Hlirmi daga yu zarzar ra ?	ɫɪrmi dəga ju zarzar ra
	I work on my farm	Nai uvir yuhlirarfa giya	nai uvɪr ju ɫɪrarfa giˁja
123.	I am going away	Nia mai	nia məi
	I am hoeing	Nayu uvra za	naju uvra za
	I am going away to hoe	Nia mai aluza	nia məi aluza
	I am going away to my farm	Nia mai alufa giya	nia məi alufa giˁja
124.	The woman comes	Mal uvra shiri (or mala ayi shiri)	mal uvra ʃiri (or mala aji ʃiri)
	She comes	Naja uvra shiri	nadʒa uvra ʃiri
	The woman laughs	Mala nggushi	mala ŋguʃi
	The woman weeps.	Mala ti	mala ti
125.	I ask the woman	Nia jogbwa ara mala	nia dʒogbwa ara mala
126.	Why do you laugh ?	Ga mingu di ga nggushi ra ?	ga mɪŋu di ga ŋguʃi ra
127.	Why do you cry ?	Ga mingu di ga nggushi ti ?	ga mɪŋu di ga ŋguʃi ti
128.	My child is dead	Ubzir giya ga mtu	ubzɪr gɪˁja ga mtu

129.	It is not dead	Ai nda mtu mai	ai nda mtu məi
130.	Are you ill ?	Naga kila ngga ya ?	nagə kɪla ŋga ja
131.	My children are ill	Musha giya kila ngga	muʃa gɪˤja kɪla ŋga
132.	Her child is better	Ubzir ginda a nar boshang	ubzɪr gɪnda a nʌr boʃʌŋ
133.	Yes	I	i
	No	Au	əu
134.	A fine knife	Nyihya minagu	njihja mɪnagu
	Give me the knife	Narda nyihya	narda njihja
	I give you the knife	Nia nang nyihya	nia naŋ njihja
135.	I am a European	Nayu nasara	naju nasara
	You are a black man	Nagu mdu kingkyer	nagu mdu kɪŋkjɛr
	You are a Margi	Nagu Margi	nagu margi
136.	Name	Hlim	ɬɪm
	My name	Hlimda	ɬɪmda
	Your name	Hlimangu	ɬɪmaŋu
	What is your name ?	Wa hlimang ra ?	wa ɬɪmʌŋ ra
137.	There is water in the gourd	Imi wuḍa pilla	imi wuḍa pɪlla
	The knife is on the stone	Nyihya a dan tsikka	njihja a dan tsɪkka
	The fire is under the pot	Uu ira ntim	uu ira ntɪm
	The roof is over the hut	Kirimbwa a derim bwa	kɪrɪmbwa a dɛrɪm bwa
138.	You are good	Nagu minagu	nagu mɪnagu
	This man is bad	Mduku dumi	mduku dumi
139.	The paper is white	Kakadu pirtu	kakadu pɪrtu
	This thing is black	Saku kengkyer	səku kɛŋkjɛr
	This thing is red	Saku dazu	səku dəzu
140.	This stone is heavy	Insika ku ai tada bu	ɪnsɪka ku ai tədə bu
	This stone is not heavy	Insika ku ai tada mai	insika ku ai tədə məi
141.	I write	Nai arubotsini	nai arubɔtsɪni
	I give you the letter	Nia nang kakadu	nia nʌŋ kaka:du
	Carry the letter to the town	Mai da kakadu a lu milimu	məi də kaka:du a lu mɪlɪmu
142.	Go away	Mai ja (or mai)	məi dʒa (or məi)
	Come here	Azugu ufku	azugu ufku
143.	Where is your house ?	Mwar kiginyi ra ?	mwar kiginji ra
144.	My house is here	Kigi ya ayi vû	kɪgi ja aji vû
	My house is there	Kigi ya ayi vuta	kɪgi ja aji vuta
145.	What have you to sell ?	Mîga adil la ?	mîga adɪl la
146.	I want to buy fish	Nia yu dilba kifi	nia ju dɪlba kifi

147.	The fish which you bought is bad	Kifi daga dilba dumi	kifi dəga dɪlba dumi
148.	Where is the man who killed the elephant ?	Mwar mdu tsa chuwa ra ?	mwar mdu tsa tʃuwʌ ra
	He has killed many elephants	A tsiar ja chuwar wadi	a tsiar dʒa tʃuwʌr wadi
	How many elephants were killed yesterday ?	Chuwar idagu dim mdu tsi umna ra ?	tʃuwʌr idagu dɪm mdu tsi umna ra
149.	Untie it	Ampillnâ nyi	ampɪllnâ nji
	Tie this rope	Imbe asii ku	ɪmbe əsii ku
	Make the boy untie the goat	Fi abzir kaja mpillna ku	fi abzɪr kədʒa mpɪllna ku
150.	My brothers and I, we are going but no one else	Naya kaka zamda yer na amai izhiriya	naja kaka zamda jɛr na aməi iʒɪrija
	Brothers, let us go and tell the chief	Zamda yer mirimai anu ana ptil	zamda jɛr mɪrɪməi anu ana ptɪl
151.	This tree is bigger than that	Wuku dagal angwara tata	wuku dəgal aŋwara tata

NOTES ON MARGI GRAMMAR

Number.—Plural is formed by suffixing -er.
There is no grammatical gender.
Abstract nouns are formed by suffixing -kur.
The genitive is formed by inserting " nir " or by suffixing " r " ;
e.g. taku nir ptil = the horse of the king or takur ptil.
Disjunctive Pronouns are :—

	Singular	Plural
1.	Nayu	Namir or naya
2.	Nagu	Nanyi
3.	Naja	Nanda

Conjunctive :—

	Singular	Plural
1.	Ni or niya or -yu	Namir or -mir, naya or -ya
2.	Nagu or gu or -gu	Nanyi or -nyi
3.	Naja or ja or -ja	Nanda or -nda

Possessive pronouns are formed by infixing ki ; thus mine =
nikiya.
The accusative form of the first personal singular pronoun is " da ".
Interrogative pronouns are mi = what ? and wa = who ? (as in
Hausa).

The Verb

Incomplete action is indicated by suffixing " a " to the stem.

Continuous action is indicated by adding the particle uvra.

Completed action is indicated by suffixing the particle " ri ", and also by placing the subject pronoun after the verb, e.g. I went = amai -ri- yu. (But in negative sentences the subject comes before the verb.)

The future tense may be formed by inserting " adzugwa " between the subject and the verb.

Imperative singular = stem plus " ja " (thou).

Imperative plural = stem plus the particle " mu ".

MARGI (OF MINTHLA) VOCABULARY AND PHRASES

1.	Head	Kir	kɪr
2.	Hair	Chichi	tʃɪtʃɪ
3.	Eye	Nja	ndʒa
	Two eyes	Nji sudai	ndʒi suɗai
4.	Ear	Hlim	ɬɪm
	Two ears	Hlim suda	ɬɪm suɗa
5.	Nose	Umchir	umtʃɪr
6.	One tooth	Umshir duku	umʃɪr duku
	Five teeth	Mshir tufu	mʃɪr tufu
7.	Tongue	Kinyedu	kɪnjɛdu
8.	Neck	Wuya	wuja
9.	Breast (woman's)	Wa	wa
10.	Heart	Diffu	dɪffu
11.	Belly	Tumpwi	tumpwi
12.	Back	Khi	xi
13.	Arm	Chai	tʃai
14.	Hand	Chai	tʃai
	Two hands	Che sudai	tʃe suɗai
15.	Finger	Ngulandá	ngulanda
	Five fingers	Ngulandam tufu	ngulandam tufu
16.	Finger nail	Simpil	sɪmpɪl
17.	Leg	Shil	ʃɪl
18.	Knee	Kir unji	kɪr undʒi
19.	Foot	Pile shil	pɪle ʃɪl
	Two feet	Pile shil suda	pɪle ʃɪl suɗa
20.	Man (person)	Mda	mda or mdə
	Ten people	Mdu kume	mdu kumɛ
21.	Man (not woman)	Sal	sal
	Two men	Sal sudai	sal sudai
22.	Woman	Mwala	mwala
	Two women	Mwala sudai or mwɛnkɪgi	mwala suɗai or mwɛnkɪgi suɗai
23.	Child	Wozha	wɔʒa
24.	Father	Ada	ada
25.	Mother	Iya	ija
26.	Slave	Fari	fari

27. Chief	Mpsile	mpsɪlɛ
28. Friend	Umvwa	umvwa
29. Smith	Yiha or yiha ble	jɪha or jɪha blɛ
30. Doctor	Yiha or yiha kuzugu	jɪha or jɪha kuzugu
31. One finger	Gulanda duku	gulanda duku
32. Two fingers	Gulanda sudai	gulanda suɗai
33. Three fingers	Gulanda magir	gulanda magɪr
34. Four fingers	Gulanda fodu	gulanda fɔɗu
35. Five fingers	Gulanda tufu	gulanda tufu
36. Six fingers	Gulandan kwa	gulandan kwa
37. Seven fingers	Gulanda mudufa	gulanda mudufa
38. Eight fingers	Gulandan chisu	gulandan tʃisu
39. Nine fingers	Gulanda imle	gulanda ɪmlɛ
40. Ten fingers	Gulanda kume	gulanda kumɛ
41. Eleven fingers	Gulanda kum kab chatan	gulanda kum kab tʃatan
42. Twelve fingers	Gulandan kum kap-umya sudai	gulanda kum kap-umja suɗai
Thirteen fingers	Gulanda kum kap-umya māgir	gulanda kum kap-umja magɪr
43. Twenty fingers	Gulanda pindi	gulanda pɪndi
44. A hundred fingers	Gulanda miya	gulanda mija
45. Two hundred fingers	Gulanda yero sudai	gulanda jɛro suɗai
46. Four hundred fingers	Gulanda yero fodu	gulanda jɛro fɔɗu
47. Sun	Biji	bɪdʒi
God	Tambi	tambi
48. Moon	Shiya	ʃija
Full moon	Shiyambile	ʃijambɪlɛ
New moon	Mzirmzir shiya	mzirmzir ʃija
49. Day	Atabiji	atabɪdʒi
Night	Amvwi	amvwi
Morning	Tishigudu	tɪʃɪgudu
50. Rain	Yimi	jimi
51. Water	Yimi	jimi
52. Blood	Mungzhi	muŋʒi
53. Fat	Malkum	malkum
54. Salt	Kagila	kagɪla
55. Stone	Paya	paja
Iron	Yia	jia
56. Hill	Gar	gar
57. River	Manda (stream = gwoya)	manda (stream = gwoja)
58. Road	Khwole	xwɔlɛ
59. House	Mbwa	mbwa
Two houses	Mbwa sudai	mbwa suɗai
Many houses	Mbwa hang	mbwa haŋ
All the houses	Mbwa pitikam	mbwa pɪtɪkʌm
60. Roof	Kirambwa	kɪrambwa
61. Door	Nyarimbwa	njarɪmbwa

62.	Mat	Buchirpi	butʃırpi
63.	Basket	Adlambila	adlambıla
64.	Drum	Gangá	gaŋga
65.	Pot	Mtuhum	mtuhum
66.	Knife	Insha	ınʃa
67.	Spear	Mwashi	mwaʃi
68.	Bow	Lilei	lıləi
69.	Arrow	Kafa	kafə
	Five arrows	Kafin tufu	kafın tufu
70.	Gun	Binduku	bınduku
71.	War	Lida	lıdə
72.	Meat (animal)	Kum	kum
73.	Elephant	Chuwar	tʃuwar
74.	Buffalo	Fur	fur
75.	Leopard	Tugvwa	tugvwa
76.	Monkey	Dagil	dagıl
77.	Pig	Gadu	gadu
78.	Goat	Kwe	kwɛ
79.	Dog	Kia	kia
80.	Bird	Yaku	jaku
	Feather	Chichir yaku	tʃitʃir jaku
81.	Crocodile	Ngillim	ngıllım
	Fulani	Pulassar	pulassar
	Hausa	Abuno	abuno
82.	Fowl	Imdiga	ımdıga
83.	Eggs	Shishimdiga or shishi	ʃiʃımdıga or ʃiʃi
84.	One egg	Shishi duku	ʃiʃi duku
85.	Snake	Pwabu	pwabu
86.	Frog	Hwǫmbe	hwɔmbɛ
87.	Spider	Tautau	təutəu
88.	Fly	Chidi	tʃidi
89.	Bee	Chidi mime	tʃidi mımɛ
	Honey	Mime	mımɛ
90.	Tree	(Im) fwe	fwɛ
	Ten trees	Fu kume	fu kumɛ
91.	Leaf	Sali	sali
92.	Guinea-corn	—	—
93.	Maize	Apanau	apanəu
94.	Ground nut	Wine	winɛ
95.	Oil	Mal	mal
96.	The tall woman	Mwala sābil	mwala sabıl
	The tall women	Mwenkigi sabil sabil	mwɛnkıgi sabıl sabıl
97.	Large dog	Gazim keya	gazım keja
98.	Small dog	Keya kuturu, or, kuturu keya	keja kuturu, or, kuturu keja
99.	The dog bites	Keyegi wo kale	kejɛgi wo kalɛ
100.	The dog bites me	Keyegi wo kalida	kejɛgi wo kalıda
101.	The dog which bit me yesterday	Keyegi ta kari dandaha	kejɛgi ta kari dandaha
102.	I flog the dog	I ka cha keya	i kə tʃa keja
103.	The dog which I have flogged	Keye ti cha	kejɛ ti tʃa

104.	I see him or her	Igu wulen	igu wulɛn
	He sees you	Jagu wulange	dʒagu wulaŋɛ
	He sees us	Jagu wulamuri	dʒagu wulamuri
	We see you (pl.)	Ya gu wulagiri	ja gu wulagɪri
	We see them	Murku wi diri (or ya gu wulanda)	murku wi dɪri (or ja gu wulanda)
105.	Beautiful bird	Yaku mna	jaku mna
106.	Slave	Fari	fari
	My slave	Farida	farida
	Thy slave	Faringe	farɪŋɛ
	Our slaves	Fariyamuri	farijamuri
107.	The chief's slave	Farim hlile	farɪm ɬilɛ
	His slave	Farini	farini
108.	We see the slave	Murku wi fari (or ya gu wu fari)	murku wi fari (or ja gu wu fari)
109.	We call the slave	Murku ha fari (or ya gu hu fari)	murku ha fari (or ja gu hu fari)
110.	The slave comes	Fari ta si	fari ta si
111.	He came yesterday	Ja ka si ndaha	dʒa kə si ndaha
	He is coming today	Ja ta se shina	dʒa ta se ʃina
	He will come tomorrow	Ja ta si ashikudu	dʒa ta si aʃikudu
112.	The slaves go away	Fariagiri ka tira	fariagɪra kə tɪra
113.	Who is your chief?	Waie mpsilagiri?	waie mpsɪlagɪri
114.	The two villages are making war on each other	Milmagir sudai atamba tikan vwoni	mɪlmagɪr sud̃ai atamba tɪkan vwɔni
115.	The sun rises	Buji ta siba	budʒi ta sɪba
	The sun sets	Buji ka di	dudʒi kə di
116.	The man is eating	Mda ta sime	mdə ta sɪmɛ
117.	The man is drinking	Mda ta sa	Mdə ta sa
118.	The man is asleep	Mda ta hangi	mdə ta haŋi
119.	I break the stick	I ka bulu zuwa	i kə bulu zuwa
	The stick is broken	Zuwa ku buluji	zuwa ku buludʒi
	This stick cannot be broken	Zuwan kin gila bile	zuwan kɪn gɪla bɪlɛ
	Break this stick for me	Bilcheli zuwangi	bɪltʃeli zuwangi
120.	I have built a house	I kin bwi mbwa	i kɪn bwi mbwa
121.	My people have built their houses yonder	Injaa kimbwi mbwadar a vinda	ɪndʒaꞔa kɪmbwi- mbwa dar a vinda
122.	What do you do every day?	Mi ti gamwa anvui rugi?	mi ti gamwa anvui rugi

	I work on my farm	Iya mọ kisir akwọ fọda	ija mọ kɪsɪr akwɔ fɔda
123.	I am going away	I ta tira	i ta tɪra
	I am hoeing	I yen chuhwe	i jɛn tʃuhwɛ
	I am going away to hoe	I talan chuhwe	i talan tʃuhwɛ
	I am going to my farm	I ta liba akwọ fọda	i ta lɪba akwɔ fɔda
124.	The woman comes	Mwala ta si	mwala ta si
	He or she comes	Je ta si (she has come = ja ka si)	dʒɛ ta si (she has come = dʒa kə si)
	The woman laughs	Mwala ga nggushi	mwala ga ŋguʃi
	The woman weeps	Mwala ga towa	mwala ga towa
125.	I ask the woman	I ka jau mwala	i kə dʒəu mwala
126.	Why do you laugh ?	Ga nggushi ka mi ?	ga ŋguʃi ka mi
127.	Why do you cry ?	Ga tuwa mi ?	ga tuwa mi
128.	My child is dead	Mzida kamte	mzɪda kʌmtɛ
129.	It is not dead	Je tam tu we	dʒɛ tʌm tu wɛ
130.	Are you ill	Gi ngga wa ?	gɪ ŋga wa
131.	My children are ill	Wazheda ngga wa	waʒeda ŋga wa
132.	Her child is better	Mzinda kammwa bozhem	mzɪnda kʌmmwa boʒɛm
133.	Yes	I	i
	No	Aa	aɕa
134.	A fine knife	Insha imna	ɪnʃa ɪmna
	Give me the knife	Nai insha	nai nɪʃa
	I give you the knife	I ka naga insha	i kə ŋga ɪnʃa
135.	I am a European	I bature	i bature
	You are a black man	Gam mda mungil	gʌm mdə mungɪl
	You are a Margi	Ga Margi	gə margi
136.	Name	Hlim	łim
	My name	Hliman	łiman
	Your name	Hlimaga	łimagə
	What is your name ?	Wai hlimaga ?	wai łimagə
137.	There is water in the gourd	Yimi akwọ pila	jɪmi akwɔ pɪla
	The knife is on the stone	Insha ta kira paya	ɪnʃa ta kira paja
	The fire is under the pot	Au a kudan tuhum	aɕu a kudan tuhum
	The roof is over the hut	Mbwa ta ka kir	mbwa tə ka kɪr
138.	You are good	Gim mna	gɪm mna
	This man is bad	Imdigi imna we	ɪmdɪgi ɪmna wɛ
139.	The paper is white	Kakadu mimiya	kakadu mɪmija
	This thing is black	Su gi mungil	su gi mungɪl
	This thing is red	Su ga môza	su gə môza

140. This stone is heavy	Payagi ga gubu	pajagi gə gubu
This stone is not heavy	Payagi ka kafu	pajagi kə kafu
141. I write	I ga rubwǫchin.	i gə rubwɔtʃini
I give you the letter	I ga naga kakadu	i gə nagə kakadu
Carry the letter to the town	Aburte kakadu akwa milminda	aburtɛ kakadu akwa mɪlmɪnda
142. Go away	Abure	aburɛ
Come here	Asire	asɪrɛ
143. Where is your house ?	Kinga ama ?	kɪŋa ama
144. My house is here	Mbwada avugi (or kinga avugi)	mbwada avugi (or kɪŋa avugi)
My house is there	Mbwada avinda	mbwada avɪnda
145. What have you to sell ?	Gwa dil mi ?	gwa dɪl mi
146. I want to buy fish	I tuwa ki sukim kilfa	i tuwa ki sɪkɪm kɪlfa
147. The fish which you bought is bad	Kilfagi ti ga sikime mna we	kɪlfagi ti gə sɪkɪmɛ mna wɛ
148. Where is the man who killed the elephant ?	Amam diga ta che chuwargi ?	amam digə ta tʃe tʃuwargi
He has killed many elephants	Ja ga che chuwar hang	dʒa gə tʃe tʃuwar haŋ
How many elephants were killed yesterday ?	Chuwar dau tinde che dahagi ?	tʃuwar dau tɪndɛ tʃe dahagi
149. Untie it	Mpili ni	mpɪli ni
Tie this rope	Imbwi sugi	ɪmbwi sugi
Make the boy untie the goat	Vum zigi kajam mpili kugi	vum zɪgi kadʒam mpɪli kugi
150. My brothers and I, we are going but no one else	Ya kaka wojera mada yer ta tira shaa	ja kaka wɔdʒɛra mada jɛr ta tɪra ʃaʕa
Brothers, let us go and tell the chief	Wǫjera mada mura lampsile kambur la noalane	wodʒɛra mada mura lampsɪlɛ kambur la noalanɛ
151. This tree is bigger than that	Fugi ngata ndahe	fugi ngata ndahɛ

CHIBBAK VOCABULARY AND PHRASES

1. Head	Kir	kɪr
2. Hair	Chichi	tʃitʃi
3. Eye	Ntsa	ntsaʕ
Two eyes	Ntsa sasada	ntsaʕ səsədə

4. Ear	Hlima	ɬimə
Two ears	Hlimi sada	ɬimi sədə
5. Nose	Kuchir	kutʃɪr
6. One tooth	Khir dugu	xɪr dugu
Five teeth	Khir ntufu	xɪr ntufu
7. Tongue	Kanyer	kanjɛr
8. Neck	Wiya	wija
9. Breast (woman's)	Uwa	uˤwa
10. Heart	Dafu	dəfu
11. Belly	Kota	kotaˤ
12. Back	Khi	xi
13. Arm	Tsai	tsai
14. Hand	Hudur tsai	hudur tsai
Two hands	Hudur tsai sada	hudur tsai sədə
15. Finger	Kwai itsai	kwəi ɪtsai
Five fingers	Kwai itsai ntufu	kwəi ɪtsai ntufu
16. Finger nail	Mpaku	mpaku
17. Leg	Hlila	ɬila
18. Knee	Bunji	bundʒi
19. Foot	Khir hlil	xɪr ɬɪl
Two feet	Khir hlil sada	xɪr ɬɪl sədə
20. Man (person)	Nda	nda
Ten people	Nju kume	ndʒu kumɛ
21. Man (not woman)	Sal	sal
Two men	Sal sada	sal sədə
22. Woman	Mwala	mwala
Two women	Mwala sada	mwala sədə
23. Child	Izir	ɪzɪr
24. Father	Bana	bana
25. Mother	Mana	mana
26. Slave	Mafa	mafa
27. Chief	Kuhi	kuhi
28. Friend	Pazhi	paʒi
29. Smith	Igha	iga
30. Doctor	Ndir wunzim	ndɪr wunzɪm
31. One finger	Kwai itsai digu	kwəi ɪtsai dugu
32. Two fingers	Kwai itsai sada	kwəi ɪtsai sədə
33. Three fingers	Kwai itsai makir	kwəi ɪtsai makɪr
34. Four fingers	Kwai itsai fǫdu	kwəi ɪtsai fɔdu
35. Five fingers	Kwai itsai ntufu	kwəi ɪtsai ntufu
36. Six fingers	Kwai itsai nkwa	kwəi ɪtsai nkwa
37. Seven fingers	Kwai itsai murfe	kwəi ɪtsai murfɛ
38. Eight fingers	Kwai itsai nchis	kwəi ɪtsai ntʃis
39. Nine fingers	Kwai itsai mihle	kwəi ɪtsai mɪɬe
40. Ten fingers	Kwai itsai kume	kwəi ɪtsai kumɛ
41. Eleven fingers	Kwai itsai kume ka puchetam	kwəi ɪtsai kumɛ ka putʃɛtam
42. Twelve fingers	Kwai itsai kume ka pusada	kwəi ɪtsai kumɛ ka pusədə
Thirteen fingers	Kwai itsai kume ka makir	kwəi ɪtsai kumɛ ka makɪr

43.	Twenty fingers	Kwai itsai sa hlani	kwəi ɪtsai sə łani
44.	A hundred fingers	Kwai itsai haru	kwəi ɪtsai haru
45.	Two hundred fingers	Kwai itsai hari sada	kwəi ɪtsai hari sədə
46.	Four hundred fingers	Kwai itsai haru fǫdu	kwəi ɪtsai haru fǫdu
47.	Sun	Chichi	tʃitʃi
	God	Hyal	Hjal
48.	Moon	Hya	hja
	Full moon	Hya diembille	hja diɛmbɪllɛ
	New moon	Hya hyeteshina	hja hjɛtɛʃina
49.	Day	Chichi	tʃitʃi
	Night	Avirvir	avɪrvɪr
	Morning	Kulakula	kulakula
50.	Rain	Yimi	jimi
51.	Water	Yimi	jimi
52.	Blood	Mashi	maʃi
53.	Fat	Mal	mal
54.	Salt	Kagila	kagɪla
55.	Stone	Paya	paja
	Iron	Ngulam	ngulam
56.	Hill	Paya	paja
57.	River	Kyaha	kjaha
58.	Road	Uhwala	uhwala
59.	House	Fir (compound = ki)	fɪr (compound = ki)
	Two houses	Fir sada	fɪr sədə
	Many houses	Fir hang	fɪr haŋ
	All the houses	Fir tippu	fɪr tɪppu
60.	Roof	Maguzam	maguzʌm
61.	Door	Nyavir	njavɪr
62.	Mat	Kachi	kətʃi
63.	Basket	Kosar	kosʌr
64.	Drum	Gangga	gaŋga
65.	Pot	Tugum	tugum
66.	Knife	Ngazha	ngəzha
67.	Spear	Mwasu	mwasu
68.	Bow	Lilai	lɪlai
69.	Arrow	Hafa	hafə
	Five arrows	Hafintufu	hafɪntufu
70.	Gun	Bindigu	bɪndɪgu
71.	War	Mpa	mpa
72.	Meat (animal)	Kum	kum
73.	Elephant	Chuwar	tʃuwʌr
74.	Buffalo	Kufir	kufɪr
75.	Leopard	Wula	wula
76.	Monkey	Dagil	dagɪl
77.	Pig	Gadu	gadu
78.	Goat	Kwai	kwəi
79.	Dog	Hya	hja
80.	Bird	Ika	ika
	Feather	Chichi	tʃitʃi

81.	Crocodile	Ngillim	ngɪllɪm
	Horse	Tagu	tagu
	Sheep	Timma	tɪmma
82.	Fowl	Tika	tɪka
83.	Eggs	Hihin tika	hihɪn tɪka
84.	One egg	Hihin tika dugu	hinɪn tɪka dugu
85.	Snake	Pwọpu	pwɔpu
86.	Frog	Hwọmba	kwɔmnə
87.	Spider	—	—
88.	Fly	Chidi	tʃidi
89.	Bee	Chidi mame	tʃidi məmɛ
	Honey	Mame	məmɛ
90.	Tree	Unzim	unzɪm
	Ten trees	Unzim kume	unzɪm kumɛ
91.	Leaf	Sukwar	sukwʌr
92.	Guinea-corn	Wuhi	wuhi
93.	Maize	Masar	masar
94.	Ground nut	Awada	awada
95.	Oil	Mal	mal
96.	Beriberi	Uvwa	uvwa
	Bura	Bura	bura
	Hausa	Hausa	hausa
	Kilba and some Margi groups	Pella	pɛlla

PLAIN MARGI VOCABULARY AND PHRASES

1.	Head	Kir	kɪr
2.	Hair	Shishir kir	ʃiʃirkɪr
3.	Eye	Ighi	ɪɡi
	Two eyes	ghi miso	ɡi mɪso
4.	Ear	Hlimi	ɬimi
	Two ears	Hlimi miso	ɬimi mɪso
5.	Nose	Mchir	mtʃɪr
6.	One tooth	Khir tato	xɪr təto
	Five teeth	Khir tafo	xɪr təfo
7.	Tongue	Kyer	kjɛr
8.	Neck	Wiya	wija
9.	Breast (woman's)	Kharso	xarso
10.	Heart	Mọdufo	mɔdufo
11.	Belly	Wodo	wodo
12.	Back	Dagiri	dagɪri
13.	Arm	Itsi	ɪtsi
14.	Hand	Wod itsi	wod ɪtsi
	Two hands	Wod itsi modo	wod ɪtsi mɪso
15.	Finger	Zirtsi	zɪrtsi
	Five fingers	Mushartsi tafo	muʃartsi təfo
16.	Finger nail	Pil	pɪl
17.	Leg	Ikhi	ɪxi
18.	Knee	Wundi	wundi
19.	Foot	Wod ikhi	wod ɪxi
	Two feet	Wod ikhi miso	wod ɪxi mɪso

20.	Male (person)	Mdo	mdo
	Ten people	Mdip kumo	mdɪp kumo
21.	Man (not woman)	Sal	sal
	Two men	Sal miso	sal mɪso
22.	Woman	Mala	mala
	Two women	Mala miso	mala mɪso
23.	Child	Bzir	bzɪr
24.	Father	Tada	tada
25.	Mother	Mama	mama
26.	Slave	Mafa	mafa
27.	Chief	Ptil	ptɪl
28.	Friend	Mwal	mwal
29.	Smith	Inkyago	ɪnkjago
30.	Doctor	Mdil lawo	mdɪl lawo
31.	One finger	Tsi titro	tsi tɪtro
32.	Two fingers	Tsi miso	tsi mɪso
33.	Three fingers	Tsi makir	tsi makɪr
34.	Four fingers	Tsi fọt	tsi fɔt
35.	Five fingers	Tsi tafo	tsi təfo
36.	Six fingers	Tsi kwa	tsi kwa
37.	Seven fingers	Tsi madafo	tsi madəfo
38.	Eight fingers	Tsi sis	tsi sis
39.	Nine fingers	Tsi mizo	tsi mɪzo
40.	Ten fingers	Tsi kumo	tsi kumo
41.	Eleven fingers	Tsi kumo ligitan	tsi kumo lɪgɪtan
42.	Twelve fingers	Tsi kum ga pa miso	tsi kum ga pa mɪso
	Thirteen fingers	Tsi kum ga pa makir	tsi kum ga pa makɪr
43.	Twenty fingers	Tsi kum miskumi	tsi kum mɪskumi
44.	A hundred fingers	Tsi aharo	tsi aharo
45.	Two hundred fingers	Tsi haro miso	tsi haro mɪso
46.	Four hundred fingers	Tsi haro fọt	tsi haro fɔt
47.	Sun	Bichi	bɪtʃi
	God	Ijo	idʒo
48.	Moon	Hya	hja
	Full moon	Hyer asato	hjɛr asato
	New moon	Hyer wago	hjɛr wago
49.	Day	Da bichi	də bɪtʃi
	Night	Do wago	do wago
	Morning	Kulakula	kulakula
50.	Rain	Yimi	jimi
51.	Water	Yimi	jimi
52.	Blood	Mamchi	mamtʃi
53.	Fat	Mal	mal
54.	Salt	Uno	uno
55.	Stone	Inska	inska
	Iron	Iyang	ijaŋ
56.	Hill	Ungwo	uŋwo
57.	River	Dil	dɪl
58.	Road	Lago	lago

59.	House	Mbwa (compound = iki)	mbwa (compound = ɪki)
	Two houses	Mbwa miso	mbwa mɪso
	Many houses	Mbwa wadi	mbwa wadi
	All the houses	Mbwa cha	mbwa tʃa
60.	Roof	Mezham	meʒam
61.	Door	Mia di mbwa	mia dɪ mbwa
62.	Mat	Itifo	ɪtɪfo
63.	Basket	Ipyago	ɪpjago
64.	Drum	Kangga	kaŋga
65.	Pot	Etim	ɛtɪm
66.	Knife	Nizha	niʒa
67.	Spear	Maso	maso
68.	Bow	Laga	laga
69.	Arrow	Ghafo	gafo
	Five arrows	Ghafo tafo	gafo təfo
70.	Gun	Birnding	bɪrndɪŋ
71.	War	Mpa	mpa
72.	Meat (animal)	Kum	kum
73.	Elephant	Pir	pɪr
74.	Buffalo	Fir	fɪr
75.	Leopard	Mapilao	mapɪlao
76.	Monkey	Cho	tʃo
77.	Pig	Fusho	fuʃo
78.	Goat	Ko	ko
79.	Dog	Hya	hja
80.	Bird	Sivir	sɪvɪr
	Feather	Shishir sivir	ʃɪʃir sɪvɪr
81.	Lion	Alveri	alvɛri
	Crocodile	Kham	xʌm
	Sheep	Timakho	tɪmaxo
	Horse	Tago	tago
	Cow	hla	ɬa
82.	Fowl	Intika	ɪntɪka
83.	Eggs	Inhyim tika	ɪnhjɪm tɪka
84.	One egg	Inhyim tika titro	ɪnhjɪm tɪka tɪtro
85.	Snake	Pabo	pabo
86.	Frog	Hwambo	hwambo
87.	Spider	Tautau	təutəu
88.	Fly	Chidi	tʃidi
89.	Bee	Chidi mamo	tʃidi məmo
	Honey	Mamo	məmo
90.	Tree	Shiruu	ʃɪruu
	Ten trees	Shiruu komo	ʃɪruu komo
91.	Leaf	Iskwar	ɪskwʌr
92.	Ground nut	Kwalchi	kwaltʃi
93.	Guinea-corn	Okhi	oxi
94.	Maize	Masar	masar
95.	Oil	Mal	mal
96.	Beriberi	Uvwa	uvwa
	Hausa	Khausa	xausa
	Fulani	Pulasar	pulasʌr

CHAPTER V

SOME MANDATED TRIBES

The Higi.—The term Higi is applied to a large group of people inhabiting the slopes of the Mandara Hills between Wuba (Uba) and Madagali. It was first conferred by the Margi in the sense of " aboriginals ", and has been adopted by the Fulani, in the form Hiji. It has been accepted by the people so described (in the form Higi), who, however, commonly refer to themselves as Kamun or Kakhumu. The word Kamun is probably the same word as occurs in the tribal titles Kamu (Bauchi Province), Kam (Muri Emirate), and Kamu-ku (Niger Province), the meaning being " the people ". Kakhumu means " The people of the mountains ". The Higi are sometimes described as " The Hill Margi " ; and it will be seen from my notes on the Margi that there is some justification for this description, as there is a definite linguistic connection between the Higi and the Margi. The Higi language may in fact be included in the large group represented by Bura, Kilba, Chibak, and Margi. The Higi also follow the characteristic Kilba and Margi customs of removing the epidermis from the bodies of old people, and of burying their chiefs in charcoal, the latter custom being practised also by the Bura and Pabir. Their word for God, viz. Hyel, is the same as that of the Bura, Kilba, and some of the Margi groups. There is also among the Higi clear evidence that they, in spite of their mountainous position, had come under the influence of Bornu. Kanuri is widely understood and spoken, and their word for maize is " The guinea-corn of the Kanuri ". The characteristic facial mark of the Kanuri (down the centre of the forehead to the tip of the nose) is everywhere seen.[1]

On the other hand there is a traditional connection between most of the Higi groups and Gudur [2] (or Shakiri) in the French Cameroons, and it is on account of this connection that the Higi assert that they and the people of Sukur (Madagali district) are

[1] Many of the Higi were enslaved by the Kanuri. See *Barth's Travels*, vol. ii, pp. 406 and 417.
[2] The Higi are still accustomed to send regular gifts to the priest-chief Gudur.

one and the same, Sukur being an offshoot of Gudur. The people of Sukur are not included in the description "Higi", but if the Sukur vocabulary is compared with that of the Higi it will be seen that the two languages are closely related. There is considerable inter-marriage between the Higi and the people of Sukur, and the Higi have always regarded the chief of Sukur as a person of out-standing spiritual importance. It may be possible in the future to extend the administrative authority of the chief of Sukur on these grounds. Separate notes on the Sukur are attached to this paper, and it will be seen that the chiefs of Sukur claim a Kanuri origin. But it will be observed that the Sukur word for maize is " The guinea-corn of the Pabir ", an indication that the influence of the Pabir extended into the Mandara Hills

To the south of the Higi there are groups of so-called " Fali ", an unsatisfactory title, as it is applied to peoples who differ widely among themselves. I mention this here because one of the " Fali " groups (represented by the villagers of Kiria, Mijilu, Miza, Manzul, Dugoba, Jombula, and Kaskufa) is as closely related to the Higi as some of the Higi groups are to each other. They speak a language which is so akin to Higi that it might be described as a Higi dialect. It is much more closely related to Higi than to the language of the " Fali " of Mubi who live a few miles further south. Separate notes on both the Fali groups are attached.

The term Higi is applied to the inhabitants of the following villages : Kamalle, Magǫdi (Fr. Cameroons), Sinna Komde, Sinna Galla, Sinna Mala, Gur, Wumsike, Ja, Humsi, Wuria, Futu, Mukaba, Njido Boka, Yamu, Muzugu, Laka, Moda, Mukulu, Jigalumbu, Maninga, Wobazhi, Hwamildo, Hlirie, Sokomo, and Lapu. These do not form a single homogeneous whole, but fall into a number of groups, between whom there are considerable differences both in customs and in dialect. The groups might be loosely described as clans. Thus all the villages in the vicinity of Mukulu (Baza) form a single clan known as the Ngwalo, a word which is found as a tribal or sub-tribal title in other parts of Adamawa Province, and which means " The Men ".[1] The people of the Kamalle area call themselves the Kapsiki, those of Mukaba the Nkafa. Other groups are the Kamilda and Kafwe, etc.

---

[1] One of the principal tribes of the Wurkun district is called the Walo. In most of the Bata-speaking communities of Adamawa division, all of whom claim to have come from the region of Baza, there are groups who call themselves Ngwalo and are probably, therefore, of Higi origin.

In most but not all groups chiefs are buried in charcoal. In some groups the epidermis is removed, in others not. Initiation rites are held in some groups, and not in others. In some groups the birth of one child cancels the bride-price, in others two children are necessary. The variations in dialect are indicated in the vocabularies attached, and it need only be added that important dialectical differences may be found between villages which are no further than 6 miles apart. Thus at Moda the first personal pronoun is "*yira*", while at Mikulu it is "*zhe*".

It is not difficult to understand these variations in view of the fact that, until a few years ago, there was constant enmity between the various clans and even between villages of the same clan. Indeed all villages, except those which used the same water supplies and market, regarded each other as enemies. It is a tribute to the British administrative officers who have worked in this region that the roads are now safe for all and that the markets are crowded with people, who until recently could not have met each other without bloodshed.

The plains at the foot of the hills occupied by the Higi were formerly held by Margi who contained Pabir, Kanuri, and Mandara elements. The original centre of these Margi was a large town a few miles to the north of Wuba. The remains of this town can still be seen. It was succeeded by Baza, a town of great importance in pre-Fulani times, and the centre from which numerous groups of peoples were distributed to become rulers of Demsa, Holma, Zumu, Malabu, and various other communities. It is probable that some at least of the Higi chiefs are descended from the same stock. Baza was disrupted by the Fulani, who established settlements at Wuba, Michika, Moda, Duhu, and Madagali [1]; and the Higi are now governed (on behalf of the Emir of Adamawa) by the Fulani district heads of Wuba, Michika, and Madagali.

The Higi never had, like the Kilba and Margi, any system of secular chieftainship. The unit of government was the kindred. But the collection of kindreds who formed the local group recognized the spiritual authority of the local chief priest, i.e. of the person who owned the cult by which successful harvests were

---

[1] Several of the Higi villages became subservient to the Fulani to whom they paid gifts of cloth at sowing-time, and of sheep, goats, and honey at the Muhammadan festivals, in order to exempt themselves from slave-raids.

PLATE 25

A VIEW AT MICHIKA

[face p. 254

obtained, childbirth promoted, and epidemics diverted. Though the chief priest had no executive power, he served as a unifying agent and exercised considerable control. To offend the chief priest was to offend the gods he served and to endanger the public welfare. He was, therefore, an adviser and arbiter on all matters of importance. We even find that at Mukulu the chief priest was accustomed to confer the secular chieftainship on the heads of the Margi villages of Baza, Dille, and Mutaro. The chief-elect of each of these villages proceeded to Mukulu and, having given the priest of Mukulu a gift of a goat, was required to sit for an entire day on the sacred stone at Mukulu. He was then given an iron staff to which a number of iron hooks, such as are worn by Margi and Kilba women, were attached. (These hooks often form part of the religious paraphernalia among the Margi and Kilba.) On returning to his town the Margi chief went into seclusion for a period of seven days. When he emerged a cow was killed and the royal drum was beaten. His hair-lock was then re-plaited, and into the plait was woven the hair-lock of his predecessor. The sacred staff was sent back to the priest of Mukulu, together with a leg of the cow which had been killed.

When the priest-chief of Mukulu died his successor was brought before the corpse, and spoke as follows : " You have been chief, and you kept the people together in health, and have passed on. May I do likewise." He then stepped across the body and returned to his own home. On the conclusion of the burial rites the priest-chief-elect was required to spend seven days sitting on the sacred stone from sunrise to sunset, returning to his own house each evening. On the eighth day his head was shaven by the senior woman of the " Killa " or blacksmith kindred, a patch being left on the back of the head. This patch was plaited, and into the plait was inserted the hair-lock of his father or uncle who had formerly held the position of priest-chief. At a later period the father's lock was removed and preserved by the priest-chief in an antelope's horn which was kept, together with other hair-locks of more distant ancestors, in a leather bag. I have remarked in several reports that in ancient Egypt members of the royal family were distinguished by the wearing of a hair-lock, and that in Nigeria the Jukun, who practise much of the ritual which was followed in ancient Egypt and who regard themselves as a royal people, treat their hair-lock as a sacred thing. Among the

Pabir, Kilba, and Margi the hair-locks of chiefs are carefully preserved by their descendants ; and among the Sukur the chief's hair-lock is so sacred that it must never be seen. The chief of Sukur, therefore, wears a double cap during the day-time, and during the night continues to wear the under-cap. I would suggest that the preservation of the hair-lock may be a substitute for an anterior custom of preserving the skull. There is clear evidence among the Jukun that the use of rounded stones and fragments of corn-rubbers as symbols of forefathers are substitutes for skulls, and ultimately, perhaps, for mummified bodies.

It may be of interest to describe at this stage the burial ceremonial followed in the case of priest-chiefs and (with slight modifications) of old and important men and women. When the chief died his sons immediately seized their arms and proceeded to the confines of some neighbouring hostile village where they slew a grown-up male member of that village. For it was considered necessary that when the chief died one of his enemies should also die. Failing an enemy a cow or dog might be killed. When the sons returned home a drum was beaten and a horn was blown. This was the first public announcement of death, and the people then began to mourn. The body was set in a sitting position over a hole in the ground, and was washed with soap and water. The deceased's son massaged the abdomen in order to expel fæcal matter. The head was shaven and the hair-lock handed to the eldest son. The mouth was bound with a cloth to keep out flies. This cloth was removed before burial, and subsequently worn as a cummerbund by the youngest son ; if this were not done the youngest son would be pursued by his father's ghost. On the day of burial also a ring was placed on the dead man's finger, and after the body had been deposited in the grave the ring was removed by the youngest son and worn by him for the rest of his life. (The reason for the special position accorded to the youngest son is that, among the Higi, the youngest son inherits his father's house and the major part of his property, the other sons having already been provided with wives and established in homes of their own.)

The body was then set on a platform in a sitting position, with the back resting against the wall of a granary. The right hand was placed in a bowl filled with guinea-corn, and the left in a bowl of ground-nuts. In the evening the corn and nuts were removed, being replaced in the morning. After the burial the corn and nuts were cooked and given to the children of the household to eat. It is said that if these rites were not performed the dead person would take away with him the blessings of the crops. But it is possible that the custom was originally bound up with the idea of resurrection, and is related to the ancient Egyptian custom of placing in the grave a figure of Osiris filled with silt in which corn was planted.

On the evening of the second day the body was placed in a hole in the ground and covered with sand, with the intention of hastening decomposition and facilitating the subsequent removal of the epidermis. It was dug up on the following morning and set on the ground. In the case of a chief a fire was lighted close by, and pieces of meat were thrown on the fire in order to allay the odour of the body and drive away flies. The epidermis was then completely peeled off by a member of the blacksmith kindred. The nails on the fingers and toes were not removed. The skin was thrown into a pot and subsequently buried in a midden. The denuded body was then washed in a preparation of acacia juice, and the bark of the *Boswellia dalzielii* tree, and when dry, was smeared with some boiled goat-fat. It was then clothed in a leather loin-covering, gown, and red fez. A leather covering was also bound round the waist ; but this was removed before burial and appropriated by the deceased's younger brother.

Dancing had been begun on the second night, and was kept up until the inhumation. If the deceased had not been a chief the dressed-up body was taken on the shoulders of a man who joined in the dance, followed by all the senior men. When they tired they laid the body against a tree and went and regaled themselves with beer, the women and children continuing the dance. Immediately before burial the dead chief's " shafa " or talisman [1] was placed in his hands. It was then taken by the senior official and handed to the chief-elect. The dead man, if he had been a chief, was carried to the grave on the back of a man, held as a mother holds her child. If not a chief he was carried on the shoulders. If a chief, the body was closely surrounded by the senior men ; for no one might see a chief being carried to his grave. Indeed the whole of the ceremonial for burying a chief was carried out in strict privacy. The grave was of the shaft and recess type,

[1] See p. 225.

S

the body sitting on a stool in the shaft, with the legs extending into the recess. The head was supported with a piece of forked iron, the prong being stuck into the wall of the grave. The hands and feet also rested on forked iron, for no part of the body was allowed to touch the ground. The body was then (in the case of a chief) completely covered with charcoal.[1]

In some groups the chief was buried immediately on death, without the removal of the epidermis. This was the general rule also among the Kilba and certain sections of the Margi and Fali, the charcoal form of burial being reserved for chiefs, while the removal of the epidermis was confined to old and important commoners. The custom of removing the epidermis and treating the body with a tanning agent is no doubt a degraded form of mummification ; for in ancient Egypt the body was immersed in a saline bath in order to preserve it and remove adipose tissues. In the course of this bath the epidermis peeled off automatically.

The only rite subsequent to burial was the pouring, during the dry season, of libations over the grave by sons, who said : " Here is your share (of the funeral feast). To-day we part with you for ever." Widows then shaved their heads and were free to re-marry. These rites are still followed except, of course, as regards the custom of slaying an enemy on the death of a chief.

The Supreme Being among the Higi, as among the Bura, Kilba, and some groups of Margi, is known as Hyel. Similar views to those described in the notes on the Margi are held as regards the origin of the world and of death. The Earth is known as Ikhi, and though not definitely personified is vaguely regarded as the female counterpart of Hyel, it being held that Hyel fertilizes Ikhi by sending rain upon her. No rites are offered directly to Hyel, but in all shrines, when rites are performed to the local deities, the name of Hyel is invoked.

There are numerous cults. Thus at Mukulu the chief priest is the servitor of six different deities, viz. Peazguta, Wata Sira, Fi, Khildaka, Ta, and Soko Chilti. Peazguta is primarily connected with fertility. The symbols of the cult are said to be three pots, one of which has a number of iron hooks fastened round the neck. It is also said that the posts supporting the shrine are made of iron. During the full moon which immediately precedes the first

---

[1] In some groups, e.g. at Moda, the chief was not buried in charcoal, this form of burial being confined to members of the blacksmith kindred.

PLATE 26

A Woman and Man of the Higi Tribe

[face p. 258

rains the priest fills the sacred pots with sweet beer, and, having called on the deity to grant them a successful agricultural season and to promote childbirth amongst them, he comes out to join the senior men. With the seniors are assembled all youths and maidens who are to become husbands and wives that year. The priest takes a hoe, digs up a little earth, and sprinkles each of the young couples with the earth. He then enters his hut and remains in strict seclusion for three nights. On the fourth day all the members of his family, including small children, assemble ; and when the priest emerges he administers some of the sacred sweet beer to each person present. No one may sow before these rites are carried out ; for it is believed that any one breaking this rule would die before the harvest. The priest himself must remain unshaven throughout the wet season and until he has carried out similar rites at harvest.

The second cult, viz. that of Wata Sira, is of peculiar interest on account of the title of the deity. In my Jukun monograph[1] reasons have been given for believing that the common Nigerian (and African) root *chi*, *shi*, *usi*, in the sense of god, sun, or moon, embodies the same root as the Egyptian word Usiri, the Greek form of which is Osiris. The Higi, Kilba, Margi, and Bura word for sun is *va-chi*, and a few miles to the south of the Higi we find (among the Cheke) the form *usi-ra* = sun. It was stated by the Higi that the expression Wata Sira meant " The house of Sira ", i.e. " the house of the Sun ", it being said that *wata* meant " thatched roof ". This may be so ; but it is noteworthy that *watshir* means " the sun " in the language of the Gamergu who are not distant neighbours of the Higi. Moreover, in the prayers Wata Sira is addressed as such. In any case there can be little doubt that *sira* = the sun ; and it is probable, therefore, that the cult of Wata Sira was originally a sun cult. At the present time there is no association of Wata Sira with the sun ; he is regarded as a spirit or godling by whom successful harvests, increase of numbers, and general health can be obtained. His symbols, like those of Peazguta, are pots ; and regular rites are carried out thrice annually. Immediately before the preparation of the farms for sowing, sweet beer is placed in the pots by the priest, who says : " Wata Sira, we received our worship of you from our forefathers. Grant that all my people may have health.

---

[1] See *A Sudanese Kingdom*, pp. 180 et seq.

May they marry and get children, may they sow and get corn, may they get prosperity in all things." Three days later the priest re-enters the shrine and says : " By your grace I am about to give this beer to our children that they may grow up strong and marry and beget children, and be kept safe from all evil. Let those who love us not perish." The priest then drinks some of the beer, and afterwards administers small quantities to all male children born since last year. No farms may be prepared for sowing until these rites have been performed.

Later in the year when the maize crops have ripened the priest slays a goat at the door of the shrine, saying : " I pour out to you the blood of this goat. May I continue to serve you for many years. May I and my people have health. May our children marry and beget children." The flesh of the goat is then cooked. Some is eaten by the priest and some is thrown into the shrine. The remainder is consumed by the senior men present. These rites permit the people to eat of the new maize ; but the priest himself must abstain until all the crops have been harvested.

The concluding rites are carried out at the guinea-corn harvest. The priest sends to the Margi chief of Baza in order to obtain first-fruits of the new corn, together with the first-fruits of beans, ground-nuts, and pumpkins. The corn is milled and made into porridge by male members of the priest's family, and the other first-fruits are used to make the sauce which accompanies the porridge at every evening meal. When all is prepared the priest goes with the viands to the door of the shrines of Wata Sira and of Suko Chilti, and says : " By the grace of Wata Sira and by the grace of Suko Chilti may we partake of this new corn in health. Let no evil befall us." He then throws some of the porridge into the shrine, and having eaten a few fragments himself he hands the remainder to junior members of his family to consume. When these rites, which are carried out at the new moon, are completed the priest is permitted to shave, and the people to use their new guinea-corn.

Disputes are commonly settled by an appeal to the gods. Thus the Higi follow the Kilba and Margi custom of settling all minor disputes by swearing on the sacred symbol known as " shafa ", a description of which is given in my notes on the Margi tribe. Major matters are referred to the ordeal of " Guti " at Wuba, or of " Khumhla " at Kamalle. The procedure followed at Wuba is described in my notes on the Margi. " Khumhla " is enshrined in a grove and symbolized by a pot. The disputants, one of whom may have accused the other of witchcraft, go to the priest of " Khumhla ", each provided with a pullet. The priest addresses the godling, saying : " By thy grace, and by the grace of Hyel who gave you to us that you might reveal to us those that speak the truth and those that lie, and that you might catch those that lie, may he who speaks the truth in this matter return to his home in health, without so much as stumbling by the wayside. But may the liar be caught by you and delivered to me." The two pullets are then released, and if one climbs on to the sacred pot his owner is declared to have won the ordeal. This pullet is killed by slitting its throat, the blood being poured over the sacred symbol and the flesh being eaten by the priest and the senior men present. The other pullet is beaten to death by sticks and is eaten by immature persons, for the young are considered to be (in these matters) safe from the jealousy of the gods. The loser is arrested by the priest, and kept in custody until his relatives have redeemed him by paying to the priest a fine of one goat. The loser has also to pay compensation to the winner. If neither pullet mounts on to the sacred pot both parties are declared to be liars. The decision can be manipulated by the priest, who contrives to give drink secretly to the pullet of the man whom he adjudges to be guilty. The other chicken, impelled by thirst, mounts the pot which has been previously filled with water.

I did not inquire further into the religious beliefs of the people, but it was stated that during an epidemic it was customary to slay a black goat and spread the skin between two posts at a cross-roads. After sunset all the people came out with firebrands in order to drive the spirit of disease out of the town. The Higi have not the Yungur and Gabin custom of relegating disease-inducing spirits to pots or other material objects. There is no strict taboo against menstruous women, but most Higi men who are the owners of amulets or talismans avoid eating food cooked by a woman in this condition. It is said also that if a woman who is still subject to menstruation looks on the body of a dead priest chief she will meet with a speedy death. The custom by which all foods used in sacrificial rites must be prepared by men instead of women is probably to be referred to the menstruation taboo (as among the Jukun). It is noteworthy that most of the cults are described as " Hyela ", i.e. as " gods ". This is also the Bura, Kilba, and Margi practice, and it is clear that ancestor worship is of small account among these groups of peoples. Nor is there any evidence (as among the Jukun-speaking people) that deceased chiefs attain the rank of gods.

Social Organization.—As already indicated the Higi consist of a number of units which might roughly be described as clans, on grounds of a common dialect and common customs. But there is no clan organisation, for the social unit is the kindred, and the political unit is the village group. A number of villages may be united, either through the fact that all look to the same priest as the guarantor of their welfare, or that all use the same water supplies and markets, and must therefore live in a state of comparative friendliness (which results in intermarriage). There is no wider allegiance ; and in fact there was, until recent years, a definite hostility to all others, especially to the next-door neighbour. Within the restricted group itself there may be recurrent hostility between kindreds, even between related kindreds. Thus two kindreds, the founders of whom were half-brothers by the same father, are commonly at daggers drawn. Normally two kindreds whose founders were full brothers will act together against those whose founders were only half-brothers. (But a case came to my notice of a feud which had lasted for many years between two kindreds, the founders of whom were reputed to be full brothers.) Inter-kindred combats, however, seldom entailed loss of life, for the use of the more lethal weapons was taboo, each side fighting with clubs only.

The kindreds are patrilineal, and each kindred is exogamous, i.e. no man may marry a woman of his own kindred. But the rule of exogamy is not applied further ; for a man may marry a woman of a kindred which is reputed to be related to his own. A man may not marry a woman known to be related to him on his mother's side. It will be seen later, when we come to review the marriage regulations, that households are frequently of a mixed character owing to the custom by which children may be adopted by their mother's second or third husband.

But such adoption does not invalidate the rule of exogamy which is based on consanguinity, and great care is taken by fathers who may have lost the custody of some of their children to warn those children of the impossibility of marrying anyone

PLATE 27

A HIGI MARKET

belonging to his own kindred. When those children themselves bear children the latter regard themselves as members of their father's adopted kindred, and they neither marry into that kindred nor yet into the kindred of the paternal grandfather. But beyond that stage the rule of exogamy is only applied as regards the kindred into which the forefather had been adopted.

It may be noted, incidentally, that among the Higi there is no prohibition against eloping with the wife of a member of any kindred of the local group (other than of one's own kindred), provided the woman is not a member of one's own kindred.[1] This is of interest because among the Margi,[2] who are closely associated with the Higi, there is a strict rule that no one may elope with the wife of a member of his own local group, as the kindreds of the local group exchange their daughters in marriage. Among the Jirai, on the contrary, daughters must be married outside the local group ; but within the local group there is an interchange of wives. The existence of these two opposing (apparently) principles within a small area is very striking.

Inheritance follows the patrilineal principle, i.e. the eldest surviving brother, or in his absence the eldest son, inherits all property and uses it on behalf of the members of the whole family whether they are living with him or not. But unmarried sons have a special claim, and it is incumbent on the heritor to use the deceased's property primarily to provide the deceased's unmarried sons with wives. As married sons have established (usually) separate compounds for themselves it frequently happens that a young unmarried boy inherits his father's compound. The establishment of separate compounds, however, does not ordinarily entail a breach within the family, and by family I mean the extended family as compared with the wider unit, the kindred. For a younger brother will normally follow the directions of an elder brother in all matters, social, religious, and economic, unless the elder brother has proved himself to be unworthy of leadership. It may be noted that among the Higi, in spite of the fact that women can change their husbands without difficulty, all wives are expected to work vigorously on the farms of their husbands, and that they have no farms of their own, except the " cabbage

---

[1] But it is unusual to elope with the wives of neighbours who use the same water supplies and roads.
[2] I.e. in those groups of Margi among whom elopement marriages are a recognized institution.

patches " round their husbands' compounds. Widows are heritable (if they so desire) by senior or junior brothers or cousins ; but sons do not inherit the young widows of their fathers. There is, however, no objection to a son inheriting the young widow of a paternal uncle.

The following are the terms of relationship :—

Ta (possessive *ta-ra*) is applied to a father and his brothers and any male of a senior generation.

Mma = mother, mother's sister, father's sister, father's brother's wife, and any female of a senior generation.

Zugwi = son, daughter or any of a junior generation.

Siga = is a special term for maternal uncle.

Shi = all grandparents and all grandchildren.

Gwasama = full brother or sister or half brother or sister by the same mother. It is applied generally to anyone of the same generation.

Gwasata = half brother or sister by the same father.

An elder brother is called *dokule* (possessive = *dokulra*).

An elder sister is called *kuve* (possessive = *kuvra*).

A younger brother is called *sake* (possessive = *sakara*).

A younger sister is called *sake* (possessive = *sakara*).

Mala (*ra*) = wife.

Za (*ra*) = husband.

Mokwo (*ra*) = parents-in-law and children-in-law.

Mive = brothers-in-law and sisters-in-law.

There is nothing of particular interest about this system. But it is noteworthy that, though the junior levirate is practised, the Higi do not follow the common custom by which a woman addresses her husband's younger brother as " my husband " (and he addresses her as " my wife "). A number of the terms (viz. *siga, mala, za*) are the same as those used by the Margi.

In most of the Higi groups there is some form of puberty rites for boys. These rites, which are held before the planting of the crops, are of a simple character and only last for three or four days. The boys are collected in an enclosure, and each is attended by a senior who has no sons of his own undergoing the rites. The boys are given a special loin-covering of cow-hide, and are taught a new dance which is known as Putta. They are well fed and are not subjected to any form of chastisement. But on the con-clusion of the rites they are told that they have now become men and must behave as such and make a home for themselves. They are also required to assist their guardian in the work of clearing his farm and planting his crops. No boy may marry until he has gone through the rites ; but the rites are not, as among the Kilba and Margi, regarded as a form of betrothal, nor is the boy smeared with ochre. But among the Higi of the Moda area (who have no puberty rites) it is customary for a man and his virgin bride to smear themselves with ochre for a period of two months after their marriage. The Higi do not practise circumcision. There are no puberty rites for girls, but no girl may marry until she has had one set of bodily marks incised (the remainder are incised after marriage).

Virgin girls are usually given in marriage to youths of their own local group (but not of course to men of their own kindred). The father of the suitor makes a preliminary gift of from three to twenty pieces of iron currency, together with some tobacco snuff to the father or guardian of the girl. If these are accepted the boy and girl are regarded as betrothed, and the boy's father sends at intervals further gifts of beer, meat, a goat, and fifteen lumps of natron. The boy's father has also to assist the girl's father or guardian at certain periods of the agricultural year, until the boy is old enough to farm by himself. The final payments follow on the puberty rites described above, and consist of two gowns and one goat payable to the girl's father or guardian, and ten pieces of iron currency and one lump of natron payable to her mother. The girl is then captured by the bridegroom's friends, but is immediately reclaimed by her father on the pretext that the bridegroom has not completed his farm-work : but in due course the father sends the girl to her husband's home, having received further gifts of beer and of goats. It is to be noted that the father or guardian of a girl always uses the bride-price received to provide a wife for his own son.

We come now to the most interesting feature of the social life of the Higi, viz. the customs connected with secondary marriages and the custody of children. The general principle appears to be that in a primary marriage the birth of two children[1] cancels the bride-price, even if the children die on the day of their birth. From this it follows that a wife who has borne two children to her husband can, without prejudice, leave him for someone else ; and if she has borne more than two children the excess children belong theoretically to her and her family. It is customary, therefore, for a husband who obtains more than two

---

[1] But in the Sinna group the birth of one child cancels the bride-price.

children from his wife to give a gift of a goat and of salt to her father or brother for each child in excess of two. Otherwise the wife's father would urge her to abandon her husband and seek another, taking the excess children with her.

A secondary husband, therefore, is not required to compensate a primary husband if his wife had borne two children to the primary husband. But he is expected to give a gift of one goat and some salt and corn to his wife's father or brother. If he obtains a child by his wife he is under no obligation to give anything to his wife's guardian, the child being considered as compensation for his initial gift. But if he obtains a second child he is required to give a further gift of a goat and gown to his wife's guardian ; otherwise the latter will restore the woman to her first husband or give her to a third.

We have said that a wife who has borne more than two children to her first husband is at liberty to take the excess children with her, if she leaves her first husband. But the first husband may obtain the custody of the excess children by payments to his wife's guardian. On the other hand the wife's guardian may refuse these payments (if offered) and hand the children over to the custody of the second husband, should the second husband be prepared to make the necessary payments (viz. one goat and gown for each child). If neither the first nor second husband is prepared to make the payments for the children the wife's father may claim the children himself, using the bride-price obtained for the female children to obtain wives for the male children. But male children can always, when they grow up, go back to their father's home, should they so desire.

Actually many children are brought up, not in their father's home, but in the home of their mother's second or possibly third husband. They are in fact adopted by him and remain with him, even if their mother does not. They are at liberty to return later to their father's home ; but in this case the father would have to compensate their adopter (who had made payments in order to obtain custody). Many children prefer to remain on in the home of their adopter. It is said that a man treats adopted sons better than his own in order that both they and their mother may continue to live with him. They are entitled to inherit equally with any other member of the family, and an adopted son may even inherit the priestly office, though a priest would be careful not to disclose the secrets of the cult to an adopted son unless he were certain that the latter would not return to his father's home.

If a wife leaves her first husband without having borne him any children the second husband must refund the whole of the bride-price paid by the first husband. If she had borne him one child the bride-price is reduced by half. But if the child accompanies the mother to her new husband the bride-price is repayable in full. For the child may insist on accompanying the mother, or may be so young that he cannot be parted from the mother. But if the child eventually returns to his father's home the father is required to refund to the second husband half the bride-price he had received from him.

If a secondary husband is under an obligation to repay part or the whole of the first husband's bride-price, and fails to make the payments, the first husband can claim the first child or the first two children born to the second husband. Many secondary husbands postpone making any payments until they see how the marriage is likely to turn out; for the wife's guardian may disapprove of the secondary husband and urge her to return to the first. It is not uncommon for a woman's guardian to allow her to live with a secondary husband until she conceives or bears a child and then compel her to return to her first husband, by whom she had borne no children. If the woman subsequently bears two children to her first husband then the second husband can reclaim his child (but he would have to make the customary gift to the woman's father).

It is obvious from the above rules that many Higi households are by no means of the purely patriarchal type, and might be described as bilateral. The wife's father or brother occupies a dominating position in the social life of the people. It is also clear that disputes over women and the custody of children are endless and the main cause of the inter-village hostility which is so pronounced among the Higi. An alteration in the marriage laws is always justifiable under such circumstances, and is in fact an essential step towards creating the wider solidarity aimed at by the Administration. A rule has, therefore, been introduced that all children over seven years of age must remain with their fathers, and that in all cases the bride-price for a girl is receivable by fathers and not by adopted fathers. My notes unfortunately do not reveal how these rules are applied to all the circumstances, but it is now possible for any father to be assured of the custody of his children (should he so desire and be able to make the necessary payments).

Material Culture.—The most noteworthy feature about Higi villages is the large neatly-built stone walls which surround the compounds and home-farms. These walls may be anything from 3 to 5 feet high. Huts are made of sun-dried mud and thatch, the peak of the thatch being covered with a cap of plaited straw. The mud for building is strengthened by the admixture of chopped straw. Rafters are not used in thatching, the roof being supported by a concave shell of plaited straw. Each wife has three huts joined together by a rectangular enclosure of matting, one hut being used for sleeping, one for milling, and the third for cooking. The enclosure is used as a sitting-room in dry weather. Husbands usually have a hut of their own. The bedstead is a single wooden plank laid on the ground or on a foundation of stones. But many Higi have adopted the Fulani custom of sleeping on straw mats. In most of the huts there are shelves made of bamboos or guinea-corn stalks. Granaries are not usually built inside the huts, as they are among the Kilba. A noteworthy feature, only observed elsewhere among the Verre and Chamba, is the use of wooden mallets for beating corn. Bows are of the single eyelet type found among most of the Northern Adamawa tribes, but the technique is different, the string being tightened at the eyelet end. The Higi also use spears and shields (of buffalo hide), and many have adopted the Margi type of throwing-iron. Among musical instruments the single membrane drum known to the Hausa as "*kutunku*" is used (especially at the puberty dances). Flutes and whistles are played by boys and young men, but playing is forbidden while the crops are ripening, lest the corn-spirit should be offended by the noise. A flute with four stops and a horn fixed on to the end is blown when a priest-chief or member of his family dies. A few Higi have harps of the West African type.

As regards clothing and ornaments the senior men wear goat-skins slung from the shoulder, but a number of the more important men now wear gowns on special occasions. The younger men wear a loin-covering consisting of two cloths. One is worn behind and the flap is brought forward between the legs to cover the genital organs. The triangular cloth worn in front hangs down

PLATE 28

WALL OF A HIGI VILLAGE

A HIGI WOMAN

[face p. 268

like an apron. Leather loin-coverings are also worn, especially by the senior men. Women wear leather fringes in front, and string fringes or a bunch of leaves behind. When the women are young the leather fringes are adorned with brass rings, but these are discarded when they become mothers. As among the Margi, babies are protected from the sun and rain while being carried by a covering of basketry.

The following designs of facial markings were observed :—

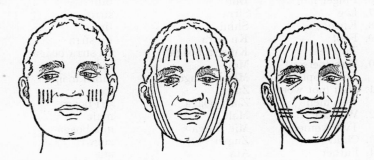

Attached is a full schedule of words and phrases together with short vocabularies illustrating dialectical differences. The schedule should be compared with (a) Margi, (b) Sukur, and (c) the language of the " Fali " of Kiria. There are some resemblances in vocabulary with Mandara (Wandala), and a Mandara vocabulary is, therefore, attached.

The vocabularies of " Hidji " and " Kapsiki," obtained by Dr. Strumpell, the German philologist, will be found to coincide with those given here, " Kapsiki " being the language spoken by the Higi of Kamalle.

THE HIGI LANGUAGE

Moda dialect Vocabulary and Phrases

1.	Head	Ikha	ıxa
2.	Hair	Shinti	ʃınti
3.	Eye	Intsa	ıntsə
	Two eyes	Intsa boaga	ıntsa boagə
4.	Ear	Hlime	ɬımɛ
	Two ears	Hlim boaga	ɬım boagə
5.	Nose	Nchi	ntʃi
6.	One tooth	Hline kute	ɬınɛ kutɛ
	Five teeth	Hlinim chiffe	ɬınım tʃıffɛ
7.	Tongue	Ane	anɛ

8.	Neck	Wure	wure
9.	Breast (woman's)	Wa	waꞎ
10.	Heart	Mni	mni
11.	Belly	Uhwi	uhwi
12.	Back	Mbwi	mbwi
13.	Arm	Pilla	pɪlla
14.	Hand	Hu	hu
	Two hands	Hu boaga	hu boagə
15.	Finger	Rihi ipilla	rihi ɪpɪlla
	Five fingers	Rihi ipilla chiffe	rihi ɪpɪlla tʃɪffɛ
16.	Finger nail	Billi	bɪlli
17.	Leg	Sirra	sɪrra
18.	Knee	Shini	ʃini
19.	Foot	Ku sirra	ku sɪrra
	Two feet	Ku sira boaga	ku sɪrra boagə
20.	Man (person)	Mdi	mdi
	Ten people	Mbiri monge	mbiri mɔŋɛ
21.	Man (not woman)	Za	za
	Two men	Zhiri boaga	ʒiri boagə
22.	Woman	Male	malɛ
	Two women	Mie boaga	miɛ boagə
23.	Child	Zugwi	zugwi
24.	Father	Ata	əta
25.	Mother	Mama	mama
26.	Slave	Mava	mava
27.	Chief	Mbage	mbəgɛ
28.	Friend	Mchera	mtʃɛra
29.	Smith	Rihye	rihje
30.	Doctor	Ndufwe	ndufwɛ
31.	One finger	Rihi kute	rihi kutɛ
32.	Two fingers	Rihi boaga	rihi boagə
33.	Three fingers	Rihi makinne	rihi makinnɛ
34.	Four fingers	Rihi fware	rihi fwarɛ
35.	Five fingers	Rihi chiffe	rihi tʃɪffɛ
36.	Six fingers	Rihi kwange	rihi kwaŋɛ
37.	Seven fingers	Rihi murfunge	rihi murfuŋɛ
38.	Eight fingers	Rihi tikisse	rihi tɪkɪssɛ
39.	Nine fingers	Rihi tiyi	rihi tiji
40.	Ten fingers	Rihi monge	rihi mɔŋɛ
41.	Eleven fingers	Rihi monge kutene kute	rihi mɔŋɛ kutɛnɛ kutɛ
42.	Twelve fingers	Rihi monge boaga	rihi mɔŋɛ boagə
	Thirteen fingers	Rihi monge makinne	rihi mɔŋɛ makinnɛ
43.	Twenty fingers	Rihi bakimsi	rihi bakɪmsi
44.	A hundred fingers	Rihi mong nimsi	rihi mɔŋ nɪmsi
45.	Two hundred fingers	Rihi boaga monge	rihi boagə mɔŋɛ
46.	Four hundred fingers	—	—
47.	Sun	Vachi	vətʃi
	God	Hyela tumwe	hjɛla tumwɛ

48. Moon	Tirre	tɪrrɛ
Full moon	Tirre latidide	tɪrrɛ lətɪkɪde
New moon	Tirr lawa	tɪrr lawa
49. Day	Ka vachi	kə vətʃi
Night	Ivre	ɪvrɛ
Morning	Makinne	makɪnnɛ
50. Rain	Va	va
51. Water	Yiemi	jiɛmi
52. Blood	Mimi	mimi
53. Fat	Mabgye	mabgje
54. Salt	Omne	ɔmnɛ
55. Stone	Pirre	pɪrrɛ
Iron	Ere	ɛre
56. Hill	Mwe	mwɛ
57. River	Hlirre	ɬɪrrɛ
58. Road	Hungkwa	huŋkwa
59. House	Impea	ɪmpea
Two houses	Impea boaga	ɪmpea boagə
Many houses	Impea bwabwa	ɪmpea bwa bwa
All the houses	Impea cheche	ɪmpea tʃetʃe
60. Roof	Eche	etʃe
61. Door	Nyim pea	njim pea
62. Mat	Bitu	bitu
63. Basket	Kwachika	kwatʃɪka
64. Drum	Kangga	kaŋga
65. Pot	Dugu	dugu
66. Knife	Hwa	hwa
67. Spear	Mbaga	mbəga
68. Bow	Rigi	rigi
69. Arrow	Have	havɛ
Five arrows	Havim chiffe	havɪm tʃɪffɛ
70. Gun	Birdengi	bɪrdɛŋi
71. War	Mpa	mpa
72. Meat (animal)	Ti	ti
73. Elephant	Chuwe	tʃuwɛ
74. Buffalo	Kilfe	kɪlfe
75. Leopard	Puke	pukɛ
76. Monkey	Lukwi	lukwi
77. Pig	Girdi	gɪrdi
78. Goat	Ukwe	ukwɛ
79. Dog	Kirre	kɪrrɛ
80. Bird	Gie	giɛ
Feather	Shinshe gie	ʃɪnʃɛ giɛ
81. Crocodile	Ikilimi	ɪkɪlɪmi
Lion	Makogula	makɔgula
Cow	Hla	ɬa
Sheep	Timi	tɪmi
82. Fowl	Kangka	kaŋka
83. Eggs	Tihle	tɪɬe
84. One egg	Tihle	tɪɬe
85. Snake	Shishi	ʃiʃi

86. Frog	Gwambe	gwambɛ
87. Spider	Tatamba	tatamba
88. Fly	Zhuwi	ʒuwi
89. Bee	Unze	unzɛ
Honey	Unze	unzɛ
90. Tree	Ipchi	ɪptʃi
Ten trees	Ipchi monge	ɪptʃi mɔŋɛ
91. Leaf	Ɖeri	ɖeri
92. Guinea-corn	Kha	xa
93. Maize	Khavwa	xavwa
94. Ground nut	Kula koche	kula kɔtʃe
95. Oil	Gi	gi
Horse	Giduwi	gɪduwi
96. The tall woman	Male de hye	malɛ dɛ hjɛ
The tall women	Mi dehyu heni	mi dehju hɛni
97. Large dog	Kirre bwa	kɪrrɛ bwa
98. Small dog	Kirre bate	kɪrre bate
99. The dog bites	Kirre halungkwa	kɪrre haluŋkwa
100. The dog bites me	Kirre halira	kɪrre halɪra
101. The dog which bit me yesterday	Kirre hal vira mbara	kɪrre hal vira mbəra
102. I flog the dog	Yira hlivante kirre	jira ɬivənte kɪrre
103. The dog which I have flogged	Kirre asa yira hlivante	kɪrre asa jira ɬivənte
104. I see him or her	Yira nata ndi	jira nata ndi
He sees you	Nji kin nata na	ndʒi kin nata na
He sees us	Nji kin nata mi	ndʒi kɪn nata mi
We see you (pl.)	Nayi kin nata ye	naji kɪn nata jɛ
We see them	Nayi kin nata hya	naji kɪn nata hja
105. Beautiful bird	Ye dandara	jɛ dandara
106. Slave	Mava	mava
My slave	Mava tara	mava tara
Thy slave	Mava ranga	mava raŋa
Our slaves	Mava raye	mava rajɛ
107. The chief's slave	Mavara mbage	mavara mbəge
His slave	Mavara nje	mavara ndʒɛ
108. We see the slave	Yi kin nata mava (or mi in the dual)	ji kɪn nata mava (or mi in the dual)
109. We call the slave	Iyi ka mava (or mi in the dual)	iji ka mava (or mi in the dual)
110. The slave comes	Na mava su kwa	na mava su kwa
111. He came yester-day	Nji sukwa mbira	ndʒi sukwa mbɪra
He is coming to-day	Nja sukwa beshi	ndʒa sukwa beʃi
He will come to-morrow	Sukwa shinje khah-lime	sukwa ʃindʒe xa-ɬimɛ
112. The slaves go away	Mavari cha sukwa	mavari tʃa sukwa
113. Who is your chief ?	Wa mbagang a re ?	wa mbəgaŋ a rɛ

114. The two villages are making war on each other	Millime boaga mpa limburi hya	mɪllɪmɛ boagə mpa lɪmburi hja
115. The sun rises	Vachi sime	vətʃi sɪmɛ
The sun sets	Vachi zuga	vətʃi zuga
116. The man is eating	Mde zime sukiz zume	mdɛ zɪmɛ sukɪz zumɛ
117. The man is drinking	Mde sa yami	mdɛ sa jami
118. The man is asleep	Mdi ta hya	mdi ta hja
119. I break the stick	Yira bilimte dilla	jira bɪlɪmte dɪlla
The stick is broken	Dilla ka bille	dɪlla kə bɪlle
This stick cannot be broken	Dilla derva bille	dɪlla dɛrva bɪlle
Break this stick for me	Bilimtira dillasa	bɪlɪmtɪra dɪllasa
120. I have built a house	Yira ane tumpea	jira anɛ tumpea
121. My people have built their houses yonder	Mbiri ra ane tumpea she kwaba	mbiri ra anɛ tumpea ʃɛ kwaba
122. What do you do every day?	Wa sina milina ala nza?	wa sɪna mɪlɪna ala nza
I work on my farm	Hlina vwǫra sa milira	łɪna vwɔra sa mɪlɪra
123. I am going away	Yira li	jira li
I am hoeing	Yirab za	jirab za
I am going away to hoe	Yira zugu za	jira zugu za
I am going away to my farm	Yira zugu avwe	jira zugu avwɛ
124. The woman comes	Mala sukwa	mala sukwa
She comes	Inja sukwa	ɪndʒa sukwa
The woman laughs	Male gushi	malɛ guʃi
The woman weeps	Male nnte huni	malɛ nntɛ huni
125. I ask the woman	Yira yu male	jira ju malɛ
126. Why do you laugh?	Timburuwa ushi nare?	tɪmburuwa uʃi nare
127. Why do you cry?	Timburuwa tahuni nare?	tɪmburuwa tahuni nare
128. My child is dead	Zugutara amte	zugutara amte
129. It is not dead	Vam tue	vam tuɛ
130. Are you ill?	Nagama kuringa na?	nagama kuriŋa na
131. My children are ill	Ngwasara ma kuringe	ngwasara ma kuriŋɛ
132. Her child is better	Zuguranji bǫ zhange	zugurandʒi bɔ ʒaŋɛ
133. Yes	I	i
No	Au	əu
134. A fine knife	Hwa ndirre	hwa ndɪrrɛ

T

	Give me the knife	Ngara hwa	ngara hwa
	I give you the knife	Yira kinggina hwa	jira kɪŋgina hwa
135.	I am a European	Yira bature	jira bature
	You are a black man	Na ndinggire	na ndɪŋgɪre
	You are a Higi	Na Kamun na	na kamun na
136.	Name	Hli	łi
	My name	Hlira	łira
	Your name	Hlinga	łiŋa
	What is your name ?	Wa hlinga re ?	wa łiŋa re
137.	There is water in the gourd	Yiemi kwa pi	jiɛmi kwa pi
	The knife is on the stone	Nahwa ta pille	nahwa tə pɪlle
	The fire is under the pot	Uhu tabta	uhu tabta
	The roof is over the hut	Wata mbekhi mpea	wata mbɛxi mpea
138.	You are good	Nane dirna	nanɛ dɪrna
	This man is bad	Mdene tamenje	mdɛnɛ təmendʒɛ
139.	The paper is white	Derewol ne bianginje	dɛrɛwol nɛ biaŋindʒɛ
	This thing is black	Sene danggiressa	sɛnɛ daŋgɪrɛssa
	This thing is red	Sene da khimatsa	sɛnɛ da xɪmatsa
140.	This stone is heavy	Pillene dedeki	pɪllɛnɛ dɛdɛki
	This stone is not heavy	Pillene dedeku we	pɪllɛnɛ dɛdɛku wɛ
141.	I write	Yira dafe	jira dafɛ
	I give you the letter	Yirang gina derewol	jiraŋ gɪna dɛrɛwol
	Carry the letter to the town	Me id zugwa milimi le derewoli	me id zugwa mɪlimi lɛ dɛrɛwɔli
142.	Go away	Mei	mei
	Come here	Nde	ndɛ
143.	Where is your house ?	Kimai yanga ?	kɪmai jaŋa
144.	My house is here	Nayera tsa	najera tsa
	My house is there	Nayera cha kwoɓa	najera tʃa kwoɓa
145.	What have you to sell ?	Wuso pana ri ?	wuso pana ri
146.	I want to buy fish	Yira pa kilpe	jira pa kɪlpɛ
147.	The fish which you bought is bad	Kilpe na pashatsa ntime	kɪlpɛ na paʃatsa ntimɛ
148.	Where is the man who killed the elephant ?	Kamandi ka pilti chuwe atsa ?	kəmandi kə pɪlti tʃuwɛ atsa
149.	He has killed many elephants	Njim pamti chuwe kukulle	ndʒɪm pamti tʃuwɛ kukullɛ

150. How many elephants were killed yesterday?	Kuni pamti chuwe hyam mbira re?	kuni pamti tʃuwɛ hjam mbɪra re
151. Untie it	Pillimtunje	pɪllɪmtundʒe
Tie this rope	Putta zuwe	puttə zuwɛ
Make the boy untie the goat	Gasha zugu a pillim tukwe nje	gəʃa zugu a pɪllɪm tukwɛ ndʒɛ
152. My brothers and I, we are going but no one else	Yira hlimblera a yeli kala ka	jira ɬimblera a jeli kala kə
153. Brothers, let us go and tell the chief	Hlimblera jigowa yira sukwa gate tim mbage	ɬimblera dʒigowa jira sukwa gəte tɪm mbəgɛ
154. This tree is bigger than that	Chiene bwomanje ta sukwa ba cha	tʃiɛnɛ bwomandʒe tə sukwa ba tʃa
Margi	Ka Mirikwe	ka mirikwɛ
Beriberi	Ka-Uvwa	ka-uvwa
Fulani	Ka-Blisini	ka-blisini
Hausa	Ka-Hausa	ka-hausa
I	Yira	jira
Thou	Na	na
He	Nje	ndʒɛ
We	Mi or yi	mi or ji
You	Yie	jiɛ
They	Hya	hja

THE HIGI LANGUAGE

Humsi dialect (showing variations from the Moda dialect)

1. Two eyes	Intsa baka	ɪntsə bakə
2. Ear	Sime	sɪmɛ
Two ears	Sim baka	sɪm bakə
3. One tooth	Hlene kutane	ɬenɛ kutanɛ
Five teeth	Hlenim chiffe	ɬenɪm tʃɪffɛ
4. Tongue	Akhane	axanɛ
5. Belly	Hu	hu
6. Back	Mbu	mbu
7. Man (person)	Ndi	ndi
Ten people	Viri monge	vɪri mɔŋɛ
8. Man (not woman)	Isa	isa
Two women	Mali baka	mali bakə
9. Child	Izru	ɪzru
10. Chief	Mbaghe	mbəgɛ
11. Friend	Mshera	mʃɛra
12. Smith	Karhye	karhje
13. Doctor	Ohwe	ohwɛ
14. One finger	Rihi kutana	rihi kutana
15. Two fingers	Rihi baka	rihi bakə
16. Three fingers	Rihi maka	rihi makə
17. Four fingers	Rihi fwọr	rihi fwɔr

18. Six fingers	Rihi ngkwange	rihi ŋkwaŋɛ
19. Seven fingers	Rihi berfonge	rihi bɛrfoŋɛ
20. Eight fingers	Rihi dikhsa	rihi dɪxsə
21. Nine fingers	Rihi mti	rihi mti
22. Ten fingers	Rɪhi mọnga	rihi mɔŋə
23. Twelve fingers	Rihi mọnga baka	rihi mɔŋə bakə
Thirteen fingers	Rihi mọnga maka	rihi mɔŋə makə
24. Twenty fingers	Rihi bakimsi	rihi bəkɪmsi
25. Two hundred fingers	Rihi bakim mọnga	rihi bəkɪm mɔŋə
26. God	Hyel letkhume	hjɛl lɛtxumɛ
27. Rain	Iva	ɪva
28. Water	Yemi	jɛmi
29. Stone	Pere	pere
Iron	Ere	ere
30. Hill	Qrame	ɔramɛ
31. River	Thirre	ɗirre
32. House	Eche	etʃe
Two houses	Iche baka	ɪtʃe bakə
33. Roof	Kwashaba	kwaʃaba
34. Door	Mijige	midʒige
35. Mat	Ichi	itʃi
36. Drum	Gangga	gaŋga
37. Pot	Dugwi	dugwi
38. Knife	Ohwa	ohwa
39. Spear	Mbakha	mbaxa
40. Leopard	Upuke	upukɛ
41. Dog	Ikirre	ɪkɪrrɛ
42. Bird	Ige	ige
Feather	Shinshege	ʃɪnʃɛˤge
43. Cow	Ihla	ɪɬa
44. Guinea-corn	Ikha	ixa

THE HIGI LANGUAGE

Makulu dialect (showing variations from the Moda dialect)

1. Two eyes	Intsa bogun	ɪntə bogun
2. Ear	Hlima	ɬima
Two ears	Hlim bogun	ɬim bogun
3. One tooth	Hlena hlimu	ɬena ɬimu
4. Neck	Wuri	wuri
5. Heart	Mnu	mnu
6. Belly	Hu	hu
7. Back	Mbu	mbu
8. Finger nail	Billa	billə
9. Man (person)	Mdu	mdu
Ten people	Mbiri mọnga	mbiri mɔŋa
10. Man (not woman)	Za	zə
11. Woman	Mala	mala
Two women	Mi bogun	mi bogun

12.	Child	Izgu	ızgu
13.	Chief	Mbaga	mbəga
14.	Friend	Ovwara	ovwara
15.	Doctor	Ndufwọ	ndufwɔ
16.	Smith	Rihyi	rihji
17.	One finger	Rihi hlimu	rihi łımu
18.	Two fingers	Rihi bogun	rihi bogun
19.	Three fingers	Rihi maka	rihi makə
20.	Four fingers	Rihi foo	rihi foo
21.	Five fingers	Rihi chiffa	rihi tʃıffa
22.	Six fingers	Rihi nkwa	rihi nkwa
23.	Seven fingers	Rihi milife	rihi mılıfɛ
24.	Eight fingers	Rihi tikhissa	rihi tıxıssa
25.	Nine fingers	Rihi mti	rihi mti
26.	Ten fingers	Rihi mọnga	rihi mɔŋa
27.	Twelve fingers	Rihi mọnga bogun	rihi mɔŋa bogun
	Thirteen fingers	Rihi mọnga maka	rihi mɔŋa makə
28.	Twenty fingers	Rihi bakimsi	rihi bakımsi
29.	Two hundred fingers	Rihi bogun mọnga	rihi bogun mɔŋa
30.	God	Hyel akhama	hjɛl axama
31.	Morning	Maska	maskə
32.	Water	Iyemi	ijɛmi
33.	Fat	Mavgye	məvgje
34.	Salt	Khọna	xɔnə
35.	Stone	Pirye	pırjɛ
	Iron	Iri	iri
36.	River	Dilla	dılla
37.	Road	Kwongkwa	kwɔŋkwa
38.	House	Impeâ	ımpeâ
	Two houses	Impeâ bogun	ımpeâ bogun
39.	Roof	Echea	etʃea
40.	Door	Nyim peâ	njım peâ
41.	Basket	Wochike	wotʃıkɛ
42.	Pot	Dugû	dugû
43.	Knife	Gilla	gılla
44.	Spear	Gari	gari
45.	Bow	Guchika	gutʃıka
46.	Arrow	Hava	havə
47.	Buffalo	Funu	funu
48.	Leopard	Upuka	upuka
49.	Monkey	Lukû	lukû
50.	Pig	Vusû	vusû
51.	Goat	Okwa	okwa
52.	Bird	Gi	gi
	Feather	Shinte gi	ʃıntɛ gi
53.	Horse	Giduwa	gıduwa
54.	Sheep	Tima	tımə
55.	Fowl	Wantwa	wantwa
56.	Eggs	Tilta	tıltə
57.	Snake	Zazû	zəzû

58. Frog	Kwamba	kwamba
59. Fly	Izguna	ɪzguna
60. Bee	Imza	ɪmzə
61. Ground nut	Kulǫ wǫcha	kulɔ wɔtʃə
62. Lion	Liveri	lɪvɛri

MANDARA (WANDALA) VOCABULARY
per Bukr of Mandara

1. Head	Irē	ire
2. Hair	Ugje	ugdʒe
3. Eye	Iche	itʃe
Two eyes	Aniji bua	anidʒi bua
4. Ear	Khima	xima
Two ears	Khim bua	xɪm bua
5. Nose	Aktare	əktare
6. One tooth	Sere (palle)	sɛrɛ (pallɛ)
Five teeth	Seri zibe	sɛri zɪbe
7. Tongue	Ara	ara
8. Neck	Iye	ije
9. Breast (woman's)	Wube	wubɛ
10. Heart	Irvǫngde	ɪruɔŋde
11. Belly	Huḍe	huḍɛ
12. Back	Iga	iga
13. Arm	Riva	riva
14. Hand	Hu darva	hu darva
Two hands	Hu darva bua	hu darva bua
15. Finger	Gulan darva	gulan darva
Five fingers	Gulandi zibe	gulandi zɪbe
16. Finger nail	Sirba	sɪrba
17. Leg	Sira	sɪra
18. Knee	Ugjé	ugdʒe
19. Foot	Iga sira	iga sɪra
Two feet	Iga sir bua	iga sɪr bua
20. Man (person)	Ura	ura
Ten people	Ur kilawa	ur kɪlawa
21. Man (not woman)	Zala	zala
Two men	Zala bua	zala bua
22. Woman	Muksa	muksə
Two women	Muksa bua	muksə bua
23. Child	Agzire	əgzɪrɛ
24. Father	Dada	dada
25. Mother	Mama	mama
26. Slave	Ave	ave
27. Chief	Hlikse	ɬikse
28. Friend	Hlakati	ɬakati
28. Smith	Aghla	əgɬa
30. Doctor	Matsame	matsame
31. One finger	Gulanda palle	gulanda pallɛ

32. Two fingers	Gulandi bua	gulandi bua
33. Three fingers	Gulandi kiye	gulandi kiˤje
34. Four fingers	Gulandi ufade	gulandi ufade
35. Five fingers	Gulandi izibe	gulandi izɪbe
36. Six fingers	Gulandi ungkwehe	gulandi uŋkwɛhɛ
37. Seven fingers	Gulandi vuye	gulandi vuje
38. Eight fingers	Gulandi tise	gulandi tise
39. Nine fingers	Gulandi masilmane	gulandi masɪlmane
40. Ten fingers	Gulandi kilawa	gulandi kɪlawa
41. Eleven fingers	Gulandi kilawa jim tukwe	gulandi kɪlawa dʒɪm tukwe
42. Twelve fingers	Gulandi kilawa ju bua	gulandi kɪlawa dʒu bua
Thirteen fingers	Gulandi kilawa ju kiye	gulandi kɪlawa dʒu kiˤje
43. Twenty fingers	Gulandi kulbua	gulandi kulbua
44. A hundred fingers	Gulandi dirim ka	gulandi dɪrɪm kə
45. Two hundred fingers	Gulandi dirim ku bua	gulandi dɪrɪm ku bua
46. Four hundred fingers	Gulandi dirim ku fade	gulandi dɪrɪm ku fade
47. Sun	Vachia	vatʃia
God	Dada miya	dada mija
48. Moon	Tirre	tɪrrɛ
Full moon	Tir langna	tɪr laŋnə
New moon	Jeja tirre	dʒedʒa tɪrrɛ
49. Day	Vachia	vatʃia
Night	Vakiya	vakiˤja
Morning	Anghya	əŋhja
50. Rain	Yewe	jɛwɛ
51. Water	Yewe	jɛwɛ
52. Blood	Uzhe	uʒɛ
53. Fat	Gilla	gɪlla
54. Salt	Izhe	iʒɛ
55. Stone	Nọkwa	nɔkwa
Iron	Iré	ire (high falling tone)
56. Hill	Uwa	uwa
57. River	Guwa	guwa
58. Road	Ungule	uŋulɛ
59. House	Bire	bɪrɛ
Two houses	Bir bua	bɪr bua
Many houses	Bir kwottya	bɪr kwottja
All the houses	Bir baḍimme	bɪr baɗɪmmɛ
60. Roof	Bire	bɪrɛ
61. Door	Wọbire	wɔbɪrɛ
62. Mat	Buche	butʃɛ
63. Basket	Ilila	ilila
64. Drum	Gangga	gaŋga
65. Pot	Gehe	gɛhɛ
66. Knife	Uwọshe	uwɔʃɛ
67. Spear	Wupa (pl. = wupaha)	wupa (pl. = wupaha)

68. Bow	Ilka	ɪlka
69. Arrow	Gurme	gurmɛ
Five arrows	Gurmi izibe	gurmi izɪbɛ
70. Gun	Karam masere	karam masɛrɛ
71. War	Ungwa	uŋwa
72. Meat (animal)	Hyuwa	hjuwa
73. Elephant	Guwe	guwɛ
74. Buffalo	Sakile	sakile
75. Leopard	Ubilla	ubɪlla
76. Monkey	Agulla	agulla
77. Pig	Abzhe	abʒɛ
78. Goat	Nauwe	nəuwɛ
79. Dog	Kare	kərɛ
80. Bird	Ghiye	gijɛ
Feather	Ugje	ugdʒe
81. Crocodile	Kirwe	kɪrwɛ
Horse	Bilsa	bɪlsa
Sheep	Kewe	kɛwɛ
82. Fowl	Ukulla	ukulla
83. Eggs	Hlaya	łaja
84. One egg	Hlayi palle	łaji pallɛ
85. Snake	Zehe	zɛhɛ
86. Frog	Mugdza	mugdza
87. Beriberi	Mufaka	mufaka
Hausa	Hausa	hausa
Fulani	Pilataha	pɪlataha
Gamergu	Malgwa	malgwa
88. Fly	Njungwa	ndʒuŋwa
89. Bee	Njungwa nama	ndʒuŋwa nʌma
Honey	Nama	nʌma
90. Tree	Khala	xala
Ten trees	Khaldi kilawa	xaldɪ kɪlawa
91. Leaf	Hlapa	łapa
92. Guinea-corn	Khiya	xija
93. Maize	Khiya masere	xija masɛrɛ
94. Ground nut	Ghina	gina
95. Oil	Waiye	wəije

HIGI-WULA DIALECT

1. Head	Kha	xa
2. Hair	Shinta	ʃɪntə
3. Eye	Intsa	ɪntsə
Two eyes	Intsa bak	ɪntsə bak
4. Ear	Hlima	łimə
Two ears	Hlim bak	łɪm bak
5. Nose	Nshi	nʃi
6. One tooth	Hli kutang	łi kutaŋ
Five teeth	Hli nchaf	łi ntʃaf

7.	Tongue	Ekhannyi	exannji
8.	Neck	Wuri	wuri
9.	Breast (woman's)	Ngwa	ŋwaʔ
10.	Heart	Wunaf	wunəf
11.	Belly	Khali	xali
12.	Back	Wumba	wumbə
13.	Arm	Zava	zəvə
14.	Hand	Daba	daba
	Two hands	Daba bak	daba bak
15.	Finger	Pilla	pɪlla
16.	Finger nail	Piri	piri
17.	Leg	Silla	sɪlla
18.	Knee	Shini	ʃini
19.	Foot	Wumba silla	wumba sɪlla
	Two feet	Wumba silla bak	wumba sɪlla bak
20.	Man (person)	Wunda	wundə
	Ten people	Wunda gumang	wundə gumaŋ
21.	Man (not woman)	Zza	zza
	Two men	Zza bak	zza bak
22.	Woman	Mala	malə
	Two women	Mali bak	mali bak
23.	Child	Humba	humba
24.	Father	Ita	ita
25.	Mother	Mma	mma
26.	Slave	Mava	mava
27.	Chief	Mbagha	mbəgə
28.	Friend	Gia	gia
29.	Smith	Irgi	ɪrgi
30.	Doctor	Shawu	ʃawu
31.	One finger	Pilla kutang	pɪlla kutaŋ
32.	Two fingers	Pilla bak	pɪlla bak
33.	Three fingers	Pilla makhkin	pɪlla maxkɪn
34.	Four fingers	Pilla ofat	pɪlla ɔfat
35.	Five fingers	Pilla nchaf	pɪlla ntʃaf
36.	Six fingers	Pilla nkwang	pɪlla nkwaŋ
37.	Seven fingers	Pilla marfang	pɪlla marfaŋ
38.	Eight fingers	Pilla dighas	pɪllas dɪgas
39.	Nine fingers	Pillas mahli	pɪlla məɬi
40.	Ten fingers	Pilla gumang	pɪlla gumaŋ
41.	Eleven fingers	Pilla gumang tan	pɪlla gumaŋ tan
42.	Twelve fingers	Pilla gumang bak	pɪlla gumaŋ bak
	Thirteen fingers	Pilla gumang makhkin	pɪlla gumaŋ maxkɪn
43.	Twenty fingers	Pilla bak kimsak	pɪlla bak kɪmsək
44.	A hundred fingers	Pilla gumsak	pɪlla gumsək
45.	Two hundred fingers	Pilla ba gumsak	pɪlla ba gumsək
46.	Four hundred fingers	Pilla far gumsak	pɪlla far gumsək
47.	Sun	Vachi	vətʃi
	God	Shella	ʃɛlla
48.	Moon	Tirri	tɪrri

HIGI-SINNA DIALECT

1.	Head	Ghi	gi
2.	Hair	Shinshi	ʃinʃi
3.	Eye	Intsi	ɪntsi
	Two eyes	Intsi bak	intsi bak
4.	Ear	Hlima	ɬɪmə
	Two ears	Hlim bak	ɬɪm bak
5.	Nose	Nshi	nʃi
6.	One tooth	Hlina kutang	ɬɪnə kutaŋ
	Five teeth	Hlina nchaf	ɬɪnə ntʃaf
7.	Tongue	Ghrene	grɛnɛ
8.	Neck	Wure	wurɛ
9.	Breast (woman's)	Ngwe	ŋwɛ
10.	Heart	Hwi	hwi
11.	Belly	Zhumbi	ʒumbi
12.	Back	Umbwi	umbwi
13.	Arm	Zava	zəvə
14.	Hand	Daba	daba
	Two hands	Daba bak	daba bak
15.	Finger	Wara ka ziv	wara ka zɪv
16.	Finger nail	Bille	bɪllɛ
17.	Leg	Sida	sɪda
18.	Knee	Reshini	rɛʃini
19.	Foot	Hu sida	hu sɪda
	Two feet	Hu sida bak	hu sɪda bak
20.	Man (person)	Mbiri	mbiri
	Ten people	Mbiri mọng	mbiri mọŋ
21.	God	Hyele	hjɛlɛ
22.	Man (not woman)	Mala	malə
	Two men	Mali bak	mali bak

THE NJAI OR NZANGI

The people known to the Fulani and surrounding tribes as the Njai or Jenge, but who call themselves the Nzangi (Nzaŋi) or Nzangyi, are located in the Vokuna and Maiha districts of British Cameroons, their principal villages being Maiha, Paka, Hudu, Ligudira, Nguli, Furkwa i, and Ndeekwe. The main group lives across the border in French Cameroons (at Kobochi, Dazal, Mbui, Wurme, Furkwa ii, etc.). Those in the British Cameroons are administered by the Emir of Adamawa through the Fulani district heads of Vokuna and Maiha.

Their language closely resembles that spoken by the Jirai (of Holma, Zumu, Malabu, etc.) and of the various Bata

communities. It may be described as a Bata dialect. It displays
affinities, therefore, with the language of the so-called Gudu
groups, as well as with Margi and with the " Fali " dialect
of Mubi.

A schedule of words and phrases is attached. This schedule
corresponds (a) with Barth's " Zany " (Umbutubi), and (b) with
Strumpell's " Njei " and " Koboci ". I am not aware if Strumpell
has identified his " Njei " with Barth's " Zany ".

Barth visited the Nzangi of Mbutubi (Paka) in 1851, and
records that they went so far as to do him the honour of identifying
him with their god " Fete " who, they thought, might have come
to spend a day with them, to make them forget their oppression
and misfortunes. For the Nzangi had fallen under the heel of the
Fulani. Incidentally, Barth mentions that he received a proposal
of marriage from a Fulani girl at Mbutudi.[1]

The following brief notes were obtained on the main points of
cultural interest.

There is no tribal organization. Each local group is an
independent political unit, the relations between the groups
being governed by a code of customary law, or at least by a code
which is supposed to be customary. Thus (in former days) if a
man of one group eloped with a married woman of another group
he was normally bound to recoup the first husband for his pre-
marriage payments. Failure to do this might lead to a state of
war between the two villages. In some cases disputes between
individuals of different villages were and are determined by
reference to the magico-religious authority, viz. Gogue, whose
shrine is located at Ligudira. (The symbol of the godling is said
to be an image with human features which is kept in a hole in the
ground. The image is not produced when oaths are sworn, but
when the local chief is elected it is shown to him.) The Nzangi also
use the " shafa " cult of the Kilba and southern Margi for settling
disputes.[2] Each village has its own chief who is a court of appeal
in all matters which cannot be settled amicably by the head of the
kindred (if the dispute is between members of the same kindred),
or by the heads of the respective kindreds (if the dispute is between
members of different kindreds). The chief had also, in former

---

[1] Barth's *Travels*, vol. ii, pp. 428–30. In his *Travels* he uses the spelling
" Zani " and " Mbutudi ". In his vocabularies these words are given as " Zany "
and " Umbutudi ".

[2] See p. 225.

times, considerable executive authority. If a murder were committed he took immediate action by requiring the murderer's kindred to recoup that of the murdered man with the gift of a girl (that her child would provide a substitute for the murdered man). In addition he exacted a heavy fine which he divided with the senior men of the local group. In cases of proved theft he directed the chief or members of his kindred to refund the stolen goods, and he also levied a fine, which he shared with the elders. He could fine any member of the community for making advances to his wives or for using language abusive of himself. His position was independent of any authority he might exercise as the custodian of a cult. He was not in any strict sense a " divine " ruler. The Nzangi, therefore, though their chiefs have only a purely local authority, have a more developed sense of chieftain-ship than many other pagan tribes, among whom the chief priest is the head of the community. For normally the executive authority of the chief priest is confined to matters involving the prestige of the gods.

There is a distinct social difference between members of a chief's kindred and others. Thus in the past offences against members of the royal family were severely punished (by the chief), whereas similar offences committed between members of peasant families were held to be of small account. The body of a deceased wife who belonged to the royal kindred has to be sent back to that kindred for burial, but that of a woman who was a commoner is buried by the husband in the grave of his own family. The form of burial for a chief is also different from that of a commoner ; for whereas a commoner is buried in a recumbent position (in a flagon-shaped grave, each kindred having three or four of such graves which are used for all sexes, young or old), the chief is buried sitting on a stool in a grave (also flagon-shaped) which is not used again. His body is not (as among the Pabir, Kilba, and some groups of Margi) covered with charcoal, but a few handfuls of charcoal are deposited in the grave. This charcoal is not inserted with a view to preservation of the body (as among the Pabir), but appears to be typical of the blacksmith's profession. For a blacksmith's hammer and tongs are also set beside the dead body (together with a slab of salt). The rites would seem to imply that originally chiefs belonged to the blacksmiths' caste ; but on the other hand blacksmiths are, as among many Nigerian tribes, regarded as social inferiors, so that no man will marry the daughter of a kindred which practises smithing. For this reason most blacksmith kindreds are endogamous. Among the neighbouring Fali tribe there is a similar taboo against marrying the daughter of a blacksmith, but chiefs do not observe this taboo.

It is noteworthy that, throughout the area we are reviewing, the grave-diggers are always members of the smithing kindred, and they are also the priests. The inference would seem to be that the invading groups were peoples to whom smithing was taboo. They were probably cattle-owning nomads, possibly Fulani. But the aboriginal groups knew how to work iron. In certain areas (e.g. at Duhu in Madagali) there is a definite tradition that " Higi " invaders who owned cattle coalesced with " Margi " aboriginals who were blacksmiths. It would be natural that the aboriginals should be left in charge of the cults ; for invaders commonly seek to pacify the local gods, many of whom are the deified ancestors of the indigenous inhabitants.

It may be added that the Nzangi chiefs wear a hair-lock and that although the lock of the preceding chief is not plaited into their own (in the Pabir and Kilba fashion) it is placed against their forehead on the day that they are formally shaven and given the chieftainship. The predecessor's lock is then buried in the grave of its former owner.

Religious beliefs were not investigated closely, but it appeared that among the hill groups some attention was paid to spirits and ancestors, while among the plain groups, which have been brought into close association with the Fulani, religion scarcely exists. At Paka there are two public cults (a) of Herere and (b) of Darba, the former being in the hands of the blacksmith kindred, the latter in those of the chief, though individual householders may also have a " Darba " cult. Both these cults seem to be used primarily to avert epidemic illnesses. The sacrificial animal, which is generally a goat, must have been owned by some member of the community. It may not be bought from a stranger. At sowing time all farmers visit the graves of their dead fathers, accompanied by an old man who had known the father in his life-time. This old man offers a prayer to the deceased for the success of his son's farm-work and for his general health. Libations are not poured over the grave, but the old man and the dead man's son drink some beer together on the conclusion of the prayer. The Nzangi do not practise circumcision and, unlike all the neighbouring tribes, have no initiation ceremonies.

As regards social organization they, like all the tribes in this section of Nigeria, are strictly patrilineal. Inheritance is governed by the rule of primogeniture ; but it was stated that, nowadays, it is customary to give younger sons a share in the inheritance on the ground that the family organization no longer possesses its former solidarity, younger sons being able to go off and settle where they please. Until recently it was dangerous to leave the confines of the village, but now anyone can go anywhere. Similarly, in former times, there was a strict rule of kindred exogamy ; but nowadays a man may marry a woman of his own kindred, provided she is not a first cousin. The reason for this change was stated to be that children nowadays do as they please. Contact with the Fulani has, no doubt, changed opinion. It is interesting in such cases to ascertain the views of the people as to the reasons for the former practice of exogamy. For where natives still adhere to the rule of exogamy and are unaware of any other state, they are usually unable to express any opinions on the subject. But when confronted by people, like the Fulani, who practise cousin marriages, they begin to discuss their own system and to discover reasons for their own practice. In most cases which have come to my notice the primary reason given for exogamy is that marriage within the kindred tends to disrupt the kindred on account of the disputes which necessarily arise between a man and his wife, just as most disputes between villages arise over women. The reclaiming of a debt by one individual from another leads to friction. The reclaiming of a bride-price from a member of one's own kindred would, it is said, cause ill-feeling within the kindred. Any quarrel between a husband and wife might result in a dispute between one section of a kindred and another. These reasons have less application at the present time as a man can leave his local group and go and reside anywhere he likes. But even among peoples like the Fulani who practise first-cousin marriage it is admitted that the practice frequently leads to a breach in the kindred solidarity. The idea that inter-breeding may be attended with evil physical results is not put forward as an argument for exogamy ; but it is sometimes held that exogamy is a good institution on the ground that women from other groups are more desirable sexually than women of one's own group. It is a common saying among the Fulani that cousin-wives are seldom the favourite wives.

Among the Nzangi marriage is by purchase plus agricultural service. Girls are not, as among the Jirai, sought at an early age and taken to the husband's home before they have reached the age of puberty. It is customary, therefore, for a lad to make personal advances to a girl, by presenting her with six rings and some strips of red leather ; if these are accepted by her, and his suit is approved by her parents and maternal uncle, the boy sends a gift of salt, and later of meat, to the girl's mother. He is also called upon to lend his services and those of his friends to the girl's father at sowing, mid-season hoeing, and reaping. His agricultural bondage lasts until the girl has attained puberty, and until the boy has completed his main marriage-payments which consist of two gowns and two blocks of salt, these gifts being appropriated by the father. For the wedding feast the boy's father has to provide a goat, basket of corn, and three pots of beer, and on the conclusion of the feast the girl goes to her husband's home for a period of six nights. During this period the husband is not entitled to have sexual relations, and he has to give numerous gifts to the girl, each gift being regarded as conferring permission on the girl to assume some function of her new life. Thus when she enters her husband's home she must be given a gift. She will not speak, or eat, or lie down until she has been given a gift. This custom appears to be parallel with the form of initiation for girls practised by the Yungur-speaking peoples immediately prior to marriage, and to the Kilba-Margi-Higi custom by which girls go into seclusion and are smeared with oil when they are formally betrothed. Among the Nzangi it may be regarded as a transition rite. The Fali of Mubi area have the same custom.

On the seventh day she returns to her own home where she remains for a week. She is then free to go to her husband's home with whom she may now have sexual relations. If the husband finds his wife a virgin he sends a gift of meat to her mother, but if not he sends a dish of dirt, and the girl is beaten by her parents. Throughout the first year of her married life the girl spends four successive nights in her husband's home and five in that of her parents. Every time she goes home she is given a gift of meat to take to her parents. Her husband is also required to build a new hut for his mother-in-law, and to continue his agricultural service on the father-in-law's farm.

A wife bears her first child in her parent's home, and if the child is a girl the husband presents his wife with four cloth belts, and her mother with four chickens and the leg of a cow. If the child is a boy three cloth belts, three chickens, and the leg of a cow are given. Subsequent children are born in the husband's home.

As regards the dissolution of marriage the rule is that if a wife abandons her husband without having borne him a child he can reclaim the bride-price in full. If she has borne him one child the amount of the bride-price reclaimable is reduced, the reduction being greater if the child is a girl. The birth of two children is held to cancel the bride-price *in toto*. The Nzangi do not follow the Higi custom by which children in excess of two are permitted to accompany the mother ; for all children belong to the father. But if a man's wife bears him a third child he is required to give a gift of a gown to his wife's father. This gift is not regarded as a ransoming of the child, but as a bribe to the wife's father to allow her to continue living with him. If the gift were not given the woman's father would encourage her to seek another husband, in order that he (the father) might derive the advantage of a second bride-price.

It may be noted that the rules governing the dissolution of marriage were not always meekly followed. For until recently it was not unusual for a man who was devoted to his wife to kill her second husband and set fire to his house.

It has been said that the Nzangi are strictly patrilineal. Maternal uncles have no authority over children. But it would be unusual for a man to give his daughter in marriage without first obtaining the consent of his wife's brother. A boy is privileged to make inroads on his maternal uncle's property during the latter's life-time, and it is also customary for sisters' sons to receive a trifling share of his estate at his death, the amount being determined by the deceased's eldest son. Sons inherit and become the husbands of their fathers' widows (except of course their own mothers), but no one may inherit the widow of his maternal uncle. Boys do not, as among many Nigerian tribes, go and live with their maternal uncle, unless their father has died. In this case they are free to take up residence with a maternal rather than a

PLATE 29

A NZANGI VILLAGE

paternal uncle, and the maternal uncle would sponsor the boy's marriage.

The following are the principal terms of relationship :—

Bagi is applied to a father and his brothers and male cousins.
Mogi is applied to a mother and her sisters and female cousins. It is also applied to a father's sister.
Zuegi is a reciprocal term used between a man (or woman) and his (or her) maternal uncles.
Jijigi is applied (male or female speaking) to male grandparents.
Kakagi is applied (male or female speaking) to female grandparents.
Jejei is applied (male or female speaking) to all grandchildren.
Matikai (fem. = *matikin*) is a reciprocal term used between parents-in-law and children-in-law.
Mashigi is a reciprocal term used between brothers-in-law and sisters-in-law.
Masinai is a general term for brother or cousin.
An elder brother is called *gahon*.
An elder sister is called *gahoking*.
A younger brother is called *dareng*.
A younger sister is called *daraking*.

Many of these titles are found among other Bata-speaking peoples. But the term *mashi* has, apparently, been adopted from the Fulani.

Material Culture.—Nzangi huts vary in character, some being of mud, some of grass, some having rafters, and some not. A bride's hut is always thatched over a bell-shaped inner shell of woven grass, no rafters being used. Two or three huts may be connected by an enclosure of grass-matting (the common type of compound in North-Eastern Nigeria). A wife has usually three huts, one for sleeping, one for milling, and the third for cooking. Some of the huts contain small bins (as among the Kilba), and others have mud screens, the tops of which are used as receptacles for pots. The bedsteads are mud platforms supported by pedestals of mud. During cold weather a fire is kept burning at night close to the bed. All compounds are surrounded by stone walls, a common feature of the hill villages in this part of Nigeria. Another feature of every village is the circular throne of loose stones on which the chief sits on official occasions and during dances. These stone thrones resemble the flat-topped cairns of the Gongola valley, and it may be that some of those cairns were the thrones of the chiefs of former tribes. The Nzangi practise terrace cultivation. Hoes are fitted by the socket method. The axes used by women are also socketed, but those of the men are tanged. Bows are rather short, and have a single eyelet, the bow-string passing direct from the back through the eyelet and made fast at the other end over a notch which is cut laterally, the loose string being made fast lower down on the stave. It is at this end that the string is tightened for use. Throwing and thrusting spears are also used, but those observed had been purchased from the Fulani. For close combat sticks, covered with leather and weighted at the end with a coil of iron, are used.

The principal musical instruments are flutes with four stops. A horn resonator is fixed at the base. A trumpet, 5 feet long, with a calabash resonator at the base, is also used. Drums are small double membrane drums, or single membrane drums of the hour-glass pattern. The membranes are made from the skin of the monitor lizard.

Men wear cloth garments, but women go nude except for a bunch of leaves worn over the pubes and buttocks. Grown-up women frequently tie a thin strip of cloth round the abdomen. Younger women wear a series of iron or brass rings fitted tightly together on the lower leg. All except mad women shave the head.

Children are carried in leather satchels on the back, and mothers who are nursing children smear their bodies with red earth and oil.

NZANGI VOCABULARY

1.	Head	Kirre	kɪrrɛ
2.	Hair	Shewe	ʃɛcwɛ
3.	Eye	Di	di
	Two eyes	Di bek	di bɛk
4.	Ear	Lekwǫdi	lɛkwɔdi
	Two ears	Lekwǫdi bek	lɛkwɔdi bɛk
5.	Nose	Chine	tʃinɛ
6.	One tooth	Line hide	linɛ hidɛ
	Five teeth	Line tuf	linɛ tuf
7.	Tongue	Gyana	gjana
8.	Neck	Wura	wura
9.	Breast (woman's)	Unechi	unɛtʃi
10.	Heart	Gbanduve	gɓanduvɛ
11.	Belly	Sikke	sɪkkɛ
12.	Back	Bii	bii
13.	Arm	Tivi	tivi
14.	Hand	Sikke tivi	sɪkkɛ tivi
	Two hands	Sikke tivi bek	sɪkkɛ tivi bɛk

15. Finger	Gele	gɛlɛ
Five fingers	Gele tuf	gɛlɛ tuf
16. Finger nail	Pape	papɛ
17. Leg	Shiḍe	ʃɩɗɛ
18. Knee	Magirshe	magɩrʃɛ
19. Foot	Bii shiḍe	bii ʃɩɗɛ
Two feet	Bii shiḍe bek	bii ʃɩɗɛ bɛk
20. Man (person)	Minde	mɩndɛ
Ten people	Gbari pu	gbari pu
21. Man (not woman)	Mure	murɛ
Two men	Muri bek	muri bɛk
22. Woman	Madichi	madɩtʃi
Two women	Madi bek	madi bɛk
23. Child	Inza	ɩnzə
24. Father	Bagi	bagi
25. Mother	Mọgi	mɔgi
26. Slave	Fali	fali
27. Chief	Mọn	mɔn
28. Friend	Nduogi	nduogi
29. Smith	Gudange	gudaŋɛ
30. Doctor	Ndukushe	ndukuʃɛ
31. One finger	Gele hiḍe	gɛlɛ hiɗɛ
32. Two fingers	Geli bek	gɛli bɛk
33. Three fingers	Geli midfim	gɛli mɩdfɩm
34. Four fingers	Geli fwat	gɛli fwat
35. Five fingers	Geli tuf	gɛli tuf
36. Six fingers	Geli kwa	gɛli kwa
37. Seven fingers	Geli miskata	gɛli mɩskata
38. Eight fingers	Geli fwọfwade	gɛli fwɔfwade
39. Nine fingers	Geli tambide	gɛle tambide
40. Ten fingers	Geli pu	gɛli pu
41. Eleven fingers	Geli pu ka hiḍe	gɛli pu ka hiɗɛ
42. Twelve fingers	Geli pu midi bek	gɛli pu mɩdi bɛk
Thirteen fingers	Geli pu midi midfim	gɛli pu mɩdi mɩdfɩm
43. Twenty fingers	Geli bem masheshi	gɛli bɛm maʃɛʃi
44. A hundred fingers	Geli gharu	gɛli garu
45. Two hundred fingers	Geli gharu ọg bek	gɛli garu ɔg bɛk
46. Four hundred fingers	Geli gharu ọ fwat	gɛli garu ɔ fwat
47. Sun	Fete	fɛtɛ
God	Fitte	fɩtte
48. Moon	Ligide	ligɩdɛ
Full moon	Ligide ma birre	ligɩdɛ mə bɩrrɛ
New moon	Kura ligide	kura ligɩdɛ
49. Day	Nda feten	nda fɛtɛn
Night	Vade	vədɛ
Morning	Put	put
50. Rain	Fame	famɛ
51. Water	Mbii	mbii
52. Blood	Bize	bizɛ

53.	Fat	Kupe	kupɛ
54.	Salt	Fitse	fıtsɛ
55.	Stone	Kwaa	kwaa
	Iron	Renge	rɛŋɛ
56.	Hill	Kiremwe	kırɛmwɛ
57.	River	Gere	gɛrɛ
58.	Road	Rugwa	rugwa
59.	House	Vine (compound = hoɗe)	vinɛ hoɗɜ
	Two houses	Vene gi bek	vɜnɛ gi bɜk
	Many houses	Vene gi bwǫng	vɛnɛ gi bwǫŋ
	All the houses	Vene gi dugba	vɛnɛ gi dugba
60.	Roof	Gidda	gıdda
61.	Door	Bafke	ɓafkɛ
62.	Mat	Dagwe	dagwe
63.	Basket	Silla	sılla
64.	Drum	Gangga	gaŋga
65.	Pot	Wuda	wuda
66.	Knife	Ngilla	ngılla
67.	Spear	Wudime	wudimɛ
68.	Bow	Rage	ragɛ
69.	Arrow	Ave	avɛ
	Five arrows	Ave tuf	avɛ tuf
70.	Gun	Bunduke	bundukɛ
71.	War	Kǫnue	kǫnuɛ
72.	Meat	Lyuwe	ljuwɛ
73.	Elephant	Chuware	tʃuwarɛ
74.	Buffalo	Mbiermachi	mbiɛrmatʃi
75.	Leopard	Boangya	boaɲja
76.	Monkey	Burame	buramɛ
77.	Pig	Dagilla (pl. = dagilla)	dagilla
78.	Goat	Hoe (pl. = hoi)	hoɛ
79.	Dog	Yangba	jaŋba
80.	Bird	Kodeke	kodɛkɛ
	Feather	Sheo kodeke	ʃɛ°o kodɛkɛ
81.	Crocodile	Gadange	gadaŋɛ
82.	Fowl	Deke	dɛkɛ
83.	Eggs	Kurei	kurɛi
84.	One egg	Kurei hiɗe	kurɛi hiɗɜ
85.	Snake	Ise	isɛ
86.	Frog	Gwanda	gwanda
87.	Horse	Kara (plural = karai)	kara
	Sheep	Pekede (plural = pekedi)	pɛkɛdɛ
	Cow	Nakwe	nakwe
88.	Fly	Jeɗe	dʒɛɗɛ
89.	Bee	Mwa zinga	mwa ziŋa
	Honey	Mwa zinga	mwa ziŋa
90.	Tree	Kadi	kadi
	Ten trees	Kadi pu	kadi pu
91.	Leaf	Gase	gase

92.	Guinea-corn	Kwama	kwama
93.	Maize	Mapinawe	mapɪnawɛ
94.	Ground nut	Masare	masare
95.	Oil	Mare	mare
96.	I am a Jenge or Njai	khin Nzange	xɪn nzaŋɛ
	We are Jenge or Njai	khinin Nzangyin	xɪnɪn nzaŋjɪn
	I	khin	xɪn
	You	Khi	xi
	He	Khichi	xɪtʃi
	We	Khine	xinɛ
	You (pl.)	Khune	zunɛ
	They	Khikyin	xɪkjɪn
	We are going (incl. person addressed)	Zimin	zɪmɪm
	We are going (excl. person addressed)	Zigine	zɪginɛ
	Batta	Gboati	gboati
	Hausa	Nji Hausa	ndʒi hausa
	Kanuri	Ufwahi	ufwahi
	Fulani	Pirsali	pɪrsali
	Cheke	Mapodi	mapodi

THE CHEKE (MUBI DISTRICT)

The Cheke of Mubi district inhabit the villages of Muvi (Mubi), Muda, Gela, Kwoja, Duvu, Gimru, Dirbishi, Gandira, Mujara, Wudili, Monua, and Tantila. Across the border in French Cameroons there are Cheke groups at Bukura, Zakura, and a number of other villages.

Their language which closely resembles that of the " Fali " of Mubi may be classed as a dialect of Bata. They differ from the Fali in that they practise circumcision, wear cloth garments, have no facial or bodily marks, and do not pierce the ears or lower lip. Though they have not yet become professing Muslims they have clearly a large Fulani admixture, and are likely to become full-fledged Muhammadans within the next generation. But their women still go about with no other loin-covering than bunches of leaves.

They differ from their Higi and Margi neighbours in that they do not remove the epidermis from the dead bodies of the aged, do not practise kindred exogamy, have no puberty rites for

boys, do not recognise any authority over children save that of
the father, do not preserve the hair-lock of chiefs, and do not
bury their chiefs in charcoal.

Marriage is permissible between all classes of cousins once
removed. Descent is reckoned patrilineally, and heritors are
sons. Sisters' sons have no legal share ; but if a sister's son is able
by stealth to appropriate any article of his maternal uncle's
property he is allowed to keep it. If the article appropriated is an
heirloom it may be redeemed by negotiation. Formerly
inheritance was by primogeniture ; but at the present time,
owing to the lessened solidarity of the family by reason of increase
of individualism, younger sons are permitted to claim forthwith
the share of the inheritance which was formerly held in trust for
them by their eldest brother.

A brother of the deceased only inherits in the capacity of
administrator on behalf of sons who have not reached an age of
discretion. But brothers may inherit the deceased's widows, if
the widows so desire. Sons may also inherit the young widows of
their father. But all widows are free to re-marry outside the
family group of their late husband. If they had borne a child to
their late husband the new husband is under no obligation to
compensate the late husband's heritors ; but if she had not
borne a child the heritors can claim a bride-price.

There are no puberty rites for boys, as there are among all the
surrounding tribes ; but every affianced girl is, at puberty,
required to go to the house of her betrothed and remain there for
twelve days during which she is smeared each day with ochre by a
girl-friend. Her fiancé has to give her a gift when she enters his
father's compound, when he addresses her, when she eats, and
when she retires for the night. He may not have sexual relations
with her. But at the end of the twelve days, when the girl has
been restored to her own home, and the youth's father or guardian
has sent gifts of beer and meat to the girl's parents, the young
man assumes all the rights of a husband. But his wife continues
to reside in her own home for a period of two years. If she bears
a child she continues to reside in her parent's home until the child
is weaned. The birth of one child, incidentally, cancels the
bride-price (which is higher among the Cheke than the Fali) ; and
if the woman subsequently abandons her first husband for a
second, the second husband is under no financial obligation to the

first (but he must pay a minor bride-price to the woman's father or brother).

The Jirai custom of the interchange of wives (without a reclaim of bride-price) within a group of associated kindreds is not practised by the Cheke, and would in fact be impossible, owing to the absence of exogamy.

The following are some of the principal terms of relationship (which are also used by the " Fali " of the Mubi district) :—

Dada = father, paternal uncle, or any male of a senior generation. (A father's younger brother or cousin is referred to as *unzi dada* = little father.)

Yai = mother, mother's sister, father's sister, or any female of a senior generation. (A father's or mother's younger sister is referred to as *unzi yai* = little mother).

A mother's brother is distinguished by the Fulani term *kawo*.

Uzin = son or daughter or any person of a junior generation.

Zukunwun is a general term for brother, sister, or relative. An elder brother or sister is called *gawak* ; a younger brother or sister is called *madzu gawak*. The Cheke commonly call an elder sister by the Fulani term *ada*.

Zidza = male grandparents.

Kaka = female grandparents.

Jiji = all grandchildren.

Suruhwa is a reciprocal term used between parents-in-law and children-in-law.

Mashi is a reciprocal term used between brothers-in-law, or sisters-in-law, or brothers-in-law and sisters-in-law. It is a Fulani term, but is widely used among the pagan tribes of Adamawa Province.

As regards religion a few scanty notes only were obtained. The Cheke have long been under the Muslim influence of the Fulani and do not concern themselves much with their inherited pagan cults. One of the principal public cults is known as Hlima, which is symbolized by a pot. Harvest rites are carried out in November, the corn for the rites being supplied to the priest by the chief. The corn is converted into sweet beer, and a libation is poured by the priest into the sacred pot, with a prayer that all may derive the advantage of their agricultural labours, that their numbers may be increased, and that they may be brought safely to the harvest of next year. On the following morning the remnants of the beer are drunk ceremonially by the senior men. The chief kills a cow, and a festival is held, which lasts for several days. Similar rites are carried out before planting. There is another cult known as Ulimin which is used principally for swearing oaths.

The Cheke call the sun " Usira ". This word is of great interest, as it has been shown in my monograph on the Jukun-speaking people [1] that the root *Chi, Shi, Si,* or *Usi* is widespread throughout Africa as a name for the moon, sun, or Supreme Being, and that it probably means " the lord ". " Usira," therefore, would presumably mean " the lord Ra ", i.e. the Cheke call the sun by the same name as the Ancient Egyptians called their great Sun-god. It is possible, however, that the termination " *Ra* " merely means " above ", so that the Cheke word for sun would mean " the lord above " and would be the equivalent of the Jukun expression " Chi-dô " (*Chi* being = *usi* and *dô* = above). The name of the Egyptian Sun-god, viz. Ra, may itself be a shortened form of an original expression meaning " the lord above ". The Cheke word is almost the equivalent of the Egyptian name for Osiris, which was " Usir " or " Usiri ". It may indeed be the identical word, as the vowel-sounds in the Egyptian word cannot be determined with certainty. The earliest form of the word Osiris may, therefore, have been Usira, and the word may merely have meant " the lord above ", being applied to the moon, as Osiris was originally a moon-god. The data before us suggest the conclusion either that Egypt propagated the name and cult of Osiris all over Africa, or that the Egyptians adopted as a name for their great deity a widespread African word which merely meant " the lord above ".

The Cheke do not now practise any sun-rites, but such rites are practised among the Jukun-speaking peoples, and were probably general at one time in this part of West Africa. The root *Si* or *Usi* appears among the Margi, Higi, and other tribes bordering on the Cheke, in the form *va-chi* = sun.

In a number of Adamawa tribes (e.g. among the Gabin) it is customary to throw corn over the body of any old man or woman. This custom is not associated by those who practise it with any idea of resurrection, but it recalls the Egyptian practice of placing a germinating figure of Osiris in the tomb of the deceased, i.e. a figure filled with silt and seed which sprouted. The Cheke have not this custom of throwing corn over the body, but they lay a line of corn between the body and the door of the hut, all friends and relatives who attend the funeral rites bringing gifts of corn for this

[1] See *A Sudanese Kingdom*, pp. 180–3.

purpose. The reason assigned for the custom is that the dead man should not leave the world in a hungry condition. The corn is subsequently collected and appropriated by the members of the grave-digging kindred. The custom is not followed in the case of chiefs. As already stated it is not the Cheke practice to preserve the hair-lock of a chief. The lock is shaven off at death and buried separately, Men are buried in rectangular graves of the usual Muslim type, but women are buried in the flagon-shaped graves common in this part of Nigeria. The only difference between the mode of burial of a chief and a commoner is that the former is carried out secretly.

The Cheke official titles corresponding with those of the Hausa and Fulani are as follows :—

Chief	= Ngwongwa.
Kaigama	= Berkuma.
Sarkin Fada	= Hledima.
Galadima	= Birma.
Sarkin Yaki	= Kadala.

The first embodies the common Bantu and Sudanic root " *gwam* ". The second is new to me, but the last three are common all over North-Eastern Nigeria.

A short vocabulary is attached. It corresponds with Strumpell's " Mubi ".

CHEKE OF MUVI (MUBI) VOCABULARY
per Kaigama of Muvi

1.	Head	Na	na
2.	Hair	Shinkin	ʃinkɪn
3.	Eye	Gin	gɪn
	Two eyes	Gin barai	gɪn bərəi
4.	Ear	Limin	limɪn
	Two ears	Limin barai	limɪn bərəi
5.	Nose	Shina	ʃina
6.	One tooth	Linyin erung	linjɪn ɛruŋ
	Five teeth	Linyin tuf	linjɪn tuf
7.	Tongue	Gana	gana
8.	Neck	Wura	wura
9.	Breast (woman's)	Wan	wan
10.	Heart	Idzimba	ɪdzɪmba
11.	Belly	Sikka	sɪkka
12.	Back	Baa	baa
13.	Arm	Chin	tʃin
14.	Hand	Sika chin	sɪkə tʃin
	Two hands	Sika chin barai	sɪkə tʃin bərəi
15.	Finger	Moji chin	mɔdʒi tʃin
	Five fingers	Moji chin tuf	mɔdʒi tʃin tuf

16.	Finger nail	Gahla	gə┼a
17.	Leg	Sida	sɪda
18.	Knee	Ida	ɪda
19.	Foot	Sika sida	sɪkə sɪda
	Two feet	Sika sida barai	sɪkə sɪda bərəi
20.	Man (person)	Nda	nda
	Ten people	Nji pu	ndʒi pu
21.	Man (not woman)	Inggura	ɪŋgura
	Two men	Wirim barai	wirɪm bərəi
22.	Woman	Min	mɪn
	Two women	Maikin barai	məikɪn bərəi
23.	Child	Uzin	uzɪn
24.	Father	Dada	dadə
25.	Mother	Iyai	ijai
26.	Slave	Mava	məva
27.	Chief	Ngwǫngwa (pl. = memin)	ŋwǫŋwa (pl. = mɛmɪn)
28.	Friend	Guvak	guvak
29.	Smith	Nghya	ŋhja
30.	Doctor	Nghya	ŋhja
31.	One finger	Mǫji chin erung	mǫdʒi tʃin ɛruŋ
32.	Two fingers	Mǫja chin barai	mǫdʒi tʃin bərəi
33.	Three fingers	Mǫji chin maka	mǫdʒi tʃin maka
34.	Four fingers	Mǫji chin angfwat	mǫdʒi tʃin ʌɲfwat
35.	Five fingers	Mǫji chin tuf	mǫdʒi tʃin tuf
36.	Six fingers	Mǫji chin kuwa	mǫdʒi tʃin kuwa
37.	Seven fingers	Mǫji chin midif	mǫdʒi tʃin mɪdɪf
38.	Eight fingers	Mǫji chin tikhis	mǫdʒi tʃin tɪxɪs
39.	Nine fingers	Mǫji chin illing	mǫdʒi tʃin ɪlliŋ
40.	Ten fingers	Mǫji chin pu	mǫdʒi tʃin pu
41.	Eleven fingers	Mǫji chin pu amin tang	mǫdʒi tʃin pu amɪn taŋ
42.	Twelve fingers	Mǫji chin pu aji barai	mǫdʒi tʃin pu adʒi bərəi
	Thirteen fingers	Mǫji chin pu aji mak	mǫdʒi tʃin pu adʒi mak
43.	Twenty fingers	Mǫji chin pupusir	mǫdʒi tʃin pupusɪr
44.	A hundred fingers	Mǫji chin guya	mǫdʒi tʃin gujaˤ
45.	Two hundred fingers	Mǫji chin guya barai	mǫdʒi tʃin gujaˤ bərəi
46.	Four hundred fingers	Mǫji chin guya ang- fwat	mǫdʒi tʃin gujaˤ ʌɲfwat
47.	Sun	Usira	usɪra
	God	Intauf	ɪntauf
48.	Moon	Ligida	ligɪda
	Full moon	Kibir ligida	kɪbɪr ligɪda
	New moon	Umza ligida	umzə ligɪda
49.	Day	Usira	usɪra
	Night	Vida	vɪda
	Morning	Derin	derɪn
50.	Rain	Vina	vɪna

51. Water	Main	main
52. Blood	Idina	ıdına
53. Fat	Mava	maːva
54. Salt	Jetena	dʒɛtɛnə
55. Stone	Fara	fara
Iron	Tivisa	tivisa
56. Hill	Gyungwa	gjuŋwa
57. River	Kagirma	kagɪrma
58. Road	Irwa	ɪrwa
59. House	Kuva (pl. = kuvinyin)	kuva (pl. = kuvɪnjɪn)
Two houses	Kuv barai	kuv bərəi
Many houses	Kuva langa	kuva laŋa
All the houses	Kuva pata	kuva pata
60. Roof	Gwaa kuva	gwaa kuva
61. Door	Makuva	makuva
62. Mat	Buncha	buntʃa
63. Basket	Lava	ləva
64. Drum	Gangga	gaŋga
65. Pot	Uda	uda
66. Knife	Ngilla	ngɪlla
67. Spear	Uduma	uduma
68. Bow	Raga	raga
69. Arrow	Ava	ava
Five arrows	Ava tuf	avə tuf
70. Gun	Bunduka	bunduka
71. War	Pan	pan
72. Meat (animal)	Luwa	luwa
73. Elephant	Choana	tʃoana
74. Buffalo	Ngwia	ngwia
75. Leopard	Bȯya	bȯja
76. Monkey	Hurba	hurba
77. Pig	Dagilla	dagɪlla
78. Goat	Ohwa (pl. = ohin)	ohwa (pl. = ohɪn)
79. Dog	Idda	idda
80. Bird	Eginna	ɛgɪnna
Feather	Shinkin ga ginna	ʃɪnkɪn ga ginna
81. Crocodile	Kirma	kɪrma
Horse	Tuhwa (pl. = tahin)	tuhwa (pl. = təhɪn)
Sheep	Baga (pl. = bagin)	baga (pl. = bagin)
82. Fowl	Gyagya	gjagja
83. Eggs	Alin	alin
84. One egg	Alin rung	alin ruŋ
85. Snake	Rahun	rəhun
86. Frog	Mugumba	mugumba
87. Horse of the chief	Tuhwa ga ngwǫngwa	tuhwa ga ŋwɔŋwa
88. Fly	Jiin	dʒiɪn
89. Bee	Mo zinga	mo ziŋa
Honey	Mo zinga	mo ziŋa
90. Tree	Ushigin	uʃigɪn
Ten trees	Ushigin pu	uʃigɪn pu
91. Leaf	Ba	ba

92. Guinea-corn	Sukungwa	sukuŋwa
93. Maize	Nggule	ŋgulε
94. Ground nut	Inyen	ɪnjɛn
95. Oil	Mara	mara
Beriberi	Uva	uva
Fulani	Pirsana	pɪrsana
Hausa	Hausa	hausa
Margi	Margi	margi
Kilba	Wuding	wudiŋ
Higi	Hiji	hidʒi

THE FALI

A. *The Fali of Wuba District*

The term Fali is applied to various tribal groups which have no apparent connection with each other. Thus the Fali of the Kiria area in Wuba District differ both in language and in customs from the Fali a few miles further south in the district of Mubi. When Barth visited Adamawa he placed the northern limit of the Fali at Badanijo 25 miles south of Mubi [1] (in the Sorau area) and he records a Fali vocabulary which is totally different from that of either the Fali of Wuba or of Mubi. Elsewhere he speaks of the town of Batema or Baguma, eleven days' journey from Yola (on the Mora road) as being the principal centre of the Fali [2] and he also applies the name Fali to the Tufuri or Tuburi group.[3] Strumpell says that Fali is widely spoken between Dama-Grenze in the south and Gider and Mubi in the north.[4] Strumpell's vocabulary has a good deal in common with Barth's, though it is not by any means identical. But it has nothing in common with the Fali of Mubi or of Wuba. Barth remarks that his Fali is entirely distinct from Bata, Zani, and Margi, but I find that the Fali spoken in the Wuba and Mubi districts has a very definite connection with Bata, Margi, and Nzangi. The term Fali is also, I believe, applied to certain groups of peoples in Bauchi Province who speak a dialect of Bolewa.

It is possible that the various so-called Fali groups are offshoots of a former homogeneous tribe (centred in French Cameroons), which while retaining the tribal title, lost their language and customs. In this case the word may be a form of Bali =

---

[1] *Travels*, vol. ii, p. 436. [2] *Travels*, vol. ii, p. 594.
[3] *Travels*, vol. ii, p. 611. [4] *Zeitschrift für Ethnologie*, iii–iv, 1910, p. 450.

men or people. On the other hand, the word Fali may have come to be used as a general term for any immigrants irrespective of their tribe. It was possibly a term of contempt meaning "slaves", for among the Nzangi the word for "slave" is "fali".

The following short notes concern the Fali of Wuba district who occupy the villages of Kiria, Kiria Mongo, Mijilu, Kaskufu, Jombula, Manzul, Dugoba, etc. These people are close neighbours of the Higi and Margi, and if the vocabulary of their language, which is attached, is compared with that of the Higi and Margi it will be apparent that there is a close linguistic connection. The language of the Fali of Mubi, on the other hand, shows very much less connection. The Fali of Wuba also display many of the cultural features characteristic of the Higi and southern Margi. Thus they follow the practice of removing the epidermis of those who had died at a ripe age. The body is, in the first instance, given a temporary burial in sand so as to hasten the decomposition which facilitates the removal of the cuticle.[1] It is then placed on a platform and the epidermis is peeled off,[2] the denuded body being smeared with mahogany oil. A cow is killed and the skin is used to make coverings for the arms, legs, head, and body of the corpse. After being sewn up in these coverings the dead man is further clothed in a gown and trousers. If he had been a person of standing and wealth four red fezes are fastened round his temples, porcupine quills being inserted between the fezes and the temples. Two types of grave are employed, one being flagon-shaped and the other having a recess at the bottom of the shaft. The former is not filled up with earth, the mouth of the grave being sealed with a stone, over which a mound is raised. This type may be re-used, the bones of the former occupant being removed and given a separate, perfunctory burial. In the second type the shaft is filled in with earth which does not touch the body as the body lies protected in the recess. This is the type used for those who have the epidermis removed. There are variations also as regards the position of the body, members of the oldest families being laid so as to face the north, those of the families which came later being faced towards the west.

As among the Kilba, some groups of the Margi and the Pabir,

---

[1] See the papers on the Kilba, Margi, and Higi.
[2] The epidermis is deposited in a pot and is subsequently buried in a midden. But the eldest son of the deceased keeps the pot, and it is said that he eats his food from this pot in order to obtain his father's blessing.

chiefs or priests are given a special form of burial, the body being interred on the same day as death in a sitting position and covered with charcoal (in a flagon-shaped grave). The hair-lock is cut off and given to the eldest son who, if he becomes chief, has the lock plaited into a patch of his own hair. After burial a dog is killed and dressed-up to represent the chief, and dancing is maintained round this symbol for a period of three days. The body of the dog is then thrown away into the bush. The dog is possibly a substitute for a mummy. Among some Jukun groups a mock body is used in the burial rites.[1]

After an interval of a year the chief's successor is chosen by the official known as the Mazu, who ties a turban round the new chief's head and then takes him to his own house for a period of five nights. The sixth night is spent in the house of another official, and the seventh in the house of a third. In the early morning of the eighth day this third official takes the chief out to the bush, where he leaves him. Returning himself to the town he shouts out : " My slave has run away, and is lost in the bush." At this all the male members of the community seize their arms and set off to search the bush. When they find the new chief they bring him back with acclamations.

This custom is paralleled among the Jukun ; for at a certain stage of his chieftainship the Jukun king has to undergo rites in the course of which he is lost in the bush and found again by his people, symbolical it would seem of the death and rebirth which chiefs are supposed to undergo both at election and at a later stage when the renewal of their chieftainship is considered necessary (perhaps in consequence of an earlier rule that chiefs could only reign for a fixed period, after which they were put to death).[2]

Two years after the appointment of a new chief it was customary, in former times, to slay an enemy whose head was paraded before the chief, and then deposited in the skull-hut which stood outside the chief's compound. A festival followed, and it was at this festival that the hair-lock of his father was plaited into that of the chief.

The chief is known as the Nga, a word which appears to be a shortened form of the word " *ingale* " = chief among the Kuka

[1] See *A Sudanese Kingdom*, p. 254 et seq.
[2] See *A Sudanese Kingdom*, p. 140.

of the Fittri region.[1] It is noteworthy that one group of the Fali of Wuba claim to have come from the east into Bornu, and that it is on account of this traditional connection with Bornu that members of this group are buried facing the north. The other official titles are (in order of precedence) (a) Mazu, (b) Tufu, (c) Riga, and (d) Wunchido.

The social system of these Fali is much the same as that of the Higi, but inheritance is primarily by primogeniture. Younger sons are not, as among the Higi, entitled to inherit on their own account. The marriage customs differ little from those of the Higi. There are puberty rites, but these last only for one day (and not for three days as among the Higi). The boy is smeared with ochre, and, as among some groups of the Margi, the puberty rites are a form of betrothal ceremony. The boy thereby becomes affianced to a girl, to whose parents or guardians he becomes an agricultural bondsman for a period of four years. Gifts of corn and other articles are made at regular intervals to the girl's guardians, and the marriage is finally concluded by a feast, for which a cow is killed by the boy's father who sends the beef to the girl's guardians. Children born to a girl before she had gone to her husband's home or before she had her final marks incised (immediately after marriage), were until recently put to death, being regarded as bastards. It is customary for a husband to make a gift of a gown to his wife's guardian on the birth of the first child. This gift is said to be in the nature of a bribe to the father to permit his daughter to remain with her husband. For the birth of one child cancels the bride-price and the mother is then free to choose a different husband, without placing the new husband under any financial obligation to the old. If a woman has borne more than one child to her first husband she can take the excess children to the home of her second husband, who is permitted to adopt them, in accordance with the system indicated in my notes on the Higi.

B. The Fali of Mubi District

The Fali of Mubi district fall roughly into two groups, viz. those of Uvin and the vicinity,[2] and those of Jilbu. There are definite dialectical differences between the two groups. Both

---

[1] See Barth's *Travels*, iii, pp. 427, 451, and 543.
[2] I.e. of the villages of Mazarin, Gbwa, Hule (Ba), and Vimtim.

languages are closely related to those of the Jirai and Gudu, and
may be considered dialects of Bata. There is little difference
between the Uvin dialect and that of the so-called " Cheke " of
Mubi. But both dialects differ considerably from the Fali of
Wuba district, which has been influenced by Higi and Margi.
In customs also the Fali of Mubi district differ in certain important
respects from the Fali of Wuba. Thus the former do not remove
the epidermis from the dead bodies of the aged, nor is it
permissible for children to be adopted by their mother's second
husband (as among the Fali of Wuba and the Higi). All children
belong to the legal father.

On the other hand, the customs of the Fali of Mubi district are
almost identical with those of their so-called " Cheke " neighbours,
with the exception that the Fali do not practise circumcision,
whereas the Cheke do. The Fali men, also, wear leather loin-
coverings, whereas the Cheke wear garments of cloth. The Fali
men pierce their ears and lips and wear facial marks,[1] but the
Cheke do not. But the marriage system, the rules of inheritance,
the relationship terms, the official ranks, and the religious practices
of the Fali are the same as those of the Cheke.

There is no strict form of family exogamy, as all second cousins
are permitted to inter-marry. There is no totemism ; but certain
kindreds abstain from eating certain animals or groups of animals
on the ground that those animals are sacred to the cults. The
grave-digging kindreds, who are also the blacksmiths, do not
intermarry with members of other kindreds. This is a general
rule throughout a large part of Adamawa Province.

The Fali are strictly patrilineal. A man's property descends
to his sons. Formerly primogeniture was the invariable rule, the
eldest son taking complete charge of the property and using it as
he thought fit on behalf of all his brothers. But nowadays, as
sons are able to go and settle where they please, it has become
customary to give each grown-up son control of his own share of
his father's property. Brothers only inherit as administrators on
behalf of immature sons. A sister's son has no definite share in
property, but he is permitted to retain any article of property
which he is able to secure by his own adroitness. Widows are

---

[1] The marks consist of three parallel rows of punch marks on the forehead.
Pieces of guinea-corn stalk of cassava are inserted in the ear-lobes.

heritable by brothers (senior or junior) and by sons according to their age and wishes.

The relationship terms are given in the notes on the Cheke.

There is a form of puberty rite for boys, but details were not obtained. The boys are segregated for four days in an enclosure and on being released they are given a new loin-covering. There are no corresponding puberty rites for girls ; but the Fali have a custom by which an affianced girl spends a period of one month in the home of her fiancé, during which she is smeared with ochre each day by a girl friend. Her betrothed has to give her a gift when she enters his home for this purpose, and other gifts when she partakes of her first meal, and retires for the night. If he wishes to converse with her he must also give her a gift. At the end of the period a cow is killed and the beef is sent to the girl's father. The youth may then have sexual relations with the girl, but the girl does not remain in his home. She returns to her own home for a period of two or three years (being still young) and is there visited at night by her betrothed who is now regarded as her husband. If she conceives a child she must remain in her own home until the child is weaned. As these rites are carried out soon after puberty they may be regarded as puberty rites, but they are intimately bound up with marriage. The Cheke have no puberty rites for boys, but in the case of girls they follow the Fali custom described above.

Old men are buried in the Muslim fashion (rectangular graves), but young men, women, and children are buried in large flagon-shaped graves, which are used over and over again, the grave being cleared periodically of the remains of the former occupants.

Short vocabularies of both dialects are attached.

FALI (OF KIRIA) VOCABULARY

1.	Head	Khin	xɪn
2.	Hair	Chinchi	tʃɪntʃi
3.	Eye	Nchi	ntʃi
	Two eyes	Nchi bak	ntʃi bək
4.	Ear	Hlim	ɬɪm
	Two ears	Hlim baka	ɬɪm bəkə
5.	Nose	Nchin	ntʃɪn
6.	One tooth	Hlai gutan	ɬai gutan
	Five teeth	Hlai nchif	ɬai ntʃɪf

x

7. Tongue	Nggana	ŋganə
8. Neck	Wuri	wuri
9. Breast (woman's)	Uwa	uwaˁ
10. Heart	Naffa	nəffə
11. Belly	Kur	kur
12. Back	Mbul	mbul
13. Arm	Pilla	pɪlla
14. Hand	Mbila pilla	mbɪla pɪlla
Two hands	Mbila pilla baka	mbɪla pɪlla bəkə
15. Finger	Eska pilla	ɛskə pɪlla
Five fingers	Eska pilla nchif	ɛskə pɪlla ntʃɪf
16. Finger nail	Getin	gɛtɪn
17. Leg	Silla	sɪlla
18. Knee	Kumaishin	kumaiʃɪn
19. Foot	Mbila silla	mbɪla sɪlla
Two feet	Mbila silla baka	mbɪla sɪlla bəkə
20. Man (person)	Mde	mdɛ
Ten people	Mbiri gum	mbɪri gum
21. Man (not woman)	Zal	zal
Two men	Zal baka	zal bəkə
22. Woman	Malka	malkə
Two women	Malka baka	malkə bəkə
23. Child	Uzga	uzgə
24. Father	Ita	ita
25. Mother	Mma	mma
26. Slave	Mava	məvə
27. Chief	Nga	ŋgə
28. Friend	Ntuva	ntuva
29. Smith	Inje	indʒe
30. Doctor	Ulla	ullə
31. One finger	Eska pilla tan	ɛskə pɪlla tan
32. Two fingers	Eska pilla baka	ɛskə pɪlla bəkə
33. Three fingers	Eska pilla makin	ɛskə pɪlla makɪn
34. Four fingers	Eska pilla nfwǫr	ɛskə pɪlla nfwɔr
35. Five fingers	Eska pilla nchifa	ɛskə pɪlla ntʃɪfə
36. Six fingers	Eska pilla nkwang	ɛskə pɪlla nkwaŋ
37. Seven fingers	Eska pilla birfung	ɛskə pɪlla bɪrfuŋ
38. Eight fingers	Eska pilla tikhis	ɛskə pɪlla tɪxɪs
39. Nine fingers	Eska pilla mti	ɛskə pɪlla mti
40. Ten fingers	Eska pilla gum	ɛskə pɪlla gum
41. Eleven fingers	Eska pilla gum na tang	ɛskə pɪlla gum na taŋ
42. Twelve fingers	Eska pilla gum na mabaka	ɛskə pɪlla gum na mabəkə
Thirteen fingers	Eska pilla gum na makin	ɛskə pɪlla gum na makɪn
43. Twenty fingers	Eska pilla sillamsaka	ɛskə pɪlla sɪllamsəkə
44. A hundred fingers	Eska pilla gumsak	ɛskə pɪlla gumsək
45. Two hundred fingers	Eska pilla gumsaka baka	ɛskə pɪlla gumsəkə bəkə
46. Four hundred fingers	Eska pilla gumsaka fwǫr	ɛskə pɪlla gumsəkə fwɔr

47.	Sun	Vachi	vətʃi
	God	Yatagum	jatəgum
48.	Moon	Tirri	tɪrri
	Full moon	Tirri a biriva	tɪrri a bɪrivə
	New moon	Tirri tarkha	tɪrri tarxa
49.	Day	Vachi	vətʃi
	Night	Ville	vɪllɛ
	Morning	Pillim	pɪllɪm
50.	Rain	Van	van
51.	Water	Yiami	jiami
52.	Blood	Mimi	mimi
53.	Fat	Mavira	mavirə
54.	Salt	Piri	piri
55.	Stone	Ghum	ɡum
	Iron	Iring	iriŋ
56.	Hill	—	—
57.	River	Tala	tala
58.	Road	Ngkwal	ŋkwal
59.	House	Chiki (compound = khe)	tʃɪki (compound = xɛ)
	Two houses	Chiki bak	tʃɪki bək
	Many houses	Chiki bwe	tʃɪki bwɛ
	All the houses	Chiki kyikya	tʃɪki kjikja
60.	Roof	Chiki	tʃɪki
61.	Door	Midiga	mɪdɪga
62.	Mat	Nshir	nʃɪr
63.	Basket	Ngwan	ngwan
64.	Drum	Dang	daŋ
65.	Pot	Dagum	dəgum
66.	Knife	Nggilla	ŋgɪlla
67.	Spear	Ngwassa	ngwassə
68.	Bow	Ngin	ngɪn
69.	Arrow	Hava	havə
	Five arrows	Havo chif	havo tʃɪf
70.	Gun	Vinding	vɪndɪŋ
71.	War	Dapwoi	dapwoi
72.	Elephant	Chun	tʃuŋ
73.	Meat (animal)	Tii	tii
74.	Buffalo	Nfun	nfun
75.	Leopard	Mvu	mvu
76.	Monkey	Luku	luku
77.	Pig	Girdim	gɪrdɪm
78.	Goat	Ku	ku
79.	Dog	Kirri	kɪrri
80.	Bird	Ika	ikə
	Feather	Chinchika	tʃɪntʃikə
81.	Crocodile	Khilim	xɪlɪm
82.	Fowl	Kamtaka	kamtəka
83.	Eggs	Hlihli	ɬiɬi
84.	One egg	Hlihli gutan	ɬiɬi gutan
85.	Snake	Shishi	ʃiʃi

86. Frog	Gwambəka	gwambəkə
87. Horse	Tuku	tuku
Sheep	Timbaka	tɪmbəkə
Cow	Hla	ła [1]
88. Fly	Zhu	ʒu
89. Bee	Umzǫho	umzɔho
Honey	Umzǫho	umzɔho
90. Tree	Otsum	otsum
Ten trees	Otsuma gum	otsuma gum
91. Leaf	Chikəfu	tʃɪkəfu
92. Guinea-corn	Ikha	ɪxa
93. Maize	Khavwa	xavwa
94. Ground nut	Kanachi	kanatʃi
95. Oil	Yii	jii
96. Beriberi	Uvwa	uvwa
Hausa	Hausa	hausa
Fulani	Baji	badʒi
Margi	Mirki	mɪrki
Kilba	Khibba	xɪbba

FALI (OF MUBI) VOCABULARY
Per Kaigama of Yimtin

1. Head	Wǫnin	wɔnɪn
2. Hair	Shimkin	ʃɪmkɪn
3. Eye	Gin	gɪn
Two eyes	Gin bik	gɪn bik
4. Ear	Limin	lɪmɪn
Two ears	Limin bik	lɪmɪn bik
5. Nose	Shinin	ʃɪnɪn
6. One tooth	Lingin erun	liŋɪn ɛrun
Five teeth	Lingin tuf	liŋɪn tuf
7. Tongue	Genin	gɛnɪn
8. Neck	Wuran	wuran
9. Breast (woman's)	Wakin	wakɪn
10. Heart	Inggilarin	ɪŋgɪlarɪn
11. Belly	Sikin	sɪkɪn
12. Back	Baan	baan
13. Arm	Chiin	tʃiin
14. Hand	Sika chiin	sɪkə tʃiin
Two hands	Sika chiin bik	sɪkə tʃiin bik
15. Finger	Uji chiin	udʒi tʃiin
Five fingers	Uji chiin tuf	udʒi tʃiin tuf
16. Finger nail	Gisin	gisɪn
17. Leg	Sidin	sɪdɪn
18. Knee	Wǫni idin	wɔni ɪdɪn
19. Foot	Sika sidin	sɪkə sɪdɪn
Two feet	Sika sidin bik	sɪkə sɪdɪn bik
20. Man (person)	Imdin	ɪmdɪn
Ten people	Wonji pu	wɔndʒi pu

[1] This lateral has an "s"-like quality.

21.	Man (not woman)	Morin	morɪn
	Two men	Morin bik	morɪn bik
22.	Woman	Imkin	ɪmkɪn
	Two women	Mathyin bik	mathjɪn bik
23.	Child	Uzikin	uzɪkɪn
24.	Father	Dada	dada
25.	Mother	Aya	aja
26.	Slave	Mavin	mavɪn
27.	Chief	Momin	momɪn
28.	Friend	Guvan	guvan
29.	Smith	Kilakin	kɪlakɪn
30.	Doctor	—	—
31.	One finger	Uji chiin erum	udʒi tʃiɪn ɛrum
32.	Two fingers	Uji chiin bik	edʒi tʃiɪn bik
33.	Three fingers	Uji chiin makh	udʒi tʃiɪn max
34.	Four fingers	Uji chiin fwat	udʒi tʃiɪn fwat
35.	Five fingers	Uji chiin tuf	udʒi tʃiɪn tuf
36.	Six fingers	Uji chiin kuwa	udʒi tʃiɪn kuwa
37.	Seven fingers	Uji chiin midif	udʒi tʃiɪn mɪdif
38.	Eight fingers	Uji chiin tikhis	udʒi tʃiɪn tɪxɪs
39.	Nine fingers	Uji chiin miling	udʒi tʃiɪn mɪlɪŋ
40.	Ten fingers	Uji chiin pu	udʒi tʃiɪn pu
41.	Eleven fingers	Uji chiin pu a katang	udʒi tʃiɪn pu a kataŋ
42.	Twelve fingers	Uji chiin ahiji bik	udʒi tʃiɪn ahidʒi bik
	Thirteen fingers	Uji chiin ahiji makh	adʒi tʃiɪn ahidʒi max
43.	Twenty fingers	Uji chiik pupusir	udʒi tʃiɪn pupusɪr
44.	A hundred fingers	Uji chiik gya	udʒi tʃiɪn gjaˤ
45.	Two hundred fingers	Uji chiik gya a bik	udʒi tʃiɪn gjaˤ a bik
46.	Four hundred fingers	Uji chiik gya a fwat	udʒi tʃiɪn gjaˤ a fwat
47.	Sun	Fetin	fetɪn
	God	Imtaf	ɪmtʌf
48.	Moon	Ligidin	lɪgɪdɪn
	Full moon	Kiwir ligidin	kɪwɪr lɪgɪdɪn
	New moon	Umza ligidin	umzə lɪgɪdɪn
49.	Day	Fetin	fetɪn
	Night	Vidin	vɪdɪn
	Morning	Putkin	putkɪn
50.	Rain	Vonin	vonɪn
51.	Water	Main	maɪn
52.	Blood	Idinin	ɪdɪnɪn
53.	Fat	Mavin	mavɪn
54.	Salt	Jetanin	dʒɛtanɪn
55.	Stone	Farin	farɪn
	Iron	Tibisin	tibɪsɪn
56.	Hill	Gimin	gimɪn
57.	River	Mirin	mirɪn
58.	Road	Rugwon	rugwɔn
59.	House	Kivin	kivɪn
	Two houses	Kivin bik	kivɪn bik

	Many houses	Kivin lang	kivɪn laŋ
	All the houses	Kivin pet	kivɪn pɛt
60.	Roof	Gidan	gɪdan
61.	Door	Makavin	makəvɪn
62.	Mat	Khidzin	xɪdzɪn
63.	Basket	Divin	divɪn
64.	Drum	Bambada	bambada
65.	Pot	Wudan	wudan
66.	Knife	Nggillan	ŋgɪllan
67.	Spear	Wudimin	wudɪmɪn
68.	Bow	Ragin	ragɪn
69.	Arrow	Avin	avɪn
	Five arrows	Avin tuf	avɪn tuf
70.	Gun	Bondikin	bondikɪn
71.	War	Pakin	pakɪn
72.	Meat (animal)	Luwin	luwɪn
73.	Elephant	Chuwan	tʃuwan
74.	Buffalo	Lumein	lumeɪn
75.	Leopard	Daguvan	dəguvan
76.	Monkey	Horuvin	horuvɪn
77.	Pig	Dagillan	dagɪllan
78.	Goat	Khun	xun
79.	Dog	Khiddan	xɪddan
80.	Bird	Auvginin	auvgɪnɪn
	Feather	Shimkiv gin	ʃɪmkɪv gɪn
81.	Crocodile	Kirmin	kɪrmɪn
82.	Fowl	Iikin	iikɪn
	Horse	Tuhun	tuhun
	Sheep	Bagan	bagan
83.	Eggs	Alin	alɪn
84.	One egg	Alin rung	alɪn ruŋ
85.	Snake	Ruhunin	ruhunɪn
86.	Frog	Kọkwaran	kɔkwaran
87.	Beriberi	Uvan	uvan
88.	Fly	Jiin	dʒiɪn
89.	Bee	Mo zungan	mo zuŋan
	Honey	Mo zungan	mo zuŋan
90.	Tree	Shikun	ʃi kun
	Ten trees	Shikun pu	ʃi kun pu
91.	Leaf	Ban	ban
92.	Guinea-corn	Mbwaran	mbwaran
93.	Maize	Nggulia	ŋgulia
94.	Ground nut	Nyaakin	njaakɪn
95.	Oil	Marin	marɪn

Fali (of Jilbu) Vocabulary

1.	Head	Yini	jini
2.	Hair	Shimchin	ʃɪmtʃin
3.	Eye	Jin	dʒɪn
	Two eyes	Jin sil	dʒɪn sɪl

4. Ear	Limin	lɪmɪn
Two ears	Limin sil	lɪmɪn sɪl
5. Nose	Shingye	ʃɪŋje
6. One tooth	Linge lim	liŋe lim
Five teeth	Linge mukhtie	liŋe muxtie
7. Tongue	Genan	gɛnan
8. Neck	Wulan	wulan
9. Breast (woman's)	Wakin	wakɪn
10. Heart	Khadikin	xadɪkɪn
11. Belly	Sika	sɪkə
12. Back	Mbule	mbule
13. Arm	Chivin	tʃɪvɪn
14. Hand	Sika a chivin	sɪkə a tʃɪvɪn
Two hands	Sika a chivin sil	sɪkə a tʃɪvɪn sɪl
15. Finger	Wuzhi shiga chivin	wuʒi ʃɪgə tʃɪvɪn
Five fingers	Wuzhi shiga chivin mukhtie	wuʒi ʃɪgə tʃɪvɪn muxtie
16. Finger nail	Gitin	gitɪn
17. Leg	Sidin	sɪdɪn
18. Knee	Idin	idɪn
19. Foot	Tapapaanga sidi	tapapaaŋa sɪdi
Two feet	Tapapaanga sidi sil	tapapaaŋa sɪdi sɪl
20. Man (person)	Mindi	mɪndi
Ten people	Mindi gamo	mɪndi gʌmo
21. Man (not woman)	Mwille	mwɪlle
Two men	Nggwire sil	ŋgwire sɪl
22. Woman	Majikin	madʒɪkɪn
Two women	Mashkin sil	maʃkɪn sɪl
23. Child	Zikin	zɪkɪn
24. Father	Dig	dig
25. Mother	Mig	mig
26. Slave	Mavan	məvan
27. Chief	Mongwin	mɔŋwin
28. Friend	Inchil	ɪntʃil
29. Smith	Mihin	mihɪn
30. Doctor	Madang gumin	madaŋ gumɪn
31. One finger	Wuzhi shiga chivin lim	wuʒi ʃɪgə tʃɪvɪn lim
32. Two fingers	Wuzhi shiga chivin sil	wuʒi ʃɪgə tʃɪvɪn sɪl
33. Three fingers	Wuzhi shiga chivin makhka	wuʒi ʃɪgə tʃɪvɪn maxkə
34. Four fingers	Wuzhi shiga chivin fwoi	wuʒi ʃɪgə tʃɪvɪn fwɔi
35. Five fingers	Wuzhi shiga chivin mukhtie	wuʒi ʃɪgə tʃɪvɪn muxtie
36. Six fingers	Wuzhi shiga chivin nkwa	wuʒi ʃɪgə tʃɪvɪn nkwa
37. Seven fingers	Wuzhi shiga chivin mbirifing	wuʒi ʃɪgə tʃɪvɪn mbɪrɪfɪŋ
38. Eight fingers	Wuzhi shiga chivin tikhis	wuʒi ʃɪgə tʃɪvɪn tɪxɪs
39. Nine fingers	Wuzhi shiga chivin mili	wuʒi ʃɪgə tʃɪvɪn mɪli

40. Ten fingers	Wuzhi shiga chivin gamo	wuʒi ʃɪgə tʃɪvɪn gʌmo	
41. Eleven fingers	Wuzhi shiga chivin da lim	wuʒi ʃɪgə tʃɪvɪn də lim	
42. Twelve fingers	Wuzhi shiga chivin siltinig	wuʒi ʃɪgə tʃɪvɪn sɪltinig	
Thirteen fingers	Wuzhi shiga chivin makhkatinig	wuʒi ʃɪgə tʃɪvɪn maxkə ti nig	
43. Twenty fingers	Wuzhi shiga chivin silamsak	wuʒi ʃɪgə tʃɪvɪn sɪlamsək	
44. A hundred fingers	Wuzhi shiga chivin juwa	wuʒi ʃɪgə tʃɪvɪn dʒuwa	
45. Two hundred fingers	Wuzhi shiga chivin sil juwanig	wuʒi ʃɪgə tʃɪvɪn sɪl dʒuwanig	
46. Four hundred fingers	Wuzhi shiga chivin fwọi	wuʒi ʃɪgə tʃɪvɪn fwọi	
47. Sun	Fiti	fiti	
God	Fitiduf	fiti duf	
48. Moon	Ligide	lɪgɪde	

THE SUKUR GROUP

This group, which numbers about 1,300 persons, occupies a mountainous site some 12 miles south of Madagali. It appears to be an offshoot of the Mpsakali or Gudur group of the French Cameroons. Their language shows many resemblances in vocabulary and phonology with Higi, Fali, and Margi, and may be included in the Bura-Kilba-Margi group, a group which is closely related to Gamergu, Nghala, and numerous Cameroon dialects. The Sukur have the same word for God (Jigilla) as the Gamergu.

It was not possible to pay a visit to the Sukur, and the following notes were obtained as a result of a short conversation at Madagali with the chief and two of his sons. The chief asked to be excused staying in Madagali more than a few hours, on the ground of his religious duties.

The chiefs of Sukur claim to be descendants of a slave of the Mai of Bornu, who obtained an ascendancy over the people of Sukur owing to his wealth and power. The stranger was given the control of the local cult which had formerly been in the hands of an immigrant family from Mpsakali (Gudur) in the French Cameroons. There is a story which is sometimes told of the stranger from Bornu and sometimes of the leader of the immigrant family from Mpsakali. He arrived near Sukur with a

PLATE 30

MARKET SCENES AT MADAGALI

[face p. 312

ram, and was met by the daughter of a blacksmith who gave him some water to drink, because he was thirsty. The girl then ran home to spread the news, and the men of the town came out to find the stranger. But they could not see him ; they only heard his voice saying that he would become visible to them when they summoned the blacksmith's daughter. So they sent for the girl, and he became visible and was escorted to the town, where the blacksmith's daughter was given to him in marriage. The priests of the local cult had been dying every year, so the people decided to make the stranger their priest-chief. The stranger thereupon slew the ram at the door of the palace, and stepping over its body entered the palace and ruled for many years, during which the people never lacked an abundance of corn.

The chief [1] is regarded as the pivot of the people's prosperity : he is the source of their corn and rain and health. His person is sacred, and he is subject to numerous taboos. He must attend constantly on the cult, and on account of this constant association his own person is regarded as charged with divinity. Being a divine person he must not eat in public. His meals are cooked and served to him by a specially selected wife, and the dishes may not touch the ground. This is also a Jukun custom ; and as among the Jukun, when the chief has finished eating he announces the fact by a cough. When the favourite wife is in a menstruous condition the chief lives entirely on beer. In former times the chief never left Sukur ; but nowadays if he is summoned by the Fulani district head to Madagali he lives wholly on beer during his absence from home. The Jukun rule is similar. It is indecorous to say of him that he eats or sleeps. No one may go near his lavatory ; and if he is absent from home the water which he passes is caught in a dish and taken back to Sukur. It was formerly also the custom for the chief of Sukur's spittle to be caught in a dish and disposed of secretly, a custom which was common among the Jukun and Yoruba. As among the Pabir and Jukun the chief wears a hair-lock, which is regarded as sacred. It may not be seen ; and for this reason the chief never removes his cap, not even, it is said, during sleep. Into this lock is plaited that of his father. There is no taboo against his feet touching the ground or against picking up anything from the ground (as among

---

[1] The word for chief, viz. *hlidi*, contains the root *hli* which is found among the Bura and Pabir in the form *ku-hli*.

the Jukun), but certain parts of the road are taboo to him, and he is not allowed to go in among the crops or to do any form of manual work, for it is said that if he scratched himself, so that blood flowed, he would die. The royal farms were formerly cultivated by his slaves and servants; but for the planting, mid-season hoeing, harvesting, and beating of the corn the entire people of Sukur took part, and each of these four operations had to be completed in a single day. It was also the custom for small quantities of seed from the royal farm to be distributed among the more prominent members of the community at sowing time, for this seed was believed to have special magical power.

The chief of Sukur carries out religious rites every day of the year, except for the period of a month or so corresponding to the interval between the Muslim festivals of *Îd al-Fitr* and *Îd al-Adhâ*, a period known to the Hausa as the slave's month. It was stated that the reason for this cessation was to give an opportunity to the owners of the various minor cults to perform their rites; rites which could not be performed while those of the royal cult were being observed. It is to be noted that during this month no member of the royal family may withdraw any corn from his granary. At dawn each day the chief enters the royal shrine and there makes an oblation of beer before the monolith which serves as the symbol of the cult of Son. This stone has a hollow at the apex. As the priest-chief tilts out the beer (which he does six times, thrice to the right and thrice to the left) he recites the following prayer : " I give to you my father ; I give to you my grandfather. O Son, give me health ; O Son, give all my people health ; O Son, give us guinea-corn ; O Son, grant me length of days that I may continue to make offerings to thee ; and when I come to die may my children inherit my office and perform their duty to thee. O Son, give them health, even as you have given health to me." This prayer is intoned exactly as prayers are intoned by Christian priests ; and when it is concluded the senior members of the chief's entourage who are assembled outside clap their hands in reverence, just as among the Jukun the attendant congregation slap their thighs.[1] Unlike the Jukun chiefs the chief of Sukur wears a gown during the performance of the rites. As he retires from the shrine he covers his sandal-prints by sweeping the ground with a brush. The rites are repeated in the evening. I have suggested that among the Jukun

---

[1] See *A Sudanese Kingdom*, p. 161.

the fact that the rites are performed at sunrise and at sunset may indicate they were originally sun-rites. But the Sukur explanation is that the rites are performed at sunrise with a view to securing the blessing of the gods throughout the day, and at sunset to secure their protection during the night.

The chief's compound has two entrances each of which is guarded by a eunuch. During the dry season he uses the main entrance to salute his people, but during the wet season he may only use the minor entrance which passes close to the shrine. On ceremonial occasions he sits on a stone throne to receive his people, and during the Yawal festival[1] he sits behind a curtain to protect his countenance from the gaze of strangers.

The chiefs of Sukur are buried in the Pabir fashion. The grave is flagon-shaped, and the body is placed on an iron bier in a sitting position, the head being kept erect by means of an iron prong, the spike of which is stuck into the wall of the grave. The arms are extended, and an iron prong is placed under each elbow and each knee. The body is fully clothed in gown, trousers, and sandals, and is covered over with leather shields. The grave is then filled with charcoal which reaches to the dead chief's shoulders. The mouth of the grave is blocked with a stone, the edges being filled in with smaller stones and covered with plaster. A mound of loose earth is built over the stone, the top of the mound being hardened with plaster. A circle of stones is then built round the mound.

The body is not subjected to any form of mummification, and the interval between death and burial is only three days. The Sukur chiefs were not apparently judicially murdered at the end of a fixed period, but it was not uncommon for a powerful relative to kill the chief and reign in his stead. This would occur most frequently after a drought, when the people believed that their chief had been repudiated by the gods. The chief's favourite wife was killed and buried with him.

The chiefs of Sukur had at one time considerable territorial authority.[2] Though they never personally took part in warfare they could raise a fairly large force, and many of the warriors were mounted. From their mountain fastness they raided the

---

[1] See p. 227.
[2] Barth (vol. ii, pp. 397 and 398) says : " The prince of Sugur overawes all the petty neighbouring chiefs; and he is said to possess a great many idols, small round stones to which the people sacrifice fowls of red, black, and white colour, and sheep with a red line on the back."

surrounding country, the roads down to the plains being paved
with stone to permit an easy descent for the horses. Even at the
present day the chiefs of Wula Vemgo and a number of other
villages receive their formal appointment from the chief of Sukur,
who ceremonially shaves the head of the nominee.

A few notes only were obtained as regards the form of social
organization. The Sukur are strictly patrilineal. The patrilineal
kindred is exogamous, i.e. no man may marry a woman who is
known to be a blood relative on the father's side. It is also
forbidden to marry a relative known to be related to one's mother.
There is no totemism ; but the people of Sukur have a custom
which is, I believe, unique. They may not kill any game-animal ;
for they believe that if they were to do so their wives, if enceinte,
would abort, or, if mothers of young children, that the young
children would die within a month.

The wife's family has no claim on children ; and inheritance is
by primogeniture, i.e. the eldest son, if sufficiently old, inherits all
property and uses it on behalf of himself and his younger brothers.
The deceased's brother only inherits as an administrator on
behalf of a son who is too young to assume the responsibilities.
Wives are reckoned as part of the heritable estate, and sons may
therefore inherit their father's young widows ; but the son of a
chief may not inherit his father's widows unless he himself
succeeds his father as chief.

Young boys undergo a form of initiation in the spring when
the crops are beginning to sprout ; but the initiation rites do not
entail any of the forms of physical hardship which are common
among most other tribes. The rites are the occasion of a general
festival, during which the relatives of the boys consume a great
deal of liquor. The rites last for five days only. On the first
evening the boys, stripped naked, are paraded before the chief ;
and on the following morning before sunrise they are escorted to
the peak of a hill where they spend the day sitting idly and
without being required to dance (as is usual among other tribes).
Instead of having to live on scanty meals they are specially well
fed. But their seclusion must not be disturbed, and if they descry
the presence of any unauthorized person they can, without
prejudice, attack him and rob him of anything he happens to
possess. Each night they return home and occupy special
quarters. On the evening of the fifth day they are escorted to the

palace of the chief, and each boy is given (by his father or guardian) a loin-covering of hide in its natural state. The boys are then addressed by the chief who tells them that they are no longer boys but men, that they must put aside the reckless behaviour of children, and assume the character of men, each becoming responsible for his own behaviour. They must give themselves to farm-work, and must marry, establish homes, and become the fathers of children.

The initiation of girls is a preliminary to marriage. For before an affianced girl goes to her husband's home she is required to live a life of retreat for a period of four days. She abstains from all physical work and is given an abundance of food, so that she may go to her husband in the pink of condition. This custom recalls the " fattening " practices found among tribes of the Southern Provinces. Among the Sukur it appears to be a transition rite, marking the stage between the old and the new form of life. It is a puberty rite.

Marriage is arranged on the so-called " purchase " system, the father appropriating two-thirds of the bride-price, and the mother one-third. But the suitor is also required to give agricultural service, the advantage of which is mainly derived by the bride's father. The young wife, having gone to her husband's home, bears her children there. If she has borne a child or even has had a miscarriage her husband has no further claim on her, should she elect to become the wife of someone else. In this the Sukur present a striking contrast to some of their " Higi " neighbours.

SUKUR VOCABULARY

1.	Head	Ka	kə
2.	Hair	Shimbut	ʃɪmbut
3.	Eye	Is	is
	Two eyes	Is bak	is bak
4.	Ear	Limai	lɪməi
	Two ears	Limai bak	lɪməi bak
5.	Nose	Shin	ʃin
6.	One tooth	Liin kili	liɪn kɪli
	Five teeth	Liin hlam	liɪn ɫam
7.	Tongue	Ghanai	ɡanai
8.	Back	Woi	wɔˁi
9.	Breast (woman's)	Wa	waˁ
10.	Heart	Mindiv	mɪndɪv

11.	Belly	Khut	xut
12.	Back	Jakh	dʒax
13.	Arm	Iri	ɪri
14.	Hand	Khut ri	xut ri
	Two hands	Khut ri bak	xut ri bak
15.	Finger	Virshin ri	vɪrʃɪn ri
	Five fingers	Virshin ri hlam	vɪrʃɪn ri łam
16.	Finger nail	Pilak	pɪlak
17.	Leg	Nas	naːs
18.	Knee	Kirim	kɪrɪm
19.	Foot	Jakh nas	dʒax naːs
	Two feet	Jakh nas bak	dʒax naːs bak
20.	Man (person)	Mdu	mdu
	Ten people	Mdu wọng	mdu wɔŋ
21.	Man (not woman)	Malakh	malax
	Two men	Maijikha bak	məidʒɪxə bak
22.	Woman	Zir	zɪr
	Two women	Ziri bak	ziri bak
23.	Child	Rui juu	rui dʒuu
24.	Father	Fanga	faŋa
25.	Mother	Manga	maŋa
26.	Slave	Vai	vəi
27.	Chief	hlidi	łidˈi
28.	Friend	Meenga	meɛŋa
29.	Smith	Dai	dˈəi
30.	Doctor	Bilaga	bɪlaga
31.	One finger	Ruri kili	ruri kɪli
32.	Two fingers	Riri bak	riri bak
33.	Three fingers	Riri makin	riri makɪn
34.	Four fingers	Riri fwọt	riri fwɔt
35.	Five fingers	Riri hlam	riri łam
36.	Six fingers	Riri mukwa	riri mukwa
37.	Seven fingers	Riri madaf	riri madaf
38.	Eight fingers	Riri tigiz	riri tɪgɪz
39.	Nine fingers	Riri mikhi	riri mɪxi
40.	Ten fingers	Riri wọng	riri wɔŋ
41.	Eleven fingers	Riri wọng hlam kimba	riri wɔŋ łam kɪmbə
42.	Twelve fingers	Riri wọng ba kimba	riri wɔŋ bə kɪmbə
	Thirteen fingers	Riri wọng makin kimba	riri wɔŋ makɪn kɪmbə
43.	Twenty fingers	Riri sara sak	riri sara sək
44.	A hundred fingers	Riri wọ sak	riri wɔ sək
45.	Two hundred fingers	Riri du wọ sak	riri du wɔ sək
46.	Four hundred fingers	Riri fwọt wọ sak	riri fwɔt wɔ sək
47.	Sun	Pis	pis
	God	Jigilla	dʒigɪlla
48.	Moon	Tea (Earth = Khat)	tea (Earth = xat)
	Full moon	Akhi ma hyen	axi mə hjɛn
	New moon	Andas tea	andas tea

49.	Day	Kavak	kavaːk
	Night	Vat	vət
	Morning	Mashin	maʃin
50.	Rain	Yiam	jiam
51.	Water	Yiam sata	jiam sətə
52.	Blood	Mumbus	mumbus
53.	Fat	Mazama hyen	məzamə hjɛn
54.	Salt	Nyerga	njɛrga
55.	Stone	Iyim	ijɪm
	Iron	Chukuri	tʃukuri
56.	Hill	Ngwa	ŋwa
57.	River	Llan	llan
58.	Road	Chive	tʃive
59.	House	Ir	ɪr
	Two houses	Ir bak	ɪr bak
	Many houses	Ir king	ɪr kɪŋ
	All the houses	Ir papa	ɪr papa
60.	Roof	Jik	dʒɪk
61.	Door	Mu ir	mu ɪr
62.	Mat	Patta	pətta
63.	Basket	Migissa	mɪgɪssa
64.	Drum	Dang	daŋ
65.	Pot	Du	du
66.	Knife	Kap	kəp
67.	Spear	mbaghaz	mbaɡaz
68.	Bow	Rai	rai
69.	Arrow	Va	va
	Five arrows	Va hlam	va ɬam
70.	Gun	Banding	bandɪŋ
71.	War	Khip	xɪp
72.	Meat (animal)	Lwi	lwi
73.	Elephant	Riveri	rɪvɛri
74.	Buffalo	Gammak	gammʌk
75.	Leopard	Dugavak	dugavʌk
76.	Monkey	Billam	bɪllam
77.	Pig	Vagis	vəgɪs
78.	Goat	Yuk	juk
79.	Dog	Kirra	kɪrra
80.	Bird	Yak	jak
	Feather	Shimbut yak	ʃɪmbut jak
81.	Crocodile	Kilim	kɪlɪm
	Horse	Duk	du
	Sheep	Gammak	gammak
	Cow	Hla	ɬə
82.	Fowl	Takur	takur
83.	Eggs	Danggal lai	daŋgal lai
84.	One egg	Danggal lai kili	daŋgal lai kili
85.	Snake	Sisi	sisi
86.	Frog	Gumbak	gumbak
87.	Beriberi	Uvwa	uvwa
	Fulani	Pilasar	pɪlasar

	Margi	Bukhidim	buxɪdɪm
	Hausa	Hausa	hausa
	Pabir	Babir	babɪr
88.	Fly	Jui	dʒui
89.	Bee	Ju mam	dʒu mam
	Honey	Mam	mam
90.	Tree	Shiku	ʃiku
	Ten trees	Shuku wǫng	ʃuku wɔŋ
91.	Leaf	Dui	ɗui
92.	Guinea-corn	Khui	xui
93.	Maize	Khlabir	xlabɪr
94.	Ground nut	Kolakochi	kolakotʃi
95.	Oil	Mir	mir
96.	The tall woman	Zir zabir	zɪr zəbɪr
	The tall women	Zhiri zibir	ʒiri zəbɪr
97.	Large dog	Kirra di	kɪrra di
98.	Small dog	Kirra juhǫi	kɪrra dʒuhɔi
99.	The dog bites	Kirra mi kinba	kɪrra mi kɪnbə
100.	The dog bites me	Kirra mi kinga	kɪrra mi kɪŋa
101.	The dog which bit me yesterday	Kirrai a kingar binna	kɪrra a kɪŋar binna
102.	I flog the dog	Adzin kirra	adzin kɪrra
103.	The dog which I have flogged	Kirra adarni	kɪrra adarni

THE VILLAGERS OF WOGA, VEMGO, VIZIK, AND TUR (MADAGALI DISTRICT)

The inhabitants of these villages, which are situated a few miles to the east and north of Madagali, speak a language which is fairly closely related to the " Higi " dialects, and may be included in the Bura-Kilba-Margi-Higi group.   There are some resemblances also (a) with Gamergu, (b) with Wandala (Mandara), and (c) with the Bata dialects.   The language is very guttural, and a noteworthy feature is that numerals are commonly placed before the noun instead of after.

The dialect of Tur differs slightly from that of Woga, Vemgo, and Vizik, and there are considerable cultural differences between the Tur and those of the other three villages.

The Woga,[1] Vemgo, and Vizik villagers, who number just over 1,600, appear to belong to a tribal group the main part of which is located in the French Cameroons (round Mabas, Mekshi,

[1] The people of Woga call themselves the Wudir.

PLATE 31

WOMEN OF THE TUR TRIBE

[face p. 320

etc.). It was said also that there was a Woga settlement at Patawa (in Bornu Province).

They have a number of customs in common with the Margi and Higi. Thus they observe the festival known as Yawal which is described in my notes on the Margi ; and at Vizik and Vemgo [1] they practise also the form of initiation by smearing with oil (which is practised in some Margi and Higi groups). They do not practise circumcision, and they have not the Kilba-Margi-Higi custom of removing the epidermis from the bodies of those who had died at a ripe age. They have not the *shafa* cult of the Margi and Higi,[2] but they regard as sacred a certain grass known as " *lidzo* ". Thus when a man dies his sons make bracelets of this grass and tie them round their wrists. His daughters fasten bands of the grass round their heads. If this were not done the dead man's ghost would pursue them, and they would go raving mad. During the Yawal festival also every householder wears a bracelet of " *lidzo* ", and bunches of the grass are laid in the centre of the dancing circle. Oaths are sworn at a sacred spring known as Holula Hahe.

The villages are composed of a number of patrilineal kindreds, each of which is an exogamous unit. But intermarriage between kindreds which are distantly related is permissible. There are no kindred totems ; but it was stated that all the people of Woga avoid killing or injuring crocodiles, as, if they broke this taboo, they would become lepers.

Inheritance is by primogeniture, the eldest son taking charge of his father's property on behalf of himself and his younger brothers. But if the eldest son is under age the property is administered by a brother of the deceased. A sister's son only inherits in the absence of patrilineal relatives. A youth may go and reside with his maternal uncle if he pleases and in such a case the uncle would see that he was provided with a wife ; but this is unusual, and the fact of having been adopted into his maternal uncle's home would not entitle him to a share in the latter's estate.

A widow may marry outside the family group of her late husband ; or she may marry a brother or cousin of the deceased. In the former case a bride-price, the amount of which is dependent on the number of children (if any) which she had borne to her first husband, is demanded by the deceased's eldest son. In the latter case the deceased man's sons can go at any time to the

---

[1] But not at Woga. [2] See pp. 197, 225.

Y

house of the paternal relative who had married their father's widow and appropriate any small articles of property they require : but a bride-price would not be demanded. If the re-married woman is a spinner she gives a proportion of all her earnings to her late husband's eldest son (who may be her own son).

Girls are sought in marriage at an early age ; and once the bride-price is fully paid a girl can be taken off to her husband's home, even if she is still under the age of puberty. But sexual relations do not occur until after her third menstruation. If she leaves her husband without having borne a child the full bride-price is recoverable. But if she had borne children the bride-price recoverable is reduced in proportion to the number of children borne.[1] The new husband is sometimes unable to meet his obligations, and in such a case the first husband (as among the Higi) has a claim on children born by the second husband. Male children can, however, be subsequently redeemed by the father, by the payment of one gown and cow. If the second husband has not paid a bride-price to the first husband and begets a child which dies, he is required by custom to compensate the first husband for the loss of that child. If the wife dies in the home of the second husband before she had borne children to the second husband, her body is sent back for burial to the first husband's home, and the first husband claims a goat and gown in lieu of the unpaid bride-price.

The following are the principal features of the relationship terminology :—

There is a special term, viz. *desen*, for maternal uncle, who addresses his sister's son as " my son " (*uzanada*). Parents-in-law and grandparents are classed together under the single term *jiji*. Brothers-in-law (male speaking) are addressed as *madza* ; (female speaking) as *hamai*. Sisters-in-law (male speaking) as *hamai* and sisters-in-law (female speaking) as *malbo*.

The inhabitants of Vizik, Vemgo, and Woga have the Higi custom of surrounding their compounds with large stone walls. They have a curious practice, which is also followed by the people of Sukur, of keeping bulls in underground pits for two years before killing them. A mud wall, covered by a thatched roof, is built on the surface round the mouth of the pit. The intention is to fatten the bulls by segregating them from the cows, and protecting them from flies. They never sell cattle to strangers to take away ; but

[1] At Vizik the birth of one child cancels the bride-price *in toto*.

PLATE 32

A MAN OF THE TUR TRIBE

they may sell a bull or cow provided it is killed on the spot. It is said that if the owner did not receive a piece of the beef of any of his cattle which had been killed he would die himself.

Graves are of the shaft and tunnel type, the mouth of the tunnel being sealed by a slanting wall of stones covered with plaster.

It is noteworthy that the word for maize is " *Babir*", which suggests that maize was introduced to these peoples by the Pabir.

As regards the Tur group these number only 300, the main body being in the French Cameroons. The Tur (like the Matakam of the French Cameroons) are distinguished by their helmet-shaped hats of leather. Most of them wear no clothing at all, but some wear a leather flap on the back. The women may be completely nude, or wear over the pubes an iron ring to which a chain of smaller rings is attached.

They marry on a smaller bride-price than the villagers of Woga, Vizik, and Vemgo. By the payment of a goat to the girl's brother the suitor becomes entitled to take his bride to his own home, but he must subsequently give three goats and two hoes to her father. If the girl abandons her husband without having borne him any children the husband can only reclaim the three goats. If she had borne a child there is no refund at all.

On the other hand the husband is expected to give his father-in-law a gift of some hoes whenever his wife bears a child.

The bodies of old people are not buried until the third or fourth day after death. The body is, during this period, set in a sitting position and half covered with sand. On the final day dishes of food are set before it. These are subsequently removed, and the food is given to young people of the household to eat. The body is then sewn up in a cow's skin and buried in a shaft and tunnel grave.

VIZIK, VEMGO, AND WOGA VOCABULARY

N.B.—*The Woga variations from Vizik and Vemgo are shown in parentheses.*

1. Head	Khan	xan
2. Hair	Sidi	sidi
3. Eye	Iri (ili)	iri (ili)
Two eyes	Khres iri (or khres ili or ili khresa)	xrɛs iri

4.	Ear	Hlimin	ɬımɪn
	Two ears	Khres hlimin	xrɛs ɬımɪn
5.	Nose	Khtsin	xtsin
6.	One tooth	Nding hliin (hlidin)	ndɪŋ ɬiin (ɬidin)
	Five teeth	Hliin khtaf	ɬiin xtaf
7.	Tongue	Nekhek	nɛxɛk
8.	Neck	Wurek (wulek)	wurɛk (wulɛk)
9.	Breast (woman's)	Wuwa (wuba)	wuˁwa wuˁba
10.	Heart	Ngudaf (nguduf)	ngudʌf (nguduf)
11.	Belly	Khudi	xudi
12.	Back	Khul (Ukhul)	xul (uxul)
13.	Arm	Zavu (zavo)	zǝvu (zǝvo)
14.	Hand	Papa kha zavu	papa xa zǝvu
	Two hands	Papa kha zavu khres	papa xa zǝvu xrɛs
15.	Finger	Uzi na zavu	uzi na zǝvu
	Five fingers	Khtaf uzi na zavu	xtaf uzi na zǝvu
16.	Finger nail	Dakhin	daxɪn
17.	Leg	Silla	sɪlla
18.	Knee	Karim	karɪm
19.	Foot	Papara silla	papara sɪlla
	Two feet	Khres papara silla	xrɛs papara sɪlla
20.	Man (person)	Wundu	wundu
	Ten people	Wang wundu	waŋ wundu
21.	Man (not woman)	Zaal (zgun)	zaal (zgun)
	Two men	Khres zilha (khres izgun)	xrɛs zilha (xrɛs izgun)
22.	Woman	Marakh	marax
	Two women	Khres mihaha	xrɛs mihaha
23.	Child	Uzan	uzan
24.	Father	Da	da
25.	Mother	Mama	mama
26.	Slave	Vua	vuˁa
27.	Chief	Mbagham	mbaɡam
28.	Friend	Gra	gra
29.	Smith	Dakha	dǝxa
30.	Doctor	Akhweni	axweni
31.	One finger	Nding zavu (tala)	ndɪŋ zǝvu (tala)
32.	Two fingers	Khres zavu	xrɛs zǝvu
33.	Three fingers	Khkin zavu	xkɪn zǝvu
34.	Four fingers	Ufat zavu	ufat zǝvu
35.	Five fingers	Qkhtáf zavu	ɔxtaf zǝvu
36.	Six fingers	Qngko zavu (mku)	ɔŋko zǝvu (mku)
37.	Seven fingers	Rafang zavu	rǝfaŋ zǝvu
38.	Eight fingers	Tikhas zavu	tɪxas zǝvu
39.	Nine fingers	Timbai zavu	tımbai zǝvu
40.	Ten fingers	Qwang zavu	ɔwaŋ zǝvu
41.	Eleven fingers	Qwang gili akhang zavu	ɔwaŋ gili axaŋ zevu
42.	Twelve fingers	Qwang khres akhang zavu	ɔwaŋ xrɛs axaŋ zǝvu
	Thirteen fingers	Qwang khkin akhang zavu	ɔwaŋ xkɪn axaŋ zǝvu

43. Twenty fingers	Khres sim sak zavu	xrɛs sɪm saːk zǝvu
44. A hundred fingers	Dirmak zavu	dɪrmǝk zǝvu
45. Two hundred fingers	Khres dirmak zavu	xrɛs dɪrmǝk zǝvu
46. Four hundred fingers	Ufat dirmak zavu	ufat dɪrmǝk zǝvu
47. Sun	Fitak (fiti)	fitǝk (fiti)
God	Lam za girftu (dedam bin)	lam zǝ girftu (dɛdam bɪn)
48. Moon	Tirri (tirre)	tɪrri (tɪrrɛ)
Full moon	Ntawa tirri	ntawa tɪrri
New moon	Nhla da tirri	nɬa da tɪrri
49. Day	Fitak	fitǝk
Night	Irvidak	ɪrvidǝk
Morning	Insakhdak	ɪnsǝxdǝk
50. Rain	Kuro	kuro
51. Water	Imi	imi
52. Blood	Uus (ubis)	uus (ubɪs)
53. Fat	Wevet (wuva dek)	wɛvɛt (wuva dɛk)
54. Salt	Khwunu	xwunu
55. Stone	Palak	palak
Iron	Họkhtsiri	hɔxtsiri
56. Hill	Khwá	xwá
57. River	Khwā	xwā
58. Road	Jivi	dʒivi
59. House	Khiga	xɪga
Two houses	Khres khiga	xrɛs xɪga
Many houses	Khiga kada	xɪga kada
All the houses	Khiga pet	xɪga pɛt
60. Roof	Mpsu	mpsu
61. Door	Bangbang	baŋbaŋ
62. Mat	Khtāf	xtaf
63. Basket	Wanak	wanak
64. Drum	Dang	daŋ
65. Pot	Kholam	xolam
66. Knife	Mangga	maŋga
67. Spear	Gupa	gupa
68. Bow	Lekhe	lɛxɛ
69. Arrow	Khava	xava
Five arrows	Khtaf khava	xtaf xava
70. Gun	Banding	bandɪŋ
71. War	Imtak	ɪmtaːk
72. Meat (animal)	Hlui	ɬui
73. Elephant	Giwan	giwan
74. Buffalo	Hlatiri	ɬatiri
75. Leopard	Puku	puku
76. Monkey	Lugvak	lugvaːk
77. Pig	Khivaz	xɪvaz
78. Goat	Go	go
79. Dog	Kirre	kɪrrɛ
80. Bird	Diak	ɗiaːk
Feather	Lighan a diak	liɣan a ɗiaːk

81.	Crocodile	Kirram	kɪrram
82.	Fowl	Khata kwal	xata kwal
83.	Eggs	Hlihli (hlihlo)	ɬiɬi (ɬiɬo)
84.	One egg	Nding hlihli	ndɪŋ ɬiɬi
85.	Snake	Bubu	bubu
86.	Frog	Khwa	xwa
87.	Kanuri	Mufeki	mufeki
	Fulani	Lapilasar	lapɪlasar
	Hausa	La Hausa	la hausa
	Margi	La Margi	la margi
88.	Fly	Zidak	zidək
89.	Bee	Zir ka mak	zir ka mək
	Honey	Mak	mək
90.	Tree	Udzu	udzu
	Ten trees	Uwang udzu	uwaŋ udzu
91.	Leaf	Hlwa	ɬwa
92.	Guinea-corn	Khia (Khria)	xia (xria)
93.	Maize	Babir	babɪr
94.	Ground nut	Bindan	bɪndan
95.	Oil	Khirdi	xɪrdi
96.	Horse of Chief	Piris a mbagham	pɪris a mbaɡam
97.	Big dog	Kirra kada	kɪrra kada
98.	Small dog	Kirrakh dika	kɪrrax dika
99.	The tall woman or women	Marakh fiwa	marax fiwa
100.	The dog bites	Kirr tirdita	kɪrr tɪrdita
101.	The dog bites me	Kirra nọ kirdita	kɪrra nɔ kɪrdita
102.	The dog which bit me yesterday	Kirre ridita nghwọho	kɪrrɛ rɪdita ŋhwɔho
103.	The dog which I have flogged	Kirre wurta wurteiyu	kɪrrɛ wurta wurtɛiju
104.	I flog the dog	Wurta wurti kirre	wurta wurti kɪrrɛ

TUR VOCABULARY

1.	Head	Khin	xɪn
2.	Hair	Sudi	sudi
3.	Eye	Iri	iri
	Two eyes	Iri khris	iri xrɪs
4.	Ear	Hlimang	ɬimaŋ
	Two ears	Khris hlimang	xrɪs ɬimaŋ
5.	Nose	Akhchin	axtʃin
6.	One tooth	Hliin turtuk (or turtuk hliin)	ɬiin turtuk (or turtuk ɬiin)
	Five teeth	Khtaf hliin	xtaf ɬiin
7.	Tongue	Ranik	ranik
8.	Neck	Ngurdung	ngurduŋ
9.	Breast (woman's)	Uwa	uwa
10.	Heart	Nguɗuf	nguɗuf
11.	Belly	Khudi	xudi
12.	Back	Khul	xul

13. Arm	Zavu	zəvu
14. Hand	Papa	papa
Two hands	Khres papa	xrɛs papa
15. Finger	Ndifi	ndıfi
16. Finger nail	Dakhin	daxın
17. Leg	Sirra	sırra
18. Knee	Karim	karım
19. Foot	Papara silla	papara sılla
Two feet	Khres papara silla	xrɛs papara sılla
20. Man (person)	Mindu	mındu
Ten people	Wang imdu	waŋ ımdu
21. Man (not woman)	Zaar	zaar
Two men	Zaar akhres	zaar axrɛs

CHAPTER VI

THE CHAMBA

The following notes on this tribe were made as a result of a short visit to Donga (Benue Province), additional information being obtained among scattered groups of the tribe in the Muri and Adamawa divisions (Adamawa Province). I had no opportunity of visiting the Chamba of the mandated territory. There are groups of Chamba across the French border.

The word *Chamba*, or *Tsamba* as they are sometimes called, appears to embody a root *Cham* or *Tsam* = Men. It is the same root, apparently, as is found in *Ba-Chama* and *Atsam* (the name by which the Chawe of Zaria call themselves). In other parts of Africa the root also appears as a tribal designation. The Chamba usually employ the form " *Shamabu* " or " *Sama* " when referring to themselves.

The Chamba of Nigeria do not at the present time constitute a single tribal unit, for as already indicated they are found living in scattered groups over a very large area, the scattering of the tribe being due firstly to the attacks of the Bata tribe, and later to those of the Fulani during the early decades of the last century. There is no longer even any homogeneity of social practice between the various groups, the customs of each group having been modified very considerably by those of its immediate neighbours. The Chamba of Donga in particular, through inter-course and intermixture with the Fulani, have lost most of the matrilineal practices which formerly characterized the tribe.

Linguistically there are two groups of Chamba :

Group A includes the Chamba Lekon and the Chamba of Kungana (Adamawa Province), and the Chamba of Donga, Suntai, Takum, and Rafin Kada (Benue Province). Chamba Lekon is the " Laego " of Strumpell's vocabularies. To this group must also be added (i) the Wom of the Verre district (Adamawa division), and (ii) the tribe known as the Mumbake (Adamawa). The Tikare of Takum cannot be included among the Chamba, as stated in Mrs. Temple's book, p. 79. (There are other mis-statements in Mrs. Temple's book under the heading Chamba, such as that the Chamba are of Verre descent, that they speak

328

a language closely resembling Jukun, and so on.) Strumpell's Kolbila (Cameroons) also belong to this group.

Group B includes the Chamba or " Daka " of Muri division, and of the mandated territory, the Chamba " Tsugu " of mandated territory, and, to a modified extent, the Daka of Kogin Baba (mandated territory), who claim to be the original Daka. To this group also belong the Chamba of Nasarao area, and the Lamja (both in the Adamawa Province).

The two groups of Chamba both speak a language of the same type ; but in spite of all similarities of vocabulary and grammatical structure, there are wide divergences, as will be observed from the vocabularies attached. As Mumbake is now found to be a Chamba dialect it should be included with Chamba in the Adamawa group of the Middle Zone languages, and not in the Benue group of the Central Sudanic division as shown in *Northern Nigeria*, vol. ii, p.138.

Group A : The Chamba of Donga.—The Chamba of Donga call themselves the Dinga (Diŋa), a word meaning apparently " The Men " (as *dinga* = man is found in the Wom dialect of Chamba. This word occurs with the same meaning in Barth's Bang-bay group). The Chamba of the Donga region are immigrants from the North-East. Early in the nineteenth century they occupied a region in the Cameroons which they describe as " Dindi ", their towns being Mapeo, Sapeo, and Zolba (Dollba).[1] They claim to have had authority over a people called the Lengona, which is no doubt the equivalent of the Lekon already mentioned. Here they lived in friendship with the Fulani, with whom they intermarried to some extent. It is even claimed that the mother of Modibo, the first Emir of Muri, was a Chamba. That there is considerable Fulani blood in the Chamba of Donga is evident, and it is probable that some of this Fulani mixture is due to enslavement.

Owing to a sudden and treacherous slaughter of their chiefs by

[1] It would appear that the main seat of the Chamba was originally at a town now known as Lamurde Jongum in French territory, that they were driven thence by the Bata across the Faro to the town called Chamba at the base of the Alantika hills, whence they were again driven out by the Bata (who had canoes, while the Chamba had none). In Barth's time (vol. ii, pp. 512 and 616) the town of Chamba was almost wholly occupied by Fulani. The Chamba, he says, from whom the place had derived its name, were said to have driven from this region the Kottofo, now located further to the south. On p. 616, however, he says that Mount Alantika was densely inhabited " by people of the Batta tribe ". The Chamba, driven into the hills, appear to have split into two groups, one coalescing with the Lekon to form the Chamba Lekon, and the other with the Daka to form the Chamba Daka.

the Fulani during the first half of the nineteenth century, they were forced to fly hurriedly from the Tibati district of the Cameroons, under the leadership of one Loya or Garbosa. They travelled by Gildu and the river Logara, in crossing which Loya was drowned. Loya was succeeded by Gangkwe, who brought the people to the region of the town Gangkwe (near Donga) which bears his name. Here Shimbura, son of Loya, quarrelled with Gangkwe and went to Zhenoa in the vicinity of Takum, where he built a walled town and joined the Tikare in reducing the local Zompere. He adopted the title of Gakie. At Zhenoa he again quarrelled with his brother Chambas and also with the Tikare, and proceeding to Munshi country he began raiding there, coming finally to Arafu, where he attacked the inhabitants, who were of the Jidu tribe. He then proceeded to the vicinity of Ibi. It is related that while he was living there a European expedition came up the river, and that Gakie visited the ship and was offered numerous gifts, which he refused, saying, " You offer these gifts because you wish the land, but the land is God's, not mine." Gakie's son Nubunga, however, went secretly to the Europeans and said that his father was an old man and spoke after the fashion of old men. And so Nubunga obtained the presents for himself ! This story enables us to affix a date to these events, for it is quite clear that the Gakie of the Donga history is the Garike, chief of Gankera, who is mentioned in the *Journal* of the Macgregor-Laird expedition to the Benue in 1854. " We anchored off the villages of Gandiko, whose chief was Ama, and Gankera, whose chief was Garike. Before the ship came to an anchor, intelligence had reached the chiefs of the villages, and all hands were up in arms. Their weapons were bows and poisoned arrows, and long spears, and some men carried three or four of the latter, poisoned also." Crowther then describes how they landed unarmed. " We shook hands with the Galadima, and he led us to the town. The path was full of soldiers coming out to join the Galadima ; but seeing him, they all fell back on both sides of the path, which brought us to the entrance of the town. The place was fortified with a wooden fence and a ditch around it." The journal then proceeds to describe the meeting with the two local chiefs, and how Ama tried to keep Garike from sharing in the interview and gifts. Both chiefs said that they were eager to trade with foreigners and were weary of making war. It is stated incidentally that these villages, together with Ibi, were under the suzeranity of the Fulani of Jibu, and that the Jukun chief of Wukari bore considerable resentment at this loss of territory.

The Donga account tells how Gakie, when old, said to his son : " Nubunga Dozonga, you have grown to full manhood, whereas I am old and frail. Do you go and search out a place where we may settle and build a walled town, that we may cease from our wanderings." Nubunga replied : " I have heard of Ibrahim, the Fulani governor of Bauchi ; let me go to him that I may receive a flag and become one of his chiefs. Do you abide here until I return and we shall then choose a site for our abode." So Nubunga went off to Bauchi ; and when he arrived there and found that the governor (Ibrahim) was absent on a local war he continued his journey until he came up with the governor. On being asked the object of his mission he replied that he had come for three reasons : (a) to bring gifts, (b) to obtain a flag of "greatness", and (c) to secure the assistance of the governor in finding a resting-place for himself, his father and his people. Ibrahim was busy making his plans for an attack on a local pagan tribe, and advised Nubunga to return to Bauchi, as he and his followers must be exhausted with their long journey. But Nubunga protested that if there was fighting to be done he would surely take a share. In the ensuing battles Nubunga behaved gallantly and was wounded three times. The governor then said : " You, Nubunga Dozonga, are indeed a warrior ; you have assisted me in difficult times and I perceive that you are no idler. Do you really require my help in recompense ? " Nubunga replied : " I do indeed, and may Allah lengthen your life." Ibrahim thereupon called up Barde Karijo, of the tribe of the Jafunawa, and directed him and his followers to accompany Nubunga back to his country and assist him in all his endeavours. He gave him a flag, saying : " In the name of the Shehu of Sokoto, who conferred this right on me, may the blessing of the Prophet and of the Shehu, and of Allah abide with you ; for you are a valiant man, and you will obtain the assistance of Allah in no ordinary measure. Do you now depart in peace, you and your followers, and those whom I have joined to you. I thank you for the assistance which you have rendered to me." Ibrahim presented him, in addition to the flag, with thirty horses. The present chief of Donga claims to have this flag in his possession at the present time, and produced it. It is a white flag of European manufacture attached to a bamboo pole, 11 feet long. The head of the pole is surmounted with ostrich feathers, and lower down the pole are two red cloth streamers. Further down still there is a leather case containing charms written in Arabic. At the top of the flag there is an Arabic inscription, written in ink, as follows : " This flag is of the Leader of the Believers (i.e. of the Sarkin Musulmi of Sokoto). Whosoever waits on his decisions shall not be ashamed. Allah is with those who wait patiently on him. By patience men shall overcome the host of unbelievers ; and the unbelievers themselves shall repent afterwards." This flag may have been the identical flag conferred on Nubunga (if any flag was indeed conferred), but the cloth of the flag displayed did not have the appearance of being over seventy years old, and I could not help feeling considerable doubts both as to the genuineness of the flag and also of the story by which it was said to have been conferred.

Nubunga Dozonga then rejoined his father Gakie, and together they made an unsuccessful attempt to wrest the local suzerainty of the Fulani from Bohari, the Chief of Jibu. (A variant account says that they killed the chief of Jibu, whose name was Boderi.) Thereafter they rejoined their brethren whom they had left at Gangkwe and Zhenoa. Gangkwe, the original leader of the (Donga) Chamba, died about this time, and it is related that on his death his elder sister prevented the children of Gangkwe from inheriting the chieftainship. She took the royal insignia and handed them to her husband, with the result that the Chamba broke up into a number of groups, some going to the present site of Donga under Nyonzuma or Gagbwai, others to Gaima, others to Kunabe, and others to Aka.

The story of the appropriation of the insignia by Gangkwe's elder sister is interesting, for it would seem to imply that succession by the sister's son had been the Chamba custom. When Gagbwai went to Donga he invited the wanderers Gakie and his son Nubunga Dozonga to join him there. They accepted this offer, as they were hard pressed for food ; but Nubunga pitched his camp outside Gagbwai's walled town. Gagbwai's followers refused to allow Nubunga any share in their harvest, with the result that Nubunga and his men took to pillaging the farms and preventing the townspeople from reaping the fruit of their labours. They even captured their Chamba brethren and sold them into slavery. Gagbwai then called on the Jukun, and the Ankwe allies of the Jukun, to come to their help and drive out Nubunga, who was a threat to the peace of the whole country. The assistance of the Fulani of Jibu was also solicited and obtained. Nubunga, faced with this combination, called on Burba, the Fulani chief of Kundi, to side with him. In the ensuing encounter the Jukun and their allies were routed. Possessed of local knowledge most of the Jukun escaped ; but many of the Ankwe, being ignorant of the country, were driven towards the river and were either killed or captured. There are still in Donga a number of people descended from these captured Ankwe. Nubunga then besieged Gagbwai in his walled town, and the starving people were forced to sell themselves one by one for food. Gagbwai himself, together with the remnants of his people, succeeded in making his escape to Wurio, where he died. Those Chamba who had accompanied Gagbwai in his flight, finding the taxes imposed on them by the Fulani of Wurio more than they could pay, left Wurio c.1865 and founded the present town of Suntai, paying tribute in the form of slaves to the Fulani chief of Kundi. Suntai was attacked and destroyed by the Niger Company constabulary in 1899 as a reprisal for the killing of one of the constabulary officers (Captain Parker).

Meanwhile Nubunga built the present town of Donga, calling it " Dozonga " after himself. The Fulani and Hausa, it is said, converted the name into Donga. This may be so ; but Donga is a common geographical name in other parts of Africa. Gakie died soon after the founding of the new town, but his name is still held in such reverence that oaths are sworn by Gakie, and it is believed that anyone falsely swearing by him would meet a speedy death. Nubunga took the title of Garbasa (i.e. mighty chief), the Jukun equivalent of which is Aku-sho. Nubunga is therefore known to the Jukun as Kusho, and people of Donga as Bando Kusho. The establishment of the town led to an influx of heterogeneous elements, and in addition to the Chamba there are at Donga to-day groups of Ankwe, Zompere, Kpwâtê, Hwâye, Jidu, Jafun, Kyâtô, Jibu, Abakwariga, and Hausa.

This short sketch illustrates the disorganized condition of tribal life in the Benue regions during the nineteenth century. The pagan tribes were broken up by the Fulani ; Chamba fought Chamba ; and the Fulani groups themselves were in a constant state of feud with one another. The ancient sovereignty of the Jukun chiefs became so restricted that Donga, a town situated within a day's journey of Wukari, recognized only the suzerainty of the Fulani of Kundi (though slaves were also regularly sent to the Fulani governor of Bauchi).

The Chamba of Donga call the Fulani the Puli or Pulubira ; the Hausa the Sǫnka, and the Jukun the Kpwâzǫna.

Government.—As the chiefdom of Donga comprises a small area only, the government is centred in the chief and his advisers at the capital. There are no districts, the heads of outlying villages being directly responsible to the chief. The chief is called the "Gara", and his assistant officials are known by the Jukun term of " Sokuru ". The senior official is also generally known by the Jukun title of " Abô", clear evidence of the extent of Jukun influence, despite the dominance of the Fulani. The functions of the Abô correspond with those of the Abô at Wukari, viz. that he is the adviser of the chief in all matters of importance and is the direct channel by which the people approach the chief. All disputes between local groups are settled by the chief and the Abô jointly. In the absence of the chief the Abô assumes supreme control of the town. He is also the head of one of the wards or quarters of the town. The title of Abô is confined to a single kindred, the Gbana, and in this respect the custom of the Chamba of Donga differs from the existing custom of the Jukun. As among the Jukun, however, no Abô may ever attain the chieftainship.

The next senior official is the Kpwâti, a title confined to the Janga kindred. He may be summoned by the chief to share in his deliberations with the Abô, and if any trouble arises in the out-lying villages he is sent by the chief to investigate and settle the matter, if possible, without further reference to the chief. The third senior official is known as the Kuni ; and one of his duties is to place on the shoulder of a new chief the hippo-hide whip which is the emblem of chieftainship. He is always a member of the Denkuna kindred. The Nya was the senior official for war, it being incumbent on him to see that the instructions of the chief's council as regards war operations were handed on to the Gangum, who was the leader in the field. Under the Gangum was a second Gangum, a young man who was responsible for the organization and control of the younger warriors. Minor officials were the Zarma, assistant to the Kpwâti ; Tigie, custodian of the drums ; Fawe, Kuna, and Galim, supervisors of repairs to the palace ; and Gbâ-lera or chief bandmaster.

The heir to the throne is the Yerma or Mukodashi ; and as the chieftainship is confined to the Sama clan, the Yerma must be a member of that clan, of which he is the acting head, having control over all the brothers, cousins, children, and nephews of the chief. In the absence of the chief he sees to the daily issue of beer to the members of the royal family, and the Abô reports to him any public matters on which action is necessary. On the death of any important personage, such as a village head, he is sent by the chief to offer to the relatives the royal condolences. He receives for distribution among the members of the royal family a share of the royal dues of the flesh of game-animals, and of fish caught in fishing battues. (The Abô also receives a share for himself and the other senior officials.)

One of the most important officials is the female known as the Mala. The term *mala* is ordinarily applied to any paternal aunt. The chief's Mala may, however, be either his father's sister or his own, or a woman whose mother formerly held the position. She is queen over the women, and her duties correspond to those of the Angwu Tsi among the Jukun.[1] Her intercession with the chief is sought by all who have incurred his displeasure. She also exercises important religious functions, having charge of the female cult of Vonkima and being " spokesman " at the Vara rites (to be described later). She sees to the preparation of the foods and beer required for the religious rites incumbent on the chief, and she is entitled to a share of the sacrificial animal. When the chief has to undertake a journey the Mala is summoned to perform rites for the success of his mission and a safe return. The senior women who accompany the Mala sweep the ground in front of certain sacred stones which stand before the palace gates. The Mala then recites the names of all the former chiefs and all the former Malas, and calls on them to escort the chief on his journey and to bring him safely back. She then smears the sacred stones with a mixture of flour and water. When the chief returns from the journey he is met by the Mala and all the women, as well as by the senior male officials, and is escorted to his palace. The Mala is then also escorted to her home, where her husband, if she has a husband, lives as a comparatively unimportant person. The Mala also

---

[1] See *A Sudanese Kingdom*, p. 340.

confers a personal name on all female children born to members of
the royal family. When the umbilical stump falls off, the junior
Malas assemble and confer a name on the child, but when the
child has obtained two teeth a second name is given by the senior
Mala, who also gives the child her first dish of porridge. The chief
himself also confers a third name. (In the case of male children
the name is given by the father's brothers, and an additional name
is given by the chief when the child cuts his two first upper teeth.)
On her death the Mala is buried with the same rites as those
accorded to the chief.

The male members of the royal family formally salute the
chief twice or three times daily—in the early morning, at midday,
and in the evening. Attendance at midday and in the evening is
optional. In the morning they are given beer, and in the evening
a regular meal. They share with the chief in all the royal
perquisites. When a junior member of the family reaches
marriageable age the chief provides him with a wife and establishes
him in a separate compound with two servants and a horse.
The farms of members of the chief's family were formerly worked
by slaves, while they themselves engaged in hunting (which
included the hunting of human beings, raids being made on pagan
villages or on passing travellers). They could, it is said, commit
with security any kind of extortion, appropriation, or highway
robbery.

The palace officials, i.e. those in immediate attendance on the
chief, are also favoured individuals. They receive at least one
meal per day at the chief's expense. They are the eyes and ears
of the chief. The seniors amongst them give news of the town and
country to the chief each evening, reporting what everyone says
of him, whether good or bad. People give gifts to these palace
officials in order that they may be well spoken of before the chief,
and, in former times, in order to save themselves from various
forms of extortion. The palace officials also help themselves
liberally to gifts intended for the chief. When the chief appears
in public they surround him to prevent any ill-disposed person
from approaching too closely ; and on a journey they precede the
chief, the members of the royal family following up behind. The
chief is careful to see that the palace officials do not all belong to
the same clan ; and newcomers are well tested before being
entrusted with any important duties. They are provided with

wives by the chief, and male children born are brought up to be his trusted servants. Female children are at the chief's disposal, either to marry himself or to give to members of his family.

It may be of interest to describe here the regular daily routine of saluting the chief. After his morning ablutions the chief enters the hut which serves as his council-chamber. About seven a.m. the senior members of the royal family, led by the Mukodashi, present themselves and salute the chief by clapping their hands. The chief inquires after their health and any news they may have to report. Beer is then issued by an attendant to all present and the chief may himself partake of beer specially brewed for himself. When the chief drinks all the others lay down their calabashes and sit with lowered eyes. Conversation becomes general, and occurrences of the previous evening are reported. When the calabashes have been collected by an attendant all present clap their hands in gratitude to the chief. The Abô may present himself at the chief's hut if he has anything of importance to report to the chief, but otherwise he and the other senior officials wait in another hut until the chief, followed by the members of the royal family, arrives to greet them. They salute the chief by clapping their hands, and the chief asks the Abô for his news. The Abô answers formally that all is well, and the others again clap their hands. (It is to be noted that no one ever addresses verbal salutations to the chief.) Beer is provided for the officials, and the chief passes on to the third hut to greet the palace officials, and finally to the fourth hut to greet the lesser men who have accompanied the Abô and the other senior office-holders. They also are provided with beer, and the chief may, if he feels inclined, stop and converse with them as they drink. The senior officials and members of the royal family join him there, and when he rises they escort him back to his own hut. He then dismisses them, and they withdraw in three parties, viz. members of the royal family, the senior officials, and the palace officials, the leader of each group being escorted back to his quarters by his followers. The morning salutation is a regular daily duty ; but the mid-day and evening salutations are purely optional. The Mukodashi and palace officials, however, and the younger members of the royal family, always salute the chief in the evening, the last-mentioned doing so with the practical object of obtaining a free evening meal. The Abô and Kpwâti may also present themselves in the evening

z

with a view to reporting anything that has come to their notice during the day. They are given some beer to drink while they recount their news. It will be seen that the matutinal greetings entail a considerable expenditure of beer. This expenditure is met partly by the gifts of beer sent to the chief by all who brew beer for their private religious rites, and by the gifts of corn given at harvest by farmers to the chief. These harvest gifts are no longer general, as in bygone days, and the chief has therefore, at the present time, to make considerable inroads on his small salary in order to maintain a semblance of the former prestige of Chamba chiefs. A chief who endeavours to live within his means is seldom popular with his people ; and a chief who endeavours to maintain his position by the traditional liberality soon finds himself in difficulties with the Administration.

The chief in theory had unlimited power, the power of life and death, of confiscating property at will, and of making war. In practice his powers were limited by the necessity of having regard to public opinion and of admitting the Abô and other senior officials to his counsels. At the present time the Chamba chief is a vigorous and progressive ruler. He is a professing Christian ; but, regarding himself as the father of all sections of the community, he carries out the pagan rites imposed by custom, and also provides the ram used at the Muslim festivals.

Social Organization.—The Chamba of Donga consist of a number of patrilineal " clans ", or, it might be more correct to say, of patrilineal kindreds ; for though the genealogical relationship of the component sections of some of the kindreds is not always demonstrable, it is clear that there is between the sections a real consanguinity. The kindreds are as follows :—(i) Sama, the royal kindred ; (ii) Janga ; (iii) Kwasa ; (iv) Nyera ; (v) Gbana; (vi) Pyere (or Pere) ; (vii) Nguma (ŋuma) ; (viii) Ngwana (ŋwana) ; (ix) Nupabe ; (x) Za ; (xi) Kola ; (xii) Poba.

The manner in which kindreds split up into separate entities is illustrated in the following story of the origin of the Sama and Janga kindreds. It is related that Sama and Janga were the junior and elder sons of one Longa. Longa was old and near to death ; so he summoned his sons in order to give them some parting advice. When Janga came before his father the old man addressed him as Sam Dinya, i.e. Black-bodied Chamba. This enraged Janga, who rose up and walked out without waiting to

hear his father's word. The father then called up his younger son,
saying, " Come hither, Sam Yelo," i.e. Light-skinned Chamba.
Sama replied, " I have come, my father," and he sat down
respectfully at his father's feet. And thus Sama received the
royal insignia, and he and his brother parted in anger, each
becoming the head of a separate kindred. The Kwasa[1] and Nyera
kindreds are said also to have been one originally, and so too the
Kola and Poba. It is stated that the founder of the Kwasa
kindred married the sister of Longa, and that it is for this reason
that the Kwasa are " comrades " of the Sama and Janga kindreds.
The Nyera kindred is not regarded, like Kwasa, as a sister's son
of the Sama and Janga kindreds ; but, being related to the Kwasa,
they are regarded as close friends of the Sama and Janga. There
are special rules governing the social relationship of kindreds which
are " comrades ". If a member of one kindred meets a member of a
comrade kindred he may address him as " slave ", and may make
abusive remarks about his father (but not about his mother, as she
would belong to a different kindred, the kindreds being
exogamous). It is permissible also to call any member of the
comrade-kindred by his personal name, however senior he may be
to the speaker. His gown may be seized if there is a hole in it ;
and at harvest a representative of the kindred may go to the farm
of one of the members of the comrade-kindred and appropriate
some of his corn. If a man has a sore throat one of the comrade-
kindred comes and takes a straw, which he bends into the shape
of a bow, attaching a thread as a bow-string. He passes this
straw-bow round the neck of the patient. (I was unable to get
any explanation of this custom.) Comrade-kindreds may not
fight with each other, for if they did it is said that they would all
be assailed with sores. Lastly, when religious rites are to be
performed, a special invitation to attend is issued to the comrade-
kindred.

Kindreds related to each other in the male line are not
" comrades ", but brothers, and they call each other *kumboa*.
Everything serious that happens to one kindred is the concern of
the brother-kindred. Thus if a Janga man dies he may not be
buried until the *kumboa* or representative of the Sama kindred
arrives to take an active part in the burial rites. Kindreds

---

[1] The term *kwasa* means " Slaves ". They may have earned this description
either because they contained a slave element, or more probably because they
were sisters' sons of the royal kindred.

which are *kumboa* attend each others' religious rites, and in the
prayers assist each other in recalling correctly the order of the
names of the deceased ancestors invoked. Each kindred has its
own Vara and Vonkima cults (see page 346) ; but brother-
kindreds may share a common cult. Each kindred also has its
talisman, the " spears " known as " Disakuna ". They are of two
kinds, one surmounted with an iron crescent, the other with a
round iron boss, thus :—

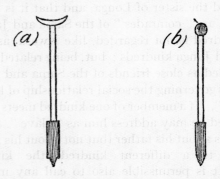

They are made entirely of iron, and have quadrilateral blades.
Type (*a*) resembles the *Ajingi* spears of the *bori* cult of the
Hausa ; and the crescent design is used by the Hausa as a
protection against the evil eye.

The spears are kept in a granary, and are produced annually
after the harvest in order that they may be redynamized by
sacrifice. The head of the kindred pours a libation of beer at the
base. He then slits the throat of a cock and smears the spear
with the blood. The cock is thrown on the ground, and as it leaps
about in its death or post-mortem struggle the women yodel, the
struggles of the cock being regarded as symbolic of the quickening
of the spear. The senior Mala or " aunt " of the kindred then
takes some oil or oil-palm grease and smears the forehead, right
arm, and left chest (over the heart) of each grown-up man of the
kindred, who is then handed a spear by the head of the kindred.
The warrior rushes off a few yards and aims a blow at some
imaginary enemy or game-animal, and then returns and shakes his
spear before the cultus-emblem.

The sacred or magical spear was carried into battle by a
specially selected warrior who, when the kindred was hard
pressed, advanced with it into the thick of the fight, dealing out

blows right and left. No foe could, it was believed, parry a blow with the sacred spear, for it rendered impotent the charms of the enemy. Were the spear to be captured, the kindred would be so completely demoralized that it would cease to exist as a social entity, scattering in all directions. The chief himself takes the principal part in the annual blooding of the sacred spear of the Sama kindred. The spear is planted in an enclosure and there, after the rites, the Mala smears the chief's forehead, right arm, and left breast with oil. The chief then takes his spear, rushes off to attack the imaginary foe, and returns to shake the spear before the royal talisman.

The head of the kindred is not necessarily the oldest or the richest or the most powerful member : he is chosen rather for his discretion and his intimate knowledge of traditional customs, religious rites, and lore. He is responsible to the chief for the good conduct of the members of the kindred, and he sees to it that burial and mourning rites, and those connected with the cults of Vara and the sacred spear, are properly carried out. If a member of the kindred dies, it is the business of the head of the kindred to summon the *kumboa* or leader of the brother-kindred, who takes charge of the distribution of beer brewed by the deceased's family for the mourning-rites. Beer brewed by friends of the deceased is distributed by the head of the kindred to the brothers and cousins of the deceased, to the women whose duty it is to sleep in the hut of the deceased for six nights, and to the Mala for the performance of the Vonkima rites.

The leader of the females of the kindred, viz. the Mala, is also chosen from among the senior women for her wisdom. As already indicated, she plays an important part in all birth, death, and religious ceremonies.

Quarrels between kindreds were not uncommon, especially in the hunting-field ; and on these occasions the kindreds involved were assisted each by its *kumboa*. Thus if a fight arose between members of the Nguma and Janga kindreds, Nguma would be joined by the Pyere, and Janga by the Sama. And so a fight, which might have arisen as a quarrel betwen two individuals, would become an affray, the combatants attacking each other with sticks or even with knives and spears. The fight might be stopped by members of a kindred unrelated to the others, or by the intervention of old men on both sides. When peace was restored the kindred which had inflicted the more injury to the other endeavoured to make amends by sending medicines to the wounded.   There was no legal redress for injuries received in hunting affrays, or in affrays arising during co-operative farm-work, or during beer festivals.   Fights between individuals of different households of the same kindred might also lead to an affray between two households.

Exogamy.—Each kindred is exogamous, e.g. no man of the Janga kindred may marry a woman of the Janga kindred.   But intermarriage is permitted between members of two related kindreds, i.e. a man of the Sama kindred may marry a woman of the Janga kindred, though these two kindreds had a common forefather.   There is therefore no " clan " exogamy   A man may also marry a woman of his mother's kindred, provided she does not come within certain prohibited degrees (which will be specified presently).   The reason assigned for the prohibition against marriage within the kindred is that such marriages would be difficult to dissolve, should the partners find that they are unsuited to each other.   The dissolution of a marriage between members of the same kindred would cause a breach within the kindred, creating an ill-feeling between two sections of the kindred which would interfere with the partnership at religious rites and would tend to destroy the kindred solidarity in a number of other ways. I have frequently, among other tribes, heard the same reason given for the custom of exogamy ; but on the other hand, among peoples who permit marriage with the daughter of the father's brother, it is asserted that this form of marriage is the best, precisely because it is difficult to dissolve.   Among the Chamba of Donga the only kind of cousin-marriages permitted are those between (*a*) a man and the daughter of his father's half-sister by the same father, (*b*) a man and the daughter of his mother's half-sister by the same father, and (*c*) a man and the daughter of his mother's half-brother by the same father.   In the case of (*a*) and (*b*) such marriages would not, of course, be permissible if the girl was a member of the same kindred as the man.   It will be observed that persons who have the same mother consider themselves more intimately related than persons who have the same father.   It is worth noting, incidentally, that among the Chamba a man must avoid having extra-marital sexual relations with a woman who is having such relations with any of his cousins or friends.   The breach of this taboo would not merely lead to quarrels and jealousies, but it is said that it would cause the death of a sick man if he were visited by a relative or friend who had shared the same woman's favours. If therefore a man discovers that he has unknowingly been having sexual relations with a woman to whom a cousin or friend has also been having access, he will avoid visiting that cousin or friend during his illness.

There is no clan or kindred totemism among the Donga Chamba. Certain animals, however, are taboo to certain cults; and the owners of the cult, together with their brothers and grown-up sons and nephews, must avoid eating those animals. Thus the priest of the Mwa Lebsa cult stated that he and all who take part with him in the rites must avoid the electric-fish. They must not touch it or eat it. The reason assigned for this taboo was that Mwa Lebsa is a lightning-cult, and the shock produced by the electric-fish was like that produced by lightning. The owner of the cult denied that all members of his kindred automatically respected the electric-fish. Sometimes the owner of a cult co-opts into the cult members of a different kindred; and where this happens the co-opted members have to observe the cult-taboos. It does not appear, therefore, that the totems are connected with the social grouping, though it is possible that they were so at one time.

Descent is reckoned patrilineally, and the household normally consists of a man, his wife and children, his brothers and their wives and children. But it is not uncommon to find a uterine descendant living in a household. Indeed, it is the regular rule for an eldest son to take up his abode with his maternal uncle. The maternal uncle can claim him to be his " fire-lighter ", i.e. to look after him as a servant looks after a master. The maternal uncle will provide the boy's bride-price; though if he is not well off he may be assisted in this respect by the boy's father, who would also be consulted as to the suitability of the marriage. The boy is not, however, at the present time a principal inheritor on his uncle's death. He may be given a small share in the estate; and, if his uncle leaves no brothers or grown-up sons, he (the nephew) may act as trustee on behalf of his uncle's young children. It is important to note that the only class of uncle entitled to claim a first-born male child is one who had the same mother as the child's mother, i.e. a half-brother by the same father cannot claim his half-sister's child.   If a first child has no maternal uncle he can be claimed by his maternal grandfather.   It is not uncommon also to find a sister's daughter living in the household, the uncle having requisitioned her services on his wife's behalf. The uncle has no absolute claim to any of his sister's daughters ; but a father will customarily hand over one of his daughters to his wife's brother if the wife's brother has no daughters of his own. If the girl were not properly treated by her uncle's wife she could be taken away by her father or mother ; or the latter might complain to her brother, who would severely rebuke his wife. It would appear that in former times the powers of the maternal uncle were even greater than they are to-day ; for it is said that in times of stress a man could pawn or sell any of his sister's children. A maternal uncle could beat his nephew to death, and no one would call him to account ; but if a father severely injured his son he was held responsible by his wife's brother.   It is also said that when anyone was convicted of witchcraft it was the uterine relatives alone who were sold into slavery or put to death, together with the witch.   For witchcraft was believed to be transmitted matrilineally.

It is difficult, nowadays, to ascertain how far the Chamba were formerly a mother-right people.[1]   They have clearly, by contact with the Fulani, lost a number of mother-right customs ; and even at the present time maternal uncles are afraid to exercise their right to the custody of the first-born nephew, believing that if they did so they might get into trouble with the Administration. Paternal uncles have much greater authority over female children than maternal uncles.   Indeed, the disposal of a girl's hand in marriage is almost entirely the affair of her father's brother by the same mother, on the principle that if two men have the same mother the property of the one is regarded as the property of the other.   The paternal uncle would, in courtesy, consult the girl's maternal uncle about her marriage, and might even give him a minor share of the bride-price ; but the right of accepting or refusing a suitor lies primarily with the paternal uncle, who is also the recipient of the bride-price, which he divides between himself, the girl's father, and her maternal uncle according as he thinks fit. He might, if the bride-price were £2, give 10s. to the maternal

---

[1] It will be shown later that the Dirrim and Taram groups of the Chamba-Daka are definitely mother-right peoples at the present time.

uncle, 10s. to the girl's father, and retain £1 for himself ; or he might give the girl's father £1 if the latter happened to be in straits for money.

As already indicated, the paternal aunt is a person of considerable importance among the Chamba. She is regarded as a second mother, and can call upon her nephew at any time to work on her farm, sweep her compound, and run messages. It is she who confers the first name on her nephew or niece, by a regular form of baptism. Taking the child from the mother's arm, she says, " You are So-and-so " (giving the name). She then dips the child's feet in palm-wine and pours some of the wine over its head. She is the first to greet her nephew on his return from the circumcision and initiation rites, anointing his head and chest with oil to soothe him after his protracted ordeal. It is on the paternal aunt also that the duty falls of instructing young boys and girls in correct behaviour and in the family and tribal traditions.

A few additional remarks may be made about the rules of inheritance. It has been suggested (pp. 332, 344) that not so long ago the Chamba of Donga may have followed the matrilineal principle. There is no clear evidence of this at the present time, though it will be seen later that in some Chamba groups certain forms of property are still heritable by sisters' sons. Among the Chamba of Donga a sister's son only inherits his uncle's property in the absence of brothers or sons. If his uncle's sons are young he may inherit the property as trustee, using it with due consideration for the benefit of the children. On the other hand, a son who inherits will generally give his father's sister's son a share, this share being known as " the share or reward of the milk ". A Chamba or Jukun will often be heard saying, " I am going to my maternal uncle's house in order to drink milk," i.e. in order to obtain the advantages of my mother's home. Among the Chamba, as among most Nigerian tribes, a boy has the right to appropriate any small articles of his maternal uncle's property during the latter's life-time.

As regards the inheritance of widows it is not permissible among the Donga Chamba for a man to inherit his father's or his paternal uncle's widows. Widows are normally inherited by younger brothers, but in some cases young widows may pass to sisters' sons (as among the Jukun). The senior levirate is taboo, and it may be for this reason that a woman who sees her husband's elder brother coming along the road turns her back, kneels on the ground, and remains in that position until he has passed her by some 50 yards or more. On the other hand a man is on terms of joking familiarity with the wife of his elder brother (and also with the wives of his maternal uncle).

Religion.—The Chamba of Donga have retained most of the ancient Chamba cults, but a number of families are in possession of Jukun cults such as Aku-ahwâ, Akwa, and Akumaga, inherited from Jukun families as a result of intermarriage. The adoption of these cults has necessitated also the adoption of the Jukun taboo which requires a menstruous woman to be segregated in a special hut for a period of six days. Even where no Jukun cults have been taken over, some Chamba villages have adopted this taboo out of respect for Jukun visitors ; for no Jukun who has charge of a cult will eat food in a village in which menstruous women are permitted to cook.

The principal Chamba cults are Tsera, Vara, Vonkima, Voma, and Mwa Lebsa. Tsera appears to be at once a spirit or godling— the tutelary genius of the town—and also the personification of the ancestral ghosts. Like the Jukun Aku-ahwâ, he enters the town at night in order to escort to the Underworld the ghost of any of his worshippers who has died. He signalizes his arrival by uttering croaks like a bull-frog, and all women and uninitiated men are required to conceal themselves in their huts until he returns to his shrine in the bush. As he goes off with the dead man's soul he beats the walls of the houses with his staff, and evidence of his visit is seen next morning in the broken branches of trees which strew the road. In times of epidemic sicknesses Tsera also enters the town to drive out the evil spirit. He beats his way through the town, and finally blocks up the gates of the wall to prevent the return of the disease-spirit. Dog and bush-cat are taboo to the cult, which is in the hands of the Ngwana and Kwasa kindreds.

Each kindred has a Vara cult in the charge of the leader of the kindred, a cult originally connected with the worship of the skulls of ancestors. The Vara is also a tutelary genius, the personification, apparently, of the first " Mala " or paternal aunt of the chief. She appears in public to mourn the death of any member of the kindred, and is personated by a man

dressed in a fibre costume surmounted by a horned mask
shaped as follows :—

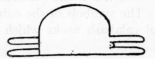

One half of the mask is painted red and the other black. Periodic
rites are performed to Vara when the head of the kindred is able to
provide the necessary beer.

The Vonkima cult is confined to females. Each kindred has
its own, the senior Mala of the kindred acting as president of the
cult. The symbol of the cult is a piece of iron resembling a hoe-
blade thus :—

When rites are about to be performed the Mala is required to
abstain from sexual relations the previous evening, and a wifeless
old man is sought to slay the sacrificial animal. No other man is
allowed to attend : any man breaking this rule or making mock
of the women during the dance would, it is said, lose his virility.
On the occasion of a mourning festival, whether for a man or a
woman, the women of the cult attend with the cultus-emblem and
an iron hand-gong. The rites of this female cult are sacred equally
with those of the men, and the orders of the priestess have to be
obeyed by the men. Thus if a drought occurred and the Vonkima
cult of the royal kindred demanded certain offerings by the
chief, the offerings would be given. Or if a man had lost his
virility, and the divining apparatus had declared that his condition
was due to Vonkima, he would have to approach the " Mala " in
charge of the cult with sacrificial gifts. The rites are secret, but it
seems that in the prayers the names of all previous " Malas " of
the kindred are recited. Initiates are taught the Vonkima dances,
and how to prepare the food for the rites. Preliminary fasting,
and the sprinkling of water on the members of the cult, form part
of the ritual, but I was unable to obtain details. Women of one
kindred may attend the Vonkima rites of another kindred ; and

non-Chamba women may be admitted to the cult on payment to the " Mala " of a chicken, some corn, and two flasks of beer.

Voma is a cult which has a wide distribution, especially in Adamawa Province. The symbols of the cult are seven horns of varying size made of calabash necks which fit into each other thus :—

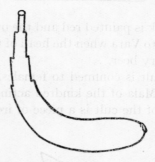

At Donga Voma is the rain-cult *par excellence*. If rain is slow in coming after the crops have been sown, the chief sends two pots of Chamba beer and a calabashful of beer-lees to the priest of Voma requesting him to have the rain-rites carried out. The priest places the horns in a row at the door of his hut, and deposits a little of the beer-lees on the outside of each instrument. Then, holding a calabash of water in his right hand and a calabash of beer in his left hand, he squats down and says : " You, my (deceased) elder brother, from whom I received this cult, come here and take your stand. If what I now do is a thing of my own invention, then do you repudiate me. But if aforetime you also did as I am about to do, then grant that rain may come to refresh our crops." He then calls on his elder brother's father, his father's sister (the Mala), and his grandfather, to bless the rites with their presence. After the prayer he pours a little water on the ground in front of the horns and then a little beer. This is done three times. The priest drinks up the remainder of the beer left in the calabash. The attendant horn-blowers are also given beer ; and when they have drunk, the priest hands to each one of the calabash horns. A little water is run through the horn in order to improve the tone. All then proceed to the chief's palace and there the horns are vigorously blown and a dance is held, the horn-players using also bell-shaped rattles made of plaited grass, with a piece of wood at the base, and pebbles inside. On the conclusion of the dance the horns are deposited in the palace, and every morning, until the rain comes, the horn-blowers arrive and blow the horns. After the first fall of rain the chief presents some corn and a sheep to the priest. The corn is made into beer which, with pieces of mutton, is divided up between the priest and the horn-blowers. There is not apparently any formal ceremony of thanksgiving to the forefathers. The cult of Voma is found among the Jukun under the name of Buhor.

Mwa Lebsa is the lightning-cult of the Chamba, and corresponds to the Achu Nyande cult of the Jukun. The symbol of the cult is a pot set between the forked branches of a *Sana*-tree in the compound of the head of the Gbana kindred. Rites are performed at the millet-harvests or whenever the divining apparatus indicates that the god requires them. If lightning strikes anyone's house or a tree on his farm and the divining apparatus declares this to be a sign that Mwa Lebsa requires food, the owner of the house or farm must forthwith offer a goat, a ram, and two chickens to the cult. When rites are performed a piece of iron is brought out and placed in front of the *Sana*-tree. The electric-fish is taboo to the priest of the cult and male members of his family.

The Purma Festival.—Among the Chamba of Donga there is an annual festival known as Purma held in October when the grain on the stalk of the guinea-corn crop first begins to burst forth. The feast seems to correspond to the Puje festival of the Jukun [1]; but among the Chamba it is associated in the minds of the people less with agricultural than with warlike operations, for the Purma festival is primarily regarded as a royal review of the warriors at the opening of the campaigning season.

The chief, in consultation with the Gangum (or Zarume), arranges the date of the festival and announces it to the people through the town-crier, who parades the streets striking a sistrum and saying : " Silence, people ! The chief bids me inform you that on such-and-such a day the first beer for the Purma festival will be set by him. Let everyone, therefore, who intends to have beer brewed, make his preparations accordingly." This announcement is also made to those living in the outlying villages, and the chief issues invitations for the feast to friendly members of neighbouring tribes. A few days later a further announcement is made as follows : " To-morrow the Gangum will set his brew of

---

[1] See *A Sudanese Kingdom*, p. 144.

the beer, and the chief will follow suit on the two succeeding days." The object in making this public announcement is that the general populace may know when to set their private brews ; for the householders arrange matters in such a way that, though the main supplies of beer are ready for the first two days of the festival, there shall not be a dearth of beer during the succeeding days.

On the evening before the Gangum's brew of beer is ready his followers assemble at his house and indulge in some preliminary dancing and singing, subsequently betaking themselves to the palace, where they salute the chief's followers by shaking their spears or other arms, a salutation which is returned in similar fashion. They dance off to a distance and return, again saluting with their spears. After doing this a third time they withdraw to the Gangum's ward and help themselves to some of the new brew of beer (which does not, however, fully mature until the following day). Next morning the Gangum, after dispatching six or seven pots of the beer to the chief, goes to the customary site behind the town, and there a war-dance is held. The warriors, girt in their war-belts of cloth or skin covered with charms, rush here and there treading down the grass and cutting off twigs of trees and plants as though they were cutting off the heads of enemies. At three in the afternoon they form a procession and return to the town, where, outside the palace, they are met by the chief and all his people. The youngest of the party first salutes the chief, then the warriors, and finally the Gangum with the older men. After being dismissed by the chief they escort the Gangum back to his ward, the drummers leading the way. There beer is distributed to all, and about 5 p.m. all again repair to the palace and receive beer from the chief's supplies. At sundown each man returns to his own home for his evening meal.

After the evening meal the chief's musicians repair to the palace and are handed their instruments by the chief's vizier. The instruments are ivory horns and iron gongs. The horns are soaked in beer and, at a given signal, are blown simultaneously. This was the old-time summons to war, and on hearing the horns every grown-up man seizes his arms and rushes with whoops and yells to the palace gate, where he salutes the principal palace officials. The chief himself does not appear ; for it is a rule in many Negro states that the chief may not be seen in public after sundown, the reason for this rule being, apparently, that chiefs were originally regarded as sons of the Sun.

On the following morning, the principal day of the festival, all the palace officials assemble at the house of the comptroller of the royal household and are escorted by him to the palace, where they are received by the chief and are given beer. The aged of the town also arrive to pay their respects, and they also are provided with beer. The chief distributes gifts of gowns or horses to the male members of his family. He then mounts his horse, and accompanied by the palace officials, all of whom are armed with swords or spears, rides out to the cleared space behind the town. Here he enters a specially prepared hut, at the door of which he receives the salutations of the people. A general dance is held and the warriors rush hither and thither, as on the previous day, trampling down the grass and lopping off the twigs and branches of trees. During the dance the chief at intervals comes out of the hut and sits watching the spectacle and engaging in conversation with the senior officials. The younger men carry swords or broad-bladed spears and wear aprons of cloth reaching from the waist to the knees. Two strips of cloth are also worn across the shoulders, the ends being made fast to a girdle of cloth or leather. A fillet of cloth is worn round the forehead. The more senior men wear sleeveless gowns, reaching to the knees and having slits in the sides. The gowns are studded with leather charms, to such an extent that they serve as a real protection against arrows. Many also carry shields of buffalo-hide. A few of the younger boys are armed with spears, but the majority have to be content with sticks.

Early in the afternoon the warriors raid some neighbouring farm. The protecting charms set on the farm are turned upside down or broken in pieces, for the festival of Purma is a Saturnalia during which the gods allow men to act as they please. A *post hoc ergo propter hoc* explanation is given of the licence permitted, for it is said that if the gods punished men for their acts during Purma so many men would be killed by the gods that the latter would have no worshippers left ! The warriors surround their heads and bodies with ground-nuts, potato-leaves, and samples of other pillaged crops, to give the impression that they are wild men who care not for gods or men. After further dancing there is a distribution of beer given by the chief. About two p.m. the chief rides back to the town, the procession being formed of the following groups : (*a*) Young unmounted boys ; (*b*) unmounted warriors ; (*c*) the Gangum and his followers ; (*d*) unmounted members of the royal family and their followers ; (*e*) palace officials (mounted) ; (*f*) royal drummers ; (*g*) personal servants of the chief ; (*h*) the chief ; (*i*) musicians and police ; (*j*) the Abô, Kpwâti, and Mukodashi ; (*k*) mounted members of the royal family ; (*l*) village headmen, and (*m*) the mounted warriors.

As the procession passes through the town two members of each group rush out at intervals, strike the ground with their swords, and return to their comrades, shaking their swords in salutation. On reaching the chief's palace they run forward and salute the chief's vizier and royal slaves who are assembled there with the three royal drums and iron gongs. Close to the vizier stands the chief Mala holding in her hands the sacred hoe of Vonkima (see page 347). Beside her stand the " Malas " of the various kindreds. The chief arrives amid a tornado of salutations, each group wheeling round and waving their spears before him as he advances to the palace. The chief himself then spurs his horse, and as he reaches the palace gate he holds up his right hand and shakes it, a salutation, apparently, to the ghosts of the royal forefathers who are believed to be assembled at the palace gates. To this salutation the vizier and royal slaves respond by holding up their right hands to the chief. The chief Mala shakes the hoe of Vonkima in front of the chief, and the other Malas yodel their greetings. The palace officials ride up and salute the door of the palace (i.e. the deceased royal ancestors), and then turn and hold up their hands in allegiance to the living chief. This they do by threes and fours until the whole company has done so. The chief and mounted warriors then ride thrice round the royal drums and gongs, followed by the Mala and the company of singing women. The chief now enters the palace, and the assembly breaks up, the junior Malas escorting the senior Mala to her home, where she issues supplies of beer. The vizier sends victuals to all members of the royal family, to invited guests, and to the poor and aged of the town. Later in the afternoon the members of the royal family assemble at the Mukodashi's compound, and the principal officials at that of the Abô. All then proceed again to the palace. They are greeted in groups by the chief, who announces, by his principal attendant, to the Abô that beer has been provided for all.

This message is passed on by the Abô to the Kpwâti, by the Kpwâti to the Turaiki, by the Turaiki to the Nya, by the Nya to the Tigye, by the Tigye to the Fawe, by the Fawe to the Gangum, and so on to all. The Turaiki then distributes the beer among those of the Chamba present, the vizier issuing supplies to the visitors. When the " Malas " arrive they take up their position in the female quarters of the palace, where they are greeted by the chief and given supplies of beer. The chief then rejoins the senior men and converses with them as they drink. The chief himself does not drink in front of the general assembly ; he may drink in the privacy of his own room, and in the presence of members of his own family and of the Abô. During the beer bout the chief may express the wish that there should be some dancing, and on this the Abô will hand the royal flutes, together with two flasks of beer, to the Gbâ Lera (or bandmaster). The Gbâ Lera takes a little of the beer and pours it on the ground, saying, " May the feet of the dancers be cold " (i.e. " May the dance be crowned with success "). This prayer is addressed to the ghosts of former bandmasters. He then spits a mouthful of beer into each flute, an offering it would seem to the spirit of the flute, the flutes being sacred instruments used only at public festivals. The musicians drink the remainder of the beer and then strike up a tune, the signal for the dance to begin. The senior officials and heir-apparent (Mukodashi) immediately rise and shake their hands in salutation to the chief ; the Mala and other women yodel, and the dance is begun by the wives of the chief, clothed in the new garments given them by the chief that day. Soon afterwards the chief withdraws to his private apartments, the ivory horns being blown to signalize his departure. The dance in front of the chief's palace is brought to a close at sundown, but is carried on elsewhere during the evening by those who prefer dancing to drinking beer.

On the following morning all the seniors of the town, including the Mala, come to the palace to salute the chief. They are given beer which has matured that morning. Later the senior Mala holds her court. She is saluted by the senior officials and members of the royal family, and she provides liberal supplies of beer for her visitors. In the afternoon dancing is recommenced, the chief attending, clothed in his royal robes. On this occasion the chief adopts a free and easy attitude with his people ; he will even

A a

occasionally beat one of the drums or blow one of the horns himself. After a short time the chief retires, and the dancing concludes at sunset. The festival is kept up spasmodically for a period of seven days.

This annual festival entails on the chief very considerable expenditure in gifts and in the provision of beer and victuals. In former times all farmers at harvest contributed two or three bundles of corn in order to assist the chief to meet the expenditure incurred in connection with the Purma festival and also with the daily supplies of beer provided for the courtiers. At the present time the gifts of corn have diminished, and the chief must experience considerable difficulty in keeping up the Purma festival.

According to the popular conception at the present time the Purma festival is a war ceremony, and when it was asked why a war ceremony should be carried out long before the guinea-corn harvest, the answer given was that it was the Chamba custom for the warriors to leave the harvesting to the youths, while they themselves harried their neighbours while the latter were engaged in gathering in the earlier crops. It is noteworthy, however, that the festival, in which the chief plays such a prominent part, is held when the guinea-corn begins to sprout, and it is possible that originally Purma was, among the forefathers of the Chamba, a kind of Sed festival in which the chief was reborn, and the chiefship renewed for a further term. Or, alternatively, is the Purma festival a symbol of Victory, the victory of the Chief as the Sun-god ? There is no clear evidence that the Chamba chief was identified with the Sun or Sun-god, but further inquiries would, I believe, prove that this was so, for it is noteworthy that in one Chamba group the members of the royal kindred call themselves " The Children of the Sun ", and that among all the Chamba groups the words for sun and god are identical.

There is a curious harvest-rite performed at the Chamba village of Rafin Kada, 14 miles from Wukari. Just before the reaping of the crops the chief of the town sends to his farm a youth of his household, who must have abstained from washing and sexual intercourse for a number of days. He takes with him a pot of beer, lights a fire at a corner of the farm, calls on the chief's ancestors to grant that during the reaping the corn may increase, and pours libations of beer here and there on the farm.

He then takes a branch of a locust-bean tree and sprinkles some of the surrounding corn with beer. Having warmed his hands at the fire, he proceeds to reap the crop. A sickle is not used, the stalk being trampled down and the head removed by hand. During the period of reaping no drumming or any kind of music is allowed in the village and corn-rubbers may not be repaired. The fire is kept burning on the farm each day until the whole of the crop has been cut. Those who bind up the sheaves must first hold their hands, and also the string used in binding, close to the flame. The intention in warming the hands is to drive away the evil spirits which are believed to have the power of diminishing the crop during the process of harvesting.

Circumcision.—All the Chamba, unlike the Bachama, practise male circumcision. The rites performed at Donga are of considerable interest and may be described in some detail. They are carried out at intervals of seven years, the boys' ages ranging from nine to sixteen. On the conclusion of the harvest in the appointed year the chief summons the principal men of the town and announces his intention of holding the septennial ceremony during the ensuing dry season. Seven days before the new moon he issues a proclamation that after the rising of the new moon all fathers of uncircumcised children of nine and over must produce their children for the customary rites. When the new moon is sighted the chief has a brew of beer set, and all other heads of households follow his example. The object of the brew is that the householder (who may be the boy's father, father's brother, or mothers' brother) may offer libations to his gods and ancestors on behalf of the lad or lads about to be circumcised. In offering these libations the prayer used is as follows : " You, So-and-so (mentioning the particular deity), I have come to find you with offerings of beer and a chicken ; for I am about to call out my son that he may be circumcised. Do you grant that he may mount the stone of circumcision and descend therefrom in safety. May he not suffer from excessive hæmorrhage. If he comes out of the ordeal safely, then I will come to you and show my gratitude with offerings of beer and a chicken. For if aught befalls him, there will be none to succeed me in the maintenance of your cult." It would appear from the character of this prayer that the object of the preliminary rites is merely to secure the physical safety of the boy about to be circumcised.   But the physical

dangers of circumcision would not seem to be so great as to demand
antecedent rites of sacrifice on the part of the whole community.
Circumcision has clearly among the Chamba a deeply religious
significance, and it will be apparent from what is said later that
initiation is nothing less than a rebirth and consecration to
the gods, though the explanations offered at the present time do
not amount to more than that circumcision is a passport to
marriage and manhood (just as in India no Brahman can marry
until he has received the sacred thread of initiation). No woman
will marry an uncircumcised man, and no uncircumcised man is
regarded as being fully a man. It is significant that no uncircumcised person may enter any shrine, and that among the Jukun-
speaking peoples of Donga and elsewhere the young acolytes,
mere children as they are, must have undergone circumcision
before they are permitted to serve as attendants on a priest or
chief, both of whom are affiliated with the gods.

When the preliminary rites have been performed the lads due
for circumcision are brought by their fathers to a shelter outside
the town. Each ward or quarter of the town has its own shelter
on the outskirts of the town, and in this all the lads of that ward
are assembled. The grouping is thus a local grouping and not a
social grouping, and members of the same kindred may be located
in different enclosures as they belong to different wards. Over
each group there is a senior male president, with one or two
assistants, known as the Nena. The Nena is responsible for the
supervision, safeguarding, and instruction of the boys throughout
the three months of circumcision and initiation. The lads of each
group, moreover, appoint a leader (the most senior amongst them
usually), and he in turn appoints a number of lieutenants, who
are given titles corresponding to those held by the principal men
of the town.

The actual operation of circumcision is performed on the first
day in order of seniority. The boy is led forward by one of the
Nena's assistants, who places his hands over the boy's eyes (with
the intention of preventing fear at the sight of blood and of the
ablated prepuces of those who had preceded him). He is set down
on a stone in front of which is a round hole in the ground. The
operator is, at the present time, a Hausa barber, but was formerly
a Chamba ; not a member of a family which specialized in circumcision, but any member of the ward who had learned the art.

The operator tells the boys that they must be plucky; and if any boy begins to whimper the attendant relative covers his mouth with his hand. One of the Nena's assistants holds the boy's hands behind his back; another holds his legs. The prepuce is removed with a razor used only for circumcision, and when severed falls into the hole in front of the patient. If the boy utters no cry of pain he is saluted by his father or brother with a slap of congratulation on the back. He then withdraws and sits down in front of a hole in the ground, into which the blood of the wound drips freely. When the bleeding becomes less active the Nena applies some astringent juice of the *gabarua*[1] tree (bark and leaves pounded). (Formerly it was the Chamba custom not to use *gabarua* juice, but to encase the penis in a leaf and then apply a juice obtained from the roots of a tree known to the Hausa as *baushen fadama*. The juice was applied hot; and the intention in using a leaf was that the fluid might be retained round the wound as long as possible. The juice of the *baushen fadama* is said to be more potent and painful than that of the *gabarua* The Nena stood behind the boy with a cane while it was being applied, and if the boy cried out he received a sharp blow. If he called out " O father ! " it was a pardonable offence ; but if he called out " O mother ! " he was beaten thoroughly, being regarded as a person wholly lacking in manhood. When the wound shows signs of healing, it is dressed with hot palm-oil administered with a chicken's feather. The penis is kept free from the legs by being placed in a triangle of wood made from the forked branches of the pepper-plant, the triangle being held in position by a string passed round the waist. During the night the Nena or one of his assistants remains awake to see that the boys do not close their legs during their sleep. It is sometimes necessary to fix a stick between the knees to prevent the closing of the legs. The boys spend each day in the shelter outside the town ; but in the evening, after it is dark, they go in a body to a large hut near the town wall, returning to the day-shelter before the sun rises ; for they must not be seen by anyone, even by initiated men. The reason assigned for the taboo is that the boys must not come in contact with persons who may have had sexual relations the previous evening. If therefore the boy's father or brother intends to visit him he must keep himself pure from women during the previous evening ; for otherwise, they say,

[1] An acacia.

the wound would not heal. On no account may any woman go near the locality where the boys are assembled. The two meals provided for the boys each day are brought by female relatives and are received by the Nena at some distance from the shelter, the boys, secluded inside, clapping their hands in salutation to the women. The morning meal consists of boiled beans and rice or ground-nuts, and the evening meal of porridge and soup. Salt must not be put into the soup until the wound is healed, as salt is believed to hinder the process of healing. They are permitted to drink *kunu* (a thin porridge), but must avoid beer and ordinary water.[1] When the wounds have healed the Nena informs the parents of the lad, and salted soup is sent, together with sweetened porridge and beer. No man is allowed to visit the boys unless he is a close relative. Anyone breaking this rule would be set upon by the boys and soundly thrashed until the Nena directed them to desist. The Nena is treated with the utmost respect and obedience. When a boy sees him approaching he claps his hands in salutation. The Nena's word is law. It is said that if he told a boy to go and beat his own father who was visiting the camp the boy would promptly get up to obey, until stopped by the Nena. If a boy were told to enter a part of the river known to be infested by crocodiles, he could not disobey. For the slightest offence he is chastised with a hippo-whip ; and an offence by one boy involves all the others. Offences would be failure to salute the Nena, failure to salute the women who bring the food, going outside the enclosure to greet one's mother, eating food without the Nena's permission, noisy conduct, quarrelling, or fighting. When the Nena decides to thrash all the boys, he directs their leader to instruct the others to go and find some straight canes suitable for the purpose, and off the boys immediately go.   Anyone bringing back an unsuitable cane would be pronounced to be evil and would be beaten with the cane until it broke. He would then be directed to go and fetch another. When the canes have been brought the lads are made to kneel down, hold out their hands, and fix their eyes on the ground. They are then each, from first to last, given one or two strokes on the back ; and if any boy shows tears in his eyes he is given some

---

[1] Initiates into the mysteries of Eleusis were required to abstain from certain foods.   The use of salt was commonly prohibited in the case of sacred foods (see *E.R.E.*, vol. v, p. 137).

additional strokes and told that he is a woman and no man. They are taught the importance of obedience to their seniors. The Nena may say to a lad, " If your father calls you, you will run to him ? " The boy replies, " Yes." " Everything he tells you to do you will do ? " The boy says, " Yes." " If he tells you to catch a bird in the sky, you will do so ? " The boy says, " Yes." The Nena says " Indeed ! How will you do it ? " The boy, nonplussed, remains silent, and is then given a blow for being stupid. Boys are also taught that henceforth they must never address their father by his personal name. They are told a good deal about the various cults, and are warned never to disclose anything pertaining thereto. On the day of circumcision the boys are given by their fathers a plaited-grass mat which they wear across the body slung over one shoulder. This protects the penis from injury when walking through grass, and also serves as a mat at night.

After the wound has healed the boys are set to do numerous tasks, such as cutting grass for thatching, collecting bamboos, weaving mats, hunting rats, and catching fish. The products of their work are, in the main, appropriated by the Nena and his assistants, but gifts are also sent to the chief and the senior men of the ward. Laziness is punished by the Nena ; and as all the boys are involved in the punishment all are careful to see that none of their number shirks his duty. They work until midday, then rest and have their midday meal. In the afternoon they engage in dancing, learning the steps peculiar to the circumcision-dance. They dance with bent body, playing the horns provided by the chief. Every now and then they suddenly straighten themselves. The Nena beats time with an iron gong, and abuses or strikes any boy who is slow in picking up the steps. During the dance the boys wear a skirt woven by themselves from the fronds of palms. They also weave for themselves head-coverings of similar material, so that if perchance they meet any woman in the bush they may conceal their features. The boys are also instructed in the art of wrestling, which in many Nigerian tribes is closely associated with religious rites (see, for example, the paper on the Bachama tribe).[1]

---

[1] Sham fights and games were a feature of the Eleusinian initiation-rites ; they were apparently the symbol of ritual combat or the victory of " good over evil ". The games may, however, be a test of qualification (of manhood or as servitors of the gods).

At the end of the three months the chief orders all house-holders to prepare beer with which to celebrate the return of the initiates to the town. The last evening is spent in dancing up to midnight, and on the following morning the chief arrives with all the senior men. The boys have previously washed themselves in the river, been shaved, and finally warned of the necessity of preserving the secrecy of the rites. Loin-cloths are distributed, the first the lads have ever worn.[1] They are tied on by the fathers or uncles, who then collect and set fire to the palm-skirts and head-coverings which the lads had worn through the period of segregation. The Nena and his assistants are required to leap over the flames, and as they do so they receive sundry slaps from the parents of the boys, in retaliation for the beatings their sons had received. The boys protest against the slapping of their " lord ". In addition to the loin-cloths the boys are tricked out in numerous ornaments such as necklaces and bells fastened round the ankle. Those of the chief's household are given special cloths and necklaces of special stones. The chief and his followers then return to the town, and soon afterwards the boys, led by the Nena and followed by his assistant, proceed to make their formal entry into the town. At the gate of the town they are met by a large assembly including a trumpet band and the tutelary genius Vara, who greets the lads by curtseying before them three times, first with his face towards them and then with his back turned to them ; for they have now become his sons, i.e. they are not human children any longer, but the grown-up sons of the gods. The Nena is again subjected to buffetings by the fathers and uncles of the boys. As the boys enter the town with head bent, the paternal aunts approach them with dishes of fried ground-nuts, beans, " *majigi* "-oil and palm-oil. The aunts anoint their heads with the " *majigi* "-oil, and smear some of the palm-oil on their foreheads, chests (over the heart), and at the base of the shoulder-blade. The intention, it is said, is to soothe the heart on the conclusion of the long period of hardship, to help them to forget. The shoulders are smeared so that evil spirits shall not settle there. The aunts keep revolving the nuts in a calabash, and as they do so some of the nuts fall out on to the

---

[1] Mr. Hocart in showing that initiation in India is regarded as a rebirth, quotes Manu (ii, 169) as saying : " According to the teaching of revelation a Twice-born's first birth is from his mother, his second on binding the girdle."

ground : the boys must not stoop to pick them up, for if any does so he is regarded as a shameless being, whose character has remained just as it was before his circumcision. The boys march on with body bent towards the chief's palace. The idea of the bent position is said to be an expression of shyness ; they are strangers entering a town they have never seen before.

On arrival at the chief's palace they are given a feast of meat and beer. They sleep three nights in the chief's compound and are treated luxuriously. During the day they go and salute their relatives (male and female on both sides), with whom, however, they refuse conversation until formal gifts are made by each. These gifts are handed to the Nena. In the evening they dance the dance learnt in the bush. On the fourth day the boys are collected by the Nena and taken again to the bush, where they set fire to the shelter which they had occupied. They are required to leap over the flames, and as they do so they receive sundry slaps from the Nena, in retaliation for those received by him from the boys' parents. The boys then return to their own homes.

Lads who are circumcised in the same group as the children of the chief consider themselves as the social superiors of the other circumcision groups, whose circumcision, they will scornfully say, was " the circumcision of a baboon ! "[1] Nevertheless all lads circumcised at the same time are friends, and a boy of nine may be rude to a boy of fifteen of his circumcision class. It is said, however, that this custom is breaking down, and that boys expect their juniors to treat them with respect, whether they belong to the same circumcision class or not. It is noteworthy that in former times two brothers by the same mother were never circumcised at the same time ; the younger had to wait for the next batch. This custom also is no longer scrupulously observed.

Death and Burial of the Chief.—If the chief falls ill he is attended by his favourite wife, a favourite servant, and the senior palace official. The assistance of a leech is sought to administer medicines. If the illness is not severe he is visited by all his brothers and children and by the Mala. If the illness is serious,

---

[1] The phrase " circumcision of a baboon " has, perhaps, a deeper significance than at first sight appears. The baboon was in Ancient Egypt a symbol of the Moon (see e.g. Briffault, *The Mothers*, ii, p. 787). The sons of chiefs are children of the Sun, but the sons of commoners are children of the Moon.

admission is only granted to brothers by the same mother and to children. The reason for excluding half-brothers by the same father is that this class of relative is considered more likely to work mischief on the chief, especially as during a severe illness poisons or magical medicines might be used without arousing any suspicion of foul play. Even a son would be refused admittance to the royal bedchamber if he was suspected of being ill-disposed to his father. During his illness the chief's food is cooked specially by his favourite wife (*wasi*) as a further safeguard against poisoning.

On the death of the chief the head of the royal kindred (Sama) is summoned, together with the heir-apparent, two paternal and maternal uncles, two brothers, and two sons. The comptroller of of the royal household is also in attendance. In the presence of these the body is washed, those not engaged in the washing standing round in a circle and handing water as required. The abdomen is massaged to drive out faecal matter, and orifices are closed with cotton-wool. These preparations for burial are carried out quietly without any outward display of grief, for the chief's death must be kept secret even from the chief's widows, who if they became aware of their bereavement would immediately begin to wail and so convey the news to the entire town. No one, therefore, except the persons indicated, may approach the hut in which the body lies. The body is clothed in trousers and two, three, or even four gowns. Shoes are put on the feet, a burnous on the shoulders, and a turban on the head. The body is then set in a chair, sitting as though alive.

During these preparations the chief's official aunt, the Mala of the Sama kindred, has been summoned, together with the head of the brother-kindred of Janga. The head of a brother-kindred is known as the " *Kumboa* " and always plays an important part in funeral rites. (The same custom has been noted among a number of other tribes, e.g. among the Bachama if a member of the Muja clan dies the burial of the body is carried out under the supervision of the local head of the Killa clan, and so on.) The senior town officials, viz. the Abô, Kpwâti, and Kuni (or Turaiki), are also summoned, and on arrival are invited to come and see the chief, i.e. to bid farewell to their royal master. When all are assembled the head of the royal kindred takes some feathers from the tail of the plantain-eater bird, and sticks them in a fold of the

dead chief's turban, so that they lie across his forehead. The
Mala then shaves his forehead, using a razor of the ancient Chamba
type shaped thus :—

She also smears his forehead with oil. The Kumboa now comes
forward holding a cock in his right hand. Addressing the dead
chief by his personal name and royal title, he says, " To-day you
have left us to go to our fathers and grandfathers. May you
depart in peace." He then plucks out some of the cock's feathers
and scatters them over the corpse. He addresses the chief's
ancestors, saying : " So-and-so has left us to-day to go to you.
Do you receive him well ; you, Suyinga, receive him and escort
him to Garbwâye, and let Garbwâye escort him to Kusho, and
Kusho to Gakie (the first chief)." As he mentions the name of
each forefather he plucks out some more feathers and scatters
them over the body. The head of the royal kindred performs a
similar rite and when he has finished the Mala steps forward and
kneels before the chief, holding a small calabashful of beer. She
calls out the names of all deceased " Malas ", saying : " Your son
is coming to you to-day ; do you each in turn receive him and
escort him to those distant forefathers whose names we can no
longer recall." She pours some of the beer from the calabash into
a cup and empties the contents of the cup in front of the corpse,
pouring a little to the right, a little to the left, and then turning
the cup upside down in the centre. This she does three times,
and in conclusion bids the chief a final farewell, saying : " Depart
in peace and find your forefathers. If the cause of your death was
due to us women, or to your brothers or your wives, do you, after
greeting your forefathers, return to earth and take the guilty one :
but if it was God who decreed that you should die, then turn your
eyes downwards and leave us in peace." The beer left over is
solemnly drunk by the two heads of kindreds (Sama and Janga),
by the brothers and other relatives. The Mala also drinks some
and hands the cup to the junior Mala. The rite is an oath of
innocence, and it is believed that if any among them had caused

the chief's death, he would speedily die after having drunk the beer, which is regarded as having become consecrated and potent, through the preliminary rite of offering some of it to the dead chief's ghost.

The body is now handed over to those who had dug the grave— a cylindrical hole 5 to 6 feet deep dug underneath one of the palace storerooms. The chief grave-digger kills a black dog and places its body in the grave. The dog is regarded as the horse of the chief which will carry him to his forefathers. (It is probable therefore that in former times a horse and not a dog was sacrificed.) The body of the chief is then lifted from the chair and deposited in the grave, the head of the royal kindred giving directions as to the precise position it shall occupy. It is buried in a standing position, the loose earth being packed in tightly all round to keep it erect. The head alone is left protruding above the earth and is covered by a pot. The Mala and other relatives are not present during the inhumation, which is carried out solely by the grave-diggers and the head of the royal kindred. When the grave has been closed in, the remainder of the Mala's beer is poured over the mound (the calabash being returned to the Mala later). The head of the royal kindred now rejoins his relatives, and after reporting that the body has been duly buried he dismisses them all. The grave-diggers, however, and certain of the late chief's slaves guard the grave day and night, until the time comes for the formal removal of the skull.

By this time the favourite wives are aware that their husband is dead, but they prepare food for him just as though he were alive. In the evening the Mala or one of her assistants comes and takes away some of the food (consisting of porridge and stew) in order to deposit it on a shelf in the late chief's hut, where, it is thought, the dead chief comes and helps himself to the substance. The remainder of the meal is handed to the juniors of the household ; for during the chief's lifetime it is the custom to hand over the remnants of the chief's meal to the members of his family, the food being turned into separate dishes, as it would be disrespectful and in fact dangerous for anyone to dip his hand into the same dish as had been used by the chief. Next morning the Mala goes to the chief's hut, empties out the food deposited the previous evening, and buries it. She washes the dishes carefully, fills them with beer and replaces them on the shelf, this being the chief's midday repast. In the evening she again leaves a meal, and so on regularly for a period of two or three weeks.

The daily custom of attending at the palace to salute the chief is continued just as though he were alive, and beer and victuals are distributed to the courtiers by the Mukodashi. The non-appearance of the chief is explained by saying that he is unwell. After some days, however, the Mukodashi instructs the Abô to inform all the seniors of the town that the chief's illness has proved " an illness indeed ". This constitutes a formal announcement of the death of the chief. As the news spreads there is a complete silence in the town and a cessation of all drumming, dancing, or any form of amusement. Six days after death the male members of the royal family shave their heads. The widows of the chief cut their hair short and don old clothes. Later, when the formal mourning festival is held, the women shave their heads completely, discard their cloth garments, and don aprons of leaves, which they wear for a year. The rites at the mourning festival are similar to those held for commoners, as described later.

Ten days or a fortnight after the burial the grave-diggers remove the head of the dead chief, clean it thoroughly, and hand it in a basket to the senior member of the royal kindred, who deposits it in the granary containing the other royal skulls, the cult of which is known as Vara (see page 346).

When the new chief enters on his chieftainship he has to perform rites in honour of his predecessor. He enters the sacred enclosure, accompanied by the priest in charge of the Vara cult and by certain favourite brothers. The skulls of former chiefs are brought out and set in a row. The priest then calls on the name of each, saying : " Your son has mounted the royal seat and assumed the royal necklace, even as you did in bygone days, and he comes to make to you offerings of beer. Grant that he and his people may have prosperity." He pours a libation of beer over the skulls, and the chief drinks the remainder of the beer, an act which confirms him in his chieftainship. The cult of the royal skulls is not merely of primary importance to the chief personally, but also to the whole community, for the royal ancestors are the presiding genii of the town, the chief protective agency and remedy for all evils. The nature of the rites performed is kept secret from the general public, for if they became a matter of common knowledge the chief's divine authority would, it is thought, be impaired, as the people would see that his special cult differed little from their own.

Coupled with the cult of the royal skulls at Donga there is another cult known by the Jukun term of *ahê*, the symbols of which are said to be a spear or arrow-head, two pots, and a bracelet. These are contained in the same enclosure as the royal skulls, and rites are performed before the eating of the new crops, before the annual hunt, and in former times, before engaging in any warlike enterprise. During the rites the chief is accompanied by his favourite brothers, his paternal aunts, certain of his grown-up sons, and his favourite wives. Others, including members of his family, are not permitted to enter the sacred enclosure, though they may take up a position just outside. The rites are, on the first day, carried out in the evening, beer and food being distributed to all in attendance. On the morning of the two succeeding days libations are again offered. The *ahê* is the special royal charm and was the talisman in time of war. As regards the preservation of skulls it is to be noted that not only is the chief's skull preserved, but it was also customary to preserve the skulls of all members of the royal family. This latter rule has since 1918 been allowed to lapse.

Mourning-rites.—A Donga Chamba is nowadays buried in a rectangular grave with a niche, reclining on a mat facing east (if a man) or west (if a woman). The opening into the niche is blocked with a mat the edges of which are plastered over with mud. The loose earth is then replaced in the rectangular shaft. This type of grave is of recent adoption, being easier to make than the cylindrical shaft with niche, the type formerly used. The body is wrapped in a cloth, which in the case of an important man or of a member of the royal kindred is presented by the chief. For three days after burial the sisters and aunts (paternal and maternal) sleep in the hut of the deceased (for a reason I was not able to ascertain). The formal mourning festival is not held, however, until the month of January or February, when the crops have been gathered in and the people have some leisure and also the supplies necessary for the rites. Two kinds of beer are prepared, (*a*) the special brew of the Chamba, and (*b*) that brewed in the Jukun fashion. The Jukun beer is that for general consumption, but the Chamba beer is preferred by connoisseurs, and is necessary when religious rites have to be performed.

The day before the beer is ready all assemble at the dead man's house, where his body is represented by a piece of matting covered with a white cloth and laid on a mat. The flute-band known as " Lera " is in attendance, and the leader of the band takes a mouthful of the Chamba beer and squirts it into each of the flutes. The head of the brother-kindred (" *kumboa* ") of the deceased then addresses the ghost of the dead man's father, saying : " You, father of So-and-so (mentioning the dead man's name), your son is going to you to-day. What it was that killed him we know not, whether it came from God, or an enemy, or some sorcerer. You know ; and do you, therefore, escort him to your father, and your father to his father, that you may take counsel together with a view to vengeance, if his death was due to foul play." As he speaks he plucks a hair from the goat which is about to be sacrificed and deposits it on the bundle representing the corpse. A similar prayer is then repeated by the senior elder brother (by the same father) of the deceased. He is followed by the deceased's Mala, i.e. his paternal aunt (or in her absence by his senior sister), who addresses her prayer to the deceased Malas of the family. The senior brother slays the goat (or sheep), and as the blood spurts out on the ground the women present burst into lamentation, and the flute-players begin blowing their instruments. The band of the Vonkima (or women's cult) also strikes up a dirge beaten on iron hand-gongs. Feasting and dancing (of a restrained character) are kept up throughout the night and during the next day. On the following evening those who had formerly buried the real corpse go through the pretence of burying the mock corpse. They carry the mat containing the bundle to the back of the house, and there, unseen by the relatives, secrete the mat and cloth for their own use. The grave-diggers are also entitled to the dead body of the goat.

This Chamba ceremony of formally handing over the dead man to the charge of his ancestors is closely paralleled by that of the Jukun of Akiri, a full account of which has been given else-where.[1] But the Chamba have a further rite performed on the same evening as that on which the mock body is formally removed ; a circumcision-comrade of the deceased goes with an adze to the door of the deceased's house, cuts down one of the posts and some

---

[1] See *A Sudanese Kingdom*, pp. 254 et seq.

of the matting at the entrance, and deposits the pieces at a cross-roads.   Next day at dawn the girls of the deceased's household carry out to the cross-roads a new three-legged pot containing some light porridge, a new calabash filled with beer-lees, and a new dish smeared with oil.   One of the deceased's sons removes the leather string from his father's bow and substitutes a string of fibre.[1]   He takes this bow and his father's quiver with him to attend the rites at the cross-roads, where all the relatives and friends are assembled, the former distinguished by a strip of hibiscus-fibre tied round the forehead.   The senior brother and Mala then utter a prayer similar to that already recorded.   On the conclusion of the prayers a man, accustomed to the duty, turns the pot, calabash and dish upside down near the pieces of stick and mat fencing which had been deposited there the previous evening.   As he does so he calls on the dead man's father, aunt, and grandfather, saying, " I have brought to you the soul of your dead son ; do you receive him joyfully."   Addressing the dead man's spirit he says, " Here is the pot in which your food was cooked, here is your feeding-dish, and here your drinking-vessel." Then taking the dead man's spear he smashes the dishes to pieces, saying, " Take these and find your forefathers."   The flute-band marches round the spot three times, and is followed by the calabash-horn band of the Voma cult, the iron-gong band of the Vonkima cult, and finally by the tutelary genius known as Vara. Then all return home.   Dancing and feasting are kept up until the following evening, when the bands and representatives of the cults are dismissed with a gift from the dead man's brother.

Rites similar to these and known as *Va ke* are, at Takum, performed in honour of a man who in his life-time had killed a leopard or lion or an enemy in war.   The officiator is a person versed in the ritual used for allaying ghosts.   He goes to the bush and obtains a certain species of grass, which he weaves so that it resembles a piece of fence-matting.   At night he sets up some sticks at a cross-roads and surrounds them with the matting. Next morning, accompanied by a few senior men who had themselves at one time slain a leopard, lion, or human being, he proceeds to the cross-roads, followed by all the warriors of the town, dressed in their war-paint and armed with spears and bows.

[1] An indication that in former times the Chamba were accustomed to use bow-strings of fibre.

PLATE 33

DONGA MARKET

VA KE SYMBOLS (Chamba)

[face p. 369

On arrival at the cross-roads the warriors shake their spears in honour of their dead comrade. The officiant takes a mouthful of beer and spits it out round the sticks and matting, with the intention, it is said, of conveying to the dead man's ghost a preliminary offering of beer by way of salutation. Then taking three dishes, one containing the Chamba beer made from maize, one the guinea-corn beer of the Jukun, and one an unguent, he smashes the dishes and their contents at the base of the tripod of sticks and matting, with the object of dispatching to the deceased the beer he was accustomed to drink himself and the ointment with which he was wont to smear his body. The Jukun beer is given for his followers in the Spirit-world ; for one who was great in this life is great also in the life hereafter.[1]

The accompanying photograph illustrates the symbols erected at a cross-roads outside the town of Takum for the performance of *Va ke* rites in honour of the late chief of Takum, who, though belonging to the Zompere tribe, had expressed the wish that on his death the Chamba rites should be performed on his behalf. This chief was much respected both by the local inhabitants and by all British administrative officials with whom he had been associated. He had, in his time, killed more than one lion ; and it was said also that in his warrior days he had accounted for many human lives. It will be seen from the photograph that a number of pieces of cloth are mixed up with fragments of the broken vessels. These bits of cloth are parts of the late chief's burnous. By tearing up the burnous and depositing the pieces at the cross-roads the burnous is conceived to be conveyed in its entirety to the dead man, who will require a burnous in the spirit-world, just as he had required one while he was a chief on earth. It is clear that the ceremony represents the formal dispatching of the dead man's soul to the spirit-world ; and that the intention of carrying out the rites at a cross-roads is that the dead man's ghost there comes into contact with friends and relatives who have departed this life and who pursue their spiritual way backwards and forwards between the town of Takum and the surrounding villages. There is also the further idea (according to those who explained the ceremony) that by conducting the ghost of the deceased to a point outside the town

---

[1] This would seem to imply that it was customary among the Chamba to slay slaves at the burial of any personage.

Death himself would be induced to leave the town ; for Death follows in the wake of anyone he has killed.

The dead man's ghost, thus dispatched, has, for the average Chamba of Donga and Takum, been got rid of finally. For among the Chamba commonalty, once the initial rites have been performed, the ancestors do not exercise a continuous predominating influence, as they do among the neighbouring Jukun. In the case of a chief, however, or of heads of clans, additional precautions have to be taken ; and secondary funerary rites, connected with the cult of Vara, have to be performed when any important person has died. These rites are carried out late in the dry season, when the beer, sufficient for the purpose, has been brewed. All relatives and friends assemble at the compound of the deceased and then proceed to the cross-roads. The brother of the deceased (or, if the brother is not acquainted with the rites, someone else who knows the ritual) deposits some beer-lees at the cross-roads and then takes a mouthful of beer and spits it out over the lees, saying, "You, So-and-so, son of So-and-so, grandson of So-and-so, we are seeking your 'Vara'; do you come to us that we may see." The beer-lees apparently attract spiders ; and so all wait until a spider, which is taken to be the embodiment of the dead man's soul, descends upon the lees. When the spider descends it is caught on a head of guinea-corn and is deposited in a new calabash. Having caught the spider they return with it to a granary in the deceased's compound. There the spider is set down on some guinea-corn in front of one of the pots that symbolize the cult of Vara. The officiant takes a new calabash, containing water, in his right hand, and a new calabash containing beer in his left hand, and pours the water and beer on the corn (on which the spider is resting). Taking a cock in his right hand he says, "To-day we have brought you to your father and your grandfather : aforetime we brought their Vara here, and now we have joined your Vara to theirs. We have given you fluid (i.e. beer), but whether you have accepted our gift or not remains to be seen." He then takes some mixed beer and water in the palm of his hand and offers it to the cock. If the cock drinks, it is a sign that the dead man's ghost has accepted the offering. The thirsty cock always drinks. Its throat is then cut and the blood is allowed to drip on the pots, the symbols of the Vara cult. The paternal aunt of the deceased (or his elder sister) then does likewise, either slitting the cock's throat with a knife, or smashing its head against the wall of a hut and opening the dead bird's beak to allow the blood to run out on to the pots. Chickens brought by other female relatives are also killed; but in the case of women who have not passed the change of life the killing is done by their husbands, as it is taboo for women who are still subject to " defilement " to offer sacrificial gifts. A sheep and goat may also be sacrificed. The flesh of the sacrificial animals is divided out, the married women taking their share home to eat with their husbands (who had provided the gifts required by the wives for the rites). On the following day all the relatives of the deceased again assemble, and the guinea-corn on which the spider had alighted is ground and mixed with water and set on two dishes, which are deposited on the pots of the Vara cult. The deceased's brother takes a fig-leaf, dips it in the floury mixture, and smears the brow of each male person present. The senior woman present (i.e. the Mala) does likewise for all the females present. (No explanation of this rite could be offered beyond that it brought good-luck and good-fellowship among those who share it.)

The precise significance of the spider in the rites described is not clear. " Vara " means " skull " in the Chamba tongue ; and there can be no doubt that among the Chamba the skulls of ancestors were preserved and used as the normal means of securing the assistance of deceased relatives. The spider would seem to take the place of the skull as the embodiment of the ghost of the ancestor. On the other hand, where the skulls of ancestors are still preserved (the Donga chiefs still preserve the ancestral skulls), the " spider " rites are also observed. Nevertheless, the spider is probably to be regarded as a later substitute for the skull. Among the Berom of the Bauchi plateau, who speak a language cognate with that of the Chamba, the spider plays a prominent part in most religious rites. It appears to be at times identified with the higher deities, particularly with *Chi*, the rain-god ; but in certain rites the priest has to search about among shrubs and leaves until he finds a rock-spider, which, when captured, is deposited in a leather bag. I have not sufficient details on this Berom custom to enable me to offer a suggestion as to whether, among the Berom, the spider is regarded as an embodiment of ancestors or of some higher departmental deity. It is possible that the rôle played by the spider in Hausa and other Negro folk-lore is due to an earlier association of the spider with ancestral ghosts. As the spider is easily attracted by the beer or beer-lees used in religious ceremonies it might easily come to be regarded as the means by which the dead reveal themselves to the living, and thus reach the stage of being considered the wisest of created things. On the other hand, there is the possibility that the spider, because of its innate ability to build intricate nets in order to capture its prey, has come to be regarded as having an intelligence so similar to that of human beings that it is considered the embodiment of the soul of some human being who has passed to the realms beyond.

CHAMBA (OF DONGA) VOCABULARY

Per Bila of Donga

1.	Head	Yilá	jila
2.	Hair	Gissá	gɪssa
3.	Eye	Nuwa	nuwa
	Two eyes	Nuwa yira	nuwa jira
4.	Ear	Tunga	tuŋa
	Two ears	Tunga yira	tuŋa jira
5.	Nose	Nyirá	njira
6.	One tooth	Nigila ningini	nɪgɪla nɪŋɪni
	Five teeth	Nigila nuna	nɪgɪla nuna
7.	Tongue	Mella	mɛlla
8.	Neck	Galá	gala
9.	Breast (woman's)	Voma	vɔma
10.	Heart	Tema	tɛma
11.	Belly	Usará	usara
12.	Back	Penga	peŋa
13.	Arm	Ngena	ŋena
14.	Hand	Ngena	ŋena
	Two hands	Ngena ti yira	ŋena ti jira
15.	Finger	Niwa yila	niwa jila
	Five fingers	Niwa yil tanuná	niwa jil tɪ nuna
16.	Finger nail	Ninkissá	nɪnkɪssa
17.	Leg	Duna	duna
18.	Knee	Dundūla	dundula
19.	Foot	Duntema	duntɛma
	Two feet	Duntem ti yira	duntɛm tɪ jira
20.	Man (person)	Noá	noa
	Ten people	Noa kup	noa kup
21.	Man (not woman)	Novánduá	no vandua
	Two men	Novando yira	no vando jira
22.	Woman	Nokendoa	no kɛndoa
	Two women	Nokendo yira	no kɛndo jira
23.	Child	Gwavella	gwavɛlla

24.	Father	Bá	ba
25.	Mother	Ná	na
26.	Slave	Kwasa	kwasa
27.	Chief	Gará	gara
28.	Friend	Wazera	wazɛr˜a
29.	Smith	Lama	lama
30.	Doctor	Nenubia	nɛnubia
31.	One finger	Niwa yila ningini	niwa jila nɪŋɪni
32.	Two fingers	Niwa yila ti yira	niwa jila ti jira
33.	Three fingers	Niwa yila ti tora	niwa jila tɪ tora
34.	Four fingers	Niwa yila ti nara	niwa jila tɪ nara
35.	Five fingers	Niwa yila ti nuna	niwa jila tɪ nuna
36.	Six fingers	Niwa yila ti nonggwá	niwa jila tɪ nɔŋgwa
37.	Seven fingers	Niwa yila ti nongsinna	niwa jila tɪ nɔŋsɪnna
38.	Eight fingers	Niwa yila ti daukat	niwa jila tɪ daukət
39.	Nine fingers	Niwa yila ti ligit	niwa jila tɪ ligɪt
40.	Ten fingers	Niwa yila ti kwop	niwa jila tɪ kwop
41.	Eleven fingers	Niwa yila ti kwop zhe ninga	niwa jila tɪ kwop ʒe nɪŋa
42.	Twelve fingers	Niwa yila ti kwop zhe yira	niwa jila tɪ kwop ʒe jira
	Thirteen fingers	Niwa yila ti kwop zhe tora	niwa jila tɪ kwop ʒe tora
43.	Twenty fingers	Niwa yila la ninga	niwa jila la nɪŋa
44.	A hundred fingers	Niwa yila la nuna	niwa jila la nuna
45.	Two hundred fingers	Niwa yila la kup	niwa jila la kup
46.	God	Nyamapá	njamapa
47.	Sun	Nyamlá	njamla
48.	Moon	Soá	soa
	Full moon	Sobida	sobida
	New moon	Sopua	sopua
49.	Day	Nyamlá	njamla
	Night	Tigilo (or limbora)	tɪgɪlo (or lɪmbora)
	Morning	Wundu (or limta)	wundu (or lɪmta)
50.	Rain	Mwana	mwana
51.	Water	Wela	wɛla
52.	Blood	Nyelima	njɛlɪma
53.	Fat	Nura	nura
54.	Salt	Mum yeba	mum jɛba
55.	Stone	Bunga	buŋa
	Iron	Basa	basa
56.	Hill	Dengsa	dɛŋsa
57.	River	Welgba (Stream = weldela)	wɛlgba or wɛldɛla
58.	Road	Kpanga	kpaŋa
59.	House	Wula (Compound = liga)	wula (lɪga)
	Two houses	Wul yira	wul jira
	Many houses	Wul kaya	wul kaja
	All the houses	Kwolle wula	kwollɛ wula

60.	Roof	Wul wabia	wul wabia
61.	Door	Wala	wala
62.	Mat	Tila	tila
63.	Basket	Pilinga	pɪlɪŋa
64.	Drum	Agangga	agaŋga
65.	Pot	Kela	kɛla
66.	Knife	Yera	jɛra
67.	Spear	Dinga	dɪŋa
68.	Bow	Tabtea	tabtea
69.	Arrow	Shira	ʃira
	Five arrows	Shira ti nuna	ʃira tɪ nuna
70.	Gun	La lebia	la lɛbia
71.	War	Buma	buma
72.	Meat (animal)	Gokha	gɔxa
73.	Elephant	Dona	dɔna
74.	Buffalo	Jella	dʒella
75.	Leopard	Gaá	gəa
76.	Monkey	Da	da
77.	Pig	Shira	ʃira
78.	Goat	Vuá	via
79.	Dog	Yekhla	jɛxla
80.	Bird	Nua	nua
	Feather	Nua gisa	nua gisa
81.	Parrot	Shingyare	ʃɪŋjare
82.	Fowl	Koá	koa
83.	Eggs	Ko bora	ko bora
84.	One egg	Bora ningini	nora nɪŋɪni
85.	Snake	Bisá	bisa
86.	Frog	Busa	busa
87.	Spider	Tamsá	tamsa
88.	Fly	Sakha	səxa
89.	Bee	Nura	nura
	Honey	Nurwela	nur wɛla
90.	Tree	Tia	tia
	Ten trees	Tia ti kwop	tia tɪ kwop
91.	Leaf	Anyisa	anjisa
92.	Banana	Kponkpono	kpɔnkpɔno
	Guinea-corn	Yera	jɛra
93.	Maize	Kpankara	kpankara
94.	Ground-nut	Kpangwara	kpaŋwara
95.	Oil	Kilima	kilɪma
96.	The tall woman	Nokendo buruwa	no kɛndo buruwa
	The tall women	Kem burobura	kɛm burobura
97.	Large dog	Yekhla gbaro	jɛxla gbaro
98.	Small dog	Yekhlan fifiwa	jɛxlan fifiwa
99.	The dog bites	Yekhl lum kiya	jɛxl lum kija
100.	The dog bites me	Yekhl lum eya	jɛxl lum eja
101.	The dog which bit me yesterday	Yekhl lum min nina	jɛxl lum mɪn nina
102.	I flog the dog	Ma yekhl li tiba	ma jɛxl lɪ tiba

103.	The dog which I have flogged	Yekhl li tibu nina	jɛxì lɪ tibu nina
104.	I see him (or her)	Ma be oya	mə be oja
	He sees you	Bemya	bemja
	He sees us	Be bi ā	be bi a:
	He sees them	Bē bi a	be: bi a
	We see you (pl.)	Mu beya	mu beja
	We see them	Mu be bia	mu be bia
105.	Beautiful bird	Nuwa sọna	nuwa sɔna
106.	Slave	Kwasa	kwasa
	My slave	Kwasa mabiya	kwasa mabija
	Thy slave	Kwasa mbia	kwasa m bia
	Our slaves	Kwasa bibiya	kwasa bibija
	Their slaves	Kwasa a babiya	kwasa a babija
107.	The chief's slave	Gar kwasa	gar kwasa
	His slave	Kwasu wobiya	kwasu wobija
108.	We see the slave	Ba bē kwasia	bə be: kwasia
109.	We call the slave	Ba ded kwasia	bə dɛd kwasia
110.	The slave comes	Kwasa titi ana	kwasa tɪ ti ana
111.	He came yesterday	Yā nina	ja nina
	He is coming to-day	Ti yai nyaio	ti njai njaio
	He will come to-morrow	Da ya kena	da ja kena
112.	The slaves have gone away	Kwasa be da ya	kwasa be da ja
113.	Who is your chief?	Garambia nere ?	gara mbija nere ?
114.	The two villages are making war on each other	Yeba yiri ti bum lana ka shi sa bebia	jɛba jiri tɪ bum lana kɪ ʃi sa bɛbia
115.	The sun rises	Nyamla ti vugiana	njamla tɪ vugiana
	The sun has set	Nyamla yimiya	njamla jɪmija
116.	The man is eating	No ti an lina	no ti an lina
117.	The man is drinking	No tu wal yina	no tu wal jina
118.	The man is asleep	No ti lem lena	no tɪ lɛm lena
119.	I break the stick	Ma ra ma kel bwasia	ma ra mə kɛl bwasia
	The stick is broken	Bwasa keria	bwasə kɛria
	This stick cannot be broken	Bwasa mwa kebia	bwasə mwə kɛbia
	Break this stick for me	En keb za bwasa yau	ɛn kɛb za bwasa jau
120.	I have built a house	Mu wo wulya	mu wo wulja
121.	My people have built their houses yonder	Nema bira wo wul abebiya wọra	nɛma bɪra wo wul abɛbija wɔra
122.	What do you do every day ?	Intini antasu ma nyema de kwọlle ?	ɪntini antəsu ma njɛma de kwɔlle ?

	I work on my farm	Mu tu antasu ma zo mil lesu	mu tu antəsu ma zo mɪl lɛsu
123.	I am going away	Ma ma dana	ma mə dana
	I am hoeing	Mu ti lese lama	mu ti lɛse lama
	I am going to my farm	Ma ra lesu	ma ra lɛsu
124.	The woman comes	Nokendo ti ana	nokɛndo ti ana
	She comes	Ti ana	ti ana
	The woman laughs	Nokendo ti lot lona	nokɛndo tɪ lot lona
	The woman weeps	Nokendo ti kpwen kpwena	nokɛndo tɪ kpwɛn kpwɛna
125.	I ask the woman	Mi ti nokendo fokha	mɪ tɪ nokɛndo fɔxa
126.	Why do you laugh ?	Amda inti lot loru ni sare ?	amda ɪntɪ lot loru ni sare ?
127.	Why do you cry ?	Amda inti kpwê pwero ni sare ?	amda ɪntɪ kpwê pwɛro ni sare ?
128.	My child is dead	Wamabe varia	wamabe varia
129.	It is not dead	Vat se	vat se
130.	Are you ill ?	Inki lam ke sene ?	ɪnki lam ke sɛne ?
131.	My children are ill	Yemabe i ki lam ke se	jɛmabe i ki lam ke se
132.	Her child is better	Wa wobe ki lam ke ya	wa wobe ki lam ke ja
133.	Yes	O	oː
	No	Aa	aˤaˤ
134.	A fine knife	Yer tsonkea	jɛr tsonkea
	Give me the knife	In pi mi yera	ɪn pi mi jɛra
	I give you the knife	Ma pim yeria	mə pɪm jɛria
135.	You are a European	Amda bature a	amda bature a
	I am a black man	Ma no dingdoa	mə no dɪŋdoa
	I am a Chamba	Ma Dinga	mə dɪŋa
136.	Name	Nigila	nɪgɪla
	My name	Nigil mabiya	nɪgɪl ma bija
	Your name	Nigil ambea	nɪgɪl ambea
	What is your name ?	Nigil ambe la ?	nɪgɪl ambe la ?
137.	There is water in the gourd	Welti bunu	wɛltɪ bunu
	The knife is on the stone	Yerta bung yilba bunga	jɛrtɪ buŋ jilba buŋa
	The fire is under the pot	La ti kel du	la tɪ kɛl du
	The roof is over the hut	Wulwambia tu wul yilba pau	wulwambia tu wul jilba pau
138.	You are good	(Amda) insonia	(amda) ɪnsɔnia
	This man is bad	No ayo son se	no ajo sɔn se
139.	The paper is white	Takarda birua	takard birua
	This thing is black	Ana yo ding doa	ana jo dɪŋ doa
	This thing is red	Ana yo ye loa	ana jo jɛ loa
140.	This stone is heavy	Bung na pia	buŋ nə pia

This stone is not heavy	Bung na pishe	buŋ nə piʃe
141. I write	Ma te an bara	mə te an bara
I give you the letter	Ma m takarda pina	mə m takarda pina
Carry the letter to the town	In ke takarda in para wulko tengo	ɪn ke takarda ɪn para wulko tɛŋo
142. Go away	Indana	ɪndana
Come here	Inyage	ɪnjagɛ
143. Where is your house ?	Liga mbe to ?	lɪga mbe to ?
144. My house is here	Liga mabe ti zom	lɪga mabe tɪ zɔm
My house is there	Liga mbe tu woda	lɪga mbe tu wɔda
145. What have you to sell ?	Impa tini lebe ?	ɪmpa tini lɛbe ?
146. I want to buy fish	Mu wọt ma dib leba	mu wɔt ma dib lɛba
147. The fish which you bought is bad	Diba lebdu sọn se	diba lɛbdu sɔn se
148. Where is the man who killed the elephant ?	Nera lo dọndo tibine ?	nera lo dɔndo tɪbɪne ?
He has killed many elephants	Lo dọn e kakeka	lo dɔn e kakɛka
How many elephants were killed yesterday ?	Dọna lo nindo tile ?	dɔna lo nindo tɪle ?
149. Untie it	Bin dau be	bɪn dau be
Tie this rope	Intabo ke kasá	ɪntabo ke kasa
Make the boy untie the goat	Impiwa ra binda vua	ɪmpiwa ra bɪnda vua
150. My brothers and I, we are going, but no one else	Mara ke ba sin dana ba ningini kunmabira	mara ke ba sɪn dana bə nɪɲini kunmabɪra
Brothers, let us go and tell the chief	Kunmabira kum je mara ba gará	kunmabɪra kum dʒe mara ba gara
151. This tree is bigger than that	Tiyao kana wọrio kangsella	tijao kana wɔrio kaŋsɛlla
Horses	Yabira	jabɪra
Horse	Ya	ja
Crocodile	Namená	namɛna
Houses	Wulbira	wulbɪra
I	Mai	mai
You	Amda	amda
He	Wora	wora
We	Ābira	abir˘a
You (pl.)	Aira	aira
They	Abebia	abɛbia

The *Chamba Lekon* of the Nasarao district, Adamawa Province, speak the same dialect as the Chamba of Donga, Benue Province. But they have preserved to a greater extent earlier customs of the Chamba. The penis-sheath, for example, is still worn by the older men, though it is never seen nowadays among the Chamba of Donga ; and in the matter of inheritance the matrilineal principle is more definitely followed than at Donga.

The Chamba Lekon of Kubi appear to consist of five social groups, viz. the Nyamkuna, Bingyela, Zamkuna, Nyerkuna, and Turkuna. The first, the Nyamkuna, are "the children of the Sun" (*Nyam* being = Sun) ; and they are also the royal kindred or clan. It is said that their ancestress bore a child who was red like the sun, and he immediately ascended to the skies and entered or became the Sun. The Nyamkuna have the women's cult of Vonkima, and it was stated that the reason why the hoe is the symbol of this cult is that the Nyamkuna first introduced hoes and seeds to the people. The children of the Sun were thus traditionally the introducers of a higher form of culture (as Dr. W. J. Perry maintains). The name of the second clan, Bingyela, means "the stones" ; and the interpretation given of this nickname is that they are hard as stones ; they survive all knocks. The Zamkuna are "the children of the mist"; for it is related that the ancestress of this clan bore a child who turned into mist and floated away to the upper air. They are the rain-makers, the rain-shrine consisting of three small white stones surrounded by monoliths. A pot is set on the top of the stones, and when the rains are due the priestly head of the clan removes the pot, fills it with beer, and pours libations on the stones, together with the blood of a pullet and a prayer that there may be a sufficiency of rain throughout the agricultural year. In the event of a drought the chief calls on the priest of the Zamkuna to perform the customary rites. As the priest pours the libation he says, "This custom I received from our forefathers, for we are the children of the mist. Let the rain therefore descend that our crops may not be withered up." A chicken is sacrificed and the blood is allowed to drip over the stones. The priest drinks some of the beer and shares with his family the flesh of the chicken. It is said that before he reaches home he is met with torrential rain. The priest may not have sexual relations for the three days preceding the rites, and it is believed that his displeasure is sufficient of itself to cause a drought. The Nyerkuna are " the children of the blind ". For their ancestor was born blind, and her descendants are permitted to behave in the irresponsible fashion which is the privilege of the blind. The word Turkuna is said to mean " the few ". For though their numbers are small they are not to be despised.

The clans are not nowadays exogamous, and there is no definite totemism, though the frog and lizard are taboo to all the Lekon. The social groups are not localized, being held together merely by the possession of a common name and common cult. Thus at the yam-harvest and sprouting of the corn each clan performs its own rites. The members of one clan may attend the dances but may not witness the rites of another clan, unless a special fee of a goat and chicken is paid. The object in being thus co-opted into the cult of another clan is to secure the assistance of that cult in addition to one's own.

The harvest-ritual in such a case is as follows. Beer and large quantities of food are prepared by the clan concerned, and after offerings have been made by the priest to the ancestors and deities, he distributes the beer and food among the senior members of the various households, saying that they are to-day permitted by the gods to eat of the new yams and also to eat new guinea-corn as soon as it ripens. The goat and chicken of the strangers are sacrificed ; and the priest addresses the strangers, saying : " To-day you have given a goat and chicken to our cult. We have shown you the rites in order that if you meet the object of our worship he shall know you and you shall know him."

All the clans have the same Voma cult, but each clan has its own special remedy for healing the diseases caused by Voma, a species of tuber or root, which the priest cuts up and smears on the sick man's face and body. Though there is a central chief for all the clans, the priest-chief of each clan is held responsible for the good conduct of the members of his own clan. He draws the attention of heads of households to any misbehaviour on the part of a member of a household, and he reports to the central chief the more serious offences, himself sitting with the chief as an assessor during the hearing of the case.

In former times, however, each clan constituted an independent political unit ; and if two clans quarrelled the matter was settled by the ordeal of sasswood, administered by a member of a third clan who understood the ritual. If the accused member of one clan was proved guilty, i.e. did not vomit the sasswood, he was generally set upon and cut to pieces by the members of the opposing clan. If the two clans were of equal strength a free fight usually ensued ; but if the accusing clan was stronger than the other the members would seize all the uterine relatives of the guilty man and sell them into slavery. Even at the present time relatives of men killed in the French Cameroons by the sasswood ordeal fly for safety to British territory.

Descent was formerly reckoned on the matrilineal principle, i.e. a person belonged to the clan of his mother. At the present time, however, the patrilineal principle is gaining ground, with the result that the old clan organization is breaking down. Children normally remain in the homes of their fathers or fathers' brothers, maternal uncles having no claim at all to the custody or economic services of their sisters' children. On the other hand a boy may, if he likes, abandon the home of his father for that of his maternal uncle, and this is so frequently done that it may be said that the Chamba Lekon are organized on a bilateral system. Any boy who gets into trouble will always seek the assistance of his maternal uncle, even though his father is a comparatively rich man.

As regards inheritance, also, there is a dual system ; for though sons inherit their fathers' compound, axe, bow, quiver, and corn, other forms of property are heritable by sisters' sons. Widows are not heritable by any class of relative, owing to the prevalence of the practice of wife-stealing. Under this system a man whose wife runs off with another man cannot reclaim his bride-price, pre-marriage gifts being only repayable in the case of betrothed girls who throw over their fiancé in favour of some-body else. Even levirate marriage is not found among the Chamba Lekon as a normal institution.

There is the usual custom that a boy may appropriate any of his maternal uncle's property during his lifetime ; but the present tendency is for uncles to discourage this practice. As regards female children the maternal uncle has little say in their upbringing, and no claim at all to their economic services or to a share in the bride-price paid on their marriage. The bride-payments are made to the father's family, the mother's family receiving only such share as the father's family thinks fit to offer. On the other hand, all boys are initiated into the religious cults of their maternal uncles as well as of those of their fathers. But it is the father and not the maternal uncle who sees to the circumcision of a boy ; and it is sons and not sisters' sons who inherit the ancestral skulls.

As regards marriage there is no strict rule of clan exogamy at the present time, it being permissible for a man to marry any second cousin. An instance was obtained of marriage with the mother's brother's daughter, but this was apparently an exceptional case, and it would appear that formerly all first-cousin marriages were taboo. Marriage with the father's sister's daughter is still taboo, for reasons which could not be stated. It may be that, as your father's sister's son is your father's inheritor, he occupies towards you the social position of a father, and his sister that of a mother. This is borne out by the relationship terminology, for a man addresses his father's sister's son as *bagira*, i.e. little father ; and his father's sister's daughter as *nagira* or " little mother ". The Chamba of Donga have the same custom, for among them a father's sister's son is addressed as *bati*, i.e. little father, while the father's sister's daughter is addressed by the honorific title of *mala* or " aunt ". Other principal terms of relationship are as follows :—

Father = *ba*.
Mother = *na*.
Son or daughter = *wama*. This term is also applied to a mother's brother's child.
Father's elder brother = *babaa*.
Father's younger brother = *bagira*.
Mother's brother = *muna*.
Father's sister = *mala*.
Mother's elder sister = *nagba*.
Mother's younger sister = *nagira*.
Elder brother or any elder cousin (except father's sister's child) = *moma*.
Younger brother or any younger cousin (except father's sister's child) = *kudvela*.

It is to be noted that among the Chamba there is an absence of the " playmate " relationship with cross-cousins (so commonly found among other tribes), and also with grandparents. Indeed, the only relatives who are really " playmates ", i.e. between whom all barriers of courtesy and respect are broken down, are a man and the wife of his elder brother. These relatives are universally playmates among all Nigerian tribes, and the explanation usually given is that they are potentially husband and wife by reason of the custom of the junior levirate. The Chamba Lekon do not, however, practise levirate marriage.

As regards religion the Chamba Lekon cults closely resemble those of the Donga Chamba described, including the cults of Voma and Vara. But, whereas among the Donga Chamba the cult of skulls is confined to the royal family, among the Chamba Lekon it is universal. The heads of fathers, paternal uncles, and paternal aunts are preserved by their descendants. The head is removed from the grave during the dry season by an old man, who addresses the skull, saying, " To-day we are going to take you to the house of your son. For it is not his wish that you should remain neglected in the bush. Do you, therefore, care for him as he cares for you. Hinder him not by bringing evil things upon him." He then hands the skull to a brother of the deceased, who puts it into a pot, which he carries to the compound of the deceased's eldest son, to whom he delivers it with words similar to those used by the old man who had removed the skull from the grave. The son never handles the skull or offers rites by himself. If he is ill or unlucky he goes to a diviner to ascertain which of his forefathers had caused his misfortune. He then summons an old man (any old man, whether he is a member of his own clan or not), who comes and removes the lid of the pot containing the skull of the ancestor indicated by the diviner. He smears the forehead of the skull with some floury water, and also the forehead of the descendant, saying, as he does so : " Your son repents of all offences committed by him against you during your lifetime. He has been unfortunate. If he goes out hunting he meets with no success ; if he plants corn it does not come up bountifully like the corn of others. If it is his neglect of you that has brought about this evil state of affairs, he asks your pardon. Hinder him no more, but let him, by your benevolence, be accounted among those whose hands turn everything to success."

A short list of words is attached for comparison with the vocabulary of the Chamba of Donga (p. 372).

CHAMBA LEKON VOCABULARY

1. Head	yila	jila
2. Hair	yilgissa	jilgɪssa
3. Eye	nuwa	nûwa
Two eyes	nuwa ira	nûwa ira

4. Ear	tunga	tuŋa
Two ears	tung ira	tuŋ ira
5. Nose	nyira	njira
6. One tooth	nigila yaham ninga	nɪgɪla jaham nɪŋa
Five teeth	nigila nuna	nɪgɪla nuna
7. Tongue	mella	mɛlla
8. Neck	gahala	gahala
9. Breast (woman's)	vuhuma	vuhuma
10. Heart	tema	tɛma
11. Belly	bakhala	baxala
12. Back	penga	pɛŋa
13. Arm	nena	nɛna
14. Hand	nen tema	nɛn tɛma
Two hands	nen tema ira	nɛn tɛma ira
15. Finger	nen yila	nɛn jila
Five fingers	nen yila nuna	nɛn jila nuna
16. Finger nail	nen gisa	nɛn gisa
17. Leg	duna	duna
18. Knee	dun lira	dun lira
19. Foot	dun penga	dun pɛŋa
Two feet	dun penga ira	dun pɛŋa ira
20. Man (person)	nenga	nɛŋa
Ten people	nenga kop	nɛŋa kop
21. Man (not woman)	ne vandua	nɛ vandua
Two men	ne vam ira	nɛ vam ira
22. Woman	keema	kɛɛma
Two women	kem ira	kɛm ira
23. Child	wa:	wa:
24. Father	ba	ba
25. Mother	naa	naa
26. Slave	kwassa	kwassa
27. Chief	gara	gara
28. Friend	wazera	wazɛrˉa
29. Smith	lama	lama
30. Doctor	gan tebia	gan tebia
31. One finger	nen yila ninga	nɛn jila nɪŋa
32. Two fingers	nen yila ira	nɛn jila ira
33. Three fingers	nen yila tora	nɛn jila tora
34. Four fingers	nen yila nara	nɛn jila nara
35. Five fingers	nen yila nuna	nɛn jila nuna
36. Six fingers	nen yila nangwos	nɛn jila nʌŋgwɔs
37. Seven fingers	nen yila nangshen	nɛn jila nʌŋʃen
38. Eight fingers	nen yila dagwa	nɛn jila dagwa
39. Nine fingers	nen yila dagogba	nɛn jila dagogɓa
40. Ten fingers	nen yila kop	nɛn jila kop
41. Eleven fingers	nen yila kop je ninga	nɛn jila kop dʒe nɪŋa
42. Twelve fingers	nen yila kop je ira	nɛn jila kop dʒe ira
Thirteen fingers	nen yila kop je tora	nɛn jila kop dʒe tora
43. Twenty fingers	nen yila la ning	nɛn jila la nɪŋ
44. A hundred fingers	nen yila la nuna	nɛn jila la nuna
45. Two hundred fingers	nen yila la kop	nɛn jila la kop

46.	God	vunera	vunɛra
47.	Sun	nyahama	njahama
48.	Moon	sua	sua
	Full moon	su bira	su bira
	New moon	su dia	su dia
49.	Day	nyahama	njahama
	Night	nyihama	njihama
	Morning	wundu lima	wundu lima
50.	Rain	wola	wola
51.	Water	nyunguna	njuŋuna
52.	Blood	nyela	njɛla
53.	Fat	nura	nura
54.	Salt	wuma	wuma
55.	Stone	banga	bəŋa
	Iron	basa	basa
56.	Hill	kolla	kɔlla

The Wom.—There is a group of 500 people inhabiting the area known as Wom, some 5 miles south-west of Nyibango in the Verre district of the Adamawa Province. These people have not hitherto been classified, but it is quite clear from their language and cults that they are Chamba, speaking the same dialect as the Chamba Lekon and Mumbake, of whom they are doubtless an offshoot. They call themselves the Pereba, a term which probably means " the Men " (compare the Jukun word *mpere* = man). They are known to the Verre as Zagai. Like their Verre neighbours they wear the penis-sheath, practise skull-worship, identify the Sun with the Supreme Being,[1] and peel the skin from corpses which swell up after death (see p. 435). Socially they consist of four groups, (*a*) Mamilo, (*b*) Pepto, (*c*) Kwolpero, and (*d*) Kaidiro. These groups are patrilineal and non-exogamous, marriage being permitted between members of the same group, including all first cousins except the father's brother's child. Monkeys and all classes of cats are taboo to all the groups ; monkeys because of their resemblance to human beings, and cats because they are sacred to the cults. (Anyone killing or eating a cat would go blind.)

The Wom have been considerably influenced by the Fulani, and it may be on this account that they display none of the matrilineal features found among the Chamba Lekon. Descent

[1] There are no definite Sun-rites, but prayers are addressed to the Sun through the mediumship of the ancestral ghosts. Four monoliths are set up, one at each corner of a rectangle, a fifth monolith occupying the centre. At harvest the priest takes some floury water in his mouth and spits it over each stone, asking the ancestors to beseech the Sun to send them prosperity. The Verre have similar rites.

and inheritance are purely patrilineal, and the mother's family has little or no say as regards the custody and control of children. As among all groups of the Chamba, the paternal aunt occupies an important social position, a position analogous to that of the maternal uncle among the more matrilineal groups. It is curious therefore to find among the Wom that the term for maternal uncle is apparently the same as that used among other Chamba groups for the father's sister. The Wom have a number of the cults (e.g. Voma) usually found among the Chamba. A short vocabulary is attached sufficient to demonstrate the close connection between the Wom language and that of (a) Chamba Lekon, and (b) Mumbake.

WOM VOCABULARY
Per Hamadiko of Wom

1.	Head	yila	jila
2.	Hair	yilgira	jilgira
3.	Eye	nora	nɔra
	Two eyes	no ira	nɔ ira
4.	Ear	tonga	tɔŋa
	Two ears	tong ira	tɔŋ ira
5.	Nose	shura or sura	ʃura
6.	One tooth	lela ninga	lɛla nɪŋa
	Five teeth	lel nona	lɛl nɔna
7.	Tongue	mella	mɛlla
8.	Neck	gara	gara
9.	Breast (woman's)	vama	vama
10.	Heart	tema	tɛma
11.	Belly	bana	bana
12.	Back	petiga	pɛtɪga
13.	Arm	nana	nʌna
14.	Hand	nan vara	nʌn vara
	Two hands	nan vaira	nʌn va ira
15.	Finger	nan vara	nʌn vara
	Five fingers	nan var nona	nʌn var nona
16.	Finger nail	pukpulla	pukpulla
17.	Leg	dona	dɔna
18.	Knee	don lingbera	dɔn lɪŋbɛra
19.	Foot	don temla	dɔn tɛmla
	Two feet	don temla ira	dɔn tɛmla ira
20.	Man (person)	ni dinga	ni dɪŋa
	Ten people	niding kop	nidɪŋ kop
21.	Man (not woman)	ned vana	nɛd vana
	Two men	nevam ira	nɛvam ira
22.	Woman	nekena	nɛkɛna
	Two women	nekem ira	nɛkɛm ira
23.	Child	wa	wa

c c

24. Father	baya	baja
25. Mother	maya	maja
26. Slave	gura	gura
27. Chief	gbana	gbana
28. Friend	veema	vεεma
29. Smith	lama	lama
30. Doctor	gisha	giʃa
31. One finger	nan va ninga	nʌn va niŋa
32. Two fingers	nan va ira	nʌn va ira
33. Three fingers	nan va tara	nʌn va tara
34. Four fingers	nan va nara	nʌn va nara
35. Five fingers	nan va nona	nʌn va nɔna
36. Six fingers	nan va nongwoi	nʌn va nɔŋgwoi
37. Seven fingers	nan va non ira	nʌn va nɔn ira
38. Eight fingers	nan va fatfat	nʌn va fatfat
39. Nine fingers	nan va ya gininga	nʌn va ja gɪnɪŋa
40. Ten fingers	nan va kop	nʌn va kop
41. Eleven fingers	nan va kop ka ninga	nʌn va kop nɪŋa
42. Twelve fingers	nan va kop ka ira	nʌn va kop ka ira
Thirteen fingers	nan va kop ka tara	nʌn va kop ka tara
43. Twenty fingers	nan va yi linga	nʌn va ji lɪŋa
44. A hundred fingers	nan va yir nona	nʌn va jir nɔna
45. Two hundred fingers	nan va yir kop	nʌn va jir kop
46. Four hundred fingers	?	?
47. Sun	ngama or ngamla	ŋama or ŋamla
47a.God	ngama	ŋama
48. Moon	shua	ʃua
Full moon	shu bimra	ʃu bɪmra
New moon	shu dia	ʃu dia
49. Day	ngamla	ŋamla
Night	lima	lima
Morning	lea	lea
50. Rain	yila	jila
51. Water	yila	jila
52. Blood	iema	iεma
53. Fat	anora	anora
54. Salt	wum vama	wum vama
55. Stone	pea	pεa
Iron	basa	basa
56. Hill	kolla	kɔlla
57. River	nga	ŋa
58. Road	kpanga	kpaŋa
59. House	wula (Compound = liga)	wula
Two houses	wul ira	wul ira
Many houses	wul dimra	wul dɪmra
All the houses	wul bi	wul bi
60. Roof	wul ngira	wul ŋira
61. Door	wul nganga	wul ŋaŋa

62. Mat	kilvonda	kilvɔnda
63. Basket	gbinga	gbɪŋa
64. Drum	shimsha	ʃimʃa
65. Pot	kela	kɛla
66. Knife	gbamsha	gɓamʃa
67. Spear	dima	dima
68. Bow	taba	taba
69. Arrow	shira	ʃira
Five arrows	shi nona	ʃi nɔna
70. Gun	bindiga	bɪndiga
71. War	bona	bona
72. Meat (animal)	namsa	namsa
Horse	sania	sania
73. Elephant	duna	duna
Crocodile	kwopta	kwɔpta
74. Buffalo	jarra	dʒarra
Sheep	mbera	mbɛra
75. Leopard	woeka	woɛka
76. Monkey	da:	da
77. Pig	teduma	tɛduma
78. Goat	vua	vua
79. Dog	iya	ija
80. Bird	noa	noa
Feather	no gibira	no gibira
81. Parrot	?	?
82. Fowl	koa	koa
83. Eggs	ko bara	ko bara
84. One egg	ko ba ninga	ko ba nɪŋa
85. Snake	bipsha	bipʃa
86. Frog	busa	busa
87. Spider	mala	mala
88. Fly	saka	saka
89. Bee	ngora	ŋora
Honey	ngorena	ŋorena
90. Tree	lara	lara
Ten trees	lat kop	lat kop
91. Leaf	ensha	ɛnʃa
92. Guinea-corn	gbera	gbera
93. Maize	diptura	dɪptura
94. Ground-nut	songwara	sɔŋwara
95. Oil	kilima	kilɪma

The next group is the *Mumbake*, who have not hitherto been identified with the Chamba. A comparison of the vocabulary attached with those of the Chamba Lekon and Chamba of Donga will demonstrate that all three groups speak a common tongue.[1]

[1] The Mumbake language is thus wrongly classed in *Northern Nigeria*, vol. ii, p. 138. It should be transferred from the Benue group of the Central Sudanic division to the Adamawa group of the Middle Zone languages.

The Mumbake also preserve the skulls of ancestors, identify the Sun with the Supreme Being, and have the Voma cult common to all Chamba groups.

They are located in the western corner of the Adamawa division. They call themselves the Nyongnepa and consist of four exogamous patrilineal localized groups, viz. Savenepa, Gonepa, Yagbajenepa, and Penepa. As among the Wom, cats and monkeys are taboo to all groups. The royal kindred of Savenepa has a number of additional taboo animals, viz. leopard, hunting-dog, donkey, and hyæna. The cat taboo, it may be noted, has a remarkably wide distribution in the Adamawa province, being found also among the Verre and groups of the Bachama and Bata. It will be observed from the notes on the Bachama tribe (p. 10) that there is among certain Bachama groups a regular cat-cult suggestive of the Ancient Egyptian worship of this animal. No Mumbake will touch any of the numerous species of cats, and if he were accidentally to shoot a wild cat at night in mistake for some other animal he would leave the arrow sticking in the body of the dead animal as a sign that his act had been unintentional. Were he to withdraw it he would go blind. The taboo on monkeys was said to be due to the observation that monkeys have five fingers like human beings.

The Mumbake, like the Wom, display few characteristics of so-called mother-right peoples. The mother's family has a definite claim on the first child born of a marriage, but it is clear that this claim is based at the present time on the bride-price idea and not on any inherent right, the extent of the claim being dependent on the extent to which the bride-payments have been paid up before the birth of the child. If the first male child's father had not completed his marriage-payments the child's economic services are placed entirely at the disposal of his maternal uncle. He has to work constantly on the farm of his uncle, to repair his uncle's house, to run messages, and to give to his uncle the principal share of all game-animals killed. He is said, in fact, to be his uncle's slave. When his services are considered to have reached a point equivalent to his father's bride-price deficiency the demands made upon him are relaxed. Even if the child's father has, before the birth of the child, fulfilled all the bride-price obligations the maternal uncle still has a special claim on the first child, though only to a modified extent. It is incumbent on the mother's family to see that the lad is duly circumcised and to bear any expenses connected with the rite. His marriage, however, is arranged by his father, but a first child can make inroads on his maternal uncle's property in order to assist his father. If the first child is a female her mother's family can in all cases claim a proportion of the bride-price given for her, the proportion being greater if the girl's father had not completed the payments. It will be seen, therefore, that the claim on the first child is considered as part of the bride-price. The claim is justified further by the custom which requires a man to live in the home of his fiancée's parents until she bears a child. The marriage is not regarded as completed until the girl becomes a mother. Looked at from this point of view the claim to the first child may be a survival of former mother-right conditions under which the husband lived in the wife's home and all children born automatically joined the mother's group. That this is more than probable is indicated by the rule that if a man's betrothed fails to bear a child in her own home after a number of years the husband is entitled to take her to his home, and if she bears a child there the wife's family has no claim on that first child. It is noteworthy also that on the death of a first child born in the mother's home the body must be buried by the mother's, and not by the father's, family. A first male also adopts the cults of his mother's family in preference to those of his father. It may be noticed in passing that abortion is practised in the case of conception by a girl who is not betrothed, or of a betrothed girl who conceives by someone other than her fiancé.

As regards the inheritance of property the patrilineal principle is followed, i.e. in the absence of brothers or half-brothers property is inherited by sons. Sons may inherit and marry their father's widows. A son is not allowed to inherit his own mother ; she is bestowed without any bride-price on some member of the son's family. If the mother elects to marry outside the kindred of her late husband a bride-price is claimed by the senior member of her late husband's family. The son would not claim the bride-price, as that would be considered to be tantamount to selling his own mother. The neighbouring Teme tribe have a similar rule. A sister's son may, as a favour, be given one of his maternal uncle's young widows.

When it is said that a man's son inherits property the term

son is used, of course, in the classificatory sense and includes sons
of brothers or paternal cousins. Brothers normally inherit
before sons. But it may happen that the deceased's elder brother's
son is older than the deceased's younger brother. In such cases
the inheritance passes to the former and not to the latter, seniority
being reckoned by years and not by generations. It is customary,
however, among the Mumbake, as among many other Nigerian
tribes, for a man to disinherit a senior son in favour of a junior
who has shown himself to be possessed of more discretion than
his elder brother. As regards a woman's property her pots and
necklaces go to her daughter ; the remainder to her mother,
mother's sister or daughter.

Authority in the family is vested primarily in the head of the
household, i.e. in a father, paternal uncle, or elder brother. The
maternal uncle has no control beyond that exercised over the
first-born child. He will, however, assist his nephew in time of
difficulties. The authority of the father's sister is less than among
other Chamba groups ; nevertheless she can requisition the
economic services of her young nephews when necessary, and
frequently acts as arbiter in disputes.

Religion.—I have a few notes only on this subject. The
circumcision rites closely resemble those of the Teme (see p. 493).
Each kindred carries out its own rites and has its own operator.
The lads are given a new name, and when they return to their
homes they cover their bodies with leaves and shroud their faces
with a curtain of ground-nuts strung on strings. They refuse all
conversation with their female relatives until the latter have
presented them with gifts. In the following spring they are
introduced to the cult of Voma, and are warned that the secrets
of the cult must not be revealed. They are also warned of the
necessity of obedience to seniors and of avoiding quarrels among
themselves.

The principal cult is that of Voma, which has already been
described. Prayers are offered to the Sun, which is identified
with the Supreme Being ; but there are no definite sun-rites, as
among some of the Jukun-speaking communities. The skulls of
old people only are preserved and pass into the custody of brothers,
paternal cousins, or sons. The skull is removed by one of the
family of grave-diggers and is handed in a calabash to the head of
the household, who deposits it under a granary. The male

members of the family are summoned and all deposit their bows on the skull. The head of the family then takes some flour and water, and addressing the skull, says : " To-day we have brought you to your home. Grant that we may have health, that our women may bear children, that our crops may be bountiful, and that when we go hunting in the bush we may find quarry in abundance." He then dips his finger in the floury water and makes a smear down the centre of the forehead of the skull. He also sprinkles the bows with a little of the porridge, using the head of a corn-stalk for the purpose.

Mumbake graves are of the same pattern as those of the Teme. The mouth of the grave is blocked by a stone, and in the case of old men the grave is marked by a monolith.

First-fruit rites are carried out by the head of the Gonepa kindred. He goes to the chief's farm and cuts some heads of corn with a knife which had been smeared in the juice of a certain tuber (" gadali ") commonly used in religious rites throughout the Benue regions. The heads of corn are deposited on a monolith. On the following morning the people assemble before the chief's residence, and the priest smears a little beer on the backs of the hands and on the shoulders of each man present. The lees of the beer are deposited at a cross-roads, and as each farmer goes out to cut his corn he takes a little of the lees and throws it into the middle of his farm. This rite is said to prevent the diminution (through the action of spirits) of the corn during the harvesting. The Mumbake have no women's cults, and in this respect they differ from other groups of Chamba-speaking peoples.

As regards material culture there are one or two noteworthy points. A square shelter made of woven grass is built out in front of the entrance hut of each compound. The bedsteads are low mud platforms without the usual fireplace underneath. At each end of the bedstead there is a well filled with sand which is used as a urinal during the night. I have not observed this elsewhere except among the neighbouring villagers of Kumba and Yofo. A further unusual feature is that in some huts there is a specially-built bedroom, a compartment shut off from the rest of the hut by a mud wall reaching to the roof. The object of this is to provide extra warmth during the cold weather. Many of the huts are decorated with representations in relief of snakes, men,

women, circles, and Arabic writing-boards, black, white, and red
pigments being used.   The pottery is similar to that of the Kona,
and in some of the huts there is a series of mud pillars used as
stands for pots, built in the Kona fashion (see *A Sudanese
Kingdom*, p. 449).   Pots are used for housing chickens at
night, being set mouth downwards with a hole pierced in the side
to serve as an entrance.   The base of the pot is surrounded with
stones, and when the chickens are housed at night the entrance is
blocked by a boulder.   The Mumbake do not nowadays wear the
penis-sheath, but it was stated that a penis-sheath of cloth was
formerly worn.   The women wear behind and in front aprons of
plaited strings of hibiscus fibre, a practice found also among the
Verre.   Leaves may be worn when it is desired to save the
aprons from excessive wear.   At festivals the younger women
wear aprons of coloured beads.

Mumbake Vocabulary

1.	Head	yila	jila
2.	Hair	yilgiba	jɪlgiba
3.	Eye	novara	novara
	Two eyes	nova ira	nova ira
4.	Ear	jinga	dʒɪŋa
	Two ears	jing ira	dʒɪŋ ira
5.	Nose	songra	sóra
6.	One tooth	nela ninga	nela nɪŋa
	Five teeth	nel nuna	nel nuna
7.	Tongue	mella	mɛlla
8.	Neck	gara	gara
9.	Breast (woman's)	vama	vama
10.	Heart	tema	tɛma
11.	Belly	bana	bana
12.	Back	mangala	maŋgala
13.	Arm	nena	nɛna
14.	Hand	nentika	nɛntɪka
	Two hands	nentika ira	nɛntɪka ira
15.	Finger	nengvara	nɛŋvara
	Five fingers	nengva nuna	nɛŋva nuna
16.	Finger nail	nengva yima	nɛŋva jima
17.	Leg	dona	dɔna
18.	Knee	dontingbila	dɔntɪŋbɪla
19.	Foot	dong vara	dɔŋ vara
	Two feet	dong vara ira	dɔŋ vara ira
20.	Man (person)	nedina	nɛdina
	Ten people	nekorokwop	nɛ korokwɔp

21.	Man (not woman)	ne venna	nɛ vɛnna
	Two men	vem kura ira	vɛm kura ira
22.	Woman	ne kenna	nɛ kɛnna
	Two women	kem kora ira	kɛm kora ira
23.	Child	wa	wa
24.	Father	ba	ba
25.	Mother	ma	ma
26.	Slave	gura	gura
27.	Chief	gbana	gbana
28.	Friend	mena	mena
29.	Smith	lama	lama
30.	Doctor	gangtia	gaŋtia
31.	One finger	nengva ninga	nɛŋva nɪŋa
32.	Two fingers	nengva ira	nɛŋva ira
33.	Three fingers	nengva tara	nɛŋva tara
34.	Four fingers	nengva nora	nɛŋva nʌra
35.	Five fingers	nengva nuna	nɛŋva nuna
36.	Six fingers	nengva nongse	nɛŋva noŋse
37.	Seven fingers	nengva non ira	nɛŋva non ira
38.	Eight fingers	nengva durtia	nɛŋva durtia
39.	Nine fingers	nengva yeningga	nɛŋva jɛnɪŋga
40.	Ten fingers	nengva kwop	nɛŋva kwɔp
41.	Eleven fingers	nengva kwop vung ninga	nɛŋva kwɔp vuŋ nɪŋa
42.	Twelve fingers	nengva kwop vung ira	nɛŋva kwɔp vuŋ ira
	Thirteen fingers	nengva kwop vung tara	nɛŋva kwɔp vuŋ tara
43.	Twenty fingers	nengva yillinga	nɛŋva jɪllɪŋa
44.	A hundred fingers	nengva ya kwop	nɛŋva ja kwɔp
45.	Two hundred fingers	nengva ya kwop jong ira	nɛŋva ja kwɔp dʒoŋ ira
46.	Four hundred fingers	nengva ya kwop jong nara	nɛŋva ja kwɔp dʒoŋ nara
47.	Sun	nyama	njama
47a.	God	nyampa	njampa
48.	Moon	sua	sua
	Full moon	su bira	su bira
	New moon	su la lina	su la lina
49.	Day	nyamila	njamɪla
	Night	limna	limna
	Morning	lena	lena
50.	Rain	yila	jila
51.	Water	yila	jila
52.	Blood	nyerima	njɛrɪma
53.	Fat	nura	nura
54.	Salt	nyung vama	njuŋvama
55.	Stone	nala	nala
	Iron	anglana	aŋlana
56.	Hill	kolla	kɔlla
57.	River	mwara	mwara
58.	Road	kpanga	kpaŋa

59. House	wutuka (Compound = liga)	wutuka (lɪga)
Two houses	wutu ira	wutu ira
Many houses	wutu kakana	wutu kakana
All the houses	wutu kudum	wutu kudum
60. Roof	nyera	njera
61. Door	wulunga	wulaŋa
62. Mat	kila	kila
63. Basket	soppa	sɔppa
64. Drum	ringgima	rɪŋgɪma
65. Pot	danglo	daŋlo
66. Knife	buma	buma
67. Spear	dima	dima
68. Bow	tapa	tapa
69. Arrow	sira	sira
Five arrows	sir ku nuna	sir ku nuna
70. Gun	bungzugaro	buŋzugaro
71. War	bonga	bɔŋa
72. Meat (animal)	nama	nʌmá
73. Elephant	duna	duna
74. Buffalo	zera	zera
75. Leopard	nambulla	nambulla
76. Monkey	da	da
77. Pig	bai	bəi
78. Goat	vua	vua
79. Dog	ya	jaː
80. Bird	nua	nua
Feather	nua gipa	nua gipa
81. Crocodile	kovra	kɔvra
82. Fowl	kua	kua
83. Eggs	kobara	kobara
84. One egg	koba ninga	koba nɪŋa
85. Snake	busa	busa
86. Frog	buza	buza
87. Horse	napanda	napanda
87a.Cow	na	naː
88. Fly	sarka	sərka
89. Bee	nora	nora
Honey	nu ila	nu ila
90. Tree	tea	tea
Ten trees	teo kwop	teo kwɔp
91. Leaf	yisa	jisa
92. Guinea-corn	tura	tura
93. Maize	izitura	ɪzitura
94. Ground-nut	kpwara	kpwara
95. Oil	kilima	kilɪma

Group B.—The second linguistic group of so-called Chamba comprises the units known as Daka or Dakha, and includes also the Chamba Tsugu, the Lamja of Maio Faram, and the Chamba of the Nasarao area. The language spoken by the members of this group is illustrated by the three schedules of words and phrases attached, the first representing the dialect spoken at Gandole, the second that spoken by the group of Daka known as the Dirrim, while the third is that of the Taram group of Daka. For purposes of comparison with the language of Group A the Gandole schedule should be compared with that of Donga.

Culturally the various units of Group B are not homogeneous ; for in some areas the social system is of a bilateral character, while in others it is definitely a mother-right system. Thus at Gandole the organization is of the same bilateral type as that of the Chamba Lekon, while among the Dirrim and Taram groups of Daka there are matrilineal clans, with a matrilocal system of marriage. The inference to be drawn from this is that aboriginal mother-right peoples, whom we may call " Daka ", were invaded by groups of " Chamba " who were a father-right people, or had become so as a result of close association with the Fulani. In some areas a fusion occurred ; in others the aboriginals accepted the authority of the invading groups, without finding it necessary to accept their father-right principles.

At Gandole and among the Lamja of Maio Faram the family is normally organized on the patrilocal and patrilineal principle, i.e. children *usually* live in their father's or paternal uncle's home, and in the absence of paternal uncles inherit the father's compound, and the father's cults and skull. A man's flint, bow, quiver, arrows, spear, axe, and sickle are also heritable by his son, it being said that a son must inherit his father's arms in order to defend the honour of his father's house. The mother's family has no claim on the custody of children, except in the case of a first child born in the mother's home. It is not essential, however, at the present time, that a woman should bear her first child in her own home ; for if the divining apparatus declares that she should bear her first child in her husband's home she does so (i.e. an inconvenient social obligation may be avoided by an appeal to religion !) The bride-price for a wife is primarily payable by a young man's father or paternal uncle, though a maternal uncle may help ; and the bride-price for a girl is primarily receivable by the girl's father or paternal uncle, the maternal uncle having no direct claim (though his permission for the marriage would usually be sought).

On the other hand descent is reckoned primarily through the mother, it being said naïvely that the mother's side is more important because a child in the womb dies if the mother dies, but does not die if the father dies ! Intermarriage with any known relatives on the mother's side is totally taboo ; but intermarriage with distant relatives on the father's side is permissible. Inheritance, moreover, with the exception noted in the previous paragraph, follows the matrilineal principle, i.e. property is heritable by brothers who had the same mother as the deceased, or, in their absence, by sisters' sons. Widows are not heritable, as they are free to return to their own homes ; but a man's concubine is heritable by his sister's son. It is the uterine relatives who are held responsible for debts and thefts, and in bygone days uterine relatives alone were involved in charges of witchcraft or when vengeance was taken for a murder.

Though the maternal uncle cannot claim the custody of his nephews, nephews may go and live in their maternal uncle's home if they wish. In times of illness they commonly do so, the maternal uncle paying the doctor's fees. A young man will always, in difficulties, appeal first to his maternal uncle. Indeed, the mother's brothers usually insist on coming to the help of their sister's son, on the ground that if this duty were left to the father's family the latter might consider that it had " bought " the child, and so could dispose of him in any way it pleased. It was stated that in bygone days a maternal uncle could sell or pawn his sister's son if he found himself in financial difficulties, and this would clearly show that, not so long ago, the group in question could quite definitely be classed as a mother-right people. Even at the present time a father will not prevent a son from obeying his maternal uncle's summons to perform a few days' work on his (the uncle's) farm. Custom also requires a young man who kills a game-animal to send what is considered the principal part (viz. the throat) as a gift to his maternal uncle.

A suitor is not nowadays necessarily obliged to work on the farm of the girl's guardians if the full bride-price has been paid. He is required to do so, however, if the payments are partial only. Abortion is procured in cases of conception by unaffianced girls, or girls who conceive by someone other than their fiancé, the means used being massage or various medicines (such as the fruit of the *Balanites ægyptiaca* tree). Unfortunately I omitted

to obtain fuller information on this subject ; to inquire, for
example, who counsels the girl to submit to this dangerous
treatment. The practice of abortion is possibly in origin a protest
against the appropriation by the mother's family of children born
in the mother's home. Among some tribes, e.g. the Kona, it is
quite common for a girl's parents to refuse to allow their daughter
to take up formal residence in her husband's home until she has
borne two or three children, all of whom are claimed by the girl's
relatives. Among the Margi, who also practise abortion, it was
stated that a child born in the mother's home never turned out
well !

Wife-stealing, or rather elopement with married women, is
practised, as among most of the other Chamba groups, the wives
being stolen from neighbouring villages (never from the same
village, and never from the kindred of one's own father or mother).
The husband who suffers the loss of his wife in this way is not
entitled to a refund of his bride-price ; he compensates himself
by stealing someone else's wife, preferably the wife of a member
of the same kindred as the man who had stolen his wife. An
enceinte wife who abandons her husband is obliged to send back
the child when born to the former husband. In some cases the
wife will return temporarily to her former husband's house in
order to bear the child !

Two other points may be noted, (a) that a husband may not
bury his wife until after the arrival of his wife's relatives ; and
(b) that menstruous women are required to follow a special path
in coming into or going out of the compound. It is said that in
former times the Chamba observed the rule still practised by the
Jukun, viz. that menstruous women are segregated in a special
hut and are not allowed to cook.   At the present time, however,
it is permissible for a woman in this condition to carry on her
cooking as usual.

Turning now to the mother-right group of Daka, viz. the
sub-tribes known as the Dirrim and Taram, these are located in
the Muri Emirate and in the mandated districts of Tongo and
Gashaka. The Dirrim are found at Kwagiri, Ganadere, Gati,
Garke, Gatijum, Zore, Gangume, Gambô, Duna, Gankushi,
Tukurua, and Jamtari. The Taram are found at Jamtari,
Kogin Baba, Gumti, and Adagoro. As some of these villages
are located in Nigeria and some in the mandated territory,

the sub-tribal grouping is not coadunate with the political boundaries.[1]

Socially the Dirrim and Taram are composed of matrilineal clans which are known as " *kona* ", " *kwon* ", or " *kon* ", a word which suggests that the tribal term of " *Kona* " means (as commonly in Africa) " The clansmen ". The Dirrim consist of the following clans : the Gbâdarakon, Gazangakon, Shirikon, Nyangakon, Yamkon, Chakon, Chinukon, Jiekon, Zungnakon, Uzhokona, Kwookon, Jangkon, Piekona, Gangkon, Sunkon, Tabakon, and Dungkon.

The Taram consist of the following clans : the Kokona, Lekona, Dampukona, Chakona, Toakona, Pikona, Kwakona, Waningkona, Mamkona, Zaukona, Ganguwakona, and Mazanakona.

These clans are not localized, as we may find (for example) groups of Lekona at Jamtari, Kogin Baba, and Adagoro. They are matrilineal, exogamous, and non-totemic. Marriage follows the matrilocal principle. The Dirrim and Taram Daka are, therefore, a mother-right people, like the Longuda, the Wurbo of Kundi, and the Jibu at the present time, and all the Jukun groups and also the Kam at the beginning of last century.

As the clan is matrilineal and exogamous it is totally taboo for anyone to marry any member of his mother's clan. Among most Nigerian tribes which practise kindred or clan exogamy the rule of exogamy is applied both to the relatives of the father and of the mother. But among the Dirrim and Taram Daka it is permissible for a man to marry the daughter of his father's brother or half-sister (by different mothers). In fact marriage with these classes of cousin is considered the best form of marriage. The reason for this is not difficult to discover. Under the matrilocal system a man is compelled to take up residence in his wife's home, and he loses close touch with his father's relatives. But if he marries the daughter of his father's brother or half-sister he can continue to live in his own home. Among the Kentu a similar reason is given for consanguineous marriages.[2]

Marriage with the daughter of the father's half-sister might possibly involve a breach of the rule of exogamy : for the respective mothers of the father and his half-sister might have

[1] Gatijum, Zore, Gangume, Gambô, Duna, Gankushi, Tukurua, Adagoro, and Jamtari are all located in the mandated territory.

[2] See the notes on the Kentu or Kyâtô, Vol. II, chap. xvi.

belonged to the same clan. In such cases the marriage would not be allowed. It is not even permissible, as a normal rule, for a man to marry a woman or even to have sexual relations with a woman who belongs to his wife's clan. A breach of this rule would, it is thought, entail an outbreak of leprosy among the woman's relatives. If a woman unwittingly had had sexual relations with a man whose wife belonged to her own clan she would demand a goat from her paramour, and give it to her maternal uncle in order that he might perform religious rites by which the consequences of the incest would be annulled. It was stated, however, that at the present time if a man evinces a strong determination to marry a woman belonging to his deceased wife's clan he may do so, provided he gives a goat to the senior member of the woman's group. But in this case it would not be possible for the child of his son to marry the child of his daughter.

It follows from these rules, coupled with the rule of matrilocality, that the Daka are, practically speaking, a mono-gamous people ; and they view with considerable contempt the polygynous unions permitted among other Nigerian tribes. It is claimed also that adultery is almost unknown. For women have little opportunity for committing adultery, as they live under the close supervision of their own relatives. The same reason operates to prevent wives seeking a constant change of husbands. From the point of view of sexual morality, therefore (in the European sense), the matrilocal system of marriage, as practised by the Daka, is infinitely superior to the patrilocal system of other tribes, whether pagan or Muhammadan.

A short account may now be given of the mode of arranging marriage. The suitor initiates his suit by presenting to the girl a ring and bracelet which the girl displays to her mother. The mother consults her husband and brother, and if it is agreed that the suitor is an eligible person the girl is told that she may wear the ring and bracelet. The suitor then sends a gift of salt to the mother, and after an interval he sends also a girdle which the mother ties round her daughter's waist. At harvest he sends two bundles of corn, followed later by a third bundle. These may be kept by the mother and shared with the father, or one or two of the bundles may be handed to her brother. On every occasion on which the suitor kills a game-animal he sends gifts of meat to the mother of his fiancée. When the girl reaches the age of puberty the young lad is invited by her father to come and take up permanent residence in his home, i.e. in the compound of his wife's relatives. The lad, thereupon, builds for himself and his fiancée or wife a hut in the compound of his parents-in-law, and when this is done he begins to have sexual relations. There is no formal bride-price. For the first year of his married life his conduct is scrutinized by the girl's father and mother and by her mother's relatives, especially as regards his industry in agricultural work. He is required to work during this year on the farm of his wife's father, and if he shows himself to be a lazy person he may be dismissed without any form of compensation. During his second year he is set to cultivate a farm on his own account, being assisted in this work by all the younger members of his wife's group. If in this year, or in the two or three succeeding years, he acts in a perfunctory manner he is subjected to general ridicule which will eventually force him to leave the group, unless he mends his ways. If he leaves the group he cannot take his wife with him ; and he has no claim on any children which may have been born. A man's worth is reckoned by his farming ability and not by any other form of wealth. It is said that a rich man may be wifeless, but an industrious farmer never. It is also said that no hard-working man need ever be afraid of unfair treatment by his parent-in-law. If quarrels arise between himself and his wife the wife's relatives will take the husband's part rather than the wife's. It is a proverbial saying that parents show greater consideration to their sons-in-law than to their own children. It is to be noted that if a chief marries he does not observe the matrilocal rule.

As regards the custody of children the strict rule formerly was that children belonged to the mother's group. The father had custody of the children as long as he continued to live with the mother, but if he abandoned her he was not at liberty to take his children with him. On his death his wife and children might continue to live in the home of her parents if they were still alive, and she might even elect to live there if her parents were dead and the headship of the household had passed to her elder sister's husband. But normally she would betake herself to the home of her maternal uncle or brother if she had not done so previously. If a man's wife died he might abandon his late wife's home and seek a wife elsewhere ; but the children remained in his wife's home or joined that of his wife's brother. If a husband and wife were childless, and the husband wished to leave his wife's group and take her with him, he could do so, provided the wife's father or maternal uncle agreed. But the latter would only agree if he had another son-in-law to look after him in his old age.

At the present time the rules governing the custody of children have been relaxed, and it is now possible for children, if they so desire, to accompany a father who decides to abandon his wife's home. Two reasons are assigned for this change. Firstly, it is maintained that, as travelling is now safe in all directions, children who accompany their father are able to maintain contact with their mother's home. And secondly, a refusal to allow children to accompany their father might be misinterpreted by the Administration as trafficking in children and as a breach of the laws against slavery. In actual practice, however, most children would refuse to accompany their father, not merely because they would be unwilling to leave their mother, but also because they would be loath to abandon the home they had known from birth for a new home among strangers. A man's relatives in the fullest sense are his mother's and not his father's relatives. An additional reason for children remaining with the mother's group is that inheritance still follows the matrilineal principle, i.e. children are entitled to inherit from their maternal uncles, but not from their fathers.

The normal rule of inheritance is that property passes to brothers by the same mother or to sisters' sons. Sons inherit nothing but what the father's brother or sister's son is prepared to give them. In practice it is usual to hand over some of the deceased's corn to his son, together with the deceased's axe, bow, hoes, and spears. The reason given for this concession is that sons are required to perform religious rites in honour of their dead father, and as this entails expense it is but fitting that they should be given a small proportion of the inheritance. Among the Dirrim the deceased's cults generally pass to his son, who takes them away to the home of his wife and establishes them there ; but among the Taram cults are inherited matrilineally like other property. Nevertheless, the Taram offer sacrifice to their dead fathers and paternal uncles as well as to their maternal uncles. If the heritor is living in some other village than that of the deceased he may leave the cults in charge of the head of the deceased's household, and come and perform the rites there when necessary. Similarly he may leave the flock of sheep or goats which he has inherited in the home of his late brother or maternal uncle, using them as necessity arises. The sheep and goats would, in such a case, be tended by the children of his late brother's daughters or of his sister. Widows are not heritable. The headship of a compound may be inherited by a brother (by the same mother) or by a sister's son, or by the senior son-in-law. Chieftainship is inherited matrilineally.[1] A woman's property is inherited by her sister (by the same mother), or daughter, or mother's sister's daughter.

The following is a list of the principal terms of relationship :

Da is applied to a father, father's brother, father's sister's son, and any male of a senior generation. A father's elder brother is referred to as *da bori*, and a father's younger brother as *da tirere*.

Nya is applied to a mother, mother's sister, father's sister, father's sister's daughter, or any female of a senior generation. A mother's or father's elder sister is described as *nya bori*, and her younger sister as *nya tirere*.

Kawo is a special term applicable to a mother's brother (m.s. or f.s.).

Sangko or *mie* is applied to a son, brother's son, sister's son (f.s.), mother's brother's son, and any male of a junior generation.

Sangko is applied to a daughter, brother's daughter, sister's daughter (f.s.), mother's brother's daughter, and any female of a junior generation.

Pwa vi is a special term applied by a man to his sister's son.

Pwa me is a special term applied by a man to his sister's daughter.

Biari is applied to a brother, a father's brother's son, a mother's sister's son, and any male of the same generation.

Biangwu is applied to a sister, a father's brother's daughter, a mother's sister's daughter, and any female of the same generation.

Karim = male grandparent (m.s. or f.s.).

Kari = female grandparent (m.s. or f.s.).

Kangme = any grandchild.

Gwom is a reciprocal term used between parents-in-law and children-in-law ; and also between a man and his wife's elder brother or elder sister, and between a woman and her husband's elder brother or sister.

Mashi is a reciprocal term used between a man and his wife's younger brother or younger sister, and between a woman and her husband's younger brother or younger sister.

Mangwashi or *Nuwô* (= lady) is a special term applicable to a maternal uncle's wife.

Shoa = husband.

Ngwo = wife.

---

[1] But recently the people of Gangume have adopted the Fulani rule of patrilineal inheritance.

The most noteworthy feature about this system is the classification of the father's sister's sons and daughters with fathers and mothers. This is due to the circumstance that the father's sister's son is the father's heritor, and therefore the social superior of the father's son. The father's sister is not distinguished by any special term, but the utmost deference is shown to her. Every time a man kills a game-animal he must send a gift of some meat to his father's sister.

CHAMBA (DAKA) VOCABULARY. (GANDOLE DIALECT)
Per Adamu of Gandole

1. Head	tii	tii
2. Hair	ti nusa	ti nusa
3. Eye	tuki	tuki
Two eyes	tuka bara	tuka bara
4. Ear	ta	ta
Two ears	ta bara	ta bara
5. Nose	nuuni	nuuni
6. One tooth	nyine nuni	njinɛ nuni
Five teeth	nyinbe tuna	njinbɛ tuna
7. Tongue	hlaa	łəə
8. Neck	guu	guu
9. Breast (woman's)	nyesa	njɛsa
10. Heart	teemi	tɛɛmi
11. Belly	gbella	gbɛlla
12. Back	dimma	dɪmma
13. Arm	wa	wa
14. Hand	wa temi	wa tɛmi
Two hands	wa teme bara	wa tɛmɛ bara
15. Finger	wamiti	wamiti
Five fingers	wamiti tuna	wamiti tuna
16. Finger nail	wanusa	wanusa
17. Leg	dingi	dɪŋi
18. Knee	ding luri	dɪŋ luri
19. Foot	ding temi	dɪŋ tɛmi
Two feet	ding teme bara	dɪŋ tɛmɛ bara
20. Man (person)	ne	nɛ
Ten people	nebo kum karara	nɛbo kum kərərə
21. Man (not woman)	lerimi	lɛrɪmi
Two men	lerim bo bara	lɛrɪm bo bara
22. Woman	uengwu (or nengu)	uɛŋwu (or nɛŋu)
Two women	uengwu bo bara	uɛŋwu bo bara
23. Child	miri	miri
24. Father	da	da
25. Mother	nya	nja
26. Slave	kaseni	kəsɛni
27. Chief	gangi	gʌŋi

28. Friend	mana	mana
29. Smith	kperi	kperi
30. Doctor	ne ganti	nɛ ganti
31. One finger	wamiti nuni	wamiti nuni
32. Two fingers	wamiti bara	wamiti bara
33. Three fingers	wamiti tara	wamiti tara
34. Four fingers	wamiti nasa	wamiti nasa
35. Five fingers	wamiti tuna	wamiti tuna
36. Six fingers	wamiti tuni	wamiti tuni
37. Seven fingers	wamiti ditim	wamiti ditim
38. Eight fingers	wamiti ditim karara	wamiti ditim kərərə
39. Nine fingers	wamiti kum	wamiti kum
40. Ten fingers	wamiti kum karara	wamiti kum kərərə
41. Eleven fingers	wamiti kum banuni	wamiti kum banuni
42. Twelve fingers	wamiti kum ba bara	wamiti kum ba bara
Thirteen fingers	wamiti kum ba tara	wamiti kum ba tara
Eighteen fingers	wamiti kum dutim karara	wamiti kum dutim kərərə
Nineteen fingers	wamiti mumnoni mi noni te be	wamiti mumnoni mi noni te be
43. Twenty fingers	wamiti mumnoni	wamiti mumnoni
44. A hundred fingers fingers	wamiti nu tuna	wamiti nu tuna
45. Two hundred fingers	wamiti nu kum	wamiti nu kum
46. God	suu (or wurumi)	suu (or wurumi)
47. Sun	suu	suu
48. Moon	su banani	su banani
Full moon	su banan tari	su banan tari
New moon	su banan pashi	su banan paʃi
49. Day	su tari	su tari
Night	takha	taxa
Morning	takh shinani	tax ʃinani
50. Rain	duri	duri
51. Water	wokhi	wɔxi
52. Blood	nyangi	njaŋi
53. Fat	beibi (or bebi)	beɪbi (or bebi)
54. Salt	gun nyenemi	gun njɛnɛmi
55. Stone	vani	vani
Iron	biebi	biɛbi
56. Hill	bumyosung	bumjosuŋ
57. River	danuri	danuri
58. Road	bono tiemi	bono tiɛmi
59. House	wuu (Compound = ya)	wuu (ja)
Two houses	wua bara	wua bara
Many houses	wua goonje	wua goondʒe
All the houses	wuje dot	wudʒe dot
60. Roof	wuti	wuti
61. Door	isa mume	isa mume
62. Mat	kirilami	kirilami
63. Basket	pilangi	pilaŋi

64. Drum	ganga	gaŋga
65. Pot	ji (or duu)	dʒi (or duu)
66. Knife	yakhi	jaxi
67. Spear	sami	səmi
68. Bow	tami	təmi
69. Arrow	wari	wəri
Five arrows	war tuna	wər tuna
70. Gun	bindiga	bɪndɪga
71. War	gakhi	gaxi
72. Meat (animal)	kaka	kaka
73. Elephant	kongla	kɔŋla
74. Buffalo	songi	sɔŋi
75. Leopard	gbe	gbe
76. Monkey	keemi (or pani)	kɛɛmi (or pə̃ni)
77. Pig	chii	tʃii
78. Goat	vini	vini
79. Dog	wona	wɔna
80. Bird	sa	sa
Feather	sa gibshi	sa gɪbʃi
81. Parrot	nameni	namɛni
82. Fowl	kpa	kpa
83. Eggs	baga	baga
84. One egg	baga noni	baga noni
85. Snake	ye	je
86. Frog	koyo	kojo
87. Spider	nyani	njani
87a. Crocodile	namani	namʌni
88. Fly	ge	ge
89. Bee	shino	ʃino
Honey	shiri	ʃiri
89a. Horse	nyani	njani
Horses	nyanbu	njanbu
90. Tree	timi	timi
Ten trees	tim kum karara	tim kum kərərə
91. Leaf	ya	ja
92. Banana	pantang	pəntəŋ
93. Maize	kai	kai
94. Ground nut	pangi	pʌŋi
95. Oil	momi	momi
96. The tall woman	nengu deri	nɛŋu deri
The tall women	nengu deri bu	nɛŋu deri bu
97. Large dog	wona wari	wɔna wari
98. Small dog	wona miri	wɔna miri
99. The dog bites	wona lomsheni	wɔna lomʃɛni
100. The dog bites me	wona lomete	wɔna lomɛtɛ
101. The dog which bit me yesterday	wona den lom nyemani	wɔna dɛn lom njɛmani
102. I flog the dog	nok vat wona	nɔk vat wɔna

(The " v " in vat is pronounced by drawing in the lower lip and exploding it against the upper lip.)

103.	The dog which I have flogged	wona den nokun varani	wɔna dɛn nɔkun varani
104.	I see him	n nyen kuri	n njɛn kuri
	I see her	n nyen kuri	n njɛn kuri
	He sees you	gon nyen ari	gɔn njɛn ari
	He sees us	gon nyen rari	gɔn njɛn rari
	We see you (pl.)	wora nyen buri	wɔra njɛn buri
	We see them	wora nyen i	wɔra njɛn i
105.	Beautiful bird	sha shemeni	ʃa ʃɛmeni
106.	Slave	kaseni	kəsɛni
	My slave	kasen me	kəsɛn me
	Thy slave	kasen we	kəsɛn we
	Our slaves	kasen wo bu	kəsɛn wo bu
	Their slaves	kasen	kəsɛn
107.	The chief's slave	gang kaseni	gʌŋ kəsɛni
	His slave	kasen ke	kəsɛn ke
108.	We see the slave	wora nyen kaseni	wɔra njɛn kəsɛni
109.	We call the slave	wora vit kaseni	wɔra vɪt kəsɛni
110.	The slave comes	kasen baroni	kəsɛn baroni
111.	He came yesterday	gon ba nyemi	gɔn ba njɛmi
	He is coming to-day	gon ba bani morani	gɔn ba bani mɔrani
	He will come tomorrow	gon ma ban takshini	gɔn ma ban takʃini
112.	The slaves have gone away	kasenbo gereni	kəsɛnbo gɛrɛni
113.	Who is your chief?	gang we ga mare ?	gʌŋ we ga mare ?
114.	The two villages are making war on each other	kam bara be wa gak nongani ding be	kam bara be wa gʌk nɔŋani dɪŋ be
115.	The sun rises	su yeroni	su jeroni
	The sun has set	su gbe nyeneni	su gbɛ njɛnɛni
116.	The man is eating	ne be wa li ni	nɛ bɛ wa li ni
117.	The man is drinking	ne be wa so ni	nɛ bɛ wa so ni
118.	The man is asleep	ne be wa lam lani	nɛ bɛ wa lam lani
119.	I break the stick	m bat timi	m bət timi
	The stick is broken	tim barani	tim bərani
	This stick cannot be broken	timan ma baranen so	timan ma bəranɛn so
	Break this stick for me	a bat timan dim nok ti	a bət timan dim nɔk ti
120.	I have built a house	n makhi wu	n maxi wu
121.	My people have built their houses yonder	ne me bu imakhi wu ba guri	nɛ mɛ bu imaxi wu ba guri
122.	What do you do every day ?	wi nakshi nya mogonane ?	wi nakʃi nja mogonane ?

I work on my farm	n tom pen tom be ban me	n tɔm pɛn tɔm bɛ ban me
123. I am going away	m be gereni	m bɛ gɛrɛni
I am hoeing	m be wa pen baneni	m bɛ wa pɛn banɛni
I am going away to hoe	m be gereni pen baneni	m bɛ gɛrɛni pɛn banɛni
I am going to my farm	m be gereni ban me	m bɛ gɛrɛni ban me
124. The woman comes	nengo be bani	nɛŋo bɛ bani
She comes	gon baroni	gɔn baroni
The woman laughs	nengo be zoneni	nɛŋo bɛ zonɛni
The woman weeps	nengo be kpani	nɛŋo bɛ kpani
125. I ask the woman	n vishi nengo	n viʃi nɛŋo
126. Why do you laugh ?	wi zoon be dim ya ti re ?	wi zoon bɛ dɪm ja ti re ?
127. Why do you cry ?	wi kpan nyare ?	wi kpan njare ?
128. My child is dead	mi me wu ri	mi mɛ wu ri
129. It is not dead	gon wu so	gɔn wu so
130. Are you ill ?	wi ga penwosatere ?	wi ga pɛnwosatɛre ?
131. My children are ill	memebu be wa pen-wosheni	mɛmɛbu be wa pɛn-woʃɛni
132. Her child is better	mi ke den tongi	mi ke dɛn tɔŋi
133. Yes	e	ɛ
No	aa	aꞩaꞩ
134. A fine knife	yakh shemani	jax ʃɛmani
Give me the knife	nyem yakhani	njɛm jaxani
I give you the knife	n nyara yakhi	n njara jaxi
135. I am a European	nok bature	nɔk bature
You are a black man	wi ne viri	wi nɛ viri
You are a Chamba	wi Sama	wi Sama
136. Name	yiri	jiri
My name	yirime	jirimɛ
Your name	yiriwe	jiriwe
What is your name ?	yiri we nyare ?	jiri we njare ?
137. There is water in the gourd	wok be na buni	wɔk bɛ na buni
There is a knife lying on the stone	yakh ba na bani	jax bɛ na bani
There is fire under the pot	ishi be tim ji	iʃi bɛ tɪm dʒi
138. You are good	wi shemani ba	wi ʃɛmani ba
This man is bad	neran ne ve	nɛram nɛ ve
139. The paper is white	saga burki	saga burki
This thing is black	penan be virki	pɛnan bɛ virki
This thing is red	penan be ji	pɛnan bɛ dʒi
140. This stone is heavy	vanan be ding dingi	vanan bɛ dɪŋ dɪŋi

This stone is not heavy	vanan ding men so	vanan dɪŋ mɛn so
141. I am writing	m bindiri	m bɪndiri
I give you the letter	n nyara saga ri	n njara saga ri
Carry the letter to the town	a te saga a geri yabara	a te saga a gɛri jabara
142. Go away	gen (or gyen)	gɛn (or gjɛn)
Come here	gera a beni	gɛra a bɛni
143. Where is your house ?	ya we be gore ?	ja we bɛ gore ?
144. My house is here	ya me ba beni	ja mɛ ba bɛni
My house is there	ya me ba guri	ja mɛ ba guri
145. What have you to sell ?	wi lepki nyare ?	wi lɛpki njare ?
146. I want to buy fish	n wo wuk lebeni	n wo wuk lɛbɛni
147. The fish which you bought is bad	wuk den wi lebeni wuk shemin so	wuk dɛn wi lɛbɛni wuk ʃɛmɪn so
148. Where is the man who killed the elephant ?	ne den but kongla ran ga gon be gore ?	nɛ dɛn but kɔŋla ran ga gɔn bɛ gore ?
He has killed many elephants	gon but kongla gonje	gɔn but kɔŋla gɔndʒə
How many elephants were killed yesterday ?	e but nyem konglabu nyakhare ?	e but njɛm kɔŋlabu njaxare ?
149. Untie it	a bishi kun	a biʃi kun
Tie this rope	tang ishi rani	taŋ iʃi rani
Make the boy untie the goat	a tap mi ku bushi vini	a tʌp mi ku buʃi vini
150. My brothers and I, we are going, but no one else	nok be ku mebu a ma ti gereni, ne don ti so	nck bɛ ku mɛbu a ma ti gɛrɛni, nɛ dɔn ti so
Brothers, let us go and tell the chief	be mebu verje a ma gang ma sarani	bɛ mɛbu vɛrdʒe a ma gʌŋ ma sarani
151. This tree is bigger than that	timan kanen timan gurani yi wari	tɪman kanɛn tɪman gurani ji wari

152. Last night I was in my house with a white man ; we heard a movement outside ; he said " You hear that ; they are thieves ; let us go and see ". We went, and I said " Who are you ? "and they answered " Nothing " ; but I said " You are thieves " ; so we called the police, and put them in prison.
nyem takha nokbe nyem noki a be bature pe ; wora wu pe dongshi ga ; gon saren " wi wuk penane ; i yilenbu ; a ve je ma ba zukeni ". wora gere n saren " von mabu re ? " i dingeri " tebe " ; n saren " voni yilenbu " ; wora vit dan sanda, pak bu yawu ri.

TARAM DIALECT

1. Head	shie (Sie)	ſie
2. Hair	she gibshi	ſe gıbſi
3. Eye	tuwi	tuwi
Two eyes	tu bara	tu bara
4. Ear	ta	ta
Two ears	ta bara	ta bara
5. Nose	ngwun	ŋwun
6. Tooth	nyin nuan	njın nuan
Five teeth	nyin tongona	njın tɔŋona
7. Tongue	lie	lie
8. Neck	mie	mie
9. Breast (woman's)	yisa	jisa
10. Heart	songo	sɔŋo
11. Belly	fu	fu
12. Back	kwom	kwɔm
13. Arm	wa	wa
14. Hand	wa na	wa na
Two hands	wa na bara	wa na bara
15. Finger	wa nyim	wa njım
Five fingers	wa nyim tongona	wa njım tɔŋona
16. Finger nail	wa missa	wa mıssa
17. Leg	gying	gjıŋ
18. Knee	gying kọọkhi	gjıŋ kɔɔxi
19. Foot	gying nana	gjıŋ nana
Two feet	gying nana bara	gjın nana bara
20. Man (person)	ni	ni
Ten people	ni kum	ni kum
21. Man (not woman)	lorom	lɔrɔm
Two men	lorom bara	lɔrɔm bara
22. Woman	nangwo	naŋwo
Two women	nangwo bara	naŋwo bara
23. Child	nyie	njie
24. Father	da	da
25. Mother	na	na
26. Slave	kasim	kəsım
27. Chief	gang	gaŋ
28. Friend	mana	mana
29. Smith	pie	pie
30. Doctor	jib gen	dʒıb gɛn
31. One finger	wa nyim noan	wa njım noan
32. Two fingers	wa nyim bara	wa njım bara
33. Three fingers	wa nyim tara	wa njım tara
34. Four fingers	wa nyim nasa	wa njım nasa
35. Five fingers	wa nyim tongona	wa njım tɔŋona
36. Six fingers	wa nyim kanoan	wa njım kənoan
37. Seven fingers	wa nyim kimbara	wa njım kımbara
38. Eight fingers	wa nyim dufwo	wa njım dufwo
39. Nine fingers	wa nyim kpanoan	wa njım kpanoan
40. Ten fingers	wa nyim kum	wa njım kum
41. Eleven fingers	wa nyim kum ba noan	wa njım kum ba noan

42. Twelve fingers	wa nyim kum ba bara	wa njɪm kum ba bara
Thirteen fingers	wa nyim kum na tara	wa njɪm kum ba tara
43. Twenty fingers	no noan	no noan
44. A hundred fingers	no tongona	no tɔŋona
47. Sun	suu	suu
God	Wurum	wurum
48. Moon	su balang	su balaŋ
Full moon	su kangkan	su kaŋkaŋ
New moon	su pashi	su paʃi
49. Day	su nuri	su nuri
Night	jokha	dʒɔxa
Morning	bong peren	bɔŋ peren
50. Rain	duri	duri
51. Water	wokhai	wɔxəi
52. Blood	nyang	njaŋ
53. Fat	bakhe	baxe
54. Salt	gum	gum
55. Stone	van	van
56. Hill	dori	dori
57. River	wogbari	wogbari
58. Road	baku	baku
Iron	babi	bəbi
59. House	wu	wu
Two houses	wu bara	wu bara
Many houses	wu changan	wu tʃaŋan
All the houses	wu piam	wu piam
60. Roof	wushe	wuʃe
61. Door	wu yishi	wu jiʃi
62. Mat	kiri	kiri
63. Basket	tangati	taŋati
64. Drum	bambane or gying	bambane or gjɪŋ
65. Pot	ji	dzi
66. Knife	yakhe	jaxe
67. Spear	sem	sɛm
68. Bow	temti	tɛmti
69. Arrow	weri	wɛri
	(lower lip placed against teeth to pronounce the " w ")	
Five arrows	wer tongona	wɛv tɔŋona
70. Gun	buingare	buɪngare
71. War	gakhe	gaxe
72. Meat (animal)	kyenna	kjɛnna
73. Elephant	kongla	kɔŋla
74. Buffalo	nam	nam
75. Leopard	gbeê	gbɛê
76. Monkey	gbin	gbɪn
77. Pig	sikhe	sɪxe
78. Goat	jun	dʒun
79. Dog	mwanin	mwanɪn
80. Bird	sa	sa
Feather	sa gibshi	sa gɪbʃi

81.	Crocodile	dokho	ɔxɔ
82.	Fowl	kpa	kpa
83.	Eggs	kpaga	kpaga
84.	One egg	kpaga noan	kpaga noan
85.	Snake	yie	jie
86.	Frog	kwoi	kwɔi
88.	Fly	ga	ga
89.	Bee	shi	ʃi
	Honey	shi wokhe	ʃi wɔxe
90.	Tree	ngwun	ŋwun
	Ten trees	ngwun kum	ŋwun kum
91.	Leaf	ya	ja
92.	Horse	nyia	njia
	Cow	nakha	naxa
	Sheep	temdi	tɛmdi
93.	Maize	ka yiri	ka jiri
	Guinea	yiri	jiri
94.	Ground nut	kpa goma	kpa gɔma
95.	Oil	mum	mum
	Jukun	Jukun	dʒukun
	Jibu	Kpaan	kpaan
	Hausa	Kausa	kausa

DIRRIM DIALECT
(As spoken at Kwagiri)

1.	Head	tie	tie
2.	Hair	tie lunshi	tie lunʃi
3.	Eye	tuwi	tuwi
	Two eyes	tugbara	tugbara
4.	Ear	ta	ta
	Two ears	ta bara	ta bara
5.	Nose	viene	viɛne
6.	One tooth	nyin nuan	njɪn nuan
	Five teeth	nyin toona	njɪn toona
7.	Tongue	hlere	ɬere
8.	Neck	gure	gure
9.	Breast (woman's)	nyisa	njisa
10.	Heart	cham	tʃʌm
11.	Belly	pu	pu
12.	Back	kom or dimma	kom or dɪmma
13.	Arm	wa	wa
14.	Hand	wa na	wa na
	Two hands	wa na bara	wa na bara
15.	Finger	wati	wati
	Five fingers	wati toona	wati toona
16.	Finger nail	wa nyisha	wa njiʃa
17.	Leg	ding	dɪŋ
18.	Knee	ding lung	dɪŋ luŋ
19.	Foot	ding na	dɪŋ na
	Two feet	ding na bara	dɪŋ na bara

20.	Man (person)	nyi	nji
	Ten people	nyi kum	nji kum
21.	Man (not woman)	lerim	lɛrɪm
	Two men	lerim bara	lɛrɪm bara
22.	Woman	nungwo	nuŋwo
	Two women	nungwo bara	nuŋwo bara
23.	Child	me	me
24.	Father	da	da
25.	Mother	nya	nja
26.	Slave	kasen	kəsɛn
27.	Chief	jang	dʒaŋ
28.	Friend	mana	mana
29.	Smith	kperi	kperi
30.	Doctor	jubjiê	dʒubdʒiê
31.	One finger	wati nuan	wati nuan
32.	Two fingers	wati bara	wati bara
33.	Three fingers	wati tara	wati tara
34.	Four fingers	wati nasa	wati nasa
35.	Five fingers	wati toona	wati toona
36.	Six fingers	wati tini	wati tɪni
37.	Seven fingers	wati tum bara	wati tum bara
38.	Eight fingers	wati dupo	wati dupo
39.	Nine fingers	wati kpânuan	wati kpânuan
40.	Ten fingers	wati kum	wati kum
41.	Eleven fingers	wati kum ba nuani	wati kum ba nuani
42.	Twelve fingers	wati kum ba bara	wati kum ba bara
42a.	Thirteen fingers	wati kum ba tara	wati kum ba tara
43.	Twenty fingers	no nuan	no nuan
44.	A hundred fingers	chingnoa	tʃɪŋnoa
46.	Four hundred fingers	wurum	wurum
47.	Sun	sun or shun	sun or ʃun
48.	Moon	su or shu barang	su or ʃu baraŋ
	Full moon	su barang tava	su baraŋ tava
	New Moon	su barang pashi	su baraŋ paʃi
49.	Day	su tawari	su tawari
	Night	takhara	taxara
	Morning	takh shino	tax ʃino
50.	Rain	duri	duri
51.	Water	wokhi	wɔxi
54.	Salt	gum	gum
59.	House	wu	wu

PLATE 34

A YOUNG MAN (Verre)

MEN OF THE VERRE TRIBE

[face p. 413

CHAPTER VII

THE VERRE

The following notes are the result of ten days' work among various groups of the Verre tribe with the object of ascertaining in a general way the character of the social organization of the tribe. The variations found between the different groups are so marked that they furnish a typical example of the danger, both in anthropological and administrative work, of generalizing from the group to the tribe. They also seem to suggest that matrilineal and patrilineal principles may exist side by side, being static rather than dependent on changing conditions (due, for example, to the result of the contact of a purely matrilineal people with a patrilineal). The Verre have been in contact with the patrilineal Fulani in recent times, but there is no evidence that the groups which have been brought most closely into contact with the Fulani are the least matrilineal. On the other hand the circumstance that one of the patrilineal groups has the principle of ultimogeniture (or inheritance by the youngest son), a principle totally unknown to me among any other people in Nigeria, is conclusive proof that in their case the patrilineality is not derived from the Fulani but is an ancient institution. Indeed, it is a boast of all the Verre groups that they have adhered to their ancient customs, and it is a fact that the patrilineal groups on the Verre hills have only come into close contact with the Fulani during the last decade.

As regards administration it is obvious that where the tribe is composed of groups displaying great variations in social practice the difficulties of administration are very much increased. Coalescence between the groups is harder to achieve, and the work of the Native Court becomes infinitely complicated. It is not surprising, therefore, that the Verre do not refer to the Muslim Alkali any disputes relating to marriage, debt, or inheritance.

The title Verre is said to have been conferred by the Fulani, but it may have been used originally by others than Fulani, and possibly by the Verre themselves, as the word means " friend " in

the Verre language. In the Mumuye language Verre means
" men ", and as many tribes call themselves " The men " I am
inclined to think that this is the real meaning of the term.[1] In the
ordinary way each group calls itself by its local name ; and if they
use a generic term they simply call themselves Jiri or men,
differentiating the Jiri Gwage or Plain Verre from the Jiri Pai
or Hill Verre. The tribe numbers between nine and ten thousand
people, and the hill groups have only been brought under effective
administration during the last decade.

The local groups on which inquiries were made were the
following :—

A. *Gweri* (consisting of the villages of Masupa, Nati, Gezipa
   Sejipa, Gurumbe, Manipa, Wolupa, Deladi, Guriga, Batipa,
   and Zampa).
B. *Ugi* (consisting of Ugi, Bati, Zagrumpa, Zelago).
C. *Bai* (consisting of Bai, Kobsufa, Dogzai).
D. *Boi* (consisting of Boi and Wari).
E. *Marki* (consisting of Kura, Ningki, Girmago, Zamapa, Sambi,
   and Vomni).
F. *Togi* or *Tuki* (consisting of the villages of Tuki, Soli, Gurumpa,
   and Sheeba).
G. *Wom* (consisting of Wom and its hamlets).
H. *Zango.*
I. *Kwoi.*
J. *Lima* and *Donggorong.*

Of these the first six are situated in the Marafa's district (Verre),
the second two in the Yibango district, and the last two in that
of Mai Ini.

The existing mode of government is that the district,
comprising a large number of local groups or village-areas, is
supervised by a Fulani district head who is directly responsible to
the Fulani Emir of Adamawa. The district head acts through a
Verre village-area head, who in turn transmits orders to the
hamlet head. This system is not based on any pre-existing Verre
system, for the reason that the Verre, so far from having had a
central tribal government, had not even a local group government,
the highest centre of authority being merely the hamlet priest.
Even when a number of local groups combined for purposes of
war there was, as far as I could gather, no definitely recognized
central authority.

All the groups with the exception of Wom speak the same

[1] Vere is the more correct spelling. Compare the Jukun word *mpere* = man.

language. The Wom people are regarded as Verre, intermarry with their Verre neighbours, identify the Sun with the Supreme Being, wear the penis-sheath, preserve the skulls of ancestors, and follow all the most characteristic Verre customs, such as peeling the skin off bodies which swell up after death. But they speak a Chamba dialect, and it is clear that they are of Chamba Lekon origin. The majority of the local groups are also, each of them, a social group, i.e. follow a uniform system of social practice ; but the Wari villagers included in the Boi group belong socially to the Marki group. The Togi local group is, from the social point of view, a heterogeneous collection : for the village of Gurumpa is of Wom (and therefore of Chamba) origin, and the villagers of Soli, being blacksmiths, only intermarry with fellow blacksmiths of the hamlets of Bubabiriji, Bopa, and Belimpa.

Before proceeding to examine the social constitution of each group it may help to clarify the position if the following rough summary is given of the main characteristics of each group, under the heads of exogamy, totemism, inheritance of property, and custody of children. Firstly, as regards exogamy, there is no " clan " organization. In the first four and ninth groups intermarriage with all known relatives on both the father's and mother's side is avoided, i.e. the exogamous unit is the bilateral kindred. In the Zango group marriage is prohibited with all known relatives of the mother's family. In the other groups there is no exogamous unit, marriages being permitted between at least second cousins on both sides of the family. Totemism is not associated with exogamy in any group. However many features of mother-right the group may display the totem is always inherited patrilineally. Matrilineal succession to property is the rule in varying degrees in all the groups except Marki and Wom, in the former of which there is the remarkable custom of inheritance by the youngest son. In some of the matrilineal groups an exception is made in favour of the son as regards the inheritance of a compound. In all cases residence in marriage is patrilocal, and in most cases children remain in the custody of their fathers. Under certain circumstances, however, in a number of the more " mother-right " groups, the maternal uncle has a claim on one or more of the children born.[1] It will be seen from

[1] There are, as far as I know, only three tribes in the Northern Provinces in which children belong to the mother's group. They are (1) the Gure, (2) the Dirrim and Taram groups of Daka, and (3) the Hill Longuda.

this short summary that there is great diversity, and that in considering the matter in further detail the characteristics of most of the groups will have to be dealt with separately.

The first four groups may be reviewed together as they display greater uniformity than any of the other groups. They believe themselves in fact to be related in some vague way, and were accustomed to combine for purposes of war against such neighbouring groups as the Marki. In these four groups the exogamous unit is the bilateral kindred, that is to say that no one may marry into the kin of either his father or his mother, by kin being meant all those with whom there is a known genealogical relationship. Owing to a dual system of marriage (a) by a small bride-price which entitles the wife's family to the custody of children, and (b) by a large bride-price which entitles the father to the custody of the children, the kin are scattered about in various hamlets and villages and even local groups. The knowledge of one's kin is maintained by the meeting of all the members of the kin at circumcision and funeral ceremonies, and also by the custom which requires a woman who bears a child to present the child to his various relatives as soon as he is able to walk. In a hamlet or village you may find members of several kindreds ; the kindred is not, as among some tribes, co-terminous with the hamlet or village, and is therefore of small importance from the administrative point of view, the kindred head being over-shadowed by the hamlet priest.

With each kindred is associated one or more animal emblems or totems which are transmitted patrilineally, but as most of the kindreds in any given group share the same totem or combination of totems it is clear that the totemism has at the present time no connection with exogamy. Kindreds and individuals having the same totem may and do intermarry. It was stated that the totem animals were taboo to the local hamlet cult, but this would not explain why certain species of animals should be associated with certain kindreds in a large group of hamlets. I did not pursue this matter further, as it would have involved much work in taking genealogies without the prospect of arriving at any satisfactory conclusions. It is possible that the local group at one time constituted a single exogamous clan and that this organization broke down when the custom of a high bride-price was introduced—a custom which deprived the wife's

family of the custody of the children. But this is merely
assumption, and is not supported by evidence from other groups
where the custom of a higher bride-price as against a lower is not
found, and where the totemic grouping is always patrilineal,
though matrilineal conditions predominate.

The animals most generally respected in the Gweri group are
the bush-cat and monkey, both of them taboo to sections of
various other groups also. No particular species of monkey was
indicated, and it was stated that the taboo was due to the
resemblance which monkeys bear to human beings ! In the Ugi
group many kindreds refrain from hunting or killing reed buck or
hunting dogs. Any one breaking the taboo would, it is believed,
be stricken with blindness.

As regards mother-right conditions it is clear that in the
groups we are considering the wife has a social status superior to
that among purely patrilineal peoples. To take a few examples—
a husband would never think of selling any of his own or the
household property such as corn or stock without first obtaining
his wife's permission. He would not even buy anything with his
own money without first asking his wife ; otherwise she might
say that she would not have the article bought brought into the
house ! Or again, if a stranger comes to the house and asks for
accommodation for the night, the husband would normally refer
the matter to his wife. If the husband's brother pays a visit the
husband would not give him a gift such as a chicken without first
receiving the special permission of the wife ; whereas if the wife's
brother visits the compound she would give him a gift without
reference to her husband. Women assist their husbands in
agricultural work doing the sowing and reaping. They have their
own ground-nut farms, and a husband is required by custom to
help his wife in cultivating these. If he refused she would leave
him. They have their own religious cults from which men are
totally excluded. If a man introduced himself to the shrine of
the women, he would, it is said, lose his virility. The reason
assigned by the natives for the high position occupied by the wife
is that wives are difficult to obtain and have to be kept humoured.
This does not cover all the ground, as we shall see. It is noteworthy that if anyone is asked who are his kin he usually, in the
first instance, specifies the kin of his mother, on the ground that
(a) it is customary to do so, (b) that inheritance is mainly

E e

matrilineal, and (c) in times of stress it is to your mother's family
you look rather than your father's.

As regards the custody and control of children this is, in
theory at least, dependent on the form of marriage contract.
For as among the Munshi, Bade, and some other tribes, a wife
may be obtained either (a) by the payment of a small bride-price
such as ten hoes, or (b) by the payment of a large bride-price
such as 40 hoes or more, plus a long period of agricultural and
other economic services rendered to the parents of the girl. In
the former case the wife's parents or brothers have a claim on all
children born of the marriage, though they may not and commonly
do not exercise their rights so long as the husband and wife
continue to live together, and the husband keeps on good terms,
by means of gifts, with the wife's parents. But, owing to the
prevalence of the custom of wife-stealing, marriages are easily
dissolved, and the runaway wife is then entitled to take the
children of the marriage with her to her new house or to send them
to the home of her parents.

In the form of marriage in which the bride-price is high the
position is reversed, for the father retains the custody of the
children. The wife and her fertility are purchased, though it is an
offence for a husband to say to a wife that he has " bought " her
and can do as he pleases with her. (In such a case she would lay
a complaint with the priest, and her family might, if strong enough
and wealthy enough, take her away from the husband, repaying
all the marriage expenses.) In spite of the above general rules
boys and girls often decide for themselves whether they will live
in the home of their parents or of their mother's relatives.

Where the bride-price is high the duty of circumcising sons
and introducing them to the cult falls on the father ; but where
the bride-price is small the maternal uncle is primarily responsible
for these duties, though the father also bears a share in the
expenses. But whatever is the form of marriage it is the maternal
relatives who perform the burial rites. It would be a gross offence
for a father to bury a son without summoning the deceased boy's
maternal uncle. Vice versa, however, it would also be an offence
for a maternal uncle to bury a nephew who had died in his
compound without summoning the lad's father. A suitor for the
hand of a girl who is living with her parents presents his gifts to
them ; but if the girl's parents had married on a small bride-price

PLATE 35

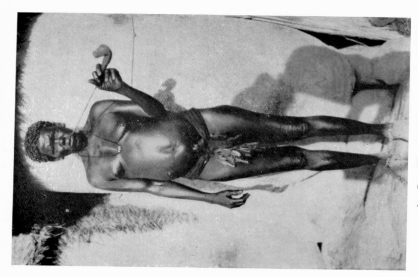

Men wearing Penis-sheath (Verre)

An Old Woman (Verre)

[face p. 418

her maternal uncle could, if he liked, appropriate all the gifts. Even if the parents had married on the high bride-price, the permission of the girl's maternal uncle had to be obtained, and he would also receive some share of the gifts. Similarly, the marriage of a boy whose parents had married on the small bride-price is arranged primarily by his maternal uncle, the father contributing to the best of his ability. But if the boy's parents had married on the larger bride-price the father is primarily responsible ; in this case, however, the maternal uncle actually meets a considerable amount of the lad's marriage expenses, for the fact that the lad's parents had married on the larger dowry does not rob him of his right to invade his maternal uncle's home and appropriate anything he can lay his hands on, a privilege which he uses to the full during the period of courtship.

In the matter of inheritance matrilineal succession is (with the exception noted below) the normal rule ; that is to say, that a man's compound, farm, corn, and other property including widows are inherited by the most senior of his sister's sons. An exception is made as regards the spear and axe of the deceased which are heritable by sons and not by sisters' sons. A sister's son who inherits his maternal uncle's compound becomes responsible for the young children of the deceased and arranges their marriage. He is, of course, responsible also for any debts his uncle may have left, just as in his lifetime the uncle was bound to pay his nephew's debts and come to his assistance in any difficulties which overtook him. It was by reason of the maternal uncle's responsibility for his nephew that he (the uncle) was said to have the right of selling his nephew into slavery, a right which a father could not exercise. For a worthless nephew who, by crime or reckless living, was constantly causing his mother's family to be mulcted in damages, became a burden too heavy to bear and the only remedy was to sell him out of the community. It is to be noted also that a conviction for witchcraft involved not merely the witch[1] but all his uterine relatives. The reason for this was said to be, not that witchcraft was transmitted through the mother (as the Jukun and Chamba believe), but because the witch's property was seizable, and it was advisable to get rid of his relatives (i.e. his uterine relatives). This statement would seem to indicate that matrilineal succession was the ancient normal Verre custom. But at the present time succession to property is not always

---

[1] A witch in Nigeria may be either a male or female.

wholly matrilineal. For where a man's father had married his wife on the higher bride-price system the sister's son may waive his claim to the compound in favour of the son and may also allow the son some share in his father's property.

The reason assigned for this was that a woman married on the higher scale is regarded as having in a sense been bought out of her own family group together with any children she may bear, and that her position is to some extent analogous to that of a slave wife whose children, having no maternal uncle to look to, depend for their inheritance on their father. The analogy is not of course exact, but it would seem to be clear that the object of the higher bride-price is to redeem the children from servitude to the wife's group. It has not followed as a consequence in these Verre groups that the children thereby lose the sister's sons privileges of inheritance, but there is a tendency in that direction, and I know of other tribes (e.g. the Bade) where children who are the result of a marriage on the higher bride-price system are totally excluded from sharing in the inheritance of their maternal uncle.

The analogy of the slave wife is interesting, as throwing light on the factors that may operate to transform a matrilineal into a patrilineal people. It is even possible that the system of the higher bride-price, as compared with a lower, has its origin in slavery practices.

Summing up the evidence for these four groups we may say that though totems and cults are inherited patrilineally and though the exogamous group is as much that of the father as of the mother, and that in certain cases the father retains the custody of the children, nevertheless it is the mother's family which is the stronger social influence.

The next group, that of Marki, presents a striking social contrast to the groups just considered. It is wholly patrilineal and there is no exogamy, marriage of second cousins on both sides of the family being permissible (and several instances of such marriages were given). The maternal uncle has no claim on any children. He cannot as in the previous groups requisition at will the economic services of his nephews ; if he wishes their assistance he must first obtain the father's consent. The nephew, however, may, as is usual throughout Nigeria, appropriate any of his maternal uncle's property. Wives have less authority in the household, and any property they have at death is heritable by the husband. Society is divided into a number of local groups the members of each of which are united by a belief that they are of one patrilineal stock. Each group has its own cult and its totem associated with the cult. Thus at Kura there are five local groups as follows :—

Verni	. .	totem goat.
Kuri	. .	,, bush-cat and all monkeys.
Kambi	. .	,, bush-cat and baboon.
Vomni	. .	,, pig.
Marasi	. .	,, sheep.

The most remarkable feature about this group is the custom of ultimogeniture or inheritance by the youngest son, a custom I have not elsewhere encountered in the Northern Provinces ; and it is interesting to speculate whether this is an instance of independent origin or transmission ; whether it originated from the consideration that, as a man has already provided for his elder sons during his lifetime, he is in duty bound to provide for his youngest son after his death (the origin no doubt of the rule in Borough English) ; or whether the Verre were at one time in contact with some foreign people—Semites, perhaps (if we remember the story of Benjamin)—who introduced the custom.

Among the Marki Verre the youngest son inherits not merely his father's compound, but all his property including his father's widows (whom, however, he does not himself marry). It may be asked how in practice the principle works, for it must frequently happen that the youngest son is a mere boy incapable of taking control of the inheritance. Among the Marki it is the rule that as soon as a son is old enough to marry he leaves his father's compound and establishes a compound and farm of his own. But where the youngest son is still unmarried the next senior brother remains in the father's compound in order to look after the younger brother. On the father's death the elder brother continues to act as his guardian until his younger brother marries and is able to take control of his inheritance. In the absence of a son a man's property is inherited by his brother, but here again it is not, as normally, the next senior brother but the most junior brother of all (provided he had the same father and mother).

Not only does the youngest son inherit his father's property but he also inherits his father's social position—he becomes head of the household. If he wishes to discuss some matter with his elder brothers he summons them to his house. If he decides to have one of his cows killed it is the elder brothers who perform the duty of killing, skinning, and cutting up, he himself taking no part beyond the actual division of the meat. If an elder brother gets into trouble he looks for assistance to his youngest brother, just as he would have looked to his father during his father's life-time. If he is unmarried and wishes to obtain a wife he expects his youngest brother to provide the major part of the bride-price. Moreover, it is the youngest son who inherits the family cult and becomes the custodian of his deceased father's skull. An elder son, therefore, who wishes to make a petition to his dead father must do so through the agency of his youngest brother, to whom he brings a gift of beer ; accompanied by his elder brother the youngest brother goes to the skull and stating the object of his visit pours some beer on the skull—the elder brother then repeating the petition on his own account. Further, the youngest son who has inherited settles disputes between his brothers, and it is to him that the village chief sends orders directed to the family as a whole. It may be noted in conclusion that if the youngest son who has inherited dies childless he is succeeded by his next senior brother.

As regards relationship terminology the noteworthy features are that (as in all the Verre groups) there is a special term for the father's elder sister (*mama*) and mother's brother (*man*). Great respect is shown to the father's elder sister who is in fact regarded as a female father. She may order you to perform any duty on her behalf. Every time you brew beer you are bound to send her a pot and she is entitled to the neck and part of the back of every animal shot. The playmate relationship is not a well-developed institution among the Verre, and it is noteworthy that in the Marki group one applies to male grandparents the same distant title of respect, viz. *domda*, that one applies to a father's elder brother and to male parents-in-law. This is unusual, but I have noted the same practice among the Bata, Bachama, and other Benue tribes. In the same way the term *baba* is applied to a father's younger sister, a female grandparent, and a mother-in-law. There is no playmate relationship with any cousin except the children of the mother's brother.

The next group is the Togi, and in this I confined my inquiries to the village of Soli which, as already stated, consists of black-smiths (known as Tibei). Blacksmiths are commonly in Nigeria an endogamous caste and the people of Soli only marry black-smiths of Soli or of the hamlets of Buba, Bopa, and Belimpa. There is among them no exogamous unit as all kinds of first cousin marriage are permitted except that with the mother's sister's child, a form of cousin marriage which is universally taboo in Nigeria (the reason given by the natives is that you may not " join two milks "). All respect the black cat and the monitor lizard, it being said that if these animals were eaten they would lose their skill in smithing. The rules governing inheritance and the custody of children are of the matrilineal type described for the first four groups.

The next group, that of Wom, consists of people who call themselves Pereba and are known to the Verre as Zagai. They speak a dialect of Chamba and are clearly of Chamba Lekon origin, having the well-known Chamba cult of Voma. They consist of four patrilineal divisions, viz. Mamilo, Pepto, Kwolpero, and Kaidiro. There is no exogamy, marriage being permitted between all first cousins except the children of two brothers by the same father. The inheritance of property is purely patrilineal, and the maternal uncle has no claim on, and very little authority over, his nephews. The father's sister, however, has great authority and occupies a position somewhat analogous to that of the maternal uncle among matrilineal peoples. It is of interest there-fore to find that the term for father's sister is the same as that for mother's brother among their Chamba relatives of Donga who, though not wholly a mother-right people, have succession in the female line. This might suggest that the Wom, who have come under Fulani (and therefore patrilineal) influence to a considerable extent, have changed in recent times from matrilineal to patrilineal conditions. The argument is not, however, convincing, for the importance of the father's sister is not a social factor confined to patrilineal peoples : in fact it has its most logical explanations under matrilineal conditions. You give great respect to your father's sister because her eldest son is the heritor of your father's property, and also of his social prestige.

The next group is the Verre of Yibango who call themselves Zango and are remarkable in that, unlike all the other Verre, they do not wear the penis-sheath, having had cloth garments from ancient times. In this group there is a mixture of father and mother-right conditions. Children reside with their father and sons inherit their father's compound. The maternal uncle has no claim on children under any circumstances. Cults are inherited from the father and no attention is paid to the cult of the mother's family. A man's skull is inherited by his eldest son, and prayers are addressed to paternal ancestors. A woman's skull is not inherited by a son but by a brother's son, for among these Verre also the father's sister is regarded as a female father; she can call on the economic services of her nephew at any time, and if he shoots beef in the bush he is bound to give her a share (the liver).

Totems, or the animal emblems associated with the cult of the kindred, are transmitted patrilineally. Marriage with second cousins on the father's side is permissible provided the second cousins had not a common great-grandmother. Intermarriage, however, with any of the mother's relatives however distant is taboo. Totemism has therefore nothing to do with exogamy, for the totemic group is patrilineal, while the exogamic group is matrilineal. The totemic group, it may be noted, may be regarded as a clan, scattered, frequently, over a number of villages. But the bond uniting the clan is religious rather than social—there was no clan government or union for purposes of war and no community of social functions, the clan merely consisting of a number of patrilineal kindreds united by the possession of a common cult and cult emblem. The maternal uncle has little or nothing to do with his nephew's circumcision or with the arrangement of his first marriage; and the bride-price for a girl is receivable by the father, though he may give a share of as much as he thinks fit to his daughter's maternal uncle.

On the other hand, the whole of a man's property (except his compound and a few arrows) is heritable by his sister's son, to the exclusion of his son, and the Verre of Yibango regard the mother's relatives as of more importance than the father's. In times of stress it is to his mother's relatives that a man looks. In cases of witchcraft the whole of the uterine relatives were involved, and it was stated that if a man was a witch he used his sister's son as food for his fellow witches! If a boy shoots beef in the bush he is bound to give his maternal uncle the shoulder. He is also bound to give a share of beef killed to his deceased father's sister's son who has inherited his father's property, even though

PLATE 36

WOMEN AND CHILDREN (Verre)

[face p. 424

he is senior in years to his cousin. It is for this reason that a sister's son who inherits his uncle's property hands a few of his uncle's arrows to his uncle's son.

Finally, he has the usual privilege of appropriating any of his maternal uncle's property, and if he wishes to marry a second wife he looks for assistance to his maternal uncle and not to his own father. If he died he could not be buried until after the arrival of the maternal uncle, who played a principal part in the matter of the funeral expenses.

In the next group, that of the Verre of Kwoi, the conditions approximate closely to those of the group we have just been considering (the Verre of Yibango) with the main exception that intermarriage with the father's relatives is avoided just as much as intermarriage with those of the mother. The totemic grouping is larger than the patrilineal exogamic unit (the kindred), for the totemic grouping includes a number of kindreds who believe themselves to be related. The totemic grouping is mainly religious, but the head of the group also exercises certain social functions, being the director of hunting operations and the arbiter in minor quarrels. As in the Yibango group children live in their father's home, follow their father's cult, and are circumcised at the instance of their father (or in the absence of a father at that of the father's brother). The maternal uncle has no claim to the custody of his sister's children; but a man may, if he pleases, hand over one of his children to his wife's brother (or father) if he has none of his own. Moreover a boy may, if he desires, abandon his father's home for that of his maternal uncle.

On the other hand, the mother's family is considered of more importance than the father's, and if a person is asked who his relatives are he will name the family of his mother, only naming that of his father if he is specifically asked who begat him. If he gets into difficulties it is to his mother's family that he looks. It is his mother's family who is primarily responsible for his burial. He can appropriate any of the property of his maternal uncle, who can in return requisition at any time the economic services of his nephew. Moreover the sister's son inherits all property, including widows (but excluding the compound which is heritable by a brother or son). The inheritor even appropriates all standing corn, giving to the maternal uncle's son merely sufficient seed corn for the following year. He also gives him his father's pipe and five arrows (in order that when he shoots beef the son may bring to him, as his father's heritor, a share of the quarry).

Owing to the inheritance of the uncle's widows (accompanied by their young children) many children grow up in the home of their father's sister's son. If the sister's son has a child by his uncle's widow curious relationships result, e.g. a boy may be a half-brother of one whose father is his own first cousin, or to put it differently a man may be first cousin to the half-brother of his son.

Interesting facts about the bride-price emerged. For the marriage of a virgin girl the bride-price is payable in three instalments as follows :.—

(i) One hoe, a new calabash, a necklace—all payable to the girl's mother on first soliciting the hand of her daughter.
(ii) Two to four goats payable to the father, and a similar payment to her maternal uncle, as the time for marriage approaches.
(iii) A final payment of one hoe to the girl's mother.

It was said that the payments to the girl's father were a recompense for the trouble and expense of bringing up the girl. The noteworthy point is that if the girl contracts a second or third marriage the bride-price is wholly payable to her maternal relatives. Similarly, the expenses of a boy's first marriage are met by his father as a reward for the economic services the boy had rendered. But for any subsequent marriage he is dependent on his own resources or on those of his maternal uncle.

In this group the predominant position occupied by the father's sister was emphasized. She can call on her nephew's services without reference to his father. She can strike him if she thinks fit, and if she sees him fighting may intervene and beat him. She is a boy's chief counsellor in the days preceding his circumcision, encouraging him to be brave and not to bring disgrace on the family. On the conclusion of the rites if her nephew has acquitted himself well she climbs on to a platform and yodels with delight, proclaiming to all that her nephew had not flinched.

The principal relationship terms in this group are as follows :—

Dam is applied to a father, father's brother, father's sister's husband. The corresponding term is *wa* = son, a term which is by all Verre also applied by grandparents to grandsons.
Bam is applied to a mother, mother's sister, father's brother's wife. *Mama* is a special term confined to the father's sister and *Umam* to mother's brother. *Umtia* is a special term confined to

cross-cousins. The term means " playmate ", but the remarkable thing is that there is no playmate relationship between those who use the term—a circumstance which suggests that formerly the group was organized on a purely matrilineal basis. Parallel cousins merely address each other as " brother ", and there is, of course, no playmate relationship.

Woke is a special term applied by a man to his sister's son.

Damang is applied to grandfathers on both sides, and *Ba* is applied to grandmothers on both sides. Parents-in-law are described as *Ungunu* and brothers and sisters-in-law as *Ungyanchi*.

We come now to the final group—that of Lima and Dongorong (Mai Ini district)—a group which displays stronger mother-right features than any of those quoted above. There is no exogamous unit, and specific instances were obtained of the marriage of second cousins on both sides of the family. Totems, or rather cult emblems, are inherited patrilineally, but descent is reckoned primarily through the mother's family, which is considered as of superior importance to the father's for the following reasons :—

(*a*) Inheritance is matrilineal, and the matrilineal rule extends to all forms of property, including compound and widows of suitable age. The heritors are brothers by the same mother or sisters' sons (but never brothers by the same father only and never sons).

(*b*) The duties connected with a lad's circumcision fall on his maternal uncle, and not on his father.

(*c*) A boy who is living with his father's family may appropriate any of his maternal uncle's property, but if he is living with his maternal uncle he cannot appropriate any of his father's property (and still less any of his paternal uncle's property).

(*d*) Even though a boy elects to remain with his father, his maternal uncle can still requisition his economic services when required.

(*e*) If a boy is living with his father and his father dies, he would always abandon his father's home in favour of that of his maternal uncle—i.e. he would not consent to live with his paternal uncle.

(*f*) If a person gets into difficulties he applies for help to his mother's and not his father's relatives.

(*g*) Funeral arrangements are made by the mother's, and not by the father's relatives.

(*h*) A girl's first marriage is arranged by her father and her mother's sister, who divide the bride-price. (The reason why the mother's sister receives a share of the bride-price is that she is primarily responsible for the girl's marriage outfit.) But the girl's secondary and subsequent marriages are arranged by her maternal uncle, who appropriates the bride-price *in toto* if he thinks fit. It was stated that the father's right to the bride-price in a primary marriage was compensation for the expenditure he had himself incurred in marrying the mother of his daughter.

This throws an interesting light on the whole question of the bride-price.

(i) The authority of the wife's brother is so great that he is entitled to take his sister's children out of the custody of a husband whom he considers to be an unworthy father. Moreover, children can choose for themselves whether they will continue to live in their father's home. If they decide to abandon it in favour of that of their maternal uncle, the father cannot prevent them.

The wife's father has a special claim on his daughter's first child. This has nothing to do with mother-right conditions, but is regarded as compensation to the father for part of the expenditure he had incurred in marrying the mother of the girl. The father may redeem his first-born by the payment of two goats.

It will be seen that the Verre of Mai Ini are strongly mother-right. Speaking generally we may say that among all the Verre groups, with the exception of Marki, the mother's family is the stronger social group.

The following are a few notes on general matters. They refer primarily to the Gweri and Soli groups. First of all, as regards the functions of the hamlet priest, it is a mistake to regard the priest purely from the religious point of view. Religion and law are so inextricably interwoven among primitive peoples that they cannot be separated. Religion is the engine of the law. Thus if two kindreds in a village started fighting it was the priest who stopped the fighting ; he had merely to appear with the sacred horns, and the combatants, awed by the mystic symbols, became ready to listen to reason. The priest then called up the leaders of each kindred and after inquiry gave his decisions in the name of the mystic powers ; a goat was offered by each kindred, and the dispute settled. Or, if two members of the same kindred fought, the head of the kindred appealed to the priest, who summoned the combatants. Taking some beer in his mouth and spitting it on the ground, as a sign that he was in touch with or summoning higher powers, he would inquire into the matter ; and on giving his decision would require the disputants to drink beer together from the same calabash, thereafter giving beer to the seniors present and drinking some himself. A quarrel between two wards was settled by a meeting of the respective priests of the ward concerned and a sacrifice of goats. Murderers were put to death by means of the religious machinery—they were " taken by

PLATE 37

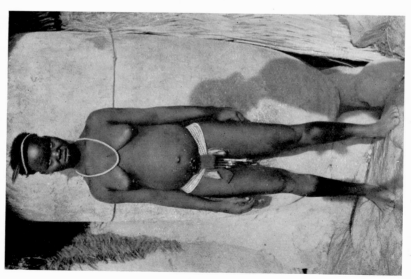

A YOUNG WOMAN (Verre)

A PRIEST (Verre)

[face p. 428

Doos ". A thief was brought before the priest, and if he did not make restitution and a gift to the cult he became virtually an outlaw ; he was excluded from all rites and dances and his position became so intolerable that he had to leave the village. Debt and witchcraft disputes were similarly settled by the priest who conducted, if necessary, a trial by ordeal.

On the other hand, disputes as to the paternity of a child were settled by the diviner (*lams*). The method of divination is worth recording as it is practised by the Chamba and some groups of Jukun. The medium of divination is the land crab, round whose hole in the ground a segment of pieces of the pulp of shea-nuts is set—each piece being soaked in oil and water, in order to induce the crab to come out and drink. Inside the segment, grass straws, representing each of the disputing parties, are set. The diviner addresses the crab and asks him to show which of the parties is speaking the truth. Whosoever's straw is taken by the crab into his hole is declared to be the winner of the action. It is interesting to note that no Fulani may be present during the test ; otherwise the crab would die.

It is apparent, therefore, that the priest was also the law-giver, and the question arises how far it is possible or desirable that the Administration should recognize and utilize the existing legal system among these primitive peoples. The Administration says summarily that legal actions can only be determined in properly constituted courts and, as far as I can gather, the properly constituted court among the Verre is that presided over by a Muslim judge, resident at what (to Verre) is some distant town. Actually, therefore, none but the most serious criminal cases are ever brought to the cognizance of the recognized legal authority. In practice all ordinary matters are still settled by the priest who nowadays protects himself by securing the goodwill and assistance of the " arnado " or head of the hamlet. Thus all disputes as to inheritance and marriage, etc., are still settled illegally (from the point of view of the Administration). This is, of course, known to the Fulani District Head. If prosecutions were made for the illegal exercise of judicial powers the result would be, in my opinion, a complete alienation of the people, who are of the opinion that the reference to the Alkali of every legal action would mean a direct attack on the authority not merely of the priest, but of all the seniors who support him in accordance with tribal custom, and a consequent breakdown of all authority within the local group. With this view I heartily agree (in so far as the primitive Verre are concerned), and I should be inclined to regard all cases settled in this customary way as "settled out of court". Provided trials by inhuman practices are avoided there should be no objection made to the local groups disposing of cases in accordance with their own customs, for the meantime at any rate. As to whether it is possible or desirable for the Administration to give formal recognition to a legal system which is contrary to all modern ideas of justice I am not prepared to express an opinion. It would of course be impossible to attempt to divorce native religion from native law and to try and enlist the services of the priest without acknowledging the religious sanction. The policy should be, I think, "to wait and see," avoiding all prosecutions for illegal exercise of judicial functions except in cases of flagrant inhuman decisions. Witchcraft charges should always be made referable to the Alkali, for in cases of this kind a very definite line has to be taken.

In religion the prevalence of stone cults is noticeable, monoliths and circular stone altars like dolmens being found in most hamlets. They are vaguely associated with deceased ancestors and are smeared by the priest with porridge as a first-fruit offering. The Verre also follow the practice (common in the semi-Bantu speaking tribes of Zaria) of smearing with porridge the lintel of the doors of their houses before partaking of the new grain. Some of these altars are solid throughout, others are hollow inside. In the latter the priest deposits over-night an offering of beer, and on the following day takes some of the beer in his mouth and spits it over the altar, asking the ancestors to intercede for them that crops may be abundant, women fertile, and bush quarry plentiful. The ancestors are regarded as being intermediaries between man and the Supreme Being, who among the Verre appears to be identified with the Sun. (The words for God and the Sun are identical in one group. In another group the word for God is *Bil*, and it is interesting to find that this word is used for Sun among the Bantu-speaking Buma of the Congo.) The Verre do not, like some of the Jukun peoples, offer definite rites to the Sun. But oaths are sworn by the Sun. A Verre who is charged with some offence will snatch his bow and looking at the Sun will say: " If I have done this thing, then on the day that

PLATE 38

A SACRED SYMBOL (Verre)

DOLMEN-LIKE SHRINE (Verre)

[face p. 431

I go hunting in the bush may the Sun deliver me into the clutches of a leopard." Before a hunt all the hunters bring their bows and deposit them at the feet of the priest, who, taking some "gadali" juice in his mouth, turns to the East and spitting some of the juice on the ground says : " May the Sun give us meat to-day." This he repeats towards each of the other three points of the compass, and finally he spits some beer also on the bows.

The accompanying photograph illustrates one of the dolmen shrines. This shrine was observed at the village of Masupa, and close to it there stood a mud pillar of phallic appearance. The shrine is known as *Kogur* and the mud pillar as *Woops*. Both are used in connection with the first-fruit rites in honour of *Doos*, a word which is employed as a personification of all the occult powers.

The rites are carried out in the middle of January and are as follows :— The priest of *Doos* prepares a small supply of beer from the newly harvested guinea-corn. He goes to the shrine of *Doos* and pours some beer over the stone symbols of the deity or deities. He then repairs to the " dolmen " known as *Kogur*, and having removed one of the stone slabs which serves as a door, he pushes in a pot of beer. He creeps in himself and pours out a libation of the beer, emptying the pot completely. He remains inside the " dolmen " for some considerable time, holding converse (it is said) with the spirits. On emerging he carefully replaces the stone slab and leaves the empty pot beside it. No one may see the priest performing these rites. He then returns to the shrine of *Doos*, where the senior men are assembled. He takes some beer in his mouth and spits it over the symbols. This he does twice. Turning to the elders he says : " I have been to the spirits and am bidden to tell you that the ensuing year will be prosperous. We shall obtain corn in plenty and have success in hunting. We shall beget children, and those who die will have sons to succeed them." The priest's assistant then takes some beer in his mouth and spits it over the symbols.

On the conclusion of these rites, which permit all to eat the new guinea-corn, the priest directs the elders to return home and set about the preparation of beer for the Siki harvest festival. When the beer is ready the festival is begun at sunrise by a dance which is carried out by women round the mud pillar known as *Woops*. The priest of *Woops*, who bears the title of *Yazoo*, first deposits a pot of beer on the top of this symbol, and he eventually hands this pot of beer to the woman who had shown herself to be the best dancer. This woman drinks some of the beer, and hands the rest to those who had taken part in the dance. While the women are dancing the men stand looking on, but some of them provide the music, with flutes which are only used on this occasion. On the conclusion of the dance all join in a procession round the village, led by the *Yazoo*. Thereafter feasting and dancing is carried out in groups.

The festival of Siki held at Masupa is attended by crowds from other villages, and on its conclusion similar rites are observed in other groups, and are attended by the villagers of Masupa.

It was impossible to obtain any information which would explain the dolmen-like character of the shrine of *Kogur*. The shrine is regarded as a " house " of the spirit or spirits of the crops, and is thus parallel to the similar but smaller shrines found among the Yungur-speaking peoples, which are set up on farms and at cross-roads as the abode of the corn-spirit.[1] It is to be noted that on the first day of the Siki festival all the interstices between the stones of the shrine are blocked with leaves to prevent people from seeing inside. The vulgar gaze would, it is said, cause the spirits to depart in anger. It will be observed that the shrine is surmounted by a pole. Heads of new corn are fastened to this pole before the corn has fully ripened, i.e. before the formal rites are performed. This early offering to the spirits safeguards children who in their ignorance break the taboo against eating new corn before the formal rites have been carried out.

The symbol known as *Woops* clearly represents a circumcised penis. This is recognised by the people themselves, but there is no conscious association of the symbol with fertility.

The priests are the guardians of the life or soul of the crops, and perform rites annually which recall the myths of Osiris and Adonis. When the crops begin to sprout or flower the priest takes a few of the new leaves and flowers and wrapping them up in a leaf of the wild *paw-paw* tree buries them ceremonially in the bush, together with a tuber of the sacred " gadali " plant. He believes that he is thus preserving the life of the crops for the ensuing year. Next year when he again comes to perform the rites he digs up the old leaves and flowers. After this formal

---

[1] See Vol. II, ch. xiv.

burial the priest abstains from eating any corn until the conclusion of the harvest and the first-fruit rites. He lives entirely on ground-nuts, beans, etc. A breach of this taboo would cause the spirit of the crops to die in the ground. If the crops fail or are poor the people are not slow to blame the priest, it being presumed that he had either deliberately neglected to observe the necessary taboos, or that his heart had not been single when he performed the rites. The custom of burying the corn spirit is still observed by the Arabs of Moab. When the harvesters have nearly finished their task and only a small portion of the field remains to be reaped, the owner takes a handful of wheat tied up in a sheaf. A hole is dug in the form of a grave : then the sheaf of wheat is laid at the bottom of the grave, and the Sheikh pronounces these words : " The old man is dead. " Earth is afterwards thrown in to cover the sheaf, with a prayer " May Allah bring us back the wheat of the dead." (*Golden Bough*, abridged edition, page 372.) In ancient Egypt " an effigy of the corn-god (Osiris) moulded of earth and corn was buried with funeral rites in the ground in order that, dying there, he might come to life again with the new crops. The ceremony was in fact a charm to ensure the growth of the corn by sympathetic magic, and we may conjecture that as such it was practised in a simple form by every Egyptian farmer on his fields long before it was adopted and transfigured by the priests in the stately ritual of the Temple " (*Golden Bough*, page 378).

The custom of burying the corn-spirit is not found among all the Verre groups. The Verre of Yibango, for example, do not observe it. In that group the harvest thanksgiving is combined with rites to secure a successful hunting season. Headed by the priest all proceed to a cross-roads outside the village. There the priest takes his stand with a pot of beer and says : " We are now about to perform the custom performed by our forefathers. What I am about to do they did, and had prosperity. May we reap the advantage of the crops sown and harvested, and may we be successful in our hunting during the dry season." He then collects the bows of all present and holding them by the strings spits beer on the grip of each. He scatters the bows on the ground and each man rushes to recover his weapon. The idea of throwing the bows on the ground is to secure an equal distribution of the magical power conferred by the ritual. For if the priest blessed each bow and handed it back to its owner the man whose bow was first blessed and given back to him would alone receive the magical power and become the sole master of all the beef in the bush.

Among the principal cults of the Soli Verre are Do Gupse and Do Tibas, the former symbolised by a bag of cow's skin and the latter by a number of long curved horns made of pieces of calabash fitted into each other. When blown these horns make a deep awe-inspiring sound. Both cults are used to terrorise women and children ; and Do Gupse was, and still is, a principal means of disciplining the general community. In by-gone days, it is said, those committing offences against religion and law were put to death by Do Gupse, apparently in some cases by being buried alive. At the present time anyone offending any of the cults (*doos*), e.g. by disclosing to his wife the religious secrets, would have to pay a fine to the priest ; otherwise, conscious of his unatoned offence, he would fall into a semi-paralysed condition and waste away. Trial by ordeal was carried out by Do Gupse, and this cult was also used to control the activities of witches.

At Soli I was roused up in the middle of the night by the arrival of Do Gupse and Do Tibas. All the women of the village had withdrawn to their huts, and the young boy attendants of the cult kept making weird ghostly cries exactly like those of the Jukun *aku ahwâ* (ancestral cult). Their shouts were accompanied by the whirring of the bull-roarer, which the Verre call *baranga* and which is specially employed in rain-making rites. (The use of the bull-roarer in connection with religion appears to be confined to tribes speaking languages of the Semi-Bantu type.) The lads also used rattles, and shook with their hands bunches of metal tubes which made a clanging sound, intended to represent the weird shuffling footsteps of departed spirits. Four men kept blowing the calabash horns, the hoarse sound emitted being intended to simulate the cry of the spirits. The Do Tibas cult, which is prominent at funeral ceremonies, appears to be the same in all essential respects as the Verre cult of the Chamba.[1]

The burial rites of the Verre are of particular interest. In former times apparently the tribe was well supplied with cattle (pagan), and it was customary to wrap the body in the skin of a cow specially killed for the purpose. Burial was deferred until the third day so as to permit of the assembly of all the relatives ; and, as already noted, the burial rites were carried out by the deceased's maternal relatives. It was not apparently the custom of the

[1] See p. 348.

Masupa Verre to fumigate the body or peel off the skin except in the case of a corpse which had swelled up after death. This was taken as a sign that the person had been a witch. The peeled skin was buried separately from the rest of the body, which was washed in beer. The idea apparently was that, when the deceased went to the next world, all departed spirits would recognise him for what he was, and he would also be unable to show his face on earth again.

The grave is a deep circular pit, with lateral extensions thus :—

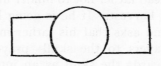

The body is set lying flat on the back and is then addressed by the priest : " You have lived long. Go now to the Sun and declare that you are the last of living men, and that it is useless to send for any more of us. And do you bear us no malice—return not to earth to interfere with our crops or prevent our women bearing children." It is noteworthy that the Verre believe that a dead man's ghost goes up to Heaven and does not remain in the ground, according to the conception of most Benue tribes. The ghosts are believed, however, to return to the world in order to attend the annual harvest festival. The grave is not filled in with earth, the mouth being blocked with a stone plastered over with mud. Some months later the funeral feast is held, at which the priest presides and performs the interesting rite of depositing seeds of various crops on the grave saying : " We give you seeds that you may go to your brethren and make a farm " (the intention being to provide him with all that he requires, so that he will not hover round the earth and spoil the crops of living human beings). The priest then pours some thick beer over the grave.

Some two months or so after the funeral ceremony the immediate paternal and maternal relatives meet and hold a private dance, and then present the priest with a gift of pounded ground-nuts, asking for permission to remove from the grave the head of the deceased. The grave is opened, the head removed, cleaned, washed with beer, and smeared with shea-nut oil. It becomes the property of the deceased's son and not of the sister's son. He tends it carefully, places it close to his head at night, and at every festival sets beside it a pot of beer. On the conclusion of the festival the beer is sent to the priest to drink. When he goes to his farm, the son places his father's skull under the care of a younger brother or other paternal relative. If anything befell the skull, the spiritual powers, represented by the priest, would drive the culprit owner out of the town ; for it is said that the Supreme Being, i.e. the Sun, would demand where the skull was, and, not finding it, would send evil spirits into the community.

At sowing time the son takes some seed, and, holding it before the skull, asks his dead father not to hinder him from reaping the fruit of a bountiful harvest. If he is going hunting he lays his bow on the skull and asks that his father may assist him. He makes constant prayers to the skull—prayers for health and children—for he regards the skull as an intermediary between himself and the Supreme God. A man may have in his keeping a large number of the skulls of his forefathers. An old woman's skull is taken by her daughter,[1] and that of a priest by his successor, who offers prayers to the skull before performing public rites. The skulls of young people are not preserved. They are nevertheless removed and deposited in a cave.

The skull cult is found also among the Chamba, who have a good deal in common with the Verre : and among the Bata, Bachama, Kam, and Kwona it was customary (as in other parts of Africa, notably Uganda) to preserve the head or some other part of the body of the chief.

The Verre, like most of the peoples who speak languages of the middle zone type (i.e. who are linguistically most nearly related to the Bantu-speaking peoples), have initiation rites which in the case of the Verre are associated with circumcision. The rites are performed at intervals of anything from five to eight years, and the initiates may therefore be boys of 10 or 11 or married men of 18 or 19. The boys are assembled and segregated, spending the day in the bush and sleeping at night in the village, not in their homes but in the vicinity of the local shrine. This happens during the dry season, and the rites extend over a period of two months. The lads are subjected to the usual discipline of physical and moral chastisement, the local priest being the Mentor. The actual operation of circumcision is not performed until the beginning of the second month, and it appears to be quite clear that by the operation the initiates are regarded as having been regenerated.

[1] Or in some cases by her brother's son.

PLATE 39

THE PHALLIC SYMBOL KNOWN AS WOOPS

A DOOR-FRAME

It was stated that, just as a man may not be present at the birth of his child, so women may not be present at the circumcision of a youth ; the idea clearly being that circumcision is a re-birth, and that the excised foreskin is a symbol of association with mystic powers. It is most noteworthy that women are not even supposed to know anything of the mode of removing the foreskin. It is even said that the intention of wearing the penis-sheath is to conceal the fact that the foreskin has been excised. This circumstance, I think, throws a new light on circumcision.

The Verre, especially the women, are notable dancers, and I was particularly struck with the similarity of many of the musical refrains with those of the Chamba of Donga. The dance steps also are remarkably like those of the Chamba, the women dancing in a circle round the male flute players from left to right, and then backwards again from right to left. They then turn their backs to the men in the centre. The flutes are of the two-stop type used by the Chamba. Double hand-gongs of iron, the double membrane drum (beaten with the hands), and the hour-glass drum with bracing strings between the membranes for altering the tone, are also used at dances.

As regards material culture the thickness of the pottery and thinness of the walls of the houses and bins are noteworthy. The latter are built on a base of stones, and the builder draws up the mud of the walls by compression with the palms of the hands, spitting water on to the mud as he works. I have only once before seen such thin walls, among the Zompere of Benue Province. The door frame is also peculiar, being a circular bundle of twisted grass plastered over with mud :—as shown in the accompanying photograph.

The compounds are small, consisting of a kitchen, two or three sleeping huts, and a large number of tall narrow granaries built on a foundation of stones and shaped thus :—

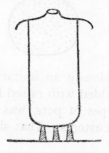

There are no special huts as among the Chamba and Jukun for the segregation of women during their menses. There is, however, a special hut for brewing the beer used in religious rites. The roofs of the huts are not made on the ground and then set on the walls as is usually done among other tribes. When the walls are made some logs of wood are laid across them to serve as a platform from which the rafters are put into position. When this is done the thatch is put on, and in this the Verre are economical, using alternate bundles of old and new grass. The peak of the roof is commonly crowned with a pot. The sleeping huts frequently have two doors, one of which was used as an emergency exit in case of surprise attack. Beds are either logs of wood or a mud platform covered with a mat, or, more commonly still, merely a plaited grass mat laid on the floor of the hut. Small wooden seats are used and shaped thus :—

Head rests of the same shape as the seats are also used. Wicker baskets plastered inside and out with cow's dung are employed for carrying grain, etc. They are of the pattern commonly seen between Yola and Ibi. The Verre bows are of the usual bamboo pagan pattern with a hole in each horn for fastening the string, i.e. there is no side notch (as in Jukun and Hausa bows). The bow-string puller is of a kind I had not previously observed. It is a piece of cane bent round to pass over the knuckles—the ends being bound together with fibre.

Of pottery the following unusual types were noticed :—

Of these No. 3 is obviously an imitation of a calabash water bottle. No. 1 was studded with raised lumps of earth and, as is common with such types of pots, was employed in connection with certain religious customs. That shown above was used by the owner for drinking beer after he had killed an oribi—an animal which is believed to have a peculiarly powerful pursuing ghost.

We may note in conclusion that the Verre wear the penis-sheath—a feature which suggests, as their language indicates, an ancient connection with the Bantu and semi-Bantu speaking peoples of the Plateau Province. The men also now-a-days commonly wear leaves before and behind, as they appear to have become ashamed of the penis-sheath in the presence of strangers.

A vocabulary of the Sǫli dialect is attached. It will be observed that there is a tendency towards monosyllabism which prevents the inclusion of Verre in the Semi-Bantu group. One of the effects of this monosyllabism is seen in the peculiar double consonantal termination—*ns*, *bs*, *nz*, etc.—a feature which I have not observed in any other Nigerian language. The alliterative concord, characteristic of the middle zone language groups, is present to some extent. Verre is thus either an early form of the classifying prefix languages, or else, having originally been one of those languages, has now become worn down by contact, perhaps, with peoples speaking languages of the monosyllabic or suffix type.

VERRE (OF SHǪLI) VOCABULARY

1.	Head	Jur	dʒur
2.	Hair	Suk	suk
3.	Eye	Nǫr	nɔr
	Two eyes	Nǫ ite	nɔ ite
4.	Ear	Tǫk	tɔk
	Two ears	Tǫ ite	tɔ ite
5.	Nose	Mi	mi
6.	One tooth	Nur mula	nur mulə
	Five teeth	Nu gbanara	nu gbanarə
7.	Tongue	Mel	mɛl
8.	Neck	Duk	duk
9.	Breast (woman's)	Wa	wa
10.	Heart	Teme	tɛme
11.	Belly	Bar	bar
12.	Back	Kur	kur
13.	Arm	Na	na
14.	Hand	Tagana	taɡana
	Two hands	Tagana ite	taɡana ite
15.	Finger	Deins	deɪns
	Five fingers	Dendi gbanara	dɛndi gbanarə
16.	Finger nail	Bunuk	bunuk

17. Leg	Da	də
18. Knee	Ruktuk	ruktuk
19. Foot	Tagada	tagadə
Two feet	Taga dan ite or taga dantitila	taga dən ite or taga dəntitıla
20. Man (person)	Jiz or mas	dʒiz or mas
Ten people	Ejiri komna	ɛdʒiri komna
21. Man (not woman)	Ya jiz	ja dʒiz
Two men	Eya jiri ite or ituko	eja dʒiri ite or ıtuko
22. Woman	Kiz	kiːz
Two women	Ki ituko	ki ituko
23. Child	Uwas	uwas
24. Father	Da	da
25. Mother	Bei	bei
26. Slave	Seens	seɛns
27. Chief	Gwanz	gwanz
28. Friend	Vere	vɛrɛ
29. Smith	Tibas	tibas
30. Doctor	Rumbas	rumbas
31. One finger	Den muzo	dɛn muzo
32. Two fingers	Dendi ituko	dɛndi ituko
33. Three fingers	Dendi tariko	dɛndi tariko
34. Four fingers	Dendi narko	dɛndi narko
35. Five fingers	Dendi gbanara	dɛndi gbanarə
36. Six fingers	Dendi bamburo	dɛndi bamburo
37. Seven fingers	Dendi bancha	dɛndi bantʃa
38. Eight fingers	Dendi samsara	dɛndi samsara
39. Nine fingers	Dendi piti muzo	dɛndi piti muzo
40. Ten fingers	Dendi komna	dɛndi komna
41. Eleven fingers	Dendi komna na muzo	dɛndi komna na muzo
42. Twelve fingers	Dendi komna na itukwe	dɛndi komna na itukwe
Thirteen fingers	Dendi komna na tarukwe	dɛndi komna na tarukwe
43. Twenty fingers	Dendi jur	dɛndi dʒur
44. A hundred fingers	Dendi ju gbanara	dɛndi dʒu gbanarə
45. Two hundred fingers	Dendi ju komna	dɛndi dʒu komna
46. God	Bil (high tone)	bil
47. Sun	Ula	ula
48. Moon	She	ʃɛ
Full moon	She puputuk	ʃɛ puputuk
New moon	She detako	ʃɛ ɗetako
49. Day	Ula	ula
Night	Tuks	tuks
Morning	Rut	rut
50. Rain	Mam	mam
51. Water	Mam	mam
52. Blood	Kwal	kwal
53. Fat	Wangkh	waŋx
54. Salt	Jingp	dʒiŋp

55.	Stone	Bil (low tone)	bil
	Iron	Wes	wɛs
56.	Hill	Kar	kar
57.	River	Ma	ma
58.	Road	Bila	bila
59.	House	Rur	rur
	Two houses	Ru ite	ru ite
	Many houses	Ru tuma	ru tuma
	All the houses	Rǫ pǫi	rɔ pɔi
	Compound	Gwak	gwaːk
60.	Roof	Eku rur	ɛku rur
61.	Door	Dangka	daŋka
62.	Mat	Kiik	kiik
63.	Basket	Bens	bɛns
64.	Drum	Bik	bik
65.	Pot	Dens	dɛns
66.	Knife	Weik	weɪk
67.	Spear	Tǫma	tɔma
68.	Bow	Tap	taːp
69.	Arrow	Che	tʃɛ
	Five arrows	Cher gbanara	tʃɛ gbanarə
70.	Gun	Ra	ra
71.	War	Yaab	jaab
72.	Meat (animal)	Gala	gala
73.	Elephant	Dangs	daŋs
74.	Buffalo	Mokpir	mɔkpɪr
75.	Leopard	Gooz	gooz
76.	Monkey	Tonggus	tɔŋgus
77.	Pig	Iyabs	ijabs
78.	Goat	Buz	buːz
79.	Dog	Zas	zas
80.	Bird	Nos	nɔs
	Feather	Gǫbi	gɔbi
81.	Crocodile	Zabs	zabs
	Horse	Nams or pirims	nams or pɪrɪms
	Sheep	Maas	maas
	Cow	Nangs	naŋs
82.	Fowl	Kǫkus	kɔkus
83.	Eggs	Bari	bari
84.	One egg	Bal mulo	mal mulo
85.	Snake	Biks	biks
86.	Frog	Dogur	dogur
87.	Spider	Barabus	barabus
88.	Fly	Gunkus	gunkus
89.	Bee	Wǫsi	wɔsi
	Honey	Wangga wosi	waŋga wɔsi
90.	Tree	Rap	raːp
	Ten trees	Rat komna	rat komna
91.	Leaf	Dangs	daŋs
92.	Guinea-corn	Kowǫp	kowɔp
93.	Maize	Resara	resara

94.	Ground nut	Go sambi	go sambi
95.	Oil	Wangkh	waŋx
	Fulani	Bure	bure
	Hausa	Hausai	hausai
	Beriberi	Siratazoe	siratazoe
96.	The tall woman (or women)	Ki riez	ki riɛz
97.	Large dog	Gbi zas	gbi zas
98.	Small dog	Wa jas	wa dʒas
99.	The dog bites	Zas rǫm rǫn	zas rɔm rɔn
100.	The dog bites me	Zas rǫm me rǫn	zas rɔm mɛ rɔn
101.	The dog which bit me yesterday	Zas rǫm me ninka ula	zas rɔm mɛ nɪnka ula
102.	I flog the dog	Min zinzǫb zas	mɪn zɪnzob zas
103.	The dog which I have flogged	Zas in zobu pu	zas ɪn zɔbu pu
104.	I see him or her	Mi oksa pu(ur)	mi ɔksa pu(ur)
	He sees you	(Ur) ǫga pu (mǫ)	(ur) ɔga pu (mɔ)
	He sees us	A ǫksa ka, or ur oga pu(e)	a ɔksa kə, or, ur ɔga pu(ɛ)
	We see you (pl.)	E ogim pu, or e ogim pu i	ɛ ɔgɪm pu, or ɛ ɔgɪm pu i
	We see them	E ǫksi pu, or e ǫksi pu iai	ɛ ɔksi pu, or ɛ ɔksi pu iai
105.	Beautiful bird	Nǫr wo	nɔr wo
106.	Slave	Seens	seɛns
	My slave	Seenja mingaras	seɛndʒa mɪngaras
	Thy slave	Seenja mos	seɛndʒa mos
	Our slaves	Seenja es	seɛndʒa ɛs
107.	The chief's slave	Seens sa gwanzis	seɛns sə gwanzɪs
	His slave	Seenja uras	seɛndʒa uras
108.	We see the slave	E ǫksa seenjo	ɛ ɔksa seɛndʒo
109.	We call the slave	E derapu seenjo	ɛ dɛra pu seɛndʒo
110.	The slave comes	Seenjo pu zakir	seɛndʒo pu zakɪr
111.	He came yesterday	Za ningka	za nɪŋka
	He is coming to-day	Pu za akiro	pu za akɪro
	He will come to-morrow	Za gbo ota	za gbo ota
112.	The slaves go away	Sheni reka pu	ʃɛni rɛ ka pu
113.	Who is your chief ?	Ne gwanza mǫs ?	nɛ gwanza mɔs ?
114.	The two villages are making war on each other	Dǫl iturǫ i pu gwalo	dɔl iturɔ i pu gwalo
115.	The sun rises	Ula pu butpur	ula pu butpur
	The sun sets	Ula ka sa pu	ula ka sa pu
116.	The man is eating	Mas pur rentu	mas pur rɛntu

117.	The man is drinking	Mas pur bo mam	mas pur bo mam
118.	The man is asleep	Mas ro sa pu	mas ro sa pu
119.	I break the stick	Mi kaa sa pu gbala	mi kaa sa pu gbala
	The stick is broken	Gbala kaa sa pu	gbala kaa sa pu
	This stick cannot be broken	Gbala mu sa pu kaa ka	gbala mu sa pu kaa ka
	Break this stick for me	Re a kaa se gbala as	rɛ a kaa se gbala as
120.	I have built a house	Mi wǫm sa pu rǫl	mi wɔm sa pu rɔl
121.	My people have built their houses yonder	Jiri eraai i wǫm sa pu gwam	dʒiri ɛraai i wɔm sa pu gwam
122.	What do you do every day ?	Arna o abortǫms naya	arna o abortɔms naja
	I work on my farm	Mi pu tǫmso a ba aro	mi pu tɔmso a ba aro
123.	I am going away	Mi re ka pu	mi rɛ ka pu
	I am hoeing	Mi pu banto	mi pu banto
	I am going away to hoe	Mi re ka pu banto	mi rɛ ka pu banto
	I am going away to my farm	Mi re ka pu minga baro	mi rɛ ka pu mɪŋga baro
124.	The woman comes	Kiz pu zakir	kiːz pu zakɪr
	She comes	Pu zakir	pu zakɪr
	The woman laughs	Kiz pu mandikir	kiːz pu mandɪkɪr
	The woman weeps	Kiz pu wǫrar	kiːz pu wɔrar
125.	I ask the woman	Mi desa pu kiz	mi dɛsa pu kiːz
126.	Why do you laugh ?	Anabo ra sea mandi-kiya ?	anabo ra sea mandi-kija ?
127.	Why do you cry ?	Anabo ra sea goeya	anabo ra sea goeja
128.	My child is dead	Was a mingara wor	was a mɪngara wor
129.	It is not dead	Wor pa	wor pa
130.	Are you ill ?	Jǫk pu omi pa ya ?	dʒɔk pu omi pa ja ?
131.	My children are ill	Yangi omingarai pu omi pa	jangi omɪngarai pu omi pa
132.	Her child is better	Jǫk weng su pu	dʒɔk wɛŋ su pu
133.	Yes	E	e
	No	A'a	aˤaˤ
134.	A fine knife	Wek o kapa	wɛk o kapa
	Give me the knife	Ise wek	ɪsɛ wɛk
	I give you the knife	Mi iksa pu monga wek	mi ɪksa pu mɔŋga wɛk
135.	You are a European	Moa bature as	moa bature as
	I am a black man	Minga jiz wiji	mɪŋga dʒiz widʒi
	I am a Verre	Minga jiri Gwa (i.e. Plain Verre)	mɪŋga dʒiri gwa
136.	Name	Ril	ril
	My name	Rira mingaral	rira mɪŋgaral

	Your name	Rira mọl	rira mɔl
	What is your name ?	Rira mọnggaral ?	rira mɔŋgaral
137.	There is water in the gourd	Mam pu zọbzur	mam pu zɔbzur
	The knife is on the stone	Wek pu bilọr	wɛk pu bilɔr
	The fire is under the pot	Ra pu gidar denra	ra pu gɪdar dɛnrə
	The roof is over the hut	Fir pu pa rọl	fir pu pa rɔl
138.	You are good	Mọnggya a o	mɔŋgja a o
	This man is bad	Jiz as ọpa	dʒiz as ɔpa
139.	The paper is white	Takarda bule	takarda bulɛ
	This thing is black	Inan pu wini	inan pu wini
	This thing is red	Ina bim nan	ina bɪm nan
140.	This stone is heavy	Bila al mo	bila al mo
	This stone is not heavy	Bila al mo pa	bila al mo pa
141.	I write	Mi rubutu	mi rubutu
	I give you the letter	Mi iksa pu mọ derau-wal	mi ɪksa pu mɔ dɛrau-wal
	Carry the letter to the town	Kam derauwal wuro	kam dɛrauwal wuro
142.	Go away	Rem	rɛm
	Come here	Zam ari	zam ari
143.	Where is your house ?	Gwa ga mos pu orea ?	gwa ga mos pu ɔrea ?
144.	My house is here	Gwak mingarak pi	gwak mɪngarak pi
	My house is there	Gwak mingarak pu ari	gwak mɪngarak pu ari
145.	What have you to sell ?	Ayikpa naya ?	ajikpa naja ?
146.	I want to buy fish	Mi i yikpa duk	mi i jikpa duk
147.	The fish which you bought is bad	Duk a yiksa pu o pa	duk a jiksa pu ɔ pa
148.	Where is the man who killed the elephant ?	Jiz yo dang pọ rea ?	dʒiz jo daŋ pɔ rea ?
149.	He has killed many elephants	Eyo dang banshi	ejo daŋ banʃi
150.	How many ele-phants were killed yester-day ?	Ningka ula dang i yu dang kugaya ?	nɪŋka ula daŋ i ju daŋ kugaja ?
151.	Untie it	Bin sumu	bɪn sumu
	Tie this rope	Dọgdum nagura	dɔgdum nagura
	Make the boy un-tie the goat	Rim atọng was na bin bus	rɪm atɔŋ was na bɪn bus

152.	My brothers and I, we are going but no one else	Minga re ka pu na buya as enge muyo	mɪnga rɛ ka pu na buja as ɛŋgɛ mujo
153.	Brothers, let us go and tell the chief	Buya as dam are a do tu gwanz	buja as dam arɛ a do tu gwanz
154.	This tree is bigger than that	Te araku te a di ak non karak	te araku te a di ak non karak

CHAPTER VIII

THE MUMUYE AND NEIGHBOURING TRIBES (INCLUDING THE GÔLA, YENDANG, WAKA, TEME, KUMBA, GENGLE, AND KUGAMA)

The following notes are the result of a short survey made of the Mumuye-speaking peoples.

The term Mumuye is a generic description for various groups of peoples in the Adamawa Province, occupying the hill country between Jalingo and the districts of Maio Belwa and Maio Faran. It is said to have been conferred by the Fulani, the various groups having no common term and each group using merely its own local group-title. It is improbable that the Fulani invented the term Mumuye, as the root is found in other parts of Africa in the sense of " Man ". Thus the Tikari word for man is "mum", and the form "muume", meaning man, occurs in one of the Nyasaland languages. We may conclude, therefore, that Mumuye means " the people ", like so many other African tribal titles.

In its strictest application the description " Mumuye " includes the following units ;—

(1) *Pugû* = (a) Kasheri (Sawa, Ungkpa, Nyaja, Langko, Kajong Lankaviri, Hoai or Gulung, Zavô, Gongô or Gḅata, Kpezang, and Lesheki).
   (b) Mika, Mana, Kwoji (half), Bamga, Sa.
(2) (a) Jega Maunde, Sô-ri, and Jole.
   (b) Apawa, Jimleri, and Yusa.
(3) *Yoro* = Dangkô, Kassa, Shara, Gba, Môkin, Nyelle, Dambô, Dabambô, Dan Seri, Sagbwe, Sensidô (half), Dingki, Kugô, Gangoro, Lampo, Jangari, Ganleri.
(4) *Rang* = Lama, Dendi Jarendi, Dendi Manga, Bansi, Sensidô (half), Kusum, Duki, Ḍuḍung, Batiso, Sakoro.
(5) *Zin (Zinna)* = Kpana, Zang, Kakuru, Zandi, Kǫkǫ, Dosa, Didongko, Labma, Karago, Lapu, Bubong, Yongko, Labo, Bitako, Kwoji (half), Je (Din-Ding).
(6) *Ya (Yakoko)* = Zang Ratong, Lambong, Gudubong, Takumba, Dopa, Yukpa, Voduka, Kodari.
(7) *Gôla (Gongla)* = (Jeren, etc.).

Of these the first three groups are administered by the Emir of Muri (whose mother was a Mumuye), and the second three [1]

[1] But the Rang villages of Kusum, Duki, Dudung, and Batiso, are included in the Chamba district of Adamawa Emirate, and the village of Sokoro is included in the Maio Faran district. Jangari and Ganleri (Yoro Group) are also included in the Chamba district.

PLATE 40

THE CHIEF OF ZINNA

by the Chief of Zinna, who is a Mumuye. The Gôla, who contain a Jukun element from Kona, are included in the Emirate of Adamawa.

There are dialectical differences between these groups, particularly between the first two and last five, but the differences are slight and all can be regarded as speaking the same language. There are also differences in custom. Thus the Rang and Gôla groups have abandoned the characteristic leather loin-coverings worn by males, and have adopted garments of cloth. Their women also no longer pierce the nasal septum. The members of the second group differ from all the other groups in that they do not practise circumcision. In some groups the tutelary genius known as *Vabô* may be seen by women, in other groups not, and so on. But in spite of these differences all the seven groups can be regarded as forming a single tribe. All look to the priest of Yoro as the chief rain-maker, and most of the groups claim to be offshoots of Yoro.

The term "Mumuye" is not, however, always confined to the seven groups enumerated above, for it is frequently applied also to the Yendang and Waka, who occupy a belt of country to the East of Zinna. I have also heard it applied to the villagers of Kumba, Yofo, Sate, and Kuseki in the Maio Belwa district, and even to the groups known as the Bali and Passam. The Yendang and Waka accept the description of "Mumuye" and they claim Yoro as their original home. But the language of the Yendang and Waka, though connected with the Mumuye group, diverges widely from Mumuye, and even though they may contain a Mumuye stratum, it is clear, both on grounds of physical appearance and of culture, that the Yendang and Waka are a distinct people. The same remarks apply to the Kumba group of villages (which have fused with the Chamba-speaking Mumbake), and even more so to the Bali and Passam. If the term Mumuye is extended to these three groups (viz. Yendang, Waka, Kumba, Bali-Passam) then it should also be extended so as to include the Gengle, Kugama, and Teme, for there is a close linguistic connection between

(a) Yendang-Waka,
(b) Gengle-Kugama,
(c) Teme,
(d) Kumba.

A noteworthy feature of this group is the common use of the word *Lu* or *Ru*, meaning God (as contrasted with the Mumuye *La*). It is also to be noted that the Yendang and Waka do not (like the Mumuye) practise circumcision, and that both they and the Gengle and Kugama (unlike the Mumuye) wear penis sheaths. This latter custom suggests that there has been an infusion into this area of groups of Chamba and Verre.

The principal common features connecting the Mumuye with the other tribal units enumerated above may be summarized as follows :—

(*a*) A close linguistic connection, so that all the languages spoken can be classed together in a single group, which for convenience may be called the Mumuye group, a group connected (1) with Chamba, and (2) with Verre.

(*b*) The use by all of the skins of bush-cats or goats as bags.

(*c*) The identification of the Sun with the Supreme Being.

(*d*) The preservation and cult of skulls.

(*e*) The use by all of the calabash horn cult known as Vadôsu.

(*f*) A general similarity in the form of social organization, inheritance, and marriage. All groups are strictly patrilineal.

This group of tribes presents a striking contrast to neighbours such as the Mbula and Bili, who speak a language of the Bantu type, and have matrilineal and totemic customs.

The following notes apply generally to the Mumuye in the strict sense of the term, but notes on the Gôla are given separately, as the Gôla group of Mumuye has diverged rather more than the others and is located in the Adamawa Division (the other groups being located in the Muri division).[1] Separate notes are also attached on

(*a*) The Yendang-Waka,
(*b*) The Teme,
(*c*) The villages of Kumba and Yofo,
(*d*) The Gengle and Kugama.

Though most of the Mumuye groups claim to have sprung from Yoro, there is a tradition among the Pugû that they are an

---

[1] The Mumuye in the strict sense of the term number at least 60,000, of whom 57,000 are situated in the Muri Division. In the Muri Division they are distributed as follows :—

(1) Mumuye District	.	.	.	26,476
(2) Zinna District	.	.	.	16,544
(3) Jalingo District	.	.	.	3,663
(4) Daka District	.	.	.	1,940
(5) Kona District	.	.	.	1,730
(6) Lau District	.	.	.	7,065

offshoot of the Kam, and it is even said that Yoro itself was founded from Kam.[1] It will be remembered that the Kam were closely associated with the Jukun and formed part, in fact, of the Jukun confederacy. It may have been in this way that the Mumuye obtained their two principal cults, viz. Vabô and Vadôsu, which correspond to the Akuma and Buhor cults of the Jukun.[2] On the other hand, these cults may have been obtained directly from the Jukun of Kona, with whom the Mumuye have long been close friends. It is noteworthy that the word *Va* is the Kona word "to pray". Many of the Mumuye villages in the vicinity of Kona recognized the suzerainty of Kona and were accustomed to send annual gifts to the Kona chief. It is even said that the influence of the Jukun extended as far East as Zinna, and that the appointment of the chief priest of the Zin received formal confirmation from Kona. One of the Zin villages is still known as Kpana, that is Kona. It would be misleading, however, to suggest that the Mumuye as a whole were ever subject to the Kona or anyone else. Most of the hill groups maintained their independence even of the Fulani right down to the time of the British occupation. The Fulani never made any organized attack owing to the strength of the Mumuye positions, and in consequence some of the Mumuye chiefs (e.g. of Kasheri) entered into friendly relations with the Emir of Muri. But when Kona was attacked by the Fulani the Kona were assisted by a large body of Mumuye. Some of the South-easterly groups of Mumuye were at various times during the nineteenth century subjected, like most of the surrounding tribes, to attacks by the Chamba. The Je, Yakoko, Zinna, and Yoro village groups were all raided by the Chamba, while the Sagbwe, Lampo, Sharo, and Gongoro groups became definitely subject to the Chamba. The cultural influence of the Chamba is very marked throughout the whole of the South-eastern area.[3]

In pre-British times the Mumuye had no form of central

---

[1] The Mumuye appear to contain a Dirrim element. The Dirrim are neighbours of the Kam.

[2] Some of the Kasheri villages have the buffalo-horn or "Aku" cult of the Jukun. See Meek, *A Sudanese Kingdom*, pp. 238 et seq.

[3] The most famous Chamba conqueror was Damashi, who swept the whole south bank of the Benue river prior to the rise of the Muri Fulani. This chief is credited with having caused the disruption of the Jukun capital of Kororofa. It was possibly through the Chamba (and not the Jukun) that the Mumuye obtained the cults of Vabô and Vadôsu, as these cults are also found among the Chamba (under the names of Vara and Voma).

administration. Though all the groups recognized the priest of Yoro as the supreme rain-maker for the tribe, this personage's authority was confined entirely to his magico-religious duties. He could summon representatives from all other Mumuye groups to attend at Yoro for the performance of special rain-making rites, and each of these representatives was required to bring with him some gift. But in other matters the priest of Yoro was of no account outside his own local group.

The system of government will become clearer when we have given some account of the form of social organization which is set forth in the following paragraphs.

Social Organization.—The Mumuye live in hamlets, a number of hamlets forming the village-area or local group. Thus the village of Mika consists of twelve hamlets as follows :—

Lanapu Boro	with a population of	350
Lanapu Takolo	,, ,,	170
Shomman	,, ,,	400
Dimhe	,, ,,	68
Pawuno	,, ,,	135
Kakulu	,, ,,	230
Kapuli	,, ,,	115
Dansa	,, ,,	150
Danyusa	,, ,,	105
Zahan	,, ,,	270
Lanapu Koron	,, ,,	275
Lanapu Wareham	,, ,,	200

Each hamlet is a self-contained unit, being composed usually of a number of extended families which are related to each other. But two or more hamlets which are close neighbours will take common action against a number of hamlets farther removed. Thus at Mika the hamlets of Lanapu Boro, Lanapu Tokolo, Kapuli, and one other (whose name I have forgotten) form a confederacy vis-à-vis the other hamlets. In the village-area of Sawa four of the hamlets, viz. Sawa, Kwoga, Tako and Dambu, form a union for purposes of offence and defence against the remaining nine hamlets. And so on. The basis of this union is primarily the local association, but the sense of relationship also plays a part, as hamlets which are situated close to one another usually claim that the founders of the hamlets had a common forefather. In some cases the blood relationship can be proved, but in others it is too remote to be capable of proof, while in a few cases it is capable of disproof. Anyhow a confederacy of hamlets

PLATE 41

A Young Mother (Mumuye)

A Mumuye Woman at Work in the Fields

[face p. 450

has none of the characteristics of a clan, for it is not an exogamous unit and has no central organization.

In the past, if a member of a hamlet murdered a fellow-member of his hamlet, the matter was arranged peacefully between the two families concerned, a fine of a bull being exacted from the family of the guilty man. But if a member of one hamlet murdered a member of another hamlet open warfare resulted between the two hamlets. If the two hamlets belonged to different groups or confederacies of hamlets the other hamlets might be drawn into the quarrel on each side. Fights between hamlets or groups of hamlets were frequent until a few years ago, and if they proceeded too far, that is, if they led to considerable loss of life, the senior priest of the whole village area intervened. He went to the hamlets concerned and swore in the name of the god he served that if any man drew another arrow that man would die within the year and his crops would be blasted. Less serious disputes between hamlets might also be referred to the chief priest, and anyone who had committed accidental homicide fled automatically for refuge to him. Even in those groups which in pre-British times acknowledged the suzerainty of the Fulani, the local *arnado*, or headman appointed by the Fulani, could not lay hands on a man who had sought refuge with the senior priest of the Vabô. The chief priest could also fine any members of the local group for real or fictitious offences against the gods. Thus he could fine a man for eating new corn before the first-fruit rites had been performed, or for speaking indiscreetly about the cults in the presence of women.

At Mika the chief priest belongs to the hamlet of Shomman. He is the priest of the principal Vabô or cult of the whole village-area, viz. of the male and female deities known as *Vawuya* and *Kwonjakalangyako*. There are other Vabô at Mika ; in fact each family has a Vabô of its own. But all Vabô are subservient to the Vabô of the priest of Shomman, who is, in consequence, the real controller of the community. By the rites performed to his Vabô he secures the success of the yam harvest for the whole village-area. All families also possess a cult of Vadôsu, but the two senior Vadôsu are in the hands of the headman of the Lanapu and Dan Yusa hamlets respectively, the Vadôsu of the former being known as *Sisero* and the latter as *Nyala*. The possession of these senior cults confers upon their owners authority over all other

Vadôsu and gives them a political and social, as well as a religious status which is inferior only to that of the senior priest of the Vabô. Among the Pugû the Vabô cult is more important than that of Vadôsu, but among the Zin the Vadôsu is the more important, while in other areas both are of equal importance. In some areas the chief priest is the rain-maker.

It will be seen, therefore, that for administrative purposes it is necessary to secure in each village-area the goodwill and co-operation of the senior priest, if possible by appointing him as the executive head of the community. In many cases the chief priest is unwilling to be protruded in this way, and to be at the beck and call of the Administration, which may require him to assume duties which are neither consistent with his dignity nor years, and may call upon him to make distant journeys at a time when he should be carrying out religious rites. In such cases some member of the community, preferably from his own family, should be chosen by him as his executive deputy, and in all cases of visits by officials of the British or Native Administrations, the chief priest should be invited to take an active part in the discussions. It is not sufficient that the " power behind the throne " should remain in the background on such occasions.

Turning now to the constitution of the hamlet (using this term in the sense of a section of a village-area) this consists of a number of extended families which are usually, but not always, related to one another. Where the extended families are related they constitute what may be described as a kindred or small clan. Thus, to take an example, the hamlet of Lanapu Boro at Mika consists of nine family groups, each with a local name. These are :—

(a) Lanapu Boro, the senior family group, from which the whole hamlet takes its name, consisting of 40 people ;
(b) Shaja (43) ;
(c) Danzin (32) ;
(d) Dakoza (34) ;
(e) Dakoko (35) ;
(f) Wawa (35) ;
(g) Dan Zahan (49) ;
(h) Kasha Nyanyi (38) ;
(i) Kanyaja (54).

The total population is 350, and there are 159 males as against 191 females. With the exception of Dakoza, Dan Zahan, and

PLATE 42

A MUMUYE YOUTH

RETURNING FROM THE FARM (Mumuye)

[face p. 453

Kanyaja, all the family groups are related to each other genealogically.

The family group or extended family is known as a " dola ", and is a social and economic unit. It has a recognized head who is the arbiter in all matters pertaining to the family, and is the custodian of the skulls of deceased members of the family. It is an economic unit to the extent that, although each householder has a farm of his own, all the householders of the "dola" combine to assist each other at those special times of the agricultural season when co-operative effort is called for. On these occasions the farmer who has called on the fellow members of his " dola " to assist him is required to supply them with beer, and on this account the co-operative family group is commonly called a " dolassa ", that is, " the beer-drinking group." The term " dolassa " is thus normally coincident with the extended family group. But sometimes a " dolassa " may be a smaller or larger unit than the extended family ; for if two senior half-brothers or cousins do not agree together one may leave the " dolassa " of his brother or cousin and join that of a friend or else establish a " dolassa " of his own. In the latter case the extended family becomes divided, and it is in this way that a kindred composed of two or more extended families is commonly formed. Sometimes a man will join the " dolassa " of another family group, because that " dolassa " is more numerous than his own and he will be able, therefore, to farm on a larger scale. A man may take this step when he is contemplating marriage and considers that his own "dolassa " is too small to render all the assistance he requires. He may even find it necessary to abandon not merely his own " dolassa " but also his " dola " or family group.

The extended family group is composed of several households, each household containing a husband, wife, and their children, and possibly also the husband's unmarried younger brother or his sister's son. The households are small, for as soon as a youth marries he establishes a household of his own. Thus the family group of Lanapu Boro at Mika contains six households with an average of under seven persons per household. These six households form a single social group and a single " dolassa" or agricultural group. If any male member of the group arrives at the age of marriage he is assisted in his pre-marriage expenses by members of his own " dolassa ", that is, by his father primarily, and by those paternal uncles, elder brothers, and cousins who belong to his " dolassa ".   He would not be assisted by other patrilineal relatives who belong to another " dolassa ".   The only other relatives who take an active interest in his welfare are maternal relatives, such as his mother's father and brothers.

Summarizing the system of social grouping, we may say that the Mumuye live in village groups, each of which is independent of the other.   The village group is composed of a number of hamlet groups, each of which consists of a number of kindreds which are generally related patrilineally, and may be loosely described as a clan, though there is no typical clan organization. The kindreds are composed of two or more related extended families.   Each extended family is also an agricultural unit, but a large extended family tends to break up into two or more agricultural groups, and this fission converts the extended family into a kindred, that is, into two or more extended families each independent of the other.   It may be added that when two or more kindreds or extended families become geographically separated contact is maintained by a return to the parent group for the annual performance of religious rites.   It is possible to discover which kindreds are related by finding out which join together to form a single initiation group, when lads are first introduced to the Vabô of the parent kindred.   At the present time, owing to the security conferred by the British Administration, there is a growing tendency for kindreds and extended families to break up, each householder setting up a farm for himself in the bush many miles away, perhaps, from the nearest member of his extended family or kindred.   This growth of individualism necessarily tends to the breakdown of authority within the family group, and is one of the most serious problems with which the Government has to cope.   It is counteracted to some extent by the " dolassa " organization, but it is probable that in time this organization will become based not on kinship ties, but on local association : that is, that the " dolassa " will be composed not necessarily of relatives, but of any persons who happen to farm in the same locality.

The head of the senior extended family is the head of the kindred, and the arbiter in all inter-family disputes.   As an acknowledgment of his authority any male member of the kindred who kills a game-animal must send a portion of the kill to the kindred-head. At the present time the kindred-head may live in some outlying farm or hamlet ; but even so his authority continues, and on the occasion of religious or initiation ceremonies he is bound to return to the parent village and take a directing part in the rites. Each kindred has its own private Vabô which is largely used to keep the young uninitiated lads in order, the masker appearing from time to time armed with a whip and chastising recalcitrant boys or any who has the effrontery to remain within his reach. Each kindred also has its own Vadôsu, the calabash-horn cult which is found along the whole South bank of the Benue from the Chamba Lekon and Verre tribes to Wukari. To this cult boys of the kindred are introduced about the age of ten. It is secret from the women, and one of its main purposes is to keep the women of the kindred on their good behaviour. A man who is constantly being abused by his wife will request the head of his kindred to send the masker to his house at night. The masker, speaking through the horn, will accuse the woman of despising the " dôsu " because she despises her husband, and warn her to mend her ways. The members of one kindred occasionally escort their masker to the quarters of another kindred, from which they exact gifts in the name of the genius. The other kindred in due course returns the compliment !

Intermarriage between relatives on both sides of the family is taboo, up to and including the third generation. It is not permissible, therefore, for a man to marry a woman of his own extended family, and it is not usually permissible for him to marry a woman of his own kindred. But if a kindred has split in two, and the two halves live in different localities, it is permissible for a man in one half to marry his second cousin in the other half.

There is a certain amount of promiscuity within the kindred and family groups, for it is not uncommon for sons and nephews to have sub-rosa sexual relations with the wives of their fathers or uncles, and for younger brothers or cousins with the wives of elder brothers or cousins. This is rendered possible when a man has more than one wife, especially as among the Mumuye there is no rule which requires a husband to distribute his favours equally among his wives : he may neglect a wife for a considerable period. Though sexual relations between persons within the kindred who are not formally married to each other are carried on sub-rosa, they are not regarded as incestuous ; for if detected there is merely a formal protest, based not on their incestuous character, but rather on the impropriety of a senior and a junior openly sharing anything on equal terms, just as it is improper for seniors and juniors to eat together. This is emphasised in the rule that while a younger brother may have *sub-rosa* sexual relations with an elder brother's wife, on no account may an elder brother have sexual relations with a younger brother's wife.

Sexual relations between a man and the wife of a member of a closely related kindred are pardonable ; but if detected the husband claims seven goats from his wife's concubitant, and these are eaten with great gusto by all the members of the husband's kindred. No resentment, apparently, is harboured by the husband. But if one of an unrelated kindred has sexual relations with a wife the matter is very different : the life of the adulterer would be sought, or a feud between the kindreds would arise which might last for generations.

Wife-stealing or secondary marriages are not permissible between members of the same kindred, and are avoided between related kindreds. But wives may be stolen from unrelated kindreds provided a bride-price is paid. There is no organized system of wife-stealing among the Mumuye as there is among, for example, the Malabu or the tribes of the Zaria and Plateau provinces.

Inheritance is purely patrilineal, the administrator of a man's estate being the eldest surviving brother or half-brother by the same father. The brother appropriates all corn, yams, and cattle. But he gives some of the yams to the deceased's sons, that is to say, three rows of yams to the eldest son, two to the second, and one to the third. Half of the deceased's goats may also be given to the eldest son, who will, however, be required to use some of these to pay part of the marriage expenses of his younger brother. The property taken over by the deceased's brother is used in the general interest of the family group. Sisters have no specified share, but they can appropriate any reasonable amount of their brother's property. Sisters' sons have no claim, but they may be given a small gift as an act of grace. The gift would be greater if a sister's son had grown up in the house of his maternal uncle. As regards the inheritance of widows, the normal rule is that brothers inherit all widows who have borne children, and sons inherit all widows who have not borne children. A son may,

PLATE 43

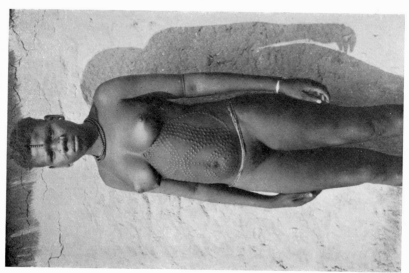

YOUNG WOMEN (MUMUYE)

however, inherit one of his father's widows who had borne a child which had died. But he would only do so if he was wifeless. Both the senior and junior levirate are practised. If the widows are disinclined to marry a brother the brother can marry them off into some other kindred and appropriate the bride-price for his own use. In the absence of brothers a son marries off widows who have borne children by his father and appropriates the bride-price.

In the matter of the arrangement of marriage it is noteworthy that among the Mumuye the young lad makes his own advances to the maid of his choice through a friend. If she is inclined to consider his suit the young people spend the evening and night together and she then gives her answer. If she accepts, the lad gives her a gift of two currency bars [1] which she shows to her mother, saying that she has accepted so-and-so as her suitor. If the mother is satisfied that her daughter is genuinely fond of the lad no objection is offered, and the lad then presents a further gift of two currency bars to the girl's father who, if he has an elder brother or cousin, passes them on to him. For among the Mumuye, as among other pagan tribes, the person who has the chief authority over children is the head of the extended family. This is an important matter which is frequently overlooked, for a native uses the term " father " when he means the social rather than biological father. The boy then announces to his father that he has sought a girl in marriage and been accepted, and the father duly reports the matter to the head of his family group. The latter takes immediate steps to clinch the engagement by providing the first instalment of the bride-price, the boy's father adding to it according to his ability. The bride-price demanded may be anything from twenty to forty goats, and this or the major part may be paid at once, or distributed over a number of years. It is received by the father of the girl, but is passed on by him to his elder brother or cousin who appropriates most of it, giving his younger brother a minor share, and perhaps also giving a small gift to the girl's maternal uncle. The girl's mother is not entitled to any share, and the maternal uncle can only claim a share under conditions which will be specified later.

---

[1] These iron bars are called *taji*. They are 14 inches long, and have a central bulb which has a diameter of 1 inch and a thickness of $\frac{1}{4}$ in. Their weight usually is about one half-pound.

As soon as the boy has been formally accepted (by the second gift of currency bars) he spends most evenings and nights in his fiancée's home, provided she does not reside at some very distant village.   Though he sleeps with her, sexual relations are taboo until the girl has passed the age of puberty and has received her final set of bodily marks.   The lad then builds a hut for himself in his fiancée's compound and is liable to be called on by the head of the compound to take part in all the co-operative farming operations held from time to time.   Normally, however, he spends the time working on his own or his father's or paternal uncle's farm.   The girl's mother may also require him to work on her farm, run messages for her, and so on.

The final cicatrization [1] of the girl constitutes the marriage ceremony, and when it is completed she is made the recipient of two currency bars from the bridegroom and of numerous bracelets from her girl friends.   The bridegroom is also required at this time to present a number of currency bars to the bride's mother.   The bridegroom now assumes the full status of husband. Should he find that his wife had had previous sexual intercourse he can demand to know the name of her paramour, who is compelled to pay a fine of seven goats.   If the husband had completed the bride-price payments he is at liberty to take his wife to his own home, but normally a wife remains in the home of her parents until the birth of her first child.

Among the hill Mumuye the mother's family has no automatic claim on the first child born of a marriage such as is exercised among the associated tribes.   If the bride-price has not been fully paid, the first child, if a male, is required, on growing up, to hand over the major part of all quarry to his maternal uncle until his father's debt has been cancelled.   If the first child is a female the maternal uncle is entitled on her marriage to receive a proportion of the bride-price equivalent to the deficiency of her father's payments.   The only case in which a maternal uncle has an absolute claim on a child is if the child is born as a result of relations between his widowed sister (or a sister whose marriage has been dissolved) and a man who has not formally married her.

---

[1] Girls have their ears pierced without ceremony between the age of 7 and 10.   The first set of abdominal marks are incised a year later.   The final marks are incised after the second menstruation.   A girl usually keeps the fact of her first menstruation secret, but informs her mother after the second menstruation.

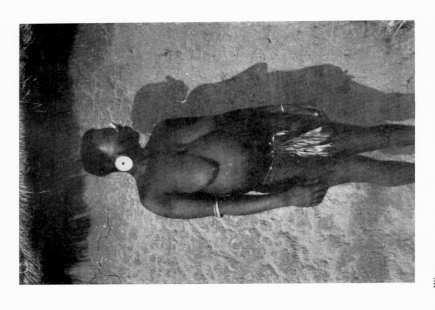

PLATE 44

MUMUYE WOMEN

But even in such a case the father may redeem the child from the maternal uncle by subsequently marrying the child's mother, that is by paying a bride-price to the woman's brother. On the other hand it is to be noted that any Mumuye may, if he pleases, abandon his father's home for that of his maternal uncle, and in such a case the maternal uncle would make himself responsible for a part or the whole of his nephew's marriage expenses. Children often accompany their mother if she returns to her own home on the death of her husband. Mumuye boys have the usual privilege of being able to appropriate small articles of property, such as chickens or even a goat, from their maternal uncle's home. A boy also treats his maternal uncle with the greatest respect. If he meets his father and uncle he will take the load of the latter. Boys have been known to strike their fathers, but it would be an unheard-of thing for anyone to strike his maternal uncle. Maternal uncles could not sell or pledge their sisters' sons, nor were uterine relatives involved in cases of witchcraft (as among the Jukun, Chamba, and numerous other Benue tribes).

The social position of the father's sister is also high. If short of children she can call on her brother to hand over to her one of his children. If the child is a male she will assist in providing him with a part of his marriage expenses : if a female she receives the girl's bride-price, but hands it on to her brother. She can call on the economic services of her brother's sons at any time, and her nephews are bound to send her a share of all their quarry. The position of women generally among the Mumuye is high, in spite of the fact that the bride-price is high. Each wife has her own quarters, her own farm, and her own corn bins : she reserves to herself the right to issue corn from her own stock for the general use of the household as she feels inclined. It is said that, as among the Verre, husbands will not dispose of any of their property in a manner displeasing to their wives. Women, it may be noted, are not segregated during their menses (as among the Jukun, Chamba, etc.), but there is the usual rule that husbands may not eat food cooked by women in this condition.

As regards the dissolution of marriage the normal rule is that if a wife leaves her husband for another man the bride-price is repayable in full, should she have borne no children. But if she had borne children the amount of bride-price repayable is reduced in proportion to the number of children born.

The following is a list of the principal terms of relationship :—

Mada (or *mai* or *dida*) = father, paternal uncle, or, in a general way, any male of a senior generation.

nja (possessive = *minja*) = son, daughter, brother's son, or, generally, any of a junior generation ; also any grandchild.

masha = maternal uncle or sister's son.

mana = mother, mother's sister, father's sister, or, generally, any female of a senior generation. A father's sister, though addressed as *mana*, is referred to as *momba*.

manzung = brother, sister, father's brother's or sister's child, mother's sister's child.

dabang (i.e. big father) = a male grandparent.

nabang (i.e. big mother) = a female grandparent.

makpang is a reciprocal term used between a person (male or female) and his parents-in-law, or senior brother-in-law or senior sister-in-law. If the persons addressing each other are of opposite sexes the term *mingkping* is used.

mama is a reciprocal term used between a man and his wife's younger brother or sister, and between a woman and her husband's younger brother or sister.

Religion.—The name of the Supreme Being among the Mumuye, properly so-called, is *La*. This name is possibly, and indeed probably, another form of the name of the Egyptian sun-god *Ra*. The Mumuye identify the sun with the Supreme Being. Elsewhere in Nigeria the same root occurs. Among the Cheki of Mubi, for example, the word for sun is *usira*, and I have suggested that this word is the equivalent of " lord (*usi*) Ra."[1] Among the Chamba Lekon we find the form *vune-ra*, and so on. It did not appear, during my short visit to the Mumuye, that any sun-rites are performed, but it is quite probable that in some groups there are analogous rites to those practised by the Kona, their close neighbours.[2]

Religious practice, however, is not much concerned with high-gods, but centres principally around two cults (*vaka*) which are known as Vadôsu and Vabô respectively. It is not clear what manner of gods these are, but we may say generally that they represent the unseen powers, the intermediaries between man and *La*, whether they are godlings or spirits or the souls of human ancestors. The symbol of the Vadôsu cult is a curved calabash horn. It is the same cult as is found among the Chamba under the name of *Voma*, among the Verre as *Doos*, and among the Jukun as *Buhor*. Among the Chamba and Verre the horns are

---

[1] See p. 296.   [2] See *A Sudanese Kingdom*, p. 186.

made of a series of calabash tubes fitted into each other, the resultant horn being anything from two to three feet long.[1] But among the Mumuye the horn is a single calabash. When blown it emits a deep awe-inspiring sound, and for this reason is regarded with the same fear as the bull-roarer among the semi-Bantu speaking peoples. The notes of the horn are, in fact, regarded as the cries of the spirits or ancestral ghosts. In some groups (for example, at Zinna) the Vadôsu is the principal Mentor of the community ; but among most of the hill Mumuye Vadôsu is an accessory cult to that of Vabô. Indeed it is little more than a men's drinking-club. Each kindred has its own Vadôsu and uses it from time to time to pay ceremonial visits to another kindred, from whom gifts are extracted in the name of the cult. On all occasions when the Vadôsu is produced there is much drinking and dancing, and it is noteworthy that the dance-step used is precisely the same as that used in the *Voma* rites of the Chamba and the *Doos* rites of the Verre. Conical rattles of plaited grass, iron gongs and drums with compression strings are all employed, as described in my paper on the Verre tribe.

The senior cult among most of the Mumuye groups is, however, that known as Vabô, which is symbolized usually by a horned mask, smeared with red earth, the nose and eyes and chin being indicated by white marks thus :—

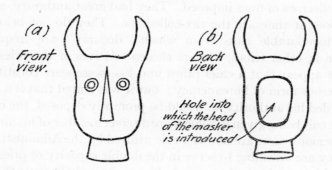

The mask resembles the Jukun mask of Akuma, and is used in much the same way, being regarded as the abode or potential abode of a spirit or spirits. The spirit symbolized is considered to be of the male sex ; but Vabô generally has a wife, who, in some cases, is represented by a pole surmounted by a human head.

[1] A sketch of the horn is given on p. 348.

This pole, which has the appearance of a totem-pole, is illustrated in the accompanying photograph. It is planted in the centre of the village; and during the rites, when Vabô descends from his shrine on the hillside, his fibre dress is hung up on the pole. Each kindred or group of related kindreds has its own Vabô, and the custodians of the cult can always be distinguished by their twin string necklaces to which a couple of beads are attached. But in every village there is always one Vabô which overshadows all the others, that to which the people resort in times of drought or epidemics, and the production of which speedily puts a stop to any armed conflict between sections of the community, the combatants being compelled to throw down their bows before the sacred mask. The priest or custodian of the superior Vabô is thus, as already stated, the chief centre of authority in the community.

In pre-Administration times if a man-slayer fled to the priest, and it appeared that the homicide was accidental, the priest could intervene to save the man from the fury of the dead man's kindred, imposing a fine of goats which were divided between the seniors of the community and the kindred which had lost one of its members. It is interesting to note that the present system of " dogarai " or native policeman, which is found among many of the Mumuye groups, is based on the Vabô cult, the " dogarai " being, in reality, the attendants and messengers of the cult and the collectors of fines imposed. They had great authority, and at the present time are the tax-collectors. They do not belong to the disreputable class from which " dogarai " are frequently drawn in other tribes, but are chosen relatives of the priest. It might appear that a chief priest and his messengers constitute a dangerous form of bureaucracy; but it was stated that if a priest exceeded his authority he would be promptly deposed, the charge of the cult being given to some more discreet member of his kindred. The senior priests are not as a rule utilized by the Administration, as they are unwilling to serve in the double capacity of priest and civil chief, partly on the ground of age and partly because they are expected to give their undivided attention to the cult, carefully guarding the mask from destruction by ants or the weather, and producing it in times of sickness or drought. Just as a masker who tripped in public when wearing the mask was heavily fined by the priest, so the priest himself was heavily fined by the seniors if anything untoward happened to the mask.

PLATE 45

A VABÔ SYMBOL

[face p. 462

A HAMLET (Mumuye)

Some account may now be given of the method of initiation into these cults. In some groups (for example, among the Gôla) initiation rites centre round circumcision; but, generally, circumcision is a purely private affair carried out when the lad is young, the initiation rites being performed at a later stage, in connection with the cults of Vadôsu and Vabô. There is considerable variation in practice, for in some groups initiation into the cult of Vadôsu is a minor matter carried out privately when a boy is ten or eleven, the main public initiation rites, i.e. those of Vabô, being carried out later. In other groups (for example, at Zinna) the main rites are those of Vadôsu. A description of the former will be given first.

When a boy is nearing the age of puberty the head of his family takes him to the hut of his Vadôsu. Here he shows the boy the sacred horn, and after pulling his ears, pinching him severely, and warning him not to reveal to women the nature of the mysterious sounds produced by the horn, he shows him how the sounds are produced. After this informal introduction the boy is considered to be a responsible member of the community, and is no longer required to conceal himself with the women and children when the sacred horns are brought forth.

The main initiation rites, i.e. those connected with a boy's introduction to the Vabô, are held every seven years. All the boys of the related kindreds bring gifts of corn to the custodians of the cult and these are brewed into beer, a process which occupies nine days instead of the six usual in the lower reaches of the Benue. On the evening before the beer is ready the attendants of the cult take the cult symbols, viz. the mask of Vabô and the horn of Vadôsu, to the stream where the boys are to assemble on the following morning. A new fringe skirt is prepared and fixed on to the mask, and the custodians then return to the town. Next morning all the seniors escort the lads to a small hill beside the stream. The boys are shaved by an attendant of the cult. A chicken is then demanded by the attendant, who takes it to the spot where the priest is concealed with the mask. The priest, holding the chicken in his right hand, addresses the mask, saying: " Vabô, you are lying before us on the ground. Our forefathers brought you here from the East, for La (God) gave you to us to help us to obtain rain and corn, and to drive illness away from our village. To-day we are going to permit our sons to look on

you and to know you, that they too may receive your protection."
The priest then cuts the throat of the chicken and allows the
blood to drip on the mask. An attendant dons the mask, his body
being concealed in the fibre garment attached to the mask. He
advances towards the boys, wagging his head and glaring at them.
The boys hang their heads in fear. The masker then returns to
the priest, doffs the costume and summons the lads to come and
see Vabô. The boys advance and take up their position in front of
the priest, each holding a stick with both hands over his head.
The attendant then openly dresses himself in the costume, and,
followed by the priest, strikes each boy a sharp blow with a whip.
The priest does likewise, and then all members of the previously
initiated grade freely belabour the boys, those who had been
especially badly behaved receiving an extra thrashing. The
marks of the chastisement received sometimes remain for lifetime,
and are regarded by the women as the outward and visible sign
of the spiritual affiliation with Vabô. The boys cover the weals
with charcoal, so that on their return to the town the mode in
which the weals had been produced may not be evident to the
women. The boys' leader is then told to bring the dead chicken
to the Vabô, and is there asked by one of the initiates of the
previous grade what the name of the mask is. The boy's uncle
(paternal or maternal) says to him : " Do not be afraid—that
which you see is Vabô." The priest then addresses the boys
saying : " You have all become grown-up men to-day. Let none
of you mention to any woman anything that you have seen. If
you do Vabô will send sickness upon you. You must respect
your father and your mother, your uncles and aunts and all
senior people. If you see them carrying a load, you must take the
load. If you fail in these duties you will be assailed by Vabô."
The masker then strikes the leader of the boys with his whip and
begins dancing. All the boys dance round him with shouts of joy
calling out " Vabô, Vabô." The boys' leader, who becomes the
attendant of the cult for the ensuing seven years, escorts the
Vabô back to the town, playing his flute in front of him.

On returning to the headquarters of the cult they deposit the
mask on the ground, and the priest kneeling before it, says : " *La*
took you and gave you to our forefathers. They brought you
from the East from Yoro. May we have rain and food by your
graciousness. *La* has permitted these young persons to see you

to-day, and we tender to you our thanks." The priest then pours a libation of beer on the mask, drinks some himself, and hands some to the masker. Beer is then drunk by all, being issued out in order of initiation-group seniority. The novices are allowed to drink beer for the first time from the same calabash as the other initiates.

After initiation the young lads, who are given new names by their parents, lead a life of semi-seclusion in grass enclosures near their homes. They remain there in idleness, being well fed with food brought to them by small boys. They eschew the society of women, and when they appear in public their faces are shrouded with a fringe of horse's hair. They are at liberty to chastise any woman who approaches them. If they join in dances they cover their mouths with their hands as they murmur the refrain of their song, for women must not see their mouths or hear their voices. At the end of the month's seclusion the boys are given bows, arrows, and knives by their fathers or uncles, and formally re-enter society, all female relatives being obliged to give them each a chicken and two iron currency bars before they will consent to lay aside their veils and hold conversation with them.

It does not appear that among the Mumuye initiation is a necessary antecedent to marriage, as among some other tribes, for, in some groups at least, initiates may be married men. A boy's initiation is often postponed owing to the rule that two brothers by the same mother may not be initiated simultaneously. The younger, even though he has passed the age of puberty, must wait for the succeeding batch seven years later ; for all persons initiated together are regarded as being on the same social footing, and it would be improper that a younger brother should be given social equality with an elder.

It is worthy of remark also that the revelation of the secret of the cult does not cause the initiates to lose their respect for the cult. Though they now know that the masker is a human being the mask itself remains sacred—the symbol of the occult powers by whose agency the well-being of the community is secured. The most solemn oath, therefore, that any man can take is by the Vabô or Vadôsu to which he has been initiated.

At Zinna the initiation procedure is as follows. When children reach the age of twelve they are introduced to the Vabô of their own ward. The rites are held every third year. The children are divided into two groups of equal number, each with a leader. During the ceremony the leaders thrash each other turn about, with the utmost severity. The others then thrash each other, also in pairs. If any boy shows fear or runs away he is expelled from the initiation group and has to come up with the next group three years later. All the boys of the village-area who pass the initiation together become a single company. They are assigned a special Vabô mask of their own and they adopt a special cry as their signal. The company becomes a unit for fighting, and the members take vengeance on any outside village for any injury done to one of their company. At the annual beer feasts held in connection with the Vabô the various companies occupy separate quarters. In addition to its uses for purposes of warfare the initiation into Vabô is regarded as a means of separating men from women, and the cult is used to browbeat women.

After the lapse of anything from fifteen to twenty-seven years three successive companies are initiated together into the senior cult of Vadôsu, each ward group being shown the Vadôsu of its own ward. The leader of the senior group is blindfolded and led backwards into a hut by two senior men. There two other men suddenly blow the calabash horns of Vadôsu, and at the same time stab the legs of the blindfolded novice with thorns. The covering is then removed from his eyes, and he rushes straight out of the hut. The leaders of the second and third group are similarly treated. They are followed by their seconds-in-command, that is to say, the two senior men of each group are subjected to this treatment. Similar treatment is accorded later to the others in a body in an enclosure outside the hut; but these are not blindfolded, as the sacred calabash horns are not used in the enclosure, cow's horns being substituted. In the evening after dark the members of the cult, accompanied by the novices, visit the various sections of the town, and are given beer; but the novices are not allowed to drink. It is during this nocturnal progression that the novices first ascertain the character of the symbols of Vadôsu. For the next seven days and nights there is continual dancing. No time is allowed for sleep, and the respite for the evening meal is made as short as possible.[1] It is a test of

---

[1] If a man turned up late he would involve the whole of his "company" in a fine.

endurance, and many youths or grown-up men become overcome with sleep and have to be carried to their homes. As soon as they wake up they must rejoin the dance.

On the eighth day a brew of beer is set in every ward, each novice being required to provide seven bundles of corn. When the beer matures dancing is resumed. Libations of beer are offered to the Vadôsu, and all initiated members of the cult partake liberally of beer. They entertain visitors from other wards, and are themselves entertained by other wards. But the novices are only allowed to drink water.

Initiation into the cult of Vadôsu entitles a man to be regarded as a " senior ", a person to be treated with respect. It confers upon him a social and religious distinction. It also admits him to a species of " night-club " in which age-seniority is considered of more importance than any other qualification.

In addition to the superior Vabô, which is only publicly brought out every seven years at the initiation rites or in cases of grave emergency, there are other masks, with fibre costumes attached, which belong to certain kindreds. These are known as *Va shenti*, and are used principally in connection with first-fruit rites. When the corn is ripe the masker appears with his attendants and makes a tour of all the farms. He is preceded by an attendant who plays on a whistle, and is followed by another who plucks heads of new corn here and there. These are taken back to the village, and on the following day all who have been initiated assemble. The custodian of the mask takes some beer in a calabash cup and holding it in his right hand speaks as follows : " By the blessing of the grave of my father, grandfather, and ancestors, I beseech you to help us before *La*, that *La* may grant us health and food. This cult is not one which I stole ; it was handed down to me by my forefathers. To-day I offer food to you, my forefathers, through the medium of the *va* (mask) ; refuse it not, but grant us your assistance." He then pours a libation of beer on the mask, and taking some of the new corn in his mouth he chews it and spits it out over the mask. Again he takes some more corn, chews it, and spits it over the masker, who in his turn also spits some of the new corn on the mask. All the senior men do likewise, and after that a feast and dance are held, the masker using the occasion to chastise with his whip the last batch of initiates, who in turn beat each other with sticks after the fashion of the Fulani " Shero ". No one may use the new corn until these rites have been performed.

Another cult found in a few Mumuye villages is that known as Aku, which is a general Jukun term for " cult ". The symbols used, viz. seven buffalo horns, are those employed by the Jukun in their Aku-Ahwâ rites. The Mumuye, however, have no rites corresponding to the Aku-Ahwâ cult of the Jukun. No details of the Aku cult were obtained beyond that, at harvest, libations of beer are poured on the horns, and that in one or two villages the horns are placed on farms as a talisman against thieves. A village chief stated that one of his sons wished to introduce the cult into his village, but his father forbade it, on the ground that it was not a Mumuye cult, and that if it were introduced it would probably bring disaster in its train.

The local Vabô may be appealed to in cases of a shortage of rain, but in some groups there are special rain cults. Thus at Mika there is a rain-cult the symbols of which are five pieces of iron with bent heads placed in the centre of four or five specially made pots. The priest enters the shrine and standing before the symbols says : " This cult is not of my own fashioning. I received it from my forefathers who brought it from Yoro. When they sought rain you gave it to them. Behold the land is all dried up and our crops are dying. By the graciousness of La (God) and of you Sô-pi (the ancestral skulls) we beseech you to send us rain." The priest then takes a stalk of the vitis quadrangularis creeper and strikes off a section with a piece of wood. " Quick as lightning " (this was the informant's expression) he rubs one of the iron rods with the juice of the creeper. He then darts across to a small pile of millet husks and sets it on fire. He leaves the hut, hastily closing the door, and it is said that a storm of rain immediately bursts.

These rites are clearly of the sympathetic-magic order, the speed with which they are carried out being likened to the speed of lightning, and the smoke being a representation of the thunder-storm clouds.

But the rain cult par excellence for all the Mumuye and surrounding tribes is that centred at Yoro. When a serious drought occurs all the senior priests of the tribe proceed with gifts to the rainmaker at Yoro. To this cult even the chief of Kona appeals as a last resort, by sending numerous gifts. The rites are said to be as follows. The priest (the *kpanti mi*, i.e. rain-chief) removes from a large pot the symbol of the cult, which is a piece of iron fashioned like a snake. It is kept rolled up in a curtain of black string. The priest unwinds the curtain and fastens it to two pegs on opposite walls of the hut. Then, taking a blacksmith's hammer in his right hand and a pair of iron scissors in his left, he says: " What I am about to do my fore-fathers did before me. Grant that this drought may cease, and that we may have corn to eat." He then chews a piece of the *vitis quadrangularis* creeper and spits it out on the implements, which he lays on the ground. Picking up the iron snake he says, " You we received from Yoro in the East : a drought has come upon us, and if we do not have rain, how shall we obtain food to eat ? Grant, therefore, that by your graciousness we may have rain in abundance, and that in due course we may reap a sufficient harvest." He again takes a piece of the creeper, chews it and spits it out on the iron snake. He then hurls the snake against the hammer and the scissors, and it is said that as soon as this is done the first peal of thunder is heard. It is a sympathetic rite, the clanging of the iron being a simulation of thunder. In case of excessive rains similar rites are performed, but the string curtain used on this ocasion is red, with the idea apparently that red is the colour of the rainbow which the Mumuye (like most Negroes) believes to be "a licker-up of rain". The priest of the cult is treated with the utmost respect, for any annoyance caused him is sufficient to produce a drought.

Though the Vadôsu and Vabô symbols are regarded as being the material abode not only of spirits of inferior status, but also of departed ancestral ghosts, this does not prevent a Mumuye from practising the more purely personal form of ancestor worship by the preservation of the skulls of dead forefathers. Among some of the units the heads of old men and women only are preserved and venerated, but among the hill Mumuye it is generally customary to preserve the heads of all adults. The heads are removed by brothers or cousins of the deceased about a year after burial, and are deposited in a skull pot which is in the keeping of the senior member of the household, viz. a brother or son of the deceased. Sons may not, however, claim the skulls of mothers ; for a married woman is buried by her own family and her skull becomes the property of her family. But when the head is removed it is first handed to the son, who delivers it, together with the gift of a chicken, into the keeping of his maternal uncle. When rites are performed before the skull the maternal uncle summons his nephew, who makes his own personal offering and prayer before his mother's skull.

The skull rites are performed immediately before the harvest, the head of the household bringing out the skulls, offering a prayer for a successful harvest, and pouring the blood of a chicken and some beer on the skulls. Similar rites are performed before the annual hunt in the dry season, all depositing their bows on the skulls. The head of a priest is inherited by his successor ; the heads of enemies were deposited in the hut of Vabô.

Women are not allowed to be present at rites performed before the skulls, and in this respect the hill Mumuye differ from some other groups ; for among the Gôla, a man will summon his father's sister when he wishes to make a prayer before his father's skull.

Re-incarnation ideas are not prominent, though it is commonly believed that some ghosts enter into the wombs of the wives of their best friend and so return to the world.

Graves are shafts with lateral extensions. As skulls are removed and the graves are used over and over again, the graves are not filled in with earth, the mouth of the shaft being merely blocked by a stone plastered over with mud.

We may conclude this section on religion by noting that dwarfs are believed to have a special relationship with the unseen powers and are treated with the utmost veneration.

The material culture of the Mumuye is of an inferior character. The huts, even of the chiefs, are devoid of any of the artistic decorations such as are found among the better class huts of the Kona to the West or of the Mumbake to the East. They are crude, circular mud huts with conical thatch, without any internal adornment and devoid even of the raised mudstead which is common among most tribes of the Adamawa province. The bedstead is a collection of logs over which is placed a mat of plaited grass. A notable feature is that the sleeping hut is usually the most remote, and is approached by a series of other huts, between each of which and the surrounding fence there is a partition of plaited grass with an aperture so small that a broad shouldered man can only struggle through with difficulty. This is a protection against robbery at night. Valuable articles are

PLATE 46

A DWARF

[face p. 470

stored in the sleeping hut, and if a robber made his way in and the alarm were given, he would find considerable difficulty in making his escape, as the small apertures could easily be blocked by members of the family arriving from a different section of the compound.

Another noteworthy feature, which I have not observed elsewhere, is that some of these partitions are constructed of logs of firewood which are only used in cases of emergency. The following sketch illustrates the method :—

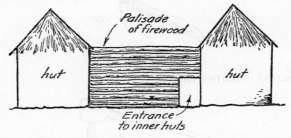

In pottery also the Mumuye are inferior to their neighbours. The three-legged small, black, glazed pot, which is found Eastwards from the Kona, is found also among the Mumuye ; but the prevalent type of pot is the following :—

The crossbands are imprinted with a pointed stick. The impressions on the lower part are made with a piece of sacking.

As regards basketry, the most common type is that of woven grass reinforced with withies and hibiscus fibre, thus :—

Farming implements are :—

(a) The Yam Hoe
(b) The Corn Hoe.

Both of these tanged implements are remarkably small. The first has a blade of about eighteen inches only and is shaped thus :—

The second is shaped thus :—

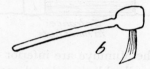

Women play a principal part in all farming operations.

As regards weapons of warfare, the Mumuye do not use the spear. Their bows are of the pattern usual in these regions : i.e. the bamboo stave, which is about $3\frac{1}{2}$ feet long, has an eyelet for the attachment of the knotted string at one end, the other end of the string being fastened by a slipknot round a terminal notch. There is no lateral notch. The iron arrow heads are fixed loosely in the shaft, the binding being smeared with strophanthus poison, which on impact is broken up and set free in the blood stream. The most noteworthy feature is the characteristic iron bow-string puller used in all the groups. It may be anything from 1 to 2 feet in length, and is usually tipped with horse-tail hair, thus :—

PLATE 47

MUMUYE MEN

The photograph accompanying the notes on the Yendang shows the method of use, and also the peculiar mode of carrying arrows sticking up out of the quiver. (See p. 488.)

Axes are carried at the side, stuck through a cloth girdle. They are shaped as follows :—

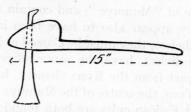

Short knives in wooden sheaths tipped with iron are also used. Another characteristic weapon of the Mumuye is a wooden stick, weighted at the end with a strip of iron and used for killing a wounded opponent.

As a defence against approaching enemies the Mumuye set mantraps in the form of concealed holes in which poisoned stakes are set. These holes are about a foot long and half a foot broad, and 1 to 2 feet deep. Thus :—

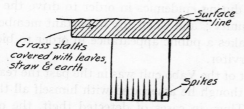

The spikes used are of hard wood, or iron, and are stuck into the ground to a depth of about four inches : poisoned porcupine quills are also used.

As regards clothing the characteristic dress of males is a small leather apron cut into strips. This is suspended from a leather girdle. In addition a goat skin is worn behind, the hind legs of the skin being fastened at the waist to the leather girdle. The other end of the skin is passed between the legs to the front, underneath the apron and girdle, and is kept in position by having the ends attached to a stick. Loin coverings of cloth are now common among the Mumuye-speaking groups to the East. They smear their heads with a charcoal made of burnt ground-nuts. The dress of the women, such as it is, is illustrated in the photographs.

THE GÔLA

The Gôla, or Gomla, are a small group of Mumuye-speaking people who are located in the districts of Yendang, Mafaran, and Nasarao. They are sometimes referred to as " The Gori ". They repudiate the title of "Mumuye", and contain a Jukun element from Kona. They appear also to have been influenced by the Chamba. Nevertheless, they must be classed as Mumuye, as they speak a Mumuye dialect, have the same religious cults as the Mumuye, and, apart from the Kona element, have a traditional connection with Yoro, the centre of the Mumuye tribe.

The Vabô and Vadôsu cults are both found among the Gôla, the Vabô being regarded as the tutelary genius of the community, whereas the Vadôsu represents the ancestral spirits. The masker of the former cult appears in public at the yam and ground-nut harvests. On these occasions, attended by his followers, he visits the farms and appropriates some of the produce of each farm, a feast being subsequently held. This practice is regarded as an offering of the first-fruits to the gods, and no one is permitted to harvest his crops until the custom has been carried out. Vabô also appears during epidemics in order to drive the sickness out of the community ; and when any important member of the cult dies Vabô makes a public appearance in order to bid farewell to his former servitor.

The priest of the Vabô cult was in the past the real chief of the community, though he associated with himself all the important old men. Thus, in cases of detected theft, the owner of the stolen property would report the theft to the priest, who would thereupon authorize the plaintiff's family to destroy the thief's house and confiscate his property. Creditors would also appeal to the priest for the recovery of a debt. The priest would send a masker at night to the debtor's house and demand the instant payment of the debt, part of which the priest and his followers would appropriate. In cases of murder the murderer's family was required to pay a fine of one cow, which the priest divided with the family of the murdered man.

As regards the calabash-horn cult of Vadôsu, this has not the same importance as among some of the Mumuye groups, being little more than a drinking club. But it is used in conjunction with the Vabô cult, and has some disciplinary value, especially

PLATE 48

THE INITIATION COSTUME

A GROUP OF NOVICES

[face p. 475

for controlling refractory boys who may be fined for their ill-behaviour.

The initiation rites among the Gôla are of peculiar interest, and differ from those of the other Mumuye groups in that they are primarily associated with circumcision and not with the cults of Vabô and Vadôsu. The rites are carried out every ten years, but it is said that in former times the interval was longer—so much so that a father and son might undergo circumcision at the same time. This is hard to believe, for in the other Mumuye groups it is not even permissible for a younger brother to be initiated at the same time as an elder brother. At the present time a group of novices includes male children from the age of one to eleven. Those under three are merely circumcised, but all children over three are required to undergo the whole of the initiation ritual.

In the spring of the initiation year the parents of children due for circumcision must work for a few days on the farms of the oldest men of the community. By doing so they are said to obtain " the knife of circumcision ". Later in the year, when the millet crops begin to ripen, some of the stalks are cut and laid aside for the construction of the special enclosure in which the boys are to be segregated. This work must be carried out in one day. The grass for thatching must be collected in one day, and prepared in one day. The enclosure is built early in the dry season, and, on its completion, the father or guardian of each boy kills a goat outside the enclosure, and cooks and eats the flesh. The boys are then assembled by local, and not kinship, groups, and are shaven by their fathers (or in the case of an eldest son, by his maternal uncle, for reasons which will be explained later). It was stated that the boys are shaved because corpses are shaved. This remark shows clearly that circumcision and initiation are regarded as a death to one's former self and a rebirth. They also wash themselves, just as a corpse is washed before burial. They then proceed to the enclosure, taking care to avoid contact with women, and are given a good meal. Any food left over is eaten up by the senior men present. Next morning they are all circumcised. A boy of strong personality is done first and becomes the leader of his initiation group. After the operation children under three years of age are sent back to their mothers, but the others are taken out to the bush and spend the day there quietly, returning to the enclosure in the evening.

They are given food and water at dawn, midday, and in the evening. The water is brought by girls who have not yet reached the age of puberty, and the food by women who are suckling children. Mothers of unweaned children lead a life of sexual abstinence, and it might be concluded, therefore, that the reason for the above regulation is that newly circumcised boys must be protected from the excitement which might be caused by the visit of women with whom sexual intercourse was possible. But this reason is insufficient, for in many tribes there is an additional rule that the men who attend on novices must abstain from sexual intercourse during the period of their attendance. Sexual intercourse is regarded as entailing a pollution or contagion which must not be communicated to boys undergoing initiation ; for initiation is, like Confirmation among Christians, a putting-away of all the " filth "[1] of life. It is a form of affiliation with the gods.

The newly circumcised boys must not eat meat or any form of food containing a savouring of salt, as meat and salt are thought to hinder the process of healing. Every third day at dawn they wash themselves until the wound is completely healed. They are then allowed to eat meat and dishes savoured with salt, and they begin also to learn the special dances of initiation. They are not subjected to any hardships, and may spend their spare time in idling or in hunting the smaller game-animals. Their clothing consists of skirts of leaves, but when they return to the town in the evening they wear a special costume which completely disguises them. For no one, particularly a woman, must recognize them. This costume, which is made by their fathers and guardians, consists of a cloak of plaited grass, adorned with pieces of guinea-corn stalks which rattle as they dance along the road. The cloak is surmounted with two horns made of rolls of grass smeared with clay. The dance-step is intended to imitate that of the antelope or other horned animal represented by the costume worn.

The boys are required to maintain their life of segregation until the crops have been completely harvested and stored in the granaries, that is to say, they live a life of seclusion for at least a month. On the conclusion of this period they are given a new skirt of leaves and are escorted back to the town, where they are received with great acclamation. Their bodies are smeared with oil by women to " soothe their afflictions ". They are entertained

---

[1] This is the actual native expression.

PLATE 49

A VERY YOUNG INITIATE

[face p. 477

SALUTING

with a feast. But they must not speak to anyone, least of all to a woman. On the following morning each father presents his son with a loin-cloth, or, if old enough, with a gown and trousers. He confers upon him a new name, and induces him to speak by a gift of a chicken. The boys then visit all their relatives and friends. The paternal aunt of each boy presents her nephew with a goat, and he is then at liberty to speak to her. The mother gives her son a chicken ; maternal and paternal uncles present him with arrows. The circumcisors and custodians of the lads are paid with gifts of beer and chickens, and they are also allowed to appropriate the food-calabashes which the boys had used during their term of segregation.

After an interval those boys who are considered old enough are formally introduced to the cults of Vabô and Vadôsu.[1] The priest produces the symbols of the cults and says to the boy : " What are these ? " The uncle of the boy says to him : " Do not be afraid. What you see is Vabô and Vadôsu." The priest then addresses the boys saying : " Until recently you were boys, irresponsible persons. But now you have become grown-up men. Let none of you mention to any woman what you have seen to-day : for if you do Vabô and Vadôsu will take vengeance on you. You must henceforth show the utmost respect to your father and mother and their brothers and sisters, and to all seniors. If you meet them with a load you must take that load. And if you fail in any of your duties towards your elders you will be prostrated with sickness." Each boy is then dressed in the costume of the genius, and is shown the dance-steps of the cult. If he is slow to pick them up he is subjected to ridicule and abuse.

As in the other Mumuye groups the skulls of the dead are preserved. They are removed from the grave during the dry season by a special family of grave-diggers, who receive a fee of one goat and a chicken in return for their services. The grave-digger cleans the head and places it in a calabash, which he hands to the brother or eldest son of the deceased. The latter leaves the head on the top of his granary for five days to dry and then places it in a pot, covered with a lid, which he secretes under his granary. If at any time he falls ill or is unlucky he seeks the assistance of his paternal aunt, who takes a white chicken and accompanies her nephew to the pot containing his father's skull.

---

[1] The introduction to Vadôsu may be postponed.

There, addressing her dead brother, she speaks as follows : " If it is you and I who have caused your son's illness (or misfortune) we must release him that we be not shamefaced before the people." She then holds out the chicken to her nephew, who slits its throat, the blood being allowed to drip on to the skull. Having performed this rite the aunt goes home, cooks the chicken, and eats it, sending some of the meat to any brothers who may be surviving.

The important position assigned to the father's sister appears to be a characteristic of the Chamba peoples, and the Gôla have seemingly absorbed this trait, as well as others, from the Chamba, who were dominant in these regions prior to the advent of the Fulani. The reason assigned for the special position held by a paternal aunt is that she is a master of witchcraft and sorcery. She can resolve a spell imposed by her brothers ; but the latter, and no one else apparently, can resolve her spell. But the real reason would appear to be that the father's sister is a potential mother-in-law, as marriage with the father's sister's child is considered the best form of marriage. During times of drought it is a Gôla custom for some senior man, acting on behalf of the community, to offer a prayer for rain before the skull of some man who was reputed to have been a centenarian. The petitioner holds a chicken up to the midday sun and speaks as follows : " Da (god) gave you food so that you lived for a hundred years. You had a long life and left the world joyfully. Da took you, not we. May we also have food and live to a ripe old age. Behold, our crops are parched for want of rain. We beseech you to ask Da to send us rain, so that we and our children may not perish. You cannot speak to us, but you can see us ; so help us, we beseech you." He then slays the chicken and pours the blood over the pot containing the skull. Subsequently he cooks and eats the flesh.

The Gôla believe in re-incarnation, those who are reborn being born into the family of either their father or mother. It is noteworthy that if a person is believed to be a re-incarnated ancestor he is not given the name of that ancestor until he has undergone initiation. For if the name were conferred earlier the returned ancestor would leave the world in wrath.

It is not a Gôla practice to segregate menstruous women in a special hut, but when a woman's menses begin the husband

PLATE 50

[face p. 479

THE INITIATION DANCE

smears the juice of a certain species of tuber over the lintel of the door. The woman must abstain from cooking. If these rules are not observed it is believed that the husband would have no success in hunting, that his poisons would lose their effect, and that he himself would stumble and break some of his bones.

The graves used by the Gôla are pits widened out at the base. A single grave may contain the remains of many people. When it becomes full the bones of the former occupants are removed and given a separate burial. Men and women are buried in the same grave, but people who die young are buried in a special grave dug beneath a granary.

The Gôla form of social organization differs from that of the other Mumuye groups in that the mother's family has a controlling interest over some of the children in certain circumstances. There are two modes of contracting marriage, (a) by the payment of a large bride-price, and (b) by the payment of a small bride-price. The large bride-price is one hundred goats or the equivalent, and the small fifteen goats. If the large bride-price has been paid the woman is considered to have been bought out of her own group, and her relatives have no claim to any of her children.[1] She cannot normally re-marry during her husband's lifetime. But if the smaller bride-price only has been paid the wife's relatives have an automatic claim to the custody of the first male child born of the marriage, and to a major share of the bride-price payable for the first two female children. If no male children are born of the marriage the wife's relatives can claim the custody of the eldest daughter. Under the small bride-price system it is easy for a woman to change her husband if she feels so disposed.

It will be seen from these regulations that there is an element of what may properly be called " purchase " in the higher bride-price system. The status of the wife becomes the same as that of one married under a system of exchange, and it is possible that marriage on the higher bride-price is a substitute for a former system of marriage by exchange. For among most tribes who practise marriage by exchange there is usually also an alternative system of marriage on a small bride-price. In the case of marriage by exchange the wife and her offspring virtually become the property of the husband, whereas in that of marriage of a small

---

[1] But a maternal uncle is entitled to a share in the bride-price of the first female child.

bride-price the wife's relatives retain control over her and her children. The Gôla system of marriage is practised by the Jukun of Kona, and was probably introduced by the immigrants from Kona. It may be noted that the dual system of marriage described is not confined to the Benue regions, for I have found it also as far North as the Bade tribe in Bornu.

When a maternal uncle receives a bride-price for his sister's daughters he may be required to give a share of it to his own maternal uncle if his own mother had been married on a small bride-price. It is also a rule that all male children born under the small bride-price system must send to their mother's relatives the major part of quarry obtained by them in hunting. On the other hand a maternal uncle is primarily responsible for arranging the marriage of a sister's son, whose custody he had claimed (under the small bride-price rule).

As regards inheritance this normally follows the patrilineal rule, but a sister's son is generally given, as an act of grace, one unit of each form of property left by the deceased. But the share of a sister's son who had been brought up by his uncle would be greater, in view of the economic advantages which the uncle had derived from his nephew's labour.

The following are the principal terms of relationship :—

> *da* = father, paternal uncle, or any male of a senior generation.
> *na* = mother, mother's sister, father's sister, or any female of a senior generation. A mother's sister is referred to as *na-zumbi*, a father's sister as *njimi*.
> *masa* = a special term for mother's brother or sister's child.
> *nja* = son, daughter, sister's or brother's child, or any of a junior generation.
> *mazung* = brothers, sisters, and all classes of cousin.
> *maibo* = male grandparents.
> *maibô* = female grandparents.
> *maja* = any grandchild.
> *makpang* = fathers-in-law, husband's elder brother, wife's elder brother.
> *makpî* = mothers-in-law, husband's elder sister, wife's elder sister.
> *mama* = a reciprocal term used between a man and his wife's younger sister, and between a woman and her husband's younger brother.

THE YENDANG AND WAKA

The Yendang.—The Yendang and Waka, who are found near Zinna in the Bajama district of the Adamawa Emirate and in the

North-East of the Muri Emirate, may be classed together as a single ethnic unit. Both speak the same dialect of a language which is closely related to that of the Mumuye and still more so to that of the people of Gengle, Kugama, and Teme. But this language is by no means identical with Mumuye, nor is the culture of the Yendang and Waka uniform with that of the Mumuye. Nevertheless some groups of Yendang and Waka accept the designation of Mumuye, and it would appear that they contain a Mumuye stratum which has fused with an aboriginal element bearing a resemblance to the Verre and, in some respects also, to the semi-Bantu speaking peoples of the Bauchi Plateau. Thus the Yendang and Waka wear penis-sheaths and use short swords. They appear to have had a duodecimal system of numeration ; for in some groups of Yendang the word for 9 is " kop " less three, and it was stated that " kop" was formerly twelve, and not ten as at the present time. It was also stated that in former times bundles of corn were always counted by twelves and not by tens. The same phenomenon has been found among numerous semi-Bantu speaking peoples of Northern Nigeria, most of whom wear some form of penis sheath and carry short swords.[1] The Yendang and Waka use a different word for the Sun and Supreme Being from the Mumuye, and their religious conceptions are different. Their relationship terminology is also different, and we shall see later that as regards material culture they present a striking contrast to the Mumuye.

The Yendang claim, like many of the tribal units in this area, to have sprung originally from Yoro, the rain-making centre of the Mumuye. This tradition probably means no more than that they contain a Mumuye element. Indeed the process of fusion with the Mumuye has been continuous. The Wagule kindred of Bajama, for example, are recent immigrants from Zinna. It is probable also that the Yendang, like the Gôla, contain elements of Jukun origin from Kona. This is suggested by the title of one of the kindreds or clans, viz. the Wakpani.[2] The Yendang, like most of the surrounding tribes, were overcome by the Fulani, and their leader, who belonged to the Wagwubi kindred, was subsequently recognized by the Fulani, being given the title of Alkali Manga. It was stated that when the British assumed direction of the

---

[1] See Meek, *The Northern Tribes of Nigeria*, vol., i, pp. 41, 307, and vol. ii, p. 142.
[2] The Jukun call themselves the Wapâ.

Administration the headman of the village of Dapanti was put forward as being the tribal chief, the Alkali Manga being timorous of too close an association with the British at that time. This may be an *ex parte* statement ; but the head of the Wagwubi kindred appears to have been, at least, the religious leader of the community.[1]

In the Bajama districts the following clans or kindreds are found :—

    (1) Wa-Gwubi, Wa-Kpani, Wa-Kabe.
    (2) Wa-Dindele, Wa-Taji, Wa-Kpuri.
    (3) Wa-Girim, Wu-Yanga.
    (4) We-Kumbe.
    (5) Wo-Daku, Wo-Gure, Wa-Kuti, Wa-Taku.
    (6) Wa-Gule.

Those which are classed together believe themselves to be descendants of a common forefather, but there is no clan organization for marriage purposes, as all classes of cousins may intermarry.[2] Father-right conditions prevail, but the mother's family enjoys certain privileges as regards children born of a marriage, particularly the first child. The first child is normally born in the home of the wife's parents, it being the Yendang custom that a young bridegroom sleeps with his bride in her own home until she becomes a mother. The first child is regarded as belonging to the mother's family. If a male he is required to give the first three game-animals he kills to his mother's father or brother, and thereafter for the rest of his life he must give every alternate animal. He normally lives with his maternal grandfather or uncle, who utilizes his services until he marries, the grandfather or uncle being primarily responsible for arranging the marriage-payments. On his marriage he is at liberty to join his father's group, but he may prefer to remain with his mother's relatives from whom he can inherit a substantial share of property left. If he rejoins his father's group his body at death must be sent back for burial at his mother's home.

[1] Court cases of major importance are at the present time referred to the Alkali of Maio Belwa. Minor cases are apparently settled by the Fulani district head, sitting with one or two important Yendang as assessors. This latter arrangement, though not legal, may work satisfactorily if scrutinized. But the senior men of Yendang should be able to carry out such work without the intervention of the district head.

[2] Cousin-marriages are considered the best form of marriage, on the ground that they keep wealth within the father's and mother's family.

PLATE 51

YENDANG GIRLS

[face p. 483

If the first male child is born in the husband's home (the woman having failed to conceive in her own home) the obligations of the child towards his mother's family are reduced. He remains in his father's home and when he dies he is buried there. But he must give a substantial part of all his quarry to his mother's father or brother. If, however, young male children are born after him one of these has to perform all the obligations which he himself would have had to perform had he been born in his mother's home, i.e. the younger brother must give the first three game-animals killed to his maternal grandfather, must place his services at his grandfather's disposal when required, and though he does not necessarily take up his abode with his mother's relatives his body, at death, must be buried by them.

If the first child born of a marriage is a female her mother's relatives claim a major part of her bride-price when she is given in marriage, but the amount claimed is considerably reduced had the girl been born in her father's home.

It is clear that the privileges enjoyed by the mother's family are, as among the Mumuye, intimately connected with the bride-price, and it may be noted that it was never a Yendang rule that a maternal uncle could pawn or sell his sister's children, nor was he held responsible for his debts. But a sister's child can appropriate any of his maternal uncle's property during his lifetime. A wife at death is always buried in her own home.

The Yendang do not practise marriage by exchange, all marriages being contracted on the bride-price system. A plurality of suitors is not permitted (as in many tribes), and if an accepted suitor should finally be repudiated he is entitled to the refund of all payments previously made. Secondary marriages may be contracted by elopement, but in such cases the first husband must be compensated. It is a general rule (as in most tribes, though not among many Bata-speaking peoples) that no one may elope with a woman who is married to a member of his own local group. It is also customary for the new husband to present a chicken to the former husband, who sacrifices it in order to allay any ill-feeling which might have arisen between them. Widows are heritable and may be married by senior or junior brothers or cousins or even by sisters' sons of their late husband. In some groups at least sons can inherit their father's young widows (other than their own mothers).

The following is a summary of the principal relationship terms :—

Da = father, father's brother, or any male of a senior generation. A father's elder brother may be called *zoda* and his younger brother *vada*.

Nene = mother, mother's sister, father's sister, or any female of a senior generation. A father's elder sister may be addressed as *yimamang*, but a mother's elder sister is always addressed as *nene*. A father's sister is referred to as *vasure da*, and a mother's sister as *va yinang*.

Wiyina = maternal uncle or sister's child.

Vaban = brother or any male cousin.

Vasurang = sister or any female cousin.

Mimvawe or *Vadi* = son, daughter, or any person of a junior generation.

Yirbamang = all grandparents.

Vadivadi mang = all grandchildren.

Kpâsang = male parents-in-law, senior brothers-in-law, and male children-in-law.

Konang = female parents-in-law, senior sisters-in-law, and female children-in-law.

Nyansang = junior brothers-in-law and sisters-in-law.

The Yendang did not in the past practise circumcision, but the custom is now spreading. They have a form of initiation for boys which is carried out every three years during the dry season. The boys are assembled in a special enclosure, and clothed in a costume of locust-bean tree leaves, which they wear for an entire year. The formal rites last ten days, They spend the day in the bush and sleep at night in the enclosure. Every morning and evening they are smeared with oil by girl friends, a custom which is also followed by the Margi tribe, among whom initiation is directly connected with entry into the married state.[1] For the first four days the boys are provided with food by their fathers, but for the succeeding six days they have to fend for themselves by hunting in the bush, the quarry being cooked for them by their girl friends. At the end of the ten days the boys return to their own homes, but they speak to no one save senior men for a period of one month. They continue to anoint themselves daily with oil until the first fall of the rains, the oil being sent to them by their girl friends.

In the following year the boys discard their leaf-costumes and each is presented by his father with a cloth loin-covering or,

[1] See p. 230.

until recently, a penis-sheath made of string or hide. He is also given a bow, arrows, quiver, knife, and iron bracelets, and is told that he is now a man and must behave as such. He must be brave on all occasions, especially when hunting : if he shows fear he will fall a prey to the animal, but if he keeps cool the animal will become his prey. He must take a wife and found a home for himself. He must avoid stealing, and treat his seniors with respect. After receiving these injunctions the boys are carried round on the shoulders of the senior men, a dance is begun, and a feast follows.

The Yendang identify the Supreme Being with the Sun under the name of *Ru*,[1] but they do not practise any sun-rites. Such rites as they do practise are directed mainly towards securing agricultural fertility. Thus at sowing-time the members of each hamlet proceed to a cross-roads, headed by an old man who acts as the officiating priest. Holding a chicken in his right hand the priest circumambulates behind the people saying : " The rites which I am about to perform were received by my forefathers from Yoro and from Yongko. They were handed down to my father who, after a lengthy life, left the world. But though he is dead he sees us now, and I ask for corn from his hands. I ask him to beseech *Ru* to send us sufficient rain for our crops. I ask him to send us guinea-corn, ground-nuts, beans, and hibiscus that we may not die of hunger or be dispersed among strangers." He then enters into the centre of the group where the elders are assembled and places some wild *paw-paw* leaves on a stone. He cuts off the head of the chicken which, as it jumps about before falling dead, sprinkles with its blood the feet of those who are near to it. The priest allows some of the blood to drip on the leaves and places the stone over the leaves. A forked branch is set in the ground beside the stone and to this the chicken's head is attached. The chicken is plucked and the feathers are deposited at each cross-roads on the outskirts of the village. The priest then takes the chicken home, cooks it and eats it.

When the corn begins to sprout these rites are repeated with the added words : " The crops are rising, and shall suffice, even though the farmer has but a small farm. May we all derive the full benefit of every seed planted."

---

[1] This word occurs as *Lu* among the Kumba, Teme, and Gengle, and also among the Warwar groups of Mambila (British Cameroons).

When the crops have been gathered the priest prepares a special brew of beer and goes to the grave of his father, where he pours a libation saying: " The food which we sought at your hand has been given to us in plenty. We thank you, and we bring you your share." He goes also to the grave of his mother and pours a libation there. All heads of households do likewise, a dance and feast are held, and the people are then at liberty to use the new corn. In some groups the first-fruit rites are marked by the priest chewing a few grains of new millet and spitting them out over a sacred pot and also over his bow, all senior men following his example.

The use of stones in these rites is interesting, and it would appear that the stones serve the same purpose as the miniature dolmens or *kist vaens* which are used by the Yungur, Gabin, and Longuda tribes as the abode of the corn-spirit, the stone being thought to serve the double purpose of providing a cool retreat and preventing the spirit from wandering away into the bush. It may be remembered that among the Yungur and Gabin there are definite Osiris-like conceptions (e.g. the throwing of corn over dead bodies) and mummification practices, and it may, therefore, be that the *kist vaens* of the corn-spirit were in origin a simulacrum of the tomb of the dying and rising man-god who was identified with the corn. The Yendang, incidentally, are firm believers in re-incarnation.

The usual type of grave found among the Yendang is a circular hole with lateral extensions. The body is wrapped in strips of cloth, and after it has been interred the grave is not filled up, the mouth being merely blocked with a stone or pot. If the deceased had been a female a stick is planted over the grave and all her calabashes and cooking utensils are stuck on to the stick (as shown in the photograph). Her pots are left lying on the grave. A funeral dance is held and at the end of five or six days a libation of beer is poured over the grave by a woman.

The graves are used over and over again, and when they are opened to receive a new body the skull of the former occupant is removed, cleaned, wrapped in strips of cloth and buried separately near the grave. If a son or younger brother of the deceased is at any time unfortunate he deposits some porridge on the stone that marks the spot where the skull is buried and says : " I come to you, my father (or mother or brother) to seek your

A Man's Grave

A Woman's Grave

[face p. 486

assistance. Everything I touch goes wrong. Hinder me no more, but permit me to have success."

It may be noted, incidentally, that the Yendang were formerly head-hunters. Heads of enemies slain were brought home and a dance was held, the heads being subsequently buried. Those who obtained heads had to have their bodies washed in beer by an old man in order to safeguard themselves from pursuit by the ghosts of their victims. It is also the Yendang custom to send annually to the Mumuye priest of Yoro for seed, and in times of drought all the village heads assemble and proceed to Yoro, taking with them gifts which include a dog, goat, and chickens.

As regards material culture the most striking feature is the costume worn by young girls. This mode of dressing, which is illustrated in the photographs, is quite unique. The white headgear is nothing more than white beads of European manufacture threaded on to the hair. Grown up women wear a bunch of leaves over the pubes and buttocks, but during dances their loin-coverings consist of short aprons decorated with white beads and suspended from a girdle of blue beads. Behind they wear a string fringe which is also decorated with white beads. Large iron rings are worn in the ears, and some women wear wisps of grass in the septum of the nose. A large number of brass bracelets may be carried on the left arm, and garters of white or yellow beads on the legs below the knee. Over the ankles iron rattles, containing a small stone or piece of metal, are worn at dances, and during dances also most grown-up women carry on the shoulder a scythe-like implement shaped as follows :—

Women smoke pipes, the mouth-pieces of which are decorated with red and white beads.

The men wear waist-coverings consisting of cloth-flaps suspended, at the back and front, from a leather girdle. But some Yendang affect the leather aprons of the Mumuye. Iron bracelets are worn on the left arm, and bronze on the right. Warriors wear wooden helmets, on the top of which is set a four-eared straw-hat surmounted with feathers. The principal weapon of the Yendang is a bow of the Mumuye type. The Yendang are not a spear-using people like some of their neighbours. The bowstrings are pulled by means of an iron puller as shown in the photograph. A noteworthy feature is the absence of shields. But they possess short swords about two feet in length shaped thus :—

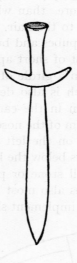

The houses are of similar pattern to those of the Yungur, Gabin, and Hona tribes, in that the hut of each married woman is approached through an enclosure made of matting, the doorway being cut out of the matting (see photograph, p. 490). The bedsteads consist of planks (as among the Mumuye). The mills for grinding corn have no well (like those of the Kona and surrounding tribes).

PLATE 53

YENDANG BOWMEN

[face p. 488

Pots of the following type were observed :—

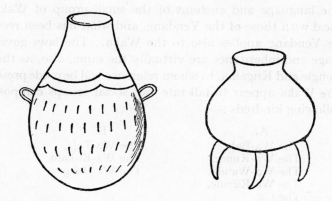

Among musical instruments single-membrane drums of the following type were observed :—

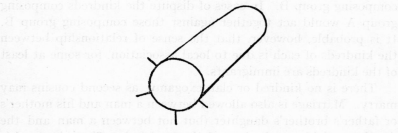

They are beaten on the ground with the hand. Whistles of bamboo and iron hand-gongs are also employed. Baskets are made of plaited straw and reinforced with withies in the following style :—

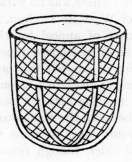

The Waka

The language and customs of the small group of Waka are identical with those of the Yendang, and what has been recorded of the Yendang applies also to the Waka. The laws governing marriage and inheritance are virtually the same, also, as those of the Gengle and Kugama, to whom reference will be made presently.

The Waka appear to fall into two social groups composed of the following kindreds :—

A.	B.
The Wa-Bale.	The Wa-Taja.
The Wa-Kuure.	The Wa-Kakalu.
The Wa-Wande.	The Wa-Bongru.
The Wa-Kileule.	
The Ga.	
The Pokare.	

The kindreds composing group A believe themselves to be descendants of a common forefather, and so also do those composing group B. In cases of dispute the kindreds composing group A would act together against those composing group B. It is probable, however, that the sense of relationship between the kindreds of each is due to local association, for some at least of the kindreds are immigrants.

There is no kindred or clan exogamy, as second cousins may marry. Marriage is also allowed between a man and his mother's or father's brother's daughter (but not between a man and the daughter of his mother's or father's sister). There is no clan totemism ; but the Wa-Bale kindred avoid eating the flesh of monkeys, while the other kindreds of group A, as well as those of group B, avoid eating the flesh of leopards. The Wa-Bale are considered the senior and ruling kindred in group A, and the Wa-Bongru in group B. There was no paramount chief in former times, but the head of Wa-Bale kindred, being the rain-maker, was regarded as a court of appeal for the whole community. Anyone charged with an offence could appeal to the priest, whose decision was final. For it was felt that a refusal to accept the ruling of the priest might lead to a drought. The priest also intervened to prevent fighting between two kindreds, by laying some *paw-paw* leaves between the combatants and ordering them to desist. No one would dare to cross these leaves. At the present time the local chief, though belonging to the Wa-Bale

PLATE 54

A GROUP OF YENDANG

WOMEN AT WORK IN THE FIELDS

[face p. 490

kindred, is not the priest : but he consults the priest in all matters of importance.

In times of drought the senior men of the Wa-Bale kindred assemble at the rain-shrine, where a goat is slain and eaten by them, the priest having first called on the ancestors to ask *Ru* (the Sun) to send them rain. The skin of the goat is hung up in the shrine. The symbol of the cult is said to be a drum in which are deposited samples of the seeds of the various crops. These seeds are changed at intervals, for it is believed that if they were allowed to decay the harvest would fail. At sowing-time the priest takes a hoe, turns up some of the soil beside the drum, deposits a few seeds of guinea-corn, and replaces the soil. This rite permits all the Waka to begin sowing. At harvest the priest takes three or four heads of corn from the farm of any member of his own kindred, and makes from it a brew of unfermented beer. Having assembled all the grown-up male members of the kindred he sprinkles some of the beer on the head and mouth of each person present. On the conclusion of this rite all farmers may begin to reap their crops.

Each kindred is represented at the shrine by an arrow stuck into the body of the drum. At the beginning of the hunting season it is the priest's duty to inspect the arrow of each kindred and repair it, if necessary. For if an arrow-head were left loose the members of the kindred represented by the arrow would have no success in their hunting.

The Waka, and Yendang also, have the Vadôsu calabash horn-cult of the Mumuye. The horns must never be produced during the period between the ripening of the corn and the planting in the following spring.

THE TEME

The Teme are a small group of people located in the Maio Belwa district, who speak a language which is virtually the same as that of the Waka, with whom they were formerly associated on the same group of hills. Generally speaking, their customs and culture are the same as those of the Yendang and Waka. The social organization is the same, and the religious conceptions are approximately the same, with the exception that the Teme have long practised circumcision and use a different type of grave. The houses and clothing are identical, and Teme girls follow the Yendang fashion of adorning the hair with a cap of white beads.[1]

The Teme consist of six localized kindreds, viz. Adong, Ahagam, Akotele, Adokwin, Ajago, and Akoja. These kindreds, which are patrilineal groupings, are not exogamous. The marriage of all classes of cousins is permissible, and cousin-marriages are considered the best form of marriage on the ground of their permanence. It was maintained by the Teme also that there is less quarrelling between the partners of cousin-marriages. There is no general totemism, but no one of the Adong kindred will kill or eat the flesh of a water-buck, it being said that a breach of this taboo would entail deafness.

The head of each kindred settles all minor disputes within the kindred, but major complaints are referred to the head of the Adong kindred, who is the official head of the community. Cases of serious crime would ultimately, at the present time, be referred to the court of the Muslim Alkali.

Authority within the family is mainly father-right, but we find among the Teme (as among the Yendang and Waka) that the mother's family has a special claim on the first-born child of a marriage, if that child had been born in the home of the mother's family, as is usually the case. The first child, if a male, has to give a leg of every animal he shoots to his maternal grandparents, and, if a female, her bride-price is appropriated by the mother's relatives. The reason assigned by the Teme for this custom is that the mother's relatives must receive compensation for the trouble and expense which they had incurred at the time of the child's birth and during the early years of his life. But the first-born child usually returns to the father's home as soon as he is weaned.

The authority of the mother's family is not, however, very extensive, for inheritance follows the patrilineal principle. There is the usual rule that a sister's children may appropriate any minor form of property from their uncle during his lifetime, and children may even go and reside with their maternal uncle, should they so desire. But this is uncommon. The Teme also follow the Yendang and Waka custom by which the body of a

---

[1] A piece of thread is rolled into one or two hairs, and the beads are then attached to the thread.

married woman is sent to her own home for burial. The husband provides one of the burial shrouds, and the woman's family the other. The husband and the children attend the burial rites, and the children remain with their mother's kin until all the rites, including the funeral feast, have been completed.

Property is inherited by brothers or in their absence by sons. When a younger brother who has inherited from an elder brother dies the eldest son of the elder brother divides the property with the eldest son of the younger brother, and each becomes responsible for the maintenance and marriage of his own younger brothers. The headship of the household is inherited by the son who is most senior in years ; but if two sons by different brothers are approximately of the same age the headship will be conferred on the more sensible of the two.

Widows are heritable, and both the senior and junior forms of levirate marriage are practised. Sons may inherit their father's widows, and may marry the younger widows if the widows agree. Or they may allow the widows to marry one of their cousins, without demanding a bride-price. But a bride-price is demanded if the widow remarries outside her late husband's family group.

Among the Teme initiation rites are associated with circumcision, and in this respect the Teme resemble their neighbours the Gôla (q.v.). The rites are preceded by a three months course of dancing, on the conclusion of which the boys are shaven and circumcised. As among the Gôla the circumcision is followed by a period of retreat, during which they spend the day hunting in the bush, and the night in a special enclosure. They are well fed, and the reason given for this was that good food was necessary in order to make the boys into new beings. At the end of the two months, when they return to the town concealed in their circumcision costumes, they are led in a body by their superintendent to the hut of the mother of each boy in rotation. The mother, looking along the line of boys, says to the superintendent : "Where is my son ?" He replies : "Look and see if he is here." She approaches the first boy with a gift, and he opens his costume so as to reveal his face. And so she passes down the line until at last she discovers her son, when, with a cry of joy, she embraces him shouting out : " My son has come back

safely. Thanks be to *Lui* (God) who has restored him to us."
But the boy remains silent, for he is a new being who knows not
his former mother, and he remains silent until the ceremonies are
finally concluded three days later.

At the end of three days, when all the boys have visited their
relatives, they take farewell of the enclosure in which they had
slept for two months, discard their costumes, and are received
in the town with great acclamation. The father of each boy
presents him with a bow, arrow, and knife, and bids him use
these for hunting animals, and not for robbing or injuring his
fellow men.

The Teme describe the Supreme Being, whom they identify
with the Sun, as *Lui*, which is a variant of *Lu* and *Ru*. No
Sun-rites are performed, and the Teme, indeed, have few cults of
any kind. Religious practice centres round the ancestors. When
anyone dies he is buried in a shaft and tunnel grave, the mouth of
which is then blocked with sticks covered with a mat and a
plaster of clay. If the deceased had been a grown-up male a
monolith is set up over the grave. A few days later the elders
of the group proceed to the grave, accompanied by the brother
and sons of the deceased, and by the two grave-diggers (who
always belong to the Adong kindred). The senior grave-digger
addresses the dead man saying : " We have cared for you and
accorded to you a proper burial. Do you care also for us. Hinder
us not in our labours, and prosper us in all things." He then
deposits on the grave some food-offerings and also pours a libation
of beer. It is customary also for a senior brother or son to make
periodic offerings at the grave of his dead relative at hoeing-time
and harvest, or on any occasion when he happens to have made a
brew of beer. Before he goes out hunting he visits the grave of his
ancestor, and with a petition for success deposits on the grave a
few pieces of porridge.

In times of drought there are no formal rites, but it
is customary for all to make gifts to the old women of the
community, who in their own homes utter some such prayer as the
following : " Men may be strong as elephants, but it is a woman
that gives birth to every man. Spirits of our forefathers behold
us ! We are old and tired. Grant that we and our children may
have rain, that we die not of hunger."

Kumba and Yofo

In the Maio Belwa district also there are groups of people found at the villages of Kumba, Yofo, Sate, and Kuseki, who speak a language which is closely related to that of the people of Gengle and Kugama, as well as of the Teme, Waka, and Yendang. They pass as " Mumbake ", but their language is different from that classed as Mumbake in my paper on the Chamba tribe. Culturally they resemble the Mumbake on the one hand and the Yendang on the other. Their houses are of the Mumbake pattern, and young girls wear the white caps of the Yendang. Grown-up women wear aprons of plaited hibiscus string, which is also the custom of the Mumbake and Verre tribes. In bygone days the men wore penis-sheaths of cloth.

They are a father-right people, with patrilineal descent ; but, as among the Yendang and Mumbake, the mother's family has a claim on the first child born of a marriage, and the first child is so far regarded as belonging to the mother's and not to the father's group that, when he dies, he must be buried in his mother's home. The mother's relatives are also responsible for the circumcision of a male first-child. The circumcision rites are similar to those of the Teme.

There is no strict exogamy, but intermarriage with close relatives on either side of the family is not favoured. It was stated that if a woman marries outside her own local group and bears a female child it is considered a point of honour that some male member of the mother's local group (who is not a close relative of the mother) should endeavour to marry the girl in order to bring her back to her mother's group. For by doing this the strength of the group will, it is said, be maintained. This statement is interesting as it reveals the attitude of mind which leads to exogamy, or at least to local exogamy.

Secondary marriages by elopement are practised, but no man may elope with a woman who is married to a member of his own local group, nor may he elope with the wife of a member of a family from which he or any of his relatives had previously obtained a virgin girl as a wife. Moreover, the first husband must receive compensation in the form of a bride-price. Widows are inherited, and married according to the rules indicated in the notes on the Teme.

As regards religion the Supreme Being is equated with the physical sun and is known as *Lu* (compare Teme, Gengle and Kugama, Yendang and Waka). But the ancestors are the principal objects of worship or propitiation, the skulls of old men being preserved and rites offered at harvest and before hunting.

It is noteworthy that the word for manufactured salt among these peoples is *ta Konan*, i.e. the ash-salt of the Kona, and that the word for maize is " the guinea-corn of the Apa." Both these expressions are evidence of the influence of the Jukun in these regions.

THE GENGLE AND KUGAMA

The inhabitants of the villages of Gengle and Kugama, which are situated in the Maio Balwa district of the Adomawa Emirate, call themselves the Wegele and the Wegam respectively, these terms meaning " The people of Gele " and " The people of Gam ". Gengle (Geŋle) or Gele is the parent settlement, Kugama being an offshoot : so that there does not appear to be any reason for describing the whole group as " The Kugamma ", the description given in Mrs. Temple's " Tribes, Emirates, etc." (page 244). If a common title is required Gengle would be more suitable than Kugama.

They claim to be immigrants from the Verre hills, and they have a number of customs which suggest that they may have formerly belonged to one of the Verre-speaking groups. Thus the wearing by men of a penis-sheath, and by women of loose string loin-coverings, are both Verre practices. They have also the Verre belief that if a body swells up after death the dead man had practised witchcraft in his lifetime, the swelling being due to the presence of his victims.

On the other hand they lack many of the characteristic customs of the Verre, such as the removal and preservation of the skulls of those who had died at a ripe old age, and the use of " dolmen " shrines and phallic emblems. Their language, moreover, is intimately connected with that of their neighbours the Yendang, Waka, Teme, and Bali, and belongs to the Mumuye group rather than to the Verre (though there is a definite connection between the Mumuye and Verre linguistic groups). The conclusion would seem to be that the Gengle and Kugama are Verre who have fused with Yendang, adopting the language of the latter. But there is a possibility that they are Chamba who have fused with Yendang ; for groups of Chamba became associated with the Verre in the past, and at the present time the people of Wom, who are commonly classed as Verre, are in reality Chamba. The use of the word *Lu* or *Ru*, meaning the Supreme Being, by the Gengle and Kugama (and also by the Yendang, Waka, and Teme) suggests a connection with the Chamba.[1]

Soon after descending from the Verre Hills to their present location the Gengle and Kugama became subservient to the Bata of Demsa, who were masters of the plain-country in this region, until their territory was reduced to its present dimensions by the extension of the power of the Fulani governors of Yola. But even at the present day the local chief of the Gengle and Kugama groups is a Bata appointed by the Bata chief of Demsa. All the senior men of Gengle and Kugama speak Bata as well as their own language ; but not all speak Fulani. In addition to the Bata chief both the Gengle and Kugama have their own traditional leader in the person of the chief priest who is known as the " Ba ", a title which is found among the Kona Jukun.

Socially the Gengle and Kugama consist of six divisions, viz. the We-Passe, We-Gaure, We-Guda, We-Kena, We-Gu, and We-Jatugi. These divisions are not localized ; groups of We-Passe, for example, being found in numerous hamlets mixed up with groups of the other social divisions. The divisions are not exogamous, and can hardly be described as " clans " if we follow current terminology. They may perhaps be described as kindreds. They are composed of a number of " extended families ", which believe themselves to be related to each other, though the relationship is not usually capable of proof genealogically. It is probable that the reputed relationship merely means that at one time (not very long ago) all those who called themselves by the same name occupied a single village : that is to say, the bond joining the various families is that created by local association and not necessarily by consanguinity.

The sense of kinship is, at the present time, maintained by the custom of assembling (*a*) for the funeral rites of any distinguished member of the kindred, and (*b*) for the performance of rites in

---

[1] Some groups of Chamba use *Ru* or *Ruma* as the name of the Supreme Being. But the normal Chamba word is *Ngama*, which is typical of the Western Bantu.

times of especial stress, such as drought. Otherwise the kindred organization has little significance. But before the British Administration it was of considerable importance in cases of local feuds. At that time the kindreds were more localized, and the members of one kindred would unite against those of another. Or two kindreds would unite against two others. Thus the We-Passe and We-Gaure acted as one against the We-Kenna and We-Guda. It was stated also that the We-Passe and We-Gaure attended the more important religious rites of each other, and that members of the We-Kenna and We-Guda could attend each others' religious rites.

It appeared that formerly each kindred had its own sacred or taboo animal. Thus the We-Passe avoided eating the flesh of bush pigs, the We-Gaure of rock coney, the We-Kenna of jackal, and the We-Guda of bush-cat. Anyone breaking the taboo would be assailed by leprosy. Little importance is attached to these taboos nowadays, and there is no prohibition against marrying a person whose taboo animal is the same as his own. For the rule of exogamy is only carried out as far as second cousins, so that a We-Passe man may marry a We-Passe woman provided she is not a first or second cousin. It is said that if a man particularly desires to marry his second cousin he may do so without much difficulty, as in these days the former rules are no longer stringently applied. But in no case would anyone be permitted to marry his first cousin, as first-cousin marriages are liable to destroy the family solidarity : but second-cousin marriages would not have this effect, the family group being no longer completely localized as heretofore. Farming is now safe in all directions, and the social unit has therefore become the extended family instead of the kindred. In due course, with the growth of individualism consequent upon the new economic conditions, the extended family organization will give place to that of the biological family, as in Europe. The breakdown of the social organization among African tribes is not, therefore, always to be ascribed to the introduction of modern " education " and the new ideas propagated by Governments and missions. It follows automatically on the freedom to farm or trade with safety in any direction.

The extended families composing the kindred are formed on the patrilineal principle : that is to say that they consist of full brothers or half-brothers by the same father, father's brother's sons, sons, brothers' sons, and the wives of these relatives. The presence of a sister's son [1] is abnormal, but a sister's son may, if he is not happy in his own home, take up formal residence with his maternal uncle.[2] We shall see presently also that a man has a special claim on the first of his sister's children, the extent of this claim being dependent on the amount of bride-price originally paid for the sister. Inheritance also follows the patrilineal principle, the inheritor being the head of the extended family, who uses the property on behalf of the whole family. Brothers and cousins, therefore, inherit before sons or brothers' sons. Sisters' sons are not entitled to any of the inheritance, but it is usual to give one goat to a sister's son who had been a first-born child, for that sister's son had (as we shall see) rendered special services to his maternal nucle. If the sister's son had taken up permanent residence with his maternal uncle and was still unmarried at the time of his uncle's death, he might be given a larger proportion of the estate to enable him to marry, or he might even be given one of his uncle's young widows (if she were agreeable). But normally widows are inherited by brothers (or cousins) and sons (or brothers' sons). A woman's property is heritable by her sister, who may hand some of it over to her deceased sister's female children.

We come now to the interesting question of the position of children as regards the mother's family. The general rule is that the mother's family (represented by her father, father's brother, or brother) has a special claim on her first-born child. If the first-born child is a male he is required during his boyhood to place his economic services at the disposal of his mother's father or brother, and to hand over to him the first two game-animals he kills. In return his maternal grandfather or uncle provides the major part of his circumcision expenses and also assists him to obtain a wife (by presenting him with five goats or pieces of cloth). If the boy's father had been deficient in his marriage payments the obligations of the boy are extended pro rata, so that he may have to give the first four game-animals he kills to his mother's relatives, or even every game-animal. If the boy has younger

---

[1] Or father's daughter's son.
[2] If a young man eloped with someone's wife, and his father's family refused to assist him in repaying the bride-price, he would appeal to his maternal uncle and take up permanent residence with him.

brothers, he may be assisted by them in carrying out the obligations imposed. If the eldest son dies before discharging the obligations his younger brother must discharge them in his stead.

If the first-born child is a female her maternal grandfather or uncle is entitled to a proportion of the bride-price paid for her, the proportion being higher if her father had been deficient in his marriage payments. Or, in the latter case, he may also claim a share of the second daughter's bride-price.

It would appear from these data that the claim on the first-born child, which is found in many Nigerian tribes, is based on bride-price considerations. It is noteworthy that a child's value is reckoned at twenty pieces of cloth. It is also worth adding that the Gengle and Kugama insist that the first child shall, on death, be buried by the mother's and not the father's family. A man who buries his first child among his own relatives lays himself open to an action for damages.

The pre-marriage payments, when fully made, are comparatively high. They are begun by a gift of an anklet to the girl, and a pot of beer, dish of corn, a bar of iron (currency), and some string to her father. At a later stage the suitor (or his father) has to build a new hut and enclosure for the girl's mother. Every second year he has to farm a crop of ground-nuts for his fiancée, and he has also to make an annual gift of two bundles of corn to her father, this gift being increased to five bundles as the girl approaches the age of puberty. There are also annual gifts of two goats and two pieces of cloth, payable to the girl's father, or to her maternal uncle if she had been a first-born child.[1] These payments are increased to three pieces of cloth and three goats when the suitor begins to have sexual relations with his fiancée (soon after the girl has reached the age of puberty). A careful tally (in the form of stalks of grass) is kept of all these payments, each stalk representing one piece of cloth or its equivalent. It may be noted that a suitor sleeps with his fiancée prior to her puberty, with a view to holding his claim against other would-be suitors. If the suitor is already a married man he sleeps with his wife and fiancée on alternate nights. Brides bear their first child in their parents' home, proceeding to the husband's home when the child is weaned.

---

[1] The lad would be assisted in making these gifts by his maternal uncle if he had been a first-born child.

If an affianced girl repudiates her suitor the suitor can reclaim all his payments from the girl's father, who recovers them from her new suitor. And if a married woman abandons her husband the latter becomes entitled to a refund less twenty pieces of cloth for each child his wife had borne him (provided he had not been deficient in his pre-marriage payments).

These rules are similar to those of most of the surrounding group of tribes, and may be compared, for example, with those of the Gôla or of the Waka (with whom the Gengle and Kugama inter-marry). It is, perhaps, worth adding that if a wife, who had lived with her husband for a considerable number of years, dies childless, the husband may obtain a second wife (if available) from his late wife's family group on advantageous terms, that is to say, he would not be called upon to make the full quota of payments normally demanded.

It might appear, at first sight, as though female members of a family were sold for money. But this would be a mistaken view. The money received is always used to provide the male members of the family with wives, so that the whole system boils down to one of exchange. Wherever the so-called " purchase " system obtains among pagan tribes parents of girls are always insistent that the payment of a bride-price does not imply " purchase ", and if a wife is ill-treated by her husband her relatives immediately interfere and ask the husband if he thinks he has " bought " their daughter. If the husband fails to amend his ways the wife's relatives remove her from his home and give her to some other man. Or the wife herself may choose a new husband. Among most pagan tribes in Nigeria wives are able to change their husbands for the slightest of reasons, and there is no greater fallacy than the common conception among Europeans that Negro women are the mere chattels of their husbands and that, because payments are made for wives, wives, therefore, become the property of husbands.

Among the Gengle and Kugama there are no initiation or puberty rites for girls, as there are among most of the tribes north of the Benue (and also among the Kona and others south of the Benue who regard the final incision of bodily marks as the passport to marriage). But all boys have to undergo rites of circumcision. These are prolonged over a considerable period. They are begun at sowing, and the boys are required to engage in dancing throughout the following wet season. They are segregated by kindreds and have to sleep in the open, except on wet nights. They have no dealings with women, have their own calabashes of food, and are attended by youths of the previous circumcision-class. They are circumcised during the ensuing dry season, and on the concluding day they arrive in the town clothed in a costume of leaves, receive a new name (conferred by their fathers or in some cases by their maternal uncles), are given a penis-sheath (of woven string), a bow, arrows, quiver, knife, and bag of goat's or cat's skin. The boys, who have now become men, are expected to go hunting in the bush and so display their prowess during the remainder of the dry season, and in due course to show their manhood by becoming fathers and establishing homes of their own.

The following is a list of the relationship terms.

Da (possessive = *dada*) means father or father's brother (or cousin) or any male of a senior generation. A father's elder brother (or cousin) is, if necessary, described as *beanda* (i.e. elder brother of my father), and a father's younger brother (or cousin) as *vavada* (or younger brother of my father).

Naa is the term of address for mother, mother's sister, or any female of a senior generation. These relatives are referred to as *yenang*.

Va = son, daughter, sister's child, or any person of a junior generation.

Variyenang (i.e. son of my mother) is the general term for brother or sister. A half-brother or sister by the same father is called *varida*. An elder brother or sister is called *beam*, a younger brother or sister *vavam*. A father's brother's child or father's sister's child is *varida*. A mother's sister's child is *variyenang*. A mother's brother's child is *virkenang*.

Tubama = father's father, mother's father.

Yebama = father's mother, mother's mother.

Kenang = mother's brother.

Konang = all parents-in-law, a wife's elder brother or elder sister, and a husband's elder brother or elder sister. A wife's younger sister and younger brother are addressed as " my wife " (*suang*), and a husband's younger sister as *vaka* (a special term). *Nyashi* is a special term used between a woman and her husband's younger brother.

No close enquiries were made on the subject of religious beliefs. As among all the neighbouring tribes the Supreme Being and the sun are identified under the title of *Lu*. No sun rites are performed (as they are among the Kona Jukun). The word for Moon is *shi*, a term widespread throughout Africa and probably meaning "Lord."[1] Such religious rites as are observed are connected with agriculture. Thus before sowing the chief priest places in a forked branch beside his granary a new calabash containing some benniseed oil and a number of small stones. This is regarded as an offering both to the spirits and the ancestral ghosts. He then goes to his farm and formally plants some seed. In the evening a meal of a semi-sacred character is eaten in each household, and on the following morning all farmers begin sowing. The priest leaves the calabash of benniseed beside or under his granary throughout the agricultural season. When the corn begins to sprout he takes a few of the shoots and rolling them up in leaves of the wild *paw-paw* tree he deposits them under some stones at a cross-roads. In the presence of the senior men of the community he cuts the throat of a fowl over the stones and then swings the bleeding fowl round his head so that all present are sprinkled with the blood. At harvest the priest is the first to reap and he deposits the first heads of corn on the forked branch beside his granary.

The Gengle have an interesting method of settling disputes by an imprecation made on the bow. If a man suspects another of having committed some offence such as theft he will invite the suspected person to swear innocence on his bow. The person charged takes his bow and says: "If I have done this thing may *Lu* hinder me from killing game-animals when I go hunting." If he is successful during the ensuing week or two in killing some game-animal his kill is taken to the chief by the senior member of his family, and the person who made the charge is required to pay damages of two or three goats to the person charged, and a fine of one hoe to the chief. But if he is consistently unsuccessful he will be required by public opinion to pay damages to his accuser. He may know that he was guiltless of the offence with which he was charged, but he will pay gladly, if only to break the spell of his ill-success. He will explain the matter to himself by thinking that, although he had not committed the offence specified, he had committed some other offence, and the gods or ancestors were taking vengeance on that account. He may be regarded as a thief by other members of the community, but those of his own household (who know that he is not a thief) will consider that he is

---

[1] See *A Sudanese Kingdom*, chap. iv. The title would seem to imply an earlier Moon-worship.

being persecuted by some spirit or dead relative whom he had offended, on account of some breach of taboo or of some neglect. Such an one would, among the Chamba or Jukun, endeavour to ascertain by divination the identity of the offended spirit or ancestor, and would then make amends by sacrifice. But I had no opportunity of enquiring further into the Gengle procedure. The Gengle are not much interested in religion. They are living in close association with their Muslim overlords, and it is probable that they will all become professing Muslims within the next generation.

As regards material culture the Gengle and Kugama employ the usual type of round hut, with baked mud walls and conical thatched roof. The all-grass hut is not seen. The bedsteads are raised platforms of baked mud. The granaries are also of sun-dried mud, the entrance at the apex being capped with a thatching of grass. Three-legged pots, such as are found among the Kona Jukun, are commonly seen. A peculiar type of pottery dish not observed elsewhere is a soup-dish with two horns or handles attached to the rim. Hoes are fitted solely by the tanged method. Bows have an eyelet at one end and a circular notch at the other. Spears were not used in warfare.

Men wear loin-coverings of cloth and sleeveless shirts. As already noted a penis-sheath is worn. It is made of cotton threads woven together, and has a fringe at the point. It is kept in position by a string attachment fastened round the waist. The custom of wearing the sheath is now being given up, but all youths wear it for a year or two after circumcision. It was stated that the object of wearing the sheath was to conceal the fact of circumcision from women. During the circumcision rites the novices wear rattles on the calves of the leg for dancing purposes, a pad being placed above the ankle to prevent the rattles from rubbing the ankles. Males do not wear any tribal marks, but it is customary to pierce the ears and insert discs of guinea-corn stalk.

Women wear fringed aprons of cloth over the pubes, and bundles of loose string on the buttocks. They pierce the lower lip and insert discs of guinea-corn stalk. The aprons worn by young girls are sometimes decorated with beads. Some Gengle and Kugama girls also decorate the head with white beads in the Yendang fashion. Men and women, when they go abroad, carry on the shoulder bags made of the skins of goats and bush-cats.

MUMUYE (PUGÚ) VOCABULARY

Per Kong of Kajong

1.	Head	Yu	ju
2.	Hair	Suyu	suju
3.	Eye	Jing	dʒiŋ
	Two eyes	Jing ziti	dʒiŋ zɪti
4.	Ear	Shu	ʃu
	Two ears	Shu ziti	ʃu zɪti
5.	Nose	Sung	suŋ
6.	One tooth	Têri gbitte	têri gbɪtte
	Five teeth	Têri mani	têri maːni
7.	Tongue	Riti	riti
8.	Neck	Turu	turu
9.	Breast (woman's)	Mí	mí (contrast mī = water)
10.	Heart	Sissing	sɪssɪŋ
11.	Belly	Buru	buru
12.	Back	Dakî	dakî
13.	Arm	Na	na
14.	Hand	Na	na
	Two hands	Na ziti	na zɪti
15.	Finger	Sa na	sa na
	Five fingers	Sa na mani	sa na maːni
16.	Finger nail	Yu sa na	ju sa na
17.	Leg	Du (or do)	du (or do)
18.	Knee	Butú	butu
19.	Foot	Dakî du	da kî du
	Two feet	Dakî du ziti	da kî du zɪti
20.	Man (person)	Shonzê or zê	ʃonzê or zɛ
	Ten people	Shonzê kupi	ʃonzê kupi
21.	Man (not woman)	Vere	vɛre
	Two men	Zan vere ziti	zʌn vɛre zɪti
22.	Woman	Suru	suru
	Two women	Zin suru ziti (or suru ziti)	zɪn suru zɪti
23.	Child	Nja	ndʒa
24.	Father	Mada	mada
25.	Mother	Mana	mana
26.	Slave	Jafu	dʒafu
27.	Chief	Kpanti	ɓanti (impl. p)
28.	Friend	Masâ	masâ
29.	Smith	Zê vi sana	zê vi sana
30.	Doctor	Zê gana	zɛ gana
31.	One finger	Sana gbitte	sana gbɪtte
32.	Two fingers	Sana ziti	sana zɪti
33.	Three fingers	Sana tati	sana tati
34.	Four fingers	Sana deti	sana deti
35.	Five fingers	Sana mani	sana maːni
36.	Six fingers	Sana manggbitte	sana maŋ gbɪtte
37.	Seven fingers	Sana mangziti	sana maŋ zɪti

38.	Eight fingers	Sana mangtati	sana maŋ tati
39.	Nine fingers	Sana mangdeti	sana maŋ deti
40.	Ten fingers	Sana kupi	sana kupi
41.	Eleven fingers	Sana kupi tu gbitte	sana kupi tu gbɪtte
42.	Twelve fingers	Sana kupi tu ziti	sana kupi tu zɪti
	Thirteen fingers	Sana kupi tu tati	sana kupi tu tati
43.	Twenty fingers	Sana mbati (or la gbitte)	sana mbati (or la gbɪtte)
44.	A hundred fingers	Sana la mani	sana la mani
45.	Sun	La	la
	God	La	la
46.	Moon	Shela	ʃɛla
	Full moon	Shela puru	ʃɛla puru
	New moon	Shela sho	ʃɛla ʃo
47.	Day	Nô la ge	nô la ge
	Night	Nô zî	nô zî
	Morning	Nô gandi	nô gandi
48.	Rain	Mi	mĩ (contrast mí = breast)
49.	Water	Mi	mĩ
50.	Blood	Zî (or Kpa)	Zî (or kpa)
51.	Fat	Nû	nû
52.	Salt	Tâ	tâ
53.	Stone	Vutu	vutu
	Iron	Tsaka	tsʌka
54.	Hill	Kopo	kɔpo
55.	River	Iyâ (Stream = erang)	ijâ (ɛraŋ)
56.	Road	Gbalâ	gbalâ
57.	House	Jaka (Compound = gâ)	dʒaka
	Two houses	Jaka ziti	dʒaka zɪti
	Many houses	Jaka doli	dʒaka doli
	All the houses	Jaka piti	dʒaka pɪti
58.	Roof	Ta gâ	ta gâ
59.	Door	Nya gâ	nja gâ
60.	Mat	Siri	siri
61.	Basket	Butu	butu
62.	Drum	Dan	dan
63.	Pot	Gbari (or bauwa or bê)	gbari, bauwa or bɛ̂
64.	Knife	Yere	jere
65.	Spear	Shellang	ʃɛllaŋ
66.	Bow	Ta	ta
67.	Arrow	Shong	ʃɔŋ
	Five arrows	Shong mani	ʃɔŋ mani
68.	Gun	Wa	wa
69.	War	Sêri	sêri
70.	Meat (animal)	Yopo	jopo
71.	Elephant	Bɔ̧	bɔ
72.	Buffalo	Baka	baka
73.	Leopard	Gɓê	gɓê (implosive b)

74. Monkey	Kono (baboon = gbigbii)	kono (baboon = gbɪgbii)
75. Pig	Gangnya (warthog)	gaŋnja
76. Goat	Ja	dʒa
77. Dog	Za	za
78. Bird	Ja nû	dʒa nû
Feather	Shenti	ʃenti
79. Crocodile	Shenshen	ʃenʃen
80. Fowl	Kî	kî
81. Eggs	âka kî	âka kî
82. One egg	âka kî gbitte	âka kî gbɪtte
83. Snake	Sǫkó	sɔko
84. Frog	Vǫkó	vɔko
85. Spider	Langlang	laŋlaŋ
86. Fly	Pû	pû
87. Bee	Were	wɛrɛ
Honey	Mi were	mi wɛrɛ
88. Tree	Lá	lá
Ten trees	Lá kupi	lá kupi
89. Leaf	Gǫpo	gɔpo
90. Banana	Kâ	kâ
91. Maize	Za kî	zakî
92. Ground-nut	Daâ	daâ
93. Guinea-corn	Ze	ze
94. Sheep	Mere	mere
Horse	Gbâtang	gbâtaŋ
Cow	Napu	napu
95. Oil	Núng	nuŋ
96. The tall woman	Suru be gbâ	suru be gbâ
The tall women	Shosuṛu be gbâ	ʃɔ suru be gbâ
97. Large dog	Za gbâ	za gbâ
98. Small dog	Za tokolo	za tokolo
99. The dog bites	Za yong kuto	za joŋ kuto
100. The dog bites me	Za yong kina	za joŋ kɪna
101. The dog which bit me yesterday	Za bo wô boro be	za bo wô boro be
102. I flog the dog	N nyo za	n njo za
103. The dog which I have flogged	Za bo n nyo u be	za bo n njo u be
104. I see him or her	N zi wu to (I know you = N zu mu to)	n zi wu to
He sees you	U zi mo to	u zi mo to
He sees us	U zi ru to	u zi ru to
We see you (pl.)	Uru zi no to	uru zi no to
We see them	Uru zi ri to	uru zi ri to
105. Beautiful bird	Janu tôtô	dʒanu tôtô
106. Slave	Jafu	dʒafu
My slave	Jafu me	dʒafu me
Thy slave	Jafu babe	dʒafu babe
Our slaves	Jafu gburube	dʒafu gburube

107.	The chief's slave	Jafu kpanti	dʒafu ɓanti
	His slave	Jafu gɓibe	dʒafu gɓibɛ
108.	We see the slave	Ru zi jafu to	ru zi dʒafu to
109.	We call the slave	Ru ba nya jafu	ru ba nja dʒafu
110.	The slave comes	Jafu a ke nâ	dʒafu a kɛ nâ
111.	He came yesterday	U a boro	u a boro
	He is coming to-day	A le ko	a le ko
	He will come to-morrow	Gburu a re (or gburu a ki to)	gburu a rɛ (or gburu a ki to)
112.	The slaves go away	Jafu ri da'a to	dʒafu ri daˁa to
113.	Who is your chief ?	Gɓu kpanti munu wiya ?	gɓu ɓanti munu wija ?
114.	The two villages are making war on each other	Dola gâ ziti ri ta sîri na zo	dola gâ zɪti ri ta sîri nə zo
115.	The sun rises	La wang to	la waŋ to
	The sun sets	La ye to	la je to
116.	The man is eating	Zin sha vi ri	zɪn ʃa vi ri
117.	The man is drinking	Zin gbo mi	zɪn gbo mi
118.	The man is asleep	Zin ru koto	zɪn ru koto
119.	I break the stick	N ka laɓalang	n ka laɓalaŋ
	This stick is broken	Laɓalang kube ka kito	laɓalaŋ kube ka kito
	This stick cannot be broken	Laɓalang kube bê kana kito	laɓalaŋ kube bê kana kito
	Break this stick for me	Kâ la balang kube	kâ la balaŋ kube
120.	I have built a house	N ma jaka	n ma dʒaka
121.	My people have built their houses yonder	Zim me ri ma jaka biribe ki kaa ba	zɪm me ri ma dʒaka biribe ki kaa ba
122.	What do you do every day ?	Mu pale vi diki viya ?	mu pale vi diki vija ?
	I work on my farm	N pale vi ki ja me	n pale vi ki dʒa me
123.	I am going away	N da kito	n da kito
	I am hoeing	N lang ja	n laŋ dʒa
	I am going away to hoe	N da lang ja	n da laŋ dʒa
	I am going to my farm	N da ja me	n da dʒa me
124.	The woman comes	Zan suru a kina	zan suru a kina
	She comes	U a kina	u a kina
	The woman laughs	Suru la ta beé	suru la ta bee
	The woman weeps	Suru ka nya vo	suru ka nja vo
125.	I ask the woman	N he suru	n he suru
126.	Why do you laugh ?	Mu la ra viya ?	mu la rə vija ?

127.	Why do you cry ?	Mu ka viya	mu ka vija ?
128.	My child is dead	Ja me vọ kuto	dʒa me vɔ kuto
129.	It is not dead	Vo kpâ	vo kpâ
130.	Are you ill ?	Mu laka kpai ya ?	mu laka kpəi ja
131.	My children are ill	Wujeme laka kpâ	wudʒeme laka kpâ
132.	Her child is better	Ja bebe bi vale to	dʒa bebe bi valɛ to
133.	Yes	N	n
	No	Aa	əçə
134.	A fine knife	Ire wa sê	ire wa sê
	Give me the knife	Anyere	anjere
	I give you the knife	N a mu yere	n a mu jere
135.	I am a European	N ko bature	n ko bature
	You are a black man	Mu ko in viri	mu ko ɪn viri
	You are a Mumuye	Mu ko shọng Pugû (Hill Mumuye) or Shọndi = Plain Mumuye)	mu ko ʃɔŋ Pugû
136.	Name	Nung	nuŋ
	My name	Nungme	nuŋme
	Your name	Nungbabe	nuŋ babe
	What is your name ?	Zin ba mu nung na viya ?	zɪn ba mu nuŋ nə vija ?
137.	There is water in the gourd	Mi ki zaang	mi ki zaaŋ
	The knife is on the stone	Yere ki yu tari	jere ki ju tari
	The fire is under the pot	Wa ki di bari	wa ki di bari
	The roof is over the hut	Yu sâ ki yu binting	ju sû ki ju bɪntɪŋ
138.	You are good	Mo zê tô	mo zê tô
	This man is bad	Zeng ku be shi kpâ	zɛŋ ku be ʃi βâ
139.	The paper is white	La bena puru	la bena puru
	This thing is black	Vu ku be vîri	vu ku be vîri
	This thing is red	Vu ku be mweri	vu ku be mweri
140.	This stone is heavy	Tari ku be kpi ti kito	tari ku be βi ti kito
	This stone is not heavy	Tari ku be kpi ti kpâ	tari ku be βi ti βa
141.	I write	N bela	n bela
	I give you the letter	N a mu la bena	n a mu la bena
	Carry the letter to the town	Tu la bena mo danon ki ga ba	tu la bena mo danon ki ga ba
142.	Go away	Di ta	di ta
	Come here	Are	arɛ
143.	Where is your house ?	Ga babe kiya	ga babe kija

144. My house is here   Ga me ka ni   ga me kə ni
     My house is there   Ga me ka ka   ga me kə ka
145. What have you to   Mo ho ru viya?   mo ho ru vija?
     sell?
146. I want to buy fish N kasse n hu jazî n kassɛ n hu dʒazî
147. The fish which you Jazî gbo mo hu be shik dʒazî gbo mo hu be
     bought is bad   kpâ   ʃik kpâ
148. Where is the man   Zê bo nyo gbo kiya? zê bo njo gbo kija?
     who killed the
     elephant?
     He has killed   U nyo gbo do li   u njo gbo do li
     many elephants
     How many ele-   Ne yo gbo ki boro ne jo gbo ki boro
     phants were   neya?   neja?
     killed yester-
     day?
149. Untie it   Kalla wu ta   kalla wu ta
     Tie this rope   Maso kube ta   maso kube ta
     Make the boy un-   Ko ja ukalla ja   ko dʒa u kalla dʒa
     tie the goat
150. My brothers and   Ingko indi da ne ri ɪŋko ɪndi da ne ri
     I, we are going   manzung she li   manzuŋ ʃe li
     but no one else
     Brothers, let us   Manzung ru dei rudi manzuŋ ru dei rudi
     go and tell the   ko kpanti   ko βanti
     chief
151. This tree is bigger La kube bawọba gbana la kube bawɔ ba gbana
     than that   katō   kəto
     Hausa   Makpa
     Fulani   Kata
     Beriberi   Bọrno
     Kona   Kpê
     I   Nko
     We   Ruko
     You   Nuko
     Thou (disj.)   Muko
     He   Uko
     They   Riko

Possessive   My = bome   Ours = burube
               Thy = babe   Yours = mono
               His = bibe   Theirs = biribe

Imperative   Go = data (singular)
                    ndata (plural)

Tell him to come   = Ko ta u arri
I want to build a house here   = Nkasse ma gâ kinukubi
We want to build a house here   = Rukasse ma gâ kinukubi
I do not want to build a house here = Nkasse ma gâ kinukube kpâ

ZINNA DIALECT OF MUMUYE

1. Head   Yu   ju
2. Hair   Sisse yu   sɪsse ju

3.	Eye	Nung	nuŋ
	Two eyes	Nung zit	nuŋ zit
4.	Ear	Shu	ʃu
	Two ears	Shu zit	ʃu zit
5.	Nose	Sǫng	sɔŋ
6.	One tooth	Târi goro	târi goro
	Five teeth	Târi man	târi maːn
7.	Tongue	Rete	rete
8.	Neck	Turu	turu
9.	Breast (woman's)	Min	min
10.	Heart	Sîsî	sîsî
11.	Belly	Buru	buru
12.	Back	Kuku	kuku
13.	Arm	Na	na
14.	Hand	Zhe na	ʒɛ na
	Two hands	Zhe na zit	ʒɛ na zit
15.	Finger	Tsa na	tsa na
	Five fingers	Tsa na man	tsa na maːn
16.	Finger nail	Sari na	sari na
17.	Leg	Dǫ	dɔ
18.	Knee	Gbwinti	gbwɪnti
19.	Foot	Kuku dǫ	kuku dɔ
	Two feet	Puku dǫ zit	kuku dɔ zit
20.	Man (person)	Shǫzeng	ʃɔzɛŋ
	Ten people	Shǫzeng kop	ʃɔzɛŋ kop
21.	Man (not woman)	Shǫvaiye	ʃɔ vəije
	Two men	Shǫvaiye zit	ʃɔ vəije zit
22.	Woman	Suye	suje
	Two women	Suye zit	suje zit
23.	Child	Wuzha	wuʒa
24.	Father	Yibi	jɪbi
25.	Mother	Mana	mana
26.	Slave	Fu (or jafu)	fu or dʒafu
27.	Chief	Kpanti	ɓanti
28.	Friend	Mâsâ	masâ
29.	Smith	Ranti	ranti
30.	Doctor	Shǫ gang	ʃɔ gaŋ
31.	One finger	Tsa na guru	tsa na guru
32.	Two fingers	Tsa na zit	tsa na zit
33.	Three fingers	Tsa na tat	tsa na tat
34.	Four fingers	Tsa na neru	tsa na nɛru
35.	Five fingers	Tsa na man	tsa na maːn
36.	Six fingers	Tsa na manggo	tsa na maŋgo
37.	Seven fingers	Tsa na manzit	tsa na manzit
38.	Eight fingers	Tsa na nauatat	tsa na nəuatat
39.	Nine fingers	Tsa na nukobeguru	tsa na nukobɛ guru
40.	Ten fingers	Tsa na kop	tsa na kop
41.	Eleven fingers	Tsa na kop a tu goro	tsa na kop a tu goro
42.	Twelve fingers	Tsa na kop a tu zit	tsa na kop a tu zit
	Thirteen fingers	Tsa na kop a tu tat	tsa na kop a tu tat
43.	Twenty fingers	Tsa na mat	tsa na maːt

44.	A hundred fingers	Tsa na ta man	tsa na tĭ man
45.	Sun	Da	da:
	God	Da	da:
46.	Moon	Shele	ʃɛlɛ
	Full moon	Shele puru	ʃɛlɛ puro
	New moon	Shele sho	ʃɛlɛ ʃo
47.	Day	Rinti	rɪnti
	Night	Zi	zi
	Morning	Gandi	gandi
48.	Rain	Me dapa	me dapa
49.	Water	Me buni	me buni
50.	Blood	Zin	zɪn
51.	Fat	Zhenû	ʒenû
52.	Salt	Tâ	tâ
53.	Stone	Tara	tara
	Iron	Tsakha	tsaxa
54.	Hill	Dondong	dondoŋ
55.	River	Yang	jaŋ
56.	Road	Dǫnǫng	dɔnɔŋ
57.	House	Zhakha	ʒaxa
	Two houses	Zhakha zit	ʒaxa zit
	Many houses	Zhakha dori	ʒaxa dori
	All the houses	Zhakha pit	ʒaxa pit
58.	Roof	Yu zhakha	ju ʒaxa
59.	Door	Nyǫwa ne zhakha	njɔwa ne ʒaxa
60.	Mat	Silong	siloŋ
61.	Basket	Biti	biti
62.	Drum	Ganggang	gaŋgaŋ
63.	Pot	Vizhê	viʒê
64.	Knife	Yere	jere
65.	Spear	Shallang	ʃallaŋ
66.	Bow	Ta	ta
67.	Arrow	Shǫng	ʃɔŋ
	Five arrows	Shǫng man	ʃɔŋ ma:n
68.	Gun	Ya	ja
69.	War	Si	si
70.	Meat (animal)	Wopǫ	wopɔ
71.	Elephant	Bǫng	bɔŋ
72.	Buffalo	Bakha	baxa
73.	Leopard	Gḫê	ɓê
74.	Monkey	Kǫng	kɔŋ
75.	Pig	Gangnya	gaŋnja
76.	Goat	Zha	ʒa
77.	Dog	Za	za
78.	Bird	Nung	nuŋ
	Feather	Shent nung	ʃent nuŋ
79.	Crocodile	Shashang	ʃaʃaŋ
80.	Fowl	Kî	kî
81.	Eggs	Wǫnka kî	wɔnka kî
82.	One egg	Wǫnka kî guru	wɔnka kî guru
83.	Snake	Sǫkhǫ	sɔxɔ

84.	Frog	Vǫkhǫ	vɔxɔ
85.	Horse	Gbantang	gbantaŋ
86.	Cow	Napo	napo
87.	Fly	Pû	pû
88.	Bee	Wera	wɛra
	Honey	Wera	wɛra
89.	Tree	Lá	la
	Ten trees	Lá kop	la kop
90.	Leaf	Bala	bala
91.	Guinea-corn	Ze	ze
92.	Maize	Zagin	zagɪn
94.	Ground nut	Danung	danuŋ
94.	Oil	No	no

DING-DING DIALECT OF MUMUYE

Per Nyavoshata

1.	Head	Yu	ju
2.	Hair	Sûri yu	sûri ju
3.	Eye	Nung	nuŋ
	Two eyes	Nung ziti	nuŋ ziti
4.	Ear	Cho	tʃo
	Two ears	Cho ziti	tʃo ziti
5.	Nose	Sung	suŋ
6.	One tooth	Târi goro	târi goro
	Five teeth	Târi mani	târi mani
7.	Tongue	Dete	dete
8.	Neck	Kǫrǫ	kɔrɔ
9.	Breast (woman's)	Min	min
10.	Heart	Sising	sisiŋ
11.	Belly	Buru	buru
12.	Back	Sang	sʌŋ
13.	Arm	Na	na
14.	Hand	Narang	naraŋ
	Two hands	Narang ziti	naraŋ ziti
15.	Finger	Ji nang	dʒi naŋ
	Five fingers	Ji nang man	dʒi naŋ man
16.	Finger nail	Sa nang	sa naŋ
17.	Leg	Dǫ	dɔ
18.	Knee	Kpwina	kpwina
19.	Foot	Dǫ rang	dɔ raŋ
	Two feet	Dǫ rang ziti	dɔ raŋ ziti
20.	Man (person)	Chǫ zin	tʃɔ zɪn
	Ten people	Chǫ zin kop	tʃɔ zɪn kop
21.	Man (not woman)	Veye	veje
	Two men	Veye ziti	veje ziti
22.	Woman	Soye	soje
	Two women	Soye ziti	soje ziti
23.	Child	Ja	dʒa
24.	Father	Da	da

25. Mother	Na	na
26. Slave	Fo	fo
27. Chief	Kwanti	kwanti
28. Friend	Masâ	masâ
29. Smith	Ranti	ranti
30. Doctor	Chọ gâ	tʃɔ̂ gâ
31. One finger	Ji nang guru	dʒi naŋ guru
32. Two fingers	Ji nang ziti	dʒi naŋ ziti
33. Three fingers	Ji nang tati	dʒi naŋ tati
34. Four fingers	Ji nang neru	dʒi naŋ neru
35. Five fingers	Ji nang man	dʒi naŋ man
36. Six fingers	Ji nang manguru	dʒi naŋ manguru
37. Seven fingers	Ji nang manzit	dʒi naŋ manzit
38. Eight fingers	Ji nang mantat	dʒi naŋ mantat
39. Nine fingers	Ji nang manneru	dʒi naŋ manneru
40. Ten fingers	Ji nang kop	dʒi naŋ kop
41. Eleven fingers	Ji nang kopi tu goro	dʒi naŋ kopi tu goro
42. Twelve fingers	Ji nang kopi tu zit	dʒi naŋ kopi tu zit
Thirteen fingers	Ji nang kopi tu tat	dʒi naŋ kopi tu tat
43. Twenty fingers	Ji nang mat	dʒi naŋ maːt
44. A hundred fingers	Ji nang la man	dʒi naŋ la man
45. Two hundred fingers	Ji nang la kop	dʒi naŋ la kop
46. Sun	Ḍa	ɗa
47. God	Ḍa	ɗa

N.B.—This Mumuye dialect is spoken by the villagers of Ding-ding, Mokin, Nyele, Dakwanti, Bibo, etc. It closely resembles that of the Zinna Mumuye q.v.

YAKỌKỌ (JAKƆKƆ) DIALECT OF MUMUYE

1. Head	Yu	ju
2. Hair	Sisi yu	sɪsɪ ju
3. Eye	Nong	noŋ
Two eyes	Nong zit	noŋ zit
4. Ear	Shu	ʃu
Two ears	Shu zit	ʃu zit
5. Nose	Sọ	sɔ̂
6. One tooth	Târi goro	târi goro
Five teeth	Târi man	târi man
7. Tongue	Lete	lete
8. Neck	Turu	turu
9. Breast (woman's)	Mî	mî
10. Heart	Sisî	sisî
11. Belly	Buru	buru
12. Back	Kuku or sang or damba	kuku or sʌŋ or damba
13. Arm	Na	na
14. Hand	Yari na	jari na
Two hands	Yari na zit	jari na zit

15. Finger	Jau na	dʒau na
Five fingers	Jau na man	dʒau na man
16. Finger nail	Sari na	sari na
17. Leg	Do	do
18. Knee	Binti	bɪnti
19. Foot	Narido	narido
Two feet	Narido zit	narido zit
20. Man (person)	Shǫzin	ʃɔzɪn
Ten people	Shǫzin kop	ʃɔzɪn kop
21. Man (not woman)	Vire	vɪre
Two men	Vire zit	vɪre zit
22. Woman	Sure	sure
Two women	Sure zit	sure zit
23. Child	Jauje	dʒaudʒe
24. Father	Da	da
25. Mother	Na	na
26. Slave	Jafo	dʒafo
27. Chief	Kpanti	ɓanti
28. Friend	Masâ	masâ
29. Smith	Ranti	ranti
30. Doctor	Shǫ gana	ʃɔ gana
31. One finger	Jau na gbiti	dʒau na gbiti
32. Two fingers	Jau na zit	dʒau na zit
33. Three fingers	Jau na tak	dʒau na taːk
34. Four fingers	Jau na neru	dʒau na neru
35. Five fingers	Jau na man	dʒau na man
36. Six fingers	Jau na toman gbiti	dʒau na toman gbiti
37. Seven fingers	Jau na toman zit	dʒau na toman zit
38. Eight fingers	Jau na toman tak	dʒau na toman taːk
39. Nine fingers	Jau na toman neru	dʒau na toman neru
40. Ten fingers	Jau na kop	dʒau na kop
41. Eleven fingers	Jau na kop tu gbiti	dʒau na kop tu gbiti
42. Twelve fingers	Jau na kop tu zit	dʒau na kop tu zit
Thirteen fingers	Jau na kop tu tak	dʒau na kop tu taːk
43. Twenty fingers	Jau na mak	dʒau na maːk
44. A hundred fingers	Jau na la man	dʒau na la man
45. Two hundred fingers	Jau na la kop	dʒau na la kop
46. Sun	La	la
God	La	la
47. Moon	Shilla	ʃɪlla
Full moon	Shilla puru	ʃɪlla puru
New moon	Shilla tîri	ʃɪlla tîri
48. Day	Runtung	runtuŋ
Night	Tirizin	tirizin
Morning	Gandi	gandi
49. Rain	Me	me
50. Water	Me	me
51. Blood	Kpa	ɓa
52. Fat	Nǫ	no
53. Salt	Tâ	ta

54. Stone	Vuturu	vaturu
Iron	Tsaka	tsʌka
55. Hill	Dundun	dundun
56. River	Iyang	ijaŋ
57. Road	Mara	mara
58. House	Jaka	dʒaka
Two houses	Jaka zit	dʒaka zit
Many houses	Jaka doile	dʒaka dɔɪle
All the houses	Jaka pit	dʒaka pit
59. Roof	Pirra	pɪrra
60. Door	Nyọ wara jaka	njɔ̀ wara dʒaka
61. Mat	Suruna	suruna
62. Basket	Bura	bura
63. Drum	Ganggang	gaŋgaŋ
64. Pot	Biri	biri
65. Knife	Yera	jɛra
66. Spear	Shellang	ʃɛllaŋ
67. Bow	Takha	taxa
68. Arrow	Shọng	ʃɔŋ
Five arrows	Shọng man	ʃɔŋ man
69. Gun	Bitigaru	bitigaru
70. War	Sira	sɪra
71. Meat (animal)	Yopo	jopo
72. Elephant	Bọng	bɔŋ
73. Buffalo	Baka	baka
74. Leopard	Gbê	gbɛ̂
75. Monkey	Kọ	kɔ̀
76. Pig	Ganying	ganjɪŋ
77. Goat	Ja	dʒa
78. Dog	Za	za
79. Bird	Nọng	nɔŋ
Feather	Shenti	ʃenti
80. Crocodile	Shanshang	ʃanʃaŋ
81. Fowl	Kî	kî
82. Eggs	Yan ka kî	jan ka kî
83. One egg	Yan ka kî gbiti	jan ka kî gɓiti
84. Snake	Sọkọ	sɔkɔ
85. Frog	Vọkọ	vɔkɔ
86. Horse	Gbantang	gɓantaŋ
Cow	Napu	napu
87. Fly	Pung	puŋ
88. Bee	Wọra	wɔra
Honey	Wọra	wɔra
89. Tree	La	la
Ten trees	La kop	la kop
90. Leaf	Balang	balaŋ
91. Guinea-corn	Ze	ze
92. Maize	Zakin	zakɪn
93. Ground nut	Danô	danô
94. Oil	No	no

GÔLA (OR GOMLA) VOCABULARY
Per Dadingdi

1.	Head	Yu	ju
2.	Hair	Zere yu	zere ju
3.	Eye	Nung	nuŋ
	Two eyes	Nung zit	nuŋ zit
4.	Ear	So	so
	Two ears	So zit	so zit
5.	Nose	Sung	suŋ
6.	One tooth	Tangri guru	taŋri guru
	Five teeth	Tangri mani	taŋri mani
7.	Tongue	Lete	lɛtɛ
8.	Neck	Vongre	vɔŋrɛ
9.	Breast (woman's)	Min	min
10.	Heart	Sisi	sisi
11.	Belly	Yati	jati
12.	Back	Kukuru	kukuru
13.	Arm	Na	na
14.	Hand	Teli na	tɛli na
	Two hands	Teli na zit	tɛli na zit
15.	Finger	Jina	dʒina
	Five fingers	Jina mani	dʒina mani
16.	Finger nail	Sari nang	sari naŋ
17.	Leg	Dọ	dɔ
18.	Knee	Kpwinang	kpwinaŋ
19.	Foot	Teli do	tɛli do
	Two feet	Teli do zit	tɛli do zit
20.	Man (person)	Sọn zing	sɔn ziŋ
	Ten people	Sọn kup	sɔn kup
21.	Man (not woman)	Vee	veɛ
	Two men	Vee zit	veɛ zit
22.	Woman	Suye	sujɛ
	Two women	Su zit	su zit
23.	Child	Ja	dʒa
24.	Father	Da	da
25.	Mother	Na	na
26.	Slave	Fo	fo
27.	Chief	Kpanti	ɓanti
28.	Friend	Masan	masan
29.	Smith	Aranti	aranti
30.	Doctor	Sọn gana	sɔn gana
31.	One finger	Jina guru	dʒina guru
32.	Two fingers	Jina zit	dʒina zit
33.	Three fingers	Jina tat	dʒina tat
34.	Four fingers	Jina nero	dʒina nero
35.	Five fingers	Jina mani	dʒina mani
36.	Six fingers	Jina mangguru	dʒina maŋguru
37.	Seven fingers	Jina nanotat	dʒina nanotat
38.	Eight fingers	Jina nakuneru	dʒina nakuneru
39.	Nine fingers	Jina nukubeguru	dʒina nukubɛguru

40. Ten fingers	Jina kup	dʒina kup
41. Eleven fingers	Jina kuata guru	dʒina kuatə guru
42. Twelve fingers	Jina kuata zit	dʒina kuatə zit
Thirteen fingers	Jina kuata tat	dʒina kuatə tat
43. Twenty fingers	Jina mat	dʒina mat
44. A hundred fingers	Jina lamanin	dʒina la manın
45. Two hundred fingers	Jina laman ja zit	dʒina la man dʒa zit
46. Four hundred fingers	Jina laman ja neru	dʒina la man dʒa neru
47. God	Ɗa	ɗa
Sun	Ɗa	ɗa
48. Moon	Sılla	sılla
Full moon	Se purɛba	se purɛba
New moon	Se kirɛba	se kirɛba
49. Day	Da belaba	da bɛlaba
Night	Bonggoreva	boŋgorɛva
Morning	Bwendiki	bwɛndiki
50. Rain	Min	min
51. Water	Min	min
52. Blood	Kpa	kpa
53. Fat	Nunja	nundʒa
54. Salt	Tanyang	tanjaŋ
55. Stone	Tari	tari
Iron	Saka	saka
56. Hill	Kọpọ	kɔpɔ
57. River	Iyang	ijaŋ
58. Road	Dọna	dɔna
59. House	Jeka (Compound = yere)	dʒeka (Compound = jere)
Two houses	Ja zit	dʒa zit
Many houses	Ja sinsin	dʒa sınsın
All the houses	Ja pit	dʒa pit
60. Roof	Pera	pɛra
61. Door	Nye jeka	nje dʒɛka
62. Mat	Siri	siri
63. Basket	Buti	buti
64. Drum	Dang	daŋ
65. Pot	Gberi	gberi
66. Knife	Yira	jira
67. Spear	Tsalang	tsalaŋ
68. Bow	Taka	taka
69. Arrow	Sọng	sɔŋ
Five arrows	Sọng mani	sɔŋ mani
70. Gun	Ya	ja
71. War	Tsira	tsira
72. Meat (animal)	Wọpọng	wɔpɔŋ
73. Elephant	Bọng	bɔŋ
74. Buffalo	Baka	baka
Lion	zingga	zıŋga
75. Leopard	Gbe	gbɛ

76.	Monkey	Kọng	kɔŋ
77.	Pig	Gengya	gɛŋja
78.	Goat	Ja	dʒa
79.	Dog	Za	za
80.	Bird	Nung	nuŋ
	Feather	Senti nung	senti nuŋ
81.	Horse	Gbangtang	gbaŋtaŋ
	Cow	Napu	napu
	Sheep	Mere	mɛrɛ
	Crocodile	Sansang	sansʌŋ
82.	Fowl	Kin	kɪn
83.	Eggs	Anka kin	anka kɪn
84.	One egg	Anka kin guru	anka kɪn guru
85.	Snake	Sọkọ	sɔkɔ
86.	Frog	Vọkọ	vɔkɔ
87.	Fly	Pung	puŋ
88.	Bee	Nungwara	nuŋwara
	Honey	Wara	wara
89.	Tree	Nyala	njala
	Ten trees	Nyala kop	njala kop
90.	Leaf	Bala	bala
91.	Guinea-corn	Zie	zie
92.	Maize	Zagin	zagɪn
93.	Ground nut	Daa	daa
94.	Oil	Nung	nuŋ
95.	Fulani	Fulahadi	fulhadi
96.	Hausa and Beri-beri	Wangpa	waŋpa

YENDANG (OF BAJAMA DISTRICT) VOCABULARY

Per Dada of Bajama

1.	Head	U	u
2.	Hair	Sûri	sûri
3.	Eye	Nọng	nɔŋ
	Two eyes	Nọng ka ini	nɔŋ ka ini
4.	Ear	To	to
	Two ears	To ka ini	to ka ini
5.	Nose	Sọ	sɔ̂
6.	One tooth	Ruu ko bindi	ruu ko bindi
	Five teeth	Ruu ginang	ruu gɪnʌŋ
7.	Tongue	Lakha	laxa
8.	Neck	Turi	turi
9.	Breast (woman's)	Nyọka	njɔka
10.	Heart	Nọsarang	nɔsarʌŋ
11.	Belly	Iyang	ijaŋ
12.	Back	Gọtta	gotta
13.	Arm	Na	na
14.	Hand	Ya na	ja na
	Two hands	Ya na ini	ja na ini
15.	Finger	So na	so na
	Five fingers	So na ginang	so na gɪnʌŋ

16. Finger nail	Kulu	kulu
17. Knee	Yenungga	jɛnuŋga
18. Leg	Ho	ho
19. Foot	Yaho	jaho
Two feet	Yaho ini	jaho ini
20. Man (person)	Wêjiki	wɛ dʒɪki
Ten people	Wenu kop	wɛnu kop
21. Man (not woman)	Wêveiwê	wɛ veɪwɛ
Two men	Wêveiwê ini	wɛ veɪwɛ ini
22. Woman	Wêsowê	wɛ sowɛ
Two women	Wêsowene ini	wɛ so wɛnɛ ini
23. Child	Vawe	vawɛ
24. Father	Da	da
25. Mother	Yinu	jinu
26. Slave	Fo	fo
27. Chief	Ҟpâ	βâ
28. Friend	Bâsâ	basâ
29. Smith	Wensâ	wɛnsâ
30. Doctor	Wensọra	wɛnsọra
31. One finger	So na binti	so na bɪnti
32. Two fingers	So na ini	so na ini
33. Three fingers	So na tat	so na tat
34. Four fingers	So na nat	so na nat
35. Five fingers	So na ginang	so nan gɪnʌŋ
36. Six fingers	So na ga indi	so na ga ɪndi
37. Seven fingers	So na gina tini	so na gɪna tini
38. Eight fingers	So na gbọlanat	so na gbɔlanat
39. Nine fingers	So na nọkmọitat	so na nɔkɔmɪtat
40. Ten fingers	So na kop	so na kop
41. Eleven fingers	So na kop di bindi	so na kop di bindi
42. Twelve fingers	So na kop ti ini	so na kop ti ini
Thirteen fingers	So na kop ti tat	so na kop ti tat
43. Twenty fingers	So na miminti	so na miminti
44. A hundred fingers	So na min ginang	so na min gɪnʌŋ
45. Two hundred fingers	So na min ginang ra ini	so na min gɪnʌŋ ra ini
46. Four hundred fingers	So na min ginang ra nat	so na min gɪnʌŋ ra nat
47. Sun	Ru	ru
God	Ru	ru
48. Moon	Se	se
Full moon	Se bulum bulum	se bulum bulum
New moon	Se pep	se pɛp
49. Day	Rubi	rubi
Night	Dase	dase
Morning	Hiri	hɪri
50. Rain	Me	me
51. Water	Me	me
52. Blood	Li	li
53. Fat	Fọra bi	fɔra bi
54. Salt	Tandiri	tandiri

55.	Stone	Tari	tari
	Iron	Nomo	nomo
56.	Hill	Gǫro (or gǫrobi)	gǫro
57.	River	Bǫngkǫ	bǫŋkɔ
58.	Road	Deri	dɛri
59.	House	Wat	wat
	Two houses	Wata ini	watɪ ini
	Many houses	Wata nonǫk	watɪ nonǫk
	All the houses	Wata bambam	watɪ bambam
60.	Roof	Lang	laŋ
61.	Door	Yawari	jawari
62.	Mat	Yuri	juri
63.	Basket	Nak	nak
64.	Drum	Vin	vɪn
65.	Pot	Tang	taŋ
66.	Knife	Tuka	tuka
67.	Spear	Yaho	jaho
68.	Bow	Tak	tak
69.	Arrow	Su	su
	Five arrows	Su ni ginang	su ni gɪnʌŋ
70.	Gun	Bindigaru	bɪndɪgaru
71.	War	Sit	sit
72.	Meat (animal)	Wuk	wuk
73.	Elephant	Bǫng	bɔŋ
74.	Buffalo	Bak	bak
75.	Leopard	Kpe	ƥe
76.	Monkey	Ta	ta
77.	Pig	Geba	geba
78.	Goat	Bi	bi
79.	Dog	Kǫ	kɔ
80.	Bird	Nyǫ	njɔ
	Feather	Pung nyǫ	puŋ njɔ
81.	Crocodile	Name	name
82.	Fowl	Teng	tɛŋ
83.	Eggs	Ha teng	ha tɛŋ
84.	One egg	Ha teng bindi	ha tɛŋ bindi
85.	Snake	Nyalahê	njalahê
86.	Frog	Vǫ	vɔ
87.	Horse	Kpantang	kpantaŋ
	Cow	Naki	naki
88.	Fly	Kû	kû
89.	Bee	Fǫro	fɔri
	Honey	Fǫri	fɔri
90.	Tree	Tihê	tihê
	Ten trees	Tihê kop	tihê kop
91.	Leaf	Nyâ ka hê	njâ ka hê
92.	Guinea-corn	Kǫng	kɔŋ
93.	Maize	Si kon	si kon
94.	Ground nut	Binima	bɪnɪma
95.	Oil	Nǫk	nɔk

WAKA VOCABULARY
Per Vori of Waka

1.	Head	U	u
2.	Hair	Sûri	sûri
3.	Eye	Nung	nuŋ
	Two eyes	Nung ini	nuŋ ini
4.	Ear	To	to
	Two ears	To ini	to ini
5.	Nose	Sung	suŋ
6.	One tooth	Ru bindi	ru bindi
	Five teeth	Ru ginang	ru gɪnʌŋ
7.	Tongue	Willo	wɪllo
8.	Neck	Turi	turi
9.	Breast (woman's)	Nyenyogel	njɛnjogɛl
10.	Heart	Saro	saro
11.	Belly	Iyang	ijaŋ
12.	Back	Gorang	goraŋ
13.	Arm	Nang	nʌŋ
14.	Hand	Ya nang	ja nʌŋ
	Two hands	Ya nang ini	ja nʌŋ ini
15.	Finger	Da nang	da nʌŋ
	Five fingers	Da nang ginang	da nʌŋ gɪnʌŋ
16.	Finger nail	Yu kune (nang)	ju kune
17.	Leg	Huang	huaŋ
18.	Knee	Yerunga	jɛruŋa
19.	Foot	Yerhuang	jɛr huaŋ
	Two feet	Yerhuang ini	jɛr huaŋ ini
20.	Man (person)	Wê	wɛ
	Ten people	Wenu kop	wɛnu kop
21.	Man (not woman)	Weveungwe	we veuŋ we
	Two men	Weveungwe ini	we veuŋ we ini
22.	Woman	Wêsôwi	wɛ sôwi
	Two women	Wêsôwe ini	wɛ sôwi ini
23.	Child	Vagi	vagi
24.	Father	Da	da
25.	Mother	Nene	nɛnɛ
26.	Slave	Fu	fu
27.	Chief	Kpâ	ɓâ
28.	Friend	Bajang	badʒaŋ
29.	Smith	Wê shau	wɛ ʃau
30.	Doctor	Wê shora bi	wɛ ʃora bi
31.	One finger	Da nang bindi	da nʌŋ bindi
32.	Two fingers	Da nang ini	da nʌŋ ini
33.	Three fingers	Da nang tat	da nʌŋ tat
34.	Four fingers	Da nang nat	da nʌŋ nat
35.	Five fingers	Da nang ginang	da nʌŋ ginʌŋ
36.	Six fingers	Da nang gatindi	da nʌŋ gatɪndi
37.	Seven fingers	Da nang ginatini	da nʌŋ gɪnatini
38.	Eight fingers	Da nang balanat	da nʌŋ balanat
39.	Nine fingers	Da nang nokorombindi	da nʌŋ nɔkɔrombindi

40.	Ten fingers	Da nang kop	da nʌŋ kop
41.	Eleven fingers	Da nang kop ta bindi	da nʌŋ kop tə bindi
42.	Twelve fingers	Da nang kop ta ini	da nʌŋ kop tə ini
	Thirteen fingers	Da nang kop ta tat	da nʌŋ kop tə tat
43.	Twenty fingers	Da nang mi bindi	da nʌŋ mi bindi
44.	A hundred fingers	Da nang min ginang	da nʌŋ min gɪnʌŋ
45.	Two hundred fingers	Da nang min kop	da nʌŋ min kop
46.	Four hundred fingers	Da nang min koranat	da nʌŋ min koranat
47.	Sun	Ru	ru
	God	Ru	ru
48.	Moon	Shi	ʃi
	Full moon	Shi hwiyebe	ʃi hwijɛbe
	New moon	Shi sarube	ʃi sarubɛ
49.	Day	Ru	ru
	Night	Dai	dai
	Morning	Dere	dere
50.	Rain	Me	me
51.	Water	Me	me
52.	Blood	Di	ɗi
53.	Fat	Nô	nô
54.	Salt	Tâ	tâ
55.	Stone	Tari	tari
	Iron	Numu	numu
56.	Hill	Gọrọ	gɔrɔ
57.	River	Banggo	baŋgo
58.	Road	Dari	dari
59.	House	Wari	wari
	Two houses	Wari ini	wari ini
	Many houses	Wari nunu	wari nunu
	All the houses	Wari kâri	wari kâri
60.	Roof	Dang	daŋ
61.	Door	Nya wari	nja wari
62.	Mat	Yuri	juri
63.	Basket	Na	naς
64.	Drum	Vî	vî
65.	Pot	Tang	tʌŋ
66.	Knife	Tuge	tuge
67.	Spear	Yaho	jaho
68.	Bow	Ta	taς
69.	Arrow	Sung	suŋ
	Five arrows	Sung ginang	ginʌŋ
70.	Gun	Nora	nora
71.	War	Chiri	tʃiri
72.	Meat (animal)	Wu	wu
73.	Elephant	Dang	daŋ
64.	Buffalo	Ba	baς
75.	Leopard	Kpe	ɓe
76.	Monkey	Tâ	ta
77.	Pig	Geba	gɛbə

78. Goat	Bi	bi
79. Dog	Za	za
80. Bird	Nyô	njô
Feather	Pong	poŋ
81. Crocodile	Ting	tiŋ
82. Fowl	Teng	tɛŋ
83. Eggs	Ha teng	ha tɛŋ
84. One egg	Ha teng bindi	ha tɛŋ bindi
85. Snake	Nyale	njalɛ
86. Frog	Vuọ	vuɔ
87. Horse	Gbanang	gbanaŋ
Cow	Nagi	nagi
88. Fly	Kû	kû
89. Bee	Vọri	vôri
Honey	No vọri	no vôri
90. Tree	Te	te
Ten trees	Te kop	te kop
91. Leaf	Nyanga	njaŋa
92. Guinea-corn	Kọng	kɔŋ
93. Maize	Jekî	dʒɛkî
94. Ground nut	Gbenemo	gbɛnɛmo
95. Oil	No	no

TEME VOCABULARY
Per Murum

1. Head	U	u
2. Hair	Sûri	sûri
3. Eye	Nọru	nɔru
Two eyes	Nọru iri	nɔru iri
4. Ear	Toro	toro
Two ears	Toro iri	toro iri
5. Nose	Sûru	sû ru
6. One tooth	Sû bini	sû bini
Five teeth	Sû ginang	sû gɪnʌŋ
7. Tongue	Lem (or lemdang)	lɛm
8. Neck	Tuli	tuli
9. Breast (woman's)	Nyô	njô
10. Heart	Sa (or sawang)	sa or sawʌŋ
11. Belly	Gyang	gjʌŋ
12. Back	Gya (or gyawang)	gja (or gjawʌŋ)
13. Arm	Na (or nang)	na (or nʌŋ)
14. Hand	Gya na	gja na
Two hands	Gya na iri	gja na iri
15. Finger	Zu na (or zu nang)	zu na (or zu nʌŋ)
Five fingers	Zu na ginang	zu na gɪnʌŋ
16. Finger nail	Kobe	kobe
17. Leg	Hoang	hoʌŋ
18. Knee	Lung	luŋ
19. Foot	Gya hoang	gja hoʌŋ
Two feet	Gya hoang iri	gja hoʌŋ iri

20. Man (person)	Nyem	njɛm
Ten people	Nyem kop	njɛm kop
21. Man (not woman)	Nyevem	njevɛm
Two men	Nyene iri	njɛnɛ iri
22. Woman	Nyesu	nje su
Two women	Nyesu iri	nje su iri
23. Child	Vage	vage
24. Father	Ɖia	ɗia
25. Mother	Na	na
26. Slave	Sam	sam
27. Chief	Gɓam	gɓam
28. Friend	Dumle	dumlɛ
29. Smith	Yemsaui	jɛmsəui
30. Doctor	Sehî	sehî
31. One finger	Zu nang bini	zu nʌŋ bini
32. Two fingers	Zu nang iri	zu nʌŋ iri
33. Three fingers	Zu nang tat	zu nʌŋ tat
34. Four fingers	Zu nang nat	zu nʌŋ nat
35. Five fingers	Zu nang ginang	zu nʌŋ gɪnʌŋ
36. Six fingers	Zu nang gadibini	zu nʌŋ gadɪbini
37. Seven fingers	Zu nang ginteni	zu nʌŋ gɪnteni
38. Eight fingers	Zu nang gbǫlana	zu nʌŋ gbɔlana
39. Nine fingers	Zu nang no kom nang bini	zu nʌŋ no kom nʌŋ bini
40. Ten fingers	Zu nang kop	zu nʌŋ kop
41. Eleven fingers	Zu nang kop ta bini	zu nʌŋ kop tə bini
42. Twelve fingers	Zu nang kop ta iri	zu nʌŋ kop tə iri
Thirteen fingers	Zu nang kop ta tat	zu nʌŋ kop tə tat
43. Twenty fingers	Zu nang ma bingti	zu nʌŋ mə bɪŋti
44. A hundred fingers	Zu nang ma ginang	zu nʌŋ mə gɪnʌŋ
45. Two hundred fingers	Zu nang ma ginang la iri	zu nʌŋ mə gɪnʌŋ la iri
46. Four hundred fingers	Zu nang ma ginang la nat	zu nʌŋ mə gɪnʌŋ la nat
47. Sun	Lui	lui
God	No toang	no toaŋ
48. Moon	See	see
Full moon	Se hwi	se hwi
New moon	Se sagi	se sagi
49. Day	Lui	lui
Night	Gyase	gjase
Morning	Iya	ija
50. Rain	Me	me
51. Water	Me	me
52. Blood	Ɖe	ɗe
53. Fat	Noe	noe
54. Salt	Tnakwe	tnakwe
55. Stone	Tale	tale
Iron	Esaui	esəui
56. Hill	Bugel	bugɛl
57. River	Ɓanggwe	ɓʌŋgwɛ

58.	Road	Gyabe	gjabe
59.	House	Ge	ge
	Two houses	Ge iri	ge iri
	Many houses	Ge kpama	ge ɓama
	All the houses	Ge kâ˙	ge kâ
60.	Roof	Heke	heke
61.	Door	Gaiye	gaije
62.	Mat	Joge	dʒoge
63.	Basket	Ne	nɛ
64.	Drum	Vim	vɪm
65.	Pot	Tang	tʌŋ
66.	Knife	Tǫe	tɔe
67.	Spear	Hǫge	hɔge
68.	Bow	Tee	tɛɜ
69.	Arrow	Suam	suʌm
	Five arrows	Soni ginang	soni gɪnʌŋ
70.	Gun	Nole	nolɛ
71.	War	Kǫng	kɔŋ
72.	Meat (animal)	Jue	dʒue
73.	Elephant	Gyang	gjaŋ
74.	Buffalo	Bake	bake
75.	Leopard	Johi	dʒohi
76.	Monkey	Ta	ta
77.	Pig	Gangkalang	gaŋkalaŋ
78.	Goat	Bi (or ebi)	bi or ɛbi
79.	Dog	Ze	ze
80.	Bird	Nyǫng	njɔŋ
	Feather	Gban nyǫng	gbʌm njɔŋ
81.	Crocodile	Tim	tim
82.	Fowl	Tem	tɛm
83.	Eggs	Habe	habɛ
84.	One egg	Habe bingti	habɛ bɪŋti
85.	Snake	Nyale	njalɛ
86.	Frog	Gbagang	gbagʌŋ
87.	Horse	Gbanang	gbanʌŋ
	Cow	Nagge	nagge
88.	Fly	Kû	kû
89.	Bee	Vǫbe	vɔbe
	Honey	Nǫe	nɔɛ
90.	Tree	Te	te
	Ten trees	Te kop	te kop
91.	Leaf	Jangga	dʒaŋga
92.	Guinea-corn	Kǫm	kɔm
93.	Maize	Kofá	kofa
94.	Ground nut	Namo	naːmo
95.	Oil	Noe	noe

KUMBA VOCABULARY

| 1. | Head | Ul | ul |
| 2. | Hair | Sur | sur |

3. Eye	Nǫr	nɔr
Two eyes	Nǫ tiri	nɔ tiri
4. Ear	To	to
Two ears	To tiri	to tiri
5. Nose	Hǫ́ka	hɔ́ka
6. One tooth	Dusi hindi	dusi hindi
Five teeth	Dusi nǫng	dusi hindi nɔŋ
7. Tongue	Wiji	widʒi
8. Neck	Kǫ̂r	kɔ̂r
9. Breast (woman's)	Seem	sɛɛm
10. Heart	Susu	susu
11. Belly	Yer	jɛr
12. Back	Gul	gul
13. Arm	Tir	tɪr
14. Hand	Tutir	tutɪr
Two hands	Tuti tiri	tuti tiri
15. Finger	Vatir	vatɪr
Five fingers	Vati nǫng	vati nɔŋ
16. Finger nail	Hungatir	huŋgatɪr
17. Leg	Jang	dʒʌŋ
18. Knee	Ninggi	niŋgi
19. Foot	Tujang	tudʒʌŋ
Two feet	Tujang tiri	tudʒʌŋ tiri
20. Man (person)	Hungguen	huŋguɛn
Ten people	Wǫri kǫp	wɔri kɔp
21. Man (not woman)	Vewen	vewɛn
Two men	Vere tiri	vere tiri
22. Woman	Howen	howɛn
Two women	Howere tiri	howere tiri
23. Child	Va	va
24. Father	Da	da
25. Mother	Na	na
26. Slave	Gura	gura
27. Chief	Kpan (plural = kpâri)	ƥan
28. Friend	Vatǫngga	vatɔŋga
29. Smith	Saa	saa
30. Doctor	Paa	paa
31. One finger	Vatir hindi	vatɪr hundi
32. Two fingers	Vati tiri	vati tiri
33. Three fingers	Vati sat	vati saːt
34. Four fingers	Vati nat	vati naːt
35. Five fingers	Vati nǫng	vati nɔŋ
36. Six fingers	Vati nogendi	vati nogɛndi
37. Seven fingers	Vati nǫnggitiri	vati nɔŋgitiri
38. Eight fingers	Vati nǫnggisat	vati nɔŋgisaːt
39. Nine fingers	Vati nǫngginyat	vati ncŋginjat
40. Ten fingers	Vati kǫp	vati kɔp
41. Eleven fingers	Vati kǫp ki hwindi	vati kɔp ki hwindi
42. Twelve fingers	Vati kǫp ki utiri	vati kɔp ki utiri
Thirteen fingers	Vati kǫp ki usat	vati kɔp ki usaːt
43. Twenty fingers	Vati mila hindi	vati mila hindi

44. A hundred fingers	Vati mida kǫp	vati mida kɔp
45. Two hundred fingers	Vati mida kǫp tiri	vati mida kɔp tiri
46. Four hundred fingers	Vati mida kǫp nat	vati mida kɔp naːt
47. Sun	Lu	lu
God	Lu	lu
48. Moon	Sii	sii
Full moon	Si po biling	si po bɪlɪŋ
New moon	Si nǫrǫ	si nɔrɔ
49. Day	Delu	dɛlu
Night	Jim	dʒɪm
Morning	Nyare	njare
50. Rain	Lee	lee
51. Water	Mem	mem
52. Blood	Deim	deɪm
53. Fat	Nǫm	nɔm
54. Salt	Takonam	ta konam
55. Stone	Tal	taːl
Iron	Shishashi	ʃɪʃaʃi
56. Hill	Bukam	bukʌm
57. River	Yagi	jagi
58. Road	Padǫnggi	padɔŋgi
59. House	Bam (Compound = ḍeere)	baːm (Compound = ɗɛɛre)
Two houses	Bam tiri	baːm tiri
Many houses	Bam pǫi	baːm pɔi
All the houses	Bam dum	baːm dum
60. Roof	Bampiji	bampidʒi
61. Door	Nyapa	njapa
62. Mat	Barau	barəu
63. Basket	Sukul	sukul
64. Drum	Vim	vim
65. Pot	Tanggi	taŋgi
66. Knife	Kuji	kudʒi
67. Spear	Kǫkǫ	kɔkɔ
68. Bow	Tau	tau
69. Arrow	Zuo	zuo
Five arrows	Zuo nǫng	zuo zɔŋ
70. Gun	Gbindigaru	gbɪndigaru
71. War	Heir	heɪr
72. Meat (animal)	Wati	wʌti
73. Elephant	Ndaji	ndadʒi
74. Buffalo	Wirra	wɪrra
75. Leopard	Sigere	sɪgere
76. Monkey	Ta	ta
77. Pig	Giriji	gɪridʒi
78. Goat	Wii (plural = wiir)	wii (plural = wiɪr)
79. Dog	Za	za
80. Bird	Nǫ̂	nɔ̂
Feather	Kǫbnǫ̂	kɔbnɔ̂

81. Crocodile	Jele	dʒɛle
82. Fowl	Tiji	tidʒi
83. Eggs	Pa tiji	pa tidʒi
84. One egg	Pa tiji hindi	pa tidʒi hindi
85. Snake	Soo	soo
86. Frog	Vuko	vuko
87. Horse	Gbaji (plural = Gbari)	gbadʒi (plural=gbari)
Cow	Na (plural = Nar)	na: (plural = na:r)
88. Fly	Ku	ku
89. Bee	Vǫri	vôri
Honey	Vǫri	vôri
90. Tree	Ya	ja:
Ten trees	Ya kǫp	ja: kɔp
91. Leaf	Waɗi	waɗi
92. Guinea-corn	Sori	sori
93. Maize	Sopa	sopa
94. Ground nut	Nǫgbir	nɔgbɪr
95. Oil	Nǫm	nɔm

GENGLE AND KUGAMA VOCABULARY

1. Head	U	u
2. Hair	Akum	akum
3. Eye	Nô	nô
Two eyes	Nô kiri	nô kiri
4. Ear	Tua	tua
Two ears	Tuang kiri	tuaŋ kiri
5. Nose	Hwang	hwaŋ
6. One tooth	Rumang bini	rumaŋ bini
Five teeth	Rumang kanǫng	rumaŋ kanɔŋ
7. Tongue	Wim	wim
8. Neck	Kôang	kôaŋ
9. Breast (woman's)	Nyiang	njiaŋ
10. Heart	Kalang	kalaŋ
11. Belly	Viram	viram
12. Back	Guang	guaŋ
13. Arm	Nang	naŋ
14. Hand	Dinange	dinaŋɛ
Two hands	Dinang kiri	dinaŋ kiri
15. Finger	Vanang	vanaŋ
Five fingers	Zanang kanǫng	zanaŋ kanɔŋ
16. Finger nail	Kôu vanang	kôu va naŋ
17. Leg	Jang	dʒaŋ
18. Knee	Rung	ruŋ
19. Foot	Jang	dʒaŋ
Two feet	Dijang kiri	didʒaŋ kiri
20. Man (person)	Wem	wɛm
Ten people	Wene kup	wɛne kup
21. Man (not woman)	Wevebi	wɛvebi
Two men	Wevere kiri	wɛ vere kiri
22. Woman	Wesubi	wɛsubi
Two women	Sesuri kiri	sesuri kiri

23. Child	Ava	ava
24. Father	Da	da
25. Mother	Naa	naꞔa
26. Slave	Sam	sam
27. Chief	Kpwaam	kpwaam
28. Friend	Uradungla	uraduŋla
29. Smith	Wesasi	we sasi
30. Doctor	Wepa	wepa
31. One finger	Vanang bini	vanaŋ bini
32. Two fingers	Zanang kiri	zanaŋ kiri
33. Three fingers	Zanang kasat	zanaŋ kasat
34. Four fingers	Zanang kaîyat	zanaŋ kaîjat
35. Five fingers	Zanang kanǫng	zanaŋ kanɔŋ
36. Six fingers	Zanang kanǫng ti bini	zanaŋ kanɔŋ ti bini
37. Seven fingers	Zanang ǫgan nyat ǫgasat	zanaŋ ɔgan njat ɔgasat
38. Eight fingers	Zanang ǫgan nyat ǫkanyat	zanaŋ ɔgan njat ɔkanjat
39. Nine fingers	Zanang ǫgan nyat ǫkanung	zanaŋ ɔgan njat ɔkanuŋ
40. Ten fingers	Zanang kup	zanaŋ kup
41. Eleven fingers	Zanang kup tu ba bini	zanaŋ kup ta ba bini
42. Twelve fingers	Zanang kup tu ga iri	zanaŋ kup ta ga iri
Thirteen fingers	Zanang kup tu ga sat	zanaŋ kup ta ga sat
43. Twenty fingers	Zanang mi bini	zanaŋ mi bini
44. A hundred fingers	Zanang mi nǫng	zanaŋ mi nɔŋ
45. Sun	Lu	lu
God	Lu	lu
46. Moon	Shi	ʃi
Full moon	Shi kalla	ʃi kalla
New moon	Shi zarasan	ʃi zarasan
47. Day	Dalu	dalu
Night	Dajê	dadʒê
Morning	Adzura	adzura
48. Rain	Leatimi	leatimi
49. Water	Me	me
50. Blood	Adi	adi
51. Fat	Anong	anoŋ
52. Salt	Ta kpwam	ta kpwam
53. Stone	Tabi	tabi
Iron	Sisasi	sisasi
54. Hill	Gora	gora
55. River	Abonggi	abɔŋgi
56. Road	Dakpwa	dakpwa
57. House	Ade (Compound = bǫm)	ade (Compound = bɔm)
Two houses	De kiri	de kiri
Many houses	De mata	de mata
All the houses	De matik	de matik
58. Roof	Abǫm piri	abɔm piri
59. Door	Nya bǫm	nja bɔm

60. Mat	Yuga	juga
61. Basket	Asheê	aʃɛɛ̂
62. Drum	Avim	avɪm
63. Pot	Tang	taŋ
64. Knife	Nokum	nokum
65. Spear	Pugi	pugi
66. Bow	Poro	poro
67. Arrow	Ajugi	adʒugi
Five arrows	Zugi kaṇǫng	zugi kanɔŋ
68. Gun	Bindigaru	bɪndɪgaru
69. War	Kǫng	kɔŋ
70. Meat (animal)	Awo	awo
71. Elephant	Adang	adaŋ
72. Buffalo	Abaki	abaki
73. Leopard	Awosi	awosi
74. Monkey	Ata	ata
75. Pig	Agiring	agiriŋ
76. Goat	Ayi	aji
77. Dog	Ja	dʒa
78. Bird	Nô	nô
Feather	Kum nô	kum nô
79. Crocodile	Tim	tim
80. Fowl	Tiim	tiim
81. Eggs	Kpa tiim	kpa tiim
82. One egg	Kpa tiim bini	kpa tiim bini
83. Snake	Sogi	sogi
84. Frog	Vǫgǫ	vɔgɔ
85. Cow	Naki	naki
86. Sheep	Dâ	dâ
87. Horse	Gbana	gbana
88. Fly	Kû	kû
89. Bee	Vǫri	vɔ̂ri
Honey	Ano vǫri	ano vɔ̂ri
90. Tree	Aya	aja
Ten trees	Aya kup	aja kup
91. Leaf	Wari	wari
92. Guinea-corn	Som	som
93. Maize	Som kiva	som kiva
94. Ground nut	Gbere	gɓɛrɛ
95. Oil	Anǫ	anɔ̂
96. The tall woman	Wesubi wehem	wɛsubi wehɛm
The tall women	Wesuran ḍi wehem	wɛsuran di wehɛm
97. Large dog	Go ja	go dʒa
98. Small dog	Ava ja	ava dʒa
99. The dog bites	Ja bosi yungchi	dʒa bosi juŋtʃi
100. Fulani	Pillaserre	pɪllasɛrrɛ
Beriberi	Wekolejo	wɛ koledʒo
Hausa	Wefofǫn	wɛ fofɔn
Bachama and Bata	Dunu	dunu

CHAPTER IX

THE MAMBILA

The Mambila tribe, in so far as the British Cameroons is concerned, numbers about 13,000 people and occupies the major part of the plateau west of Banyo, which is known as the Mambila Plateau. The term "plateau" is hardly suitable, as it is anything but flat. It is hilly country with deep gullies, and the traveller is constantly passing from one panoramic view to another. According to Captain Izard, who has surveyed the district, the plateau has a mean level of about 5,000 feet above the sea. But most of the villages are situated on hills which must be at least 6,000 feet above sea level, and the highest hills probably attain an altitude of 9,000 feet. The Mambila Plateau presents a distinct contrast in appearance to the Bauchi Plateau in that it is completely covered with soil, outcrops of granite occurring only at long intervals of travelling. The subsoil is of a heavy broken-down laterite type, and in certain areas is composed of chalk. The infertility of the soil forces the natives to use fertilizing agents in the form of leguminous pigeon-pea plants specially cultivated for the purpose. But the plateau is eminently suitable for grazing cattle, and on this account, and also on account of the absence of noxious flies, is well patronized by the cattle-owning Fulani. It is covered with bracken, and there is a great variety of flowers, including orchids. There is a complete absence of trees, except in the gullies, and the dearth of firewood entails great hardship on the inhabitants, who have not yet become accustomed to the use of clothing. The Mambila men wear a loin covering of cloth ; the women are completely nude. Strong winds prevail throughout the day, and the rainy season lasts from the middle of March until close on the end of December. The severity of the climate has taught the Mambila peoples, primitive as they are, to evolve a technique of house-building which is superior to anything seen in the Northern Provinces of Nigeria.

The term Mambila is stated generally to have been conferred by the Fulani. But this can hardly be accepted. The Mambila themselves pronounce the word as Mabila, which is probably a variant of Mbula, a common tribal title in Nigeria (in the form Mbula, Bura, etc.) and meaning "The Men". The title has long been applied by neighbouring tribes to the group classed as Mambila, and it is no doubt from them that it was adopted by the Fulani of Banyo, who succeeded in reducing many of the Mambila groups during the latter half of the nineteenth century. The Mambila have no common title for themselves. Each village group calls itself by the name of its own locality or by that of the founder of the village or by that of some specially distinguished chief. There was and is no tribal organization, and the next-door neighbour was usually the principal enemy, in spite of inter-marriage. (Intermarriage commonly creates hostility. Indeed a Mambila, if asked who are his traditional enemies, will answer : "The members of such-and-such a village, for we marry their daughters and they marry ours.") The only common title that the Mambila admit is that of "Nǫr", i.e. "The Men", a term which was formerly sufficient to describe all the people they knew, viz. those who inhabited the Mambila Plateau and spoke dialects of the same language. But this generic term is now seen to be unsuitable, for the Mambila have come to know other "men" than those who share their own language and culture.

Certain groups describe themselves collectively as Torbi, and it was asserted that the Torbi are quite distinct from the Mambila, all the Torbi speaking a common dialect and having common customs. Investigation, however, showed that the so-called Torbi (viz. the villagers of Kuma, Jabu, Gikaum, Jeke, Titong, Kabri, Barrat, Baso, Yurum, Wa, Nyege, Ngubin, Tem, and Genbu) had not a uniform dialect or uniform customs, and that not all of the villages so described accepted the term of Torbi. Moreover, the term appeared to be applied to villages which had accepted the suzerainty of the Fulani, those described as "Mambila" being those who had maintained their independence of the Fulani.

In view of the Fulani-sounding suffix in the term "Torbi" it seemed probable that this term was invented by the Fulani to describe those groups which had accepted Fulani domination.

It was suggested, therefore (by me), that the term "Torbi" was a Fulani term, and in most of the villages visited this suggestion was, after discussion, accepted.[1] I note that Captain Izard, who has made a close study of the Mambila (and if I may say so has done work of outstanding value), confines the use of the term " Torbi " to the villagers of Kuma. In this, I think, he is mistaken.

The Mambila groups all speak dialects of the same language ; but there are variations by which we can make a rough classification into two groups, a Northern and Southern. The Northern group uses the words *Mwandi* for Sun and *Nama* for God, whereas the Southern group uses the words *Lu* and *Chang* respectively. There are other variations which will be seen by a study of the vocabularies (e.g. that *wuni* = head in the Northern group and *gur* in the Southern group) and it will appear later also that there are cultural distinctions between the two groups (e.g. in house building). In some cases (e.g. at Kabri) there is a fusion between the two groups. On this basis we may include the following villages in the Northern group : Jabu, Gikaun, Kuma, Baso, Yurum, Ngubin, Dembi, Tem, Titong, and Kabri. The Southern group would include (*a*) Warwar, Vakude, Tamnyang, and Mbamgam, and (*b*) Wa, (Leme), Genbu, Mverrip, Bou, Bar, Teb, and San. This latter section is known collectively as Tagbo (Lagubi) or Tongbo.

All these groups are administered by the Emir of Adamawa, through the district head of Gashaka, who is also a Fulani. But formerly the Mambila had no relations either with Gashaka or with the Emirs of Adamawa. Those who became subject to the Fulani acknowledged only the Fulani governors of Banyo, which is now included in French Cameroons (but the Fulani of Banyo were to some extent subordinate to the Emirs of Adamawa).

It is stated that there are other groups of Mambila in the French Cameroons (viz. at Sangkola, Shone, Ata, Lingam, and Kakara), and also in the Bamenda division of British Cameroons (viz. at Nyoro, Gongkor and Birpa).

Closely connected with the Mambila, though not described as Mambila, are the villagers of Kamkam and Magu. This group formerly occupied the site which is now the Fulani settlement of Guroje. When attacked by the Fulani of Banyo one group fled

---

[1] The blacksmith groups who are an immigrant caste describe the Mambila as Tu-turu. The Fulani may have adopted this term from the blacksmiths, dropping the prefix " Tu " and adding their suffix " be ".

PLATE 55

DISTANT VIEW OF THE MAMBILA PLATEAU

westwards to Magu and the other southwards to the Mambila country. Their language is intimately related to Mambila, though it can hardly be described as a Mambila dialect. Culturally they can scarcely be distinguished from the Mambila, having the same religious cults and the same methods of house-building, etc. They were formerly a matrilineal people, lacking the exchange system of marriage which among the Mambila has, coupled with the so-called " purchase " system, resulted in a bilateral form of social organization (as will be explained later).

Reference has been made to the presence among the Mambila of groups of blacksmiths. These groups, who are known as Kila, speak a language of their own which is intimately connected with the Bute and Wawa languages of the French Cameroons. It has some affinities with Mambila which belongs to the same linguistic group as Bute and Wawa. The fact that the blacksmiths have preserved their own language would indicate that their immigration is of recent date, and this is borne out by the Mambila tradition that formerly the Mambila had no iron weapons, their arrows being wooden pointed, and their agricultural work being carried out by means of digging-sticks. Their bowstrings, it is said, were made of fibre and not of leather. On the other hand it is difficult to square this tradition with the fact that the Mambila claim to have been a spear-using people from ancient times, and that they are the possessors of a short unpointed cutting sword of scimitar type unknown in Nigeria. It would appear to be probable that the Mambila have long been accustomed to the use of iron, but that when iron was unobtainable they had resort to the instruments described. They say that if they had no knives they cut up meat with a piece of guinea-corn stalk, the bark of the stalk serving as a blade. This primitive form of knife is still used by children among Nigerian tribes which have attained a high standard of civilization.

A feature of the blacksmith groups is their insistence that all male children born to one of their caste, whether male or female, shall become blacksmiths. For this reason blacksmiths are commonly endogamous. But they are not averse, when associated with matrilineal peoples, to allow their daughters to marry outside of their own group. Among the Mambila, therefore, they are quite ready to allow their daughters to marry Mambila men on the " purchase " (but not on the exchange) system, for under the purchase system the children (according to Mambila rules) belong to the mother's group.

The social system of the Mambila is of great interest and must be thoroughly understood if the tribe is to be properly administered. As already stated there is no tribal organization, nor is there any clan organization.

A number of villages might form a confederacy for fighting purposes,[1] based on the possession of a common territory and dialect, or on a common origin from some parent village, but each village group considered itself politically independent of any other village group, and inter-village fights were of frequent occurrence. There was and is no banding-together of villages for marriage purposes, for the exogamous unit is merely the kindred. At the present time, as the people are more scattered than formerly, two separate villages may be composed of two branches of a single kindred, and this will produce the impression that local exogamy is the rule ; but in the larger villages where there may be two or more kindreds occupying a single village intermarriage between the kindreds is permitted, though in practice it is unusual. It may be noted that the taboo against marriage with close relatives (e.g. second cousins) applies to both sides of the family, and that greater care would be taken by a man contemplating marriage to ascertain that the woman he proposed to marry was not a close relative if she and her parents were members of his own village, than would be taken if she were a member of another village. In fact it was stated that a man might marry his second cousin if her parents belonged to another village, whereas he could not do so if they belonged to his own village, the underlying idea being that the introduction of new blood into the stock was desirable.

There is no totemism connected with the exogamy, nor should we expect it. But there are a number of family taboos against eating the flesh of certain animals at all times or on special occasions. To this reference will be made later.

The social unit is thus the family group which we may call the kindred. This group is bilateral, that is to say, that it is composed of both patrilineal and matrilineal relatives. This

---

[1] E.g. the villagers of Wa, Genbu, Mverrip, Bou, Bar, Teb, and San would assist each other in repelling the Fulani or in beating off an attack by the villagers of Kuma, Baso, Ngubin, and Tem. Mbamgam, Tamnyang, Barrip, and Yakude (Vokude) also united for purposes of defence.

condition is produced by a dual system of marriage. A man may obtain a wife (*a*) by exchanging one of his own female relatives, or by buying a slave girl, or (*b*) by paying a small bride-price. In the former case the children of the marriage belong to the family group of the father, in the latter they belong to the family group of the mother. An exchange wife is regarded as absolute property, whereas a wife obtained by a bride-price is regarded as merely lent by her family group. This exemplifies the misleading character of the term " purchase " where a bride-price is payable. But on the other hand it is a mistake to suppose that in Negro society the wife is never regarded as " bought ", for among the Mambila the social status of an exchange wife does not differ from that of a slave wife. As many false views on this subject are being put forward by anthropologists it may be pointed out that among some tribes (e.g. the Bade of Bornu) there is a system of marriage by which a bride is obtained by (*a*) a large bride-price or (*b*) a small bride-price. Under the former the woman is regarded as bought out of her own group ; under the latter as loaned. Under the former the children belong to the father's group, under the latter to the mother's. Among the Mambila an exchange wife loses her freedom, dissolution of marriage being practically impossible. Her property becomes at her death the property of her husband, and her relatives have no influence with nor concern in her children. But a woman married under the purchase system is free to leave her husband when she pleases, and can take her children with her. Her children are, in fact, at the disposal of her relatives. Her property (and Mambila women acquire property, so much so that in former times a woman might be the owner of several slaves) cannot be taken on her death by her husband ; it is claimed by her own relatives. A woman married under the exchange system loses contact with her own relatives. A woman married under the " purchase " system remains in constant contact with her relatives. Indeed, she spends much of her time in her father's or maternal uncle's home. She bears her children there. She will assist her husband on his farm, but she will also, in the same year, carry on a farm of her own in her father's village. For if she has reason for leaving her husband she is unwilling to be dependent on her relatives for her food and for that of her children.

It will be seen, therefore, that the Mambila are both a

patrilineal and matrilineal people.   Captain Izard has stated that
formerly there was no other form of marriage than that by
exchange, but this is clearly incorrect, as the whole of the social
system is based on the dual form of marriage.   Captain Heath
reports that the Mambila are wholly patrilineal.   It is very easy
to be misled in these matters, as tribes which still adhere to
matrilineal practices or even to some of their matrilineal customs
are averse to admitting that they do so.   The reasons are obvious.
They think that a claim by a man on his sister's children will be
construed by the Government as an infringement of the laws
against slavery, for during the Fulani régime a man could sell
his sister's child [1] into slavery in order to redeem himself.   Under
the British régime, therefore, we usually find that (*a*) matrilineal
or semi-matrilineal peoples are forced to abandon their customs
as regards the custody of children, as the father will threaten
an action in court if the children are taken from him, and (*b*) that
the exchange system of marriage is automatically dropped,
as girls will threaten a court action if they are forced to marry
against their will.

The Mambila have accommodated themselves to the new
conditions (i) by abandoning marriage by exchange, and (ii) by
making it optional whether the offspring of a marriage by purchase
join their mother's group or not.   Formerly the offspring of
a marriage by exchange inherited property patrilineally, while
the offspring of a marriage by purchase inherited matrilineally.
Now that marriage by purchase is the only form of marriage
inheritance should be wholly matrilineal, but there is a tendency
towards revising this rule.   For it is illogical that a man should
inherit from his maternal uncle if he has lived with his father
and has rendered no services to his maternal uncle.

The following account of the former system of marriage will
assist in making the position clearer.

(*a*) *Marriage by exchange.*—In this form of marriage two men
agree to exchange as wives one of their female relatives.

When the arrangement has been made one of the men invites
the other to his house, having made preparations to celebrate the
occasion.   The host introduces his friend to the girl and the
young couple become friendly.   A few days later the other man
likewise invites his friend to come to his house to meet his future

---

[1] If his sister had been married under the bride-price system.

wife. A date is then fixed for the exchange, and each man performs the following rites in order that his sister (in the classificatory sense) may remain happily with her husband: The man takes his sister to the family shrine in the bush. (If he is himself the son of a woman married under the exchange system the shrine will be that of his father's family, but if he is the son of a woman married under the purchase system the shrine will be that of his mother's family.) The shrine consists of three stones, one large and two small. The large stone represents the senior ancestor of the family, while the smaller stones represent a deceased grandfather and grandmother respectively. The man then produces fire (by drilling), and lighting a bundle of grass places it on the large stone and says: " My forefathers, I follow the custom of ancient times. From you we derive all our welfare in life. My sister's daughter is about to go to her husband's house. Do you care for her there. Grant that she may reside there happily, protected from witchcraft and other evils." He then places another bundle of smouldering grass on each of the other stones and offers a similar prayer. The couple now close their eyes and place their hands on the smouldering grass and extinguish the fire, the man blowing an antelope's horn and shouting " Kaukau, kaukau, kaukau ", i.e. " Good luck, good luck, good luck ". The idea of the fire is to give warmth to the ancestors, and the idea of blowing the horn is to drive the ancestral ghosts to accompany the girl. The man then takes a chicken, slits its lips with a knife, and presses the bleeding mouth against each of the stones, repeating his former prayer. He holds the chicken to the mouth of the girl, who licks a little of the blood, and he then places the chicken's bleeding mouth against her forehead and each temple. Plucking out three small feathers from the chicken's head he sticks one on each of the bloody patches on the girl's face. He also pulls out four larger feathers and sticks two on the large stone and one each on the smaller stones. The girl now goes home and prepares some porridge which she brings back to the shrine, the man in the meantime killing the chicken by twisting its neck, and parching it over a fire which has to be produced by the drill method. He takes some of the flesh and porridge and, closing his eyes, throws it to the West, saying: " May our forefathers who have gone West look after this girl in her married life." A similar offering is thrown Eastwards with the words : " May our forefathers who have gone East look after this girl in her married life." He closes his eyes in order to avoid looking on the ancestors as they take the offerings. The rite is concluded by the man binding two iron anklets on each of the girl's legs.

The girl is then escorted to her husband's home by an aged female relative. On arrival she is given a chicken and hoe by her husband as an inducement to her to enter the compound. She must be given another hoe before she enters his hut, another before she sits down, another before she partakes of food, and two before she permits him to have sexual relations. Before she washes next morning she must be presented with a chicken. Each morning for a period of a month she is smeared with red earth and oil by female relatives of her husband. During this month she does no work of any kind, the intention being to make her contented with her new surroundings. She is given the best of fare.

There are certain points about the exchange form of marriage which deserve attention. The first point is that a girl cannot be used as an exchange by her mother's male relatives if her mother was herself an exchange wife, because the children of an exchange wife belong to their father's and not to their mother's group. Vice versa, a girl cannot be used by her paternal relatives as an exchange wife if her mother had been married under the purchase system, for in this case the children belong to the mother's group. Secondly, a father cannot use his own daughter as an exchange wife for himself, even if the girl's mother had been married under the exchange system. Thirdly, a man may not elope with an exchange wife. But elopement with wives married under the purchase system is permitted and is a regular practice.

Children born under the exchange system of marriage reside with their father, and inherit from him.

(b) *Marriage by Purchase.*—If a man sees a girl in the market who takes his fancy and finds that she is free to marry he buys some beer and calls the girl aside. He ascertains from her the names of her relatives, and if one of them had accompanied the girl to market he invites that one to join him in drinking beer.[1] The girl's guardian leaves the girl and young man to talk and drink

---

[1] In drinking beer it is the Mambila custom for two friends or acquaintances to drink simultaneously from the same calabash.

together, and in due course the man proposes marriage. The girl replies that she will have to consult her father and mother.[1] After a few days' interval the young man sends his friends to the girl's home with a gift of five hoes, two chickens, and a spear. The girl is asked if she agrees to the proposed marriage, and if she does the presents are handed by her to her father, the spear being given to her brother. She is then escorted to her husband's home without any further formalities, except the religious rite already described (which may, however, have been previously performed by the girl's father when she had reached marriageable age). The girl stops at frequent intervals on the road to her husband's home and is given a gift of a hoe on each occasion ; and on entering her husband's home she is made the recipient of numerous gifts as already described. Whereas an exchange wife remains idle for the first month of her married life a woman married in consideration of a bride-price remains idle for two months. It was stated that this difference is due to the fact that a woman married under the purchase system has to be shown greater consideration than one married under the exchange system. Under the purchase system the wife can terminate the marriage at her pleasure and take her children with her. The bride-price is only refunded if she has not borne a child to her first husband. This seems an anomalous rule in view of the fact that children born under the purchase system belong to the mother's group, but actually the father derives certain advantages from children even though the children are at the disposal of their maternal uncle. For the father is entitled to the first game-animal killed by his son, and he is entitled to the bride-price of a daughter (if she marries on the purchase system) for her first marriage. (Game-animals subsequently killed by sons must be given to their maternal uncle, and maternal uncles also claim the bride-price for all subsequent marriages contracted by their sisters' daughters.)

It is not an absolute rule that all children born under the purchase system must go and live in their maternal uncle's home. They can continue to live with their father if they please, or they may alternate between one home and the other. But they usually gravitate towards the maternal uncle's home for the

---

[1] But it is only the mother who can prevent her daughter marrying under the purchase system.

reason that they cannot inherit from their father, and they cannot obtain an exchange wife from their father's group. Female children born under this system can be used as marriage exchanges by their mother's male relatives but not by their father's. A son who is happy in his father's home may be provided with a wife by his father under the purchase system (but not, as already stated, under the exchange system). But a son who elects to remain with his father is liable to perform farm or other work for his mother's relatives when called upon. Female children may remain in their father's home until claimed by their mother's relatives to be used as exchanges. But if there are several female children the father may be allowed to keep one or two and give them in marriage (by purchase), receiving the bride-price. But when these girls themselves bear female children those children can be claimed by the mother's relatives to be used as exchanges.

It may be noted finally that in former times a man could redeem himself from slavery by giving to his enslaver a child born to his sister under the purchase system of marriage. He might even use for this purpose a sister's daughter who was married (under the purchase system). The husband, if he were devoted to his wife, might in such a case offer one of his own female relatives instead. If this offer were accepted the status of his wife would be altered to that of an exchange wife, i.e. all children borne by her would become his and she herself could not contract a secondary marriage.

Husbands can inherit from wives who had been married under the exchange system, but not from wives married under the purchase system. The property of the latter class is claimed by the wife's maternal relatives. Widows are heritable by brothers, sons, and sisters' sons ; but widows married under the purchase system cannot be inherited against their will. Widows who had married under the exchange system can, of course, only be inherited by a man who is the son of a woman who had married under the exchange system, or of a woman who was married as a slave.

A further point as regards inheritance of property is that if the deceased had a son by an exchange marriage and a sister's son whose mother had been married under the purchase system the property would be divided between them, both being entitled to inherit.

PLATE 56

MAMBILA TYPES

[face p. 542

As regards inheritance of chieftainship it was apparently the Mambila rule that no one could become a chief who was not the offspring of an exchange marriage.

The question of the mode of inheritance of witchcraft will be dealt with later.

Before leaving the subject of marriage reference may be made to a Mambila custom which is probably common enough among other pagan tribes, though I have only observed it among the Malabu and Jirai peoples north of the Benue. By this custom it is permissible for a man to have sexual relations with the wife of any senior member of his father's or mother's group. The custom is carried so far that a husband who has to absent himself from home will call upon a younger relative to sleep with his wife during his absence. I have discussed this subject at some length in my report on the Malabu tribe and it need only be mentioned here that among the Mambila there is no organization (as among the Malabu) by which a number of kindreds have a community (or form of community) of wives. But the Mambila observe the rule that no one may have sexual relations with the wife of a brother or half-brother, or with the wife of a father or maternal uncle. Sons frequently have sexual relations with their fathers' wives, but these relations are considered improper and are carried out *sub rosa*.

It may be of interest to give now a brief illustration of the constitution of a family group. The group chosen is that of a family at Kuma, the present head of which is Wondem. It consists of the following members :—

(1) Wondem, son of Wanbonga (deceased), by a slave wife.
(2) Tiso, son of Chembira (deceased), by a slave wife.
  Chembira was a first-cousin (paternal) of Wanbonga.
(3) Shomo, son of Chembira, by a woman married under the purchase system.

These three with their wives and children occupy a single compound.

(4) Kunu, son of Wanbonga, by a slave wife (but not the same slave wife as the mother of Wondem).
(5) Bike, son of Wankurip (deceased), by a woman married under the exchange system. Wankurip's father was a brother of Wanbonga.

These two, with their wives and children, occupy a single compound.

(6) Tam, son of Michir, a daughter of Wanbonga's younger brother Gedi.
  Michir was married under the purchase system.

(7) Waneme, son of Wanbonga's daughter, who was married under the purchase system.

The above two share a single compound.

(8) Nyine, son of Wanbonga, by a woman married under the purchase system. He has a compound of his own.

It will be seen that this household includes five patrilineal relatives and three uterine relatives. The family group is thus bilateral. Of the uterine relatives the presence of Tam and Waneme is normal, as the mothers of both were married under the purchase system. But it might be thought that Shomo and Nyine should, for the same reason, be resident in the mother's group. Both were until recently. Shomo and his two brothers and one sister had all joined their mother's group at the village of Titong. Shomo's maternal uncle had, however, come to the conclusion that it would be but fair to Shomo's aged father Chembira that one of his children should be returned to him to look after him in his old age. For Chembira had only one other son, viz. Tiso (by a slave wife). This is an illustration of the native point of view that legal rights should be modified by equity. Actually, however, Chembira died before Shomo's maternal uncle had carried out his intention. Tiso succeeded to Chembira's estate, as Tiso's mother was a slave woman. Shomo's maternal uncle then sent Shomo to keep Tiso company. Shomo is older than Tiso, but Tiso, nevertheless, as his father's heritor, takes precedence of Shomo, and Shomo must respect Tiso's wishes in all matters as long as they continue to reside together. Tiso, in a sense, has become the legal father of Shomo, and will assist Shomo in the same way as a father will assist his son. If Shomo, for example, wishes to obtain a second wife, he will look to Tiso for assistance.

It is important for Europeans to bear in mind that in Negro society social status is not entirely governed by age. I have pointed this out in numerous reports, and drawn attention to the fact that in some tribes a person may have to address another younger than himself by the title of " father ".

Nyine was until recently resident in the village of his mother's father, but owing to a violent quarrel with his mother's relatives he left the village and joined his father's group at Kuma.

It is hardly necessary to add that there are a number of children of Wanbonga and Chembira who are not residing with their paternal relatives, as they have joined their mother's group, the mother having been married under the purchase system. Thus Wanbonga's son Kumake is living with his mother's group. Shomo is at liberty to return to the home of his maternal uncle at any time.

Wanbonga was formerly the head of the household. He had inherited from his father, as his mother had been married under the exchange system. On his death Chembira inherited, as he was entitled to do, his mother having been a slave wife. Chembira became responsible for such children of Wanbonga as did not belong to their mother's group. On Chembira's death Wondem succeeded, as he was the son of a slave wife and not of a woman married under the purchase system. On Wondem's death Kunu will succeed. It may be noted that Wondem's present wife was inherited by him from Chembira. She is the mother of Tiso.

We may conclude this summary of the social organization by giving a list of the relationship terms.

Koo is applied to a father and his brothers and also to maternal uncles. A senior *koo* is described as *koo ngitane* (" big father ") and a junior as *koo buwe* (" little father ").

Descriptive terms are used when necessary to distinguish a father's brothers from a mother's brothers. A father's or mother's brothers may also be addressed (if the speaker is grown up) by the title *wan dikha*, i.e. " My big brother ". For " fathers " and elder brothers are classed together, so that a young person will address a grown-up elder brother as *koo*, i.e. as " father ".

It was surprising to find that a young man might address a paternal uncle by the same term as he addressed an elder brother, but it was stated that any grown-up man could drink from the same calabash of beer as a paternal or maternal uncle. This would be shocking to most Nigerian tribes. The Mambila do not show an excessive respect for elders, and a Mambila youth may, without any offence, sit himself down beside his seniors and join in their conversation, a practice which would never be permitted by e.g. the Hausa or Fulani of Nigeria. Another Mambila custom which in the majority of Nigerian tribes would be considered as a sign of insanity is that by which a man may drink beer simultaneously from the same calabash as a woman.

It is not permissible to address any *koo* by his personal

name, but apart from an actual father a perversion of the personal
name may be used in address.   Thus if a *koo*'s name is Shoga
he may be addressed as Gaga.

A mother is addressed as *dee* and referred to as *me ndikha*.
There is a special term, viz. *ada* for a father's sister (elder
or younger) and this term is also applied to a mother's
younger sister.   But a mother's elder sister is addressed as *baba*,
a term which normally carries the significance of " father ".   Just
as a father's and mother's brothers are classed with elder brothers,
so a father's sisters and a mother's younger sister are classed
with elder sisters, for an elder sister is called *ada*.

Younger brothers and sisters (and cousins) are addressed by
their personal names, and if very junior may be described as
buwa nya, i.e. my little son.   This is logical when it is remembered
that elder brothers rank as fathers.

Nya = son and *ngou* = daughter.

It may be noted that elder brothers may not be addressed
by their personal names.   The reason is obvious when we
remember that they rank as fathers.   But the reason given is
that if a younger brother addressed an elder brother by his
personal name, his own child might follow suit.

Male grandparents are addressed as *tamtam* and female
as *gogo*, this latter term being used by the Fulani for " father's
sister ".   But grandparents may also be described as *koom
ngitane* (i.e. big father) or *me ngitane* (big mother).   Grandchildren
are addressed by their personal names or as *tandu*.   A grandmother may playfully call her grandson " my husband ",
and a grandfather may call his granddaughter " my wife "
(and vice versa).   But there is no potential intermarriage.

Parents-in-law and children-in-law address each other as
guna, but it is usual for a woman to address her father-in-law
as *takurindi*, i.e. as " father of the house ", and her mother-
in-law as *makurindi*, i.e. as " mother of the house ".   Just as
elder brothers are classed as fathers, so elder brothers-in-law
or sisters-in-law are classed as parents-in-law, i.e. they are
addressed as *guna*.   Younger brothers-in-law   or   sisters-in-
law are addressed as *nyini*, and this term is also applied to the
wife of a maternal uncle, and is used by her towards her husband's
nephew or niece.

Husbands and wives address each other by their personal

names and refer to each other as *ndakha shi* and *ndakha bwen* respectively.

Religion.—Among the Mambila there are, as already noted, two distinct terms for the Supreme Being, viz. *Nama* and *Chang*. The former is one of the commonest terms in West Africa, occurring as *Nyam*, *Nyamba*, *Yamba*, etc. It possibly embodies the root *Ma* or *Ama* which is the name of the Jukun creator-deity. The term *Chang* is not, as far as I know, paralleled else-where in West Africa.

Neither *Nama* nor *Chang* is identified with the Sun, though the identification of the Supreme Being with the Sun is general among the tribes of the Benue basin.[1] Nor are there any Sun rites such as are found among the Jukun groups which are located at no great distance from the Mambila.

On the other hand I received from a Mambila of Kuma a remarkable account of Moon rites which, he said, were practised originally at Mbamga, and subsequently at Dembe, the officiant of the cult being at that time a woman who was a relative of the informant. I was unable to obtain any verification of the account given of these rites and I have some hesitation, therefore, in recording it, more especially as the subject of moon-worship is of exceptional importance for the study of the history of religious thought. Nevertheless, owing to the circumstantial character of the description given I feel bound to record it.

The rites are held twice monthly at the waxing and waning of the moon.

On the morning of the day on which the moon is due to appear, food, consisting of porridge and chicken's flesh, is prepared by the villagers. In the evening the priest (*mbon shǫǫ*) proceeds to the sacred grove and blows loudly on an antelope's horn. The men of the village then proceed to a cleared space in the vicinity of the shrine, taking with them the prepared food and a supply of palm-wine. Meanwhile a man who is to personate the moon-deity enters the shrine (which is shaped like a granary) and dons an animal-headed mask. He covers his body with a string costume to which are attached feathers of various kinds of birds. He is then escorted out to a wooden seat in the cleared

---

[1] It is noteworthy that in the Warwar group of Mambila the word for Sun is *Lu*. This word occurs as *Lu* or *Ru*, in the sense of Sun and Supreme Being among the Yendang, Waka, Kumba, Teme, and Gengle tribes.

space, and as he sits down all the assembled men of the village
clap their hands in salutation, and give vent to a loud hum.
The priest then takes some medicine, mixes it with a little red
earth and inserts the mixture in a calabash of palm wine.
Addressing the deity he says : " The Moon has returned to us
to-day. The custom which I am now carrying out was inherited
by me from my forefathers, and when I die will be carried on
by my successors. It is not a thing of my own invention. By
the grace of the Moon may we all enjoy health and prosperity ;
may we be defended from sickness, and may witchcraft recoil
on the heads of those who practise it. May we obtain all the
things that are necessary to our welfare."

On the conclusion of these words all the assembled people
give a grunt of assent, and the priest then applies the medicated
wine to the lips of the masker, who pushes back his mask in order
to receive it. The calabash is presented to him thrice and he
drinks a mouthful on each occasion. The priest then gives him
some chicken's flesh, which he eats. He is then given another
draught of wine. All present now light their pipes and blow
tobacco smoke into the masker's maw. Having done this they
clap their hands and sing :

" *Ee shǫ a ye, shǫ an dayi nano, ee* ", i.e. " Ah ! be careful of
the god, the god is about to rise and go on his way. Ah ! "

The masker then rises and begins to jump about and leap
into the air, imitating the actions of a bird. He goes off alone
to the village and jumps about in the open spaces, the women
and children having concealed themselves in their huts. Every
now and then he squats down near the huts and grunts, the
women clapping their hands in salutation. He then addresses
the women in a falsetto voice saying [1] : " During this moon
abide in health." The women answer " Yea ! " And again :
" During this month bear male children without mishap." The
women answer " Yea ! " He continues : " During this month
bear female children without mishap." The women answer
" Yea ! " He concludes : " During this month witchcraft shall
not come upon you." The women answer : " Yea ! "

In the meanwhile the men, assembled in age groups, are
given a meal by the priest. Beginning with the senior group

[1] The masker disguises his voice by speaking through a horn, the end of which
is covered with spider's web or the skin of a bat.

the priest places some porridge and chicken on banana leaves in front of each group. He then places in his left hand a piece of the bark of a certain sacred tree and covers it with some feathers. Next he takes a little of the porridge and chicken's flesh with his right hand and, placing it on the bark, he holds it to the mouth of the most senior man, who eats it out of the hand of the priest. The priest next passes down the line, serving each communicant. After this rite all are served with palm wine.

When the masker returns he skips about from tree to tree, leaping in the air like a bird, and when he finally comes to rest on his chair all salute him by clapping their hands. As the new moon has now disappeared all return home leaving the masker and the priest.

Similar rites are performed at the waning of the moon, but they are attended by a few only, and little food is provided, for the moon-deity is sick and about to die. The priest addresses the masker saying: "Formerly when you came we welcomed you, and during your stay we had health and prosperity. No evil befel even one of our chickens, and witchcraft entered not amongst us. Now you are about to leave us, and we beseech you to depart without anger against us, even though one of our number should, in forgetfulness, make a noise on the day of your departure. But care for us even in your absence. When you die salute for us our forefathers, and when you rise again on the third day and return to us, be not wrathful towards us."

The priest then offers him some food and wine, but the masker scarcely partakes. The people salute by clapping their hands gently, for the deity is sick unto death and cannot bear a noise. He makes a few desultory movements and then wanders slowly off to the town to bid farewell to the women. When he reaches the town he begins to utter groans and all the women wail "Alas! Alas!" Then he slowly murmurs: "I am dying and am leaving you. But on the third day I will rise again and come unto you. Meanwhile abide in peace, and when I return receive me with rejoicing and offerings of gratitude."

On returning to the grove he falls down into his chair and all the men present bid him a quiet farewell, leaving him to "die" in the care of the priest.

It will have been observed from the petitions offered to the moon-deity that the fear of witchcraft is potent among the Mambila.

Witchcraft is acquired either by heredity or by purchase or by accident. It is hereditary in the female line only. If a woman is a witch her children automatically acquire the witch soul or complex by imbibing her milk. But the mere possession of the witch-soul is not sufficient to enable the owner to practise witchcraft. The eyes of the owner have to be opened to his powers, and this is done by means of a medicine mixed by the mother or more usually by an elder sister. It is said that an elder brother will not perform this service for a younger brother, on account of the jealousy which exists between brothers.

Witchcraft is not transmitted automatically from father to son; but a father who is a witch or wizard can reveal his art to a son by taking the soul of one of his maternal relatives, cooking it after the fashion of witches, and giving a piece of soul-liver to his son, together with part of a slippery fish or a secret medicine. Or a man may purchase witchcraft from a witch who is not a relative, by making a present of the soul of one of his maternal relatives to the witch. The witch devours the gift, but gives some of the soul-liver, together with the secret medicine, to the person who wishes to become a member of the guild of witches. The souls of paternal relatives may not be taken and given as gifts to witches, for paternal relatives are not regarded as one's kith and kin. A man can do anything he likes with his kith and kin, i.e. with his maternal relatives, but if he took a paternal relative he would be taking what did not belong to him, and if detected he and all his maternal relatives would be sold into slavery. But if he is detected trafficking in the lives of his maternal relatives he is merely rebuked, the head of his wife's family pointing out out to him that if he does not desist he will have no relatives left in the world. These beliefs show that among the Mambila descent is reckoned primarily in the female line.

A person may become a witch unwittingly by partaking of food which contains the secret medicine of witchcraft, the medicine having been inserted into the food by a witch who may be an acquaintance or even a friend of the innocent man. The person who eats such tainted food soon begins to become thin and ill. The witch then goes to him and explains the reason of his illness. He offers to restore the sick man to health, and directs him to bring a " cock ", i.e. to hand over the soul of one of his maternal relatives. The sick man feels he cannot refuse, and is restored to health by eating some of the soul-liver of the victim. In this way he himself becomes a witch. If he is accused later of practising witchcraft he can put forward the plea that he was made into a witch against his will, and he indicates the name of the man who was responsible for his condition. The latter (i.e. the original witch) is then required to undergo the sasswood ordeal, and if he is found guilty the secondary witch is allowed to go scot free.

Among the Mambila it is customary to open the body and examine the heart of every person before burial, in order to see if he had practised witchcraft during his lifetime. The examination is carried out at the instance of the deceased's maternal relatives, who employ a professional examiner. One horizontal and two vertical incisions are made in the abdomen, the flap is raised and the heart pulled forward. If the heart is found to be surrounded with a rough filament it is concluded that the deceased had practised witchcraft. In this case a diviner is summoned in order to show whether the witchcraft had been obtained by heredity, purchase, or involuntarily. If it is shown that the witchcraft of the deceased had been due to heredity or purchase, nothing further is said or done. But if it is shown that the deceased had become a witch through the trickery of another witch the diviner is called on to declare the name of the other witch, who is then required to undergo an ordeal, and if he is found guilty he and some of his relatives become the slaves of the family of the deceased. The reason for this procedure is that the family of the deceased may receive compensation for the loss it had sustained through the witchcraft of the deceased, who had been forced by the machination of the other witch to make inroads on his own family.

The form of ordeal usually practised to determine the innocence or guilt of a person suspected of witchcraft was that of drinking sasswood, a method which is now illegal. If the accused vomited the poison at once, he was adjudged not guilty of the charge, and his accuser was required to pay heavy compensation for bringing a false charge.

If the accused retained the poison he soon died, and his family was required to pay compensation to the family of the accuser, which had lost one or more members as the result of the guilty man's witchcraft. It was stated that an accuser could save the life of a guilty man (i.e. of one who did not immediately vomit) by calling on the poison to leave the accused, saying : " Sasswood I thank you, you have shown his guilt ; come forth now and leave him." The accused would then vomit, but he would suffer from illness afterwards.

Compensation generally took the form of a small boy or girl, who was handed over by the family of the unsuccessful litigant to that of the successful litigant. If the unsuccessful litigant had been the offspring of an exchange marriage, then the boy or girl given as compensation had also to be the offspring of an exchange marriage, i.e. had to be a patrilineal relative of the unsuccessful litigant. But if the unsuccessful litigant had been the offspring of a marriage by purchase then the boy or girl given as compensation had to be the offspring of a marriage by purchase, i.e. had to be a matrilineal relative.

There is a charm against witchcraft which is known as *Ngub Shǫ* or the rites of the *Ngub* bark. The head of a family, in order to safeguard his household, goes out to the bush and obtains a piece of the bark of a certain tree known as *Ngub*. On reaching home he keeps the bark concealed, for if any woman should look on it it would lose its virtue. He places the piece of bark on the ground, covers it with a layer of the sacred grass known as *jiro*, lays a chicken's head across the bark and grass, and then cuts off the chicken's head. He next pares off a little of the bark, places it in the beak of the chicken, and buries the chicken's head at the entrance to his compound, together with some of the *jiro* grass and the fruit of the *Gardenia ternifolia* tree. Next he takes a bundle of straw, lights it, and begins singing the chant used at the funeral rites of a woman. At the conclusion of the chant he kneels down over the buried head of the chicken and says : " I am a lover of my fellow men and work mischief on no one. If any woman comes to this house to kill me or any of my people by witchcraft may she be killed, even as I now kill the fire of this torch." So saying, he presses the grass torch against the ground until the light is extinguished. He then lights another bundle of grass, and singing the chant used at the burial rites of a man he utters a prayer that if any

MAMBILA WARRIORS

man comes to his house to kill him or any of his people by witchcraft, he may himself be killed. And so he extinguishes the second firebrand. Lastly, he lays some *Gardenia* fruit on the ground, closes his eyes, and squashes the fruit with his foot.

It will be observed that these rites are based mainly on the principle of sympathetic magic. He closes his eyes in order that the witch visitor may be rendered blind, and he squashes the fruit in order that the witch may be reduced to pulp. Having completed these rites he erects over the spot a piece of palm cut to a point, and striped with charcoal and red earth.

The *Ngub Shǫ* symbol is also used as a means of swearing innocence of any charge. For example, if a man is accused of having practised witchcraft he will offer to swear his innocence on his accuser's *Ngub Shǫ*. He gives a piece of his wearing apparel to his accuser, who places it over the head of a chicken, and then cuts off the chicken's head. During this operation he grips in his left hand a piece of the sacred bark and grass. If the headless chicken, after jumping about for a second, falls with its right leg in the air, the accused is considered guiltless ; but if it falls with the left leg in the air, he is considered guilty ; and if he does not make atonement for his crime it is believed that he will sicken and die within a week. The test is not, however, considered infallible, for it was stated that if a guiltless man manifested undue anger during the test the chicken might fall with its left leg in the air. Moreover, if nothing happened within a week to a man who had been adjudged guilty, then it was assumed that there had been some flaw in the test, and that he had proved his innocence.

One who had been accused by another usually seeks an early opportunity of retaliating on his accuser. If he loses any small article he goes to a diviner, and by means of a small bribe obtains a pronouncement that his former accuser had stolen the article. The latter has then to swear his innocence on the former's *Ngub Shǫ*. In due course the two men may agree to become friends by drinking simultaneously from a calabash of beer. It may be noted that there are two methods of divination, viz. (*a*) by watching the action of a land crab, or (*b*) by rubbing the hands together. The former method has been described in my monograph on the Jukun. Under the second method an

affirmative answer is obtained to the question put if the hands
of the diviner suddenly spring back to back.

Oaths are commonly sworn solely on the *jiro* grass, and
every Mambila man of importance carries in his bag some of this
grass wrapped up in a bundle of leaves. In any dispute he will
produce the sacred grass, strike his breast thrice with it, and
ask that the grass may " catch " him if he is at fault, and his
opponent if the latter is at fault.

Jiro grass also plays a part in other magico-religious
rites. Thus in some groups at sowing-time the village priest
plants a small patch of millet, and then lays on the surface some
of the sacred grass. If the millet springs up well it is a sign that
the rite has been accepted, and the priest then authorizes the
people to begin planting. Otherwise the priest must perform a
second ceremony. Before harvest the priest prepares a brew of
beer from last year's millet with a few grains of the new year's
millet intermixed. When the beer is ready he spits some of it
on to a bundle of the sacred grass. A wisp of the grass is then
handed to each farmer, who plants it on his farm. This ensures
that the crop will increase and not diminish during the process
of harvesting.

At the village of Ngubin the following rites are performed in
January or February, when the harvested millets are formally
consigned to the granaries. All heads of families prepare
a brew of beer, and on the morning of the day when the beer
matures they proceed at dawn to an open space in front of the
Chief's compound, where there are three monoliths, one, regarded
as a male, facing East, and the other two, regarded as females,
facing West. There a priest proceeds to cook the flesh of a
number of bush rats, and when this is done he hands a little of
the meat to each man present, together with some porridge which
had been prepared by his assistant (and not, as usual, by a
woman). The priest then takes a calabash of beer and stands
beside the monoliths. The most senior men take hold of the right
arm of the priest. The others present place their right hands on
the shoulders of the senior man or of their nearest neighbour,
the intention being that one and all shall participate in the
rites. The priest then speaks, saying : " We have deposited
our corn in our granaries, and we beseech you to grant that,
however little it may be, it may prove sufficient for our needs

throughout the year. May it not be robbed of its goodness by
reason of the witchcraft of men or the malice of spirits (*kwiyip*).
Grant to one and all of us health and prosperity." He then
pours some beer on the stone representing the male deity, and
afterwards drinks some of the beer himself, and gives a little to
each person present. Next he rubs his finger in the beer which
he had poured on the monolith and touches the breast of each
person present. All then help themselves liberally to beer.
After an interval the tutelary genius known as Vwam appears
dancing, and sits down in their midst. He is served with beer
by a girl who has not reached the age of puberty, and as she
performs this duty she covers her eyes. The chief then presents
a bush rat to the genius, who, later on, parades the town, receiving
a dried bush rat from each householder. These offerings are
subsequently handed over to the chief, and are ceremonially
eaten immediately after the sowing of the crops.

As among most Nigerian tribes, the ancestors are the
dominating religious influence. They are known as the *kuru*,
a word which obviously embodies the Jukun root for ancestral
spirits, viz. *ku*. The cult of the dead is known as *Shǫ Kuru*.
As among the Jukun, when a man dies, the personified ancestors
or *kuru* come and take away his soul to the grove in the bush
where the ancestral souls are wont to assemble. They come and
sit by his body throughout the night, blowing trumpets, the
squeaky notes of which are intended to represent the cries of the
ancestors. The leader of the *kuru* carries a trumpet of calabash,
the end of which is covered with a bat's skin. He also carries
an iron gong suspended by a string. The trumpets of his assistants
are covered with dog skins. Before the body is taken out for
burial at dawn the *kuru* march round it three times and then
disappear into the bush, taking the dead man's soul with them.
After their departure the tutelary genius known as Mbar,
concealed inside a hut, addresses the dead man's relatives and
friends, bidding them not to break their hearts because the
kuru have taken away the dead man's soul. For it is, he says,
the custom of the *kuru* to add to their numbers. The relatives
and friends must abide in peace and beget children to take the
place of those who die. In making this announcement the
genius uses a piece of guinea-corn stalk with a hole at each
end and one in the middle. One of the end holes is covered

with spider's web, and he speaks through the central hole. His speech is interpreted by one of the members of the cult.

On the seventh day after death a funeral feast is held, during the course of which the priest of the *kuru* cult blows a whistle and calls on the people to be silent while he speaks as follows : " So-and-so has left us. But he is not dead. He is with the *kuru*, and he bids me to tell you that all is well with him and that you must abide together in peace, one with the other."

During the dry season there is an annual " feast of all souls ", palm-wine, porridge, and pieces of the flesh of game-animals being offered at the shrine of the *kuru*. First-fruit offerings are also made to the ancestors at the guinea-corn and maize harvests. It was also customary in the past to get rid of criminals and recalcitrant slaves by sacrificing them to the *kuru*.

The genius Mbar appears on other occasions besides funeral ceremonies. Thus when the maize crop has reached a height of two feet Mbar is the presiding genius at the rites which are then held. The officiant priest, holding a calabash-ful of beer, takes his stand in front of the genius and says : " We have come to-day to perform the custom of our forefathers at this season. I therefore beseech Nama (God) and Mbar that they may give us health and prosper our farm work. Let not birds rob us of the fruits of our labour, and may we have rain at appropriate times. May prosperity follow us in all that we do." He then offers some beer to the genius, and, having drunk some himself, he pours a few drops on the forefinger of the right hand of each man present. All then touch their right shoulder with the moistened finger. The intention appears to be the sanctification of the right hand which does most of the farm work. After this rite each man is given some beer to drink. Later a feast is held in the town, and during this the genius appears dancing, the women and children meanwhile hiding themselves in their huts. But sometimes Mbar's wife Yageru appears and dances with the women and children.

There are a number of other genii, all of whom appear to be personifications of the earliest ancestors. Thus there are Garmau, Bǫǫ, Nbem, and Chimbin. Mbem appears to be the guardian genius of children, and when beer is offered to him he drinks it through a tube as a child drinks from his mother's teat. Chimbin is the special genius of women and he appears on the death of any old woman. It is said that women taking part in the dances attended by this genius dress themselves in the loin coverings of men. There are other rites connected with the cult of Chimbin about which I was unable to obtain any information, as the rites are a secret of the women. It is said that if any man intrudes during these rites he will lose his virility.

The Mambila bury their dead in graves of the shaft and tunnel type. The body is buried naked, all ornaments being removed. It is laid on its side in a contracted position, with both hands holding the head. The face looks towards the west, for it is said that a man comes into the world from the east, and at death " goes west ".

The position for women is the same as that for men. Loose earth is thrown in until the shaft is filled up, no attempt being made (as is usual where the shaft and tunnel grave is employed) to protect the body from the earth. The mouth of the shaft is not blocked by a stone, nor is the grave used more than once.

Chiefs are buried under a granary, possibly because they are regarded as the personification of the corn. Their red fezzes and gowns are fastened to the walls of the granary, a custom similar to that followed by the Jibu and Okpoto tribes.

All the Mambila groups were cannibal until recently, and most of them would be cannibal still were it not for fear of the Administration. They ate the flesh of their enemies killed in war,[1] and among their enemies might be the members of a neighbouring village with whom they had intermarried when at peace. Thus it might happen that a man would kill and eat one of his own relatives. An instance was given of a man killing and eating his wife's brother during an affray between two villages. But it was stated that if a man killed and ate his father-in-law he would contract bronchitis and die !

Religious ideas were not prominent in the cannibalism of the Mambila, for those who were willing to speak on the subject confessed that they ate human flesh purely as meat. When they killed an enemy they cut pieces off his body and ate them raw *in situ*, without any formalities. Pieces were taken home and given to the old men, who ate them from sheer lust of flesh. In such cases the flesh might be eaten raw or cooked. Even the

---

[1] Apparently they, sometimes, sold their own dead for food. See Migeod, *Through British Cameroons*, p. 140.

intestines were eaten, being ripped up, cleaned and boiled. On the other hand, it was stated that young men were compelled to eat in order to make them brave, the conception being, apparently, that by eating the flesh of a slain warrior they absorbed his courage. The skulls of enemies were preserved, and when the young men first went to war they were made to drink beer and a certain medicine from one of the skulls, with a view to making them fearless. Women were not permitted to eat human flesh, and it was not permissible for married men to eat the flesh of women who were killed during an attack on a town. But wifeless old men could eat the flesh of a woman with impunity.

Blood-brother rites are not practised by the Mambila. But if two towns which had been enemies agreed to live together in peace, the chiefs of the respective towns would meet at the boundary and swear friendship. Each carried a calabash of water, and, after swearing the oath, he put some salt into the water and gave it to the other to drink.

All the Mambila practise male circumcision, but it was said that the blacksmith groups had only recently adopted the custom. The operation is performed without any elaborate ceremony when boys have reached the age of 8 or 9. After the operation the glans is covered with a grass cap in order that women may not see the wound. The cap is discarded when the wound heals, and each boy receives a gift of a chicken from his mother. It is possible that the custom among numerous other tribes of wearing a penis-sheath is connected with the rite of circumcision, and I have been told by members of a sheath-wearing tribe that their women are supposed to be ignorant of the fact of circumcision, which was regarded as a sign of secret affiliation with the gods.

There is no developed totemism among the Mambila, but most of the Torbi section refrain from eating goat's flesh and do not allow visitors to use their dishes for cooking goat's flesh. Some also refrain from killing and eating the flesh of a certain species of antelope.

There are also a number of animal-taboos connected with child-birth, each family having its own particular taboo which is inherited matrilineally. Thus in one family it may be taboo for an enceinte woman to eat mutton, in another to eat chicken

PLATE 58

TYPES OF MAMBILA HUTS

[face p. 559

or any form of bird, and so on. In one family which observes the taboo against eating any bird, it is taboo also for the woman to look on the sun for ten days after having given birth. On the tenth day her father comes with a spear and a large string bag, and standing at the door of his daughter's hut presents the head of the spear to her. The woman grasps the spearhead and is then drawn by her father to the threshold. The father then spits a certain medicine on to his daughter's temples and covers her eyes with his hands. Taking hold of her right hand he swings her round to the sun, at the same time uncovering her eyes. He then takes the infant and places him in the string bag, which he fastens to the roof of the hut. At the same time he shouts out : " Let any bird come and go." He then whistles, and if a bird appears soon afterwards, it is a sign that the woman will bear another child. If no bird appears, she will never again become a mother. This custom has the appearance of being totemic.

A husband must observe his wife's taboo until the child is weaned, when the following rites are performed. The mother takes her child to the home of her father or maternal uncle, who kills her taboo animal and gives pieces of the meat to the mother and the child to eat. A piece of the meat is also taken home by the mother for her husband, who is required to eat it out of his wife's hands without touching it with his own hands.

Material Culture.—The material culture of the Mambila is in many respects quite distinctive. This is particularly so as regards the character of the dwellings, which are built with a technique not found in Nigeria.

The site chosen for a hut is carefully levelled and covered with a floor of mud, which is beaten flat and sun-dried. The walls consist of a framework of reeds or canes which are cross-warped, ten reeds being used to each warp. When completed the frame is bent into a circle, the base being fitted into a trench made in the mud floor and cemented in with mud to a height of about one foot above the floor level. A hole three feet square is cut out of the frame to serve as a doorway. This doorway is fitted with a frame of bamboo in which the door, consisting of six to ten bamboo poles lashed closely together with fibre, slides laterally. When the door is closed it can be secured from the inside by means of wooden pegs. As an additional protection from the weather the wall framework of reeds is lined on the inside with matting, one end of which is brought across the floor of the hut behind the doorway so as to serve as a screen when the door is open, thus (in plan) :—

The upper part of the reed framework or outer-wall is reinforced by a thick band of grass bound tightly together, which runs round the circumference. The wall framework is thus strengthened to take the weight of the roof, which consists of bamboo poles covered with a thatching of tufts of short grass laid on in layers, and kept in position by fibre bindings. These tufts of grass are disposed with the roots pointing downwards, and the roots retain much of the clay in which they had grown. In re-thatching it is usual to leave on the layer, and merely add another layer.

The type of house described above is, in its essential features, typical of all the Mambila groups. But in some groups (e.g. in the Tongbo or Lagbo group) the framework of the walls composed of canes or reeds fixed vertically between wooden poles may be plastered inside [1] and out with mud.

In this class of hut the thatch is of a different character, the grass used being longer and laid on thickly in six successive layers. Evey Mambila hut has an upper storey, the floor of which consists of matting laid across bamboo poles which rest directly on the outer wall and receive additional support from bamboo uprights placed at intervals round the circumference of the wall. Entrance is obtained from the lower to the upper storey by means of a trap door which is reached by a ladder. The upper storey is used as a bedroom or as a store. When used for storing grain the upper storey can be approached from the outside through a hole in the thatch, this hole being covered with a flap of matting which swings laterally. The lower storey of the hut is used for milling flour and cooking, for storing pots, and occasionally also as a bedroom. At night a wood fire is lit in the lower storey to

---

[1] In some cases the inside is not plastered, the wall being strengthened by an inner lining of matting.

A SMALL GRANARY

A BEER BASKET

PLATE 59

keep the sleepers in the upper storey warm. Woven grass mats are used as mattresses. The only other form of furniture is a square stool made of pieces of bamboo lashed together with fibre. A noteworthy feature is the use of plaited grass funnels for filling pots with water or beer. Baskets woven with strips of bark or cane are used as receptacles for beer during the process of maturing. They are two or three feet in height, and are reinforced by four pieces of bamboo palm which serve as legs. They are rendered watertight by being smeared inside with the ashes of the fruit of the *Gardenia ternifolia* tree. Similar baskets woven from the bark of bamboo-palm are used as granaries, being set on a platform which raises them two or three feet from the ground.

The legs of the platform consist of two pieces of wood, one resting on the other. The upper piece is bamboo-palm, the smooth surface of which prevents rats from climbing up into the granary. The platform is covered with matting, and the basket which stands on it is protected from rain by a covering made of woven strips of palm-branch. There is usually also an additional outer covering consisting of pieces of palm-branch split in half and set vertically, each piece fitting closely to the other. The basket is reinforced at the base and rim with a band of grass several inches thick. It is protected at the top with a cap of thatch.

A compound consists usually of two or three huts surrounded or connected by fencing made of woven reeds or cane. Granaries as described are scattered about the compound, and there may be one or two stone pens for chickens or goats. Wooden troughs, cut out of a solid tree-trunk, are used for watering the domestic animals. All the compounds are well drained by trenches, and many contain groves of banana trees.

Two or three compounds standing close together form the hamlet of the smaller family group. More remote relatives, and other unrelated sections of the village or local group, may occupy sites as much as a mile away. In former times, however, the various families lived cheek by jowl close to the grove, into which they would fly when threatened by more powerful enemies. The trees of these groves are never cut, and where a grove is seen on high ground it is a certain sign that there is a village in the vicinity.

Most of the gullies contain trees, and every gully which has bamboo-palms is owned by some family group. In each village area there is a central site for dancing, which takes the form of a large circle of beaten mud, surrounded by a low wall which serves as seats for spectators and keeps the dancing arena free of rain-water. It may be added that villages are frequently known by the name of the person who first founded the village, or by the name of one of his more distinguished descendants. For purposes of defence the Mambila dig trenches across the main roads leading to their villages.

As regards weapons spears are used at the present time, but they are of comparatively recent introduction. Groups of blacksmiths have been associated with the Mambila for a considerable time, but they are of foreign origin and have not even yet become absorbed. The Mambila state that in ancient times they had no iron, and that their only weapon was the fibre-stringed bow and wooden-pointed arrow. They had no hoes and carried out their agricultural operations by means of digging-sticks. When they first obtained the iron hoe-head they used it without affixing a handle. At the present time the hoe head is fixed to the iron handle by the primitive method of binding with palm-fibre. Their shields are made of two layers of woven strips of palm branch, the layers being bound together with palm fibre. They are made in two sections which are woven together vertically and strengthened by a wooden cross-piece, which lies under the grip and takes the force of the blow of a spear or arrow. At the upper and lower end of the shield a circular section is cut out to permit of seeing and moving easily. A number of porcupine quills are stuck into the meshes of the shield on the inner side. These were used in retreat, being thrust into the ground to catch and injure the feet of a pursuing assailant.

The Mambila use short swords of the type illustrated in the accompanying photograph. The design is, as far as I know, characteristic of the Mambila, but it is possible and indeed probable that this type of sword was introduced from some tribe of the French Cameroons.

The Mambila are expert pipe-makers. Their pipes are characterized by a wooden plug at the base of the bowl, on the removal of which the pipe can be easily cleaned. The pipes are burnished by being put among damp grass while still hot.

Among musical instruments two types of single membrane drums were observed, one being open and the other closed at

PLATE 60

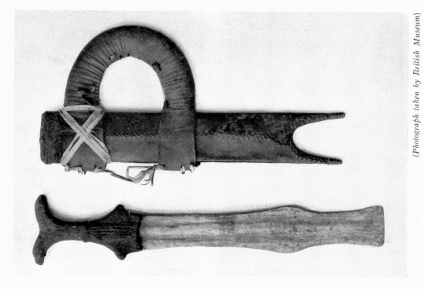

(Photograph taken by British Museum)

A MAMBILA SWORD AND SHEATH

[face p. 562

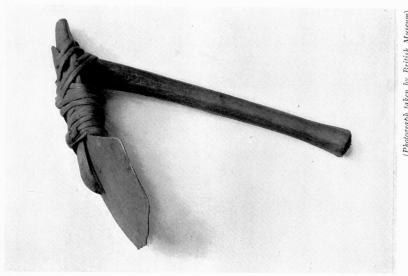

(Photograph taken by British Museum)

A MAMBILA HOE

the lower end. Those with the closed end are about three feet high and stand on a carved pedestal cut out of the solid wood. Those with the open end are about four feet high.

A flute of special design is used for giving the preliminary summons to religious rites. It is about fifteen inches long and is surmounted by a carved representation of a human head, thus :

Women and children always hide in their huts when they hear this flute blown.

As regards dress Mambila wear cloth loin coverings of the same type as those of the Yungur.[1] The women are completely nude. In the Southern group, however, women occasionally wear a loin covering of plaited strings, like the women of the Verre tribe. Both sexes chip to a point the two upper and lower incisor teeth.

It may be noted in conclusion that the Mambila have a ten-day week based on the local market system. Thus in the Northern area the days of the week are known as follows : 1, Jimini (i.e. Kuma market day) ; 2, Sambiri (Yiru) ; 3, Nderi (Tem) ; 4, Yọi (Basso) ; 5, Biga (Yana) ; 6, Suri ; 7, Bagiri (Jeke) ; 8, Bara (Ngabin) ; 9, Ndakha ; and 10, Jire. Of these Suri, Bagin, Ndakha, and Jire have now ceased to exist as markets. On the other hand markets are held at a number of villages the names of which are not included in the market week.

There are two small groups of people occupying the villages of Kamkam and Magu who live in close association with the Mambila, but clearly belong to a different stock. Their language

[1] See Vol. II, ch. xiv.

is quite distinct from Mambila, though it displays numerous points of contact, especially with the dialect of the Wa group of Mambila. There are also points of contact with the Tigong dialect of Ashaku, and the villagers of Magu are commonly classed as Tigong.

The villagers of Kamkam and Magu are said to be one and the same people, having occupied a common village in the vicinity of Guroje until they were driven out by the Fulani of Banyo, one group flying to the present site of Kamkam and the other to Magu. If this is so, and there is no reason to doubt it, it is interesting to note the rapidity with which cultural and dialectical differences have arisen between the two groups.

The Kamkam group has, for example, retained its former system of matrilineal inheritance, whereas the Magu group now follows the patrilineal principle. On the other hand the people of Kamkam have adopted many of the religious cults of the Mambila. Their language appears to have been influenced also by that of the Bute, and it is probable, therefore, that a number of Bute have joined the Kamkam group within the last fifty years.

The people of Kamkam call themselves the Bungnu, the word Kamkam being, it is said, a nickname given by the Bute and Fulani, on account of the characteristic bag woven by the Bungnu and known as a " Kamkam ".

The Bungnu differ from the Mambila in that they have no system of marriage exchange. A suitor approaches the maiden of his choice directly, and if she accepts his suit he can marry her without reference to her parents. He elopes with her, and notifies the elopement to her father by sending him a spear. But he has to give numerous gifts to the girl before he can claim the full status of husband. Thus on the journey to his house the girl stops at frequent intervals and refuses to proceed until the bridegroom gives her a hoe. She must be given a gift when she enters his compound, and another when she eats her first meal, and so on. During the first month she lives a life of seclusion, is smeared daily with oil and is given an abundance of food. At the end of this period a dance and feast are held, and the bridegroom must then send a substantial bride-price (consisting principally of hoes) to the girl's parents. One third of this bride-price is handed by the girl's father to his wife's relatives. All children born of the marriage remain normally in the father's home, but they can be called on at any time to perform services for their mother's relatives, and if one of these required continuous economic assistance the father would hand over one of his children for this purpose. Moreover, in pre-Administration days a man could redeem himself or one of his children from slavery by giving in exchange one of his sister's children. In cases of murder, also, the murdered man was replaced by one of the murderer's uterine relatives.

It is permissible for a man to dissolve his sister's marriage if he thinks that she is not being properly treated, and until recently it was the rule that in such a case the children followed the mother. Inheritance was and is by matriliny.

We may conclude, therefore, that matriarchal principles were, until the advent of the Fulani, predominant among the Bungnu.

The Bungnu employ the Mambila term *shǫ* in the sense of religious cult. They use the same rites as the Mambila in connection with the cult of the dead, which they describe as Shǫ Furu. They have the Mambila tutelary genius known as Garmau. They call the Ngub Shǫ charm " Nan " and the sacred *jiro* grass " jura ". They deny that they ever practised cannibalism, but they were headhunters. Their clothing and weapons are the same as those of the Mambila.

The Magu group differ principally from the Kamkam group in that inheritance is patrilineal. A man could, however, in former times, use his sister's children as pawns. But if he did this he was required to compensate the father of the children by giving him a gift of twenty hoes. A father could not pawn his own children unless his wife was a slave, and the reason given was that when a man marries a woman he does not buy her. The mother's relatives, in fact, were regarded as the real owners of the children.

In both the Kamkam and Magu groups marriage with close relatives on both sides of the family is forbidden. The cross-cousin marriage found among a number of neighbouring tribes is not practised. The junior but not the senior form of levirate marriage is practised among the Magu group; and it is permissible to inherit and marry a father's or paternal uncle's widows, but not those of a maternal uncle.

In the Magu group the Shǫ Kuru rites of the Mambila and

Bungnu are not observed, but the Ngubshǫ and *jiro* grass charms are used. Women wear necklaces of *jiro* grass in order to promote fertility.

The following vocabularies are attached :—

    (1) The Kuma dialect of Mambila.
    (2) The Warwar dialect of Mambila.
    (3) The Wa dialect of Mambila.
    (4) The Kila or blacksmith language.
    (5) The Kamkam language.
    (6) The Magu language.

MAMBILA VOCABULARY (KUMA DIALECT)
Per Tiso of Kuma

1.	Head	wuni	wuni
2.	Hair	shari	ʃari
3.	Eye	njire	ndʒirɛ
	Two eyes	njire wan	ndʒirɛ waːn
4.	Ear	tia	tia
	Two ears	tia yan	tia jaːn
5.	Nose	nyon	njon
6.	One tooth	nyie nyunu	njiɛ njunu
	Five teeth	nyie teen	njiɛ tɛɛn
7.	Tongue	namman	nəmman
8.	Neck	manna	mʌnna
9.	Breast (woman's)	mban	mban
10.	Heart	bingen	bɪŋgɛn
11.	Belly	tubri	tubri
12.	Back	kamo or ngata	kamo or ngata
13.	Arm	boo	boo
14.	Hand	bomban	bomban
	Two hands	bomban yan	bomban jaːn
15.	Finger	njaru	ndʒaru
	Five fingers	njaru teen	ndʒaru tɛɛn
16.	Finger nail	nyaru	njaru
17.	Leg	gure	gure
18.	Knee	neen	neɛn
19.	Foot	gurim mban	gurɪm mban
	Two feet	gurim mban iyan	gurɪm mban ijaːn
20.	Man (person)	nor	nɔr˜
	Ten people	nor yuta	nɔr juta
21.	Man (not woman)	no tira	no tɪr˜a
	Two men	no tira yan	no tɪr˜a jaːn
22.	Woman	ma bwen	ma bwɛn
	Two women	ma bwen yan	ma bwɛn jaːn
23.	Child	wunu	wunu
24.	Father	tei	tei
25.	Mother	mei	mei

26. Slave	tomo	tomo
27. Chief	mbon	mbɔn
28. Friend	mba	mba
29. Smith	shomo	ʃomo
30. Doctor	tee kangin	tee kaŋgɪn
31. One finger	njaru nyunu	ndʒaru njunu
32. Two fingers	njaru yan	ndʒaru jaːn
33. Three fingers	njaru tar	ndʒaru taːr
34. Four fingers	njaru na	ndʒaru naː
35. Five fingers	njaru teen	ndʒaru teɛn
36. Six fingers	njaru teechini	ndʒaru teɛtʃini
37. Seven fingers	njaru taniye	ndʒaru tanije
38. Eight fingers	njaru tin dariye	ndʒaru tɪn darije
39. Nine fingers	njaru tina	ndʒaru tina
40. Ten fingers	njaru yuta	ndʒaru juta
41. Eleven fingers	njaru yuta tere nyunu	ndʒaru juta tɛrɛ njunu
42. Twelve fingers	njaru yuta tere yan	ndʒaru juta tɛrɛ jaːn
Thirteen fingers	njaru yuta tere tar	ndʒaru juta tɛrɛ taːr
43. Twenty fingers	njaru noton or bingere	ndʒaru nɔtɔn or bɪŋgere
Thirty fingers	njaru noton tere yuta	ndʒaru nɔtɔn tɛrɛ juta
Thirty-one fingers	njaru noton tere yuta, yuta tere nyunu (i.e. 20 plus ten, and at the ten plus one.)	ndʒaru nɔtɔn tɛrɛ juta juta tɛrɛ njunu
Thirty-eight fingers	njaru noton tere yuta, yuta tere tindariye	ndʒaru nɔtɔn tɛrɛ juta, juta tɛrɛ tɪndarije
Forty fingers	njaru noton yan	ndʒaru nɔtɔn jaːn

N.B.—Twenty is indicated by placing the hands against the feet. Thirty by doing this and then by putting the two hands together.

44. A hundred fingers	njaru noton teen	ndʒaru nɔtɔn teɛn
One hundred and twenty fingers	njaru noton tini or noton teen terie bingere nyunu	ndʒaru nɔtɔn tini or nɔtɔn teɛn tɛrie bɪŋgere njunu
45. Two hundred fingers	njaru noton yuta	ndʒaru nɔtɔn juta
46.		
47. Sun	Mwandi	mwandi
God	Nama	nama
48. Moon	wuru	wuru
Full moon	wuru ye baran	wuru je baran
New moon	wuru aye	wuru aje
49. Day	seten	seten
Night	chimbin	tʃɪmbɪn
Morning	mene jange	mene dʒaŋge
50. Rain	nu	nu
51. Water	nimme	nɪmmɛ
52. Blood	omo	ɔmo
53. Fat	chuen	tʃuɛn

54. Salt	tomo	tɔmo
55. Stone	tan	tan
Iron	tunge	tuŋgɛ
56. Hill	kun	kun
57. River	komo	komo
58. Road	chindi	tʃindi
59. House	gon (Compound = ara)	gɔn (Compound = ara)
Two houses	gon yan	gɔn jaːn
Many houses	gon dungun	gɔn duːŋgun
All the houses	gon be	gɔn bé
60. Roof	gon jurung	gɔn dʒuruŋ
61. Door	nyu	nju
62. Mat	bere	berɛ
63. Basket	kuna	kuna
64. Drum	jongo	dʒɔŋgo
65. Pot	siene	siɛnɛ
66. Knife	bu	buː
67. Spear	gongon	goŋgon
68. Bow	nyiam	njiam
69. Arrow	koango	koaŋgo
Five arrows	koango teen	koaŋgo teɛn
70. Gun	bundigaru	bundɪgaru
71. War	tap or kawun	taːp or kawun
72. Meat (animal)	nyama	njamá
73. Elephant	njoa	ndʒoa
74. Buffalo	yar	jar
75. Leopard	ngwi	ngwi
76. Monkey	duri	duri
77. Pig	nyamgang or genderu	njamgaŋ or gɛnderu
78. Goat	mbien	mbiɛn
79. Dog	bundu	bundu
80. Bird	nunu	nunu
Feather	sheri nunu we	ʃeri nunu we
81. Crocodile	ngani	ngani
82. Fowl	chondo	tʃɔndo
83. Eggs	geen	gɛɛn
84. One egg	gen nyunu	gɛn njunu
85. Snake	nyamba	njamba
86. Frog	takura	takura
87. Horse	dang	daŋ
88. Fly	njigi	ndʒigi
Cow	nage	nage
89. Bee	noe	noe
Honey	nime noe ga	nɪmɛ noe gə
90. Tree	jar	dʒar⁓
Ten trees	jar yuta	dʒar⁓ juta
91. Leaf	wan	wan
92. Guinea-corn	yire	jirɛ
93. Maize	tap	taːp
94. Ground-nut	shingar	ʃɪngar

95. Oil	kurume	kurumɛ
Hausa	Kasakhap	kasaxap
Fulani	Dakhap (Sing. = Tabiri)	daxap (Sing. = tabiri)
96. The tall woman	mabwen turia	mabwɛn turia
The tall women	mabuno turia	məbuno turia
97. Large dog	bundu gitane	bundu gɪtane
98. Small dog	bundu buwe	bundu buwe
99. The dog bites	bundu yie numan	bundu jiɛ numan
100. The dog bites me	bundu yie me numan	bundu jiɛ me numan
101. The dog which bit me yesterday	bundu numa me ana	bundu numa me ana
102. I flog the dog	me ye bundu nimben	me je bundu nɪmbɛn
103. The dog which I have flogged	bundu me nimbe ana	bundu me nɪmbe ana
Horse	dang	daŋ
Horses	dangip	daŋɪp
House	gon	gɔn
Houses	goyip	gɔjɪp
Goat	mbien	mbien
Goats	mbinip	mbinɪp
Man	no tira	no tɪra
Men	no tirap	no tɪrap
104. I see him	me enebo	me ɛnɛbō
I see her	me enebo	me ɛnɛbō
He sees you	enewe	ɛnɛwɛ
He sees us	enebir	ɛnɛbɪr
We see you (pl.)	bir enebi	bɪr ɛnɛbi
We see them	bir enebo	bɪr ɛnɛbó
I	mi	mi
You	we	we
He	bo	bo
We	bir	bɪr
You	bi	bi
They	bo	bó
105. Beautiful bird	nunu gaam	nunu gaam
106. Slave	tomo	tomo
My slave	tomo ndiga	tomo ndɪga
Thy slave	tomo chiga	tomo tʃɪga
Our slaves	tomo bira	tomo bɪra
107. The chief's slave	tomo mbon ga	tomo mbon gə
His slave	tomo china	tomo tʃɪna
108. We see the slave	bir ene tomo	bɪr ɛnɛ tomo
109. We call the slave	bir yina tomo	bɪr jina tomo
110. The slave comes	tomo yi ororen	tomo ji ororɛn
111. He came yesterday	oro ana (or bo oro ana)	ɔrɔ ana (or bo ɔrɔ ana)
He is coming today	a oro shu (to-day = shu)	a ɔrɔ ʃu (to-day = ʃu)
He will come tomorrow	a oro mene (or bo a oro mene)	a ɔrɔ mɛnɛ (or bo a ɔrɔ mɛnɛ)

112.	The slaves go away	tomop ye yinan	tomop je jinan
113.	Who is your chief?	chigam mbon ne ane ?	tʃɪgam mbon ne ane ?
114.	The two villages are making war on each other	chire yan bum bam-abe boye kawun nean	tʃɪre jaːn bum bam-abe boje kawun nean
	with one another	bum bamabe	bum bamabe
115.	The sun rises	mwandi yie shimeren	mwandi jie ʃimɛrɛn
	The sun sets	mwandi yie toron	mwandi jie tɔrɔn
116.	The man is eating	nor yie nyarap nyan	nɔr jiɛ njarap njan
117.	The man is drinking	nor yie nime mwan	nɔr jiɛ nɪmɛ mwan
118.	The man is asleep	nor yie nyom chan	nɔr jiɛ njom tʃan
119.	I break the stick	me koro kimbu	me koro kɪmbu
	The stick is broken	kimbu keriim	kɪmbu kɛriːm
	This stick cannot be broken	kimbu ne kerie ke	kɪmbu ne kɛrie ke
	Break this stick for me	keria me kimbu ne	kɛria me kɪmbu ne
120.	I have built a house	me ma gon	me ma gɔn
121.	My people have built their houses yonder	norum diga ma bo gon gache	nɔrum dɪga ma bo gɔn gatʃe
122.	What work do you do at day-break all ?	tom chine kunde tom chie miche anda ne bingeri ?	tom tʃine kundɛ tom tʃie mitʃe anda ne bɪŋgeri ?

N.B.—Note alliteration. tom (tom) = work.

	or	tom chine kunde mwandi bingeri tom chieri ?	tom tʃine kundɛ mwandi bɪŋgeri tom tʃiɛri
	I work on my farm	me yen tom mwarim digha kunden	me jɛn tom mwarɪm dɪga kunden
	I work	me yen tom kunden	me jɛn tom kundɛn
123.	I am going away	me yen dan	me jɛn dan
	I am hoeing	me ye bor buan	me jɛ bor buan
	I am going away to hoe	min da bor ga	mɪn da bor gə
	I am going away to my farm	min dam mwarim digha	mɪn dam mwarɪm dɪga
124.	The woman comes	mabwen yien daren	mabwɛn jiɛn darɛn
	She comes	yien daren	jiɛn darɛn
	The woman laughs	mabwen ye onon	mabwɛn je ɔnɔn
	The woman weeps	mabwen ye wen	mabwɛn je wɛn
125.	I ask the woman	ma bie mabwen	me biɛ mabwɛn
126.	Why do you laugh ?	ngam che we ye onon ?	ngam tʃe we je ɔnɔn ?
127.	Why do you cry ?	ngam che we ye wen ?	ngam tʃe we je wɛn ?

128. My child is dead (N.B.—Possessive precedes noun.) — ndiga wunu kuem — ndɪga wunu kuɛm

129. It is not dead — kue ke — kuɛ kɛ

130. Are you ill ? — yie chigha jamu keen ? — jie tʃɪga dʒamu keɛn ?

131. My children are ill — nyunum ndigha jamu ke — njunum ndɪga dʒamu ke

132. Her child is better — mwona china chini dama — mwona tʃɪna tʃɪni dama

133. Yes — ee — ɛɛ

No — mm — mˤm

134. A fine knife — bu di — bu di

Give me the knife — ame bu — ame bu

I give you the knife — me awe bu — me awe bu

135. You are a European — uwe wa bature — uwe wa bature

I am a black man — min nor yirie — mɪn nɔr jiriɛ

I am a Torbi — me Tɔrbi — me tɔrbi

136. Name — yin — jin

My name — yin ndigha — jin ndɪga

Your name — yin chigha — jin tʃɪga

What is your name ? — chigha yin neche ? — tʃɪga jin netʃe ?

137. There is water in the gourd — nime te timbige — nɪmɛ tɛ timbige

The knife is on the stone — bu terier tange — bu tɛriɛr taŋge

The fire is under the pot — wuu gon kir shienege — wuu gɔn kɪr ʃiɛnɛge

The roof is over the hut — juru gonge terier gon ge — dʒuru gɔn ge tɛrɪɛr gɔn ge

138. You are good — wue giri — wuɛ giri

This man is bad — nor ne biri — nɔr nɛ biri

139. The paper is white — derewol churi ye — dɛrɛwol tʃuri je

This thing is black — ngir ne yiri — ngɪr nɛ jiri

This thing is red — ngir ne biri — ngɪr nɛ biri

140. This stone is heavy — tan ne nuwa — tan nɛ nuwa

This stone is not heavy — tan ne nuwa ke — tan nɛ nuwa kɛ

141. I write — me ye vindinin — me jɛ vindɪnɪn

I give you the letter — me auwe derewol — me auwɛ dɛrɛwol

Carry the letter to the town — ndi derewol ne kue — ndi derewol nɛ kue

142. Go away — nda ge — nda ge

Come here — na ne — na nɛ

143. Where is your house ? — chigha arin ne ke ? — tʃɪga arɪn ne ke ?

144. My house is here — ndigha arin ne — ndɪga arɪn ne

My house is there — ndigha arin gache — ndɪga arɪn gatʃe

145. What have you to sell ?	we guriche ? (sell = guri)	we guritʃe ? (sell = guri)
146. I want to buy fish	me dui me gure borop	me dui me gure bɔrɔp
147. The fish which you bought is bad	borop wue gurere ne biri	bɔrɔp wue gurere ne biri
148. Where is the man who killed the elephant ?	nor bomi wuna njua ana che ?	nɔr bomi wuna ndʒua ana tʃe ?
He has killed many elephants	wuna njua dungun	wuna ndʒua duŋgun
How many elephants were killed yesterday ?	njua me bo wuna ana ?	ndʒua me bo wuna ana ?
149. Untie it	barabo	barabo
Tie this rope	kanda wuen ne	kanda wuɛn nɛ
Make the boy untie the goat	gire wunu bonda bara bienche	gɪre wunu bɔnda bara bientʃe
150. My brothers and I, we are going but no one else	birme ndigha dimbe min dage bir nyine	bɪrme ndɪga dɪmbɛ mɪn dage bɪr njine
Brothers, let us go and tell the chief	ndigha dimbe muege min da gara mbon ge	ndɪga dɪmbɛ muɛge mɪn da gara mbon gɛ
151. This tree is bigger than that	tu bone kiri bone ye gitan ge	tu bonɛ kiri bonɛ jɛ gɪtan gɛ

Mambila Vocabulary (Warwar Dialect)

Per Kasala Warwar

1. Head	gul	gul
2. Hair	sheri	ʃeri
3. Eye	njir	ndʒɪr
Two eyes	njir fal	ndʒɪr faːl
4. Ear	tia	tia
Two ears	tia fal	tia faːl
5. Nose	nyun	njun
6. One tooth	nyi	nji
Five teeth	nyi tin	nji tin
7. Tongue	nabal	nabal
8. Neck	mana	mʌna
9. Breast (woman's)	mban	mban
10. Heart	tawal	tawal
11. Belly	lee	lee
12. Back	ngur	ngur
13. Arm	bu (u with lip rounding)	bu
14. Hand	bubal	bubal
Two hands	bubal fal	bubal faːl
15. Finger	bu kol	bu kɔl
Five fingers	bu kol tin	bu kɔl tin

16. Finger nail	njeri	ndʒɛri
17. Leg	gure	gure
18. Knee	nil	nil
19. Foot	gure bal	gure bal
Two feet	gure bal fal	gure bal faːl
20. Man (person)	nor	nɔr
Ten people	nor yura (or nor na yura)	nɔr jura (or nɔr na jura)
21. Man (not woman)	nachie	natʃie
Two men	nachie fal	natʃie faːl
22. Woman	navul	navul
Two women	navul fal	navul faːl
23. Child	nyuna	njuna
24. Father	teri	teri
25. Mother	me	me
26. Slave	kweer	kweɛr
27. Chief	ngwa	ngwa
28. Friend	bil	bil
29. Smith	la	la
30. Doctor	lel	lɛl
31. One finger	bukol chen	bukɔl tʃen
32. Two fingers	bukol fal	bukɔl faːl
33. Three fingers	bukol tar	bukɔl taːr
34. Four fingers	bokol nea	bukɔl nea
35. Five fingers	bukol tin	bukɔl tin
36. Six fingers	bukol tenjen	bukɔl tɛndʒen
37. Seven fingers	bukol tafal	bukɔl tefal
38. Eight fingers	bukol tinderi	bukɔl tɪndɛri
39. Nine fingers	bukol tara nea	bukɔl tara nea
40. Ten fingers	bukol yura	bukɔl jura
41. Eleven fingers	bukol yura tur chen	bukɔl jura tur tʃen
42. Twelve fingers	bukol yura tur fal	bukɔl jura tur fal
Thirteen fingers	bukol yura tur tar	bukɔl jura tur taːr
43. Twenty fingers	bukol wul	bukɔl wul
Thirty fingers	bukol wul tur yura	bukɔl wul tur jura
Thirty-one fingers	bukol wul tur yura tur chen	bukɔl wul tur jura tur tʃen
44. A hundred fingers	bukol wul tin	bukɔl wul tin
45. Two hundred fingers	bukol wul yura	bukɔl wul jura
46. Four hundred fingers	—	—
47. Sun	Lu	lu
God	Chang	tʃaŋ
48. Moon	wur	wur
Full moon	wur bar bar	wur bar bar
New moon	wur yurigen	wur jurɪgɛn
49. Day	suraten	suratɛn
Night	turi	turi
Morning	menaja	mɛnadʒa
50. Rain	nyu	nju

51.	Water	nim	nɪm
52.	Blood	am	aːm
53.	Fat	cheri	tʃɜri
54.	Salt	tam	taːm
55.	Stone	tal	tal
	Iron	tugu	tugu
56.	Hill	ndou	ndou
57.	River	kuum	kuum
58.	Road	chir	tʃir
59.	House	miyim (Compound = far)	mijɪm (Compound = far)
	Two houses	miyim fal	mijɪm faːl
	Many houses	miyim kakuo	mijɪm kəkuo
	All the houses	miyim shii	mijɪm ʃii
60.	Roof	ndong miyime	ndoŋ mijime
61.	Door	hor miyime	hɔr mijime
62.	Mat	ber	bɛr
63.	Basket	shaa	ʃaa
64.	Drum	juwo	dʒuwɔ
65.	Pot	sheel	ʃeɛl
66.	Knife	buu	buu
67.	Spear	gual	gual
68.	Bow	lam	lam
69.	Arrow	kuu	kuu
	Five arrows	kuu tin	kuu tin
70.	Gun	nakan	nakan
71.	War	tap	taːp
72.	Meat (animal)	nyam	njam
73.	Elephant	teen	tɛɛn
74.	Buffalo	nyar	njar
75.	Leopard	ngwi	ngwi
76.	Monkey	char	tʃaːr
77.	Pig	gunyang	gunjaŋ
78.	Goat	bil	bil
79.	Dog	bur	bur
80.	Bird	non	nɔn
	Feather	sheri none	ʃɛri nɔne
81.	Crocodile	nyam kuu	njam kuu
	Horse	nyam ale	njam ale
	Sheep	njir	ndʒir
	Cow	karnda	karnda
82.	Fowl	chor	tʃɔr
83.	Eggs	gee	gee
84.	One egg	gee chen	gee tʃen
85.	Snake	yap	jaːp
86.	Frog	tukura	tukura
87.			
88.	Fly	njige	ndʒɪge
89.	Bee	nyu	nju
	Honey	nyu	nju
90.	Tree	giar	giar
	Ten trees	giar yura	giar jura

91.	Leaf	we	we
92.	Guinea-corn	yiir	jiir
93.	Maize	koom	kɔɔm
94.	Ground-nut	shangar	ʃaŋgar
95.	Oil	kurim	kurɪm
	Fulani	Tibar	tɪbar
	Tikar	Tikar	təkar
	Hausa	Kasakh	kasax
	Beri-Beri	Kaka	kaka
	Kaka	Ya Korip	ja korɪp

DIALECT OF THE WA GROUP

1.	Head	gur	gur
2.	Hair	yur	jur
3.	Eye	nzele	nzɛle
	Two eyes	nzele fal	nzɛle faːl
4.	Ear	taa	təə
	Two ears	taa fal	təə faːl
5.	Nose	nyuon	njuon
6.	One tooth	nyie chen	njie tʃɛn
	Five teeth	nyie tin	njie tin
7.	Tongue	namal	namal
8.	Neck	manna	manná
9.	Breast (woman's)	mban	mban
10.	Heart	tamal	tamal
11.	Belly	le	lɛ
12.	Back	ngur	ngur
13.	Arm	bu	bu
14.	Hand	bubal	bubal
	Two hands	bubal fal	bubal faːl
15.	Finger	korbu	korbu
	Five fingers	korbu tin	korbu tin
16.	Finger nail	cher bu	tʃɛr bu
17.	Leg	gur	gur
18.	Knee	nil	nil
19.	Foot	gurbal	gurbal
	Two feet	gurbal fal	gurbal faːl
20.	Man (person)	nor	nɔr
	Ten people	nor yura	nɔr jura
21.	Man (not woman)	nase	nasɛ
	Two men	nase fal	nasɛ faːl
22.	Woman	nave	navɛ
	Two women	naven fal	navɛn faːl
23.	Child	mon	mon
24.	Father	ter	tɛr
25.	Mother	me	mɛ
26.	Slave	kwer	kwɛr
27.	Chief	mboon	mbɔɔn
28.	Friend	bil	bil
29.	Smith	la	la

30. Doctor	lel	lɛl
31. One finger	korbu chen	korbu tʃɛn
32. Two fingers	korbu fal	korbu faːl
33. Three fingers	korbu tar	korbu taːr
34. Four fingers	korbu na	korbu naː
35. Five fingers	korbu tin	korbu tin
36. Six fingers	korbu tenchen	korbu tɛntʃɛn
37. Seven fingers	korbu tafal	korbu təfal
38. Eight fingers	korbu tindar	korbu tɪndar
39. Nine fingers	korbu tarana	korbu tarana
40. Ten fingers	korbu yura	korbu jura
41. Eleven fingers	korbu yura chap chen	korbu jura tʃap tʃɛn
42. Twelve fingers	korbu yura cha far	korbu jura tʃa faːr
Thirteen fingers	korbu yura cha tar	korbu jura tʃa taːr
43. Twenty fingers	korbu wul	korbu wul
Sun	Laa	ləə
God	Chang	tʃʌŋ
Moon	wir	wir

DIALECT OF THE KILA OR BLACKSMITH GROUPS
Per Shoga of Kuma

1. Head	ngwa	ngwa
2. Hair	yuwo	juwo
3. Eye	ya	ja
Two eyes	ya han	ja haːn
4. Ear	tuo	tuɔ
Two ears	tuo han	tuɔ haːn
5. Nose	nyuon	njuon
6. One tooth	nyian mwe	njian mwe
Five teeth	nyian tien	njian tiɛn
7. Tongue	liam	liam
8. Neck	towo	towo
9. Breast (woman's)	sagha	saɡa
10. Heart	kikanga	kɪkaŋa
11. Belly	lara	larə
12. Back	gwii	gwii
13. Arm	kars or kar	kars or kar
14. Hand	karn jas	karn dʒas
Two hands	karn jas han	karn dʒas haːn
15. Finger	do karn jas	do karn dʒas
Five fingers	do karn jas tien	do karn dʒas tiɛn
16. Finger nail	karn jas	karn dʒas
17. Leg	gwari	gwari
18. Knee	jujungi	dʒudʒuŋi
19. Foot	gwari dibi	gwari dɪbi
Two feet	gwari dibi han	gwari dɪbi haːn
20. Man (person)	fir	fɪr˜
Ten people	fir chong	fɪr˜ tʃɔŋ
21. Man (not woman)	wumbara	wumbarə
Two men	wumbara han	wumbarə haːn

22. Woman	wuguye	wugujɛ
Two women	wuguye han	wugujɛ haːn
23. Child	onane	onane
24. Father	tata	tata
25. Mother	mawi	mawi
26. Slave	kwara	kwarə
27. Chief	tambona	tambonə
28. Friend	mambowi	mambowi
29. Smith	wawa	wawa
30. Doctor	fir kaghana	firˠ kaɡanə
31. One finger	karn mwe	karn mwe
32. Two fingers	karn han	karn haːn
33. Three fingers	karn tar	karn taːr
34. Four fingers	karn nar	karn naːr
35. Five fingers	karn tien	karn tiɛn
36. Six fingers	karn temwe	karn temwe
37. Seven fingers	karn tenar	karn tenar
38. Eight fingers	karn tentar	karn tentar
39. Nine fingers	karn tennar	karn tennar
40. Ten fingers	karn chong	karn tʃɔŋ
41. Eleven fingers	karn chong yai mwe	karn tʃɔŋ jai mwe
42. Twelve fingers	karn chong yai han	karn tʃɔŋ jai haːn
Thirteen fingers	karn chong yai tar	karn tʃɔŋ jai taːr
43. Twenty fingers	karn ngwa yire	karn ngwa jirɛ
44. A hundred fingers	karn ngwa tien	karn ngwa tiɛn
45. Sun	nyagha	njaɡa
46. God	nama	nam
47. Moon	wuer	wuɛr
48. Full moon	wuer a nomda	wuɛr a nɔmda
New moon	wuer a hara	wuɛr a harə
49. Day	nyagha tena	njaɡa tɛnə
Night	gbinna	gbɪnnə
Morning	timoko	tɪmoko
50. Rain	nii	nii
51. Water	mbum	mbum
52. Blood	jim	dʒɪm
53. Fat	dou	dou
54. Salt	mbara	mbare
55. Stone	tana	tanə
Iron	tera	terə
56. Hill	kun	kun
57. River	makuo	məkuo
58. Road	bi	bi
59. House	nyum (Compound = yiena)	njum (Compound = jiɛnə)
Two houses	nyum han	njum haːn
Many houses	nyum nyibra	njum njibrə
All the houses	nyum bangading	njum bəŋgadɪŋ
60. Roof	nyum jagha	njum dʒaga
61. Door	ona	onə
62. Mat	hana	hanə

P p

63.	Basket	sagha	sagə
64.	Drum	dana	danə
65.	Pot	siena	sienə
66.	Knife	bi	bi
67.	Spear	goghona	gogonə
68.	Bow	lou	lou
69.	Arrow	kogho	kogo
	Five arrows	kogho tien	kogo tiɛn
70.	Gun	bindiga	bɪndɪga
71.	War	mwam	mwam
72.	Meat (animal)	nyam	njam
73.	Elephant	nyam	njam
74.	Buffalo	yar	jar
75.	Leopard	luaba	luəbə
76.	Monkey	gora	gorə
77.	Pig	gaduru	gaduru
78.	Goat	biena	biɛnə
79.	Dog	ba	ba:
80.	Bird	gane	gane
	Feather	yuwo	juwo
81.	Crocodile	ngani	ngani
82.	Fowl	chowora	tʃoworə
83.	Eggs	gina	ginə
84.	One egg	ginim mwe	ginɪn mwe
85.	Snake	yuzabi	juzabi
86.	Frog	bukuova	bukuovə
87.	Horse	dowa	dowə
	Cow	nagha	nagə
88.	Fly	gingieva	gɪŋgiɛvə
89.	Bee	nui	nui
	Honey	nui m bum i	nuɪ m bum i
90.	Tree	chen	tʃɛn
	Ten trees	chen chong	tʃɛn tʃɔŋ
91.	Leaf	chi kiri	tʃi kiri
92.	Guinea-corn	yie	jiɛ
93.	Maize	mu buba	mu bubə
94.	Ground-nut	amba	ambə
95.	Oil	kum	kum
	Mambila	Katoba	kətoba
	Fulani	Tibera	tïberə
	Hausa	Kasagha	kasaga

KAMKAM VOCABULARY

1.	Head	hun	hun
2.	Hair	oru	oru
3.	Eye	yian	jian
	Two eyes	yian hwan	jian hwa:n
4.	Ear	to	tɔ
	Two ears	to hwan	tɔ hwa:n

5. Nose	nyun	njun
6. One tooth	nyan ding	njan dɪŋ
Five teeth	nyan tien	njan tien
7. Tongue	nimmin	nɪmmɪn
8. Neck	min	mɪn
9. Breast (woman's)	manim	manɪm
10. Heart	njor	ndʒɔr
11. Belly	na	na
12. Back	aszima	adzɪma
13. Arm	bi	bi
14. Hand	binbaulin	binbaulɪn
Two hands	binbaulin hwan	binbaulɪn hwaːn
15. Finger	njare	ndʒare
Five fingers	njare tien	ndʒare tiɛn
16. Finger nail	nvarin	nvarɪn
17. Leg	gol	gɔl
18. Knee	jungnin	dʒuŋnɪn
19. Foot	gol baulin	gɔl baulɪn
Two feet	gol baulin hwan	gɔl baulɪn hwaːn
20. Man (person)	wuru	wuru
Ten people	wuru yauro	wuru jauro
21. Man (not woman)	vamda	vamdə
Two men	vamda hwan	vamdə hwaːn
22. Woman	giauru	giauru
Two women	giauru hwan	giauru hwaːn
23. Child	imbi	ɪmbi
24. Father	tangne	taŋne
25. Mother	mangne	maŋne
26. Slave	njul	ndʒul
27. Chief	mbon	mbɔn
28. Friend	mba	mba
29. Smith	vel	vɛl
30. Doctor	buin	buin
31. One finger	nvarin ding	nvarɪn dɪŋ
32. Two fingers	nvarin hwan	nvarɪn hwaːn
33. Three fingers	nvarin tar	nvarɪn taːr
34. Four fingers	nvarin na	nvarɪn naː
35. Five fingers	nvarin tien	nvarɪn tiɛn
36. Six fingers	nvarin tienmo	nvarɪn tiɛnmo
37. Seven fingers	nvarin tien han	nvarɪn tiɛn haːn
38. Eight fingers	nvarin tien tar	nvarɪn tiɛn taːr
39. Nine fingers	nvarin tien na	nvarɪn tiɛn na
40. Ten fingers	nvarin yauro	nvarɪn jauro
41. Eleven fingers	nvarin yaura shin ding	nvarɪn jaura ʃɪn dɪŋ
42. Twelve fingers	nvarin yauro hwan	nvarɪn jauro hwan
Thirteen fingers	nvarin yauro tar	nvarɪn jauro taːr
43. Twenty fingers	nvarin kumin biingne	nvarɪn kumɪn biiŋne
44. A hundred fingers	nvarin shonda shuan	nvarɪn ʃɔndə ʃuan
45. Sun	nyang	nyaŋ
46. God	me	mɛ
47. Moon	vir	vɪr

48.	Full moon	vir andin popopo	vɪr andɪn popopo
	New moon	vir wulga	vɪr wulga
49.	Day	nyang	njaŋ
	Night	chimbi	tʃimbi
	Morning	sa	saː
50.	Rain	nni	nni
51.	Water	mvi	mvi
52.	Blood	jillam	dʒɪllʌm
53.	Fat	furim	furɪm
54.	Salt	mbeng	mbɛŋ
55.	Stone	tan	tan
	Iron	billa	bɪlla
56.	Hill	nang	nʌŋ
57.	River	kum	kum
58.	Road	jua	dʒua
59.	House	nim (Compound = ayame)	nim (Compound = ajamɛ)
	Two houses	nim hwan	nim hwaːn
	Many houses	nim mere mere	nim mɛrɛ mɛrɛ
	All the houses	nim bit	nim bit
60.	Roof	hunimde	hunɪmde
61.	Door	afura	afura
62.	Mat	jual	dʒual
63.	Basket	ching	tʃiŋ
64.	Drum	kimbin	kɪmbɪn
65.	Pot	nang	naŋ
66.	Knife	bie	biɛ
67.	Spear	gongin	goŋɪn
68.	Bow	luan	luan
69.	Arrow	banin	banɪn
	Five arrows	banin tien	banɪn tiɛn
70.	Gun	biudigare	bɪudɪgare
71.	War	mwam	mwam
72.	Meat (animal)	nyam	njam
73.	Elephant	ngombo	ngombo
74.	Buffalo	yiir	jiɪr
75.	Leopard	ser	sɛr
76.	Monkey	mber	mbɛr
77.	Pig	ngage	ngagɛ
78.	Goat	jin	dʒin
79.	Dog	juar	dʒuar
80.	Bird	giene	giɛne
	Feather	oru	oru
81.	Crocodile	—	—
82.	Fowl	sondu	sɔndu
83.	Eggs	gen	gɛn
84.	One egg	gen ding	gɛn dɪŋ
85.	Snake	shuambe	ʃuambe
86.	Frog	ngor	ngɔr
87.	Horse	deng	dɛŋ
	Cow	nang	naːŋ

88. Fly	jinjere	dʒɪndʒere
89. Bee	nyung	njuŋ
Honey	nyung	njuŋ
90. Tree	jaa	dʒaa
Ten trees	ja yauro	dʒa jauro
91. Leaf	faniva	fanɪva
92. Guinea-corn	ya	ja
93. Maize	fan	fan
94. Ground-nut	sangar	saŋgar
95. Oil	furim	furɪm
Mambila	Luen	luɛn
Fulani	Deim	deim
Hausa	Kasa	kasa

MVANIP VOCABULARY

As spoken by the people of Magu and Ndunda

1. Head	hun	hun
2. Hair	oru	oru
3. Eye	yian	jian
Two eyes	yian bahan	jian bəhan
4. Ear	tuu	tuu
Two ears	tuu bahan	tuu bəhan
5. Nose	nyun	njun
6. One tooth	nyian ding	njian dɪŋ
Five teeth	nyian batien	njian bətiɛn
7. Tongue	nammin	nəmmɪn
8. Neck	chongin	tʃoŋɪn
9. Breast (woman's)	manim	manɪm
10. Heart	njoru	ndʒoru
11. Belly	fun	fun
12. Back	edzima	ɛdzɪma
13. Arm	bi	bi
14. Hand	bi	bi
Two hands	bi bahan	bi bəhan
15. Finger	njare	ndʒare
Five fingers	njare batien	ndʒare bətiɛn
16. Finger nail	nvarin	nvarɪn
17. Leg	guru	guru
18. Knee	jungnun	dʒuŋnun
19. Foot	mbare gule	mbare gule
Two feet	mbare gule bahan	mbare gule bəhan
20. Man (person)	viende	viɛnde
Ten people	viende bahan	viɛnde bəhan
21. Man (not woman)	wovam	wovam
Two men	wovam bahan	wovam bəhan
22. Woman	wogie	wogie
Two women	wogie bahan	wogie bəhan
23. Child	imbi	ɪmbi
24. Father	tien	tiɛn
25. Mother	mien	miɛn

26.	Slave	ngiri	ngiri	
27.	Chief	mbon	mbɔn	
28.	Friend	mba	mba	
29.	Smith	wowuro	wowuro	
30.	Doctor	buin	buɪn	
31.	One finger	nvarin ding	nvarɪn dɪŋ	
32.	Two fingers	nvarin bahan	nvarɪn bəhan	
33.	Three fingers	nvarin batar	nvarɪn bətar	
34.	Four fingers	nvarin bana	nvarɪn bənaː	
35.	Five fingers	nvarin batien	nvarɪn bətiɛn	
36.	Six fingers	nvarin batienmo	nvarɪn bətiɛnmo	
37.	Seven fingers	nvarin batien han	nvarɪn bətiɛn han	
38.	Eight fingers	nvarin batie tar	nvarɪn bətiɛ tar	
39.	Nine fingers	nvarin batiena	nvarɪn bətiɛna	
40.	Ten fingers	nvarin yobru	nvarɪn jobru	
41.	Eleven fingers	nvarin yobriu shin ding	nvarɪn jobriu ʃɪn dɪŋ	
42.	Twelve fingers	nvarin yobriu shiru hang	nvarɪn jobriu ʃiru haŋ	
	Thirteen fingers	nvarin yobriu shir vata	nvarɪn jobriu ʃir vəta	
43.	Twenty fingers	nvarin kumin	nvarɪn kumɪn	
44.	A hundred fingers	nvarin shendi shen	nvarɪn ʃɛndi ʃɛn	
45.	Sun	nyang	njaŋ	
46.	God	Kondop	kondop	
47.	Moon	wuru	wuru	
48.	Rain	nni	nni	
49.	Water	mbuu	mbuu	
50.	Blood	nzirram	nzɪrrʌm	
51.	Salt	fangip	faŋɪp	
52.	Iron	birra	bɪrra	
53.	Guinea-corn	ya	ja	
54.	Maize	fuan	fuan	

END OF VOL. I